Python for Finance

Yves Hilpisch

Beijing · Cambridge · Farnham · Köln · Sebastopol · Tokyo

Python for Finance

by Yves Hilpisch

Printed in the United States of America.

Published by O'Reilly Media, Inc., 1005 Gravenstein Highway North, Sebastopol, CA 95472.

O'Reilly books may be purchased for educational, business, or sales promotional use. Online editions are also available for most titles (*http://safaribooksonline.com*). For more information, contact our corporate/institutional sales department: 800-998-9938 or *corporate@oreilly.com*.

Editors: Brian MacDonald and Meghan Blanchette	**Indexer:** Judith McConville
Production Editor: Matthew Hacker	**Cover Designer:** Ellie Volckhausen
Copyeditor: Charles Roumeliotis	**Interior Designer:** David Futato
Proofreader: Rachel Head	**Illustrator:** Rebecca Demarest

December 2014:   First Edition

Revision History for the First Edition:

2014-12-09:   First release

See *http://oreilly.com/catalog/errata.csp?isbn=9781491945285* for release details.

ISBN: 978-1-491-94528-5

[LSI]

Table of Contents

Preface... xi

Part I.   Python and Finance

1. Why Python for Finance?..................................... 3
What Is Python?   3
  Brief History of Python   5
  The Python Ecosystem   6
  Python User Spectrum   7
  The Scientific Stack   8
Technology in Finance   9
  Technology Spending   10
  Technology as Enabler   10
  Technology and Talent as Barriers to Entry   10
  Ever-Increasing Speeds, Frequencies, Data Volumes   11
  The Rise of Real-Time Analytics   12
Python for Finance   13
  Finance and Python Syntax   14
  Efficiency and Productivity Through Python   17
  From Prototyping to Production   21
Conclusions   22
Further Reading   23

2. Infrastructure and Tools................................... 25
Python Deployment   26
  Anaconda   26
  Python Quant Platform   32
Tools   34
  Python   34

     IPython   35

     Spyder   45

   Conclusions   47

   Further Reading   48

3. Introductory Examples. **49**

   Implied Volatilities   50

   Monte Carlo Simulation   59

     Pure Python   61

     Vectorization with NumPy   63

     Full Vectorization with Log Euler Scheme   65

     Graphical Analysis   67

   Technical Analysis   68

   Conclusions   74

   Further Reading   75

Part II.   Financial Analytics and Development

4. Data Types and Structures. **79**

   Basic Data Types   80

     Integers   80

     Floats   81

     Strings   84

   Basic Data Structures   86

     Tuples   87

     Lists   88

     Excursion: Control Structures   89

     Excursion: Functional Programming   91

     Dicts   92

     Sets   94

   NumPy Data Structures   95

     Arrays with Python Lists   96

     Regular NumPy Arrays   97

     Structured Arrays   101

   Vectorization of Code   102

     Basic Vectorization   102

     Memory Layout   105

   Conclusions   106

   Further Reading   107

5. Data Visualization. **109**
  Two-Dimensional Plotting   109
    One-Dimensional Data Set   110
    Two-Dimensional Data Set   115
    Other Plot Styles   121
  Financial Plots   128
  3D Plotting   132
  Conclusions   135
  Further Reading   135

6. Financial Time Series. **137**
  pandas Basics   138
    First Steps with DataFrame Class   138
    Second Steps with DataFrame Class   142
    Basic Analytics   146
    Series Class   149
    GroupBy Operations   150
  Financial Data   151
  Regression Analysis   157
  High-Frequency Data   166
  Conclusions   170
  Further Reading   171

7. Input/Output Operations. **173**
  Basic I/O with Python   174
    Writing Objects to Disk   174
    Reading and Writing Text Files   177
    SQL Databases   179
    Writing and Reading NumPy Arrays   181
  I/O with pandas   183
    SQL Database   184
    From SQL to pandas   185
    Data as CSV File   188
    Data as Excel File   189
  Fast I/O with PyTables   190
    Working with Tables   190
    Working with Compressed Tables   196
    Working with Arrays   197
    Out-of-Memory Computations   198
  Conclusions   200
  Further Reading   201

8. Performance Python **203**

Python Paradigms and Performance   204
Memory Layout and Performance   207
Parallel Computing   209
    The Monte Carlo Algorithm   209
    The Sequential Calculation   210
    The Parallel Calculation   211
    Performance Comparison   214
multiprocessing   215
Dynamic Compiling   217
    Introductory Example   217
    Binomial Option Pricing   218
Static Compiling with Cython   223
Generation of Random Numbers on GPUs   226
Conclusions   230
Further Reading   231

9. Mathematical Tools **233**

Approximation   234
    Regression   234
    Interpolation   245
Convex Optimization   249
    Global Optimization   250
    Local Optimization   251
    Constrained Optimization   253
Integration   255
    Numerical Integration   256
    Integration by Simulation   257
Symbolic Computation   258
    Basics   258
    Equations   259
    Integration   260
    Differentiation   261
Conclusions   262
Further Reading   263

10. Stochastics **265**

Random Numbers   266
Simulation   271
    Random Variables   271
    Stochastic Processes   274
    Variance Reduction   287

Valuation	290
European Options	291
American Options	295
Risk Measures	298
Value-at-Risk	298
Credit Value Adjustments	302
Conclusions	305
Further Reading	305

11. Statistics **307**

Normality Tests	308
Benchmark Case	309
Real-World Data	317
Portfolio Optimization	322
The Data	323
The Basic Theory	324
Portfolio Optimizations	328
Efficient Frontier	330
Capital Market Line	332
Principal Component Analysis	335
The DAX Index and Its 30 Stocks	336
Applying PCA	337
Constructing a PCA Index	338
Bayesian Regression	341
Bayes's Formula	341
PyMC3	342
Introductory Example	343
Real Data	347
Conclusions	355
Further Reading	355

12. Excel Integration **357**

Basic Spreadsheet Interaction	358
Generating Workbooks (.xls)	359
Generating Workbooks (.xslx)	360
Reading from Workbooks	362
Using OpenPyxl	364
Using pandas for Reading and Writing	366
Scripting Excel with Python	369
Installing DataNitro	369
Working with DataNitro	370
xlwings	379

Conclusions   379
Further Reading   380

13. Object Orientation and Graphical User Interfaces **381**
Object Orientation   381
Basics of Python Classes   382
Simple Short Rate Class   387
Cash Flow Series Class   391
Graphical User Interfaces   393
Short Rate Class with GUI   394
Updating of Values   396
Cash Flow Series Class with GUI   398
Conclusions   401
Further Reading   401

14. Web Integration **403**
Web Basics   404
ftplib   405
httplib   407
urllib   408
Web Plotting   411
Static Plots   411
Interactive Plots   414
Real-Time Plots   417
Rapid Web Applications   424
Traders' Chat Room   426
Data Modeling   426
The Python Code   427
Templating   434
Styling   440
Web Services   442
The Financial Model   443
The Implementation   445
Conclusions   451
Further Reading   452

Part III.   Derivatives Analytics Library

15. Valuation Framework **455**
Fundamental Theorem of Asset Pricing   455
A Simple Example   456

The General Results 457
Risk-Neutral Discounting 458
Modeling and Handling Dates 458
Constant Short Rate 460
Market Environments 462
Conclusions 465
Further Reading 466

16. Simulation of Financial Models. 467
Random Number Generation 468
Generic Simulation Class 470
Geometric Brownian Motion 473
The Simulation Class 474
A Use Case 476
Jump Diffusion 478
The Simulation Class 478
A Use Case 481
Square-Root Diffusion 482
The Simulation Class 483
A Use Case 485
Conclusions 486
Further Reading 487

17. Derivatives Valuation. 489
Generic Valuation Class 489
European Exercise 493
The Valuation Class 494
A Use Case 496
American Exercise 500
Least-Squares Monte Carlo 501
The Valuation Class 502
A Use Case 504
Conclusions 507
Further Reading 509

18. Portfolio Valuation. 511
Derivatives Positions 512
The Class 512
A Use Case 514
Derivatives Portfolios 515
The Class 516
A Use Case 520

     Conclusions   525

Conclusions 525
Further Reading 527

19. Volatility Options. **529**
   The VSTOXX Data 530
     VSTOXX Index Data 530
     VSTOXX Futures Data 531
     VSTOXX Options Data 533
   Model Calibration 534
     Relevant Market Data 535
     Option Modeling 536
     Calibration Procedure 538
   American Options on the VSTOXX 542
     Modeling Option Positions 543
     The Options Portfolio 544
   Conclusions 545
   Further Reading 546

A. Selected Best Practices. **547**

B. Call Option Class. **557**

C. Dates and Times. **563**

Index. **575**

Preface

Not too long ago, Python as a programming language and platform technology was considered exotic—if not completely irrelevant—in the financial industry. By contrast, in 2014 there are many examples of large financial institutions—like Bank of America Merrill Lynch with its Quartz project, or JP Morgan Chase with the Athena project—that strategically use Python alongside other established technologies to build, enhance, and maintain some of their core IT systems. There is also a multitude of larger and smaller hedge funds that make heavy use of Python's capabilities when it comes to efficient financial application development and productive financial analytics efforts.

Similarly, many of today's Master of Financial Engineering programs (or programs awarding similar degrees) use Python as one of the core languages for teaching the translation of quantitative finance theory into executable computer code. Educational programs and trainings targeted to finance professionals are also increasingly incorporating Python into their curricula. Some now teach it as the main implementation language.

There are many reasons why Python has had such recent success and why it seems it will continue to do so in the future. Among these reasons are its syntax, the ecosystem of scientific and data analytics libraries available to developers using Python, its ease of integration with almost any other technology, and its status as open source. (See Chapter 1 for a few more insights in this regard.)

For that reason, there is an abundance of good books available that teach Python from different angles and with different focuses. This book is one of the first to introduce and teach Python for finance—in particular, for quantitative finance and for financial analytics. The approach is a practical one, in that implementation and illustration come before theoretical details, and the big picture is generally more focused on than the most arcane parameterization options of a certain class or function.

Most of this book has been written in the powerful, interactive, browser-based IPython Notebook environment (explained in more detail in Chapter 2). This makes it possible to provide the reader with executable, interactive versions of almost all examples used in this book.

Those who want to immediately get started with a full-fledged, interactive financial analytics environment for Python (and, for instance, R and Julia) should go to *http://oreilly.quant-platform.com* and try out the Python Quant Platform (in combination with the IPython Notebook files and code that come with this book). You should also have a look at DX analytics (*http://dx-analytics.com*), a Python-based financial analytics library. My other book, *Derivatives Analytics with Python* (Wiley Finance), presents more details on the theory and numerical methods for advanced derivatives analytics. It also provides a wealth of readily usable Python code. Further material, and, in particular, slide decks and videos of talks about Python for Quant Finance can be found on my private website (*http://hilpisch.com*).

If you want to get involved in Python for Quant Finance community events, there are opportunities in the financial centers of the world. For example, I myself (co)organize meetup groups with this focus in London (cf. *http://www.meetup.com/Python-for-Quant-Finance-London/*) and New York City (cf. *http://www.meetup.com/Python-for-Quant-Finance-NYC/*). There are also For Python Quants conferences and workshops several times a year (cf. *http://forpythonquants.com* and *http://pythonquants.com*).

I am really excited that Python has established itself as an important technology in the financial industry. I am also sure that it will play an even more important role there in the future, in fields like derivatives and risk analytics or high performance computing. My hope is that this book will help professionals, researchers, and students alike make the most of Python when facing the challenges of this fascinating field.

Conventions Used in This Book

The following typographical conventions are used in this book:

Italic
: Indicates new terms, URLs, and email addresses.

`Constant width`
: Used for program listings, as well as within paragraphs to refer to software packages, programming languages, file extensions, filenames, program elements such as variable or function names, databases, data types, environment variables, statements, and keywords.

`Constant width italic`
: Shows text that should be replaced with user-supplied values or by values determined by context.

This element signifies a tip or suggestion.

 This element indicates a warning or caution.

Using Code Examples

Supplemental material (in particular, IPython Notebooks and Python scripts/modules) is available for download at *http://oreilly.quant-platform.com*.

This book is here to help you get your job done. In general, if example code is offered with this book, you may use it in your programs and documentation. You do not need to contact us for permission unless you're reproducing a significant portion of the code. For example, writing a program that uses several chunks of code from this book does not require permission. Selling or distributing a CD-ROM of examples from O'Reilly books does require permission. Answering a question by citing this book and quoting example code does not require permission. Incorporating a significant amount of example code from this book into your product's documentation does require permission.

We appreciate, but do not require, attribution. An attribution usually includes the title, author, publisher, and ISBN. For example: "*Python for Finance* by Yves Hilpisch (O'Reilly). Copyright 2015 Yves Hilpisch, 978-1-491-94528-5."

If you feel your use of code examples falls outside fair use or the permission given above, feel free to contact us at *permissions@oreilly.com*.

Safari® Books Online

 *Safari Books Online* is an on-demand digital library that delivers expert content in both book and video form from the world's leading authors in technology and business.

Technology professionals, software developers, web designers, and business and creative professionals use Safari Books Online as their primary resource for research, problem solving, learning, and certification training.

Safari Books Online offers a range of plans and pricing for enterprise, government, education, and individuals.

Members have access to thousands of books, training videos, and prepublication manuscripts in one fully searchable database from publishers like O'Reilly Media, Prentice Hall Professional, Addison-Wesley Professional, Microsoft Press, Sams, Que, Peachpit Press, Focal Press, Cisco Press, John Wiley & Sons, Syngress, Morgan Kaufmann, IBM Redbooks, Packt, Adobe Press, FT Press, Apress, Manning, New Riders, McGraw-Hill, Jones & Bartlett, Course Technology, and hundreds more. For more information about Safari Books Online, please visit us online.

How to Contact Us

Please address comments and questions concerning this book to the publisher:

O'Reilly Media, Inc.
1005 Gravenstein Highway North
Sebastopol, CA 95472
800-998-9938 (in the United States or Canada)
707-829-0515 (international or local)
707-829-0104 (fax)

We have a web page for this book, where we list errata, examples, and any additional information. You can access this page at *http://bit.ly/python-finance*.

To comment or ask technical questions about this book, send email to *bookques tions@oreilly.com*.

For more information about our books, courses, conferences, and news, see our website at *http://www.oreilly.com*.

Find us on Facebook: *http://facebook.com/oreilly*

Follow us on Twitter: *http://twitter.com/oreillymedia*

Watch us on YouTube: *http://www.youtube.com/oreillymedia*

Acknowledgments

I want to thank all those who helped to make this book a reality, in particular those who have provided honest feedback or even completely worked out examples, like Ben Lerner, James Powell, Michael Schwed, Thomas Wiecki or Felix Zumstein. Similarly, I would like to thank reviewers Hugh Brown, Jennifer Pierce, Kevin Sheppard, and Galen Wilkerson. The book benefited from their valuable feedback and the many suggestions.

The book has also benefited significantly as a result of feedback I received from the participants of the many conferences and workshops I was able to present at in 2013 and 2014: PyData, For Python Quants, Big Data in Quant Finance, EuroPython, Euro-Scipy, PyCon DE, PyCon Ireland, Parallel Data Analysis, Budapest BI Forum and

CodeJam. I also got valuable feedback during my many presentations at Python meetups in Berlin, London, and New York City.

Last but not least, I want to thank my family, which fully accepts that I do what I love doing most and this, in general, rather intensively. Writing and finishing a book of this length over the course of a year requires a large time commitment—on top of my usually heavy workload and packed travel schedule—and makes it necessary to sit sometimes more hours in solitude in front the computer than expected. Therefore, thank you Sandra, Lilli, and Henry for your understanding and support. I dedicate this book to my lovely wife Sandra, who is the heart of our family.

Yves
Saarland, November 2014

## PART I

Python and Finance

This part introduces Python for finance. It consists of three chapters:

- Chapter 1 briefly discusses Python in general and argues why Python is indeed well suited to address the technological challenges in the finance industry and in financial (data) analytics.

- Chapter 2, on Python infrastructure and tools, is meant to provide a concise overview of the most important things you have to know to get started with interactive analytics and application development in Python; the related Appendix A surveys some selected best practices for Python development.

- Chapter 3 immediately dives into three specific financial examples; it illustrates how to calculate implied volatilities of options with Python, how to simulate a financial model with Python and the array library NumPy, and how to implement a backtesting for a trend-based investment strategy. This chapter should give the reader a feeling for what it means to use Python for financial analytics—details are not that important at this stage; they are all explained in Part II.

## CHAPTER 1

Why Python for Finance?

> Banks are essentially technology firms.
>
> — Hugo Banziger

What Is Python?

`Python` is a high-level, multipurpose programming language that is used in a wide range of domains and technical fields. On the `Python` website you find the following executive summary (cf. *https://www.python.org/doc/essays/blurb*):

> Python is an interpreted, object-oriented, high-level programming language with dynamic semantics. Its high-level built in data structures, combined with dynamic typing and dynamic binding, make it very attractive for Rapid Application Development, as well as for use as a scripting or glue language to connect existing components together. Python's simple, easy to learn syntax emphasizes readability and therefore reduces the cost of program maintenance. Python supports modules and packages, which encourages program modularity and code reuse. The Python interpreter and the extensive standard library are available in source or binary form without charge for all major platforms, and can be freely distributed.

This pretty well describes *why* `Python` has evolved into one of the major programming languages as of today. Nowadays, `Python` is used by the beginner programmer as well as by the highly skilled expert developer, at schools, in universities, at web companies, in large corporations and financial institutions, as well as in any scientific field.

Among others, `Python` is characterized by the following features:

Open source
    `Python` and the majority of supporting libraries and tools available are open source and generally come with quite flexible and open licenses.

Interpreted

The reference CPython implementation is an interpreter of the language that translates Python code at runtime to executable byte code.

Multiparadigm

Python supports different programming and implementation paradigms, such as object orientation and imperative, functional, or procedural programming.

Multipurpose

Python can be used for rapid, interactive code development as well as for building large applications; it can be used for low-level systems operations as well as for high-level analytics tasks.

Cross-platform

Python is available for the most important operating systems, such as Windows, Linux, and Mac OS; it is used to build desktop as well as web applications; it can be used on the largest clusters and most powerful servers as well as on such small devices as the Raspberry Pi (cf. *http://www.raspberrypi.org*).

Dynamically typed

Types in Python are in general inferred during runtime and not statically declared as in most compiled languages.

Indentation aware

In contrast to the majority of other programming languages, Python uses indentation for marking code blocks instead of parentheses, brackets, or semicolons.

Garbage collecting

Python has automated garbage collection, avoiding the need for the programmer to manage memory.

When it comes to Python syntax and what Python is all about, Python Enhancement Proposal 20—i.e., the so-called "Zen of Python"—provides the major guidelines. It can be accessed from every interactive shell with the command import this:

```
$ ipython
Python 2.7.6 |Anaconda 1.9.1 (x86_64)| (default, Jan 10 2014, 11:23:15)
Type "copyright", "credits" or "license" for more information.

IPython 2.0.0--An enhanced Interactive Python.
?         -> Introduction and overview of IPython's features.
%quickref -> Quick reference.
help      -> Python's own help system.
object?   -> Details about 'object', use 'object??' for extra details.

In [1]: import this

The Zen of Python, by Tim Peters
```

```
Beautiful is better than ugly.
Explicit is better than implicit.
Simple is better than complex.
Complex is better than complicated.
Flat is better than nested.
Sparse is better than dense.
Readability counts.
Special cases aren't special enough to break the rules.
Although practicality beats purity.
Errors should never pass silently.
Unless explicitly silenced.
In the face of ambiguity, refuse the temptation to guess.
There should be one--and preferably only one--obvious way to do it.
Although that way may not be obvious at first unless you're Dutch.
Now is better than never.
Although never is often better than *right* now.
If the implementation is hard to explain, it's a bad idea.
If the implementation is easy to explain, it may be a good idea.
Namespaces are one honking great idea--let's do more of those!
```

Brief History of Python

Although Python might still have the appeal of something *new* to some people, it has been around for quite a long time. In fact, development efforts began in the 1980s by Guido van Rossum from the Netherlands. He is still active in Python development and has been awarded the title of *Benevolent Dictator for Life* by the Python community (cf. *http://en.wikipedia.org/wiki/History_of_Python*). The following can be considered milestones in the development of Python:

- **Python 0.9.0** released in 1991 (first release)
- **Python 1.0** released in 1994
- **Python 2.0** released in 2000
- **Python 2.6** released in 2008
- **Python 2.7** released in 2010
- **Python 3.0** released in 2008
- **Python 3.3** released in 2010
- **Python 3.4** released in 2014

It is remarkable, and sometimes confusing to Python newcomers, that there are two major versions available, still being developed and, more importantly, in parallel use since 2008. As of this writing, this will keep on for quite a while since neither is there 100% code compatibility between the versions, nor are all popular libraries available for Python 3.x. The majority of code available and in production is still Python 2.6/2.7, and this book is based on the 2.7.x version, although the majority of code examples should work with versions 3.x as well.

The Python Ecosystem

A major feature of Python as an ecosystem, compared to just being a programming language, is the availability of a large number of libraries and tools. These libraries and tools generally have to be *imported* when needed (e.g., a plotting library) or have to be started as a separate system process (e.g., a Python development environment). Importing means making a library available to the current namespace and the current Python interpreter process.

Python itself already comes with a large set of libraries that enhance the basic interpreter in different directions. For example, basic mathematical calculations can be done without any importing, while more complex mathematical functions need to be imported through the math library:

```
In [2]: 100 * 2.5 + 50
Out[2]: 300.0
In [3]: log(1)

...

NameError: name 'log' is not defined
In [4]: from math import *

In [5]: log(1)
Out[5]: 0.0
```

Although the so-called "star import" (i.e., the practice of importing *everything* from a library via from library import *) is sometimes convenient, one should generally use an alternative approach that avoids ambiguity with regard to name spaces and relationships of functions to libraries. This then takes on the form:

```
In [6]: import math

In [7]: math.log(1)
Out[7]: 0.0
```

While math is a standard Python library available with any installation, there are many more libraries that can be installed optionally and that can be used in the very same fashion as the standard libraries. Such libraries are available from different (web) sources. However, it is generally advisable to use a Python distribution that makes sure that all libraries are consistent with each other (see Chapter 2 for more on this topic).

The code examples presented so far all use IPython (cf. *http://www.ipython.org*), which is probably the most popular interactive development environment (IDE) for Python. Although it started out as an enhanced shell only, it today has many features typically found in IDEs (e.g., support for profiling and debugging). Those features missing are typically provided by advanced text/code editors, like Sublime Text (cf. *http://www.sublimetext.com*). Therefore, it is not unusual to combine IPython with one's text/code editor of choice to form the basic tool set for a Python development process.

IPython is also sometimes called the *killer application* of the Python ecosystem. It enhances the standard interactive shell in many ways. For example, it provides improved command-line history functions and allows for easy object inspection. For instance, the help text for a function is printed by just adding a ? behind the function name (adding ?? will provide even more information):

```
In [8]: math.log?

Type:       builtin_function_or_method
String Form:<built-in function log>
Docstring:
log(x[, base])

Return the logarithm of x to the given base.
If the base not specified, returns the natural logarithm (base e) of x.

In [9]:
```

IPython comes in three different versions: a *shell* version, one based on a QT graphical user interface (the QT console), and a browser-based version (the Notebook). This is just meant as a teaser; there is no need to worry about the details now since Chapter 2 introduces IPython in more detail.

Python User Spectrum

Python does not only appeal to professional software developers; it is also of use for the casual developer as well as for domain experts and scientific developers.

Professional software developers find all that they need to efficiently build large applications. Almost all programming paradigms are supported; there are powerful development tools available; and any task can, in principle, be addressed with Python. These types of users typically build their own frameworks and classes, also work on the fundamental Python and scientific stack, and strive to make the most of the ecosystem.

Scientific developers or *domain experts* are generally heavy users of certain libraries and frameworks, have built their own applications that they enhance and optimize over time, and tailor the ecosystem to their specific needs. These groups of users also generally engage in longer interactive sessions, rapidly prototyping new code as well as exploring and visualizing their research and/or domain data sets.

Casual programmers like to use Python generally for specific problems they know that Python has its strengths in. For example, visiting the gallery page of matplotlib, copying a certain piece of visualization code provided there, and adjusting the code to their specific needs might be a beneficial use case for members of this group.

There is also another important group of Python users: *beginner programmers*, i.e., those that are just starting to program. Nowadays, Python has become a very popular language at universities, colleges, and even schools to introduce students to programming.[1] A major reason for this is that its basic syntax is easy to learn and easy to understand, even for the nondeveloper. In addition, it is helpful that Python supports almost all programming styles.[2]

The Scientific Stack

There is a certain set of libraries that is collectively labeled the *scientific stack*. This stack comprises, among others, the following libraries:

NumPy *(http://www.numpy.org)*
> NumPy provides a multidimensional array object to store homogenous or heterogeneous data; it also provides optimized functions/methods to operate on this array object.

SciPy *(http://www.scipy.org)*
> SciPy is a collection of sublibraries and functions implementing important standard functionality often needed in science or finance; for example, you will find functions for cubic splines interpolation as well as for numerical integration.

matplotlib *(http://www.matplotlib.org)*
> This is the most popular plotting and visualization library for Python, providing both 2D and 3D visualization capabilities.

PyTables *(http://www.pytables.org)*
> PyTables is a popular wrapper for the HDF5 data storage library (cf. *http://www.hdfgroup.org/HDF5/*); it is a library to implement optimized, disk-based I/O operations based on a hierarchical database/file format.

---

1. Python, for example, is a major language used in the Master of Financial Engineering program at Baruch College of the City University of New York (cf. *http://mfe.baruch.cuny.edu*).

2. Cf. *http://wiki.python.org/moin/BeginnersGuide*, where you will find links to many valuable resources for both developers and nondevelopers getting started with Python.

pandas *(http://pandas.pydata.org)*

> pandas builds on NumPy and provides richer classes for the management and analysis of time series and tabular data; it is tightly integrated with matplotlib for plotting and PyTables for data storage and retrieval.

Depending on the specific domain or problem, this stack is enlarged by additional libraries, which more often than not have in common that they build on top of one or more of these fundamental libraries. However, the *least common denominator* or *basic building block* in general is the NumPy ndarray class (cf. Chapter 4).

Taking Python as a programming language alone, there are a number of other languages available that can probably keep up with its syntax and elegance. For example, Ruby is quite a popular language often compared to Python. On the language's website (*http://www.ruby-lang.org*) you find the following description:

> A dynamic, open source programming language with a focus on simplicity and productivity. It has an elegant syntax that is natural to read and easy to write.

The majority of people using Python would probably also agree with the exact same statement being made about Python itself. However, what distinguishes Python for many users from equally appealing languages like Ruby is the availability of the scientific stack. This makes Python not only a good and elegant language to use, but also one that is capable of replacing domain-specific languages and tool sets like Matlab or R. In addition, it provides by default anything that you would expect, say, as a seasoned web developer or systems administrator.

Technology in Finance

Now that we have some rough ideas of what Python is all about, it makes sense to step back a bit and to briefly contemplate the role of technology in finance. This will put us in a position to better judge the role Python already plays and, even more importantly, will probably play in the financial industry of the future.

In a sense, technology per se is *nothing special* to financial institutions (as compared, for instance, to industrial companies) or to the finance function (as compared to other corporate functions, like logistics). However, in recent years, spurred by innovation and also regulation, banks and other financial institutions like hedge funds have evolved more and more into technology companies instead of being *just* financial intermediaries. Technology has become a major asset for almost any financial institution around the globe, having the potential to lead to competitive advantages as well as disadvantages. Some background information can shed light on the reasons for this development.

Technology Spending

Banks and financial institutions together form the industry that spends the most on technology on an annual basis. The following statement therefore shows not only that technology is important for the financial industry, but that the financial industry is also really important to the technology sector:

> Banks will spend 4.2% more on technology in 2014 than they did in 2013, according to IDC analysts. Overall IT spend in financial services globally will exceed $430 billion in 2014 and surpass $500 billion by 2020, the analysts say.
>
> — Crosman 2013

Large, multinational banks today generally employ thousands of developers that maintain existing systems and build new ones. Large investment banks with heavy technological requirements show technology budgets often of several billion USD per year.

Technology as Enabler

The technological development has also contributed to innovations and efficiency improvements in the financial sector:

> Technological innovations have contributed significantly to greater efficiency in the derivatives market. Through innovations in trading technology, trades at Eurex are today executed much faster than ten years ago despite the strong increase in trading volume and the number of quotes ... These strong improvements have only been possible due to the constant, high IT investments by derivatives exchanges and clearing houses.
>
> — Deutsche Börse Group 2008

As a side effect of the increasing efficiency, competitive advantages must often be looked for in ever more complex products or transactions. This in turn inherently increases risks and makes risk management as well as oversight and regulation more and more difficult. The financial crisis of 2007 and 2008 tells the story of potential dangers resulting from such developments. In a similar vein, "algorithms and computers gone wild" also represent a potential risk to the financial markets; this materialized dramatically in the so-called *flash crash* of May 2010, where automated selling led to large intraday drops in certain stocks and stock indices (cf. *http://en.wikipedia.org/wiki/2010_Flash_Crash*).

Technology and Talent as Barriers to Entry

On the one hand, technology advances reduce cost over time, *ceteris paribus*. On the other hand, financial institutions continue to invest heavily in technology to both gain market share and defend their current positions. To be active in certain areas in finance today often brings with it the need for large-scale investments in both technology and skilled staff. As an example, consider the derivatives analytics space (see also the case study in Part III of the book):

> Aggregated over the total software lifecycle, firms adopting in-house strategies for OTC [derivatives] pricing will require investments between $25 million and $36 million alone to build, maintain, and enhance a complete derivatives library.
>
> — Ding 2010

Not only is it costly and time-consuming to build a full-fledged derivatives analytics library, but you also need to have *enough experts* to do so. And these experts have to have the right tools and technologies available to accomplish their tasks.

Another quote about the early days of Long-Term Capital Management (LTCM), formerly one of the most respected quantitative hedge funds—which, however, went bust in the late 1990s—further supports this insight about technology and talent:

> Meriwether spent $20 million on a state-of-the-art computer system and hired a crack team of financial engineers to run the show at LTCM, which set up shop in Greenwich, Connecticut. It was risk management on an industrial level.
>
> — Patterson 2010

The same computing power that Meriwether had to buy for millions of dollars is today probably available for thousands. On the other hand, trading, pricing, and risk management have become so complex for larger financial institutions that today they need to deploy IT infrastructures with tens of thousands of computing cores.

Ever-Increasing Speeds, Frequencies, Data Volumes

There is one dimension of the finance industry that has been influenced most by technological advances: the *speed* and *frequency* with which financial transactions are decided and executed. The recent book by Lewis (2014) describes so-called *flash trading* —i.e., trading at the highest speeds possible—in vivid detail.

On the one hand, increasing data availability on ever-smaller scales makes it necessary to react in real time. On the other hand, the increasing speed and frequency of trading let the data volumes further increase. This leads to processes that reinforce each other and push the average time scale for financial transactions systematically down:

> Renaissance's Medallion fund gained an astonishing 80 percent in 2008, capitalizing on the market's extreme volatility with its lightning-fast computers. Jim Simons was the hedge fund world's top earner for the year, pocketing a cool $2.5 billion.
>
> — Patterson 2010

Thirty years' worth of daily stock price data for a single stock represents roughly 7,500 quotes. This kind of data is what most of today's finance theory is based on. For example, theories like the modern portfolio theory (MPT), the capital asset pricing model (CAPM), and value-at-risk (VaR) all have their foundations in daily stock price data.

In comparison, on a typical trading day the stock price of Apple Inc. (AAPL) is quoted around 15,000 times—two times as many quotes as seen for end-of-day quoting over a time span of 30 years. This brings with it a number of challenges:

Data processing

It does not suffice to consider and process end-of-day quotes for stocks or other financial instruments; "too much" happens during the day for some instruments during 24 hours for 7 days a week.

Analytics speed

Decisions often have to be made in milliseconds or even faster, making it necessary to build the respective analytics capabilities and to analyze large amounts of data in real time.

Theoretical foundations

Although traditional finance theories and concepts are far from being perfect, they have been well tested (and sometimes well rejected) over time; for the millisecond scales important as of today, consistent concepts and theories that have proven to be somewhat robust over time are still missing.

All these challenges can in principle only be addressed by modern technology. Something that might also be a little bit surprising is that the lack of consistent theories often is addressed by technological approaches, in that high-speed algorithms exploit market microstructure elements (e.g., order flow, bid-ask spreads) rather than relying on some kind of financial reasoning.

The Rise of Real-Time Analytics

There is one discipline that has seen a strong increase in importance in the finance industry: *financial and data analytics*. This phenomenon has a close relationship to the insight that speeds, frequencies, and data volumes increase at a rapid pace in the industry. In fact, real-time analytics can be considered the industry's answer to this trend.

Roughly speaking, "financial and data analytics" refers to the discipline of applying software and technology in combination with (possibly advanced) algorithms and methods to gather, process, and analyze data in order to gain insights, to make decisions, or to fulfill regulatory requirements, for instance. Examples might include the estimation of sales impacts induced by a change in the pricing structure for a financial product in the retail branch of a bank. Another example might be the large-scale overnight calculation of credit value adjustments (CVA) for complex portfolios of derivatives trades of an investment bank.

There are two major challenges that financial institutions face in this context:

Big data

Banks and other financial institutions had to deal with massive amounts of data even before the term "big data" was coined; however, the amount of data that has to be processed during single analytics tasks has increased tremendously over time, demanding both increased computing power and ever-larger memory and storage capacities.

Real-time economy
> In the past, decision makers could rely on structured, regular planning, decision, and (risk) management processes, whereas they today face the need to take care of these functions in real time; several tasks that have been taken care of in the past via overnight batch runs in the back office have now been moved to the front office and are executed in real time.

Again, one can observe an interplay between advances in technology and financial/business practice. On the one hand, there is the need to constantly improve analytics approaches in terms of speed and capability by applying modern technologies. On the other hand, advances on the technology side allow new analytics approaches that were considered impossible (or infeasible due to budget constraints) a couple of years or even months ago.

One major trend in the analytics space has been the utilization of parallel architectures on the CPU (central processing unit) side and massively parallel architectures on the GPGPU (general-purpose graphical processing units) side. Current GPGPUs often have more than 1,000 computing cores, making necessary a sometimes radical rethinking of what parallelism might mean to different algorithms. What is still an obstacle in this regard is that users generally have to learn new paradigms and techniques to harness the power of such hardware.[3]

Python for Finance

The previous section describes some selected aspects characterizing the role of technology in finance:

- Costs for technology in the finance industry
- Technology as an enabler for new business and innovation
- Technology and talent as barriers to entry in the finance industry
- Increasing speeds, frequencies, and data volumes
- The rise of real-time analytics

In this section, we want to analyze how Python can help in addressing several of the challenges implied by these aspects. But first, on a more fundamental level, let us examine Python for finance from a language and syntax standpoint.

---

3. Chapter 8 provides an example for the benefits of using modern GPGPUs in the context of the generation of random numbers.

Finance and Python Syntax

Most people who make their first steps with Python in a finance context may attack an algorithmic problem. This is similar to a scientist who, for example, wants to solve a differential equation, wants to evaluate an integral, or simply wants to visualize some data. In general, at this stage, there is only little thought spent on topics like a formal development process, testing, documentation, or deployment. However, this especially seems to be the stage when people fall in love with Python. A major reason for this might be that the Python syntax is generally quite close to the mathematical syntax used to describe scientific problems or financial algorithms.

We can illustrate this phenomenon by a simple financial algorithm, namely the valuation of a European call option by Monte Carlo simulation. We will consider a Black-Scholes-Merton (BSM) setup (see also Chapter 3) in which the option's underlying risk factor follows a geometric Brownian motion.

Suppose we have the following numerical *parameter values* for the valuation:

- Initial stock index level $S_0 = 100$
- Strike price of the European call option $K = 105$
- Time-to-maturity $T = 1$ year
- Constant, riskless short rate $r = 5\%$
- Constant volatility $\sigma = 20\%$

In the BSM model, the index level at maturity is a random variable, given by Equation 1-1 with z being a standard normally distributed random variable.

Equation 1-1. Black-Scholes-Merton (1973) index level at maturity

$$S_T = S_0 \exp\left(\left(r - \frac{1}{2}\sigma^2\right)T + \sigma\sqrt{T}z\right)$$

The following is an *algorithmic description* of the Monte Carlo valuation procedure:

1. Draw I (pseudo)random numbers $z(i)$, $i \in \{1, 2, ..., I\}$, from the standard normal distribution.

2. Calculate all resulting index levels at maturity $S_T(i)$ for given $z(i)$ and Equation 1-1.

3. Calculate all inner values of the option at maturity as $h_T(i) = \max(S_T(i) - K, 0)$.

4. Estimate the option present value via the Monte Carlo estimator given in Equation 1-2.

Equation 1-2. Monte Carlo estimator for European option

$$C_0 \approx e^{-rT} \frac{1}{I} \sum_I h_T(i)$$

We are now going to translate this problem and algorithm into Python code. The reader might follow the single steps by using, for example, IPython—this is, however, not really necessary at this stage.

First, let us start with the parameter values. This is really easy:

```
S0 = 100.
K = 105.
T = 1.0
r = 0.05
sigma = 0.2
```

Next, the valuation algorithm. Here, we will for the first time use NumPy, which makes life quite easy for our second task:

```
from numpy import *

I = 100000

z = random.standard_normal(I)
ST = S0 * exp((r - 0.5 * sigma ** 2) * T + sigma * sqrt(T) * z)
hT = maximum(ST - K, 0)
C0 = exp(-r * T) * sum(hT) / I
```

Third, we print the result:

```
print "Value of the European Call Option %5.3f" % C0
```

The output might be:[4]

```
Value of the European Call Option 8.019
```

Three aspects are worth highlighting:

Syntax

The Python syntax is indeed quite close to the mathematical syntax, e.g., when it comes to the parameter value assignments.

Translation

Every mathematical and/or algorithmic statement can generally be translated into a *single* line of Python code.

---

4. The output of such a numerical simulation depends on the pseudorandom numbers used. Therefore, results might vary.

Vectorization

One of the strengths of NumPy is the compact, vectorized syntax, e.g., allowing for 100,000 calculations within a single line of code.

This code can be used in an interactive environment like IPython. However, code that is meant to be reused regularly typically gets organized in so-called *modules* (or *scripts*), which are single Python (i.e., text) files with the suffix .py. Such a module could in this case look like Example 1-1 and could be saved as a file named bsm_mcs_euro.py.

Example 1-1. Monte Carlo valuation of European call option

```
#
# Monte Carlo valuation of European call option
# in Black-Scholes-Merton model
# bsm_mcs_euro.py
#
import numpy as np

# Parameter Values
S0 = 100.  # initial index level
K = 105.  # strike price
T = 1.0  # time-to-maturity
r = 0.05  # riskless short rate
sigma = 0.2  # volatility

I = 100000  # number of simulations

# Valuation Algorithm
z = np.random.standard_normal(I)  # pseudorandom numbers
ST = S0 * np.exp((r - 0.5 * sigma ** 2) * T + sigma * np.sqrt(T) * z)
  # index values at maturity
hT = np.maximum(ST - K, 0)  # inner values at maturity
C0 = np.exp(-r * T) * np.sum(hT) / I  # Monte Carlo estimator

# Result Output
print "Value of the European Call Option %5.3f" % C0
```

The rather simple algorithmic example in this subsection illustrates that Python, with its very syntax, is well suited to complement the classic duo of scientific languages, English and Mathematics. It seems that adding Python to the set of scientific languages makes it more well rounded. We have

- **English** for *writing, talking* about scientific and financial problems, etc.
- **Mathematics** for *concisely and exactly describing and modeling* abstract aspects, algorithms, complex quantities, etc.
- **Python** for *technically modeling and implementing* abstract aspects, algorithms, complex quantities, etc.

Mathematics and Python Syntax

There is hardly any programming language that comes as close to mathematical syntax as Python. Numerical algorithms are therefore simple to translate from the mathematical representation into the Pythonic implementation. This makes prototyping, development, and code maintenance in such areas quite efficient with Python.

In some areas, it is common practice to use *pseudocode* and therewith to introduce a fourth language family member. The role of pseudocode is to represent, for example, financial algorithms in a more technical fashion that is both still close to the mathematical representation and already quite close to the technical implementation. In addition to the algorithm itself, pseudocode takes into account how computers work in principle.

This practice generally has its cause in the fact that with most programming languages the technical implementation is quite "far away" from its formal, mathematical representation. The majority of programming languages make it necessary to include so many elements that are only technically required that it is hard to see the equivalence between the mathematics and the code.

Nowadays, Python is often used in a *pseudocode way* since its syntax is almost analogous to the mathematics and since the technical "overhead" is kept to a minimum. This is accomplished by a number of high-level concepts embodied in the language that not only have their advantages but also come in general with risks and/or other costs. However, it is safe to say that with Python you can, whenever the need arises, follow the same strict implementation and coding practices that other languages might require from the outset. In that sense, Python can provide the best of both worlds: *high-level abstraction* and *rigorous implementation.*

Efficiency and Productivity Through Python

At a high level, benefits from using Python can be measured in three dimensions:

Efficiency
How can Python help in getting results faster, in saving costs, and in saving time?

Productivity
How can Python help in getting more done with the same resources (people, assets, etc.)?

Quality
What does Python allow us to do that we could not do with alternative technologies?

A discussion of these aspects can by nature not be exhaustive. However, it can highlight some arguments as a starting point.

Shorter time-to-results

A field where the efficiency of Python becomes quite obvious is interactive data analytics. This is a field that benefits strongly from such powerful tools as IPython and libraries like pandas.

Consider a finance student, writing her master's thesis and interested in Google stock prices. She wants to analyze historical stock price information for, say, five years to see how the volatility of the stock price has fluctuated over time. She wants to find evidence that volatility, in contrast to some typical model assumptions, fluctuates over time and is far from being constant. The results should also be visualized. She mainly has to do the following:

- Download Google stock price data from the Web.
- Calculate the rolling standard deviation of the log returns (volatility).
- Plot the stock price data and the results.

These tasks are complex enough that not too long ago one would have considered them to be something for professional financial analysts. Today, even the finance student can easily cope with such problems. Let us see how exactly this works—without worrying about syntax details at this stage (everything is explained in detail in subsequent chapters).

First, make sure to have available all necessary libraries:

```
In [1]: import numpy as np
        import pandas as pd
        import pandas.io.data as web
```

Second, retrieve the data from, say, Google itself:

```
In [2]: goog = web.DataReader('GOOG', data_source='google',
                start='3/14/2009', end='4/14/2014')
        goog.tail()
```

```
Out[2]:             Open    High    Low     Close   Volume
        Date
        2014-04-08  542.60  555.00  541.61  554.90  3152406
        2014-04-09  559.62  565.37  552.95  564.14  3324742
        2014-04-10  565.00  565.00  539.90  540.95  4027743
        2014-04-11  532.55  540.00  526.53  530.60  3916171
        2014-04-14  538.25  544.10  529.56  532.52  2568020

        5 rows × 5 columns
```

Third, implement the necessary analytics for the volatilities:

```
In [3]: goog['Log_Ret'] = np.log(goog['Close'] / goog['Close'].shift(1))
        goog['Volatility'] = pd.rolling_std(goog['Log_Ret'],
                                    window=252) * np.sqrt(252)
```

Fourth, plot the results. To generate an inline plot, we use the IPython magic command %matplotlib with the option inline:

```
In [4]: %matplotlib inline
        goog[['Close', 'Volatility']].plot(subplots=True, color='blue',
                                            figsize=(8, 6))
```

Figure 1-1 shows the graphical result of this brief interactive session with IPython. It can be considered almost amazing that four lines of code suffice to implement three rather complex tasks typically encountered in financial analytics: data gathering, complex and repeated mathematical calculations, and visualization of results. This example illustrates that pandas makes working with whole time series almost as simple as doing mathematical operations on floating-point numbers.

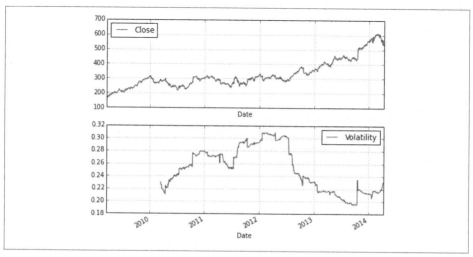

Figure 1-1. Google closing prices and yearly volatility

Translated to a professional finance context, the example implies that financial analysts can—when applying the right Python tools and libraries, providing high-level abstraction—focus on their very domain and not on the technical intrinsicalities. Analysts can react faster, providing valuable insights almost in real time and making sure they are one step ahead of the competition. This example of *increased efficiency* can easily translate into measurable bottom-line effects.

Ensuring high performance

In general, it is accepted that Python has a rather concise syntax and that it is relatively efficient to code with. However, due to the very nature of Python being an interpreted language, the *prejudice* persists that Python generally is too slow for compute-intensive tasks in finance. Indeed, depending on the specific implementation approach, Python can be really slow. But it *does not have to be slow*—it can be highly performing in almost any application area. In principle, one can distinguish at least three different strategies for better performance:

Paradigm

In general, many different ways can lead to the same result in Python, but with rather different performance characteristics; "simply" choosing the right way (e.g., a specific library) can improve results significantly.

Compiling

Nowadays, there are several performance libraries available that provide compiled versions of important functions or that compile Python code statically or dynamically (at runtime or call time) to machine code, which can be orders of magnitude faster; popular ones are Cython and Numba.

Parallelization

Many computational tasks, in particular in finance, can strongly benefit from parallel execution; this is nothing special to Python but something that can easily be accomplished with it.

Performance Computing with Python

Python per se is not a high-performance computing technology. However, Python has developed into an ideal platform to access current performance technologies. In that sense, Python has become something like a *glue language for performance computing*.

Later chapters illustrate all three techniques in detail. For the moment, we want to stick to a simple, but still realistic, example that touches upon all three techniques.

A quite common task in financial analytics is to evaluate complex mathematical expressions on large arrays of numbers. To this end, Python itself provides everything needed:

```
In [1]: loops = 25000000
        from math import *
        a = range(1, loops)
        def f(x):
            return 3 * log(x) + cos(x) ** 2
        %timeit r = [f(x) for x in a]

Out[1]: 1 loops, best of 3: 15 s per loop
```

The Python interpreter needs 15 seconds in this case to evaluate the function f 25,000,000 times.

The same task can be implemented using NumPy, which provides optimized (i.e., *precompiled*), functions to handle such array-based operations:

```
In [2]: import numpy as np
        a = np.arange(1, loops)
        %timeit r = 3 * np.log(a) + np.cos(a) ** 2

Out[2]: 1 loops, best of 3: 1.69 s per loop
```

Using NumPy considerably reduces the execution time to 1.7 seconds.

However, there is even a library specifically dedicated to this kind of task. It is called numexpr, for "numerical expressions." It *compiles* the expression to improve upon the performance of NumPy's general functionality by, for example, avoiding in-memory copies of arrays along the way:

```
In [3]: import numexpr as ne
        ne.set_num_threads(1)
        f = '3 * log(a) + cos(a) ** 2'
        %timeit r = ne.evaluate(f)

Out[3]: 1 loops, best of 3: 1.18 s per loop
```

Using this more specialized approach further reduces execution time to 1.2 seconds. However, numexpr also has built-in capabilities to parallelize the execution of the respective operation. This allows us to use all available threads of a CPU:

```
In [4]: ne.set_num_threads(4)
        %timeit r = ne.evaluate(f)

Out[4]: 1 loops, best of 3: 523 ms per loop
```

This brings execution time further down to 0.5 seconds in this case, with two cores and four threads utilized. Overall, this is a performance improvement of 30 times. Note, in particular, that this kind of improvement is possible without altering the basic problem/algorithm and without knowing anything about compiling and parallelization issues. The capabilities are accessible from a high level even by nonexperts. However, one has to be aware, of course, of which capabilities exist.

The example shows that Python provides a number of options to make more out of existing resources—i.e., to *increase productivity*. With the sequential approach, about 21 mn evaluations per second are accomplished, while the parallel approach allows for almost 48 mn evaluations per second—in this case simply by telling Python to use all available CPU threads instead of just one.

From Prototyping to Production

Efficiency in interactive analytics and performance when it comes to execution speed are certainly two benefits of Python to consider. Yet another major benefit of using Python for finance might at first sight seem a bit subtler; at second sight it might present itself as an important strategic factor. It is the possibility to use Python end to end, from *prototyping to production*.

Today's practice in financial institutions around the globe, when it comes to financial development processes, is often characterized by a separated, two-step process. On the one hand, there are the *quantitative analysts* ("quants") responsible for model development and technical prototyping. They like to use tools and environments like `Matlab` and `R` that allow for rapid, interactive application development. At this stage of the development efforts, issues like performance, stability, exception management, separation of data access, and analytics, among others, are not that important. One is mainly looking for a proof of concept and/or a prototype that exhibits the main desired features of an algorithm or a whole application.

Once the prototype is finished, IT departments with their *developers* take over and are responsible for translating the existing *prototype code* into reliable, maintainable, and performant *production code*. Typically, at this stage there is a paradigm shift in that languages like `C++` or `Java` are now used to fulfill the requirements for production. Also, a formal development process with professional tools, version control, etc. is applied.

This two-step approach has a number of generally unintended consequences:

Inefficiencies
    Prototype code is not reusable; algorithms have to be implemented twice; redundant efforts take time and resources.

Diverse skill sets
    Different departments show different skill sets and use different languages to implement "the same things."

Legacy code
    Code is available and has to be maintained in different languages, often using different styles of implementation (e.g., from an architectural point of view).

Using `Python`, on the other hand, enables a *streamlined* end-to-end process from the first interactive prototyping steps to highly reliable and efficiently maintainable production code. The communication between different departments becomes easier. The training of the workforce is also more streamlined in that there is only one major language covering all areas of financial application building. It also avoids the inherent inefficiencies and redundancies when using different technologies in different steps of the development process. All in all, `Python` can provide a *consistent technological framework* for almost all tasks in financial application development and algorithm implementation.

Conclusions

`Python` as a language—but much more so as an ecosystem—is an ideal technological framework for the financial industry. It is characterized by a number of benefits, like an elegant syntax, efficient development approaches, and usability for prototyping *and* production, among others. With its huge amount of available libraries and tools, Python seems to have answers to most questions raised by recent developments in the financial industry in terms of analytics, data volumes and frequency, compliance, and regulation, as well as technology itself. It has the potential to provide a *single, powerful, consistent framework* with which to streamline end-to-end development and production efforts even across larger financial institutions.

Further Reading

There are two books available that cover the use of Python in finance:

- Fletcher, Shayne and Christopher Gardner (2009): *Financial Modelling in Python*. John Wiley & Sons, Chichester, England.
- Hilpisch, Yves (2015): *Derivatives Analytics with Python*. Wiley Finance, Chichester, England. *http://derivatives-analytics-with-python.com*.

The quotes in this chapter are taken from the following resources:

- Crosman, Penny (2013): "Top 8 Ways Banks Will Spend Their 2014 IT Budgets." *Bank Technology News*.
- Deutsche Börse Group (2008): "The Global Derivatives Market—An Introduction." White paper.
- Ding, Cubillas (2010): "Optimizing the OTC Pricing and Valuation Infrastructure." *Celent study*.
- Lewis, Michael (2014): *Flash Boys*. W. W. Norton & Company, New York.
- Patterson, Scott (2010): *The Quants*. Crown Business, New York.

## CHAPTER 2

Infrastructure and Tools

Infrastructure is much more important than architecture.

— Rem Koolhaas

You could say infrastructure is not everything, but without infrastructure everything can be nothing—be it in the real world or in technology. What do we mean then by infrastructure? In principle, it is those hardware and software components that allow the development and execution of a simple Python script or more complex Python applications.

However, this chapter does not go into detail with regard to hardware infrastructure, since all Python code and examples should be executable on almost any hardware.[1] Nor does it discuss different operating systems, since the code should be executable on any operating system on which Python, in principle, is available. This chapter rather focuses on the following topics:

Deployment

How can I make sure to have everything needed available in a consistent fashion to deploy Python code and applications? This chapter introduces Anaconda, a Python distribution that makes deployment quite efficient, as well as the Python Quant Platform, which allows for a web- and browser-based deployment.

Tools

Which tools shall I use for (interactive) Python development and data analytics? The chapter introduces two of the most popular development environments for Python, namely IPython and Spyder.

---

1. They can, for example, in general be executed even on a Raspberry Pi for about 30 USD (cf. *http://www.raspberrypi.org*), although memory issues quickly arise for some applications. Nevertheless, this can be considered a rather low requirement when it comes to hardware.

There is also Appendix A, on:

Best practices
Which best practices should I follow when developing Python code? The appendix briefly reviews fundamentals of, for example, Python code syntax and documentation.

Python Deployment

This section shows how to deploy Python locally (or on a server) as well as via the web browser.

Anaconda

A number of operating systems come with a version of Python and a number of additional libraries already installed. This is true, for example, of Linux operating systems, which often rely on Python as their main language (for packaging, administration, etc.). However, in what follows we assume that Python is not installed or that we are installing an additional version of Python (in parallel to an existing one) using the Anaconda distribution.

You can download Anaconda for your operating system from the website *http://contin uum.io/downloads*. There are a couple of reasons to consider using Anaconda for Python deployment. Among them are:

Libraries/packages
You get more than 100 of the most important Python libraries and packages in a single installation step; in particular, you get all these installed in a version-consistent manner (i.e., all libraries and packages work with each other).[2]

Open source
The Anaconda distribution is free of charge in general,[3] as are all libraries and packages included in the distribution.

Cross platform
It is available for Windows, Mac OS, and Linux platforms.

---

2. For those who want to control which libraries and packages get installed, there is Miniconda, which comes with a minimal Python installation only. Cf. *http://conda.pydata.org/miniconda.html*.

3. There is also an Anaconda version available that contains proprietary packages from Continuum Analytics called Accelerate. This commercial version, whose main goal is to improve the performance of typical operations with Python, has to be licensed.

Separate installation

It installs into a separate directory without interfering with any existing installation; no root/admin rights are needed.

Automatic updates

Libraries and packages included in Anaconda can be (semi)automatically updated via free online repositories.

Conda package manager

The package manager allows the use of multiple Python versions and multiple versions of libraries in parallel (for experimentation or development/testing purposes); it also has great support for virtual environments.

After having downloaded the installer for Anaconda, the installation in general is quite easy. On Windows platforms, just double-click the installer file and follow the instructions. Under Linux, open a shell, change to the directory where the installer file is located, and type:

```
$ bash Anaconda-1.x.x-Linux-x86[_64].sh
```

Replacing the file name with the respective name of your installer file. Then again follow the instructions. It is the same on an Apple computer; just type:

```
$ bash Anaconda-1.x.x-MacOSX-x86_64.sh
```

making sure you replace the name given here with the correct one. Alternatively, you can use the graphical installer that is available.

After the installation you have more than 100 libraries and packages available that you can use immediately. Among the scientific and data analytics packages are those listed in Table 2-1.

Table 2-1. Selected libraries and packages included in Anaconda

Name	Description
BitArray	Object types for arrays of Booleans
Cubes OLAP	Framework for Online Analytical Processing (OLAP) applications
Disco	mapreduce implementation for distributed computing
Gdata	Implementation of Google Data Protocol
h5py	Python wrapper around HDF5 file format
HDF5	File format for fast I/O operations
IPython	Interactive development environment (IDE)
lxml	Processing XML and HTML with Python
matplotlib	Standard 2D and 3D plotting library
MPI4Py	Message Parsing Interface (MPI) implementation for parallel computation
MPICH2	Another MPI implementation

Name	Description
NetworkX	Building and analyzing network models and algorithms
numexpr	Optimized execution of numerical expressions
NumPy	Powerful array class and optimized functions on it
pandas	Efficient handling of time series data
PyTables	Hierarchical database using HDF5
SciPy	Collection of scientific functions
Scikit-Learn	Machine learning algorithms
Spyder	Python IDE with syntax checking, debugging, and inspection capabilities
statsmodels	Statistical models
SymPy	Symbolic computation and mathematics
Theano	Mathematical expression compiler

If the installation procedure was successful, you should open a new terminal window and should then be able, for example, to start the Spyder IDE by simply typing in the shell:

```
$ spyder
```

Alternatively, you can start a Python session from the shell as follows:

```
$ python
Python 2.7.6 |Anaconda 1.9.2 (x86_64)| (default, Feb 10 2014, 17:56:29)
[GCC 4.0.1 (Apple Inc. build 5493)] on darwin
Type "help", "copyright", "credits" or "license" for more information.
>>> exit()
$
```

Anaconda by default installs, at the time of this writing, with Python 2.7.x. It always comes with conda, the open source package manager. Useful information about this tool can be obtained by the command:

```
$ conda info
Current conda install:

             platform : osx-64
        conda version : 3.4.1
       python version : 2.7.6.final.0
     root environment : /Library/anaconda  (writable)
  default environment : /Library/anaconda
      envs directories : /Library/anaconda/envs
        package cache : /Library/anaconda/pkgs
          channel URLs : http://repo.continuum.io/pkgs/free/osx-64/
                         http://repo.continuum.io/pkgs/pro/osx-64/
          config file : None
    is foreign system : False
```

```
$
```

conda allows one to search for libraries and packages, both locally and in available online repositories:

```
$ conda search pytables
Fetching package metadata: ..
pytables               .  2.4.0           np17py27_0  defaults
                          2.4.0           np17py26_0  defaults
                          2.4.0           np16py27_0  defaults
                          2.4.0           np16py26_0  defaults
                       .  3.0.0           np17py27_0  defaults
                          3.0.0           np17py26_0  defaults
                          3.0.0           np16py27_0  defaults
                          3.0.0           np16py26_0  defaults
                       .  3.0.0           np17py33_1  defaults
                       .  3.0.0           np17py27_1  defaults
                          3.0.0           np17py26_1  defaults
                       .  3.0.0           np16py27_1  defaults
                          3.0.0           np16py26_1  defaults
                          3.1.0           np18py33_0  defaults
                       *  3.1.0           np18py27_0  defaults
                          3.1.0           np18py26_0  defaults
                          3.1.1           np18py34_0  defaults
                          3.1.1           np18py33_0  defaults
                          3.1.1           np18py27_0  defaults
                          3.1.1           np18py26_0  defaults
```

The results contain those versions of PyTables that are available for download and installation in this case and that are installed (indicated by the asterisk). Similary, the list command gives all locally installed packages that match a certain pattern. The following lists all packages that start with "pyt":

```
$ conda list ^pyt
# packages in environment at /Library/anaconda:
#
pytables              3.1.0              np18py27_0
pytest                2.5.2                 py27_0
python                2.7.6                      1
python-dateutil       1.5                    <pip>
python.app            1.2                   py27_1
pytz                  2014.2                py27_0
```

More complex patterns, based on regular expressions, are also possible. For example:

```
$ conda list ^p.*les$
# packages in environment at /Library/anaconda:
#
pytables              3.1.0              np18py27_0
$
```

Suppose we want to have `Python 3.x` available in addition to the `2.7.x` version. The package manager conda allows the creation of an environment in which to accomplish this goal. The following output shows how this works in principle:

```
$ conda create -n py33test anaconda=1.9 python=3.3 numpy=1.8
Fetching package metadata: ..
Solving package specifications: .
Package plan for installation in environment /Library/anaconda/envs/py33test:

The following packages will be downloaded:

    package                    |             build
    ---------------------------|-----------------
    anaconda-1.9.2             |        np18py33_0           2 KB
    ...
    xlsxwriter-0.5.2          |           py33_0           168 KB

The following packages will be linked:

    package                    |             build
    ---------------------------|-----------------
    anaconda-1.9.2             |        np18py33_0    hard-link
    ...
    zlib-1.2.7                 |               1     hard-link

Proceed ([y]/n)?
```

When you type **y** to confirm the creation, conda will do as proposed (i.e., downloading, extracting, and linking the packages):

```
******UPDATE**********

Fetching packages ...
anaconda-1.9.2-np18py33_0.tar.bz2 100% |#########| Time: 0:00:00 173.62 kB/s
...
xlsxwriter-0.5.2-py33_0.tar.bz2 100% |###########| Time: 0:00:01 131.32 kB/s
Extracting packages ...
[        COMPLETE        ] |######################| 100%
Linking packages ...
[        COMPLETE        ] |######################| 100%
#
# To activate this environment, use:
# $ source activate py33test
#
# To deactivate this environment, use:
# $ source deactivate
#
```

Now activate the new environment as advised by conda:

```
$ source activate py33test
discarding /Library/anaconda/bin from PATH
prepending /Library/anaconda/envs/py33test/bin to PATH
```

```
(py33test)$ python
Python 3.3.4 |Anaconda 1.9.2 (x86_64)| (default, Feb 10 2014, 17:56:29)
[GCC 4.0.1 (Apple Inc. build 5493)] on darwin
Type "help", "copyright", "credits" or "license" for more information.
>>> print "Hello Python 3.3"  # this shouldn't work with Python 3.3
  File "<stdin>", line 1
    print "Hello Python 3.3"  # this shouldn't work with Python 3.3
                          ^
SyntaxError: invalid syntax
>>> print ("Hello Python 3.3")  # this syntax should work
Hello Python 3.3
>>> exit()
$
```

Obviously, we indeed are now in the Python 3.3 world, which you can judge from the
Python version number displayed and the fact that you need parentheses for the print
statement to work correctly.[4]

Multiple Python Environments

With the conda package manager you can install and use multiple
separated Python environments on a single machine. This, among
other features, simplifies testing of Python code for compatibility with
different Python versions.

Single libraries and packages can be installed using the conda install command, either
in the general Anaconda installation:

```
$ conda install scipy
```

or for a specific environment, as in:

```
$ conda install -n py33test scipy
```

Here, py33test is the environment we created before. Similarly, you can update single
packages easily:

```
$ conda update pandas
```

The packages to download and link depend on the respective version of the package
that is installed. These can be very few to numerous, e.g., when a package has a number
of dependencies for which no current version is installed. For our newly created environment, the updating would take the form:

```
$ conda update -n py33test pandas
```

---

4. This is only one subtle, but harmless, change in the Python syntax from 2.7.x to 3.x that might be a bit
   confusing to someone new to Python.

Finally, conda makes it easy to remove packages with the remove command from the main installation or a specific environment. The basic usage is:

```
$ conda remove scipy
```

For an environment it is:

```
$ conda remove -n py33test scipy
```

Since the removal is a somewhat "final" operation, you might want to *dry run* the command:

```
$ conda remove --dry-run -n py33test scipy
```

If you are sure, you can go ahead with the actual removal. To get back to the original Python and Anaconda version, deactivate the environment:

```
$ source deactivate
```

Finally, we can clean up the whole environment by use of remove with the option --all:

```
$ conda remove --all -n py33test
```

The package manager conda makes Python deployment quite convenient. Apart from the basic functionalities illustrated in this section, there are also a number of more advanced features available. Detailed documentation is found at *http://conda.pyda ta.org/docs/*.

Python Quant Platform

There are a number of reasons why one might like to deploy Python via a web browser. Among them are:

No need for installation
Local installations of a complete Python environment might be both complex (e.g., in a large organization with many computers), and costly to support and maintain; making Python available via a web browser makes deployment much more efficient in certain scenarios.

Use of (better) remote hardware
When it comes to complex, compute- and memory-intensive analytics tasks, a local computer might not be able to perform such tasks; the use of (multiple) shared servers with multiple cores, larger memories, and maybe GPGPUs makes such tasks possible and more efficient.

Collaboration
Working, for example, with a team on a single or multiple servers makes collaboration simpler and also increases efficiency: data is not moved to every local machine, nor, after the analytics tasks are finished, are the results moved back to some central storage unit and/or distributed among the team members.

The `Python Quant Platform` is a web- and browser-based financial analytics and collaboration platform developed and maintained by The Python Quants GmbH (*http://www.pythonquants.com*). You can register for the platform at *http://quant-platform.com*. It features, among others, the following basic components:

File manager

> A tool to manage file up/downloads and more via a web GUI.

`Linux` *terminal*

> A `Linux` terminal to work with the server (for example, a virtual server instance in the cloud or a dedicated server run on-premise by a company); you can use `Vim`, `Nano`, etc. for code editing and work with `Git` repositories for version control.

Anaconda

> An Anaconda installation that provides all the functionality discussed previously; by default you can choose between `Python 2.7` and `Python 3.4`.

Python *shell*

> The standard `Python` shell.

`IPython` *Shell*

> An enhanced `IPython` shell.

`IPython Notebook`

> The browser version of `IPython`. You will generally use this as the central tool.

Chat room/forum

> To collaborate, exchange ideas, and to up/download, for example, research documents.

Advanced analytics

> In addition to the `Linux` server and `Python` environments, the platform provides analytical capabilities for, e.g., portfolio, risk, and derivatives analytics as well as for backtesting trading strategies (in particular, `DX` analytics; see Part III for a simplified but fully functional version of the library); there is also an `R` stack available to call, for example, `R` functions from within `IPython Notebook`.

Standard APIs

> Standard `Python`-based APIs for data delivery services of leading financial data providers.

When it comes to collaboration, the `Python Quant Platform` also allows one to define —under a "company"—certain "user groups" with certain rights for different `Python` projects (i.e., directories and files). The platform is easily scalable and is deployed via `Docker` containers (*http://docker.com*). Figure 2-1 shows a screenshot of the main screen of the `Python Quant Platform`.

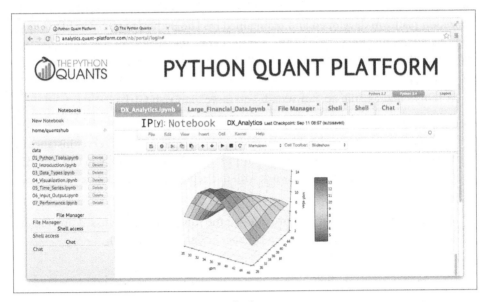

Figure 2-1. Screenshot of Python Quant Platform

Tools

The success and popularity of a programming language result to some extent from the tools that are available to work with the language. It has long been the case that Python was considered a nice, easy-to-learn and easy-to-use language, but without a compelling set of tools for interactive analytics or development. This has changed. There are now a large number of tools available that help analysts and developers to be as productive as possible with Python. It is not possible to give even a somewhat exhaustive overview. However, it is possible to highlight two of the most popular tools in use today: IPython and Spyder.[5]

Python

For completeness, let us first consider using the standard Python interpreter itself. From the system shell/command-line interface, Python is invoked by simply typing python:

```
$ python
Python 2.7.6 |Anaconda 1.9.2 (x86_64)| (default, Feb 10 2014, 17:56:29)
[GCC 4.0.1 (Apple Inc. build 5493)] on darwin
```

5. For Windows users and developers, the full integration of Python in Visual Studio is a compelling alternative. There is even a whole suite of Python tools for Visual Studio available (cf. *http://pytools.code plex.com*).

```
Type "help", "copyright", "credits" or "license" for more information.
>>> print "Hello Python for Finance World."
Hello Python for Finance World.
>>> exit()
$
```

Although you can do quite a bit of Python with the standard prompt, most people prefer to use IPython by default since this environment provides *everything* that the standard interpreter prompt offers, and *much more* on top of that.

IPython

IPython was used in Chapter 1 to present the first examples of Python code. This section gives an overview of the capabilities of IPython through specific examples. A complete ecosystem has evolved around IPython that is so successful and appealing that users of other languages make use of the basic approach and architecture it provides. For example, there is a version of IPython for the Julia language (*http://julialang.org*).

From shell to browser

IPython comes in three flavors:

Shell

> The shell version is based on the system and Python shell, as the name suggests; there are no graphical capabilities included (apart from displaying plots in a separate window).

QT console

> This version is based on the QT graphical user interface framework (cf. *http://qt-project.org*), is more feature-rich, and allows, for example, for inline graphics.

Notebook

> This is a JavaScript-based web browser version that has become the community favorite for interactive analytics and also for teaching, presenting, etc.

The shell version is invoked by simply typing ipython in the shell:

```
$ ipython
Python 2.7.6 |Anaconda 1.9.2 (x86_64)| (default, Feb 10 2014, 17:56:29)
Type "copyright", "credits" or "license" for more information.

IPython 2.0.0 -- An enhanced Interactive Python.
?         -> Introduction and overview of IPython's features.
%quickref -> Quick reference.
help      -> Python's own help system.
object?   -> Details about 'object', use 'object??' for extra details.

In [1]: 3 + 4 * 2

Out[1]: 11
```

```
In [2]:
```

Using the option --pylab imports a large set of scientific and data analysis libraries, like NumPy, in the namespace:

```
$ ipython --pylab
Python 2.7.6 |Anaconda 1.9.2 (x86_64)| (default, Feb 10 2014, 17:56:29)
Type "copyright", "credits" or "license" for more information.

IPython 2.0.0 -- An enhanced Interactive Python.
?         -> Introduction and overview of IPython's features.
%quickref -> Quick reference.
help      -> Python's own help system.
object?   -> Details about 'object', use 'object??' for extra details.
Using matplotlib backend: MacOSX

In [1]: a = linspace(0, 20, 5)  # linspace from NumPy

In [2]: a

Out[2]: array([ 0.,    5.,   10.,   15.,   20.])

In [3]:
```

Similarly, the QT console of IPython is invoked by the following command:

```
$ ipython qtconsole --pylab inline
```

Using the inline parameter in addition to the --pylab option lets IPython plot all graphics inline. Figure 2-2 shows a screenshot of the QT console with an inline plot.

Finally, the Notebook version is invoked as follows:

```
$ ipython notebook --pylab inline
```

Figure 2-3 shows a screenshot of an IPython Notebook session. The inline option again has the effect that plots will be displayed in IPython Notebook and not in a separate window.

All in all, there are a large number of options for how to invoke an IPython kernel. You can get a listing of all the options by typing:

```
$ ipython --h
```

Refer to the IPython documentation (*http://www.ipython.org/documentation.html*) for detailed explanations.

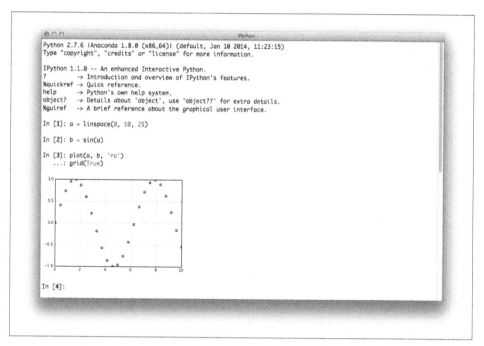

Figure 2-2. IPython's QT console

Basic usage

In what follows, we describe the basic usage of the IPython Notebook. A fundamental concept of the Notebook is that you work with different kinds of cells. These include the following types:

Code
Contains executable Python code

Markdown
Contains text written in Markdown language and/or HTML

Raw text
Contains text without formatting[6]

Heading (1-6)
Headings for text structuring, e.g., section heads

---

6. From IPython 2.0 on, these cells are called Raw NBConvert.

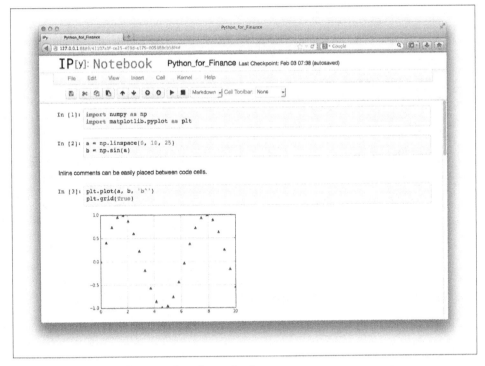

Figure 2-3. IPython's browser-based Notebook

The different cell types already indicate that the Notebook is more than an enhanced Python shell only. It is intended to fulfill the requirements of a multitude of documentation and presentation scenarios. For example, an IPython Notebook file, having a suffix of .ipynb, can be converted to the following formats:

Python *file*
> Generates a Python code file (.py) from an IPython Notebook file with noncode cells commented out.

HTML *page*
> Generates a single HTML page from a single IPython Notebook file.

HTML5 *slides*
> Making use of different cell markings for slide shows, a Notebook file is converted into a presentation with multiple HTML5 slides (using the reveal.js framework (*http://lab.hakim.se/reveal-js/*)).

LaTeX/PDF
> Such a file can also be converted to a LaTeX file, which then can be converted into a PDF document.

RestructuredText

RestructuredText (.rst) is used, for example, by the SPHINX documentation package (*http://sphinx-doc.org*) for Python projects.

Analytics and Publishing Platform

A major advantage of IPython Notebook is that you can easily publish and share your complete Notebook with others. Once your analytics project with IPython is finished, you can publish it as an HTML page or a PDF, or use the content for a slide presentation.

The format of an IPython Notebook file is based on the JavaScript Object Notation (JSON) standard. The following is the text version of the Notebook displayed in Figure 2-3—you will notice some metadata, the different types of cells, and their content, and that even graphics are translated into ASCII characters:

```
{
 "metadata": {
  "name": ""
 },
 "nbformat": 3,
 "nbformat_minor": 0,
 "worksheets": [
  {
   "cells": [
    {
     "cell_type": "code",
     "collapsed": false,
     "input": [
      "import numpy as np\n",
      "import matplotlib.pyplot as plt"
     ],
     "language": "python",
     "metadata": {},
     "outputs": [],
     "prompt_number": 1
    },
    {
     "cell_type": "code",
     "collapsed": false,
     "input": [
      "a = np.linspace(0, 10, 25)\n",
      "b = np.sin(a)"
     ],
     "language": "python",
     "metadata": {},
     "outputs": [],
     "prompt_number": 2
    },
```

```json
{
  "cell_type": "markdown",
  "metadata": {},
  "source": [
    "Inline comments can be easily placed between code cells."
  ]
},
{
  "cell_type": "code",
  "collapsed": false,
  "input": [
    "plt.plot(a, b, 'b^')\n",
    "plt.grid(True)"
  ],
  "language": "python",
  "metadata": {},
  "outputs": [
    {
      "metadata": {},
      "output_type": "display_data",
      "png": "iVBORw0KGgoAAAAN...SuQmCC\n",
      "text": [
        "<matplotlib.figure.Figure at 0x105812a10>"
      ]
    }
  ],
  "prompt_number": 3
}
],
"metadata": {}
}
]
}
```

For example, when converting such a file to LaTeX, raw text cells can contain LaTeX code since the content of such cells is simply passed on by the converter. All this is one of the reasons why the IPython Notebook is nowadays often used for the composition of larger, more complex documents, like scientific research papers. You have executable code and documenting text in a single file that can be translated into a number of different output formats.

In a finance context this also makes IPython a valuable tool, since, for example, the mathematical description of an algorithm and the executable Python version can live in the same document. Depending on the usage scenario, a web page (e.g., intranet), a PDF document (e.g., client mailings), or a presentation (e.g., board meeting) can be generated. With regard to the presentation option, you can, for example, skip those cells that may contain text passages that might be too long for a presentation.

The basic usage of the Notebook is quite intuitive. You mainly navigate it with the arrow keys and "execute" cells by using either Shift-Return or Ctrl-Return. The difference is that the first option moves you automatically to the next cell after execution while the second option lets you remain at the same cell. The effect of "executing" cells depends on the type of the cell. If it is a code cell, then the code is executed and the output (if any) is shown. If it is a `Markdown` cell, the content is rendered to show the result.

Markdown and LaTeX

The following shows a few selected examples for `Markdown` commands:

```
**bold** prints the text in bold

*italic* prints the text in italic

_italic_ also prints it in italic

**_italic_** bold and italic

bullet point lists:

* first_bullet
* second_bullet

&ndash; renders to a dash

<br> inserts a line break
```

Figure 2-4 shows the same code both in a raw text cell (which looks the same as the preceding text) and rendered in a `Markdown` cell. In this way, you can easily combine `Python` code and formatted, nicely rendered text in a single document.

A detailed description of the `Markdown` language used for `IPython Notebook` is found at *http://daringfireball.net/projects/markdown/*.

As mentioned before, the rendering capabilities of `IPython` are not restricted to the `Markdown` language. `IPython` also renders by default mathematical formulae described on the basis of the `LaTeX` typesetting system, the de facto standard for scientific publishing. Consider, for example, from Chapter 1 the formula for the index level in the Black-Scholes-Merton (1973) model, as provided in Equation 1-1. For convenience, we repeat it here as Equation 2-1.

Equation 2-1. Black-Scholes-Merton (1973) index level at maturity

$$S_T = S_0 \exp\left(\left(r - \frac{1}{2}\sigma^2\right)T + \sigma\sqrt{T}z\right)$$

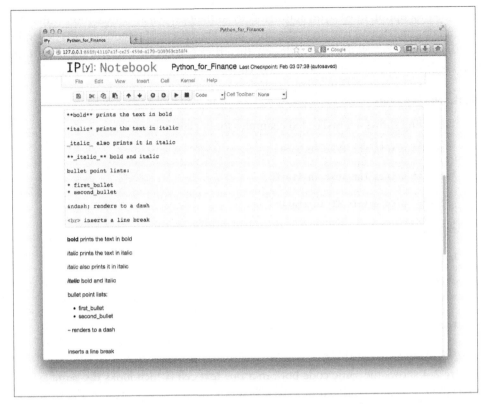

Figure 2-4. Screenshot of IPython Notebook with Markdown rendering

The LaTeX code that describes Equation 2-1 looks roughly like the following:

```
S_T = S_0 \exp((r - 0.5\sigma^2) T + \sigma \sqrt{T} z)
```

Figure 2-5 shows a raw text cell with Markdown text and the LaTeX code, as well as the result as rendered in a Markdown cell. The figure also shows a more complex formula: the Black-Scholes-Merton option pricing formula for European call options, as found in Equation 3-1 in Chapter 3.

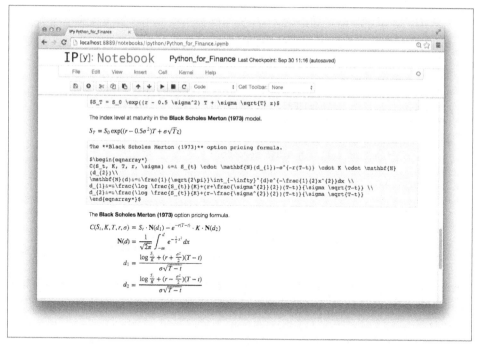

Figure 2-5. Markdown and LaTeX for financial formulae

Magic commands

One of IPython's strengths lies in its magic commands. They are "magic" in the sense that they add some really helpful and powerful functions to the standard Python shell functionality. Basic information and help about these functions can be accessed via:

```
In [1]: %magic
```

```
IPython's 'magic' functions
===============================
```

```
The magic function system provides a series of functions which allow you to
control the behavior of IPython itself, plus a lot of system-type
features. There are two kinds of magics, line-oriented and cell-oriented.
```

```
...
```

A list of all available magic commands can be generated in an IPython session as follows:

```
In [2]: %lsmagic
```

In interactive computing, magic commands can, for example, be used for simple profiling tasks. For such a use case, you might use %time or %prun:

```
In [3]: import numpy as np

In [4]: %time np.sin(np.arange(1000000))
CPU times: user 31.8 ms, sys: 7.87 ms, total: 39.7 ms
Wall time: 39 ms

Out[5]:
array([ 0.        ,  0.84147098,  0.90929743, ...,  0.21429647,
       -0.70613761, -0.97735203])

In [6]: %prun np.sin(np.arange(1000000))
         3 function calls in 0.043 seconds

   Ordered by: internal time

   ncalls  tottime  percall  cumtime  percall filename:lineno(function)
        1    0.041    0.041    0.043    0.043 <string>:1(<module>)
        1    0.002    0.002    0.002    0.002 {numpy.core.multiarray.arange}
        1    0.000    0.000    0.000    0.000 {method 'disable'
        of '_lsprof.Profiler' objects}
```

There is yet another command, %timeit or %%timeit, for timing codes in a single line
or a whole cell in the IPython Notebook:

```
In [6]: %timeit np.sin(np.arange(1000000))
10 loops, best of 3: 27.5 ms per loop
```

This function executes a number of loops to get more reliable estimates for the duration
of a function call or a snippet of code.

It is not possible to explain in detail all the magic functions that IPython provides.
However, IPython itself strives to make it as easy as possible to interactively look up
information about IPython and its commands. Among the most helpful are those listed
in Table 2-2 (cf. *http://bit.ly/ipython_tutorial*).

Table 2-2. Selected help functions included in IPython

Name	Description
?	Introduction and overview of IPython features
%quickref	Quick reference
help	Python's own help system
object?	Details about the "object"; use object?? for extra details

Another feature of IPython is that it is highly configurable. Information about the configuration capabilities is also found in the documentation (*http://ipython.org/ipython-
doc/stable/config/*).

A magic command that also helps with customizing IPython is %bookmark. This allows
the bookmarking of arbitrary directories by the use of your custom names such that
you can later—no matter where the IPython kernel is invoked from and no matter what

the current directory is—navigate to any of your bookmarked directories immediately (i.e., you do not need to use cd). The following shows how to set a bookmark and how to get a list of all bookmarks:

```
In [6]: %bookmark py4fi

In [7]: %bookmark -l
Current bookmarks:
py4fi -> /Users/yhilpisch/Documents/Work/Python4Finance/
```

System shell commands

Yet another really helpful feature is that you can execute command-line/system shell functions directly from an IPython prompt or a Notebook cell. To this end you need to use the ! to indicate that the following command should be escaped to the system shell (or %%! when a complete cell should be handled that way). As a simple illustration, the following creates a directory, moves to that directory, moves back, and deletes the directory:

```
In [7]: !mkdir python4finance

In [8]: cd python4finance/
/Users/yhilpisch/python4finance

In [9]: cd ..
/Users/yhilpisch

In [10]: !rm -rf python4finance/
```

IPython provides you with all the functions you would expect from a powerful interactive development environment. It is often the case that people, beginners and experts alike, even find their way to Python via IPython. Throughout the book, there are a plentitude of examples illustrating the use of IPython for interactive data and financial analytics. You should also consult the book by McKinney (2012), and in particular Chapter 3, for further information on how to use IPython effectively.

Spyder

While IPython satisfies all of most users' requirements for interactive analytics and prototyping, larger projects generally demand "something more." In particular, IPython itself has no editor directly built into the application.[7] For all those looking for a more traditional development environment, Spyder might therefore be a good choice.

---

7. However, you can configure your favorite editor for IPython and invoke it by the magic command %editor FILENAME.

Similar to IPython, Spyder has been designed to support rapid, interactive development with Python. However, it also has, for example, a full-fledged editor, more powerful project management and debugging capabilities, and an object and variable inspector as well as a full integration of the IPython shell version. Within Spyder you can also start a standard Python prompt session.

The built-in editor of Spyder provides all you need to do Python development. Among other features (cf. *http://code.google.com/p/spyderlib/wiki/Features*), it offers the following:

Highlighting
Syntax coloring for Python, C/C++, and Fortran code; occurrence highlighting

Introspection
Powerful dynamic code introspection features (e.g., code completion, calltips, object definition with a mouse click)

Code browser
Browsing of classes and functions

Project management
Defining and managing projects; generating to-do lists

Instant code checking
Getting errors and warnings on the fly (by using pyflakes, cf. *https://pypi.python.org/pypi/pyflakes*)

Debugging
Setting breakpoints and conditional breakpoints to use with the Python debugger pdb (cf. *http://docs.python.org/2/library/pdb.html*)

In addition, Spyder provides further helpful functionality:

Consoles
Open multiple Python and IPython consoles with separate processes each; run the code from the active editor tab (or parts of it) in a console

Variable explorer
Edit and compare variables and arrays; generate 2D plots of arrays on the fly; inspect variables while debugging

Object inspector
Display documentation strings interactively; automatically render, for example, rich text formatting

Other features

History log; array editor similar to a spreadsheet; direct access to online help; management and exploration of whole projects; syntax and code checking via `Pylint` (*http://www.pylint.org*).

Figure 2-6 provides a screenshot of `Spyder` showing the text editor (on the left), the variable inspector (upper right), and an active `Python` console (lower right). `Spyder` is a good choice to start with `Python` programming, especially for those who are used, for example, to such environments as those provided by `Matlab` or `R`. However, advanced programmers will also find a lot of helpful development functionality under a single roof.

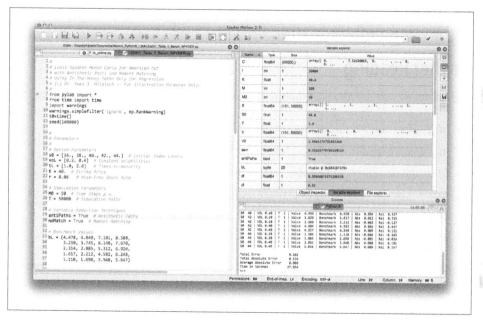

Figure 2-6. Screenshot of Spyder

Conclusions

If you are a beginner or casual `Python` developer or an expert coming from a different programming background, getting started with `Python` is generally pretty easy in that only a couple of simple steps are required. To begin, you should install an appropriate `Python` distribution, like `Anaconda`, to have a consistent `Python` environment available and also to simplify the regular updating procedures.

With a distribution like `Anaconda` you have available the most important tools to interactively practice data and financial analytics, like with `IPython`, or to develop larger applications in a more traditional implement-test-debug fashion, like with Spyder. Of course, you can add to the mix your favorite editor, which probably already has Python syntax highlighting included. If you additionally are looking for syntax and code checking capabilities, you might consider the built-in Spyder editor or any other Python-focused editor available.

Appendix A introduces a number of best practices in the areas of *syntax, documentation*, and *unit testing*. In terms of syntax, spaces and blank lines play an important role, as well as the indentation of code blocks. When it comes to documentation, you should consider including documentation strings in any function or class, providing background and help for such things as input parameters, output, and possible errors, as well as usage examples. Finally, you should include unit tests in your development process from the beginning (at least for larger projects or those shared with a broader user base) and use dedicated tools to simplify the test procedures.

Further Reading

The following web resources are helpful with regard to the topics covered in this chapter:

- *http://docs.continuum.io/anaconda/* for the Anaconda documentation
- *http://conda.pydata.org/docs/* for the conda documentation
- *http://ipython.org/ipython-doc/stable/* for the IPython documentation
- *http://daringfireball.net/projects/markdown/* for the Markdown language used by IPython Notebook
- *http://code.google.com/p/spyderlib* for information about Spyder

A good introduction to Python deployment and the use of IPython as a development environment is provided in:

- Wes McKinney (2012): *Python for Data Analysis*. O'Reilly, Sebastopol, CA.

## CHAPTER 3

Introductory Examples

> Quantitative analysis, as we define it, is the application of
> mathematical and/or statistical methods to market data.
>
> — John Forman

This chapter dives into some concrete examples from *quantitative finance* to illustrate how convenient and powerful it is to use Python and its libraries for financial analytics. The focus lies on the flow of the exposition, and a number of details that might be important in real-world applications are not touched upon. Also, details of Python usage are mainly skipped because later chapters explain them further.

Specifically, this chapter presents the following examples:

Implied volatilities
> Option quotes for certain maturity dates are taken to back out the implied volatilities of these options and to plot them—a task option traders and risk managers, among others, are faced with on a daily basis.

Monte Carlo simulation
> The evolution of a stock index over time is simulated via Monte Carlo techniques, selected results are visualized, and European option values are calculated. Monte Carlo simulation is a cornerstone for numerical option pricing as well as for risk management efforts involving value-at-risk calculations or credit value adjustments.

Technical analysis
> An analysis of historical time series data is implemented to backtest an investment strategy based on trend signals; both professional investors and ambitious amateurs regularly engage in this kind of investment analysis.

All examples have to deal in some ways with date-time information. Appendix C introduces handling such information with Python, NumPy, and pandas.

Implied Volatilities

Given an option pricing formula like the seminal one of Black-Scholes-Merton (1973), *implied volatilities* are those volatility values that, *ceteris paribus*, when put into the formula, give observed market quotes for different option strikes and maturities. In this case, the volatility is not an input parameter for the model/formula, but the result of a (numerical) optimization procedure given that formula.

The example we consider in the following discussion is about a new generation of options, namely volatility options on the VSTOXX volatility index. Eurex, the derivatives exchange that provides these options on the VSTOXX and respective futures contracts, established a comprehensive Python-based tutorial called "VSTOXX Advanced Services" (*http://www.eurexchange.com/advanced-services/*) in June 2013 about the index and its derivatives contracts.[1]

However, before proceeding with the VSTOXX options themselves, let us first reproduce in Equation 3-1 the famous Black-Scholes-Merton formula for the pricing of European call options on an underlying without dividends.

Equation 3-1. Black-Scholes-Merton (1973) option pricing formula

$$C(S_t, K, t, T, r, \sigma) = S_t \cdot N(d_1) - e^{-r(T-t)} \cdot K \cdot N(d_2)$$

$$N(d) = \frac{1}{\sqrt{2\pi}} \int_{-\infty}^{d} e^{-\frac{1}{2}x^2} dx$$

$$d_1 = \frac{\log \frac{S_t}{K} + \left(r + \frac{\sigma^2}{2}\right)(T-t)}{\sigma\sqrt{T-t}}$$

$$d_2 = \frac{\log \frac{S_t}{K} + \left(r - \frac{\sigma^2}{2}\right)(T-t)}{\sigma\sqrt{T-t}}$$

The different parameters have the following meaning:

---

1. Chapter 19 also deals with options based on the VSTOXX volatility index; it calibrates an option pricing model to market quotes and values American, nontraded options given the calibrated model.

S_t

Price/level of the underlying at time t

σ

Constant volatility (i.e., standard deviation of returns) of the underlying

K

Strike price of the option

T

Maturity date of the option

r

Constant riskless short rate

Consider now that an option quote for a European call option C^* is given. The implied volatility σ^{imp} is the quantity that solves the implicit Equation 3-2.

Equation 3-2. Implied volatility given market quote for option

$$C\left(S_t, K, t, T, r, \sigma^{imp}\right) = C^*$$

There is no closed-form solution to this equation, such that one has to use a numerical solution procedure like the Newton scheme to estimate the correct solution. This scheme iterates, using the first derivative of the relevant function, until a certain number of iterations or a certain degree of precision is reached. Formally, we have Equation 3-3 for some starting value σ_0^{imp} and for $0 < n < \infty$.

Equation 3-3. Newton scheme for numerically solving equations

$$\sigma_{n+1}^{imp} = \sigma_n^{imp} - \frac{C\left(\sigma_n^{imp}\right) - C^*}{\partial C\left(\sigma_n^{imp}\right) / \partial \sigma_n^{imp}}$$

The partial derivative of the option pricing formula with respect to the volatility is called *Vega* and is given in closed form by Equation 3-4.

Equation 3-4. Vega of a European option in BSM model

$$\frac{\partial C}{\partial \sigma} = S_t N'\left(d_1\right)\sqrt{T-t}$$

The financial and numerical tools needed are now complete—even if only roughly described—and we can have a look into the respective Python code that assumes the special case $t = 0$ (Example 3-1).

Example 3-1. Black-Scholes-Merton (1973) functions

```
#
# Valuation of European call options in Black-Scholes-Merton model
# incl. Vega function and implied volatility estimation
# bsm_functions.py
#

# Analytical Black-Scholes-Merton (BSM) Formula


def bsm_call_value(S0, K, T, r, sigma):
    ''' Valuation of European call option in BSM model.
    Analytical formula.

    Parameters
    ==========
    S0 : float
        initial stock/index level
    K : float
        strike price
    T : float
        maturity date (in year fractions)
    r : float
        constant risk-free short rate
    sigma : float
        volatility factor in diffusion term

    Returns
    =======
    value : float
        present value of the European call option
    '''
    from math import log, sqrt, exp
    from scipy import stats

    S0 = float(S0)
    d1 = (log(S0 / K) + (r + 0.5 * sigma ** 2) * T) / (sigma * sqrt(T))
    d2 = (log(S0 / K) + (r - 0.5 * sigma ** 2) * T) / (sigma * sqrt(T))
    value = (S0 * stats.norm.cdf(d1, 0.0, 1.0)
            - K * exp(-r * T) * stats.norm.cdf(d2, 0.0, 1.0))
      # stats.norm.cdf --> cumulative distribution function
      #                    for normal distribution
    return value

# Vega function
```

```
def bsm_vega(S0, K, T, r, sigma):
    ''' Vega of European option in BSM model.

    Parameters
    ==========
    S0 : float
        initial stock/index level
    K : float
        strike price
    T : float
        maturity date (in year fractions)
    r : float
        constant risk-free short rate
    sigma : float
        volatility factor in diffusion term

    Returns
    =======
    vega : float
        partial derivative of BSM formula with respect
        to sigma, i.e. Vega

    '''
    from math import log, sqrt
    from scipy import stats

    S0 = float(S0)
    d1 = (log(S0 / K) + (r + 0.5 * sigma ** 2) * T / (sigma * sqrt(T))
    vega = S0 * stats.norm.cdf(d1, 0.0, 1.0) * sqrt(T)
    return vega

# Implied volatility function


def bsm_call_imp_vol(S0, K, T, r, C0, sigma_est, it=100):
    ''' Implied volatility of European call option in BSM model.

    Parameters
    ==========
    S0 : float
        initial stock/index level
    K : float
        strike price
    T : float
        maturity date (in year fractions)
    r : float
        constant risk-free short rate
    sigma_est : float
        estimate of impl. volatility
    it : integer
        number of iterations
```

```
Returns
=======
simga_est : float
    numerically estimated implied volatility
'''
for i in range(it):
    sigma_est -= ((bsm_call_value(S0, K, T, r, sigma_est) - C0)
                    / bsm_vega(S0, K, T, r, sigma_est))
return sigma_est
```

These are only the basic functions needed to calculate implied volatilities. What we need as well, of course, are the respective option quotes, in our case for European call options on the VSTOXX index, and the code that generates the single implied volatilities. We will see how to do this based on an interactive IPython session.

Let us start with the day from which the quotes are taken; i.e., our $t = 0$ reference day. This is March 31, 2014. At this day, the closing value of the index was $V_0 = 17.6639$ (we change from S to V to indicate that we are now working with the volatility index):

```
In [1]: V0 = 17.6639
```

For the risk-free short rate, we assume a value of $r = 0.01$ p.a.:

```
In [2]: r = 0.01
```

All other input parameters are given by the options data (i.e., T and K) or have to be calculated (i.e., σ^{imp}). The data is stored in a pandas DataFrame object (see Chapter 6) and saved in a PyTables database file (see Chapter 7). We have to read it from disk into memory:

```
In [3]: import pandas as pd
        h5 = pd.HDFStore('./source/vstoxx_data_31032014.h5', 'r')
        futures_data = h5['futures_data']  # VSTOXX futures data
        options_data = h5['options_data']  # VSTOXX call option data
        h5.close()
```

We need the futures data to select a subset of the VSTOXX options given their (forward) moneyness. Eight futures on the VSTOXX are traded at any time. Their maturities are the next eight *third Fridays* of the month. At the end of March, there are futures with maturities ranging from the third Friday of April to the third Friday of November. TTM in the following pandas table represents time-to-maturity in year fractions:

```
In [4]: futures_data

Out[4]:           DATE  EXP_YEAR  EXP_MONTH  PRICE    MATURITY    TTM
        496 2014-03-31      2014          4  17.85  2014-04-18  0.049
        497 2014-03-31      2014          5  19.55  2014-05-16  0.126
        498 2014-03-31      2014          6  19.95  2014-06-20  0.222
        499 2014-03-31      2014          7  20.40  2014-07-18  0.299
        500 2014-03-31      2014          8  20.70  2014-08-15  0.375
        501 2014-03-31      2014          9  20.95  2014-09-19  0.471
```

```
          502 2014-03-31      2014      10  21.05 2014-10-17  0.548
          503 2014-03-31      2014      11  21.25 2014-11-21  0.644
```

The options data set is larger since at any given trading day multiple call and put options are traded per maturity date. The maturity dates, however, are the same as for the futures. There are a total of 395 call options quoted on March 31, 2014:

```
In [5]: options_data.info()

Out[5]: <class 'pandas.core.frame.DataFrame'>
        Int64Index: 395 entries, 46170 to 46564
        Data columns (total 8 columns):
        DATE          395 non-null datetime64[ns]
        EXP_YEAR      395 non-null int64
        EXP_MONTH     395 non-null int64
        TYPE          395 non-null object
        STRIKE        395 non-null float64
        PRICE         395 non-null float64
        MATURITY      395 non-null datetime64[ns]
        TTM           395 non-null float64
        dtypes: datetime64[ns](2), float64(3), int64(2), object(1)

In [6]: options_data[['DATE', 'MATURITY', 'TTM', 'STRIKE', 'PRICE']].head()

Out[6]:             DATE   MATURITY    TTM  STRIKE  PRICE
        46170 2014-03-31 2014-04-18  0.049       1  16.85
        46171 2014-03-31 2014-04-18  0.049       2  15.85
        46172 2014-03-31 2014-04-18  0.049       3  14.85
        46173 2014-03-31 2014-04-18  0.049       4  13.85
        46174 2014-03-31 2014-04-18  0.049       5  12.85
```

As is obvious in the pandas table, there are call options traded and quoted that are far in-the-money (index level much higher than option strike). There are also options traded that are far out-of-the-money (index level much lower than option strike). We therefore want to restrict the analysis to those call options with a certain (forward) moneyness, given the value of the future for the respective maturity. We allow a maximum deviation of 50% from the futures level.

Before we can start, we need to define a new column in the options_data DataFrame object to store the results. We also need to import the functions from the script in Example 3-1:

```
In [7]: options_data['IMP_VOL'] = 0.0
            # new column for implied volatilities

In [8]: from bsm_functions import *
```

The following code now calculates the implied volatilities for all those call options:

```
In [9]: tol = 0.5  # tolerance level for moneyness
        for option in options_data.index:
            # iterating over all option quotes
            forward = futures_data[futures_data['MATURITY'] == \
                        options_data.loc[option]['MATURITY']]['PRICE'].values[0]
```

```
                    # picking the right futures value
        if (forward * (1 - tol) < options_data.loc[option]['STRIKE']
                                < forward * (1 + tol)):
            # only for options with moneyness within tolerance
            imp_vol = bsm_call_imp_vol(
                    V0,  # VSTOXX value
                    options_data.loc[option]['STRIKE'],
                    options_data.loc[option]['TTM'],
                    r,   # short rate
                    options_data.loc[option]['PRICE'],
                    sigma_est=2.,  # estimate for implied volatility
                    it=100)
            options_data['IMP_VOL'].loc[option] = imp_vol
```

In this code, there is some pandas syntax that might not be obvious at first sight. Chapter 6 explains pandas and its use for such operations in detail. At this stage, it suffices to understand the following features:

```
In [10]: futures_data['MATURITY']
             # select the column with name MATURITY

Out[10]: 496    2014-04-18
         497    2014-05-16
         498    2014-06-20
         499    2014-07-18
         500    2014-08-15
         501    2014-09-19
         502    2014-10-17
         503    2014-11-21
         Name: MATURITY, dtype: datetime64[ns]

In [11]: options_data.loc[46170]
             # select data row for index 46170

Out[11]: DATE          2014-03-31 00:00:00
         EXP_YEAR                     2014
         EXP_MONTH                       4
         TYPE                            C
         STRIKE                          1
         PRICE                       16.85
         MATURITY      2014-04-18 00:00:00
         TTM                         0.049
         IMP_VOL                         0
         Name: 46170, dtype: object

In [12]: options_data.loc[46170]['STRIKE']
             # select only the value in column STRIKE
             # for index 46170

Out[12]: 1.0
```

The implied volatilities for the selected options shall now be visualized. To this end, we use only the subset of the options_data object for which we have calculated the implied volatilities:

```
In [13]: plot_data = options_data[options_data['IMP_VOL'] > 0]
```

To visualize the data, we iterate over all maturities of the data set and plot the implied volatilities both as lines and as single points. Since all maturities appear multiple times, we need to use a little trick to get to a nonredundant, sorted list with the maturities. The set operation gets rid of all duplicates, but might deliver an unsorted *set* of the maturities. Therefore, we sort the set object (cf. also Chapter 4):[2]

```
In [14]: maturities = sorted(set(options_data['MATURITY']))
         maturities

Out[14]: [Timestamp('2014-04-18 00:00:00'),
          Timestamp('2014-05-16 00:00:00'),
          Timestamp('2014-06-20 00:00:00'),
          Timestamp('2014-07-18 00:00:00'),
          Timestamp('2014-08-15 00:00:00'),
          Timestamp('2014-09-19 00:00:00'),
          Timestamp('2014-10-17 00:00:00'),
          Timestamp('2014-11-21 00:00:00')]
```

The following code iterates over all maturities and does the plotting. The result is shown as Figure 3-1. As in stock or foreign exchange markets, you will notice the so-called *volatility smile*, which is most pronounced for the shortest maturity and which becomes a bit less pronounced for the longer maturities:

```
In [15]: import matplotlib.pyplot as plt
         %matplotlib inline
         plt.figure(figsize=(8, 6))
         for maturity in maturities:
             data = plot_data[options_data.MATURITY == maturity]
               # select data for this maturity
             plt.plot(data['STRIKE'], data['IMP_VOL'],
                     label=maturity.date(), lw=1.5)
             plt.plot(data['STRIKE'], data['IMP_VOL'], 'r.')
         plt.grid(True)
         plt.xlabel('strike')
         plt.ylabel('implied volatility of volatility')
         plt.legend()
         plt.show()
```

2. As we are only considering a single day's worth of futures and options quotes, the MATURITY column of the futures_data object would have delivered the information a bit more easily since there are no duplicates.

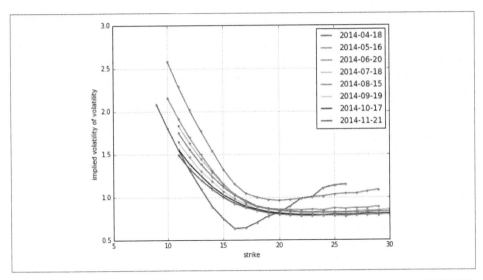

Figure 3-1. Implied volatilities (of volatility) for European call options on the VSTOXX on March 31, 2014

To conclude this example, we want to show another strength of pandas: namely, for working with hierarchically indexed data sets. The DataFrame object options_data has an *integer index*, which we have used in several places. However, this index is not really meaningful—it is "just" a number. The option quotes for the day March 31, 2014 are uniquely described ("identified") by a combination of the *maturity* and the *strike*—i.e., there is only one call option per maturity and strike.

The groupby method can be used to capitalize on this insight and to get a more meaningful index. To this end, we group by MATURITY first and then by the STRIKE. We only want to keep the PRICE and IMP_VOL columns:

```
In [16]: keep = ['PRICE', 'IMP_VOL']
         group_data = plot_data.groupby(['MATURITY', 'STRIKE'])[keep]
         group_data

Out[16]: <pandas.core.groupby.DataFrameGroupBy object at 0x7faf483d5710>
```

The operation returns a DataFrameGroupBy object.[3] To get to the data, we need to apply an aggregation operation on the object, like taking the sum. Taking the sum yields the single data point since there is only one data element in every group:

```
In [17]: group_data = group_data.sum()
         group_data.head()
```

---

3. Note that you can always look up attributes and methods of unknown objects by using the Python built-in function dir, like with dir(group_data).

```
Out[17]:                       PRICE   IMP_VOL
         MATURITY    STRIKE
         2014-04-18  9          8.85    2.083386
                     10         7.85    1.804194
                     11         6.85    1.550283
                     12         5.85    1.316103
                     13         4.85    1.097184
```

The resulting `DataFrame` object has two index levels and two columns. The following shows all values that the two indices can take:

```
In [18]: group_data.index.levels
```

```
Out[18]: FrozenList([[2014-04-18 00:00:00, 2014-05-16 00:00:00, 2014-06-20 00:00
         :00, 2014-07-18 00:00:00, 2014-08-15 00:00:00, 2014-09-19 00:00:00, 201
         4-10-17 00:00:00, 2014-11-21 00:00:00], [9.0, 10.0, 11.0, 12.0, 13.0, 1
         4.0, 15.0, 16.0, 17.0, 18.0, 19.0, 20.0, 21.0, 22.0, 23.0, 24.0, 25.0,
         26.0, 27.0, 28.0, 29.0, 30.0]])
```

Monte Carlo Simulation

Monte Carlo simulation is one of the most important algorithms in finance and numerical science in general. Its importance stems from the fact that it is quite powerful when it comes to option pricing or risk management problems. In comparison to other numerical methods, the Monte Carlo method can easily cope with high-dimensional problems where the complexity and computational demand, respectively, generally increase in linear fashion.

The downside of the Monte Carlo method is that it is per se *computationally demanding* and often needs huge amounts of memory even for quite simple problems. Therefore, it is necessary to implement Monte Carlo algorithms efficiently. The example that follows illustrates different implementation strategies in `Python` and offers three different implementation approaches for a Monte Carlo-based valuation of a European option.[4] The three approaches are:[5]

Pure Python
    This example sticks with the standard library—i.e., those libraries and packages that come with a standard `Python` installation—and uses only built-in `Python` capabilities to implement the Monte Carlo valuation.

---

4. Although not needed here, all approaches store complete simulation paths in-memory. For the valuation of standard European options this is not necessary, as the corresponding example in Chapter 1 shows. However, for the valuation of American options or for certain risk management purposes, whole paths are needed.

5. These Monte Carlo examples and implementation approaches also appear in the article Hilpisch (2013).

Vectorized NumPy
> This implementation uses the capabilities of NumPy to make the implementation more compact and much faster.

Fully vectorized NumPy
> The final example combines a different mathematical formulation with the vectorization capabilities of NumPy to get an even more compact version of the same algorithm.

The examples are again based on the model economy of Black-Scholes-Merton (1973), where the risky underlying (e.g., a stock price or index level) follows, under risk neutrality, a geometric Brownian motion with a stochastic differential equation (SDE), as in Equation 3-5.

Equation 3-5. Black-Scholes-Merton (1973) stochastic differential equation

$$dS_t = rS_t dt + \sigma S_t dZ_t$$

The parameters are defined as in Equation 3-1 and Z is a Brownian motion. A discretization scheme for the SDE in Equation 3-5 is given by the difference equation in Equation 3-6.

Equation 3-6. Euler discretization of SDE

$$S_t = S_{t-\Delta t}\exp\left(\left(r - \frac{1}{2}\sigma^2\right)\Delta t + \sigma\sqrt{\Delta t}z_t\right)$$

The variable z is a standard normally distributed random variable, $0 < \Delta t < T$, a (small enough) time interval. It also holds $0 < t \le T$ with T the final time horizon.[6]

We parameterize the model with the values $S_0 = 100$, $K = 105$, $T = 1.0$, $r = 0.05$, $\sigma = 0.2$. Using the Black-Scholes-Merton formula as in Equation 3-1 and Example 3-1 from the previous example, we can calculate the exact option value as follows:

```
In [19]: from bsm_functions import bsm_call_value
         S0 = 100.
         K = 105.
         T = 1.0
         r = 0.05
         sigma = 0.2
         bsm_call_value(S0, K, T, r, sigma)
```

---

6. For details, refer to the book by Hilpisch (2015).

```
Out[19]: 8.0213522351431763
```

This is our benchmark value for the Monte Carlo estimators to follow. To implement a Monte Carlo valuation of the European call option, the following recipe can be applied:

1. Divide the time interval $[0,T]$ in equidistant subintervals of length Δt.
2. Start iterating $i = 1, 2,..., I$.
   a. For every time step $t \in \{\Delta t, 2\Delta t,..., T\}$, draw pseudorandom numbers $z_t(i)$.
   b. Determine the time T value of the index level $S_T(i)$ by applying the pseudo-random numbers time step by time step to the discretization scheme in Equation 3-6.
   c. Determine the inner value h_T of the European call option at T as $h_T(S_T(i)) = \max(S_T(i) - K,0)$.
   d. Iterate until $i = I$.
3. Sum up the inner values, average, and discount them back with the riskless short rate according to Equation 3-7.

Equation 3-7 provides the numerical Monte Carlo estimator for the value of the European call option.

Equation 3-7. Monte Carlo estimator for European call option

$$C_0 \approx e^{-rT} \frac{1}{I} \sum_I h_T(S_T(i))$$

Pure Python

Example 3-2 translates the parametrization and the Monte Carlo recipe into pure Python. The code simulates 250,000 paths over 50 time steps.

Example 3-2. Monte Carlo valuation of European call option with pure Python

```
#
# Monte Carlo valuation of European call options with pure Python
# mcs_pure_python.py
#

from time import time
from math import exp, sqrt, log
from random import gauss, seed

seed(20000)
t0 = time()
```

```
# Parameters
S0 = 100.  # initial value
K = 105.  # strike price
T = 1.0  # maturity
r = 0.05  # riskless short rate
sigma = 0.2  # volatility
M = 50  # number of time steps
dt = T / M  # length of time interval
I = 250000  # number of paths

# Simulating I paths with M time steps
S = []
for i in range(I):
    path = []
    for t in range(M + 1):
        if t == 0:
            path.append(S0)
        else:
            z = gauss(0.0, 1.0)
            St = path[t - 1] * exp((r - 0.5 * sigma ** 2) * dt
                                    + sigma * sqrt(dt) * z)
            path.append(St)
    S.append(path)

# Calculating the Monte Carlo estimator
C0 = exp(-r * T) * sum([max(path[-1] - K, 0) for path in S]) / I

# Results output
tpy = time() - t0
print "European Option Value %7.3f" % C0
print "Duration in Seconds   %7.3f" % tpy
```

Running the script yields the following output:

```
In [20]: %run mcs_pure_python.py

Out[20]: European Option Value   7.999
         Duration in Seconds    34.258
```

Note that the estimated option value itself depends on the pseudorandom numbers generated while the time needed is influenced by the hardware the script is executed on.

The major part of the code in Example 3-2 consists of a nested loop that generates step-by-step single values of an index level path in the inner loop and adds completed paths to a list object with the outer loop. The Monte Carlo estimator is calculated using Python's list comprehension syntax (*https://docs.python.org/2/tutorial/datastructures.html*). The estimator could also be calculated by a for loop:

```
In [21]: sum_val = 0.0
         for path in S:
             # C-like iteration for comparison
```

```
        sum_val += max(path[-1] - K, 0)
    C0 = exp(-r * T) * sum_val / I
    round(C0, 3)

Out[21]: 7.999
```

Although this loop yields the same result, the list comprehension syntax is more compact and closer to the mathematical notation of the Monte Carlo estimator.

Vectorization with NumPy

NumPy provides a powerful multidimensional array class, called ndarray, as well as a comprehensive set of functions and methods to manipulate arrays and implement (complex) operations on such objects. From a more general point of view, there are two major benefits of using NumPy:

Syntax
NumPy generally allows implementations that are more compact than pure Python and that are often easier to read and maintain.

Speed
The majority of NumPy code is implemented in C or Fortran, which makes NumPy, when used in the right way, faster than pure Python.

The generally more compact syntax stems from the fact that NumPy brings powerful vectorization and broadcasting capabilities to Python. This is similar to having vector notation in mathematics for large vectors or matrices. For example, assume that we have a vector with the first 100 natural numbers, *1, ..., 100*:

$$\vec{v} = \begin{pmatrix} 1 \\ 2 \\ \vdots \\ 100 \end{pmatrix}$$

Scalar multiplication of this vector is written compactly as:

$$\vec{u} = 2 \cdot \vec{v} = \begin{pmatrix} 2 \\ 4 \\ \vdots \\ 200 \end{pmatrix}$$

Let's see if we can do this with Python list objects, for example:

```
In [22]: v = range(1, 6)
         print v
```

```
Out[22]: [1, 2, 3, 4, 5]

In [23]: 2 * v

Out[23]: [1, 2, 3, 4, 5, 1, 2, 3, 4, 5]
```

Naive scalar multiplication does not return the scalar product. It rather returns, in this case, two times the object (vector). With NumPy the result is, however, as desired:

```
In [24]: import numpy as np
         v = np.arange(1, 6)
         v

Out[24]: array([1, 2, 3, 4, 5])

In [25]: 2 * v

Out[25]: array([ 2,  4,  6,  8, 10])
```

This approach can be beneficially applied to the Monte Carlo algorithm. Example 3-3 provides the respective code, this time making use of NumPy's vectorization capabilities.

Example 3-3. Monte Carlo valuation of European call option with NumPy (first version)

```
#
# Monte Carlo valuation of European call options with NumPy
# mcs_vector_numpy.py
#
import math
import numpy as np
from time import time

np.random.seed(20000)
t0 = time()

# Parameters
S0 = 100.; K = 105.; T = 1.0; r = 0.05; sigma = 0.2
M = 50; dt = T / M; I = 250000

# Simulating I paths with M time steps
S = np.zeros((M + 1, I))
S[0] = S0
for t in range(1, M + 1):
    z = np.random.standard_normal(I)  # pseudorandom numbers
    S[t] = S[t - 1] * np.exp((r - 0.5 * sigma ** 2) * dt
                             + sigma * math.sqrt(dt) * z)
        # vectorized operation per time step over all paths

# Calculating the Monte Carlo estimator
C0 = math.exp(-r * T) * np.sum(np.maximum(S[-1] - K, 0)) / I

# Results output
tnp1 = time() - t0
```

```
print "European Option Value %7.3f" % C0
print "Duration in Seconds   %7.3f" % tnp1
```

Let us run this script:

```
In [26]: %run mcs_vector_numpy.py

Out[26]: European Option Value   8.037
         Duration in Seconds     1.215

In [27]: round(tpy / tnp1, 2)

Out[27]: 28.2
```

Vectorization brings a *speedup of more than 30 times* in comparison to pure Python. The estimated Monte Carlo value is again quite close to the benchmark value.

The vectorization becomes obvious when the pseudorandom numbers are generated. In the line in question, 250,000 numbers are generated in a single step, i.e., a single line of code:

```
z = np.random.standard_normal(I)
```

Similarly, this vector of pseudorandom numbers is applied to the discretization scheme *at once* per time step in a vectorized fashion. In that sense, the tasks that are accomplished by the outer loop in Example 3-2 are now delegated to NumPy, avoiding the outer loop completely on the Python level.

Vectorization

Using vectorization with NumPy generally results in code that is more compact, easier to read (and maintain), and faster to execute. All these aspects are in general important for financial applications.

Full Vectorization with Log Euler Scheme

Using a different discretization scheme for the SDE in Equation 3-5 can yield an even more compact implementation of the Monte Carlo algorithm. To this end, consider the log version of the discretization in Equation 3-6, which takes on the form in Equation 3-8.

Equation 3-8. Euler discretization of SDE (log version)

$$\log S_t = \log S_{t-\Delta t} + \left(r - \frac{1}{2}\sigma^2\right)\Delta t + \sigma\sqrt{\Delta t}z_t$$

This version is completely additive, allowing for an implementation of the Monte Carlo algorithm without any loop on the Python level. Example 3-4 shows the resulting code.

Example 3-4. Monte Carlo valuation of European call option with NumPy (second version)

```
#
# Monte Carlo valuation of European call options with NumPy (log version)
# mcs_full_vector_numpy.py
#
import math
from numpy import *
from time import time
  # star import for shorter code

random.seed(20000)
t0 = time()

# Parameters
S0 = 100.; K = 105.; T = 1.0; r = 0.05; sigma = 0.2
M = 50; dt = T / M; I = 250000

# Simulating I paths with M time steps
S = S0 * exp(cumsum((r - 0.5 * sigma ** 2) * dt
            + sigma * math.sqrt(dt)
                    * random.standard_normal((M + 1, I)), axis=0))
  # sum instead of cumsum would also do
  # if only the final values are of interest
S[0] = S0

# Calculating the Monte Carlo estimator
C0 = math.exp(-r * T) * sum(maximum(S[-1] - K, 0)) / I

# Results output
tnp2 = time() - t0
print "European Option Value %7.3f" % C0
print "Duration in Seconds    %7.3f" % tnp2
```

Let us run this third simulation script.

```
In [28]: %run mcs_full_vector_numpy.py

Out[28]: European Option Value   8.166
         Duration in Seconds     1.439
```

The execution speed is somewhat slower compared to the first NumPy implementation. There might also be a trade-off between compactness and readability in that this implementation approach makes it quite difficult to grasp what exactly is going on on the NumPy level. However, it shows how far one can go sometimes with NumPy vectorization.

Graphical Analysis

Finally, let us have a graphical look at the underlying mechanics (refer to Chapter 5 for an explanation of the `matplotlib` plotting library). First, we plot the first 10 simulated paths over all time steps. Figure 3-2 shows the output:

```
In [29]: import matplotlib.pyplot as plt
         plt.plot(S[:, :10])
         plt.grid(True)
         plt.xlabel('time step')
         plt.ylabel('index level')
```

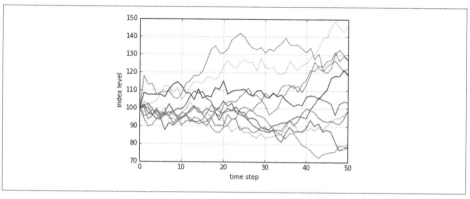

Figure 3-2. The first 10 simulated index level paths

Second, we want to see the frequency of the simulated index levels at the end of the simulation period. Figure 3-3 shows the output, this time illustrating the (approximately) log-normal distribution of the end-of-period index level values:

```
In [30]: plt.hist(S[-1], bins=50)
         plt.grid(True)
         plt.xlabel('index level')
         plt.ylabel('frequency')
```

The same type of figure looks completely different for the option's end-of-period (maturity) inner values, as Figure 3-4 illustrates:

```
In [31]: plt.hist(np.maximum(S[-1] - K, 0), bins=50)
         plt.grid(True)
         plt.xlabel('option inner value')
         plt.ylabel('frequency')
         plt.ylim(0, 50000)
```

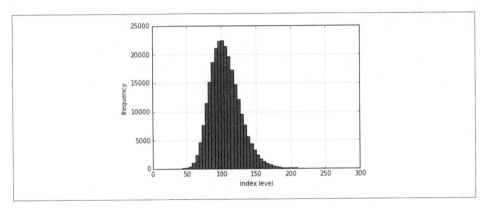

Figure 3-3. Histogram of all simulated end-of-period index level values

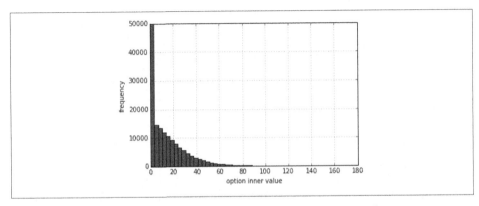

Figure 3-4. Histogram of all simulated end-of-period option inner values

In this case, the majority of the simluated values are zero, indicating that the European call option expires worthless in a significant amount of cases. The exact number is generated through the following calculation:

```
In [32]: sum(S[-1] < K)

Out[32]: 133533
```

This number might vary somewhat, of course, from simulation to simulation.

Technical Analysis

Technical analysis based on historical price information is a typical task finance professionals and interested amateurs engage in. On Wikipedia (*http://en.wikipedia.org/wiki/Technical_analysis*) you find the following definition:

In finance, technical analysis is a security analysis methodology for forecasting the direction of prices through the study of past market data, primarily price and volume.

In what follows, we focus on the study of past market data for backtesting purposes, and not too much on using our insights to predict future price movements. Our object of study is the benchmark index Standard & Poor's 500 (S&P 500), which is generally considered to be a good proxy for the *whole* stock market in the United States. This is due to the high number of names included in the index and the total market capitalization represented by it. It also has highly liquid futures and options markets.

We will read historical index level information from a web source and will implement a simple backtesting for a trading system based on trend signals. But first we need the data to get started. To this end, we mainly rely on the pandas library, which simplifies a number of related technical issues. Since it is almost always used, we should also import NumPy by default:

```
In [33]: import numpy as np
         import pandas as pd
         import pandas.io.data as web
```

Scientific and Financial Python Stack

In addition to NumPy and SciPy, there are only a couple of important libraries that form the fundamental scientific and financial Python stack. Among them is pandas. Make sure to always have current (stable) versions of these libraries installed (but be aware of potential syntax and/or API changes).

The sublibrary pandas.io.data contains the function DataReader, which helps with getting financial time series data from different sources and in particular from the popular Yahoo! Finance site (*http://finance.yahoo.com*). Let's retrieve the data we are looking for, starting on January 1, 2000:

```
In [34]: sp500 = web.DataReader('^GSPC', data_source='yahoo',
                       start='1/1/2000', end='4/14/2014')
         sp500.info()

Out[34]: <class 'pandas.core.frame.DataFrame'>
         DatetimeIndex: 3592 entries, 2000-01-03 00:00:00 to 2014-04-14 00:00:00
         Data columns (total 6 columns):
         Open         3592 non-null float64
         High         3592 non-null float64
         Low          3592 non-null float64
         Close        3592 non-null float64
         Volume       3592 non-null int64
         Adj Close    3592 non-null float64
         dtypes: float64(5), int64(1)
```

DataReader has connected to the data source via an Internet connection and has given back the time series data for the S&P 500 index, from the first trading day in 2000 until the end date. It has also generated automatically a time index with Timestamp objects.

To get a first impression, we can plot the closing quotes over time. This gives an output like that in Figure 3-5:

```
In [35]: sp500['Close'].plot(grid=True, figsize=(8, 5))
```

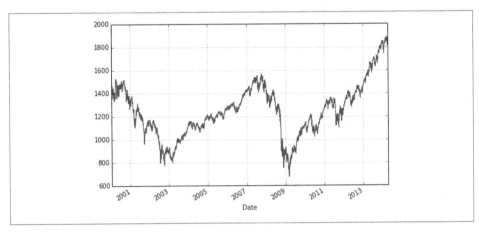

Figure 3-5. Historical levels of the S&P 500 index

The trend strategy we want to implement is based on both a *two-month* (i.e., 42 trading days) and a *one-year* (i.e., 252 trading days) *trend* (i.e., the moving average of the index level for the respective period). Again, pandas makes it efficient to generate the respective time series and to plot the three relevant time series in a single figure. First, the generation of the trend data:

```
In [36]: sp500['42d'] = np.round(pd.rolling_mean(sp500['Close'], window=42), 2)
         sp500['252d'] = np.round(pd.rolling_mean(sp500['Close'], window=252), 2)
```

In this example, the first line simultaneously *adds a new column* to the pandas DataFrame object and *puts in the values* for the 42-day trend. The second line does the same with respect to the 252-day trend. Consequently, we now have two new columns. These have fewer entries due to the very nature of the data we have generated for these columns— i.e., they start only at those dates when 42 and 252 observation points, respectively, are available for the first time to calculate the desired statistics:

```
In [37]: sp500[['Close', '42d', '252d']].tail()
Out[37]:              Close      42d     252d
         Date
         2014-04-08  1851.96  1853.88  1728.66
         2014-04-09  1872.18  1855.66  1729.79
         2014-04-10  1833.08  1856.46  1730.74
```

```
2014-04-11  1815.69  1856.36  1731.64
2014-04-14  1830.61  1856.63  1732.74
```

Second, the plotting of the new data. The resulting plot in Figure 3-6 already provides some insights into what was going on in the past with respect to upward and downward trends:

```
In [38]: sp500[['Close', '42d', '252d']].plot(grid=True, figsize=(8, 5))
```

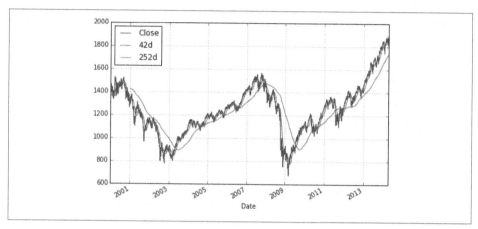

Figure 3-6. The S&P 500 index with 42d and 252d trend lines

Our basic data set is mainly complete, such that we now can devise a rule to generate trading signals. The rule says the following:

Buy signal (go long)
> the 42d trend is for the first time *SD points above* the 252d trend.

Wait (park in cash)
> the 42d trend is within a range of +/– *SD points around* the 252d trend.

Sell signal (go short)
> the 42d trend is for the first time *SD points below* the 252d trend.

To this end, we add a new column to the pandas DataFrame object for the differences between the two trends. As you can see, numerical operations with pandas can in general be implemented in a *vectorized* fashion, in that one can take the difference between two whole columns:

```
In [39]: sp500['42-252'] = sp500['42d'] - sp500['252d']
         sp500['42-252'].tail()

Out[39]: Date
         2014-04-08    125.22
         2014-04-09    125.87
         2014-04-10    125.72
```

```
2014-04-11    124.72
2014-04-14    123.89
Name: 42-252, dtype: float64
```

On the last available trading date the 42d trend lies well above the 252d trend. Although the number of entries in the two trend columns is not equal, pandas takes care of this by putting NaN values at the respective index positions:

```
In [40]: sp500['42-252'].head()

Out[40]: Date
         2000-01-03    NaN
         2000-01-04    NaN
         2000-01-05    NaN
         2000-01-06    NaN
         2000-01-07    NaN
         Name: 42-252, dtype: float64
```

To make it more formal, we again generate a new column for what we call a *regime*. We assume a value of 50 for the signal threshold:

```
In [41]: SD = 50
         sp500['Regime'] = np.where(sp500['42-252'] > SD, 1, 0)
         sp500['Regime'] = np.where(sp500['42-252'] < -SD, -1, sp500['Regime'])
         sp500['Regime'].value_counts()

Out[41]:  1    1489
          0    1232
         -1     871
         dtype: int64
```

In words, on 1,489 trading dates, the 42d trend lies more than SD points above the 252d trend. On 1,232 days, the 42d trend is more than SD points below the 252d trend. Obviously, if the short-term trend crosses the line of the long-term trend it tends to rest there for a (longer) while. This is what we call *regime* and what is illustrated in Figure 3-7, which is generated by the following two lines of code:

```
In [42]: sp500['Regime'].plot(lw=1.5)
         plt.ylim([-1.1, 1.1])
```

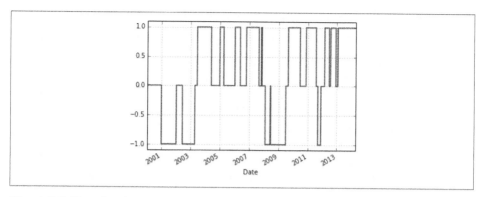

Figure 3-7. Signal regimes over time

Everything is now available to test the investment strategy based on the signals. We assume for simplicity that an investor can directly invest in the index or can directly short the index, which in the real world must be accomplished by using index funds, exchange-traded funds, or futures on the index, for example. Such trades inevitably lead to transaction costs, which we neglect here. This seems justifiable since we do not plan to trade "too often."

Based on the respective regime, the investor either is long or short in the market (index) or parks his wealth in cash, which does not bear any interest. This simplified strategy allows us to work with market returns only. The investor makes the market return when he is long (1), makes the negative market returns when he is short (–1), and makes no returns (0) when he parks his wealth in cash. We therefore need the returns first. In Python, we have the following vectorized pandas operation to calculate the log returns. Note that the shift method shifts a time series by as many index entries as desired—in our case by one trading day, such that we get daily log returns:

```
In [43]: sp500['Market'] = np.log(sp500['Close'] / sp500['Close'].shift(1))
```

Recalling how we constructed our regimes, it is now simple to get the returns of the trend-based trading strategy—we just have to multiply our Regime column, shifted by one day, by the Returns columns (the position is built "yesterday" and yields "today's" returns):

```
In [44]: sp500['Strategy'] = sp500['Regime'].shift(1) * sp500['Market']
```

The strategy pays off well; the investor is able to lock in a much higher return over the relevant period than a plain long investment would provide. Figure 3-8 compares the cumulative, continuous returns of the index with the cumulative, continuous returns of our strategy:

```
In [45]: sp500[['Market', 'Strategy']].cumsum().apply(np.exp).plot(grid=True,
                                                         figsize=(8, 5))
```

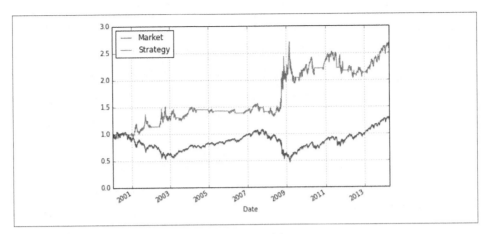

Figure 3-8. The S&P 500 index vs. investor's wealth

Figure 3-8 shows that especially during market downturns (2003 and 2008/2009) the shorting of the market yields quite high returns. Although the strategy does not capture the whole upside during bullish periods, the strategy as a whole outperforms the market quite significantly.

However, we have to keep in mind that we completely neglect operational issues (like trade execution) and relevant market microstructure elements (e.g., transaction costs). For example, we are working with daily closing values. A question would be when to execute an exit from the market (from being long to being neutral/in cash): on the same day at the closing value or the next day at the opening value. Such considerations for sure have an impact on the performance, but the overall result would probably persist. Also, transaction costs generally diminish returns, but the trading rule does not generate too many signals.

Financial Time Series

Whenever it comes to the analysis of financial time series, consider using pandas. Almost any time series-related problem can be tackled with this powerful library.

Conclusions

Without going into too much detail, this chapter illustrates the use of Python by the means of concrete and typical financial examples:

Calculation of implied volatilities

Using real-world data, in the form of a cross section of option data for a given day, we calculate numerically the implied volatilities of European call options on the

VSTOXX volatility index. This example introduces some custom `Python` functions (e.g., for analytical option valuation) and uses functionality from `NumPy`, `SciPy`, and `pandas`.

Monte Carlo simulation

Using different implementation approaches, we simulate the evolution of an index level over time and use our simulated end-of-period values to derive Monte Carlo estimators for European call options. Using `NumPy`, the major benefits of vectorization of `Python` code are illustrated: namely, *compactness of code* and *speed of execution*.

Backtesting of trend signal strategy

Using real historical time series data for the S&P 500, we backtest the performance of a trading strategy based on signals generated by 42-day and 252-day trends (moving averages). This example illustrates the capabilities and convenience of `pandas` when it comes to time series analytics.

In terms of working with `Python`, this chapter introduces interactive financial analytics (using the `IPython` interactive shell), working with more complex functions stored in modules, as well as the performance-oriented implementation of algorithms using vectorization. One important topic is not covered: namely, object orientation and classes in `Python`. For the curious reader, Appendix B contains a class definition for a European call option with methods based on the functions found in the code of Example 3-1 in this chapter.

Further Reading

The major references used in this chapter are:

- Black, Fischer and Myron Scholes (1973): "The Pricing of Options and Corporate Liabilities." *Journal of Political Economy*, Vol. 81, No. 3, pp. 638-659.

- Hilpisch, Yves (2015): *Derivatives Analytics with Python*. Wiley Finance, Chichester, England. *http://www.derivatives-analytics-with-python.com*.

- Hilpisch, Yves (2013): "Efficient Data and Financial Analytics with Python." *Software Developer's Journal*, No. 13, pp. 56-65. *http://hilpisch.com/YH_Efficient_Analytics_Article.pdf*.

- Merton, Robert (1973): "Theory of Rational Option Pricing." *Bell Journal of Economics and Management Science*, Vol. 4, pp. 141-183.

Financial Analytics and Development

This part of the book represents its core. It introduces the most important `Python` libraries, techniques, and approaches for financial analytics and application development. The sheer number of topics covered in this part makes it necessary to focus mainly on selected, and partly rather specific, examples and use cases.

The chapters are organized according to certain topics such that this part can be used as a reference to which the reader can come to look up examples and details related to a topic of interest. This core part of the book consists of the following chapters:

- Chapter 4 on `Python` data types and structures
- Chapter 5 on 2D and 3D visualization with `matplotlib`
- Chapter 6 on the handling of financial time series data
- Chapter 7 on (performant) input/output operations
- Chapter 8 on performance techniques and libraries
- Chapter 9 on several mathematical tools needed in finance
- Chapter 10 on random number generation and simulation of stochastic processes
- Chapter 11 on statistical applications with `Python`
- Chapter 12 on the integration of `Python` and `Excel`
- Chapter 13 on object-oriented programming with `Python` and the development of (simple) graphical user interfaces (GUIs)
- Chapter 14 on the integration of `Python` with web technologies as well as the development of web-based applications and web services

Financial Analytic and Development

## CHAPTER 4

Data Types and Structures

> Bad programmers worry about the code. Good programmers
> worry about data structures and their relationships.
>
> — Linus Torvalds

This chapter introduces basic data types and data structures of Python. Although the Python interpreter itself already brings a rich variety of data structures with it, NumPy and other libraries add to these in a valuable fashion.

The chapter is organized as follows:

Basic data types

The first section introduces basic data types such as int, float, and string.

Basic data structures

The next section introduces the fundamental data structures of Python (e.g., list objects) and illustrates control structures, functional programming paradigms, and anonymous functions.

NumPy data structures

The following section is devoted to the characteristics and capabilities of the NumPy ndarray class and illustrates some of the benefits of this class for scientific and financial applications.

Vectorization of code

As the final section illustrates, thanks to NumPy's array class vectorized code is easily implemented, leading to more compact and also better-performing code.

The spirit of this chapter is to provide a general introduction to Python specifics when it comes to data types and structures. If you are equipped with a background from another programing language, say C or Matlab, you should be able to easily grasp the differences that Python usage might bring along. The topics introduced here are all important and fundamental for the chapters to come.

Basic Data Types

Python is a *dynamically typed* language, which means that the Python interpreter infers the type of an object at runtime. In comparison, compiled languages like C are generally *statically typed*. In these cases, the type of an object has to be attached to the object before compile time.[1]

Integers

One of the most fundamental data types is the integer, or int:

```
In [1]: a = 10
        type(a)

Out[1]: int
```

The built-in function type provides type information for all objects with standard and built-in types as well as for newly created classes and objects. In the latter case, the information provided depends on the description the programmer has stored with the class. There is a saying that "everything in Python is an object." This means, for example, that even simple objects like the int object we just defined have built-in methods. For example, you can get the number of bits needed to represent the int object in-memory by calling the method bit_length:

```
In [2]: a.bit_length()

Out[2]: 4
```

You will see that the number of bits needed increases the higher the integer value is that we assign to the object:

```
In [3]: a = 100000
        a.bit_length()

Out[3]: 17
```

In general, there are so many different methods that it is hard to memorize all methods of all classes and objects. Advanced Python environments, like IPython, provide tab completion capabilities that show all methods attached to an object. You simply type the object name followed by a dot (e.g., a.) and then press the Tab key, e.g., a.*tab*. This then provides a collection of methods you can call on the object. Alternatively, the

---

1. The Cython library (*http://www.cython.org*) brings static typing and compiling features to Python that are comparable to those in C. In fact, Cython is a hybrid language of Python and C.

Python built-in function `dir` gives a complete list of attributes and methods of any object.

A specialty of Python is that integers can be arbitrarily large. Consider, for example, the googol number 10^{100}. Python has no problem with such large numbers, which are technically long objects:

```
In [4]: googol = 10 ** 100
        googol
```

```
Out[4]: 1000000000000000000000000000000000000000000000000000000000000000000000000
        0000000000000000000000000000000L
```

```
In [5]: googol.bit_length()
```

```
Out[5]: 333
```

Large Integers

Python integers can be arbitrarily large. The interpreter simply uses as many bits/bytes as needed to represent the numbers.

It is important to note that mathematical operations on `int` objects return `int` objects. This can sometimes lead to confusion and/or hard-to-detect errors in mathematical routines. The following expression yields the expected result:

```
In [6]: 1 + 4
```

```
Out[6]: 5
```

However, the next case may return a somewhat surprising result:

```
In [7]: 1 / 4
```

```
Out[7]: 0
```

```
In [8]: type(1 / 4)
```

```
Out[8]: int
```

Floats

For the last expression to return the generally *desired* result of 0.25, we must operate on `float` objects, which brings us naturally to the next basic data type. Adding a dot to an integer value, like in `1.` or `1.0`, causes Python to interpret the object as a `float`. Expressions involving a `float` also return a `float` object in general:[2]

---

2. Here and in the following discussion, terms like *float, float object*, etc. are used interchangeably, acknowledging that every *float* is also an *object*. The same holds true for other object types.

```
In [9]: 1. / 4
Out[9]: 0.25
In [10]: type (1. / 4)
Out[10]: float
```

A float is a bit more involved in that the computerized representation of rational or real numbers is in general not exact and depends on the specific technical approach taken. To illustrate what this implies, let us define another float object:

```
In [11]: b = 0.35
         type(b)
Out[11]: float
```

float objects like this one are always represented internally up to a certain degree of accuracy only. This becomes evident when adding 0.1 to b:

```
In [12]: b + 0.1
Out[12]: 0.44999999999999996
```

The reason for this is that floats are internally represented in binary format; that is, a decimal number $0 < n < 1$ is represented by a series of the form $n = \frac{x}{2} + \frac{y}{4} + \frac{z}{8} + \dots$. For certain floating-point numbers the binary representation might involve a large number of elements or might even be an infinite series. However, given a fixed number of bits used to represent such a number—i.e., a fixed number of terms in the representation series—inaccuracies are the consequence. Other numbers can be represented *perfectly* and are therefore stored exactly even with a finite number of bits available. Consider the following example:

```
In [13]: c = 0.5
         c.as_integer_ratio()
Out[13]: (1, 2)
```

One half, i.e., 0.5, is stored exactly because it has an exact (finite) binary representation as $0.5 = \frac{1}{2}$. However, for b = 0.35 we get something different than the expected rational number $0.35 = \frac{7}{20}$:

```
In [14]: b.as_integer_ratio()
Out[14]: (3152519739159347, 9007199254740992)
```

The precision is dependent on the number of bits used to represent the number. In general, all platforms that Python runs on use the IEEE 754 double-precision standard (i.e., 64 bits), for internal representation.[3] This translates into a 15-digit relative accuracy.

---

3. Cf. *http://en.wikipedia.org/wiki/Double-precision_floating-point_format.*

Since this topic is of high importance for several application areas in finance, it is sometimes necessary to ensure the exact, or at least best possible, representation of numbers. For example, the issue can be of importance when summing over a large set of numbers. In such a situation, a certain kind and/or magnitude of representation error might, in aggregate, lead to significant deviations from a benchmark value.

The module decimal provides an arbitrary-precision object for floating-point numbers and several options to address precision issues when working with such numbers:

```
In [15]: import decimal
         from decimal import Decimal

In [16]: decimal.getcontext()

Out[16]: Context(prec=28, rounding=ROUND_HALF_EVEN, Emin=-999999999, Emax=999999
         999, capitals=1, flags=[], traps=[Overflow, InvalidOperation, DivisionB
         yZero])

In [17]: d = Decimal(1) / Decimal (11)
         d

Out[17]: Decimal('0.09090909090909090909090909091')
```

You can change the precision of the representation by changing the respective attribute value of the Context object:

```
In [18]: decimal.getcontext().prec = 4  # lower precision than default

In [19]: e = Decimal(1) / Decimal (11)
         e

Out[19]: Decimal('0.09091')

In [20]: decimal.getcontext().prec = 50  # higher precision than default

In [21]: f = Decimal(1) / Decimal (11)
         f

Out[21]: Decimal('0.090909090909090909090909090909090909090909090909091')
```

If needed, the precision can in this way be adjusted to the exact problem at hand and one can operate with floating-point objects that exhibit different degrees of accuracy:

```
In [22]: g = d + e + f
         g

Out[22]: Decimal('0.27272818181818181818181818181909090909090909090909')
```

Arbitrary-Precision Floats

The module decimal provides an arbitrary-precision floating-point number object. In finance, it might sometimes be necessary to ensure high precision and to go beyond the 64-bit double-precision standard.

Strings

Now that we can represent natural and floating-point numbers, we turn to text. The basic data type to represent text in Python is the string. The string object has a number of really helpful built-in methods. In fact, Python is generally considered to be a good choice when it comes to working with text files of any kind and any size. A string object is generally defined by single or double quotation marks or by converting another object using the str function (i.e., using the object's standard or user-defined string representation):

```
In [23]: t = 'this is a string object'
```

With regard to the built-in methods, you can, for example, capitalize the first word in this object:

```
In [24]: t.capitalize()

Out[24]: 'This is a string object'
```

Or you can split it into its single-word components to get a list object of all the words (more on list objects later):

```
In [25]: t.split()

Out[25]: ['this', 'is', 'a', 'string', 'object']
```

You can also search for a word and get the position (i.e., index value) of the first letter of the word back in a successful case:

```
In [26]: t.find('string')

Out[26]: 10
```

If the word is not in the string object, the method returns -1:

```
In [27]: t.find('Python')

Out[27]: -1
```

Replacing characters in a string is a typical task that is easily accomplished with the replace method:

```
In [28]: t.replace(' ', '|')

Out[28]: 'this|is|a|string|object'
```

The stripping of strings—i.e., deletion of certain leading/lagging characters—is also often necessary:

```
In [29]: 'http://www.python.org'.strip('htp:/')

Out[29]: 'www.python.org'
```

Table 4-1 lists a number of helpful methods of the string object.

Table 4-1. Selected string methods

Method	Arguments	Returns/result
capitalize	()	Copy of the string with first letter capitalized
count	(*sub*[, *start*[, *end*]])	Count of the number of occurrences of substring
decode	([*encoding*[, *errors*]])	Decoded version of the string, using *encoding* (e.g., UTF-8)
encode	([*encoding*[, *errors*]])	Encoded version of the string
find	(*sub*[, *start*[, *end*]])	(Lowest) index where substring is found
join	(*seq*)	Concatenation of strings in sequence *seq*
replace	(*old, new*[, *count*])	Replaces *old* by *new* the first *count* times
split	([*sep*[, *maxsplit*]])	List of words in string with *sep* as separator
splitlines	([*keepends*])	Separated lines with line ends/breaks if *keepends* is *True*
strip	(*chars*)	Copy of string with leading/lagging characters in *chars* removed
upper	()	Copy with all letters capitalized

A powerful tool when working with **string** objects is *regular expressions*. Python provides such functionality in the module **re**:

```
In [30]: import re
```

Suppose you are faced with a large text file, such as a comma-separated value (CSV) file, which contains certain time series and respective date-time information. More often than not, the date-time information is delivered in a format that Python cannot interpret directly. However, the date-time information can generally be described by a regular expression. Consider the following **string** object, containing three date-time elements, three integers, and three strings. Note that triple quotation marks allow the definition of strings over multiple rows:

```
In [31]: series = """
         '01/18/2014 13:00:00', 100, '1st';
         '01/18/2014 13:30:00', 110, '2nd';
         '01/18/2014 14:00:00', 120, '3rd'
         """
```

The following regular expression describes the format of the date-time information provided in the **string** object:[4]

```
In [32]: dt = re.compile("'[0-9/:\s]+'")  # datetime
```

---

4. It is not possible to go into details here, but there is a wealth of information available on the Internet about regular expressions in general and for Python in particular. For an introduction to this topic, refer to Fitzgerald, Michael (2012): *Introducing Regular Expressions*. O'Reilly, Sebastopol, CA.

Equipped with this regular expression, we can go on and find all the date-time elements. In general, applying regular expressions to `string` objects also leads to performance improvements for typical parsing tasks:

```
In [33]: result = dt.findall(series)
         result

Out[33]: ["'01/18/2014 13:00:00'", "'01/18/2014 13:30:00'", "'01/18/2014 14:00:0
         0'"]
```

Regular Expressions

When parsing `string` objects, consider using regular expressions, which can bring both convenience and performance to such operations.

The resulting `string` objects can then be parsed to generate `Python` `datetime` objects (cf. Appendix C for an overview of handling date and time data with `Python`). To parse the `string` objects containing the date-time information, we need to provide information of how to parse—again as a `string` object:

```
In [34]: from datetime import datetime
         pydt = datetime.strptime(result[0].replace("'", ""),
                                  '%m/%d/%Y %H:%M:%S')
         pydt

Out[34]: datetime.datetime(2014, 1, 18, 13, 0)

In [35]: print pydt

Out[35]: 2014-01-18 13:00:00

In [36]: print type(pydt)

Out[36]: <type 'datetime.datetime'>
```

Later chapters provide more information on date-time data, the handling of such data, and `datetime` objects and their methods. This is just meant to be a teaser for this important topic in finance.

Basic Data Structures

As a general rule, data structures are objects that contain a possibly large number of other objects. Among those that `Python` provides as built-in structures are:

`tuple`
    A collection of arbitrary objects; only a few methods available

`list`
    A collection of arbitrary objects; many methods available

`dict`

   A key-value store object

`set`

   An unordered collection object for other *unique* objects

Tuples

A `tuple` is an advanced data structure, yet it's still quite simple and limited in its applications. It is defined by providing objects in parentheses:

```
In [37]: t = (1, 2.5, 'data')
         type(t)

Out[37]: tuple
```

You can even drop the parentheses and provide multiple objects separated by commas:

```
In [38]: t = 1, 2.5, 'data'
         type(t)

Out[38]: tuple
```

Like almost all data structures in `Python` the `tuple` has a built-in index, with the help of which you can retrieve single or multiple elements of the `tuple`. It is important to remember that `Python` uses *zero-based numbering*, such that the third element of a `tuple` is at index position 2:

```
In [39]: t[2]

Out[39]: 'data'

In [40]: type(t[2])

Out[40]: str
```

Zero-Based Numbering

In contrast to some other programming languages like `Matlab`, `Python` uses zero-based numbering schemes. For example, the first element of a `tuple` object has index value 0.

There are only two special methods that this object type provides: `count` and `index`. The first counts the number of occurrences of a certain object and the second gives the index value of the first appearance of it:

```
In [41]: t.count('data')

Out[41]: 1

In [42]: t.index(1)

Out[42]: 0
```

tuple objects are not very flexible since, once defined, they cannot be changed easily.

Lists

Objects of type list are much more flexible and powerful in comparison to tuple objects. From a finance point of view, you can achieve a lot working only with list objects, such as storing stock price quotes and appending new data. A list object is defined through brackets and the basic capabilities and behavior are similar to those of tuple objects:

```
In [43]: l = [1, 2.5, 'data']
         l[2]

Out[43]: 'data'
```

list objects can also be defined or converted by using the function list. The following code generates a new list object by converting the tuple object from the previous example:

```
In [44]: l = list(t)
         l

Out[44]: [1, 2.5, 'data']

In [45]: type(l)

Out[45]: list
```

In addition to the characteristics of tuple objects, list objects are also expandable and reducible via different methods. In other words, whereas string and tuple objects are *immutable* sequence objects (with indexes) that cannot be changed once created, list objects are *mutable* and can be changed via different operations. You can append list objects to an existing list object, and more:

```
In [46]: l.append([4, 3])  # append list at the end
         l

Out[46]: [1, 2.5, 'data', [4, 3]]

In [47]: l.extend([1.0, 1.5, 2.0])  # append elements of list
         l

Out[47]: [1, 2.5, 'data', [4, 3], 1.0, 1.5, 2.0]

In [48]: l.insert(1, 'insert')  # insert object before index position
         l
```

```
Out[48]: [1, 'insert', 2.5, 'data', [4, 3], 1.0, 1.5, 2.0]

In [49]: l.remove('data')  # remove first occurrence of object
         l

Out[49]: [1, 'insert', 2.5, [4, 3], 1.0, 1.5, 2.0]

In [50]: p = l.pop(3)  # removes and returns object at index
         print l, p

Out[50]: [1, 'insert', 2.5, 1.0, 1.5, 2.0] [4, 3]
```

Slicing is also easily accomplished. Here, *slicing* refers to an operation that breaks down a data set into smaller parts (of interest):

```
In [51]: l[2:5]  # 3rd to 5th elements

Out[51]: [2.5, 1.0, 1.5]
```

Table 4-2 provides a summary of selected operations and methods of the list object.

Table 4-2. Selected operations and methods of list objects

Method	Arguments	Returns/result
l[i] = x	[i]	Replaces *i*th element by *x*
l[i:j:k] = s	[i:j:k]	Replaces every *k*th element from *i* to *j* - 1 by *s*
append	(x)	Appends *x* to object
count	(x)	Number of occurrences of object *x*
del l[i:j:k]	[i:j:k]	Deletes elements with index values *i* to *j* − 1
extend	(s)	Appends all elements of *s* to object
index	(x[, i[, j]])	First index of *x* between elements *i* and *j* − 1
insert	(i, x)++	Inserts *x* at/before index *i*
remove	(i)	Removes element with index *i*
pop	(i)	Removes element with index *i* and return it
reverse	()	Reverses all items in place
sort	([cmp[, key[, reverse]]])	Sorts all items in place

Excursion: Control Structures

Although a topic in itself, *control structures* like for loops are maybe best introduced in Python based on list objects. This is due to the fact that looping in general takes place over list objects, which is quite different to what is often the standard in other languages. Take the following example. The for loop loops over the elements of the list object l with index values 2 to 4 and prints the square of the respective elements. Note the importance of the indentation (whitespace) in the second line:

```
In [52]: for element in l[2:5]:
             print element ** 2
```

```
Out[52]: 6.25
         1.0
         2.25
```

This provides a really high degree of flexibility in comparison to the typical counter-based looping. Counter-based looping is also an option with Python, but is accomplished based on the (standard) list object range:

```
In [53]: r = range(0, 8, 1)  # start, end, step width
         r

Out[53]: [0, 1, 2, 3, 4, 5, 6, 7]

In [54]: type(r)

Out[54]: list
```

For comparison, the same loop is implemented using range as follows:

```
In [55]: for i in range(2, 5):
             print l[i] ** 2

Out[55]: 6.25
         1.0
         2.25
```

Looping over Lists

In Python you can loop over arbitrary list objects, no matter what the content of the object is. This often avoids the introduction of a counter.

Python also provides the typical (conditional) control elements if, elif, and else. Their use is comparable in other languages:

```
In [56]: for i in range(1, 10):
             if i % 2 == 0:  # % is for modulo
                 print "%d is even" % i
             elif i % 3 == 0:
                 print "%d is multiple of 3" % i
             else:
                 print "%d is odd" % i

Out[56]: 1 is odd
         2 is even
         3 is multiple of 3
         4 is even
         5 is odd
         6 is even
         7 is odd
         8 is even
         9 is multiple of 3
```

Similarly, while provides another means to control the flow:

```
In [57]: total = 0
         while total < 100:
             total += 1
         print total

Out[57]: 100
```

A specialty of Python is so-called list *comprehensions*. Instead of looping over existing list objects, this approach generates list objects via loops in a rather compact fashion:

```
In [58]: m = [i ** 2 for i in range(5)]
         m

Out[58]: [0, 1, 4, 9, 16]
```

In a certain sense, this already provides a first means to generate "something like" vectorized code in that loops are rather more implicit than explicit (vectorization of code is discussed in more detail later in this chapter).

Excursion: Functional Programming

Python provides a number of tools for functional programming support as well—i.e., the application of a function to a whole set of inputs (in our case list objects). Among these tools are filter, map, and reduce. However, we need a function definition first. To start with something really simple, consider a function f that returns the square of the input x:

```
In [59]: def f(x):
             return x ** 2
         f(2)

Out[59]: 4
```

Of course, functions can be arbitrarily complex, with multiple input/parameter objects and even multiple outputs, (return objects). However, consider the following function:

```
In [60]: def even(x):
             return x % 2 == 0
         even(3)

Out[60]: False
```

The return object is a Boolean. Such a function can be applied to a whole list object by using map:

```
In [61]: map(even, range(10))

Out[61]: [True, False, True, False, True, False, True, False, True, False]
```

To this end, we can also provide a function definition directly as an argument to map, by using lambda or *anonymous* functions:

```
In [62]: map(lambda x: x ** 2, range(10))

Out[62]: [0, 1, 4, 9, 16, 25, 36, 49, 64, 81]
```

Functions can also be used to filter a list object. In the following example, the filter returns elements of a list object that match the Boolean condition as defined by the even function:

```
In [63]: filter(even, range(15))

Out[63]: [0, 2, 4, 6, 8, 10, 12, 14]
```

Finally, reduce helps when we want to apply a function to all elements of a list object that returns a single value only. An example is the cumulative sum of all elements in a list object (assuming that summation is defined for the objects contained in the list):

```
In [64]: reduce(lambda x, y: x + y, range(10))

Out[64]: 45
```

An alternative, *nonfunctional* implementation could look like the following:

```
In [65]: def cumsum(l):
             total = 0
             for elem in l:
                 total += elem
             return total
         cumsum(range(10))

Out[65]: 45
```

List Comprehensions, Functional Programming, Anonymous Functions
It can be considered *good practice* to avoid loops on the Python level as far as possible. list comprehensions and functional programming tools like map, filter, and reduce provide means to write code without loops that is both compact and in general more readable. lambda or anonymous functions are also powerful tools in this context.

Dicts

dict objects are dictionaries, and also mutable sequences, that allow data retrieval by keys that can, for example, be string objects. They are so-called *key-value stores*. While list objects are ordered and sortable, dict objects are unordered and unsortable. An example best illustrates further differences to list objects. Curly brackets are what define dict objects:

```
In [66]: d = {
             'Name' : 'Angela Merkel',
             'Country' : 'Germany',
             'Profession' : 'Chancelor',
```

```
            'Age' : 60
            }
        type(d)

Out[66]: dict

In [67]: print d['Name'], d['Age']

Out[67]: Angela Merkel 60
```

Again, this class of objects has a number of built-in methods:

```
In [68]: d.keys()

Out[68]: ['Country', 'Age', 'Profession', 'Name']

In [69]: d.values()

Out[69]: ['Germany', 60, 'Chancelor', 'Angela Merkel']

In [70]: d.items()

Out[70]: [('Country', 'Germany'),
         ('Age', 60),
         ('Profession', 'Chancelor'),
         ('Name', 'Angela Merkel')]

In [71]: birthday = True
         if birthday is True:
             d['Age'] += 1
         print d['Age']

Out[71]: 61
```

There are several methods to get `iterator` objects from the `dict` object. The objects behave like `list` objects when iterated over:

```
In [72]: for item in d.iteritems():
             print item

Out[72]: ('Country', 'Germany')
         ('Age', 61)
         ('Profession', 'Chancelor')
         ('Name', 'Angela Merkel')

In [73]: for value in d.itervalues():
             print type(value)

Out[73]: <type 'str'>
         <type 'int'>
         <type 'str'>
         <type 'str'>
```

Table 4-3 provides a summary of selected operations and methods of the `dict` object.

Table 4-3. Selected operations and methods of dict objects

Method	Arguments	Returns/result
d[k]	[k]	Item of d with key k
d[k] = x	[k]	Sets item key k to x
del d[k]	[k]	Deletes item with key k
clear	()	Removes all items
copy	()	Makes a copy
has_key	(k)	True if k is a key
items	()	Copy of all key-value pairs
iteritems	()	Iterator over all items
iterkeys	()	Iterator over all keys
itervalues	()	Iterator over all values
keys	()	Copy of all keys
poptiem	(k)	Returns and removes item with key k
update	([e])	Updates items with items from e
values	()	Copy of all values

Sets

The last data structure we will consider is the set object. Although set theory is a cornerstone of mathematics and also finance theory, there are not too many practical applications for set objects. The objects are unordered collections of other objects, containing every element only once:

```
In [74]: s = set(['u', 'd', 'ud', 'du', 'd', 'du'])
         s
Out[74]: {'d', 'du', 'u', 'ud'}
In [75]: t = set(['d', 'dd', 'uu', 'u'])
```

With set objects, you can implement operations as you are used to in mathematical set theory. For example, you can generate unions, intersections, and differences:

```
In [76]: s.union(t)  # all of s and t
Out[76]: {'d', 'dd', 'du', 'u', 'ud', 'uu'}
In [77]: s.intersection(t)  # both in s and t
Out[77]: {'d', 'u'}
In [78]: s.difference(t)  # in s but not t
Out[78]: {'du', 'ud'}
In [79]: t.difference(s)  # in t but not s
```

```
Out[79]: {'dd', 'uu'}

In [80]: s.symmetric_difference(t)  # in either one but not both

Out[80]: {'dd', 'du', 'ud', 'uu'}
```

One application of `set` objects is to get rid of duplicates in a `list` object. For example:

```
In [81]: from random import randint
         l = [randint(0, 10) for i in range(1000)]
             # 1,000 random integers between 0 and 10
         len(l)  # number of elements in l

Out[81]: 1000

In [82]: l[:20]

Out[82]: [8, 3, 4, 9, 1, 7, 5, 5, 6, 7, 4, 4, 7, 1, 8, 5, 0, 7, 1, 9]

In [83]: s = set(l)
         s

Out[83]: {0, 1, 2, 3, 4, 5, 6, 7, 8, 9, 10}
```

NumPy Data Structures

The previous section shows that `Python` provides some quite useful and flexible general data structures. In particular, `list` objects can be considered a real workhorse with many convenient characteristics and application areas. However, scientific and financial applications generally have a need for high-performing operations on special data structures. One of the most important data structures in this regard is the *array*. Arrays generally structure other (fundamental) objects in rows and columns.

Assume for the moment that we work with numbers only, although the concept generalizes to other types of data as well. In the simplest case, a one-dimensional array then represents, mathematically speaking, a *vector* of, in general, real numbers, internally represented by `float` objects. It then consists of a *single* row or column of elements only. In a more common case, an array represents an $i \times j$ *matrix* of elements. This concept generalizes to $i \times j \times k$ *cubes* of elements in three dimensions as well as to general n-dimensional arrays of shape $i \times j \times k \times l \times \ldots$.

Mathematical disciplines like linear algebra and vector space theory illustrate that such mathematical structures are of high importance in a number of disciplines and fields. It can therefore prove fruitful to have available a specialized class of data structures explicitly designed to handle arrays conveniently and efficiently. This is where the `Python` library `NumPy` comes into play, with its `ndarray` class.

Arrays with Python Lists

Before we turn to NumPy, let us first construct arrays with the built-in data structures presented in the previous section. `list` objects are particularly suited to accomplishing this task. A simple `list` can already be considered a one-dimensional array:

```
In [84]: v = [0.5, 0.75, 1.0, 1.5, 2.0]  # vector of numbers
```

Since `list` objects can contain arbitrary other objects, they can also contain other `list` objects. In that way, two- and higher-dimensional arrays are easily constructed by nested `list` objects:

```
In [85]: m = [v, v, v]  # matrix of numbers
         m

Out[85]: [[0.5, 0.75, 1.0, 1.5, 2.0],
          [0.5, 0.75, 1.0, 1.5, 2.0],
          [0.5, 0.75, 1.0, 1.5, 2.0]]
```

We can also easily select rows via simple indexing or single elements via double indexing (whole columns, however, are not so easy to select):

```
In [86]: m[1]

Out[86]: [0.5, 0.75, 1.0, 1.5, 2.0]

In [87]: m[1][0]

Out[87]: 0.5
```

Nesting can be pushed further for even more general structures:

```
In [88]: v1 = [0.5, 1.5]
         v2 = [1, 2]
         m = [v1, v2]
         c = [m, m]  # cube of numbers
         c

Out[88]: [[[0.5, 1.5], [1, 2]], [[0.5, 1.5], [1, 2]]]

In [89]: c[1][1][0]

Out[89]: 1
```

Note that combining objects in the way just presented generally works with reference pointers to the original objects. What does that mean in practice? Let us have a look at the following operations:

```
In [90]: v = [0.5, 0.75, 1.0, 1.5, 2.0]
         m = [v, v, v]
         m

Out[90]: [[0.5, 0.75, 1.0, 1.5, 2.0],
          [0.5, 0.75, 1.0, 1.5, 2.0],
          [0.5, 0.75, 1.0, 1.5, 2.0]]
```

Now change the value of the first element of the v object and see what happens to the m object:

```
In [91]: v[0] = 'Python'
         m

Out[91]: [['Python', 0.75, 1.0, 1.5, 2.0],
          ['Python', 0.75, 1.0, 1.5, 2.0],
          ['Python', 0.75, 1.0, 1.5, 2.0]]
```

This can be avoided by using the deepcopy function of the copy module:

```
In [92]: from copy import deepcopy
         v = [0.5, 0.75, 1.0, 1.5, 2.0]
         m = 3 * [deepcopy(v), ]
         m

Out[92]: [[0.5, 0.75, 1.0, 1.5, 2.0],
          [0.5, 0.75, 1.0, 1.5, 2.0],
          [0.5, 0.75, 1.0, 1.5, 2.0]]

In [93]: v[0] = 'Python'
         m

Out[93]: [[0.5, 0.75, 1.0, 1.5, 2.0],
          [0.5, 0.75, 1.0, 1.5, 2.0],
          [0.5, 0.75, 1.0, 1.5, 2.0]]
```

Regular NumPy Arrays

Obviously, composing array structures with list objects works, somewhat. But it is not really convenient, and the list class has not been built with this specific goal in mind. It has rather been built with a much broader and more general scope. From this point of view, some kind of specialized class could therefore be really beneficial to handle array-type structures.

Such a specialized class is numpy.ndarray, which has been built with the specific goal of handling n-dimensional arrays both conveniently and efficiently—i.e., in a highly performing manner. The basic handling of instances of this class is again best illustrated by examples:

```
In [94]: import numpy as np

In [95]: a = np.array([0, 0.5, 1.0, 1.5, 2.0])
         type(a)

Out[95]: numpy.ndarray

In [96]: a[:2]  # indexing as with list objects in 1 dimension

Out[96]: array([ 0. ,  0.5])
```

A major feature of the numpy.ndarray class is the *multitude of built-in methods*. For instance:

```
In [97]: a.sum()  # sum of all elements
Out[97]: 5.0
In [98]: a.std()  # standard deviation
Out[98]: 0.70710678118654757
In [99]: a.cumsum()  # running cumulative sum
Out[99]: array([ 0. , 0.5, 1.5, 3. , 5. ])
```

Another major feature is the (vectorized) *mathematical operations* defined on ndarray objects:

```
In [100]: a * 2
Out[100]: array([ 0., 1., 2., 3., 4.])
In [101]: a ** 2
Out[101]: array([ 0. , 0.25, 1. , 2.25, 4. ])
In [102]: np.sqrt(a)
Out[102]: array([ 0.       , 0.70710678, 1.       , 1.22474487, 1.41421356
          ])
```

The transition to more than one dimension is seamless, and all features presented so far carry over to the more general cases. In particular, the indexing system is made consistent across all dimensions:

```
In [103]: b = np.array([a, a * 2])
          b
Out[103]: array([[ 0. , 0.5, 1. , 1.5, 2. ],
               [ 0. , 1. , 2. , 3. , 4. ]])
In [104]: b[0]  # first row
Out[104]: array([ 0. , 0.5, 1. , 1.5, 2. ])
In [105]: b[0, 2]  # third element of first row
Out[105]: 1.0
In [106]: b.sum()
Out[106]: 15.0
```

In contrast to our list object-based approach to constructing arrays, the numpy.ndar ray class knows axes explicitly. Selecting either rows or columns from a matrix is essentially the same:

```
In [107]: b.sum(axis=0)
          # sum along axis 0, i.e. column-wise sum
Out[107]: array([ 0. , 1.5, 3. , 4.5, 6. ])
In [108]: b.sum(axis=1)
          # sum along axis 1, i.e. row-wise sum
```

```
Out[108]: array([  5.,  10.])
```

There are a number of ways to initialize (instantiate) a `numpy.ndarray` object. One is as presented before, via `np.array`. However, this assumes that all elements of the array are already available. In contrast, one would maybe like to have the `numpy.ndarray` objects instantiated first to populate them later with results generated during the execution of code. To this end, we can use the following functions:

```
In [109]: c = np.zeros((2, 3, 4), dtype='i', order='C')  # also: np.ones()
          c
Out[109]: array([[[0, 0, 0, 0],
                  [0, 0, 0, 0],
                  [0, 0, 0, 0]],

                 [[0, 0, 0, 0],
                  [0, 0, 0, 0],
                  [0, 0, 0, 0]]], dtype=int32)
In [110]: d = np.ones_like(c, dtype='f16', order='C')  # also: np.zeros_like()
          d
Out[110]: array([[[ 1.0,  1.0,  1.0,  1.0],
                  [ 1.0,  1.0,  1.0,  1.0],
                  [ 1.0,  1.0,  1.0,  1.0]],

                 [[ 1.0,  1.0,  1.0,  1.0],
                  [ 1.0,  1.0,  1.0,  1.0],
                  [ 1.0,  1.0,  1.0,  1.0]]], dtype=float128)
```

With all these functions we provide the following information:

shape

Either an `int`, a sequence of `int`s, or a reference to another `numpy.ndarray`

`dtype` *(optional)*

A `numpy.dtype`—these are NumPy-specific data types for `numpy.ndarray` objects

`order` *(optional)*

The order in which to store elements in memory: C for C-like (i.e., row-wise) or F for `Fortran`-like (i.e., column-wise)

Here, it becomes obvious how NumPy specializes the construction of arrays with the `numpy.ndarray` class, in comparison to the `list`-based approach:

- The shape/length/size of the array is *homogenous* across any given dimension.
- It only allows for a *single data type* (`numpy.dtype`) for the whole array.

The role of the `order` parameter is discussed later in the chapter. Table 4-4 provides an overview of `numpy.dtype` objects (i.e., the basic data types NumPy allows).

Table 4-4. NumPy dtype objects

dtype	Description	Example
t	Bit field	t4 (4 bits)
b	Boolean	b (true or false)
i	Integer	i8 (64 bit)
u	Unsigned integer	u8 (64 bit)
f	Floating point	f8 (64 bit)
c	Complex floating point	c16 (128 bit)
O	Object	0 (pointer to object)
S, a	String	S24 (24 characters)
U	Unicode	U24 (24 Unicode characters)
V	Other	V12 (12-byte data block)

NumPy provides a generalization of regular arrays that loosens at least the dtype restriction, but let us stick with regular arrays for a moment and see what the specialization brings in terms of performance.

As a simple exercise, suppose we want to generate a matrix/array of shape 5,000 × 5,000 elements, populated with (pseudo)random, standard normally distributed numbers. We then want to calculate the sum of all elements. First, the pure Python approach, where we make heavy use of list comprehensions and functional programming methods as well as lambda functions:

```
In [111]: import random
          I = 5000

In [112]: %time mat = [[random.gauss(0, 1) for j in range(I)] for i in range(I)]
          # a nested list comprehension

Out[112]: CPU times: user 36.5 s, sys: 408 ms, total: 36.9 s
          Wall time: 36.4 s

In [113]: %time reduce(lambda x, y: x + y,          \
                  [reduce(lambda x, y: x + y, row)  \
                       for row in mat])

Out[113]: CPU times: user 4.3 s, sys: 52 ms, total: 4.35 s
          Wall time: 4.07 s

          678.5908519876674
```

Let us now turn to NumPy and see how the same problem is solved there. For convenience, the NumPy sublibrary random offers a multitude of functions to initialize a numpy.ndarray object and populate it at the same time with (pseudo)random numbers:

```
In [114]: %time mat = np.random.standard_normal((I, I))
```

```
Out[114]: CPU times: user 1.83 s, sys: 40 ms, total: 1.87 s
          Wall time: 1.87 s
```

```
In [115]: %time mat.sum()
```

```
Out[115]: CPU times: user 36 ms, sys: 0 ns, total: 36 ms
          Wall time: 34.6 ms
```

```
          349.49777911439384
```

We observe the following:

Syntax

Although we use several approaches to compact the pure Python code, the NumPy version is even more compact and readable.

Performance

The generation of the numpy.ndarray object is roughly 20 times faster and the calculation of the sum is roughly 100 times faster than the respective operations in pure Python.

Using NumPy Arrays

The use of NumPy for array-based operations and algorithms generally results in compact, easily readable code and significant performance improvements over pure Python code.

Structured Arrays

The specialization of the numpy.ndarray class obviously brings a number of really valuable benefits with it. However, a too-narrow specialization might turn out to be too large a burden to carry for the majority of array-based algorithms and applications. Therefore, NumPy provides structured arrays that allow us to have different NumPy data types *per column*, at least. What does "per column" mean? Consider the following initialization of a structured array object:

```
In [116]: dt = np.dtype([('Name', 'S10'), ('Age', 'i4'),
                         ('Height', 'f'), ('Children/Pets', 'i4', 2)])
          s = np.array([('Smith', 45, 1.83, (0, 1)),
                       ('Jones', 53, 1.72, (2, 2))], dtype=dt)
          s
```

```
Out[116]: array([('Smith', 45, 1.8300000429153442, [0, 1]),
                 ('Jones', 53, 1.7200000286102295, [2, 2])],
                dtype=[('Name', 'S10'), ('Age', '<i4'), ('Height', '<f4'), ('Chi
          ldren/Pets', '<i4', (2,))])
```

In a sense, this construction comes quite close to the operation for initializing tables in a SQL database. We have column names and column data types, with maybe some additional information (e.g., maximum number of characters per `string` object). The single columns can now be easily accessed by their names:

```
In [117]: s['Name']
Out[117]: array(['Smith', 'Jones'],
                dtype='|S10')
In [118]: s['Height'].mean()
Out[118]: 1.7750001
```

Having selected a specific row and record, respectively, the resulting objects mainly behave like `dict` objects, where one can retrieve values via keys:

```
In [119]: s[1]['Age']
Out[119]: 53
```

In summary, structured arrays are a generalization of the regular `numpy.ndarray` object types in that the data type only has to be the same *per column*, as one is used to in the context of tables in SQL databases. One advantage of structured arrays is that a single element of a column can be another multidimensional object and does not have to conform to the basic NumPy data types.

Structured Arrays

NumPy provides, in addition to regular arrays, structured arrays that allow the description and handling of rather complex array-oriented data structures with a variety of different data types and even structures per (named) column. They bring SQL table-like data structures to Python, with all the benefits of regular `numpy.ndarray` objects (syntax, methods, performance).

Vectorization of Code

Vectorization of code is a strategy to get more compact code that is possibly executed faster. The fundamental idea is to conduct an operation on or to apply a function to a complex object "at once" and not by iterating over the single elements of the object. In Python, the functional programming tools `map`, `filter`, and `reduce` provide means for vectorization. In a sense, NumPy has vectorization built in deep down in its core.

Basic Vectorization

As we learned in the previous section, simple mathematical operations can be implemented on `numpy.ndarray` objects directly. For example, we can add two NumPy arrays element-wise as follows:

```
In [120]: r = np.random.standard_normal((4, 3))
          s = np.random.standard_normal((4, 3))

In [121]: r + s

Out[121]: array([[-1.94801686, -0.6855251 ,  2.28954806],
                 [ 0.33847593, -1.97109602,  1.30071653],
                 [-1.12066585,  0.22234207, -2.73940339],
                 [ 0.43787363,  0.52938941, -1.38467623]])
```

NumPy also supports what is called *broadcasting*. This allows us to combine objects of different shape within a single operation. We have already made use of this before. Consider the following example:

```
In [122]: 2 * r + 3

Out[122]: array([[ 2.54691692,  1.65823523,  8.14636725],
                 [ 4.94758114,  0.25648128,  1.89566919],
                 [ 0.41775907,  0.58038395,  2.06567484],
                 [ 0.67600205,  3.41004636,  1.07282384]])
```

In this case, the r object is multiplied by 2 element-wise and then 3 is added element-wise—the 3 is *broadcasted* or *stretched* to the shape of the r object. It works with differently shaped arrays as well, up to a certain point:

```
In [123]: s = np.random.standard_normal(3)
          r + s

Out[123]: array([[ 0.23324118, -1.09764268,  1.90412565],
                 [ 1.43357329, -1.79851966, -1.22122338],
                 [-0.83133775, -1.63656832, -1.13622055],
                 [-0.70221625, -0.22173711, -1.63264605]])
```

This broadcasts the one-dimensional array of size 3 to a shape of (4, 3). The same does not work, for example, with a one-dimensional array of size 4:

```
In [124]: s = np.random.standard_normal(4)
          r + s

Out[124]: ValueError
          operands could not be broadcast together with shapes (4,3) (4,)
```

However, transposing the r object makes the operation work again. In the following code, the transpose method transforms the ndarray object with shape (4, 3) into an object of the same type with shape (3, 4):

```
In [125]: r.transpose() + s

Out[125]: array([[-0.63380522,  0.5964174 ,  0.88641996, -0.86931849],
                 [-1.07814606, -1.74913253,  0.9677324 ,  0.49770367],
                 [ 2.16591995, -0.92953858,  1.71037785, -0.67090759]])

In [126]: np.shape(r.T)

Out[126]: (3, 4)
```

As a general rule, custom-defined Python functions work with numpy.ndarrays as well. If the implementation allows, arrays can be used with functions just as int or float objects can. Consider the following function:

```
In [127]: def f(x):
              return 3 * x + 5
```

We can pass standard Python objects as well as numpy.ndarray objects (for which the operations in the function have to be defined, of course):

```
In [128]: f(0.5)  # float object

Out[128]: 6.5

In [129]: f(r)  # NumPy array

Out[129]: array([[  4.32037538,   2.98735285,  12.71955087],
                 [  7.9213717 ,   0.88472192,   3.34350378],
                 [  1.1266386 ,   1.37057593,   3.59851226],
                 [  1.51400308,   5.61506954,   2.10923576]])
```

What NumPy does is to simply apply the function f to the object element-wise. In that sense, by using this kind of operation we do *not* avoid loops; we only avoid them on the Python level and delegate the looping to NumPy. On the NumPy level, looping over the numpy.ndarray object is taken care of by highly optimized code, most of it written in C and therefore generally much faster than pure Python. This explains the "secret" behind the performance benefits of using NumPy for array-based use cases.

When working with arrays, one has to take care to call the right functions on the respective objects. For example, the sin function from the standard math module of Python does not work with NumPy arrays:

```
In [130]: import math
          math.sin(r)

Out[130]: TypeError
          only length-1 arrays can be converted to Python scalars
```

The function is designed to handle, for example, float objects—i.e., single numbers, not arrays. NumPy provides the respective counterparts as so-called *ufuncs*, or *universal functions*:

```
In [131]: np.sin(r)  # array as input

Out[131]: array([[-0.22460878, -0.62167738,  0.53829193],
                 [ 0.82702259, -0.98025745, -0.52453206],
                 [-0.96114497, -0.93554821, -0.45035471],
                 [-0.91759955,  0.20358986, -0.82124413]])

In [132]: np.sin(np.pi)  # float as input

Out[132]: 1.2246467991473532e-16
```

NumPy provides a large number of such ufuncs that generalize typical mathematical functions to numpy.ndarray objects.[5]

Universal Functions

Be careful when using the from library import * approach to importing. Such an approach can cause the NumPy reference to the *ufunc* numpy.sin to be replaced by the reference to the math function math.sin. You should, as a rule, import both libraries by name to avoid confusion: import numpy as np; import math. Then you can use math.sin alongside np.sin.

Memory Layout

When we first initialized numpy.ndarray objects by using numpy.zero, we provided an optional argument for the memory layout. This argument specifies, roughly speaking, which elements of an array get stored in memory next to each other. When working with small arrays, this has hardly any measurable impact on the performance of array operations. However, when arrays get large the story is somewhat different, depending on the operations to be implemented on the arrays.

To illustrate this important point for memory-wise handling of arrays in science and finance, consider the following construction of multidimensional numpy.ndarray objects:

```
In [133]: x = np.random.standard_normal((5, 10000000))
          y = 2 * x + 3  # linear equation y = a * x + b
          C = np.array((x, y), order='C')
          F = np.array((x, y), order='F')
          x = 0.0; y = 0.0  # memory cleanup

In [134]: C[:2].round(2)

Out[134]: array([[[-0.51, -1.14, -1.07, ...,  0.2 , -0.18,  0.1 ],
                  [-1.22,  0.68,  1.83, ...,  1.23, -0.27, -0.16],
                  [ 0.45,  0.15,  0.01, ..., -0.75,  0.91, -1.12],
                  [-0.16,  1.4 , -0.79, ..., -0.33,  0.54,  1.81],
                  [ 1.07, -1.07, -0.37, ..., -0.76,  0.71,  0.34]],

                 [[ 1.98,  0.72,  0.86, ...,  3.4 ,  2.64,  3.21],
                  [ 0.55,  4.37,  6.66, ...,  5.47,  2.47,  2.68],
                  [ 3.9 ,  3.29,  3.03, ...,  1.5 ,  4.82,  0.76],
                  [ 2.67,  5.8 ,  1.42, ...,  2.34,  4.09,  6.63],
                  [ 5.14,  0.87,  2.27, ...,  1.48,  4.43,  3.67]]])
```

---

5. Cf. *http://docs.scipy.org/doc/numpy/reference/ufuncs.html* for an overview.

Let's look at some really fundamental examples and use cases for both types of `ndarray` objects:

```
In [135]: %timeit C.sum()
Out[135]: 10 loops, best of 3: 123 ms per loop
In [136]: %timeit F.sum()
Out[136]: 10 loops, best of 3: 123 ms per loop
```

When summing up all elements of the arrays, there is no performance difference between the two memory layouts. However, consider the following example with the C-like memory layout:

```
In [137]: %timeit C[0].sum(axis=0)
Out[137]: 10 loops, best of 3: 102 ms per loop
In [138]: %timeit C[0].sum(axis=1)
Out[138]: 10 loops, best of 3: 61.9 ms per loop
```

Summing five large vectors and getting back a single large results vector obviously is slower in this case than summing 10,000,000 small ones and getting back an equal number of results. This is due to the fact that the single elements of the small vectors—i.e., the *rows*—are stored next to each other. With the `Fortran`-like memory layout, the relative performance changes considerably:

```
In [139]: %timeit F.sum(axis=0)
Out[139]: 1 loops, best of 3: 801 ms per loop
In [140]: %timeit F.sum(axis=1)
Out[140]: 1 loops, best of 3: 2.23 s per loop
In [141]: F = 0.0; C = 0.0  # memory cleanup
```

In this case, operating on a few large vectors performs better than operating on a large number of small ones. The elements of the few large vectors are stored in memory next to each other, which explains the relative performance advantage. However, overall the operations are absolutely much slower when compared to the C-like variant.

Conclusions

Python provides, in combination with NumPy, a rich set of flexible data structures. From a finance point of view, the following can be considered the most important ones:

Basic data types

In finance, the classes `int`, `float`, and `string` provide the atomic data types.

Standard data structures

The classes `tuple`, `list`, `dict`, and `set` have many application areas in finance, with `list` being the most flexible workhorse in general.

Arrays

A large class of finance-related problems and algorithms can be cast to an array setting; `NumPy` provides the specialized class `numpy.ndarray`, which provides both convenience and compactness of code as well as high performance.

This chapter shows that both the basic data structures and the `NumPy` ones allow for highly vectorized implementation of algorithms. Depending on the specific shape of the data structures, care should be taken with regard to the memory layout of arrays. Choosing the right approach here can speed up code execution by a factor of two or more.

Further Reading

This chapter focuses on those issues that might be of particular importance for finance algorithms and applications. However, it can only represent a starting point for the exploration of data structures and data modeling in `Python`. There are a number of valuable resources available to go deeper from here.

Here are some Internet resources to consult:

- The `Python` documentation is always a good starting point: *http://www.python.org/doc/*.

- For details on `NumPy` arrays as well as related methods and functions, see *http://docs.scipy.org/doc/*.

- The `SciPy` lecture notes are also a good source to get started: *http://scipy-lectures.github.io/*.

Good references in book form are:

- Goodrich, Michael et al. (2013): *Data Structures and Algorithms in Python.* John Wiley & Sons, Hoboken, NJ.

- Langtangen, Hans Petter (2009): *A Primer on Scientific Programming with Python.* Springer Verlag, Berlin, Heidelberg.

## CHAPTER 5

Data Visualization

> Use a picture. It's worth a thousand words.
>
> — Arthur Brisbane (1911)

This chapter is about basic visualization capabilities of the `matplotlib` library (*http://www.matplotlib.org*). Although there are many other visualization libraries available, `matplotlib` has established itself as the benchmark and, in many situations, a robust and reliable visualization tool. It is both easy to use for standard plots and flexible when it comes to more complex plots and customizations. In addition, it is tightly integrated with `NumPy` and the data structures that it provides.

This chapter mainly covers the following topics:

2D plotting

  From the most simple to some more advanced plots with two scales or different subplots; typical financial plots, like candlestick charts, are also covered.

3D plotting

  A selection of 3D plots useful for financial applications are presented.

This chapter cannot be comprehensive with regard to data visualization with `Python` and `matplotlib`, but it provides a number of examples for the most basic and most important capabilities for finance. Other examples are also found in later chapters. For instance, Chapter 6 shows how to visualize time series data with the `pandas` library.

Two-Dimensional Plotting

To begin with, we have to import the respective libraries. The main plotting functions are found in the sublibrary `matplotlib.pyplot`:

```
In [1]: import numpy as np
        import matplotlib as mpl
```

```
import matplotlib.pyplot as plt
%matplotlib inline
```

One-Dimensional Data Set

In all that follows, we will plot data stored in NumPy ndarray objects. However, matplot lib is of course able to plot data stored in different Python formats, like list objects, as well. First, we need data that we can plot. To this end, we generate 20 standard normally distributed (pseudo)random numbers as a NumPy ndarray:

```
In [2]: np.random.seed(1000)
        y = np.random.standard_normal(20)
```

The most fundamental, but nevertheless quite powerful, plotting function is plot from the pyplot sublibrary. In principle, it needs two sets of numbers:

- **x values**: a list or an array containing the x coordinates (values of the abscissa)
- **y values**: a list or an array containing the y coordinates (values of the ordinate)

The number of x and y values provided must match, of course. Consider the following two lines of code, whose output is presented in Figure 5-1:

```
In [3]: x = range(len(y))
        plt.plot(x, y)
```

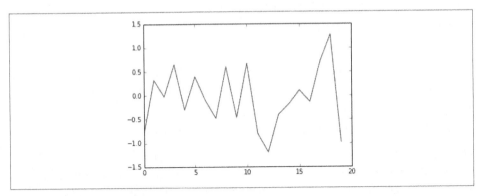

Figure 5-1. Plot given x and y values

plot notices when you pass an ndarray object. In this case, there is no need to provide the "extra" information of the x values. If you only provide the y values, plot takes the index values as the respective x values. Therefore, the following single line of code generates exactly the same output (cf. Figure 5-2):

```
In [4]: plt.plot(y)
```

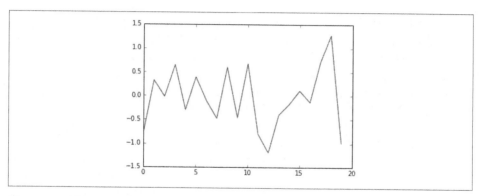

Figure 5-2. Plot given data as 1D array

NumPy Arrays and matplotlib
You can simply pass NumPy ndarray objects to matplotlib functions. It is able to interpret the data structure for simplified plotting. However, be careful to not pass a too large and/or complex array.

Since the majority of the ndarray methods return again an ndarray object, you can also pass your object with a method (or even multiple methods, in some cases) attached. By calling the cumsum method on the ndarray object with the sample data, we get the cumulative sum of this data and, as to be expected, a different output (cf. Figure 5-3):

```
In [5]: plt.plot(y.cumsum())
```

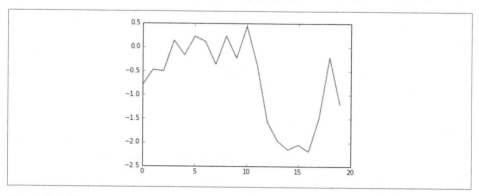

Figure 5-3. Plot given a 1D array with method attached

In general, the default plotting style does not satisfy typical requirements for reports, publications, etc. For example, you might want to customize the font used (e.g., for compatibility with LaTeX fonts), to have labels at the axes, or to plot a grid for better readability. Therefore, matplotlib offers a large number of functions to customize the plotting style. Some are easily accessible; for others one has to go a bit deeper. Easily accessible, for example, are those functions that manipulate the axes and those that add grids and labels (cf. Figure 5-4):

```
In [6]: plt.plot(y.cumsum())
        plt.grid(True)  # adds a grid
        plt.axis('tight')  # adjusts the axis ranges
```

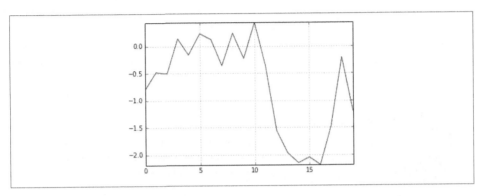

Figure 5-4. Plot with grid and tight axes

Other options for `plt.axis` are given in Table 5-1, the majority of which have to be passed as a `string` object.

Table 5-1. Options for plt.axis

Parameter	Description
Empty	Returns current axis limits
off	Turns axis lines and labels off
equal	Leads to equal scaling
scaled	Equal scaling via dimension changes
tight	Makes all data visible (tightens limits)
image	Makes all data visible (with data limits)
[xmin, xmax, ymin, ymax]	Sets limits to given (list of) values

In addition, you can directly set the minimum and maximum values of each axis by using `plt.xlim` and `plt.ylim`. The following code provides an example whose output is shown in Figure 5-5:

```
In [7]: plt.plot(y.cumsum())
        plt.grid(True)
        plt.xlim(-1, 20)
        plt.ylim(np.min(y.cumsum()) - 1,
                 np.max(y.cumsum()) + 1)
```

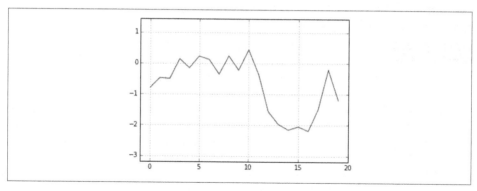

Figure 5-5. Plot with custom axis limits

For the sake of better readability, a plot usually contains a number of labels—e.g., a title and labels describing the nature of x and y values. These are added by the functions plt.title, plt.xlabel, and plt.ylabel, respectively. By default, plot plots continuous lines, even if discrete data points are provided. The plotting of discrete points is accomplished by choosing a different style option. Figure 5-6 overlays (red) points and a (blue) line with line width of 1.5 points:

```
In [8]: plt.figure(figsize=(7, 4))
        # the figsize parameter defines the
        # size of the figure in (width, height)
        plt.plot(y.cumsum(), 'b', lw=1.5)
        plt.plot(y.cumsum(), 'ro')
        plt.grid(True)
        plt.axis('tight')
        plt.xlabel('index')
        plt.ylabel('value')
        plt.title('A Simple Plot')
```

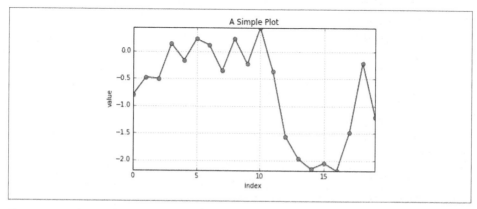

Figure 5-6. Plot with typical labels

By default, `plt.plot` supports the color abbreviations in Table 5-2.

Table 5-2. Standard color abbreviations

Character	Color
b	Blue
g	Green
r	Red
c	Cyan
m	Magenta
y	Yellow
k	Black
w	White

In terms of line and/or point styles, `plt.plot` supports the characters listed in Table 5-3.

Table 5-3. Standard style characters

Character	Symbol
-	Solid line style
--	Dashed line style
-.	Dash-dot line style
:	Dotted line style
.	Point marker
,	Pixel marker
o	Circle marker
v	Triangle_down marker
^	Triangle_up marker
<	Triangle_left marker
>	Triangle_right marker
1	Tri_down marker
2	Tri_up marker
3	Tri_left marker
4	Tri_right marker
s	Square marker
p	Pentagon marker
*	Star marker
h	Hexagon1 marker
H	Hexagon2 marker
+	Plus marker

Character	Symbol
x	X marker
D	Diamond marker
d	Thin diamond marker
		Vline marker

Any color abbreviation can be combined with any style character. In this way, you can make sure that different data sets are easily distinguished. As we will see, the plotting style will also be reflected in the legend.

Two-Dimensional Data Set

Plotting one-dimensional data can be considered a special case. In general, data sets will consist of multiple separate subsets of data. The handling of such data sets follows the same rules with matplotlib as with one-dimensional data. However, a number of additional issues might arise in such a context. For example, two data sets might have such a different scaling that they cannot be plotted using the same y- and/or x-axis scaling. Another issue might be that you may want to visualize two different data sets in different ways, e.g., one by a line plot and the other by a bar plot.

To begin with, let us first generate a two-dimensional sample data set. The code that follows generates first a NumPy ndarray of shape 20 × 2 with standard normally distributed (pseudo)random numbers. On this array, the method cumsum is called to calculate the cumulative sum of the sample data along axis 0 (i.e., the first dimension):

```
In [9]: np.random.seed(2000)
        y = np.random.standard_normal((20, 2)).cumsum(axis=0)
```

In general, you can also pass such two-dimensional arrays to plt.plot. It will then automatically interpret the contained data as separate data sets (along axis 1, i.e., the second dimension). A respective plot is shown in Figure 5-7:

```
In [10]: plt.figure(figsize=(7, 4))
         plt.plot(y, lw=1.5)
           # plots two lines
         plt.plot(y, 'ro')
           # plots two dotted lines
         plt.grid(True)
         plt.axis('tight')
         plt.xlabel('index')
         plt.ylabel('value')
         plt.title('A Simple Plot')
```

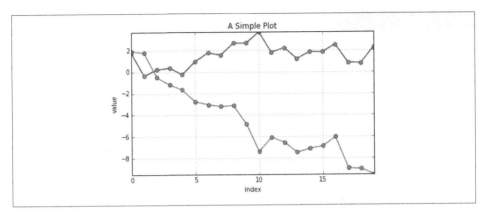

Figure 5-7. Plot with two data sets

In such a case, further annotations might be helpful to better read the plot. You can add individual labels to each data set and have them listed in the legend. plt.legend accepts different locality parameters. 0 stands for *best location*, in the sense that as little data as possible is hidden by the legend. Figure 5-8 shows the plot of the two data sets, this time with a legend. In the generating code, we now do not pass the ndarray object as a whole but rather access the two data subsets separately (y[:, 0] and y[:, 0]), which allows us to attach individual labels to them:

```
In [11]: plt.figure(figsize=(7, 4))
         plt.plot(y[:, 0], lw=1.5, label='1st')
         plt.plot(y[:, 1], lw=1.5, label='2nd')
         plt.plot(y, 'ro')
         plt.grid(True)
         plt.legend(loc=0)
         plt.axis('tight')
         plt.xlabel('index')
         plt.ylabel('value')
         plt.title('A Simple Plot')
```

Further location options for plt.legend include those presented in Table 5-4.

Table 5-4. Options for plt.legend

Loc	Description
Empty	Automatic
0	Best possible
1	Upper right
2	Upper left
3	Lower left
4	Lower right
5	Right

Loc	Description
6	Center left
7	Center right
8	Lower center
9	Upper center
10	Center

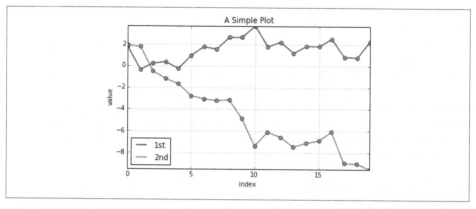

Figure 5-8. Plot with labeled data sets

Multiple data sets with a similar scaling, like simulated paths for the same financial risk factor, can be plotted using a single y-axis. However, often data sets show rather different scalings and the plotting of such data with a single y scale generally leads to a significant loss of visual information. To illustrate the effect, we scale the first of the two data subsets by a factor of 100 and plot the data again (cf. Figure 5-9):

```
In [12]: y[:, 0] = y[:, 0] * 100
         plt.figure(figsize=(7, 4))
         plt.plot(y[:, 0], lw=1.5, label='1st')
         plt.plot(y[:, 1], lw=1.5, label='2nd')
         plt.plot(y, 'ro')
         plt.grid(True)
         plt.legend(loc=0)
         plt.axis('tight')
         plt.xlabel('index')
         plt.ylabel('value')
         plt.title('A Simple Plot')
```

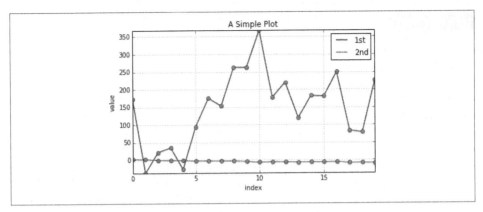

Figure 5-9. Plot with two differently scaled data sets

Inspection of Figure 5-9 reveals that the first data set is still "visually readable," while the second data set now looks like a straight line with the new scaling of the y-axis. In a sense, information about the second data set now gets "visually lost." There are two basic approaches to resolve this problem:

- Use of two y-axes (left/right)
- Use of two subplots (upper/lower, left/right)

Let us first introduce a second y-axis into the plot. Figure 5-10 now has two different y-axes. The left y-axis is for the first data set while the right y-axis is for the second. Consequently, there are also two legends:

```
In [13]: fig, ax1 = plt.subplots()
         plt.plot(y[:, 0], 'b', lw=1.5, label='1st')
         plt.plot(y[:, 0], 'ro')
         plt.grid(True)
         plt.legend(loc=8)
         plt.axis('tight')
         plt.xlabel('index')
         plt.ylabel('value 1st')
         plt.title('A Simple Plot')
         ax2 = ax1.twinx()
         plt.plot(y[:, 1], 'g', lw=1.5, label='2nd')
         plt.plot(y[:, 1], 'ro')
         plt.legend(loc=0)
         plt.ylabel('value 2nd')
```

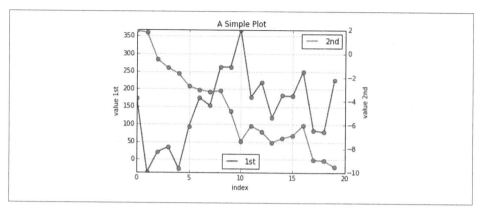

Figure 5-10. Plot with two data sets and two y-axes

The key lines of code are those that help manage the axes. These are the ones that follow:

```
fig, ax1 = plt.subplots()
    # plot first data set using first (left) axis
ax2 = ax1.twinx()
    # plot second data set using second (right) axis
```

By using the `plt.subplots` function, we get direct access to the underlying plotting objects (the figure, subplots, etc.). It allows us, for example, to generate a second subplot that shares the x-axis with the first subplot. In Figure 5-10 we have, then, actually two subplots that *overlay* each other.

Next, consider the case of two *separate* subplots. This option gives even more freedom to handle the two data sets, as Figure 5-11 illustrates:

```
In [14]: plt.figure(figsize=(7, 5))
         plt.subplot(211)
         plt.plot(y[:, 0], lw=1.5, label='1st')
         plt.plot(y[:, 0], 'ro')
         plt.grid(True)
         plt.legend(loc=0)
         plt.axis('tight')
         plt.ylabel('value')
         plt.title('A Simple Plot')
         plt.subplot(212)
         plt.plot(y[:, 1], 'g', lw=1.5, label='2nd')
         plt.plot(y[:, 1], 'ro')
         plt.grid(True)
         plt.legend(loc=0)
         plt.axis('tight')
         plt.xlabel('index')
         plt.ylabel('value')
```

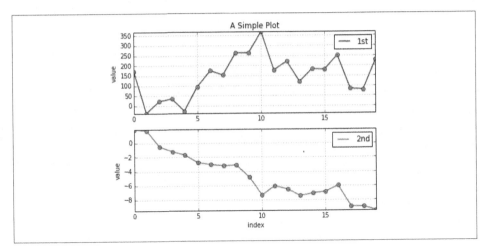

Figure 5-11. Plot with two subplots

The placing of subplots in the a `matplotlib` `figure` object is accomplished here by the use of a special coordinate system. `plt.subplot` takes as arguments three integers for `numrows`, `numcols`, and `fignum` (either separated by commas or not). `numrows` specifies the number of *rows*, `numcols` the number of *columns*, and `fignum` the number of the *sub-plot*, starting with 1 and ending with `numrows` * `numcols`. For example, a figure with nine equally sized subplots would have `numrows=3`, `numcols=3`, and `fig num=1,2,...,9`. The lower-right subplot would have the following "coordinates": `plt.subplot(3, 3, 9)`.

Sometimes, it might be necessary or desired to choose two different plot types to visualize such data. With the subplot approach you have the freedom to combine arbitrary kinds of plots that `matplotlib` offers.[1] Figure 5-12 combines a line/point plot with a bar chart:

```
In [15]: plt.figure(figsize=(9, 4))
         plt.subplot(121)
         plt.plot(y[:, 0], lw=1.5, label='1st')
         plt.plot(y[:, 0], 'ro')
         plt.grid(True)
         plt.legend(loc=0)
         plt.axis('tight')
         plt.xlabel('index')
         plt.ylabel('value')
         plt.title('1st Data Set')
         plt.subplot(122)
         plt.bar(np.arange(len(y)), y[:, 1], width=0.5,
```

---

1. For an overview of which plot types are available, visit the `matplotlib` gallery (*http://matplotlib.org/gallery.html*).

```
                color='g', label='2nd')
    plt.grid(True)
    plt.legend(loc=0)
    plt.axis('tight')
    plt.xlabel('index')
    plt.title('2nd Data Set')
```

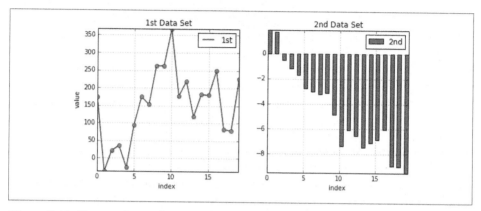

Figure 5-12. Plot combining line/point subplot with bar subplot

Other Plot Styles

When it comes to two-dimensional plotting, line and point plots are probably the most important ones in finance; this is because many data sets embody time series data, which generally is visualized by such plots. Chapter 6 addresses financial times series data in detail. However, for the moment we want to stick with the two-dimensional data set and illustrate some alternative, and for financial applications useful, visualization approaches.

The first is the *scatter plot*, where the values of one data set serve as the x values for the other data set. Figure 5-13 shows such a plot. Such a plot type is used, for example, when you want to plot the returns of one financial time series against those of another one. For this example we will use a new two-dimensional data set with some more data:

```
In [16]: y = np.random.standard_normal((1000, 2))
```

```
In [17]: plt.figure(figsize=(7, 5))
         plt.plot(y[:, 0], y[:, 1], 'ro')
         plt.grid(True)
         plt.xlabel('1st')
         plt.ylabel('2nd')
         plt.title('Scatter Plot')
```

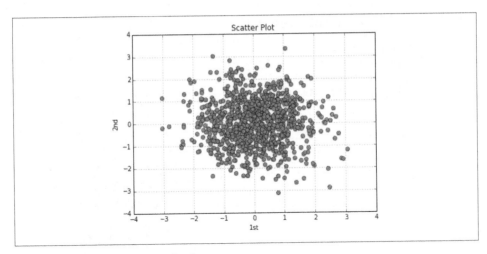

Figure 5-13. Scatter plot via plot function

matplotlib also provides a specific function to generate scatter plots. It basically works in the same way, but provides some additional features. Figure 5-14 shows the corresponding scatter plot to Figure 5-13, this time generated using the scatter function:

```
In [18]: plt.figure(figsize=(7, 5))
         plt.scatter(y[:, 0], y[:, 1], marker='o')
         plt.grid(True)
         plt.xlabel('1st')
         plt.ylabel('2nd')
         plt.title('Scatter Plot')
```

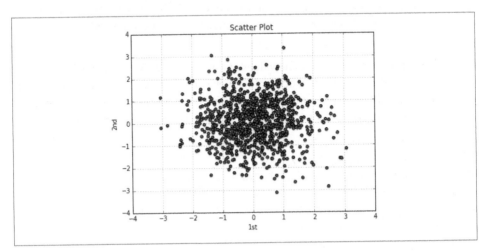

Figure 5-14. Scatter plot via scatter function

The scatter plotting function, for example, allows the addition of a third dimension, which can be visualized through different colors and be described by the use of a color bar. To this end, we generate a third data set with random data, this time with integers between 0 and 10:

```
In [19]: c = np.random.randint(0, 10, len(y))
```

Figure 5-15 shows a scatter plot where there is a third dimension illustrated by different colors of the single dots and with a color bar as a legend for the colors:

```
In [20]: plt.figure(figsize=(7, 5))
         plt.scatter(y[:, 0], y[:, 1], c=c, marker='o')
         plt.colorbar()
         plt.grid(True)
         plt.xlabel('1st')
         plt.ylabel('2nd')
         plt.title('Scatter Plot')
```

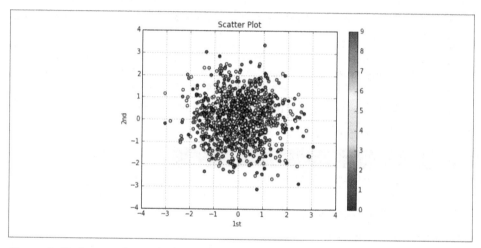

Figure 5-15. Scatter plot with third dimension

Another type of plot, the *histogram*, is also often used in the context of financial returns. Figure 5-16 puts the frequency values of the two data sets next to each other in the same plot:

```
In [21]: plt.figure(figsize=(7, 4))
         plt.hist(y, label=['1st', '2nd'], bins=25)
         plt.grid(True)
         plt.legend(loc=0)
         plt.xlabel('value')
         plt.ylabel('frequency')
         plt.title('Histogram')
```

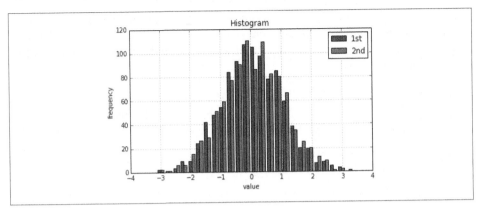

Figure 5-16. Histogram for two data sets

Since the histogram is such an important plot type for financial applications, let us take a closer look at the use of `plt.hist`. The following example illustrates the parameters that are supported:

```
plt.hist(x, bins=10, range=None, normed=False, weights=None, cumulative=False,
bottom=None, histtype='bar', align='mid', orientation='vertical', rwidth=None,
log=False, color=None, label=None, stacked=False, hold=None, **kwargs)
```

Table 5-5 provides a description of the main parameters of the `plt.hist` function.

Table 5-5. Parameters for plt.hist

Parameter	Description
x	`list` object(s), `ndarray` object
bins	Number of bins
range	Lower and upper range of bins
normed	Norming such that integral value is 1
weights	Weights for every value in x
cumulative	Every bin contains the counts of the lower bins
histtype	Options (strings): `bar`, `barstacked`, `step`, `stepfilled`
align	Options (strings): `left`, `mid`, `right`
orientation	Options (strings): `horizontal`, `vertical`
rwidth	Relative width of the bars
log	Log scale
color	Color per data set (array-like)
label	String or sequence of strings for labels
stacked	Stacks multiple data sets

Figure 5-17 shows a similar plot; this time, the data of the two data sets is stacked in the histogram:

```
In [22]: plt.figure(figsize=(7, 4))
         plt.hist(y, label=['1st', '2nd'], color=['b', 'g'],
                  stacked=True, bins=20)
         plt.grid(True)
         plt.legend(loc=0)
         plt.xlabel('value')
         plt.ylabel('frequency')
         plt.title('Histogram')
```

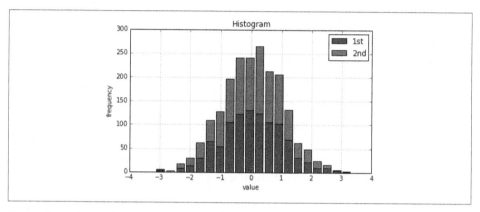

Figure 5-17. Stacked histogram for two data sets

Another useful plot type is the *boxplot*. Similar to the histogram, the boxplot allows both a concise overview of the characteristics of a data set and easy comparison of multiple data sets. Figure 5-18 shows such a plot for our data set:

```
In [23]: fig, ax = plt.subplots(figsize=(7, 4))
         plt.boxplot(y)
         plt.grid(True)
         plt.setp(ax, xticklabels=['1st', '2nd'])
         plt.xlabel('data set')
         plt.ylabel('value')
         plt.title('Boxplot')
```

This last example uses the function plt.setp, which sets properties for a (set of) plotting instance(s). For example, considering a line plot generated by:

```
line = plt.plot(data, 'r')
```

the following code:

```
plt.setp(line, linestyle='--')
```

changes the style of the line to "dashed." This way, you can easily change parameters after the plotting instance ("artist object") has been generated.

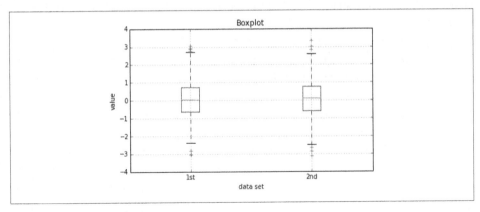

Figure 5-18. Boxplot for two data sets

As a final illustration in this section, we consider a mathematically inspired plot that can also be found as an example in the gallery for matplotlib (*http://www.matplot lib.org/gallery.html*). It plots a function and illustrates graphically the area below the function between a lower and an upper limit—in other words, the integral value of the function between the lower and upper limits. Figure 5-19 shows the resulting plot and illustrates that matplotlib seamlessly handles LaTeX type setting for the inclusion of mathematical formulae into plots:

```
In [24]: from matplotlib.patches import Polygon
         def func(x):
             return 0.5 * np.exp(x) + 1

         a, b = 0.5, 1.5  # integral limits
         x = np.linspace(0, 2)
         y = func(x)

         fig, ax = plt.subplots(figsize=(7, 5))
         plt.plot(x, y, 'b', linewidth=2)
         plt.ylim(ymin=0)

         # Illustrate the integral value, i.e. the area under the function
         # between the lower and upper limits
         Ix = np.linspace(a, b)
         Iy = func(Ix)
         verts = [(a, 0)] + list(zip(Ix, Iy)) + [(b, 0)]
         poly = Polygon(verts, facecolor='0.7', edgecolor='0.5')
         ax.add_patch(poly)

         plt.text(0.5 * (a + b), 1, r"$\int_a^b f(x)\mathrm{d}x$",
                  horizontalalignment='center', fontsize=20)

         plt.figtext(0.9, 0.075, '$x$')
         plt.figtext(0.075, 0.9, '$f(x)$')
```

```
ax.set_xticks((a, b))
ax.set_xticklabels(('$a$', '$b$'))
ax.set_yticks([func(a), func(b)])
ax.set_yticklabels(('$f(a)$', '$f(b)$'))
plt.grid(True)
```

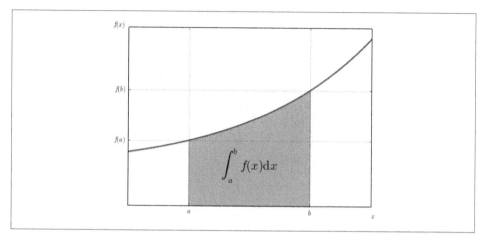

Figure 5-19. Exponential function, integral area, and LaTeX labels

Let us go through the generation of this plot step by step. The first step is the definition of the function to be integrated:

```
def func(x):
    return 0.5 * np.exp(x) + 1
```

The second step is the definition of the integral limits and the generation of needed numerical values:

```
a, b = 0.5, 1.5  # integral limits
x = np.linspace(0, 2)
y = func(x)
```

Third, we plot the function itself:

```
fig, ax = plt.subplots(figsize=(7, 5))
plt.plot(x, y, 'b', linewidth=2)
plt.ylim(ymin=0)
```

Fourth and central, we generate the shaded area ("patch") by the use of the `Polygon` function illustrating the integral area:

```
Ix = np.linspace(a, b)
Iy = func(Ix)
verts = [(a, 0)] + list(zip(Ix, Iy)) + [(b, 0)]
poly = Polygon(verts, facecolor='0.7', edgecolor='0.5')
ax.add_patch(poly)
```

The fifth step is the addition of the mathematical formula and some axis labels to the plot, using the `plt.text` and `plt.figtext` functions. LaTeX code is passed between two dollar signs ($ ... $). The first two parameters of both functions are coordinate values to place the respective text:

```
plt.text(0.5 * (a + b), 1, r"$\int_a^b f(x)\mathrm{d}x$",
         horizontalalignment='center', fontsize=20)

plt.figtext(0.9, 0.075, '$x$')
plt.figtext(0.075, 0.9, '$f(x)$')
```

Finally, we set the individual x and y tick labels at their respective positions. Note that although we place variable names rendered in LaTeX, the correct numerical values are used for the placing. We also add a grid, which in this particular case is only drawn for the selected ticks highlighted before:

```
ax.set_xticks((a, b))
ax.set_xticklabels(('$a$', '$b$'))
ax.set_yticks([func(a), func(b)])
ax.set_yticklabels(('$f(a)$', '$f(b)$'))
plt.grid(True)
```

Financial Plots

`matplotlib` also provides a small selection of special finance plots. These, like the *candlestick* plot, are mainly used to visualize historical stock price data or similar financial time series data. Those plotting capabilities are found in the `matplotlib.finance` sublibrary:

```
In [25]: import matplotlib.finance as mpf
```

As a convenience function, this sublibrary allows for easy retrieval of historical stock price data from the Yahoo! Finance website (cf. *http://finance.yahoo.com*). All you need are start and end dates and the respective ticker symbol. The following retrieves data for the German DAX index whose ticker symbol is ^GDAXI:

```
In [26]: start = (2014, 5, 1)
         end = (2014, 6, 30)

         quotes = mpf.quotes_historical_yahoo('^GDAXI', start, end)
```

Data Quality of Web Sources

Nowadays, a couple of Python libraries provide convenience functions to retrieve data from Yahoo! Finance. Be aware that, although this is a convenient way to visualize financial data sets, the data quality is not sufficient to base any important investment decision on it. For example, stock splits, leading to "price drops," are often not correctly accounted for in the data provided by Yahoo! Finance. This holds true for a number of other freely available data sources as well.

quotes now contains time series data for the DAX index starting with Date (in epoch time format), then Open, High, Low, Close, and Volume:

```
In [27]: quotes[:2]

Out[27]: [(735355.0,
           9611.7900000000009,
           9556.0200000000004,
           9627.3799999999992,
           9533.2999999999993,
           88062300.0),
          (735358.0,
           9536.3799999999992,
           9529.5,
           9548.1700000000001,
           9407.0900000000001,
           61911600.0)]
```

The plotting functions of matplotlib.finance understand exactly this format and the data set can be passed, for example, to the candlestick function as it is. Figure 5-20 shows the result. Daily *positive* returns are indicated by *blue* rectangles, and *negative* returns by *red* ones. As you notice, matplotlib takes care of the right labeling of the x-axis given the date information in the data set:

```
In [28]: fig, ax = plt.subplots(figsize=(8, 5))
         fig.subplots_adjust(bottom=0.2)
         mpf.candlestick(ax, quotes, width=0.6, colorup='b', colordown='r')
         plt.grid(True)
         ax.xaxis_date()
           # dates on the x-axis
         ax.autoscale_view()
         plt.setp(plt.gca().get_xticklabels(), rotation=30)
```

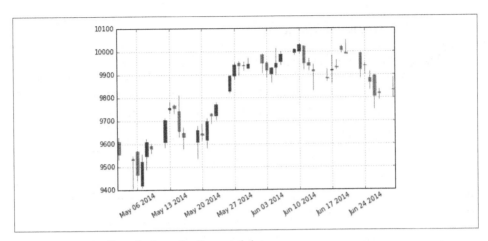

Figure 5-20. Candlestick chart for financial data

In the preceding code, `plt.setp(plt.gca().get_xticklabels(), rotation=30)` grabs the x-axis labels and rotates them by 30 degrees. To this end, the function `plt.gca` is used, which returns the current `figure` object. The method call of `get_xticklabels` then provides the tick labels for the x-axis of the figure.

Table 5-6 provides a description of the different parameters the `mpf.candlestick` function takes.

Table 5-6. Parameters for mpf.candlestick

Parameter	Description
ax	An Axes instance to plot to
quotes	Financial data to plot (sequence of `time`, `open`, `close`, `high`, `low` sequences)
width	Fraction of a day for the rectangle width
colorup	The color of the rectangle where close >= open
colordown	The color of the rectangle where close < open
alpha	The rectangle alpha level

A rather similar plot type is provided by the `plot_day_summary` function, which is used in the same fashion as the `candlestick` function and with similar parameters. Here, opening and closing values are not illustrated by a colored rectangle but rather by two small horizontal lines, as Figure 5-21 shows:

```
In [29]: fig, ax = plt.subplots(figsize=(8, 5))
         mpf.plot_day_summary(ax, quotes, colorup='b', colordown='r')
         plt.grid(True)
         ax.xaxis_date()
         plt.title('DAX Index')
```

```
plt.ylabel('index level')
plt.setp(plt.gca().get_xticklabels(), rotation=30)
```

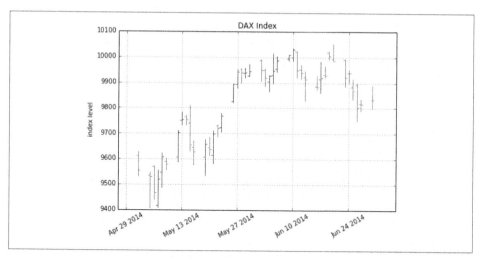

Figure 5-21. Daily summary chart for financial data

Often, stock price data is combined with volume data in a single plot to also provide information with regard to market activity. The following code, with the result shown in Figure 5-22, illustrates such a use case based on historical data for the stock of Yahoo! Inc.:

```
In [30]: quotes = np.array(mpf.quotes_historical_yahoo('YHOO', start, end))

In [31]: fig, (ax1, ax2) = plt.subplots(2, sharex=True, figsize=(8, 6))
         mpf.candlestick(ax1, quotes, width=0.6, colorup='b', colordown='r')
         ax1.set_title('Yahoo Inc.')
         ax1.set_ylabel('index level')
         ax1.grid(True)
         ax1.xaxis_date()
         plt.bar(quotes[:, 0] - 0.25, quotes[:, 5], width=0.5)
         ax2.set_ylabel('volume')
         ax2.grid(True)
         ax2.autoscale_view()
         plt.setp(plt.gca().get_xticklabels(), rotation=30)
```

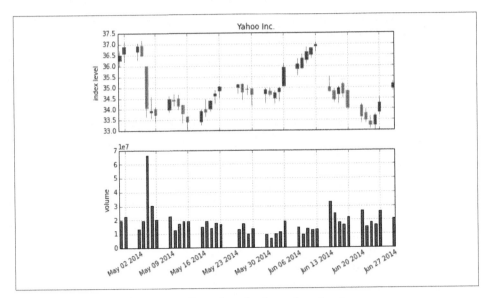

Figure 5-22. Plot combining candlestick and volume bar chart

3D Plotting

There are not too many fields in finance that really benefit from visualization in three dimensions. However, one application area is volatility surfaces showing implied volatilities simultaneously for a number of times-of-maturity and strikes. In what follows, we artificially generate a plot that resembles a volatility surface. To this end, we consider:

- *Strike values* between 50 and 150
- *Times-to-maturity* between 0.5 and 2.5 years

This provides our two-dimensional coordinate system. We can use NumPy's meshgrid function to generate such a system out of two one-dimensional ndarray objects:

```
In [32]: strike = np.linspace(50, 150, 24)
         ttm = np.linspace(0.5, 2.5, 24)
         strike, ttm = np.meshgrid(strike, ttm)
```

This transforms both 1D arrays into 2D arrays, repeating the original axis values as often as needed:

```
In [33]: strike[:2]
Out[33]: array([[  50.        ,   54.34782609,   58.69565217,   63.04347826,
                  67.39130435,   71.73913043,   76.08695652,   80.43478261,
                  84.7826087 ,   89.13043478,   93.47826087,   97.82608696,
                 102.17391304,  106.52173913,  110.86956522,  115.2173913 ,
                 119.56521739,  123.91304348,  128.26086957,  132.60869565,
```

```
        136.95652174,  141.30434783,  145.65217391,  150.           ],
    [  50.          ,   54.34782609,   58.69565217,   63.04347826,
        67.39130435,   71.73913043,   76.08695652,   80.43478261,
        84.7826087 ,   89.13043478,   93.47826087,   97.82608696,
       102.17391304,  106.52173913,  110.86956522,  115.2173913 ,
       119.56521739,  123.91304348,  128.26086957,  132.60869565,
       136.95652174,  141.30434783,  145.65217391,  150.           ]])
```

Now, given the new ndarray objects, we generate the *fake implied volatilities* by a simple, scaled quadratic function:

```
In [34]: iv = (strike - 100) ** 2 / (100 * strike) / ttm
           # generate fake implied volatilities
```

The plot resulting from the following code is shown in Figure 5-23:

```
In [35]: from mpl_toolkits.mplot3d import Axes3D

         fig = plt.figure(figsize=(9, 6))
         ax = fig.gca(projection='3d')

         surf = ax.plot_surface(strike, ttm, iv, rstride=2, cstride=2,
                                cmap=plt.cm.coolwarm, linewidth=0.5,
                                antialiased=True)

         ax.set_xlabel('strike')
         ax.set_ylabel('time-to-maturity')
         ax.set_zlabel('implied volatility')

         fig.colorbar(surf, shrink=0.5, aspect=5)
```

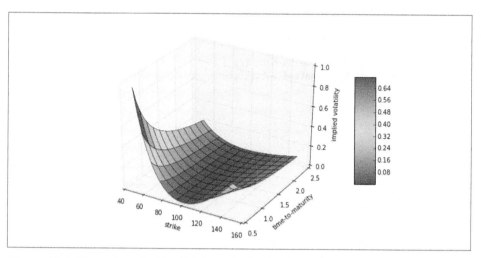

Figure 5-23. 3D surface plot for (fake) implied volatilities

Table 5-7 provides a description of the different parameters the `plot_surface` function can take.

Table 5-7. Parameters for plot_surface

Parameter	Description
X, Y, Z	Data values as 2D arrays
rstride	Array row stride (step size)
cstride	Array column stride (step size)
color	Color of the surface patches
cmap	A colormap for the surface patches
facecolors	Face colors for the individual patches
norm	An instance of Normalize to map values to colors
vmin	Minimum value to map
vmax	Maximum value to map
shade	Whether to shade the face colors

As with two-dimensional plots, the line style can be replaced by single points or, as in what follows, single triangles. Figure 5-24 plots the same data as a 3D scatter plot, but now also with a different viewing angle, using the `view_init` function to set it:

```
In [36]: fig = plt.figure(figsize=(8, 5))
         ax = fig.add_subplot(111, projection='3d')
         ax.view_init(30, 60)

         ax.scatter(strike, ttm, iv, zdir='z', s=25,
                 c='b', marker='^')

         ax.set_xlabel('strike')
         ax.set_ylabel('time-to-maturity')
         ax.set_zlabel('implied volatility')
```

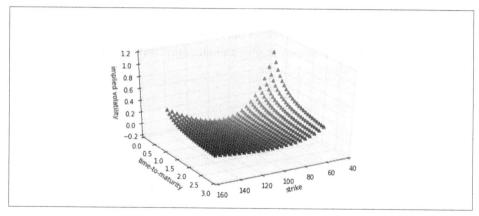

Figure 5-24. 3D scatter plot for (fake) implied volatilities

Conclusions

`matplotlib` can be considered both the benchmark and the workhorse when it comes to data visualization in `Python`. It is tightly integrated with `NumPy` and the basic functionality is easily and conveniently accessed. However, on the other hand, `matplotlib` is a rather mighty library with a somewhat complex API. This makes it impossible to give a broader overview of all the capabilities of `matplotlib` in this chapter.

This chapter introduces the basic functions of `matplotlib` for 2D and 3D plotting useful in most financial contexts. Other chapters provide further examples of how to use this fundamental library for visualization.

Further Reading

The major resources for `matplotlib` can be found on the Web:

- The home page of `matplotlib` is, of course, the best starting point: *http://matplotlib.org*.
- There's a gallery with many useful examples: *http://matplotlib.org/gallery.html*.
- A tutorial for 2D plotting is found here: *http://matplotlib.org/users/pyplot_tutorial.html*.
- Another one for 3D plotting is here: *http://matplotlib.org/mpl_toolkits/mplot3d/tutorial.html*.

It has become kind of a standard routine to consult the gallery, to look there for an appropriate visualization example, and to start with the corresponding example code. Using, for example, `IPython Notebook`, only a single command is required to get started once you have found the right example.

## CHAPTER 6

Financial Time Series

The only reason for time is so that everything doesn't happen at once.

— Albert Einstein

One of the most important types of data one encounters in finance are *financial time series*. This is data indexed by date and/or time. For example, prices of stocks represent financial time series data. Similarly, the USD-EUR exchange rate represents a financial time series; the exchange rate is quoted in brief intervals of time, and a collection of such quotes then is a time series of exchange rates.

There is no financial discipline that gets by without considering time an important factor. This mainly is the same as with physics and other sciences. The major tool to cope with time series data in Python is the library pandas. Wes McKinney, the main author of pandas, started developing the library when working as an analyst at AQR Capital Management, a large hedge fund. It is safe to say that pandas has been designed from the ground up to work with financial time series. As this chapter demonstrates, the main inspiration for the fundamental classes, such as the DataFrame and Series classes, is drawn from the R statistical analysis language, which without doubt has a strength in that kind of modeling and analysis.

The chapter is mainly based on a couple of examples drawn from a financial context. It proceeds along the following lines:

First and second steps

    We start exploring the capabilities of pandas by using very simple and small data sets; we then proceed by using a NumPy ndarray object and transforming this to a DataFrame object. As we go, basic analytics and visualization capabilities are illustrated.

Data from the Web
> pandas allows us to conveniently retrieve data from the Web—e.g., from Yahoo! Finance (*http://finance.yahoo.com*)—and to analyze such data in many ways.

Using data from CSV files
> Comma-separated value (CSV) files represent a global standard for the exchange of financial time series data; pandas makes reading data from such files an efficient task. Using data for two indices, we implement a regression analysis with pandas.

High-frequency data
> In recent years, available financial data has increasingly shifted from daily quotes to tick data. Daily tick data volumes for a stock price regularly surpass those volumes of daily data collected over 30 years.[1]

All financial time series data contains date and/or time information, by definition. Appendix C provides an overview of how to handle such data with Python, NumPy, and pandas as well as of how to convert typical date-time object types into each other.

pandas Basics

In a sense, pandas is built "on top" of NumPy. So, for example, NumPy universal functions will generally work on pandas objects as well. We therefore import both to begin with:

```
In [1]: import numpy as np
        import pandas as pd
```

First Steps with DataFrame Class

On a rather fundamental level, the DataFrame class is designed to manage indexed and labeled data, not too different from a SQL database table or a worksheet in a spreadsheet application. Consider the following creation of a DataFrame object:

```
In [2]: df = pd.DataFrame([10, 20, 30, 40], columns=['numbers'],
                          index=['a', 'b', 'c', 'd'])
        df

Out[2]:    numbers
        a       10
        b       20
        c       30
        d       40
```

---

1. Considering only daily closing prices, you have approximately 30 × 252 = 7,560 closing prices for a single stock over a period of 30 years. It is not uncommon to have more than 10,000 daily (bid/ask) ticks for a single stock.

This simple example already shows some major features of the DataFrame class when it comes to storing data:

Data

Data itself can be provided in different shapes and types (list, tuple, ndarray, and dict objects are candidates).

Labels

Data is organized in columns, which can have custom names.

Index

There is an index that can take on different formats (e.g., numbers, strings, time information).

Working with such a DataFrame object is in general pretty convenient and efficient, e.g., compared to regular ndarray objects, which are more specialized and more restricted when you want to do something link enlarge an existing object. The following are simple examples showing how typical operations on a DataFrame object work:

```
In [3]: df.index  # the index values
Out[3]: Index([u'a', u'b', u'c', u'd'], dtype='object')

In [4]: df.columns  # the column names
Out[4]: Index([u'numbers'], dtype='object')

In [5]: df.ix['c']  # selection via index
Out[5]: numbers    30
        Name: c, dtype: int64

In [6]: df.ix[['a', 'd']]  # selection of multiple indices
Out[6]:    numbers
        a       10
        d       40

In [7]: df.ix[df.index[1:3]]  # selection via Index object
Out[7]:    numbers
        b       20
        c       30

In [8]: df.sum()  # sum per column
Out[8]: numbers    100
        dtype: int64

In [9]: df.apply(lambda x: x ** 2)  # square of every element
Out[9]:    numbers
        a       100
        b       400
        c       900
        d      1600
```

In general, you can implement the same vectorized operations on a DataFrame object as on a NumPy ndarray object:

```
In [10]: df ** 2  # again square, this time NumPy-like

Out[10]:    numbers
         a      100
         b      400
         c      900
         d     1600
```

Enlarging the DataFrame object in both dimensions is possible:

```
In [11]: df['floats'] = (1.5, 2.5, 3.5, 4.5)
            # new column is generated
         df

Out[11]:    numbers  floats
         a       10     1.5
         b       20     2.5
         c       30     3.5
         d       40     4.5

In [12]: df['floats']  # selection of column

Out[12]: a    1.5
         b    2.5
         c    3.5
         d    4.5
         Name: floats, dtype: float64
```

A whole DataFrame object can also be taken to define a new column. In such a case, indices are aligned automatically:

```
In [13]: df['names'] = pd.DataFrame(['Yves', 'Guido', 'Felix', 'Francesc'],
                                    index=['d', 'a', 'b', 'c'])
         df

Out[13]:    numbers  floats     names
         a       10     1.5     Guido
         b       20     2.5     Felix
         c       30     3.5  Francesc
         d       40     4.5      Yves
```

Appending data works similarly. However, in the following example we see a side effect that is usually to be avoided—the index gets replaced by a simple numbered index:

```
In [14]: df.append({'numbers': 100, 'floats': 5.75, 'names': 'Henry'},
                   ignore_index=True)
            # temporary object; df not changed

Out[14]:    numbers  floats     names
         0       10    1.50     Guido
         1       20    2.50     Felix
         2       30    3.50  Francesc
```

```
          3       40      4.50       Yves
          4      100      5.75       Henry
```

It is often better to append a `DataFrame` object, providing the appropriate index information. This preserves the index:

```
In [15]: df = df.append(pd.DataFrame({'numbers': 100, 'floats': 5.75,
                                      'names': 'Henry'}, index=['z',]))
         df

Out[15]:    floats      names  numbers
         a    1.50      Guido       10
         b    2.50      Felix       20
         c    3.50   Francesc       30
         d    4.50       Yves       40
         z    5.75      Henry      100
```

One of the strengths of pandas is working with missing data. To this end, consider the following code that adds a new column, but with a slightly different index. We use the rather flexible join method here:

```
In [16]: df.join(pd.DataFrame([1, 4, 9, 16, 25],
                     index=['a', 'b', 'c', 'd', 'y'],
                     columns=['squares',]))
             # temporary object

Out[16]:    floats      names  numbers  squares
         a    1.50      Guido       10        1
         b    2.50      Felix       20        4
         c    3.50   Francesc       30        9
         d    4.50       Yves       40       16
         z    5.75      Henry      100      NaN
```

What you can see here is that pandas by default accepts only values for those indices that already exist. We lose the value for the index y and have a NaN value (i.e., "Not a Number") at index position z. To preserve both indices, we can provide an additional parameter to tell pandas how to join. In our case, we use how="outer" to use the union of all values from both indices:

```
In [17]: df = df.join(pd.DataFrame([1, 4, 9, 16, 25],
                           index=['a', 'b', 'c', 'd', 'y'],
                           columns=['squares',]),
                           how='outer')
         df

Out[17]:    floats      names  numbers  squares
         a    1.50      Guido       10        1
         b    2.50      Felix       20        4
         c    3.50   Francesc       30        9
         d    4.50       Yves       40       16
         y     NaN        NaN      NaN       25
         z    5.75      Henry      100      NaN
```

Indeed, the index is now the union of the two original indices. All missing data points, given the new enlarged index, are replaced by NaN values. Other options for the join operation include inner for the intersection of the index values, left (default) for the index values of the object on which the method is called, and right for the index values of the object to be joined.

Although there are missing values, the majority of method calls will still work. For example:

```
In [18]: df[['numbers', 'squares']].mean()
            # column-wise mean

Out[18]: numbers    40
         squares    11
         dtype: float64

In [19]: df[['numbers', 'squares']].std()
            # column-wise standard deviation

Out[19]: numbers    35.355339
         squares     9.669540
         dtype: float64
```

Second Steps with DataFrame Class

From now on, we will work with numerical data. We will add further features as we go, like a DatetimeIndex to manage time series data. To have a dummy data set to work with, generate a numpy.ndarry with, for example, nine rows and four columns of pseudorandom, standard normally distributed numbers:

```
In [20]: a = np.random.standard_normal((9, 4))
         a.round(6)

Out[20]: array([[-0.737304,  1.065173,  0.073406,  1.301174],
                [-0.788818, -0.985819,  0.403796, -1.753784],
                [-0.155881, -1.752672,  1.037444, -0.400793],
                [-0.777546,  1.730278,  0.417114,  0.184079],
                [-1.76366 , -0.375469,  0.098678, -1.553824],
                [-1.134258,  1.401821,  1.227124,  0.979389],
                [ 0.458838, -0.143187,  1.565701, -2.085863],
                [-0.103058, -0.36617 , -0.478036, -0.03281 ],
                [ 1.040318, -0.128799,  0.786187,  0.414084]])
```

Although you can construct DataFrame objects more directly (as we have seen before), using an ndarray object is generally a good choice since pandas will retain the basic structure and will "only" add meta-information (e.g., index values). It also represents a typical use case for financial applications and scientific research in general. For example:

```
In [21]: df = pd.DataFrame(a)
         df
```

```
Out[21]:          0          1          2          3
       0 -0.737304   1.065173   0.073406   1.301174
       1 -0.788818  -0.985819   0.403796  -1.753784
       2 -0.155881  -1.752672   1.037444  -0.400793
       3 -0.777546   1.730278   0.417114   0.184079
       4 -1.763660  -0.375469   0.098678  -1.553824
       5 -1.134258   1.401821   1.227124   0.979389
       6  0.458838  -0.143187   1.565701  -2.085863
       7 -0.103058  -0.366170  -0.478036  -0.032810
       8  1.040318  -0.128799   0.786187   0.414084
```

Table 6-1 lists the parameters that the DataFrame function takes. In the table, "array-like" means a data structure similar to an ndarray object—a list, for example. Index is an instance of the pandas Index class.

Table 6-1. Parameters of DataFrame function

Parameter	Format	Description
data	ndarray/dict/DataFrame	Data for DataFrame; dict can contain Series, ndarrays, lists
index	Index/array-like	Index to use; defaults to range(n)
columns	Index/array-like	Column headers to use; defaults to range(n)
dtype	dtype, default None	Data type to use/force; otherwise, it is inferred
copy	bool, default None	Copy data from inputs

As with structured arrays, and as we have already seen, DataFrame objects have column names that can be defined directly by assigning a list with the right number of elements. This illustrates that you can define/change the attributes of the DataFrame object as you go:

```
In [22]: df.columns = [['No1', 'No2', 'No3', 'No4']]
         df

Out[22]:        No1        No2        No3        No4
       0 -0.737304   1.065173   0.073406   1.301174
       1 -0.788818  -0.985819   0.403796  -1.753784
       2 -0.155881  -1.752672   1.037444  -0.400793
       3 -0.777546   1.730278   0.417114   0.184079
       4 -1.763660  -0.375469   0.098678  -1.553824
       5 -1.134258   1.401821   1.227124   0.979389
       6  0.458838  -0.143187   1.565701  -2.085863
       7 -0.103058  -0.366170  -0.478036  -0.032810
       8  1.040318  -0.128799   0.786187   0.414084
```

The column names provide an efficient mechanism to access data in the DataFrame object, again similar to structured arrays:

```
In [23]: df['No2'][3]  # value in column No2 at index position 3

Out[23]: 1.7302783624820191
```

To work with financial time series data efficiently, you must be able to handle time indices well. This can also be considered a major strength of pandas. For example, assume that our nine data entries in the four columns correspond to month-end data, beginning in January 2015. A DatetimeIndex object is then generated with date_range as follows:

```
In [24]: dates = pd.date_range('2015-1-1', periods=9, freq='M')
         dates

Out[24]: <class 'pandas.tseries.index.DatetimeIndex'>
         [2015-01-31, ..., 2015-09-30]
         Length: 9, Freq: M, Timezone: None
```

Table 6-2 lists the parameters that the date_range function takes.

Table 6-2. Parameters of date_range function

Parameter	Format	Description
start	string/datetime	left bound for generating dates
end	string/datetime	right bound for generating dates
periods	integer/None	number of periods (if start or end is None)
freq	string/DateOffset	frequency string, e.g., 5D for 5 days
tz	string/None	time zone name for localized index
normalize	bool, default None	normalize start and end to midnight
name	string, default None	name of resulting index

So far, we have only encountered indices composed of string and int objects. For time series data, however, a DatetimeIndex object generated with the date_range function is of course what is needed.

As with the columns, we assign the newly generated DatetimeIndex as the new Index object to the DataFrame object:

```
In [25]: df.index = dates
         df

Out[25]:                    No1       No2       No3       No4
         2015-01-31 -0.737304  1.065173  0.073406  1.301174
         2015-02-28 -0.788818 -0.985819  0.403796 -1.753784
         2015-03-31 -0.155881 -1.752672  1.037444 -0.400793
         2015-04-30 -0.777546  1.730278  0.417114  0.184079
         2015-05-31 -1.763660 -0.375469  0.098678 -1.553824
         2015-06-30 -1.134258  1.401821  1.227124  0.979389
         2015-07-31  0.458838 -0.143187  1.565701 -2.085863
         2015-08-31 -0.103058 -0.366170 -0.478036 -0.032810
         2015-09-30  1.040318 -0.128799  0.786187  0.414084
```

When it comes to the generation of DatetimeIndex objects with the help of the date_range function, there are a number of choices for the frequency parameter freq. Table 6-3 lists all the options.

Table 6-3. Frequency parameter values for date_range function

Alias	Description
B	Business day frequency
C	Custom business day frequency (experimental)
D	Calendar day frequency
W	Weekly frequency
M	Month end frequency
BM	Business month end frequency
MS	Month start frequency
BMS	Business month start frequency
Q	Quarter end frequency
BQ	Business quarter end frequency
QS	Quarter start frequency
BQS	Business quarter start frequency
A	Year end frequency
BA	Business year end frequency
AS	Year start frequency
BAS	Business year start frequency
H	Hourly frequency
T	Minutely frequency
S	Secondly frequency
L	Milliseonds
U	Microseconds

In this subsection, we start with a NumPy ndarray object and end with an enriched version in the form of a pandas DataFrame object. But does this procedure work the other way around as well? Yes, it does:

```
In [26]: np.array(df).round(6)

Out[26]: array([[-0.737304,  1.065173,  0.073406,  1.301174],
                [-0.788818, -0.985819,  0.403796, -1.753784],
                [-0.155881, -1.752672,  1.037444, -0.400793],
                [-0.777546,  1.730278,  0.417114,  0.184079],
                [-1.76366 , -0.375469,  0.098678, -1.553824],
                [-1.134258,  1.401821,  1.227124,  0.979389],
                [ 0.458838, -0.143187,  1.565701, -2.085863],
```

```
             [-0.103058, -0.36617 , -0.478036, -0.03281 ],
             [ 1.040318, -0.128799,  0.786187,  0.414084]])
```

 Arrays and DataFrames

You can generate a DataFrame object in general from an ndarray object. But you can also easily generate an ndarray object out of a DataFrame by using the function array of NumPy.

Basic Analytics

Like NumPy arrays, the pandas DataFrame class has built in a multitude of convenience methods. For example, you can easily get the column-wise sums, means, and cumulative sums as follows:

```
In [27]: df.sum()

Out[27]: No1   -3.961370
         No2    0.445156
         No3    5.131414
         No4   -2.948346
         dtype: float64

In [28]: df.mean()

Out[28]: No1   -0.440152
         No2    0.049462
         No3    0.570157
         No4   -0.327594
         dtype: float64

In [29]: df.cumsum()

Out[29]:                  No1       No2       No3       No4
         2015-01-31 -0.737304  1.065173  0.073406  1.301174
         2015-02-28 -1.526122  0.079354  0.477201 -0.452609
         2015-03-31 -1.682003 -1.673318  1.514645 -0.853403
         2015-04-30 -2.459549  0.056960  1.931759 -0.669323
         2015-05-31 -4.223209 -0.318508  2.030438 -2.223147
         2015-06-30 -5.357467  1.083313  3.257562 -1.243758
         2015-07-31 -4.898629  0.940126  4.823263 -3.329621
         2015-08-31 -5.001687  0.573956  4.345227 -3.362430
         2015-09-30 -3.961370  0.445156  5.131414 -2.948346
```

There is also a shortcut to a number of often-used statistics for numerical data sets, the describe method:

```
In [30]: df.describe()

Out[30]:            No1       No2       No3       No4
         count  9.000000  9.000000  9.000000  9.000000
         mean  -0.440152  0.049462  0.570157 -0.327594
         std    0.847907  1.141676  0.642904  1.219345
```

```
min   -1.763660 -1.752672 -0.478036 -2.085863
25%   -0.788818 -0.375469  0.098678 -1.553824
50%   -0.737304 -0.143187  0.417114 -0.032810
75%   -0.103058  1.065173  1.037444  0.414084
max    1.040318  1.730278  1.565701  1.301174
```

You can also apply the majority of NumPy universal functions to DataFrame objects:

```
In [31]: np.sqrt(df)

Out[31]:                   No1       No2       No3       No4
         2015-01-31        NaN  1.032072  0.270935  1.140690
         2015-02-28        NaN       NaN  0.635449       NaN
         2015-03-31        NaN       NaN  1.018550       NaN
         2015-04-30        NaN  1.315400  0.645844  0.429045
         2015-05-31        NaN       NaN  0.314131       NaN
         2015-06-30        NaN  1.183985  1.107756  0.989641
         2015-07-31  0.677376       NaN  1.251280       NaN
         2015-08-31        NaN       NaN       NaN       NaN
         2015-09-30  1.019960       NaN  0.886672  0.643494
```

NumPy Universal Functions

In general, you can apply NumPy universal functions to pandas Data Frame objects whenever they could be applied to an ndarray object containing the same data.

pandas is quite error tolerant, in the sense that it captures errors and just puts a NaN value where the respective mathematical operation fails. Not only this, but as briefly shown already, you can also work with such incomplete data sets as if they were complete in a number of cases:

```
In [32]: np.sqrt(df).sum()

Out[32]: No1    1.697335
         No2    3.531458
         No3    6.130617
         No4    3.202870
         dtype: float64
```

In such cases, pandas just leaves out the NaN values and only works with the other available values. Plotting of data is also only one line of code away in general (cf. Figure 6-1):

```
In [33]: %matplotlib inline
         df.cumsum().plot(lw=2.0)
```

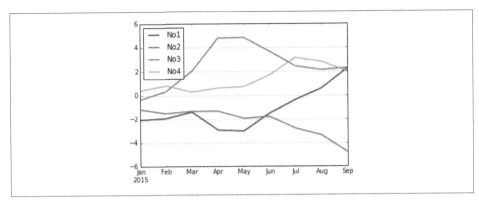

Figure 6-1. Line plot of a DataFrame object

Basically, pandas provides a wrapper around matplotlib (cf. Chapter 5), specifically designed for DataFrame objects. Table 6-4 lists the parameters that the plot method takes.

Table 6-4. Parameters of plot method

Parameter	Format	Description
x	Label/position, default None	Only used when column values are x-ticks
y	Label/position, default None	Only used when column values are y-ticks
subplots	Boolean, default False	Plot columns in subplots
sharex	Boolean, default True	Sharing of the x-axis
sharey	Boolean, default False	Sharing of the y-axis
use_index	Boolean, default True	Use of DataFrame.index as x-ticks
stacked	Boolean, default False	Stack (only for bar plots)
sort_columns	Boolean, default False	Sort columns alphabetically before plotting
title	String, default None	Title for the plot
grid	Boolean, default False	Horizontal and vertical grid lines
legend	Boolean, default True	Legend of labels
ax	matplotlib axis object	matplotlib axis object to use for plotting
style	String or list/dictionary	line plotting style (for each column)
kind	"line"/"bar"/"barh"/"kde"/"density"	type of plot
logx	Boolean, default False	Logarithmic scaling of x-axis
logy	Boolean, default False	Logarithmic scaling of y-axis
xticks	Sequence, default Index	x-ticks for the plot
yticks	Sequence, default Values	y-ticks for the plot
xlim	2-tuple, list	Boundaries for x-axis
ylim	2-tuple, list	Boundaries for y-axis

Parameter	Format	Description
rot	Integer, default None	Rotation of x-ticks
secondary_y	Boolean/sequence, default False	Secondary y-axis
mark_right	Boolean, default True	Automatic labeling of secondary axis
colormap	String/colormap object, default None	Colormap to use for plotting
kwds	Keywords	Options to pass to matplotlib

Series Class

So far, we have worked mainly with the pandas DataFrame class:

```
In [34]: type(df)

Out[34]: pandas.core.frame.DataFrame
```

But there is also a dedicated Series class. We get a Series object, for example, when selecting a single column from our DataFrame object:

```
In [35]: df['No1']

Out[35]: 2015-01-31    -0.737304
         2015-02-28    -0.788818
         2015-03-31    -0.155881
         2015-04-30    -0.777546
         2015-05-31    -1.763660
         2015-06-30    -1.134258
         2015-07-31     0.458838
         2015-08-31    -0.103058
         2015-09-30     1.040318
         Freq: M, Name: No1, dtype: float64

In [36]: type(df['No1'])

Out[36]: pandas.core.series.Series
```

The main DataFrame methods are available for Series objects as well, and we can, for instance, plot the results as before (cf. Figure 6-2):

```
In [37]: import matplotlib.pyplot as plt
         df['No1'].cumsum().plot(style='r', lw=2.)
         plt.xlabel('date')
         plt.ylabel('value')
```

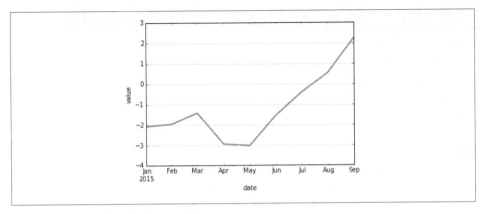

Figure 6-2. Line plot of a Series object

GroupBy Operations

pandas has powerful and flexible grouping capabilities. They work similarly to grouping in SQL as well as pivot tables in Microsoft Excel. To have something to group by, we add a column indicating the quarter the respective data of the index belongs to:

```
In [38]: df['Quarter'] = ['Q1', 'Q1', 'Q1', 'Q2', 'Q2', 'Q2', 'Q3', 'Q3', 'Q3']
         df

Out[38]:                   No1       No2       No3       No4 Quarter
         2015-01-31 -0.737304  1.065173  0.073406  1.301174      Q1
         2015-02-28 -0.788818 -0.985819  0.403796 -1.753784      Q1
         2015-03-31 -0.155881 -1.752672  1.037444 -0.400793      Q1
         2015-04-30 -0.777546  1.730278  0.417114  0.184079      Q2
         2015-05-31 -1.763660 -0.375469  0.098678 -1.553824      Q2
         2015-06-30 -1.134258  1.401821  1.227124  0.979389      Q2
         2015-07-31  0.458838 -0.143187  1.565701 -2.085863      Q3
         2015-08-31 -0.103058 -0.366170 -0.478036 -0.032810      Q3
         2015-09-30  1.040318 -0.128799  0.786187  0.414084      Q3
```

Now, we can group by the "Quarter" column and can output statistics for the single groups:

```
In [39]: groups = df.groupby('Quarter')
```

For example, we can easily get the mean, max, and size of every group bucket as follows:

```
In [40]: groups.mean()

Out[40]:               No1       No2       No3       No4
         Quarter
         Q1       -0.560668 -0.557773  0.504882 -0.284468
         Q2       -1.225155  0.918877  0.580972 -0.130118
         Q3        0.465366 -0.212719  0.624617 -0.568196

In [41]: groups.max()
```

```
Out[41]:                  No1        No2        No3       No4
         Quarter
         Q1         -0.155881   1.065173   1.037444   1.301174
         Q2         -0.777546   1.730278   1.227124   0.979389
         Q3          1.040318  -0.128799   1.565701   0.414084

In [42]: groups.size()

Out[42]: Quarter
         Q1    3
         Q2    3
         Q3    3
         dtype: int64
```

Grouping can also be done with multiple columns. To this end, we add another column, indicating whether the month of the index date is odd or even:

```
In [43]: df['Odd_Even'] = ['Odd', 'Even', 'Odd', 'Even', 'Odd', 'Even',
                           'Odd', 'Even', 'Odd']
```

This additional information can now be used for a grouping based on two columns simultaneously:

```
In [44]: groups = df.groupby(['Quarter', 'Odd_Even'])

In [45]: groups.size()

Out[45]: Quarter  Odd_Even
         Q1       Even        1
                  Odd         2
         Q2       Even        2
                  Odd         1
         Q3       Even        1
                  Odd         2
         dtype: int64

In [46]: groups.mean()

Out[46]:                          No1        No2        No3        No4
         Quarter Odd_Even
         Q1      Even       -0.788818  -0.985819   0.403796  -1.753784
                 Odd        -0.446592  -0.343749   0.555425   0.450190
         Q2      Even       -0.955902   1.566050   0.822119   0.581734
                 Odd        -1.763660  -0.375469   0.098678  -1.553824
         Q3      Even       -0.103058  -0.366170  -0.478036  -0.032810
                 Odd         0.749578  -0.135993   1.175944  -0.835890
```

This concludes the introduction into pandas and the use of DataFrame objects. Subsequent sections apply this tool set to real-world financial data.

Financial Data

The Web today provides a wealth of financial information for free. Web giants such as Google or Yahoo! have comprehensive financial data offerings. Although the quality of the data sometimes does not fulfill professional requirements, for example with regard to the handling of stock splits, such data is well suited to illustrate the "financial power" of pandas.

To this end, we will use the pandas built-in function DataReader to retrieve stock price data from Yahoo! Finance (*http://finance.yahoo.com*), analyze the data, and generate different plots of it.[2] The required function is stored in a submodule of pandas:

```
In [47]: import pandas.io.data as web
```

At the time of this writing, pandas supports the following data sources:

- Yahoo! Finance (yahoo)
- Google Finance (google)
- St. Louis FED (fred)
- Kenneth French's data library (famafrench)
- World Bank (via pandas.io.wb)

We can retrieve stock price information for the German DAX index, for example, from Yahoo! Finance with a single line of code:

```
In [48]: DAX = web.DataReader(name='^GDAXI', data_source='yahoo',
                              start='2000-1-1')
         DAX.info()

Out[48]: <class 'pandas.core.frame.DataFrame'>
         DatetimeIndex: 3760 entries, 2000-01-03 00:00:00 to 2014-09-26 00:00:00
         Data columns (total 6 columns):
         Open         3760 non-null float64
         High         3760 non-null float64
         Low          3760 non-null float64
         Close        3760 non-null float64
         Volume       3760 non-null int64
         Adj Close    3760 non-null float64
         dtypes: float64(5), int64(1)
```

Table 6-5 presents the parameters that the DataReader function takes.

---

2. For a similar example using matplotlib only, see Chapter 5.

Table 6-5. Parameters of DataReader function

Parameter	Format	Description
name	String	Name of data set—generally, the ticker symbol
data_source	E.g., "yahoo"	Data source
start	String/datetime/None	Left boundary of range (default "2010/1/1")
end	String/datetime/None	Right boundary of range (default today)

The `tail` method provides us with the five last rows of the data set:

```
In [49]: DAX.tail()
Out[49]:                Open     High      Low    Close     Volume  Adj Close
         Date
         2014-09-22  9748.53  9812.77  9735.69  9749.54  73981000    9749.54
         2014-09-23  9713.40  9719.66  9589.03  9595.03  88196000    9595.03
         2014-09-24  9598.77  9669.45  9534.77  9661.97  85850600    9661.97
         2014-09-25  9644.36  9718.11  9482.54  9510.01  97697000    9510.01
         2014-09-26  9500.55  9545.34  9454.88  9490.55  83499600    9490.55
```

To get a better overview of the index's history, a plot is again generated easily with the `plot` method (cf. Figure 6-3):

```
In [50]: DAX['Close'].plot(figsize=(8, 5))
```

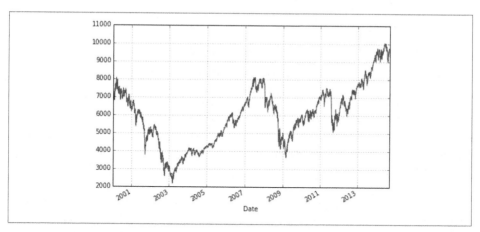

Figure 6-3. Historical DAX index levels

Retrieving data and visualizing it is one thing. Implementing more complex analytics tasks is another. Like NumPy ndarrays, pandas allows for vectorized mathematical operations on whole, and even complex, DataFrame objects. Take the log returns based on the daily closing prices as an example. Adding a column with the respective information could be achieved with the following code, which first generates a new, empty column and then iterates over all indexes to calculate the single log return values step by step:

```
In [51]: %%time
         DAX['Ret_Loop'] = 0.0
         for i in range(1, len(DAX)):
             DAX['Ret_Loop'][i] = np.log(DAX['Close'][i] /
                                         DAX['Close'][i - 1])

Out[51]: CPU times: user 452 ms, sys: 12 ms, total: 464 ms
         Wall time: 449 ms

In [52]: DAX[['Close', 'Ret_Loop']].tail()

Out[52]:               Close  Ret_Loop
         Date
         2014-09-22  9749.54 -0.005087
         2014-09-23  9595.03 -0.015975
         2014-09-24  9661.97  0.006952
         2014-09-25  9510.01 -0.015853
         2014-09-26  9490.55 -0.002048
```

Alternatively, you can use vectorized code to reach the same result without looping. To
this end, the `shift` method is useful; it shifts `Series` or whole `DataFrame` objects relative
to their index, forward as well as backward. To accomplish our goal, we need to shift
the `Close` column by one day, or more generally, one index position:

```
In [53]: %time DAX['Return'] = np.log(DAX['Close'] / DAX['Close'].shift(1))

Out[53]: CPU times: user 4 ms, sys: 0 ns, total: 4 ms
         Wall time: 1.52 ms

In [54]: DAX[['Close', 'Ret_Loop', 'Return']].tail()

Out[54]:               Close  Ret_Loop    Return
         Date
         2014-09-22  9749.54 -0.005087 -0.005087
         2014-09-23  9595.03 -0.015975 -0.015975
         2014-09-24  9661.97  0.006952  0.006952
         2014-09-25  9510.01 -0.015853 -0.015853
         2014-09-26  9490.55 -0.002048 -0.002048
```

This not only provides the same results with more compact and readable code, but also
is the much faster alternative.

Vectorization with DataFrames

In general, you can use the same vectorization approaches with pan
das `DataFrame` objects as you would whenever you could do such an
operation with two NumPy `ndarray` objects containing the same data.

One column with the log return data is enough for our purposes, so we can delete the
other one:

```
In [55]: del DAX['Ret_Loop']
```

Now let us have a look at the newly generated return data. Figure 6-4 illustrates two stylized facts of equity returns:

Volatility clustering
    Volatility is not constant over time; there are periods of *high volatility* (both *highly* positive and negative returns) as well as periods of *low volatility*.

Leverage effect
    Generally, volatility and stock market returns are *negatively correlated*; when markets come down volatility rises, and vice versa.

Here is the code that generates this plot:

```
In [56]: DAX[['Close', 'Return']].plot(subplots=True, style='b',
                                        figsize=(8, 5))
```

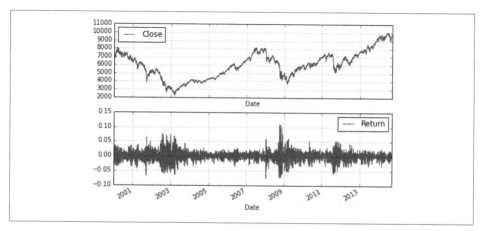

Figure 6-4. The DAX index and daily log returns

While volatility is something of particular importance for options traders, (technical) stock traders might be more interested in moving averages, or so-called *trends*. A moving average is easily calculated with the rolling_mean function of pandas (there are other "rolling" functions as well, like rolling_max, rolling_min, and rolling_corr):

```
In [57]: DAX['42d'] = pd.rolling_mean(DAX['Close'], window=42)
         DAX['252d'] = pd.rolling_mean(DAX['Close'], window=252)

In [58]: DAX[['Close', '42d', '252d']].tail()

Out[58]:                  Close         42d          252d
         Date
         2014-09-22    9749.54    9464.947143    9429.476468
         2014-09-23    9595.03    9463.780952    9433.168651
         2014-09-24    9661.97    9465.300000    9437.122381
         2014-09-25    9510.01    9461.880476    9440.479167
         2014-09-26    9490.55    9459.425000    9443.769008
```

A typical stock price chart with the two trends included then looks like Figure 6-5:

```
In [59]: DAX[['Close', '42d', '252d']].plot(figsize=(8, 5))
```

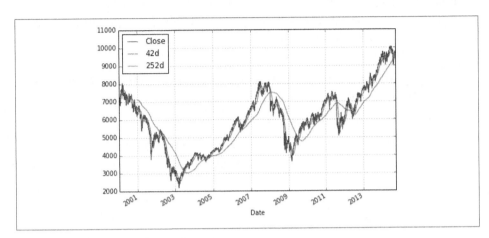

Figure 6-5. The DAX index and moving averages

Returning to the more options trader-like perspective, the moving historical standard deviation of the log returns—i.e. the moving historical volatility—might be more of interest:

```
In [60]: import math
         DAX['Mov_Vol'] = pd.rolling_std(DAX['Return'],
                                         window=252) * math.sqrt(252)
         # moving annual volatility
```

Figure 6-6 further supports the hypothesis of the leverage effect by clearly showing that the historical moving volatility tends to increase when markets come down, and to decrease when they rise:

```
In [61]: DAX[['Close', 'Mov_Vol', 'Return']].plot(subplots=True, style='b',
                                                  figsize=(8, 7))
```

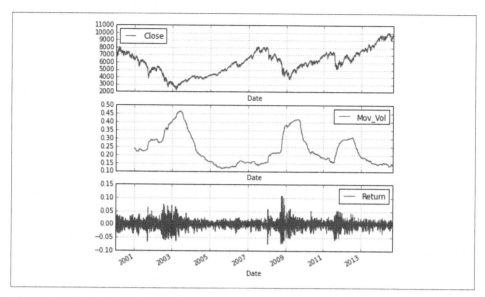

Figure 6-6. The DAX index and moving, annualized volatility

Regression Analysis

The previous section introduces the leverage effect as a stylized fact of equity market returns. So far, the support that we provided is based on the inspection of financial data plots only. Using `pandas`, we can also base such analysis on a more formal, statistical ground. The simplest approach is to use (linear) *ordinary least-squares regression* (OLS).

In what follows, the analysis uses two different data sets available on the Web:

EURO STOXX 50
> Historical daily closing values of the EURO STOXX 50 index, composed of European blue-chip stocks

VSTOXX
> Historical daily closing data for the VSTOXX volatility index, calculated on the basis of volatilities implied by options on the EURO STOXX 50 index

It is noteworthy that we now (indirectly) use *implied volatilities*, which relate to expectations with regard to the future volatility development, while the previous DAX analysis used historical volatility measures. For details, see the "VSTOXX Advanced Services" tutorial pages (*http://www.eurexchange.com/advanced-services/vstoxx/*) provided by Eurex.

We begin with a few imports:

```
In [62]: import pandas as pd
         from urllib import urlretrieve
```

For the analysis, we retrieve files from the Web and save them in a folder called data. If there is no such folder already, you might want to create one first via mkdir data. We proceed by retrieving the most current available information with regard to both indices:

```
In [63]: es_url = 'http://www.stoxx.com/download/historical_values/hbrbcpe.txt'
         vs_url = 'http://www.stoxx.com/download/historical_values/h_vstoxx.txt'
         urlretrieve(es_url, './data/es.txt')
         urlretrieve(vs_url, './data/vs.txt')
         !ls -o ./data/*.txt
         # Windows: use dir

Out[63]: -rw------- 1 yhilpisch      0 Sep 28 11:14 ./data/es50.txt
         -rw------- 1 yhilpisch 641180 Sep 28 11:14 ./data/es.txt
         -rw------- 1 yhilpisch 330564 Sep 28 11:14 ./data/vs.txt
```

Reading the EURO STOXX 50 data directly with pandas is not the best route in this case. A little data cleaning beforehand will give a better data structure for the import. Two issues have to be addressed, relating to the header and the structure:

- There are a couple of additional header lines that we do not need for the import.
- From December 27, 2001 onwards, the data set "suddenly" has an additional semicolon at the end of each data row.

The following code reads the whole data set and removes all blanks:[3]

```
In [64]: lines = open('./data/es.txt', 'r').readlines()
         lines = [line.replace(' ', '') for line in lines]
```

With regard to the header, we can inspect it easily by printing the first couple of lines of the downloaded data set:

```
In [65]: lines[:6]

Out[65]: ['PriceIndices-EUROCurrency\n',
          'Date;Blue-Chip;Blue-Chip;Broad;Broad;ExUK;ExEuroZone;Blue-Chip;Broad\
          n',
          ';Europe;Euro-Zone;Europe;Euro-Zone;;;Nordic;Nordic\n',
          ';SX5P;SX5E;SXXP;SXXE;SXXF;SXXA;DK5F;DKXF\n',
          '31.12.1986;775.00;900.82;82.76;98.58;98.06;69.06;645.26;65.56\n',
          '01.01.1987;775.00;900.82;82.76;98.58;98.06;69.06;645.26;65.56\n']
```

The above-mentioned format change can be seen between lines 3,883 and 3,990 of the file. From December 27, there suddenly appears an additional semicolon at the end of each data row:

```
In [66]: for line in lines[3883:3890]:
             print line[41:],
```

---

3. See Chapter 7 for more information on input-output operations with Python.

```
Out[66]:  317.10;267.23;5268.36;363.19
          322.55;272.18;5360.52;370.94
          322.69;272.95;5360.52;370.94
          327.57;277.68;5479.59;378.69;
          329.94;278.87;5585.35;386.99;
          326.77;272.38;5522.25;380.09;
          332.62;277.08;5722.57;396.12;
```

To make the data set easier to import, we do the following:

1. Generate a new text file.

2. Delete unneeded header lines.

3. Write an appropriate new header line to the new file.

4. Add a helper column, DEL (to catch the trailing semicolons).

5. Write all data rows to the new file.

With these adjustments, the data set can be imported and the helper column deleted after the import. But first, the cleaning code:

```
In [67]: new_file = open('./data/es50.txt', 'w')
             # opens a new file
         new_file.writelines('date' + lines[3][:-1]
                             + ';DEL' + lines[3][-1])
             # writes the corrected third line of the original file
             # as first line of new file
         new_file.writelines(lines[4:])
             # writes the remaining lines of the orignial file
         new_file.close()
```

Let us see how the new header looks:

```
In [68]: new_lines = open('./data/es50.txt', 'r').readlines()
         new_lines[:5]

Out[68]: ['date;SX5P;SX5E;SXXP;SXXE;SXXF;SXXA;DK5F;DKXF;DEL\n',
          '31.12.1986;775.00;900.82;82.76;98.58;98.06;69.06;645.26;65.56\n',
          '01.01.1987;775.00;900.82;82.76;98.58;98.06;69.06;645.26;65.56\n',
          '02.01.1987;770.89;891.78;82.57;97.80;97.43;69.37;647.62;65.81\n',
          '05.01.1987;771.89;898.33;82.82;98.60;98.19;69.16;649.94;65.82\n']
```

It looks appropriate for the import with the read_csv function of pandas, so we continue:

```
In [69]: es = pd.read_csv('./data/es50.txt', index_col=0,
                  parse_dates=True, sep=';', dayfirst=True)

In [70]: np.round(es.tail())
```

```
Out[70]:              SX5P  SX5E  SXXP  SXXE  SXXF  SXXA  DK5F  DKXF  DEL
         date
         2014-09-22  3096  3257   347   326   403   357  9703   565  NaN
         2014-09-23  3058  3206   342   321   398   353  9602   558  NaN
```

```
2014-09-24  3086  3244  344  323  401  355  9629  560  NaN
2014-09-25  3059  3202  341  320  397  353  9538  556  NaN
2014-09-26  3064  3220  342  321  398  353  9559  557  NaN
```

The helper column has fulfilled its purpose and can now be deleted:

```
In [71]: del es['DEL']
         es.info()

Out[71]: <class 'pandas.core.frame.DataFrame'>
         DatetimeIndex: 7153 entries, 1986-12-31 00:00:00 to 2014-09-26 00:00:00
         Data columns (total 8 columns):
         SX5P    7153 non-null float64
         SX5E    7153 non-null float64
         SXXP    7153 non-null float64
         SXXE    7153 non-null float64
         SXXF    7153 non-null float64
         SXXA    7153 non-null float64
         DK5F    7153 non-null float64
         DKXF    7153 non-null float64
         dtypes: float64(8)
```

Equipped with the knowledge about the structure of the EURO STOXX 50 data set, we can also use the advanced capabilities of the read_csv function to make the import more compact and efficient:

```
In [72]: cols = ['SX5P', 'SX5E', 'SXXP', 'SXXE', 'SXXF',
                  'SXXA', 'DK5F', 'DKXF']
         es = pd.read_csv(es_url, index_col=0, parse_dates=True,
                     sep=';', dayfirst=True, header=None,
                     skiprows=4, names=cols)
```

```
In [73]: es.tail()

Out[73]:             SX5P     SX5E    SXXP    SXXE    SXXF    SXXA    DK5F  \
         DKXF
         2014-09-22  3096.02  3257.48  346.69  325.68  403.16  357.08  9703.33
         564.81
         2014-09-23  3057.89  3205.93  341.89  320.72  397.96  352.56  9602.32
         558.35
         2014-09-24  3086.12  3244.01  344.35  323.42  400.58  354.72  9628.84
         559.83
         2014-09-25  3059.01  3202.31  341.44  319.77  396.90  352.58  9537.95
         555.51
         2014-09-26  3063.71  3219.58  342.30  321.39  398.33  352.71  9558.51
         556.57
```

Fortunately, the VSTOXX data set is already in a form such that it can be imported a bit more easily into a DataFrame object:

```
In [74]: vs = pd.read_csv('./data/vs.txt', index_col=0, header=2,
                     parse_dates=True, sep=',', dayfirst=True)
         vs.info()
```

```
Out[74]: <class 'pandas.core.frame.DataFrame'>
         DatetimeIndex: 4010 entries, 1999-01-04 00:00:00 to 2014-09-26 00:00:00
         Data columns (total 9 columns):
         V2TX    4010 non-null float64
         V6I1    3591 non-null float64
         V6I2    4010 non-null float64
         V6I3    3960 non-null float64
         V6I4    4010 non-null float64
         V6I5    4010 non-null float64
         V6I6    3995 non-null float64
         V6I7    4010 non-null float64
         V6I8    3999 non-null float64
         dtypes: float64(9)
```

Table 6-6 contains the parameters of this important import function. There are a multitude of parameters, the majority of which default to None; object, of course, is non-default and has to be specified in any case.

Table 6-6. Parameters of read_csv function

Parameter	Format	Description
object	String	File path, URL, or other source
sep	String, default ","	Delimiter to use
lineterminator	String (one character)	String for line breaks
quotechar	String	Character for quotes
quoting	Integer	Controls recognition of quotes
escapechar	String	String for escaping
dtpye	dtype/dict	dict of dtype(s) for column(s)
compression	"gzip"/"bz2"	For decompression of data
dialect	String/csv.Dialect	CSV dialect, default Excel
header	Integer	Number of header rows
skiprows	Integer	Number of rows to skip
index_col	Integer	Number of index columns (sequence for multi-index)
names	Array-like	Column names if no header rows
prefix	String	String to add to column numbers if no header names
na_values	List/dict	Additional strings to recognize as NA, NaN
true_values	List	Values to consider as True
false_values	List	Values to consider as False
keep_default_na	Boolean, default True	If True, NaN is added to na_values
parse_dates	Boolean/list, default False	Whether to parse dates in index columns or multiple columns
keep_date_col	Boolean, default False	Keeps original date columns
dayfirst	Boolean, default False	For European date convention DD/MM
thousands	String	Thousands operator

Parameter	Format	Description
comment	String	Rest of line as comment (not to be parsed)
decimal	String	String to indicate decimal, e.g., "." or ","
nrows	Integer	Number of rows of file to read
iterator	Boolean, default False	Return TextFileReader object
chunksize	Integer	Return TextFileReader object for iteration
skipfooter	Integer	Number of lines to skip at bottom
converters	Dictionary	Function to convert/translate column data
verbose	Boolean, default False	Report number of NA values in nonnumeric columns
delimiter	String	Alternative to sep, can contain regular expressions
encoding	String	Encoding to use, e.g., "UTF-8"
squeeze	Boolean, default False	Return one-column data sets as Series
na_filter	Boolean, default False	Detect missing value markers automatically
usecols	Array-like	Selection of columns to use
mangle_dupe_cols	Boolean, default False	Name duplicate columns differently
tupleize_cols	Boolean, default False	Leave a list of tuples on columns as is

To implement the regression analysis, we only need one column from each data set. We therefore generate a new DataFrame object within which we combine the two columns of interest, namely those for the major indexes. Since VSTOXX data is only available from the beginning of January 1999, we only take data from that date on:

```
In [75]: import datetime as dt
         data = pd.DataFrame({'EUROSTOXX' :
                             es['SX5E'][es.index > dt.datetime(1999, 1, 1)]})
         data = data.join(pd.DataFrame({'VSTOXX' :
                             vs['V2TX'][vs.index > dt.datetime(1999, 1, 1)]}))
```

We also fill missing values with the last available values from the time series. We call the fillna method, providing ffill (for *forward fill*) as the method parameter. Another option would be bfill (for *backward fill*), which would however lead to a "foresight" issue:

```
In [76]: data = data.fillna(method='ffill')
         data.info()

Out[76]: <class 'pandas.core.frame.DataFrame'>
         DatetimeIndex: 4034 entries, 1999-01-04 00:00:00 to 2014-09-26 00:00:00
         Data columns (total 2 columns):
         EUROSTOXX    4034 non-null float64
         VSTOXX       4034 non-null float64
         dtypes: float64(2)

In [77]: data.tail()
```

```
Out[77]:              EUROSTOXX   VSTOXX
         2014-09-22     3257.48  15.8303
         2014-09-23     3205.93  17.7684
         2014-09-24     3244.01  15.9504
         2014-09-25     3202.31  17.5658
         2014-09-26     3219.58  17.6012
```

Again, a graphical representation of the new data set might provide some insights. In-deed, as Figure 6-7 shows, there seems to be a negative correlation between the two indexes:

```
In [78]: data.plot(subplots=True, grid=True, style='b', figsize=(8, 6))
```

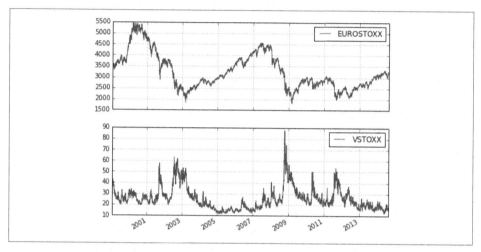

Figure 6-7. The EURO STOXX 50 index and the VSTOXX volatility index

However, to put this on more formal ground, we want to work again with the log returns of the two financial time series. Figure 6-8 shows these graphically:

```
In [79]: rets = np.log(data / data.shift(1))
         rets.head()

Out[79]:              EUROSTOXX    VSTOXX
         1999-01-04        NaN       NaN
         1999-01-05   0.017228  0.489248
         1999-01-06   0.022138 -0.165317
         1999-01-07  -0.015723  0.256337
         1999-01-08  -0.003120  0.021570

In [80]: rets.plot(subplots=True, grid=True, style='b', figsize=(8, 6))
```

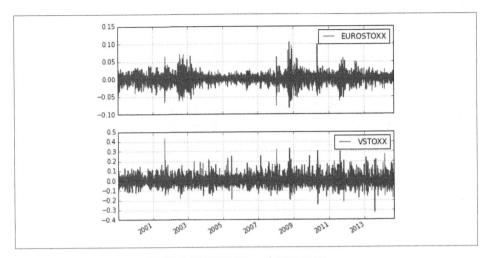

Figure 6-8. Log returns of EURO STOXX 50 and VSTOXX

We have everything together to implement the regression analysis. In what follows, the EURO STOXX 50 returns are taken as the independent variable while the VSTOXX returns are taken as the dependent variable:

```
In [81]: xdat = rets['EUROSTOXX']
         ydat = rets['VSTOXX']
         model = pd.ols(y=ydat, x=xdat)
         model

Out[81]: ------------------------Summary of Regression Analysis----------------
         ---------

         Formula: Y ~ <x> + <intercept>

         Number of Observations:          4033
         Number of Degrees of Freedom:    2

         R-squared:          0.5322
         Adj R-squared:      0.5321

         Rmse:               0.0389

         F-stat (1, 4031):   4586.3942, p-value:      0.0000

         Degrees of Freedom: model 1, resid 4031

         ----------------------Summary of Estimated Coefficients--------------
         ---------
             Variable       Coef    Std Err    t-stat    p-value    CI 2.5%
         CI 97.5%
         --------------------------------------------------------------------
         ---------
```

```
             x      -2.7529    0.0406    -67.72    0.0000    -2.8326
   -2.6732
          intercept  -0.0001    0.0006     -0.12    0.9043    -0.0013
   0.0011
---------------------------------End of Summary-----------------------
---------
```

Obviously, there is indeed a highly negative correlation. We can access the results as follows:

```
In [82]: model.beta

Out[82]: x           -2.752894
         intercept   -0.000074
         dtype: float64
```

This input, in combination with the raw log return data, is used to generate the plot in Figure 6-9, which provides strong support for the leverage effect:

```
In [83]: plt.plot(xdat, ydat, 'r.')
         ax = plt.axis()  # grab axis values
         x = np.linspace(ax[0], ax[1] + 0.01)
         plt.plot(x, model.beta[1] + model.beta[0] * x, 'b', lw=2)
         plt.grid(True)
         plt.axis('tight')
         plt.xlabel('EURO STOXX 50 returns')
         plt.ylabel('VSTOXX returns')
```

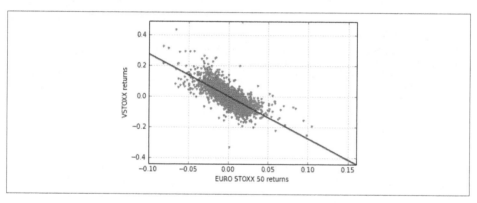

Figure 6-9. Scatter plot of log returns and regression line

As a final cross-check, we can calculate the correlation between the two financial time series directly:

```
In [84]: rets.corr()

Out[84]:             EUROSTOXX     VSTOXX
         EUROSTOXX    1.000000   -0.729538
         VSTOXX      -0.729538    1.000000
```

Although the correlation is strongly negative on the whole data set, it varies considerably over time, as shown in Figure 6-10. The figure uses correlation on a yearly basis, i.e., for 252 trading days:

```
In [85]: pd.rolling_corr(rets['EUROSTOXX'], rets['VSTOXX'],
                         window=252).plot(grid=True, style='b')
```

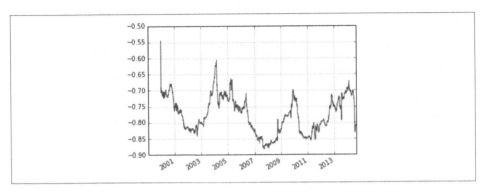

Figure 6-10. Rolling correlation between EURO STOXX 50 and VSTOXX

High-Frequency Data

By now, you should have a feeling for the strengths of pandas when it comes to financial time series data. One aspect in this regard has become prevalent in the financial analytics sphere and represents quite a high burden for some market players: *high-frequency data*. This brief section illustrates how to cope with tick data instead of daily financial data. To begin with, a couple of imports:

```
In [86]: import numpy as np
         import pandas as pd
         import datetime as dt
         from urllib import urlretrieve
         %matplotlib inline
```

The Norwegian online broker Netfonds (*http://www.netfonds.no*) provides tick data for a multitude of stocks, in particular for American names. The web-based API has basically the following format:

```
In [87]: url1 = 'http://hopey.netfonds.no/posdump.php?'
         url2 = 'date=%s%s%s&paper=AAPL.O&csv_format=csv'
         url = url1 + url2
```

We want to download, combine, and analyze a week's worth of tick data for the Apple Inc. stock, a quite actively traded name. Let us start with the dates of interest:[4]

```
In [88]: year = '2014'
         month = '09'
         days = ['22', '23', '24', '25']
           # dates might need to be updated

In [89]: AAPL = pd.DataFrame()
         for day in days:
             AAPL = AAPL.append(pd.read_csv(url % (year, month, day),
                              index_col=0, header=0, parse_dates=True))
         AAPL.columns = ['bid', 'bdepth', 'bdeptht',
                           'offer', 'odepth', 'odeptht']
           # shorter colummn names
```

The data set now consists of almost 100,000 rows:

```
In [90]: AAPL.info()

Out[90]: <class 'pandas.core.frame.DataFrame'>
         DatetimeIndex: 95871 entries, 2014-09-22 10:00:01 to 2014-09-25 22:19:25
         Data columns (total 6 columns):
         bid          95871 non-null float64
         bdepth       95871 non-null float64
         bdeptht      95871 non-null float64
         offer        95871 non-null float64
         odepth       95871 non-null float64
         odeptht      95871 non-null float64
         dtypes: float64(6)
```

Figure 6-11 shows the bid columns graphically. One can identify a number of periods without any trading activity—i.e., times when the markets are closed:

```
In [91]: AAPL['bid'].plot()
```

Over the course of a single trading day when markets are open, there is of course usually a high activity level. Figure 6-12 shows the trading activity for the first day in the sample and three hours of the third. Times are for the Norwegian time zone and you can see easily when pre-trading starts, when US stock markets are open, and when they close:

```
In [92]: to_plot = AAPL[['bid', 'bdepth']][
             (AAPL.index > dt.datetime(2014, 9, 22, 0, 0))
           & (AAPL.index < dt.datetime(2014, 9, 23, 2, 59))]
             # adjust dates to given data set
         to_plot.plot(subplots=True, style='b', figsize=(8, 5))
```

---

4. Note that the data provider only provides this type of data for a couple of days back from the current date. Therefore, you might need to use different (i.e., more current) dates to implement the same example.

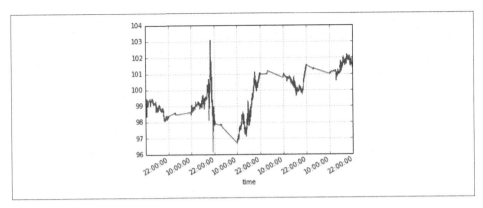

Figure 6-11. Apple stock tick data for a week

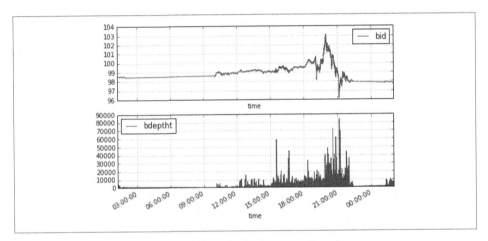

Figure 6-12. Apple stock tick data and volume for a trading day

Usually, financial tick data series lead to a `DatetimeIndex` that is highly irregular. In other words, time intervals between two observation points are highly heterogeneous. Against this background, a *resampling* of such data sets might sometimes be useful or even in order depending on the task at hand. `pandas` provides a method for this purpose for the `DataFrame` object. In what follows, we simply take the mean for the resampling procedure; this might be consistent for some columns (e.g., "bid") but not for others (e.g., "bdepth"):

```
In [93]: AAPL_resam = AAPL.resample(rule='5min', how='mean')
         np.round(AAPL_resam.head(), 2)
```
```
Out[93]:                        bid  bdepth  bdeptht   offer  odepth  odeptht
         2014-09-22 10:00:00  100.49  366.67   366.67  100.95     200      200
         2014-09-22 10:05:00  100.49  100.00   100.00  100.84     200      200
         2014-09-22 10:10:00  100.54  150.00   150.00  100.74     100      100
```

```
2014-09-22 10:15:00   100.59   200.00     200.00   100.75      1500       1500
2014-09-22 10:20:00   100.50   100.00     100.00   100.75      1500       1500
```

The resulting plot in Figure 6-13 looks a bit smoother. Here, we have also filled empty time intervals with the most recent available values (before the empty time interval):

```
In [94]: AAPL_resam['bid'].fillna(method='ffill').plot()
```

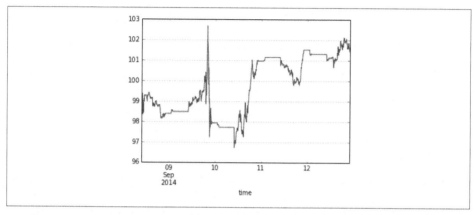

Figure 6-13. Resampled Apple stock tick data

To conclude this section, we apply a custom-defined Python function to our new data set. The function we choose is arbitrary and does not make any economic sense here; it just mirrors the stock performance at a certain stock price level (compare Figure 6-14 to Figure 6-13):

```
In [95]: def reversal(x):
             return 2 * 95 - x

In [96]: AAPL_resam['bid'].fillna(method='ffill').apply(reversal).plot()
```

Finally, let's clean up disk space by erasing all data sets saved to disk:

```
In [97]: !rm ./data/*
             # Windows: del /data/*
```

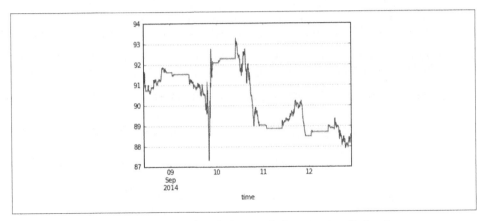

Figure 6-14. Resampled Apple stock tick data with function applied to it

Conclusions

Financial time series data is one of the most common and important forms of data in finance. The library `pandas` is generally the tool of choice when it comes to working with such data sets. Modeled after the `data.frame` class of R, the `pandas` `DataFrame` class provides a wealth of attributes and methods to attack almost any kind of (financial) analytics problem you might face. *Convenience* is another benefit of using `pandas`: even if you might be able to generate the same result by using `NumPy` and/or `matplotlib` only, `pandas` generally has some neat shortcuts based on a powerful and flexible API.

In addition, `pandas` makes it really easy to retrieve data from a variety of web sources, like Yahoo! Finance or Google. Compared to "pure" `NumPy` or `matplotlib`, it automates the management of financial time series data in many respects and also provides higher flexibility when it comes to combining data sets and enlarging existing ones.

Further Reading

At the time of this writing, the definitive resource in printed form for pandas is the book by the main author of the library:

- McKinney, Wes (2012): *Data Analysis with Python*. O'Reilly, Sebastopol, CA.

Of course, the Web—especially the website of pandas itself—also provides a wealth of information:

- Again, it is good to start on the home page of the library: *http://pandas.pydata.org*.
- There is rather comprehensive online documentation available at *http://pandas.pydata.org/pandas-docs/stable/*.
- The documentation in PDF format with 1,500+ pages illustrates how much functionality pandas has to offer: *http://pandas.pydata.org/pandas-docs/stable/pandas.pdf*.

## CHAPTER 7

Input/Output Operations

It is a capital mistake to theorize before one has data.

— Sherlock Holmes

As a general rule, the majority of data, be it in a finance context or any other application area, is stored on hard disk drives (HDDs) or some other form of permanent storage device, like solid state disks (SSDs) or hybrid disk drives. Storage capacities have been steadily increasing over the years, while costs per storage unit (e.g., megabytes) have been steadily falling.

At the same time, stored data volumes have been increasing at a much faster pace than the typical random access memory (RAM) available even in the largest machines. This makes it necessary not only to store data to disk for permanent storage, but also to compensate for lack of sufficient RAM by swapping data from RAM to disk and back.

Input/output (I/O) operations are therefore generally very important tasks when it comes to finance applications and data-intensive applications in general. Often they represent the bottleneck for performance-critical computations, since I/O operations cannot in general shuffle data fast enough to the RAM[1] and from the RAM to the disk. In a sense, CPUs are often "starving" due to slow I/O operations.

Although the majority of today's financial and corporate analytics efforts are confronted with "big" data (e.g., of petascale size), single analytics tasks generally use data (sub)sets that fall in the "mid" data category. A recent study concluded:

> Our measurements as well as other recent work shows that the majority of real-world analytic jobs process less than 100 GB of input, but popular infrastructures such as Hadoop/MapReduce were originally designed for petascale processing.
>
> — Appuswamy et al. (2013)

---

1. Here, we do not distinguish between different levels of RAM and processor caches. The optimal use of current memory architectures is a topic in itself.

In terms of frequency, single financial analytics tasks generally process data of not more than a couple of gigabytes (GB) in size—and this is a sweet spot for Python and the libraries of its scientific stack, like NumPy, pandas, and PyTables. Data sets of such a size can also be analyzed in-memory, leading to generally high speeds with today's CPUs and GPUs. However, the data has to be read into RAM and the results have to be written to disk, meanwhile ensuring today's performance requirements are met.

This chapter addresses the following areas:

Basic I/O
> Python has built-in functions to serialize and store any object on disk and to read it from disk into RAM; apart from that, Python is strong when it comes to working with text files and SQL databases. NumPy also provides dedicated functions for fast storage and retrieval of ndarray objects.

I/O with pandas
> The pandas library provides a plentitude of convenience functions and methods to read data stored in different formats (e.g., CSV, JSON) and to write data to files in diverse formats.

I/O with PyTables
> PyTables uses the HDF5 standard (*http://www.hdfgroup.org*) to accomplish fast I/O operations for large data sets; speed often is only bound by the hardware used.

Basic I/O with Python

Python itself comes with a multitude of I/O capabilites, some optimized for performance, others more for flexibility. In general, however, they are easily used in interactive as well as in large-scale deployment settings.

Writing Objects to Disk

For later use, for documentation, or for sharing with others, one might want to store Python objects on disk. One option is to use the pickle module. This module can serialize the majority of Python objects. *Serialization* refers to the conversion of an object (hierarchy) to a byte stream; *deserialization* is the opposite operation. In the example that follows, we work again with (pseudo)random data, this time stored in a list object:

```
In [1]: path = '/flash/data/'

In [2]: import numpy as np
        from random import gauss

In [3]: a = [gauss(1.5, 2) for i in range(1000000)]
          # generation of normally distributed randoms
```

The task now is to write this `list` object to disk for later retrieval. `pickle` accomplishes this task:

```
In [4]: import pickle

In [5]: pkl_file = open(path + 'data.pkl', 'w')
          # open file for writing
          # Note: existing file might be overwritten
```

The two major functions we need are `dump`, for writing objects, and `load`, for loading them into the memory:

```
In [6]: %time pickle.dump(a, pkl_file)

Out[6]: CPU times: user 4.3 s, sys: 43 ms, total: 4.35 s
          Wall time: 4.36 s

In [7]: pkl_file

Out[7]: <open file '/flash/data/data.pkl', mode 'w' at 0x3df0540>

In [8]: pkl_file.close()
```

We can now inspect the size of the file on disk. The `list` object with 1,000,000 `floats` takes about 20 megabytes (MB) of disk space:

```
In [9]: ll $path*

Out[9]: -rw-r--r-- 1 root 20970325 28. Sep 15:16 /flash/data/data.pkl
```

Now that we have data on disk, we can read it into memory via `pickle.load`:

```
In [10]: pkl_file = open(path + 'data.pkl', 'r')  # open file for reading

In [11]: %time b = pickle.load(pkl_file)

Out[11]: CPU times: user 3.37 s, sys: 18 ms, total: 3.38 s
           Wall time: 3.39 s

In [12]: b[:5]

Out[12]: [-3.6459230447943165,
           1.4637510875573307,
           2.5483218463404067,
           0.9822259685028746,
           3.594915396586916]
```

Let us compare this with the first five `floats` of the original object:

```
In [13]: a[:5]

Out[13]: [-3.6459230447943165,
           1.4637510875573307,
           2.5483218463404067,
           0.9822259685028746,
           3.594915396586916]
```

To ensure that objects a and b are indeed the same, NumPy provides the function all
close:

```
In [14]: np.allclose(np.array(a), np.array(b))

Out[14]: True
```

In principle, this is the same as calculating the difference of two ndarray objects and
checking whether it is 0:

```
In [15]: np.sum(np.array(a) - np.array(b))

Out[15]: 0.0
```

However, allclose takes as a parameter a tolerance level, which by default is set to 1e-5.

Storing and retrieving a single object with pickle obviously is quite simple. What about
two objects?

```
In [16]: pkl_file = open(path + 'data.pkl', 'w')  # open file for writing

In [17]: %time pickle.dump(np.array(a), pkl_file)

Out[17]: CPU times: user 799 ms, sys: 47 ms, total: 846 ms
         Wall time: 846 ms

In [18]: %time pickle.dump(np.array(a) ** 2, pkl_file)

Out[18]: CPU times: user 742 ms, sys: 41 ms, total: 783 ms
         Wall time: 784 ms

In [19]: pkl_file.close()

In [20]: ll $path*

Out[20]: -rw-r--r-- 1 root 44098737 28. Sep 15:16 /flash/data/data.pkl
```

What has happened? Mainly the following:

- We have written an ndarray version of the original object to disk.

- We have also written a squared ndarray version to disk, into the same file.

- Both operations were faster than the original operation (due to the use of ndarray
  objects).

- The file is approximately double the size as before, since we have stored double the
  amount of data.

Let us read the two ndarray objects back into memory:

```
In [21]: pkl_file = open(path + 'data.pkl', 'r')  # open file for reading
```

pickle.load does the job. However, notice that it only returns a single ndarray object:

```
In [22]: x = pickle.load(pkl_file)
         x
```

```
Out[22]: array([-3.64592304,  1.46375109,  2.54832185, ...,  2.87048515,
                  0.66186994, -1.38532837])
```

Calling pickle.load for the second time returns the second object:

```
In [23]: y = pickle.load(pkl_file)
         y

Out[23]: array([ 13.29275485,   2.14256725,   6.49394423, ...,   8.23968501,
                  0.43807181,   1.9191347 ])

In [24]: pkl_file.close()
```

Obviously, pickle stores objects according to the *first in, first out* (FIFO) principle. There is one major problem with this: there is no meta-information available to the user to know beforehand what is stored in a pickle file. A sometimes helpful workaround is to not store single objects, but a dict object containing all the other objects:

```
In [25]: pkl_file = open(path + 'data.pkl', 'w')  # open file for writing
         pickle.dump({'x' : x, 'y' : y}, pkl_file)
         pkl_file.close()
```

Using this approach allows us to read the whole set of objects at once and, for example, to iterate over the dict object's key values:

```
In [26]: pkl_file = open(path + 'data.pkl', 'r')  # open file for writing
         data = pickle.load(pkl_file)
         pkl_file.close()
         for key in data.keys():
             print key, data[key][:4]

Out[26]: y [ 13.29275485   2.14256725   6.49394423   0.96476785]
         x [-3.64592304  1.46375109  2.54832185  0.98222597]

In [27]: !rm -f $path*
```

This approach, however, requires us to write and read all objects at once. This is a compromise one can probably live with in many circumstances given the much higher convenience it brings along.

Reading and Writing Text Files

Text processing can be considered a strength of Python. In fact, many corporate and scientific users use Python for exactly this task. With Python you have a multitude of options to work with string objects, as well as with text files in general.

Suppose we have generated quite a large set of data that we want to save and share as a comma-separated value (CSV) file. Although they have a special structure, such files are basically plain text files:

```
In [28]: rows = 5000
         a = np.random.standard_normal((rows, 5))  # dummy data
```

```
In [29]: a.round(4)

Out[29]: array([[ 1.381 , -1.1236,  1.0622, -1.3997, -0.7374],
               [ 0.15  ,  0.967 ,  1.8391,  0.5633,  0.0569],
               [-0.9504,  0.4779,  1.8636, -1.9152, -0.3005],
               ...,
               [ 0.8843, -1.3932, -0.0506,  0.2717, -1.4921],
               [-1.0352,  1.0368,  0.4562, -0.0667, -1.3391],
               [ 0.9952, -0.6398,  0.8467, -1.6951,  1.122 ]])
```

To make the case a bit more realistic, we add date-time information to the mix and use the pandas date_range function to generate a series of hourly date-time points (for details, see Chapter 6 and Appendix C):

```
In [30]: import pandas as pd
         t = pd.date_range(start='2014/1/1', periods=rows, freq='H')
           # set of hourly datetime objects

In [31]: t

Out[31]: <class 'pandas.tseries.index.DatetimeIndex'>
         [2014-01-01 00:00:00, ..., 2014-07-28 07:00:00]
         Length: 5000, Freq: H, Timezone: None
```

To write the data, we need to open a new file object on disk:

```
In [32]: csv_file = open(path + 'data.csv', 'w')  # open file for writing
```

The first line of a CSV file generally contains the names for each data column stored in the file, so we write this first:

```
In [33]: header = 'date,no1,no2,no3,no4,no5\n'
         csv_file.write(header)
```

The actual data is then written row by row, merging the date-time information with the (pseudo)random numbers:

```
In [34]: for t_, (no1, no2, no3, no4, no5) in zip(t, a):
             s = '%s,%f,%f,%f,%f,%f\n' % (t_, no1, no2, no3, no4, no5)
             csv_file.write(s)
         csv_file.close()

In [35]: ll $path*

Out[35]: -rw-r--r-- 1 root 337664 28. Sep 15:16 /flash/data/data.csv
```

The other way around works quite similarly. First, open the now-existing CSV file. Second, read its content line by line using the readline method of the file object:

```
In [36]: csv_file = open(path + 'data.csv', 'r')  # open file for reading

In [37]: for i in range(5):
             print csv_file.readline(),

Out[37]: date,no1,no2,no3,no4,no5
         2014-01-01 00:00:00,1.381035,-1.123613,1.062245,-1.399746,-0.737369
         2014-01-01 01:00:00,0.149965,0.966987,1.839130,0.563322,0.056906
```

```
2014-01-01 02:00:00,-0.950360,0.477881,1.863646,-1.915203,-0.300522
2014-01-01 03:00:00,-0.503429,-0.895489,-0.240227,-0.327176,0.123498
```

You can also read all the content at once by using the `readlines` method:

```
In [38]: csv_file = open(path + 'data.csv', 'r')
         content = csv_file.readlines()
         for line in content[:5]:
             print line,
```

```
Out[38]: date,no1,no2,no3,no4,no5
         2014-01-01 00:00:00,1.381035,-1.123613,1.062245,-1.399746,-0.737369
         2014-01-01 01:00:00,0.149965,0.966987,1.839130,0.563322,0.056906
         2014-01-01 02:00:00,-0.950360,0.477881,1.863646,-1.915203,-0.300522
         2014-01-01 03:00:00,-0.503429,-0.895489,-0.240227,-0.327176,0.123498
```

We finish with some closing operations in this example:

```
In [39]: csv_file.close()
         !rm -f $path*
```

SQL Databases

Python can work with any kind of SQL database and in general also with any kind of NoSQL database. One database that is delivered with Python by default is SQLite3 (*http://www.sqlite.org*). With it, the basic Python approach to SQL databases can be easily illustrated:[2]

```
In [40]: import sqlite3 as sq3
```

SQL queries are formulated as `string` objects. The syntax, data types, etc. of course depend on the database in use:

```
In [41]: query = 'CREATE TABLE numbs (Date date, No1 real, No2 real)'
```

Open a database connection. In this case, we generate a new database file on disk:

```
In [42]: con = sq3.connect(path + 'numbs.db')
```

Then execute the query statement to create the table by using the method `execute`:

```
In [43]: con.execute(query)
```

```
Out[43]: <sqlite3.Cursor at 0xb8a4490>
```

To make the query effective, call the method `commit`:

```
In [44]: con.commit()
```

---

2. Another first-class citizen in the database world is MySQL, with which Python also integrates very well. While many web projects are implemented on the basis of the so-called LAMP stack, which generally stands for Linux, Apache Web server, MySQL, PHP, there are also a large number of stacks where Python replaces PHP for the P in the stack. For an overview of available database connectors, visit *https://wiki.python.org/moin/DatabaseInterfaces*.

Now that we have a database file with a table, we can populate that table with data. Each row consists of date-time information and two floats:

```
In [45]: import datetime as dt
```

A single data row can be written with the respective SQL statement, as follows:

```
In [46]: con.execute('INSERT INTO numbs VALUES(?, ?, ?)',
                      (dt.datetime.now(), 0.12, 7.3))

Out[46]: <sqlite3.Cursor at 0xb8a4570>
```

However, you usually have to (or want to) write a larger data set in bulk:

```
In [47]: data = np.random.standard_normal((10000, 2)).round(5)
```

```
In [48]: for row in data:
             con.execute('INSERT INTO numbs VALUES(?, ?, ?)',
                         (dt.datetime.now(), row[0], row[1]))
         con.commit()
```

There is also a method called executemany. Since we have combined current date-time information with our pseudorandom number data set, we cannot use it here. What we can use, however, is fetchmany to retrieve a certain number of rows at once from the database:

```
In [49]: con.execute('SELECT * FROM numbs').fetchmany(10)

Out[49]: [(u'2014-09-28 15:16:19.486021', 0.12, 7.3),
          (u'2014-09-28 15:16:19.762476', 0.30736, -0.21114),
          (u'2014-09-28 15:16:19.762640', 0.95078, 0.50106),
          (u'2014-09-28 15:16:19.762702', 0.95896, 0.15812),
          (u'2014-09-28 15:16:19.762774', -0.42919, -1.45132),
          (u'2014-09-28 15:16:19.762825', -0.99502, -0.91755),
          (u'2014-09-28 15:16:19.762862', 0.25416, -0.85317),
          (u'2014-09-28 15:16:19.762890', -0.55879, -0.36144),
          (u'2014-09-28 15:16:19.762918', -1.61041, -1.29589),
          (u'2014-09-28 15:16:19.762945', -2.04225, 0.43446)]
```

Or we can just read a single data row at a time:

```
In [50]: pointer = con.execute('SELECT * FROM numbs')
```

```
In [51]: for i in range(3):
             print pointer.fetchone()

Out[51]: (u'2014-09-28 15:16:19.486021', 0.12, 7.3)
         (u'2014-09-28 15:16:19.762476', 0.30736, -0.21114)
         (u'2014-09-28 15:16:19.762640', 0.95078, 0.50106)
```

```
In [52]: con.close()
         !rm -f $path*
```

SQL databases are a rather broad topic; indeed, too broad and complex to be covered in any significant way in this chapter. The basic messages only are:

- `Python` integrates pretty well with almost any database technology.

- The basic SQL syntax is mainly determined by the database in use; the rest is, as we say, real `Pythonic`.

Writing and Reading NumPy Arrays

`NumPy` itself has functions to write and read `ndarray` objects in a convenient and performant fashion. This saves a lot of effort in some circumstances, such as when you have to convert `NumPy` dtypes into specific database types (e.g., for `SQLite3`). To illustrate that `NumPy` can sometimes be an efficient replacement for a SQL-based approach, we replicate the example from before, this time only using `NumPy`:

```
In [53]: import numpy as np
```

Instead of `pandas`, we use the `arange` function of `NumPy` to generate an `array` object with `datetime` objects stored:[3]

```
In [54]: dtimes = np.arange('2015-01-01 10:00:00', '2021-12-31 22:00:00',
                             dtype='datetime64[m]')  # minute intervals
         len(dtimes)

Out[54]: 3681360
```

What is a table in a SQL database is a structured array with `NumPy`. We use a special `dtype` object mirroring the SQL table from before:

```
In [55]: dty = np.dtype([('Date', 'datetime64[m]'), ('No1', 'f'), ('No2', 'f')])
         data = np.zeros(len(dtimes), dtype=dty)
```

With the `dates` object, we populate the `Date` column:

```
In [56]: data['Date'] = dtimes
```

The other two columns are populated as before with pseudorandom numbers:

```
In [57]: a = np.random.standard_normal((len(dtimes), 2)).round(5)
         data['No1'] = a[:, 0]
         data['No2'] = a[:, 1]
```

Saving of `ndarray` objects is highly optimized and therefore quite fast. Almost 60 MB of data takes less than 0.1 seconds to save on disk (here using an SSD):

```
In [58]: %time np.save(path + 'array', data)  # suffix .npy is added

Out[58]: CPU times: user 0 ns, sys: 77 ms, total: 77 ms
         Wall time: 77.1 ms

In [59]: ll $path*
```

---

3. Cf. *http://docs.scipy.org/doc/numpy/reference/arrays.datetime.html*.

```
Out[59]: -rw-r--r-- 1 root 58901888 28. Sep 15:16 /flash/data/array.npy
```

Reading is even faster:

```
In [60]: %time np.load(path + 'array.npy')

Out[60]: CPU times: user 10 ms, sys: 29 ms, total: 39 ms
         Wall time: 37.8 ms

         array([ (datetime.datetime(2015, 1, 1, 9, 0), -1.4985100030899048,
         0.9664400219917297),
                 (datetime.datetime(2015, 1, 1, 9, 1), -0.2501699924468994,
         -0.9184499979019165),
                 (datetime.datetime(2015, 1, 1, 9, 2), 1.2026900053024292,
         0.49570000171661377),
                 ...,
                 (datetime.datetime(2021, 12, 31, 20, 57), 0.8927800059318542,
         -1.0334899425506592),
                 (datetime.datetime(2021, 12, 31, 20, 58), 1.0062999725341797,
         -1.3476499915122986),
                 (datetime.datetime(2021, 12, 31, 20, 59), -0.08011999726295471,
         0.4992400109767914)],
                 dtype=[('Date', '<M8[m]'), ('No1', '<f4'), ('No2', '<f4')])
```

A data set of 60 MB is not that large. Therefore, let us try a somewhat larger ndarray object:

```
In [61]: data = np.random.standard_normal((10000, 6000))

In [62]: %time np.save(path + 'array', data)

Out[62]: CPU times: user 0 ns, sys: 631 ms, total: 631 ms
         Wall time: 633 ms

In [63]: ll $path*

Out[63]: -rw-r--r-- 1 root 480000080 28. Sep 15:16 /flash/data/array.npy
```

In this case, the file on disk is about 480 MB large and it is written in less than a second. This illustrates that writing to disk in this case is mainly hardware-bound, since 480 MB/s represents roughly the advertised writing speed of better SSDs at the time of this writing (512 MB/s). Reading the file/object from disk is even faster (note that caching techniques might also play a role here):

```
In [64]: %time np.load(path + 'array.npy')

Out[64]: CPU times: user 2 ms, sys: 216 ms, total: 218 ms
         Wall time: 216 ms

         array([[ 0.10989742, -0.48626177, -0.60849881, ..., -0.99051776,
                  0.88124291, -1.34261656],
                [-0.42301145,  0.29831708,  1.29729826, ..., -0.73426192,
                 -0.13484905,  0.91787421],
                [ 0.12322789, -0.28728811,  0.85956891, ...,  1.47888978,
                 -1.12452641, -0.528133  ],
```

```
           ...,
          [ 0.06507559, -0.37130379,  1.35427048, ..., -1.4457718 ,
            0.49509821,  0.0738847 ],
          [ 1.76525714, -0.07876135, -2.94133788, ..., -0.62581084,
            0.0933164 ,  1.55788205],
          [-1.18439949, -0.73210571, -0.45845113, ...,  0.0528656 ,
           -0.39526633, -0.5964333 ]])

In [65]: data = 0.0
         !rm -f $path*
```

In any case, you can expect that this form of data storage and retrieval is much, much faster as compared to SQL databases or using the standard pickle library for serialization. Of course, you do not have the functionality of a SQL database available with this approach, but PyTables will help in this regard, as subsequent sections show.

I/O with pandas

One of the major strengths of the pandas library is that it can read and write different data formats natively, including among others:

- CSV (comma-separated value)
- SQL (Structured Query Language)
- XLS/XSLX (Microsoft Excel files)
- JSON (JavaScript Object Notation)
- HTML (HyperText Markup Language)

Table 7-1 lists all the supported formats and the corresponding import and export functions/methods of pandas. The parameters that the import functions take are listed and described in Table 6-6 (depending on the functions, some other conventions might apply).

Table 7-1. Parameters of DataFrame function

Format	Input	Output	Remark
CSV	read_csv	to_csv	Text file
XLS/XLSX	read_excel	to_excel	Spreadsheet
HDF	read_hdf	to_hdf	HDF5 database
SQL	read_sql	to_sql	SQL table
JSON	read_json	to_json	JavaScript Object Notation
MSGPACK	read_msgpack	to_msgpack	Portable binary format
HTML	read_html	to_html	HTML code
GBQ	read_gbq	to_gbq	Google Big Query format

Format	Input	Output	Remark
DTA	read_stata	to_stata	Formats 104, 105, 108, 113-115, 117
Any	read_clipboard	to_clipboard	E.g., from HTML page
Any	read_pickle	to_pickle	(Structured) Python object

Our test case will again be a large set of floating-point numbers:

```
In [66]: import numpy as np
         import pandas as pd
         data = np.random.standard_normal((1000000, 5)).round(5)
             # sample data set

In [67]: filename = path + 'numbs'
```

To this end, we will also revisit SQLite3 and will compare the performance with alternative approaches using pandas.

SQL Database

All that follows with regard to SQLite3 should be known by now:

```
In [68]: import sqlite3 as sq3

In [69]: query = 'CREATE TABLE numbers (No1 real, No2 real,\
             No3 real, No4 real, No5 real)'

In [70]: con = sq3.Connection(filename + '.db')

In [71]: con.execute(query)

Out[71]: <sqlite3.Cursor at 0x9d59c00>
```

This time, executemany can be applied since we write from a single ndarray object:

```
In [72]: %%time
         con.executemany('INSERT INTO numbers VALUES (?, ?, ?, ?, ?)', data)
         con.commit()

Out[72]: CPU times: user 13.9 s, sys: 229 ms, total: 14.2 s
         Wall time: 14.9 s

In [73]: ll $path*

Out[73]: -rw-r--r-- 1 root 54446080 28. Sep 15:16 /flash/data/numbs.db
```

Writing the whole data set of 1,000,000 rows takes quite a while. The reading of the whole table into a list object is much faster:

```
In [74]: %%time
         temp = con.execute('SELECT * FROM numbers').fetchall()
         print temp[:2]
         temp = 0.0

Out[74]: [(-1.67378, -0.58292, -1.10616, 1.14929, -0.0393), (1.38006, 0.82665, 0
         .34168, -1.1676, -0.53274)]
```

```
CPU times: user 1.54 s, sys: 138 ms, total: 1.68 s
Wall time: 1.68 s
```

Reading SQL query results directly into a NumPy ndarray object is easily accomplished. Accordingly, you can also easily plot the results of such a query, as shown by the following code and the output in Figure 7-1:

```
In [75]: %%time
         query = 'SELECT * FROM numbers WHERE No1 > 0 AND No2 < 0'
         res = np.array(con.execute(query).fetchall()).round(3)

Out[75]: CPU times: user 766 ms, sys: 34 ms, total: 800 ms
         Wall time: 799 ms

In [76]: res = res[::100]  # every 100th result
         import matplotlib.pyplot as plt
         %matplotlib inline
         plt.plot(res[:, 0], res[:, 1], 'ro')
         plt.grid(True); plt.xlim(-0.5, 4.5); plt.ylim(-4.5, 0.5)
```

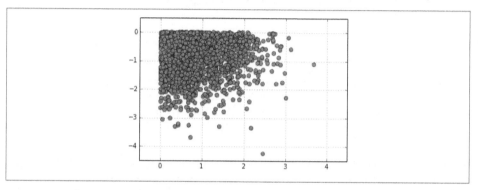

Figure 7-1. Plot of the query result

From SQL to pandas

A generally more efficient approach, however, is the reading of either whole tables or query results with pandas. When you are able to read a whole table into memory, analytical queries can generally be executed much faster than when using the SQL disk-based approach. The sublibrary pandas.io.sql contains functions to handle data stored in SQL databases:

```
In [77]: import pandas.io.sql as pds
```

Reading the whole table with pandas takes roughly the same amount of time as reading it into a NumPy ndarray object. There as here, the bottleneck is the SQL database:

```
In [78]: %time data = pds.read_sql('SELECT * FROM numbers', con)
```

```
Out[78]: CPU times: user 2.16 s, sys: 60 ms, total: 2.22 s
         Wall time: 2.23 s

In [79]: data.head()

Out[79]:        No1       No2       No3       No4       No5
         0 -1.67378 -0.58292 -1.10616  1.14929 -0.03930
         1  1.38006  0.82665  0.34168 -1.16760 -0.53274
         2  0.79329  0.11947  2.06403 -0.36208  1.77442
         3 -0.33507 -0.00715 -1.01193  0.23157  1.30225
         4 -0.35292  0.67483  1.59507 -1.21263  0.14745

         [5 rows x 5 columns]
```

The data is now in-memory. This allows for much faster analytics. The SQL query that takes a few seconds with SQLite3 finishes in less than 0.1 seconds with pandas in-memory:

```
In [80]: %time data[(data['No1'] > 0) & (data['No2'] < 0)].head()

Out[80]: CPU times: user 50 ms, sys: 0 ns, total: 50 ms
         Wall time: 49.9 ms

                 No1       No2       No3       No4       No5
         6   1.17749 -1.13017 -0.24176 -0.64047  1.58002
         8   0.18625 -0.99949  2.29854  0.91816 -0.92661
         9   1.09481 -0.26301  1.11341  0.68716 -0.71524
         18  0.31836 -0.33039 -1.50109  0.52961  0.96595
         20  0.40261 -0.45917  0.37339 -1.09515  0.23972

         [5 rows x 5 columns]
```

pandas can master even more complex queries, although it is neither meant nor able to replace SQL databases when it comes to complex, relational data structures. The result of the next query is shown in Figure 7-2:

```
In [81]: %%time
         res = data[['No1', 'No2']][(((data['No1'] > 0.5) | (data['No1'] < -0.5))
                            & ((data['No2'] < -1) | (data['No2'] > 1)))]

Out[81]: CPU times: user 49 ms, sys: 0 ns, total: 49 ms
         Wall time: 48.7 ms

In [82]: plt.plot(res.No1, res.No2, 'ro')
         plt.grid(True); plt.axis('tight')
```

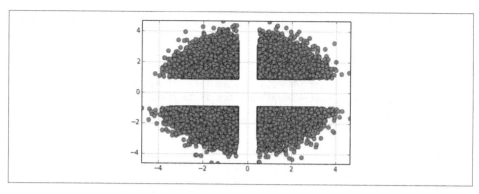

Figure 7-2. Scatter plot of complex query result

As expected, using the in-memory analytics capabilities of pandas leads to a significant speedup, provided pandas is able to replicate the respective SQL statement. This is not the only advantage of using pandas, though pandas is tightly integrated with PyTa bles, which is the topic of the next section. Here, it suffices to know that the combination of both can speed up I/O operations considerably. This is shown in the following:

```
In [83]: h5s = pd.HDFStore(filename + '.h5s', 'w')

In [84]: %time h5s['data'] = data

Out[84]: CPU times: user 43 ms, sys: 60 ms, total: 103 ms
         Wall time: 161 ms

In [85]: h5s

Out[85]: <class 'pandas.io.pytables.HDFStore'>
         File path: /flash/data/numbs.h5s
         /data              frame         (shape->[1000000,5])

In [86]: h5s.close()
```

The whole DataFrame with all the data from the original SQL table is written in well below 1 second. Reading is even faster, as is to be expected:

```
In [87]: %%time
         h5s = pd.HDFStore(filename + '.h5s', 'r')
         temp = h5s['data']
         h5s.close()

Out[87]: CPU times: user 13 ms, sys: 22 ms, total: 35 ms
         Wall time: 32.7 ms
```

A brief check of whether the data sets are indeed the same:

```
In [88]: np.allclose(np.array(temp), np.array(data))

Out[88]: True

In [89]: temp = 0.0
```

Also, a look at the two files now on disk, showing that the HDF5 format consumes somewhat less disk space:

```
In [90]: ll $path*
Out[90]: -rw-r--r-- 1 root 54446080 28. Sep 15:16 /flash/data/numbs.db
         -rw-r--r-- 1 root 48007368 28. Sep 15:16 /flash/data/numbs.h5s
```

As a summary, we can state the following with regard to our dummy data set, which is roughly 50 MB in size:

- Writing the data with SQLite3 takes *multiple seconds*, with pandas taking much *less than a second*.

- Reading the data from the SQL database takes a bit more than *a few seconds*, with pandas taking less than *0.1 second*.

Data as CSV File

One of the most widely used formats to exchange data is the CSV format. Although it is not really standardized, it can be processed by any platform and the vast majority of applications concerned with data and financial analytics. The previous section shows how to write and read data to and from CSV files step by step with standard Python functionality (cf. "Reading and Writing Text Files" on page 177). pandas makes this whole procedure a bit more convenient, the code more concise, and the execution in general faster:

```
In [91]: %time data.to_csv(filename + '.csv')
Out[91]: CPU times: user 5.55 s, sys: 137 ms, total: 5.69 s
         Wall time: 5.87 s
```

Reading the data now stored in the CSV file and plotting it is accomplished with the read_csv function (cf. Figure 7-3 for the result):

```
In [92]: %%time
         pd.read_csv(filename + '.csv')[['No1', 'No2',
                                         'No3', 'No4']].hist(bins=20)
Out[92]: CPU times: user 1.72 s, sys: 54 ms, total: 1.77 s
         Wall time: 1.78 s
```

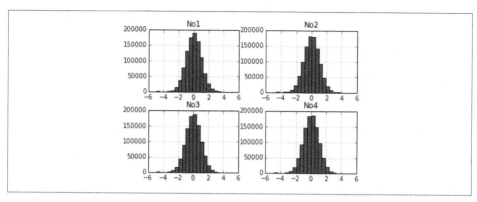

Figure 7-3. Histogram of four data sets

Data as Excel File

Although working with Excel spreadsheets is the topic of a later chapter, we want to briefly demonstrate how pandas can write data in Excel format and read data from Excel spreadsheets. We restrict the data set to 100,000 rows in this case:

```
In [93]: %time data[:100000].to_excel(filename + '.xlsx')

Out[93]: CPU times: user 27.5 s, sys: 131 ms, total: 27.6 s
         Wall time: 27.7 s
```

Generating the Excel spreadsheet with this small subset of the data takes quite a while. This illustrates what kind of overhead the spreadsheet structure brings along with it. Reading (and plotting) the data is a faster procedure (cf. Figure 7-4):

```
In [94]: %time pd.read_excel(filename + '.xlsx', 'Sheet1').cumsum().plot()

Out[94]: CPU times: user 12.9 s, sys: 6 ms, total: 12.9 s
         Wall time: 12.9 s
```

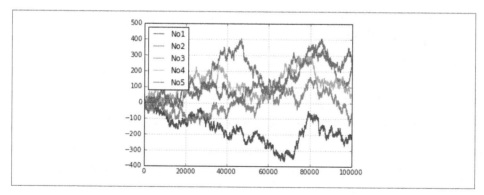

Figure 7-4. Paths of random data from Excel file

Inspection of the generated files reveals that the `DataFrame` with `HDFStore` combination is the most compact alternative (using compression, as described later in this chapter, further increases the benefits). The same amount of data as a CSV file—i.e., as a text file—is somewhat larger in size. This is one reason for the slower performance when working with CSV files, the other being the very fact that they are "only" general text files:

```
In [95]: ll $path*

Out[95]: -rw-r--r-- 1 root 48831681 28. Sep 15:17 /flash/data/numbs.csv
         -rw-r--r-- 1 root 54446080 28. Sep 15:16 /flash/data/numbs.db
         -rw-r--r-- 1 root 48007368 28. Sep 15:16 /flash/data/numbs.h5s
         -rw-r--r-- 1 root  4311424 28. Sep 15:17 /flash/data/numbs.xlsx

In [96]: rm -f $path*
```

Fast I/O with PyTables

PyTables is a Python binding for the HDF5 database/file standard (cf. *http://www.hdfgroup.org*). It is specifically designed to optimize the performance of I/O operations and make best use of the available hardware. The library's import name is `tables`. Similar to `pandas` when it comes to in-memory analytics, PyTables is neither able nor meant to be a full replacement for SQL databases. However, it brings along some features that further close the gap. For example, a PyTables database can have many tables, and it supports compression and indexing and also nontrivial queries on tables. In addition, it can store NumPy arrays efficiently and has its own flavor of array-like data structures.

We begin with a few imports:

```
In [97]: import numpy as np
         import tables as tb
         import datetime as dt
         import matplotlib.pyplot as plt
         %matplotlib inline
```

Working with Tables

PyTables provides a file-based database format:

```
In [98]: filename = path + 'tab.h5'
         h5 = tb.open_file(filename, 'w')
```

For our example case, we generate a table with 2,000,000 rows of data:

```
In [99]: rows = 2000000
```

The table itself has a `datetime` column, two `int` columns, and two `float` columns:

```
In [100]: row_des = {
              'Date': tb.StringCol(26, pos=1),
              'No1': tb.IntCol(pos=2),
```

```
        'No2': tb.IntCol(pos=3),
        'No3': tb.Float64Col(pos=4),
        'No4': tb.Float64Col(pos=5)
        }
```

When creating the table, we choose no compression. A later example will add compression as well:

```
In [101]: filters = tb.Filters(complevel=0)  # no compression
          tab = h5.create_table('/', 'ints_floats', row_des,
                                title='Integers and Floats',
                                expectedrows=rows, filters=filters)

In [102]: tab

Out[102]: /ints_floats (Table(0,)) 'Integers and Floats'
            description := {
            "Date": StringCol(itemsize=26, shape=(), dflt='', pos=0),
            "No1": Int32Col(shape=(), dflt=0, pos=1),
            "No2": Int32Col(shape=(), dflt=0, pos=2),
            "No3": Float64Col(shape=(), dflt=0.0, pos=3),
            "No4": Float64Col(shape=(), dflt=0.0, pos=4)}
            byteorder := 'little'
            chunkshape := (2621,)

In [103]: pointer = tab.row
```

Now we generate the sample data:

```
In [104]: ran_int = np.random.randint(0, 10000, size=(rows, 2))
          ran_flo = np.random.standard_normal((rows, 2)).round(5)
```

The sample data set is written row-by-row to the table:

```
In [105]: %%time
          for i in range(rows):
              pointer['Date'] = dt.datetime.now()
              pointer['No1'] = ran_int[i, 0]
              pointer['No2'] = ran_int[i, 1]
              pointer['No3'] = ran_flo[i, 0]
              pointer['No4'] = ran_flo[i, 1]
              pointer.append()
                # this appends the data and
                # moves the pointer one row forward
          tab.flush()

Out[105]: CPU times: user 15.7 s, sys: 3.53 s, total: 19.2 s
          Wall time: 19.4 s
```

Always remember to commit your changes. What the commit method is for the SQLite3 database, the flush method is for PyTables. We can now inspect the data on disk, first logically via our Table object and second physically via the file information:

```
In [106]: tab

Out[106]: /ints_floats (Table(2000000,)) 'Integers and Floats'
            description := {
            "Date": StringCol(itemsize=26, shape=(), dflt='', pos=0),
            "No1": Int32Col(shape=(), dflt=0, pos=1),
            "No2": Int32Col(shape=(), dflt=0, pos=2),
            "No3": Float64Col(shape=(), dflt=0.0, pos=3),
            "No4": Float64Col(shape=(), dflt=0.0, pos=4)}
            byteorder := 'little'
            chunkshape := (2621,)

In [107]: ll $path*

Out[107]: -rw-r--r-- 1 root 100156256 28. Sep 15:18 /flash/data/tab.h5
```

There is a more performant and Pythonic way to accomplish the same result, by the use of NumPy structured arrays:

```
In [108]: dty = np.dtype([('Date', 'S26'), ('No1', '<i4'), ('No2', '<i4'),
                          ('No3', '<f8'), ('No4', '<f8')])
          sarray = np.zeros(len(ran_int), dtype=dty)

In [109]: sarray

Out[109]: array([('', 0, 0, 0.0, 0.0), ('', 0, 0, 0.0, 0.0),
          ('', 0, 0, 0.0, 0.0),
                ..., ('', 0, 0, 0.0, 0.0), ('', 0, 0, 0.0, 0.0),
                ('', 0, 0, 0.0, 0.0)],
              dtype=[('Date', 'S26'), ('No1', '<i4'), ('No2', '<i4'), ('No3',
          '<f8'), ('No4', '<f8')])

In [110]: %%time
          sarray['Date'] = dt.datetime.now()
          sarray['No1'] = ran_int[:, 0]
          sarray['No2'] = ran_int[:, 1]
          sarray['No3'] = ran_flo[:, 0]
          sarray['No4'] = ran_flo[:, 1]

Out[110]: CPU times: user 113 ms, sys: 18 ms, total: 131 ms
          Wall time: 131 ms
```

Equipped with the complete data set now stored in the structured array, the creation of the table boils down to the following line of code. Note that the row description is not needed anymore; PyTables uses the NumPy dtype instead:

```
In [111]: %%time
          h5.create_table('/', 'ints_floats_from_array', sarray,
                          title='Integers and Floats',
                          expectedrows=rows, filters=filters)

Out[111]: CPU times: user 38 ms, sys: 117 ms, total: 155 ms
          Wall time: 154 ms

          /ints_floats_from_array (Table(2000000,)) 'Integers and Floats'
            description := {
```

```
"Date": StringCol(itemsize=26, shape=(), dflt='', pos=0),
"No1": Int32Col(shape=(), dflt=0, pos=1),
"No2": Int32Col(shape=(), dflt=0, pos=2),
"No3": Float64Col(shape=(), dflt=0.0, pos=3),
"No4": Float64Col(shape=(), dflt=0.0, pos=4)}
byteorder := 'little'
chunkshape := (2621,)
```

Being an order of magnitude faster than the previous approach, this approach achieves
the same result and also needs less code:

```
In [112]: h5

Out[112]: File(filename=/flash/data/tab.h5, title=u'', mode='w', root_uep='/',
          filters=Filters(complevel=0, shuffle=False, fletcher32=False,
          least_significant_digit=None))
          / (RootGroup) u''
          /ints_floats (Table(2000000,)) 'Integers and Floats'
            description := {
            "Date": StringCol(itemsize=26, shape=(), dflt='', pos=0),
            "No1": Int32Col(shape=(), dflt=0, pos=1),
            "No2": Int32Col(shape=(), dflt=0, pos=2),
            "No3": Float64Col(shape=(), dflt=0.0, pos=3),
            "No4": Float64Col(shape=(), dflt=0.0, pos=4)}
            byteorder := 'little'
            chunkshape := (2621,)
          /ints_floats_from_array (Table(2000000,)) 'Integers and Floats'
            description := {
            "Date": StringCol(itemsize=26, shape=(), dflt='', pos=0),
            "No1": Int32Col(shape=(), dflt=0, pos=1),
            "No2": Int32Col(shape=(), dflt=0, pos=2),
            "No3": Float64Col(shape=(), dflt=0.0, pos=3),
            "No4": Float64Col(shape=(), dflt=0.0, pos=4)}
            byteorder := 'little'
            chunkshape := (2621,)
```

We can now delete the duplicate table, since it is no longer needed:

```
In [113]: h5.remove_node('/', 'ints_floats_from_array')
```

The Table object behaves like typical Python and NumPy objects when it comes to slicing,
for example:

```
In [114]: tab[:3]

Out[114]: array([('2014-09-28 15:17:57.631234', 4342, 1672, -0.9293, 0.06343),
                 ('2014-09-28 15:17:57.631368', 3839, 1563, -2.02808, 0.3964),
                 ('2014-09-28 15:17:57.631383', 5100, 1326, 0.03401, 0.46742)],
          dtype=[('Date', 'S26'), ('No1', '<i4'), ('No2', '<i4'), ('No3',
          '<f8'), ('No4', '<f8')])
```

Similarly, we can select single columns only:

```
In [115]: tab[:4]['No4']

Out[115]: array([ 0.06343,  0.3964 ,  0.46742, -0.56959])
```

Even more convenient and important: we can apply NumPy universal functions to tables or subsets of the table:

```
In [116]: %time np.sum(tab[:]['No3'])

Out[116]: CPU times: user 31 ms, sys: 58 ms, total: 89 ms
          Wall time: 88.3 ms

          -115.34513999999896

In [117]: %time np.sum(np.sqrt(tab[:]['No1']))

Out[117]: CPU times: user 53 ms, sys: 48 ms, total: 101 ms
          Wall time: 101 ms

          133360523.08794475
```

When it comes to plotting, the Table object also behaves very similarly to an ndarray object (cf. Figure 7-5):

```
In [118]: %%time
          plt.hist(tab[:]['No3'], bins=30)
          plt.grid(True)
          print len(tab[:]['No3'])

Out[118]: 2000000
          CPU times: user 396 ms, sys: 89 ms, total: 485 ms
          Wall time: 485 ms
```

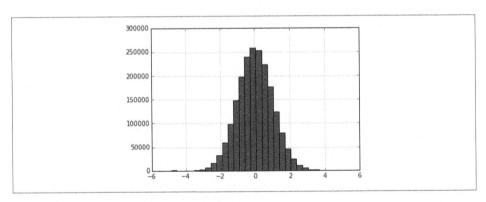

Figure 7-5. Histogram of data

And, of course, we have rather flexible tools to query data via typical SQL-like statements, as in the following example (the result of which is neatly illustrated in Figure 7-6; compare it with Figure 7-2, based on a pandas query):

```
In [119]: %%time
          res = np.array([(row['No3'], row['No4']) for row in
                tab.where('((No3 < -0.5) | (No3 > 0.5)) \
                    & ((No4 < -1) | (No4 > 1))')])[::100]

Out[119]: CPU times: user 530 ms, sys: 52 ms, total: 582 ms
          Wall time: 469 ms

In [120]: plt.plot(res.T[0], res.T[1], 'ro')
          plt.grid(True)
```

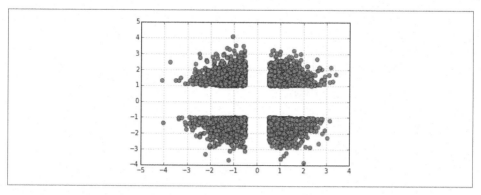

Figure 7-6. Scatter plot of query result

Fast Complex Queries

Both pandas and PyTables are able to process complex, SQL-like queries and selections. They are both optimized for speed when it comes to such operations.

As the following examples show, working with data stored in PyTables as a Table object makes you feel like you are working with NumPy and in-memory, both from a *syntax* and a *performance* point of view:

```
In [121]: %%time
          values = tab.cols.No3[:]
          print "Max %18.3f" % values.max()
          print "Ave %18.3f" % values.mean()
          print "Min %18.3f" % values.min()
          print "Std %18.3f" % values.std()

Out[121]: Max                5.152
          Ave               -0.000
          Min               -5.537
          Std                1.000
          CPU times: user 44 ms, sys: 39 ms, total: 83 ms
          Wall time: 82.6 ms
```

```
In [122]: %%time
          results = [(row['No1'], row['No2']) for row in
                        tab.where('((No1 > 9800) | (No1 < 200)) \
                                & ((No2 > 4500) & (No2 < 5500))')]
          for res in results[:4]:
              print res

Out[122]: (9987, 4965)
          (9934, 5263)
          (9960, 4729)
          (130, 5023)
          CPU times: user 167 ms, sys: 37 ms, total: 204 ms
          Wall time: 118 ms

In [123]: %%time
          results = [(row['No1'], row['No2']) for row in
                        tab.where('(No1 == 1234) & (No2 > 9776)')]
          for res in results:
              print res

Out[123]: (1234, 9805)
          (1234, 9785)
          (1234, 9821)
          CPU times: user 93 ms, sys: 40 ms, total: 133 ms
          Wall time: 90.1 ms
```

Working with Compressed Tables

A major advantage of working with PyTables is the approach it takes to compression.
It uses compression not only to save space on disk, but also to improve the performance
of I/O operations. How does this work? When I/O is the bottleneck and the CPU is able
to (de)compress data fast, the net effect of compression in terms of speed might be
positive. Since the following examples are based on the I/O of a state-of-the-art (at the
time of this writing) SSD, there is no speed advantage of compression to be observed.
However, there is also almost no *disadvantage* of using compression:

```
In [124]: filename = path + 'tab.h5c'
          h5c = tb.open_file(filename, 'w')

In [125]: filters = tb.Filters(complevel=4, complib='blosc')

In [126]: tabc = h5c.create_table('/', 'ints_floats', sarray,
                                  title='Integers and Floats',
                                  expectedrows=rows, filters=filters)

In [127]: %%time
          res = np.array([(row['No3'], row['No4']) for row in
                        tabc.where('((No3 < -0.5) | (No3 > 0.5)) \
                                & ((No4 < -1) | (No4 > 1))')])[::100]

Out[127]: CPU times: user 670 ms, sys: 41 ms, total: 711 ms
          Wall time: 602 ms
```

Generating the table with the original data and doing analytics on it is slightly slower compared to the uncompressed table. What about reading the data into an `ndarray`? Let's check:

```
In [128]: %time arr_non = tab.read()

Out[128]: CPU times: user 13 ms, sys: 49 ms, total: 62 ms
          Wall time: 61.3 ms

In [129]: %time arr_com = tabc.read()

Out[129]: CPU times: user 161 ms, sys: 33 ms, total: 194 ms
          Wall time: 193 ms
```

This indeed takes much longer than before. However, the compression ratio is about 20%, saving 80% of the space on disk. This may be of importance for backup routines or when shuffling large data sets between servers or even data centers:

```
In [130]: ll $path*

Out[130]: -rw-r--r-- 1 root 200313168 28. Sep 15:18 /flash/data/tab.h5
          -rw-r--r-- 1 root  41335178 28. Sep 15:18 /flash/data/tab.h5c

In [131]: h5c.close()
```

Working with Arrays

We have already seen that NumPy has built-in fast writing and reading capabilities for `ndarray` objects. PyTables is also quite fast and efficient when it comes to storing and retrieving `ndarray` objects:

```
In [132]: %%time
          arr_int = h5.create_array('/', 'integers', ran_int)
          arr_flo = h5.create_array('/', 'floats', ran_flo)

Out[132]: CPU times: user 2 ms, sys: 33 ms, total: 35 ms
          Wall time: 35 ms
```

Writing these objects directly to an HDF5 database is of course much faster than looping over the objects and writing the data row-by-row to a `Table` object. A final inspection of the database shows now three objects in it, the table and the two arrays:

```
In [133]: h5

Out[133]: File(filename=/flash/data/tab.h5, title=u'', mode='w', root_uep='/', f
          ilters=Filters(complevel=0, shuffle=False, fletcher32=False, least_sig
          nificant_digit=None))
          / (RootGroup) u''
          /floats (Array(2000000, 2)) ''
            atom := Float64Atom(shape=(), dflt=0.0)
            maindim := 0
            flavor := 'numpy'
            byteorder := 'little'
            chunkshape := None
```

```
          /integers (Array(2000000, 2)) ''
            atom := Int64Atom(shape=(), dflt=0)
            maindim := 0
            flavor := 'numpy'
            byteorder := 'little'
            chunkshape := None
          /ints_floats (Table(2000000,)) 'Integers and Floats'
            description := {
            "Date": StringCol(itemsize=26, shape=(), dflt='', pos=0),
            "No1": Int32Col(shape=(), dflt=0, pos=1),
            "No2": Int32Col(shape=(), dflt=0, pos=2),
            "No3": Float64Col(shape=(), dflt=0.0, pos=3),
            "No4": Float64Col(shape=(), dflt=0.0, pos=4)}
            byteorder := 'little'
            chunkshape := (2621,)

In [134]: ll $path*

Out[134]: -rw-r--r-- 1 root 200313168 28. Sep 15:18 /flash/data/tab.h5
          -rw-r--r-- 1 root  41335178 28. Sep 15:18 /flash/data/tab.h5c

In [135]: h5.close()

In [136]: !rm -f $path*
```

HDF5-Based Data Storage

The HDF5 database (file) format is a powerful alternative to, for example, relational databases when it comes to structured numerical and financial data. Both on a standalone basis when using PyTables directly and when combining it with the capabilities of pandas, you can expect to get almost the maximum I/O performance that the available hardware allows.

Out-of-Memory Computations

PyTables supports out-of-memory operations, which makes it possible to implement array-based computations that do not fit into the memory:

```
In [137]: filename = path + 'array.h5'
          h5 = tb.open_file(filename, 'w')
```

We create an EArray object that is extendable in the first dimension and has a fixed width of 1,000 in the second dimension:

```
In [138]: n = 1000
          ear = h5.createEArray(h5.root, 'ear',
                                atom=tb.Float64Atom(),
                                shape=(0, n))
```

Since it is extendable, such an object can be populated chunk-wise:

```
In [139]: %%time
          rand = np.random.standard_normal((n, n))
          for i in range(750):
              ear.append(rand)
          ear.flush()

Out[139]: CPU times: user 2.42 s, sys: 7.29 s, total: 9.71 s
          Wall time: 20.6 s
```

To check how much data we have generated logically and physically, we can inspect the meta-information provided for the object as well as the disk space consumption:

```
In [140]: ear

Out[140]: /ear (EArray(750000, 1000)) ''
            atom := Float64Atom(shape=(), dflt=0.0)
            maindim := 0
            flavor := 'numpy'
            byteorder := 'little'
            chunkshape := (8, 1000)

In [141]: ear.size_on_disk

Out[141]: 6000000000L
```

The EArray object is 6 GB large. For an out-of-memory computation, we need a target EArray object in the database:

```
In [142]: out = h5.createEArray(h5.root, 'out',
                                atom=tb.Float64Atom(),
                                shape=(0, n))
```

PyTables has a special module to cope with numerical expressions efficiently. It is called Expr and is based on the numerical expression library numexpr (*http://code.google.com/p/numexpr/*). This is what we want to use to calculate the mathematical expression in Equation 7-1 on the whole EArray object that we generated before.

Equation 7-1. Example mathematical expression

$$y = 3\sin(x) + \sqrt{|x|}$$

The following code shows the capabilities for out-of-memory calculations in action:

```
In [143]: expr = tb.Expr('3 * sin(ear) + sqrt(abs(ear))')
              # the numerical expression as a string object
          expr.setOutput(out, append_mode=True)
              # target to store results is disk-based array

In [144]: %time expr.eval()
              # evaluation of the numerical expression
              # and storage of results in disk-based array
```

```
Out[144]: CPU times: user 34.4 s, sys: 11.6 s, total: 45.9 s
          Wall time: 1min 41s

          /out (EArray(750000, 1000)) ''
            atom := Float64Atom(shape=(), dflt=0.0)
            maindim := 0
            flavor := 'numpy'
            byteorder := 'little'
            chunkshape := (8, 1000)

In [145]: out[0, :10]

Out[145]: array([-0.95979563, -1.21530335,  0.02687751,  2.88229293, -0.05596624,
                  -1.70266651, -0.58575264,  1.70317385,  3.54571202,  2.81602673
                ])
```

Given that the whole operation takes place out-of-memory, it can be considered quite fast, in particular as it is executed on standard hardware. Let us briefly compare this to the in-memory performance of the numexpr module (see also Chapter 8):

```
In [146]: %time imarray = ear.read()
              # read whole array into memory

Out[146]: CPU times: user 1.26 s, sys: 4.11 s, total: 5.37 s
          Wall time: 5.39 s

In [147]: import numexpr as ne
          expr = '3 * sin(imarray) + sqrt(abs(imarray))'

In [148]: ne.set_num_threads(16)
          %time ne.evaluate(expr)[0, :10]

Out[148]: CPU times: user 24.2 s, sys: 29.1 s, total: 53.3 s
          Wall time: 3.81 s

          array([-0.95979563, -1.21530335,  0.02687751,  2.88229293, -0.05596624,
                 -1.70266651, -0.58575264,  1.70317385,  3.54571202,  2.81602673
                ])

In [149]: h5.close()

In [150]: !rm -f $path*
```

Conclusions

SQL-based (i.e., relational) databases have advantages when it comes to complex data structures that exhibit lots of relations between single objects/tables. This might justify in some circumstances their performance disadvantage over pure NumPy ndarray-based or pandas DataFrame-based approaches.

However, many application areas in finance or science in general, can succeed with a mainly array-based data modeling approach. In these cases, huge performance improvements can be realized by making use of native NumPy I/O capabilities, a combina-

---

tion of NumPy and PyTables capabilities, or of the pandas approach via HDF5-based stores.

While a recent trend has been to use cloud-based solutions—where the cloud is made up of a large number of computing nodes based on commodity hardware—one should carefully consider, especially in a financial context, which hardware architecture best serves the analytics requirements. A recent study by Microsoft sheds some light on this topic:

> We claim that a single "scale-up" server can process each of these jobs and do as well or better than a cluster in terms of performance, cost, power, and server density.
>
> — Appuswamy et al. (2013)

Companies, research institutions, and others involved in data analytics should therefore analyze first what specific tasks have to be accomplished in general and then decide on the hardware/software architecture, in terms of:

Scaling out
Using a cluster with many commodity nodes with standard CPUs and relatively low memory

Scaling up
Using one or a few powerful servers with many-core CPUs, possibly a GPU, and large amounts of memory

Our out-of-memory analytics example in this chapter underpins the observation. The out-of-memory calculation of the numerical expression with PyTables takes roughly 1.5 minutes on standard hardware. The same task executed in-memory (using the numexpr library) takes about 4 seconds, while reading the whole data set from disk takes just over 5 seconds. This value is from an eight-core server with enough memory (in this particular case, 64 GB of RAM) and an SSD drive. Therefore, scaling up hardware and applying different implementation approaches might significantly influence performance. More on this in the next chapter.

Further Reading

The paper cited at the beginning of the chapter as well as in the "Conclusions" section is a good read, and a good starting point to think about hardware architecture for financial analytics:

- Appuswamy, Raja et al. (2013): "Nobody Ever Got Fired for Buying a Cluster." Microsoft Research, Cambridge, England, *http://research.microsoft.com/apps/pubs/default.aspx?id=179615*.

As usual, the Web provides many valuable resources with regard to the topics covered in this chapter:

- For serialization of Python objects with pickle, refer to the documentation: *http:// docs.python.org/2/library/pickle.html*.

- An overview of the I/O capabilities of NumPy is provided on the SciPy website: *http://docs.scipy.org/doc/numpy/reference/routines.io.html*.

- For I/O with pandas see the respective section in the online documentation: *http:// pandas.pydata.org/pandas-docs/stable/io.html*.

- The PyTables home page provides both tutorials and detailed documentation: *http://www.pytables.org*.

## CHAPTER 8

Performance Python

Don't lower your expectations to meet your performance.
Raise your level of performance to meet your expectations.

— Ralph Marston

When it comes to performance-critical applications two things should always be checked: are we using the right *implementation paradigm* and are we using the right *performance libraries*? A number of performance libraries can be used to speed up the execution of Python code. Among others, you will find the following libraries useful, all of which are presented in this chapter (although in a different order):

- Cython, for merging Python with C paradigms for static compilation
- IPython.parallel, for the parallel execution of code/functions locally or over a cluster
- numexpr, for fast numerical operations
- multiprocessing, Python's built-in module for (local) parallel processing
- Numba, for dynamically compiling Python code for the CPU
- NumbaPro, for dynamically compiling Python code for multicore CPUs and GPUs

Throughout this chapter, we compare the performance of different implementations of the same algorithms. To make the comparison a bit easier, we define a convenience function that allows us to systematically compare the performance of different functions executed on the same or different data sets:

```
In [1]: def perf_comp_data(func_list, data_list, rep=3, number=1):
            ''' Function to compare the performance of different functions.

            Parameters
            ==========
            func_list : list
```

```
            list with function names as strings
        data_list : list
            list with data set names as strings
        rep : int
            number of repetitions of the whole comparison
        number : int
            number of executions for every function
        '''
        from timeit import repeat
        res_list = {}
        for name in enumerate(func_list):
            stmt = name[1] + '(' + data_list[name[0]] + ')'
            setup = "from __main__ import " + name[1] + ', ' \
                            + data_list[name[0]]
            results = repeat(stmt=stmt, setup=setup,
                            repeat=rep, number=number)
            res_list[name[1]] = sum(results) / rep
        res_sort = sorted(res_list.iteritems(),
                            key=lambda (k, v): (v, k))
        for item in res_sort:
            rel = item[1] / res_sort[0][1]
            print 'function: ' + item[0] + \
                    ', av. time sec: %9.5f, ' % item[1] \
                + 'relative: %6.1f' % rel
```

Python Paradigms and Performance

In finance, like in other scientific and data-intensive disciplines, numerical computations on large data sets can be quite time-consuming. As an example, we want to evaluate a somewhat complex mathematical expression on an array with 500,000 numbers. We choose the expression in Equation 8-1, which leads to some computational burden per calculation. Apart from that, it does not have any specific meaning.

Equation 8-1. Example mathematical expression

$$y = \sqrt{|\cos(x)|} + \sin(2 + 3x)$$

Equation 8-1 is easily translated into a `Python` function:

```
In [2]: from math import *
        def f(x):
            return abs(cos(x)) ** 0.5 + sin(2 + 3 * x)
```

Using the `range` function we can generate efficiently a `list` object with 500,000 numbers that we can work with:

```
In [3]: I = 500000
        a_py = range(I)
```

As the first implementation, consider function f1, which loops over the whole data set and appends the single results of the function evaluations to a results list object:

```
In [4]: def f1(a):
            res = []
            for x in a:
                res.append(f(x))
            return res
```

This is not the only way to implement this. One can also use different Python paradigms, like *iterators* or the eval function, to get functions of the form f2 and f3:

```
In [5]: def f2(a):
            return [f(x) for x in a]
```

```
In [6]: def f3(a):
            ex = 'abs(cos(x)) ** 0.5 + sin(2 + 3 * x)'
            return [eval(ex) for x in a]
```

Of course, the same algorithm can be implemented by the use of NumPy vectorization techniques. In this case, the array of data is an ndarray object instead of a list object. The function implementation f4 shows no loops whatsoever; all looping takes place on the NumPy level and not on the Python level:

```
In [7]: import numpy as np
```

```
In [8]: a_np = np.arange(I)
```

```
In [9]: def f4(a):
            return (np.abs(np.cos(a)) ** 0.5 +
                    np.sin(2 + 3 * a))
```

Then, we can use a specialized library called numexpr to evaluate the numerical expression. This library has built-in support for multithreaded execution. Therefore, to compare the performance of the single with the multithreaded approach, we define two different functions, f5 (single thread) and f6 (multiple threads):

```
In [10]: import numexpr as ne
```

```
In [11]: def f5(a):
             ex = 'abs(cos(a)) ** 0.5 + sin(2 + 3 * a)'
             ne.set_num_threads(1)
             return ne.evaluate(ex)
```

```
In [12]: def f6(a):
             ex = 'abs(cos(a)) ** 0.5 + sin(2 + 3 * a)'
             ne.set_num_threads(16)
             return ne.evaluate(ex)
```

In total, the same task—i.e., the evaluation of the numerical expression in Equation 8-1 on an array of size 500,000—is implemented in six different ways:

- Standard Python function with explicit looping
- Iterator approach with implicit looping
- Iterator approach with implicit looping and using eval
- NumPy vectorized implementation
- Single-threaded implementation using numexpr
- Multithreaded implementation using numexpr

First, let us check whether the implementations deliver the same results. We use the IPython cell magic command %%time to record the total execution time:

```
In [13]: %%time
         r1 = f1(a_py)
         r2 = f2(a_py)
         r3 = f3(a_py)
         r4 = f4(a_np)
         r5 = f5(a_np)
         r6 = f6(a_np)
Out[13]: CPU times: user 16 s, sys: 125 ms, total: 16.1 s
         Wall time: 16 s
```

The NumPy function allclose allows for easy checking of whether two ndarray(-like) objects contain the same data:

```
In [14]: np.allclose(r1, r2)

Out[14]: True

In [15]: np.allclose(r1, r3)

Out[15]: True

In [16]: np.allclose(r1, r4)

Out[16]: True

In [17]: np.allclose(r1, r5)

Out[17]: True

In [18]: np.allclose(r1, r6)

Out[18]: True
```

This obviously is the case. The more interesting question, of course, is how the different implementations compare with respect to execution speed. To this end, we use the perf_comp_data function and provide all the function and data set names to it:

```
In [19]: func_list = ['f1', 'f2', 'f3', 'f4', 'f5', 'f6']
         data_list = ['a_py', 'a_py', 'a_py', 'a_np', 'a_np', 'a_np']
```

We now have everything together to initiate the competition:

```
In [20]: perf_comp_data(func_list, data_list)

Out[20]: function: f6, av. time sec:   0.00583, relative:    1.0
         function: f5, av. time sec:   0.02711, relative:    4.6
         function: f4, av. time sec:   0.06331, relative:   10.9
         function: f2, av. time sec:   0.46864, relative:   80.3
         function: f1, av. time sec:   0.59660, relative:  102.3
         function: f3, av. time sec:  15.15156, relative: 2597.2
```

There is a clear winner: the multithreaded numexpr implementation f6. Its speed advantage, of course, depends on the number of cores available. The vectorized NumPy version f4 is slower than f5. The pure Python implementations f1 and f2 are more than 80 times slower than the winner. f3 is the slowest version, since the use of the eval function for such a large number of evaluations generates a huge overhead. In the case of numexpr, the string-based expression is evaluated once and then compiled for later use; with the Python eval function this evaluation takes place 500,000 times.

Memory Layout and Performance

NumPy allows the specification of a so-called dtype per ndarray object: for example, np.int32 or f8. NumPy also allows us to choose from two different *memory layouts* when initializing an ndarray object. Depending on the structure of the object, one layout can have advantages compared to the other. This is illustrated in the following:

```
In [21]: import numpy as np

In [22]: np.zeros((3, 3), dtype=np.float64, order='C')

Out[22]: array([[ 0.,  0.,  0.],
                [ 0.,  0.,  0.],
                [ 0.,  0.,  0.]])
```

The way you initialize a NumPy ndarray object can have a significant influence on the performance of operations on these arrays (given a certain size of array). In summary, the initialization of an ndarray object (e.g., via np.zeros or np.array) takes as input:

shape

Either an int, a sequence of ints, or a reference to another numpy.ndarray

dtype *(optional)*

A numpy.dtype—these are NumPy-specific basic data types for numpy.ndarray objects

order *(optional)*

The order in which to store elements in memory: C for C-like (i.e., row-wise) or F for Fortran-like (i.e., column-wise)

Consider the C-like (i.e., row-wise), storage:

```
In [23]: c = np.array([[ 1.,   1.,   1.],
                       [ 2.,   2.,   2.],
                       [ 3.,   3.,   3.]], order='C')
```

In this case, the 1s, the 2s, and the 3s are stored next to each other. By contrast, consider the Fortran-like (i.e., column-wise) storage:

```
In [24]: f = np.array([[ 1.,   1.,   1.],
                       [ 2.,   2.,   2.],
                       [ 3.,   3.,   3.]], order='F')
```

Now, the data is stored in such a way that 1, 2, and 3 are next to each other in each column. Let's see whether the memory layout makes a difference in some way when the array is large:

```
In [25]: x = np.random.standard_normal((3, 1500000))
         C = np.array(x, order='C')
         F = np.array(x, order='F')
         x = 0.0
```

Now let's implement some standard operations on the C-like layout array. First, calculating sums:

```
In [26]: %timeit C.sum(axis=0)

Out[26]: 100 loops, best of 3: 11.3 ms per loop

In [27]: %timeit C.sum(axis=1)

Out[27]: 100 loops, best of 3: 5.84 ms per loop
```

Calculating sums over the first axis is roughly two times slower than over the second axis. One gets similar results for calculating standard deviations:

```
In [28]: %timeit C.std(axis=0)

Out[28]: 10 loops, best of 3: 70.6 ms per loop

In [29]: %timeit C.std(axis=1)

Out[29]: 10 loops, best of 3: 32.6 ms per loop
```

For comparison, consider the Fortran-like layout. Sums first:

```
In [30]: %timeit F.sum(axis=0)

Out[30]: 10 loops, best of 3: 29.2 ms per loop

In [31]: %timeit F.sum(axis=1)

Out[31]: 10 loops, best of 3: 37 ms per loop
```

Although absolutely slower compared to the other layout, there is hardly a relative difference for the two axes. Now, standard deviations:

```
In [32]: %timeit F.std(axis=0)

Out[32]: 10 loops, best of 3: 107 ms per loop
```

```
In [33]: %timeit F.std(axis=1)

Out[33]: 10 loops, best of 3: 98.8 ms per loop
```

Again, this layout option leads to worse performance compared to the C-like layout. There is a small difference between the two axes, but again it is not as pronounced as with the other layout. The results indicate that in general the C-like option will perform better—which is also the reason why NumPy ndarray objects default to this memory layout if not otherwise specified:

```
In [34]: C = 0.0; F = 0.0
```

Parallel Computing

Nowadays, even the most compact notebooks have mainboards with processors that have multiple cores. Moreover, modern cloud-based computing offerings, like Amazon's EC2 or Microsoft's Azure, allow for highly scalable, parallel architectures at rather low, variable costs. This brings large-scale computing to the small business, the researcher, and even the ambitious amateur. However, to harness the power of such offerings, appropriate tools are necessary. One such tool is the IPython.parallel library.

The Monte Carlo Algorithm

A financial algorithm that leads to a high computational burden is the Monte Carlo valuation of options. As a specific example, we pick the *Monte Carlo estimator for a European call option value* in the Black-Scholes-Merton setup (see also Chapter 3 for the same example). In this setup, the underlying of the option to be valued follows the stochastic differential equation (SDE), as in Equation 8-2. S_t is the value of the underlying at time t; r is the constant, riskless short rate; σ is the constant instantaneous volatility; and Z_t is a Brownian motion.

Equation 8-2. Black-Scholes-Merton SDE

$$dS_t = rS_t dt + \sigma S_t dZ_t$$

The Monte Carlo estimator for a European call option is given by Equation 8-3, where $S_T(i)$ is the ith simulated value of the underlying at maturity T.

Equation 8-3. Monte Carlo estimator for European call option

$$C_0 = e^{-rT} \frac{1}{I} \sum_I \max\left(S_T(i) - K, 0\right)$$

A function implementing the Monte Carlo valuation for the Black-Scholes-Merton set-up could look like the following, if we only allow the strike of the European call option to vary:

```
In [35]: def bsm_mcs_valuation(strike):
             ''' Dynamic Black-Scholes-Merton Monte Carlo estimator
             for European calls.

             Parameters
             ==========
             strike : float
                 strike price of the option

             Results
             =======
             value : float
                 estimate for present value of call option
             '''
             import numpy as np
             S0 = 100.; T = 1.0; r = 0.05; vola = 0.2
             M = 50; I = 20000
             dt = T / M
             rand = np.random.standard_normal((M + 1, I))
             S = np.zeros((M + 1, I)); S[0] = S0
             for t in range(1, M + 1):
                 S[t] = S[t-1] * np.exp((r - 0.5 * vola ** 2) * dt
                                         + vola * np.sqrt(dt) * rand[t])
             value = (np.exp(-r * T)
                              * np.sum(np.maximum(S[-1] - strike, 0)) / I)
             return value
```

The Sequential Calculation

As the benchmark case we take the valuation of 100 options with different strike prices. The function `seq_value` calculates the Monte Carlo estimators and returns `list` objects containing strikes and valuation results:

```
In [36]: def seq_value(n):
             ''' Sequential option valuation.

             Parameters
             ==========
             n : int
                 number of option valuations/strikes
             '''
             strikes = np.linspace(80, 120, n)
             option_values = []
             for strike in strikes:
                 option_values.append(bsm_mcs_valuation(strike))
             return strikes, option_values
```

```
In [37]: n = 100  # number of options to be valued
         %time strikes, option_values_seq = seq_value(n)

Out[37]: CPU times: user 11.7 s, sys: 1e+03 µs, total: 11.7 s
Wall time: 11.7 s
```

The productivity is roughly 8.5 options per second. Figure 8-1 shows the valuation results:

```
In [38]: import matplotlib.pyplot as plt
         %matplotlib inline
         plt.figure(figsize=(8, 4))
         plt.plot(strikes, option_values_seq, 'b')
         plt.plot(strikes, option_values_seq, 'r.')
         plt.grid(True)
         plt.xlabel('strikes')
         plt.ylabel('European call option values')
```

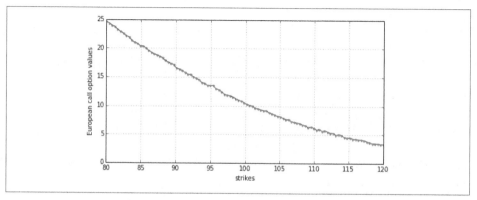

Figure 8-1. European call option values by Monte Carlo simulation

The Parallel Calculation

For the parallel calculation of the 100 option values, we use IPython.parallel and a local "cluster." A local cluster is most easily started via the Clusters tab in the IPython Notebook dashboard. The number of threads to be used of course depends on the machine and the processor you are running your code on. Figure 8-2 shows the IPython page for starting a cluster.

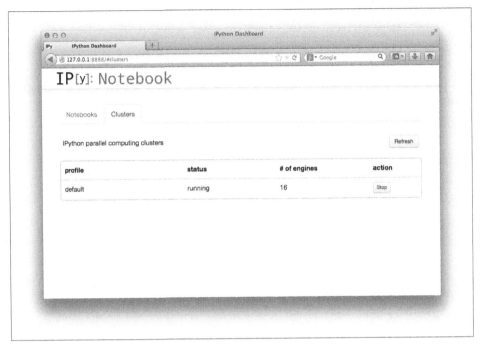

Figure 8-2. Screenshot of IPython cluster page

IPython.parallel needs the information on which cluster to use for the parallel execution of code. In this case, the cluster profile is stored in the "default" profile. In addition, we need to generate a view on the cluster:

```
In [39]: from IPython.parallel import Client
         c = Client(profile="default")
         view = c.load_balanced_view()
```

The function implementing the parallel valuation of the options looks rather similar to the sequential implementation:

```
In [40]: def par_value(n):
             ''' Parallel option valuation.

             Parameters
             ==========
             n : int
                 number of option valuations/strikes
             '''
             strikes = np.linspace(80, 120, n)
             option_values = []
             for strike in strikes:
                 value = view.apply_async(bsm_mcs_valuation, strike)
                 option_values.append(value)
```

```
c.wait(option_values)
return strikes, option_values
```

There are two major differences to note. The first is that the valuation function is applied asynchronously via `view.apply_sync` to our cluster view, which in effect initiates the parallel valuation of all options at once. Of course, not all options can be valued in parallel because there are (generally) not enough cores/threads available. Therefore, we have to wait until the queue is completely finished; this is accomplished by the `wait` method of the `Client` object `c`. When all results are available, the function returns, as before, `list` objects containing the strike prices and the valuation results, respectively.

Execution of the parallel valuation function yields a productivity that ideally scales linearly with the number of cores (threads) available. For example, having *eight* cores (threads) available reduces the execution time to maximally *one-eighth* of the time needed for the sequential calculation:

```
In [41]: %time strikes, option_values_obj = par_value(n)
```

```
Out[41]: CPU times: user 415 ms, sys: 30 ms, total: 445 ms
         Wall time: 1.88 s
```

The parallel execution does not return option values directly; it rather returns more complex result objects:

```
In [42]: option_values_obj[0].metadata
```

```
Out[42]: {'after': [],
          'completed': datetime.datetime(2014, 9, 28, 16, 6, 54, 93979),
          'data': {},
          'engine_id': 5,
          'engine_uuid': u'6b64aebb-39d5-49aa-9466-e6ab37d3b2c9',
          'follow': [],
          'msg_id': u'c7a44c22-b4bd-46d7-ba5e-34690f178fa9',
          'outputs': [],
          'outputs_ready': True,
          'pyerr': None,
          'pyin': None,
          'pyout': None,
          'received': datetime.datetime(2014, 9, 28, 16, 6, 54, 97195),
          'started': datetime.datetime(2014, 9, 28, 16, 6, 53, 921633),
          'status': u'ok',
          'stderr': '',
          'stdout': '',
          'submitted': datetime.datetime(2014, 9, 28, 16, 6, 53, 917290)}
```

The valuation result itself is stored in the `result` attribute of the object:

```
In [43]: option_values_obj[0].result
```

```
Out[43]: 24.436651486350289
```

To arrive at a results list as with the sequential calculation, we need to read the single results out from the returned objects:

```
In [44]: option_values_par = []
         for res in option_values_obj:
             option_values_par.append(res.result)
```

This could have been done, of course, in the parallel valuation loop directly. Figure 8-3 compares the valuation results of the sequential calculation with those of the parallel calculation. Differences are due to numerical issues concerning the Monte Carlo valuation:

```
In [45]: plt.figure(figsize=(8, 4))
         plt.plot(strikes, option_values_seq, 'b', label='Sequential')
         plt.plot(strikes, option_values_par, 'r.', label='Parallel')
         plt.grid(True); plt.legend(loc=0)
         plt.xlabel('strikes')
         plt.ylabel('European call option values')
```

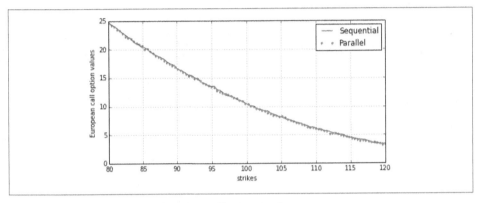

Figure 8-3. Comparison of European call option values

Performance Comparison

With the help of the `perf_comp_func` function, we can compare the performance a bit more rigorously:

```
In [46]: n = 50   # number of option valuations
         func_list = ['seq_value', 'par_value']
         data_list = 2 * ['n']
```

```
In [47]: perf_comp_data(func_list, data_list)
```

```
Out[47]: function: par_value, av. time sec:   0.90832, relative:   1.0
         function: seq_value, av. time sec:   5.75137, relative:   6.3
```

The results clearly demonstrate that using `IPython.parallel` for parallel execution of functions can lead to an almost linear scaling of the performance with the number of cores available.

multiprocessing

The advantage of IPython.parallel is that it scales over small- and medium-sized clusters (e.g., with 256 nodes). Sometimes it is, however, helpful to parallelize code execution locally. This is where the "standard" multiprocessing module of Python might prove beneficial:

```
In [48]: import multiprocessing as mp
```

Consider the following function to simulate a geometric Brownian motion:

```
In [49]: import math
         def simulate_geometric_brownian_motion(p):
             M, I = p
               # time steps, paths
             S0 = 100; r = 0.05; sigma = 0.2; T = 1.0
               # model parameters
             dt = T / M
             paths = np.zeros((M + 1, I))
             paths[0] = S0
             for t in range(1, M + 1):
                 paths[t] = paths[t - 1] * np.exp((r - 0.5 * sigma ** 2) * dt +
                         sigma * math.sqrt(dt) * np.random.standard_normal(I))
             return paths
```

This function returns simulated paths given the parameterization for M and I:

```
In [50]: paths = simulate_geometric_brownian_motion((5, 2))
         paths

Out[50]: array([[ 100.        ,  100.        ],
                [  93.65851581,   98.93916652],
                [  94.70157252,   93.44208625],
                [  96.73499004,   97.88294562],
                [ 110.64677908,   96.04515015],
                [ 124.09826521,  101.86087283]])
```

Let us implement a test series on a server with eight cores and the following parameter values. In particular, we want to do 100 simulations:

```
In [51]: I = 10000  # number of paths
         M = 100  # number of time steps
         t = 100  # number of tasks/simulations
```

```
In [52]: # running on server with 8 cores/16 threads
         from time import time
         times = []
         for w in range(1, 17):
             t0 = time()
             pool = mp.Pool(processes=w)
               # the pool of workers
             result = pool.map(simulate_geometric_brownian_motion,
                         t * [(M, I), ])
```

```
# the mapping of the function to the list of parameter tuples
times.append(time() - t0)
```

We again come to the conclusion that performance scales with the number of cores available. Hyperthreading, however, does not add much (or is even worse) in this case, as Figure 8-4 illustrates:

```
In [53]: plt.plot(range(1, 17), times)
         plt.plot(range(1, 17), times, 'ro')
         plt.grid(True)
         plt.xlabel('number of processes')
         plt.ylabel('time in seconds')
         plt.title('%d Monte Carlo simulations' % t)
```

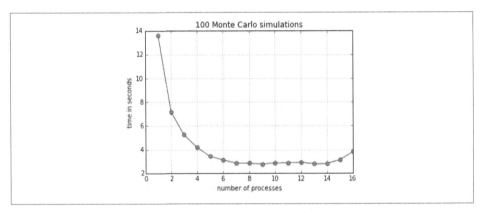

Figure 8-4. Execution speed depending on the number of threads used (eight-core machine)

Easy Parallelization

Many problems in finance allow for the application of simple parallelization techniques, for example, when no data is shared between instances of an algorithm. The `multiprocessing` module of Python allows us to efficiently harness the power of modern hardware architectures without in general changing the basic algorithms and/or Python functions to be parallelized.

Dynamic Compiling

Numba (*http://numba.pydata.org*) is an open source, NumPy-aware optimizing compiler for Python code. It uses the LLVM compiler infrastructure[1] to compile Python byte code to machine code especially for use in the NumPy runtime and SciPy modules.

Introductory Example

Let us start with a problem that typically leads to performance issues in Python: algorithms with nested loops. A sandbox variant can illustrate the problem:

```
In [54]: from math import cos, log
         def f_py(I, J):
             res = 0
             for i in range(I):
                 for j in range (J):
                     res += int(cos(log(1)))
             return res
```

In a somewhat compute-intensive way, this function returns the total number of loops given the input parameters I and J. Setting both equal to 5,000 leads to 25,000,000 loops:

```
In [55]: I, J = 5000, 5000
         %time f_py(I, J)

Out[55]: CPU times: user 17.4 s, sys: 2.3 s, total: 19.7 s
         Wall time: 15.2 s

         25000000
```

In principle, this can be vectorized with the help of NumPy ndarray objects:

```
In [56]: def f_np(I, J):
             a = np.ones((I, J), dtype=np.float64)
             return int(np.sum(np.cos(np.log(a)))), a

In [57]: %time res, a = f_np(I, J)

Out[57]: CPU times: user 1.41 s, sys: 285 ms, total: 1.69 s
         Wall time: 1.65 s
```

This is much faster, roughly by a factor of 8–10 times, but not really memory-efficient. The ndarray object consumes 200 MB of memory:

```
In [58]: a.nbytes

Out[58]: 200000000
```

---

1. Formerly, LLVM (*http://www.llvm.org*) was meant to be an acronym for Low Level Virtual Machine; now "it is the full name of the project."

I and J can easily be chosen to make the NumPy approach infeasible given a certain size of RAM. Numba provides an attractive alternative to tackle the performance issue of such loop structures while preserving the memory efficiency of the pure Python approach:

```
In [59]: import numba as nb
```

With Numba you only need to apply the jit function to the pure Python function to generate a Python-callable, compiled version of the function:

```
In [60]: f_nb = nb.jit(f_py)
```

As promised, this new function can be called directly from within the Python interpreter, realizing a significant speedup compared to the NumPy vectorized version:

```
In [61]: %time f_nb(I, J)
Out[61]: CPU times: user 143 ms, sys: 12 ms, total: 155 ms
         Wall time: 139 ms

         25000000L
```

Again, let us compare the performance of the different alternatives a bit more systematically:

```
In [62]: func_list = ['f_py', 'f_np', 'f_nb']
         data_list = 3 * ['I, J']
In [63]: perf_comp_data(func_list, data_list)
Out[63]: function: f_nb, av. time sec:   0.02022, relative:    1.0
         function: f_np, av. time sec:   1.67494, relative:   82.8
         function: f_py, av. time sec:  15.82375, relative:  782.4
```

The Numba version of the nested loop implementation is by far the fastest; much faster even than the NumPy vectorized version. The pure Python version is much slower than the other two versions.

 Quick Wins

Many approaches for performance improvements (of numerical algorithms) involve considerable effort. With Python and Numba you have an approach available that involves only the smallest effort possible—in general, importing the library and a single additional line of code. It does not work for all kinds of algorithms, but it is often worth a (quick) try and sometimes indeed yields a quick win.

Binomial Option Pricing

The previous section uses Monte Carlo simulation to value European call options, using a parallel computing approach. Another popular numerical method to value options is the binomial option pricing model pioneered by Cox, Ross, and Rubinstein (1979). In this model, as in the Black-Scholes-Merton setup, there is a risky asset, an index or stock, and a riskless asset, a bond. As with Monte Carlo, the relevant time interval from today until the maturity of the option is divided into generally equidistant subintervals, Δt. Given an index level at time s of S_s, the index level at $t = s + \Delta t$ is given by $S_t = S_s \cdot m$, where m is chosen randomly from from $\{u,d\}$ with $0 < d < e^{r\Delta t} < u = e^{\sigma\sqrt{\Delta t}}$ as well as $u = \frac{1}{d}$. r is the constant, riskless short rate. The risk-neutral probability for an up-movement is given as $q = \frac{e^{r\Delta t} - d}{u - d}$.

Consider that a parameterization for the model is given as follows:

```
In [64]: # model & option parameters
         S0 = 100.  # initial index level
         T = 1.  # call option maturity
         r = 0.05  # constant short rate
         vola = 0.20  # constant volatility factor of diffusion

         # time parameters
         M = 1000  # time steps
         dt = T / M  # length of time interval
         df = exp(-r * dt)  # discount factor per time interval

         # binomial parameters
         u = exp(vola * sqrt(dt))  # up-movement
         d = 1 / u  # down-movement
         q = (exp(r * dt) - d) / (u - d)  # martingale probability
```

An implementation of the binomial algorithm for European options consists mainly of these parts:

Index level simulation
   Simulate step by step the index levels.

Inner value calculation
   Calculate the inner values at maturity and/or at every time step.

Risk-neutral discounting
   Discount the (expected) inner values at maturity step by step to arrive at the present value.

In Python this might take on the form seen in the function binomial_py. This function uses NumPy ndarray objects as the basic data structure and implements three different nested loops to accomplish the three steps just sketched:

```
In [65]: import numpy as np
         def binomial_py(strike):
             ''' Binomial option pricing via looping.

             Parameters
             ==========
             strike : float
```

```
        strike price of the European call option
    '''
    # LOOP 1 - Index Levels
    S = np.zeros((M + 1, M + 1), dtype=np.float64)
      # index level array
    S[0, 0] = S0
    z1 = 0
    for j in xrange(1, M + 1, 1):
        z1 = z1 + 1
        for i in xrange(z1 + 1):
            S[i, j] = S[0, 0] * (u ** j) * (d ** (i * 2))

    # LOOP 2 - Inner Values
    iv = np.zeros((M + 1, M + 1), dtype=np.float64)
      # inner value array
    z2 = 0
    for j in xrange(0, M + 1, 1):
        for i in xrange(z2 + 1):
            iv[i, j] = max(S[i, j] - strike, 0)
        z2 = z2 + 1

    # LOOP 3 - Valuation
    pv = np.zeros((M + 1, M + 1), dtype=np.float64)
      # present value array
    pv[:, M] = iv[:, M]  # initialize last time point
    z3 = M + 1
    for j in xrange(M - 1, -1, -1):
        z3 = z3 - 1
        for i in xrange(z3):
            pv[i, j] = (q * pv[i, j + 1] +
                        (1 - q) * pv[i + 1, j + 1]) * df
    return pv[0, 0]
```

This function returns the present value of a European call option with parameters as specified before:

```
In [66]: %time round(binomial_py(100), 3)

Out[66]: CPU times: user 4.18 s, sys: 312 ms, total: 4.49 s
         Wall time: 3.64 s

         10.449
```

We can compare this result with the estimated value the Monte Carlo function bsm_mcs_valuation returns:

```
In [67]: %time round(bsm_mcs_valuation(100), 3)

Out[67]: CPU times: user 133 ms, sys: 0 ns, total: 133 ms
         Wall time: 126 ms

         10.318
```

The values are similar. They are only "similar" and not the same since the Monte Carlo valuation as implemented with bsm_mcs_valuation is not too precise, in that different sets of random numbers will lead to (slightly) different estimates. 20,000 paths per simulation can also be considered a bit too low for robust Monte Carlo estimates (leading, however, to high valuation speeds). By contrast, the binomial option pricing model with 1,000 time steps is rather precise but also takes much longer in this case.

Again, we can try NumPy vectorization techniques to come up with equally precise but faster results from the binomial approach. The binomial_np function might seem a bit cryptic at first sight; however, when you step through the individual construction steps and inspect the results, it becomes clear what happens behind the (NumPy) scenes:

```python
In [68]: def binomial_np(strike):
             ''' Binomial option pricing with NumPy.

             Parameters
             ==========
             strike : float
                 strike price of the European call option
             '''
             # Index Levels with NumPy
             mu = np.arange(M + 1)
             mu = np.resize(mu, (M + 1, M + 1))
             md = np.transpose(mu)
             mu = u ** (mu - md)
             md = d ** md
             S = S0 * mu * md

             # Valuation Loop
             pv = np.maximum(S - strike, 0)
             z = 0
             for t in range(M - 1, -1, -1):  # backward iteration
                 pv[0:M - z, t] = (q * pv[0:M - z, t + 1]
                                 + (1 - q) * pv[1:M - z + 1, t + 1]) * df
                 z += 1
             return pv[0, 0]
```

Let us briefly take a look behind the scenes. For simplicity and readability, consider only M=4 time steps. The first step:

```python
In [69]: M = 4  # four time steps only
         mu = np.arange(M + 1)
         mu

Out[69]: array([0, 1, 2, 3, 4])
```

The second step of the construction:

```python
In [70]: mu = np.resize(mu, (M + 1, M + 1))
         mu
```

```
Out[70]: array([[0, 1, 2, 3, 4],
                [0, 1, 2, 3, 4],
                [0, 1, 2, 3, 4],
                [0, 1, 2, 3, 4],
                [0, 1, 2, 3, 4]])
```

The third one:

```
In [71]: md = np.transpose(mu)
         md

Out[71]: array([[0, 0, 0, 0, 0],
                [1, 1, 1, 1, 1],
                [2, 2, 2, 2, 2],
                [3, 3, 3, 3, 3],
                [4, 4, 4, 4, 4]])
```

The fourth and fifth steps:

```
In [72]: mu = u ** (mu - md)
         mu.round(3)

Out[72]: array([[ 1.   , 1.006, 1.013, 1.019, 1.026],
                [ 0.994, 1.   , 1.006, 1.013, 1.019],
                [ 0.987, 0.994, 1.   , 1.006, 1.013],
                [ 0.981, 0.987, 0.994, 1.   , 1.006],
                [ 0.975, 0.981, 0.987, 0.994, 1.   ]])

In [73]: md = d ** md
         md.round(3)

Out[73]: array([[ 1.   , 1.   , 1.   , 1.   , 1.   ],
                [ 0.994, 0.994, 0.994, 0.994, 0.994],
                [ 0.987, 0.987, 0.987, 0.987, 0.987],
                [ 0.981, 0.981, 0.981, 0.981, 0.981],
                [ 0.975, 0.975, 0.975, 0.975, 0.975]])
```

Finally, bringing everything together:

```
In [74]: S = S0 * mu * md
         S.round(3)

Out[74]: array([[ 100.   , 100.634, 101.273, 101.915, 102.562],
                [  98.743,  99.37 , 100.   , 100.634, 101.273],
                [  97.502,  98.121,  98.743,  99.37 , 100.   ],
                [  96.276,  96.887,  97.502,  98.121,  98.743],
                [  95.066,  95.669,  96.276,  96.887,  97.502]])
```

From the ndarray object S, only the upper triangular matrix is of importance. Although we do more calculations with this approach than are needed in principle, the approach is, as expected, much faster than the first version, which relies heavily on nested loops on the Python level:

```
In [75]: M = 1000  # reset number of time steps
         %time round(binomial_np(100), 3)
```

```
Out[75]: CPU times: user 308 ms, sys: 6 ms, total: 314 ms
         Wall time: 304 ms

         10.449
```

Numba has proven a valuable performance enhancement tool for our sandbox example. Here, it can prove its worth in the context of a very important financial algorithm:

```
In [76]: binomial_nb = nb.jit(binomial_py)

In [77]: %time round(binomial_nb(100), 3)

Out[77]: CPU times: user 1.71 s, sys: 137 ms, total: 1.84 s
         Wall time: 1.59 s

         10.449
```

We do not yet see a significant speedup over the NumPy vectorized version since the first call of the compiled function involves some overhead. Therefore, using the perf_comp_func function shall shed a more realistic light on how the three different implementations compare with regard to performance. Obviously, the Numba compiled version is indeed significantly faster than the NumPy version:

```
In [78]: func_list = ['binomial_py', 'binomial_np', 'binomial_nb']
         K = 100.
         data_list = 3 * ['K']

In [79]: perf_comp_data(func_list, data_list)

Out[79]: function: binomial_nb, av. time sec:    0.14800, relative:    1.0
         function: binomial_np, av. time sec:    0.31770, relative:    2.1
         function: binomial_py, av. time sec:    3.36707, relative:   22.8
```

In summary, we can state the following:

- **Efficiency**: using Numba involves only a little additional effort. The original function is often not changed at all; all you need to do is call the jit function.

- **Speed-up**: Numba often leads to significant improvements in execution speed, not only compared to pure Python but also to vectorized NumPy implementations.

- **Memory**: with Numba there is no need to initialize large array objects; the compiler specializes the machine code to the problem at hand (as compared to the "universal" functions of NumPy) and maintains memory efficiency, as with pure Python.

Static Compiling with Cython

The strength of Numba is the effortless application of the approach to arbitrary functions. However, Numba will only "effortlessly" generate significant performance improvements for certain types of problems. Another approach, which is more flexible but also more involved, is to go the route of *static compiling* with Cython. In effect, Cython is a hybrid language of Python and C. Coming from Python, the major differences to be noticed are the static type declarations (as in C) and a separate compiling step (as with any compiled language).

As a simple example function, consider the following nested loop that again returns simply the number of loops. Compared to the previous nested loop example, this time the number of inner loop iterations is scaled by the outer loop iterations. In such a case, you will pretty quickly run into memory troubles when you try to apply NumPy for a speedup:

```
In [80]: def f_py(I, J):
             res = 0.  # we work on a float object
             for i in range(I):
                 for j in range (J * I):
                     res += 1
             return res
```

Let us check Python performance for I = 500 and J = 500. A NumPy ndarray object allowing us to vectorize the function f_py in such a case would already have to have a shape of (500, 250000):

```
In [81]: I, J = 500, 500
         %time f_py(I, J)

Out[81]: CPU times: user 17 s, sys: 2.72 s, total: 19.7 s
         Wall time: 14.2 s

         125000000.0
```

Consider next the code shown in Example 8-1. It takes the very same function and introduces static type declarations for use with Cython. Note that the suffix of this Cython file is .pyx.

Example 8-1. Nested loop example with Cython static type declarations

```
#
# Nested loop example with Cython
# nested_loop.pyx
#
def f_cy(int I, int J):
    cdef double res = 0
    # double float much slower than int or long
    for i in range(I):
        for j in range (J * I):
            res += 1
    return res
```

In such a simple case, when no special C modules are needed, there is an easy way to import such a module—namely, via pyximport:

```
In [82]: import pyximport
         pyximport.install()

Out[82]: (None, <pyximport.pyximport.PyxImporter at 0x92cfc10>)
```

This allows us now to directly import from the Cython module:

```
In [83]: import sys
         sys.path.append('data/')
             # path to the Cython script
             # not needed if in same directory

In [84]: from nested_loop import f_cy
```

Now, we can check the performance of the Cython function:

```
In [85]: %time res = f_cy(I, J)

Out[85]: CPU times: user 154 ms, sys: 0 ns, total: 154 ms
         Wall time: 153 ms

In [86]: res

Out[86]: 125000000.0
```

When working in IPython Notebook there is a more convenient way to use Cython—
cythonmagic:

```
In [87]: %load_ext cythonmagic
```

Loading this extension from within the IPython Notebook allows us to compile code
with Cython from within the tool:

```
In [88]: %%cython
         #
         # Nested loop example with Cython
         #
         def f_cy(int I, int J):
             cdef double res = 0
             # double float much slower than int or long
             for i in range(I):
                 for j in range (J * I):
                     res += 1
             return res
```

The performance results should, of course, be (almost) the same:

```
In [89]: %time res = f_cy(I, J)

Out[89]: CPU times: user 156 ms, sys: 0 ns, total: 156 ms
         Wall time: 154 ms

In [90]: res

Out[90]: 125000000.0
```

Let us see what Numba can do in this case. The application is as straightforward as before:

```
In [91]: import numba as nb

In [92]: f_nb = nb.jit(f_py)
```

The performance is—when invoking the function for the first time—worse than that of the Cython version (recall that with the first call of the Numba compiled function there is always some overhead involved):

```
In [93]: %time res = f_nb(I, J)

Out[93]: CPU times: user 285 ms, sys: 9 ms, total: 294 ms
         Wall time: 273 ms

In [94]: res

Out[94]: 125000000.0
```

Finally, the more rigorous comparison—showing that the Numba version indeed keeps up with the Cython version(s):

```
In [95]: func_list = ['f_py', 'f_cy', 'f_nb']
         I, J = 500, 500
         data_list = 3 * ['I, J']

In [96]: perf_comp_data(func_list, data_list)

Out[96]: function: f_nb, av. time sec:   0.15162, relative:    1.0
         function: f_cy, av. time sec:   0.15275, relative:    1.0
         function: f_py, av. time sec:  14.08304, relative:   92.9
```

Generation of Random Numbers on GPUs

The last topic in this chapter is the use of devices for massively parallel operations—i.e., *General Purpose Graphical Processing Units* (GPGPUs, or simply GPUs). To use an Nvidia GPU, we need to have CUDA (Compute Unified Device Architecture, cf. *https://developer.nvidia.com*) installed. An easy way to harness the power of Nvidia GPUs is to use NumbaPro, a performance library by Continuum Analytics that dynamically compiles Python code for the GPU (or a multicore CPU).

This chapter does not allow us to go into the details of GPU usage for Python programming. However, there is one financial field that can benefit strongly from the use of a GPU: Monte Carlo simulation and (pseudo)random number generation in particular.[2] In what follows, we use the native CUDA library curand to generate random numbers on the GPU:

```
In [97]: from numbapro.cudalib import curand
```

As the *benchmark* case, we define a function, using NumPy, that delivers a two-dimensional array of standard normally distributed pseudorandom numbers:

---

2. See also Chapter 10 on these topics.

```
In [98]: def get_randoms(x, y):
             rand = np.random.standard_normal((x, y))
             return rand
```

First, let's check if it works:

```
In [99]: get_randoms(2, 2)

Out[99]: array([[-0.30561007,  1.33124048],
                [-0.04382143,  2.31276888]])
```

Now the function for the Nvidia GPU:

```
In [100]: def get_cuda_randoms(x, y):
              rand = np.empty((x * y), np.float64)
                  # rand serves as a container for the randoms
                  # CUDA only fills 1-dimensional arrays
              prng = curand.PRNG(rndtype=curand.PRNG.XORWOW)
                  # the argument sets the random number algorithm
              prng.normal(rand, 0, 1)  # filling the container
              rand = rand.reshape((x, y))
                  # to be "fair", we reshape rand to 2 dimensions
              return rand
```

Again, a brief check of the functionality:

```
In [101]: get_cuda_randoms(2, 2)

Out[101]: array([[ 1.07102161,  0.70846868],
                 [ 0.89437398, -0.86693007]])
```

And a first comparison of the performance:

```
In [102]: %timeit a = get_randoms(1000, 1000)

Out[102]: 10 loops, best of 3: 72 ms per loop

In [103]: %timeit a = get_cuda_randoms(1000, 1000)

Out[103]: 100 loops, best of 3: 14.8 ms per loop
```

Now, a more systematic routine to compare the performance:

```
In [104]: import time as t
          step = 1000
          def time_comparsion(factor):
              cuda_times = list()
              cpu_times = list()
              for j in range(1, 10002, step):
                  i = j * factor
                  t0 = t.time()
                  a = get_randoms(i, 1)
                  t1 = t.time()
                  cpu_times.append(t1 - t0)
                  t2 = t.time()
                  a = get_cuda_randoms(i, 1)
                  t3 = t.time()
```

```
            cuda_times.append(t3 - t2)
            print "Bytes of largest array %i" % a.nbytes
            return cuda_times, cpu_times
```

And a helper function to visualize performance results:

```
In [105]: def plot_results(cpu_times, cuda_times, factor):
              plt.plot(x * factor, cpu_times,'b', label='NUMPY')
              plt.plot(x * factor, cuda_times, 'r', label='CUDA')
              plt.legend(loc=0)
              plt.grid(True)
              plt.xlabel('size of random number array')
              plt.ylabel('time')
              plt.axis('tight')
```

Let's take a look at the first test series with a *medium* workload:

```
In [106]: factor = 100
          cuda_times, cpu_times = time_comparsion(factor)

Out[106]: Bytes of largest array 8000800
```

Calculation time for the random numbers on the GPU is almost *independent* of the numbers to be generated. By constrast, time on the CPU *rises sharply* with increasing size of the random number array to be generated. Both statements can be verified in Figure 8-5:

```
In [107]: x = np.arange(1, 10002, step)
```

```
In [108]: plot_results(cpu_times, cuda_times, factor)
```

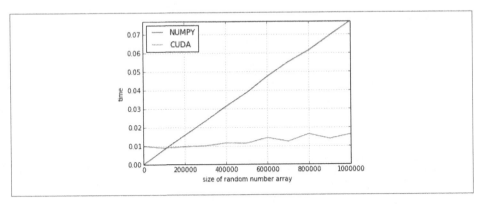

Figure 8-5. Random number generation on GPU and CPU (factor = 100)

Now let's look at the second test series, with a pretty *low* workload:

```
In [109]: factor = 10
          cuda_times, cpu_times = time_comparsion(factor)

Out[109]: Bytes of largest array 800080
```

The *overhead* of using the GPU is too large for low workloads—something quite obvious from inspecting Figure 8-6:

```
In [110]: plot_results(cpu_times, cuda_times, factor)
```

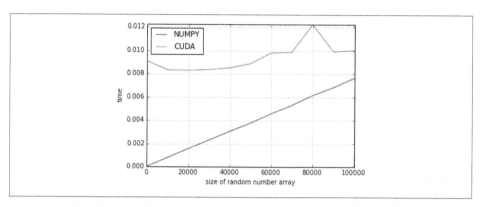

Figure 8-6. Random number generation on GPU and CPU (factor = 10)

Now let's consider a test series with a comparatively *heavy* workload. The largest random number array is 400 MB in size:

```
In [111]: %%time
          factor = 5000
          cuda_times, cpu_times = time_comparsion(factor)

Out[111]: Bytes of largest array 400040000
          CPU times: user 22 s, sys: 3.52 s, total: 25.5 s
          Wall time: 25.4 s
```

For heavy workloads the GPU clearly shows its advantages, as Figure 8-7 impressively illustrates:

```
In [112]: plot_results(cpu_times, cuda_times, factor)
```

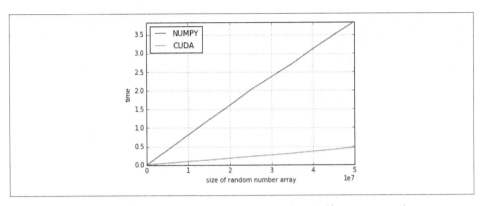

Figure 8-7. Random number generation on GPU and CPU (factor = 5,000)

Conclusions

Nowadays, the `Python` ecosystem provides a number of ways to improve the performance of code:

Paradigms
Some `Python` paradigms might be more performant than others, given a specific problem.

Libraries
There is a wealth of libraries available for different types of problems, which often lead to much higher performance given a problem that fits into the scope of the library (e.g., `numexpr`).

Compiling
A number of powerful compiling solutions are available, including static (e.g., `Cython`) and dynamic ones (e.g., `Numba`).

Parallelization
Some Python libraries have built-in parallelization capabilities (e.g., `numexpr`), while others allow us to harness the full power of multiple-core CPUs, whole clusters (e.g., `IPython.parallel`), or GPUs (e.g., `NumbaPro`).

A major benefit of the Python ecosystem is that all these approaches generally are easily implementable, meaning that the additional effort included is generally quite low (even for nonexperts). In other words, performance improvements often are low-hanging fruits given the performance libraries available as of today.

Further Reading

For all performance libraries introduced in this chapter, there are valuable web resources available:

- For details on numexpr see *http://github.com/pydata/numexpr*.
- IPython.parallel is explained here: *http://ipython.org/ipython-doc/stable/parallel*.
- Find the documentation for the multiprocessing module here: *https://docs.python.org/2/library/multiprocessing.html*.
- Information on Numba can be found at *http://github.com/numba/numba*.
- *http://cython.org* is the home of the Cython compiler project.
- For the documentation of NumbaPro, refer to *http://docs.continuum.io/numbapro*.

For a reference in book form, see the following:

- Gorelick, Misha and Ian Ozsvald (2014): *High Performance Python*. O'Reilly, Sebastopol, CA.

## CHAPTER 9

Mathematical Tools

> The mathematicians are the priests of the modern world.
>
> — Bill Gaede

Since the arrival of the so-called Rocket Scientists on Wall Street in the '80s and '90s, finance has evolved into a discipline of applied mathematics. While early research papers in finance came with few mathematical expressions and equations, current ones are mainly comprised of mathematical expressions and equations, with some explanatory text around.

This chapter introduces a number of useful mathematical tools for finance, without providing a detailed background for each of them. There are many useful books on this topic available. Therefore, this chapter focuses on how to use the tools and techniques with Python. Among other topics, it covers:

Approximation

> Regression and interpolation are among the most often used numerical techniques in finance.

Convex optimization

> A number of financial disciplines need tools for convex optimization (e.g., option pricing when it comes to model calibration).

Integration

> In particular, the valuation of financial (derivative) assets often boils down to the evaluation of integrals.

Symbolic mathematics

> Python provides with SymPy a powerful tool for symbolic mathematics, e.g., to solve (systems of) equations.

Approximation

To begin with, let us import the libraries that we need for the moment—NumPy and `matplotlib.pyplot`:

```
In [1]: import numpy as np
        import matplotlib.pyplot as plt
        %matplotlib inline
```

Throughout this discussion, the main example function we will use is the following, which is comprised of a trigonometric term and a linear term:

```
In [2]: def f(x):
            return np.sin(x) + 0.5 * x
```

The main focus is the approximation of this function over a given interval by *regression* and *interpolation*. First, let us generate a plot of the function to get a better view of what exactly the approximation shall achieve. The interval of interest shall be $[-2\pi, 2\pi]$. Figure 9-1 displays the function over the fixed interval defined via the `linspace` function. `np.linspace(start, stop, num)` returns *num* points beginning with *start* and ending with *stop*, with the subintervals between two consecutive points being evenly spaced:

```
In [3]: x = np.linspace(-2 * np.pi, 2 * np.pi, 50)
```

```
In [4]: plt.plot(x, f(x), 'b')
        plt.grid(True)
        plt.xlabel('x')
        plt.ylabel('f(x)')
```

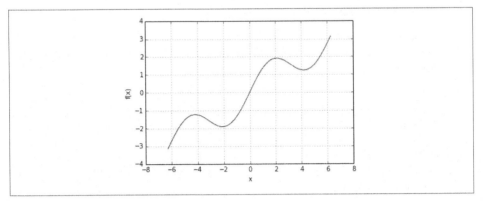

Figure 9-1. Example function plot

Regression

Regression is a rather efficient tool when it comes to function approximation. It is not only suited to approximate one-dimensional functions but also works well in higher dimensions. The numerical techniques needed to come up with regression results are easily implemented and quickly executed. Basically, the task of regression, given a set of so-called basis functions b_d, $d \in \{1,...,D\}$, is to find optimal parameters $\alpha_1^*,...,\alpha_D^*$ according to Equation 9-1, where $y_i \equiv f(x_i)$ for $i \in \{1,\cdots,I\}$ observation points. The x_i are considered *independent* observations and the y_i *dependent* observations (in a functional or statistical sense).

Equation 9-1. Minimization problem of regression

$$\min_{\alpha_1,...,\alpha_D} \frac{1}{I} \sum_{i=1}^{I} \left(y_i - \sum_{d=1}^{D} \alpha_d \cdot b_d(x_i)\right)^2$$

Monomials as basis functions

One of the simplest cases is to take monomials as basis functions—i.e., $b_1 = 1$, $b_2 = x$, $b_3 = x^2$, $b_4 = x^3$,.... In such a case, NumPy has built-in functions for both the determination of the optimal parameters (namely, polyfit) and the evaluation of the approximation given a set of input values (namely, polyval).

Table 9-1 lists the parameters the polyfit function takes. Given the returned optimal regression coefficients p from polyfit, np.polyval(p, x) then returns the regression values for the x coordinates.

Table 9-1. Parameters of polyfit function

Parameter	Description
x	x coordinates (independent variable values)
y	y coordinates (dependent variable values)
deg	Degree of the fitting polynomial
full	If True, returns diagnostic information in addition
w	Weights to apply to the y coordinates
cov	If True, covariance matrix is also returned

In typical vectorized fashion, the application of polyfit and polyval takes on the following form for a linear regression (i.e., for deg=1):

```
In [5]: reg = np.polyfit(x, f(x), deg=1)
        ry = np.polyval(reg, x)
```

Given the regression estimates stored in the ry array, we can compare the regression result with the original function as presented in Figure 9-2. Of course, a linear regression cannot account for the sin part of the example function:

```
In [6]: plt.plot(x, f(x), 'b', label='f(x)')
        plt.plot(x, ry, 'r.', label='regression')
        plt.legend(loc=0)
        plt.grid(True)
        plt.xlabel('x')
        plt.ylabel('f(x)')
```

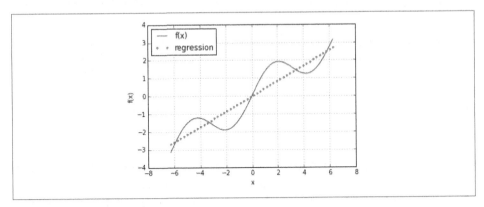

Figure 9-2. Example function and linear regression

To account for the sin part of the example function, higher-order monomials are necessary. The next regression attempt takes monomials up to the order of 5 as basis functions. It should not be too surprising that the regression result, as seen in Figure 9-3,
now looks much closer to the original function. However, it is still far away from being
perfect:

```
In [7]: reg = np.polyfit(x, f(x), deg=5)
        ry = np.polyval(reg, x)

In [8]: plt.plot(x, f(x), 'b', label='f(x)')
        plt.plot(x, ry, 'r.', label='regression')
        plt.legend(loc=0)
        plt.grid(True)
        plt.xlabel('x')
        plt.ylabel('f(x)')
```

The last attempt takes monomials up to order 7 to approximate the example function.
In this case the result, as presented in Figure 9-4, is quite convincing:

```
In [9]: reg = np.polyfit(x, f(x), 7)
        ry = np.polyval(reg, x)
```

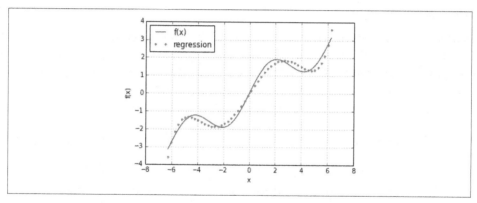

Figure 9-3. Regression with monomials up to order 5

```
In [10]: plt.plot(x, f(x), 'b', label='f(x)')
         plt.plot(x, ry, 'r.', label='regression')
         plt.legend(loc=0)
         plt.grid(True)
         plt.xlabel('x')
         plt.ylabel('f(x)')
```

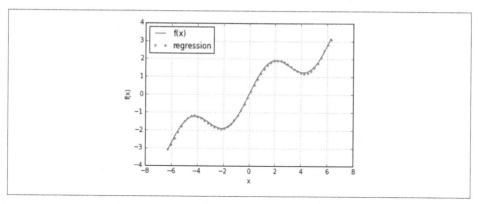

Figure 9-4. Regression with monomials up to order 7

A brief check reveals that the result is not perfect:

```
In [11]: np.allclose(f(x), ry)

Out[11]: False
```

However, the mean squared error (MSE) is not too large—at least, over this narrow range of x values:

```
In [12]: np.sum((f(x) - ry) ** 2) / len(x)

Out[12]: 0.0017769134759517413
```

Individual basis functions

In general, you can reach better regression results when you can choose better sets of basis functions, e.g., by exploiting knowledge about the function to approximate. In this case, the individual basis functions have to be defined via a matrix approach (i.e., using a NumPy ndarray object). First, the case with monomials up to order 3:

```
In [13]: matrix = np.zeros((3 + 1, len(x)))
         matrix[3, :] = x ** 3
         matrix[2, :] = x ** 2
         matrix[1, :] = x
         matrix[0, :] = 1
```

The sublibrary numpy.linalg provides the function lstsq to solve least-squares optimization problems like the one in Equation 9-1:

```
In [14]: reg = np.linalg.lstsq(matrix.T, f(x))[0]
```

Applying lstsq to our problem in this way yields the optimal parameters for the single basis functions:

```
In [15]: reg

Out[15]: array([  1.13968447e-14,   5.62777448e-01,  -8.88178420e-16,
                 -5.43553615e-03])
```

To get the regression estimates we apply the dot function to the reg and matrix arrays. Figure 9-5 shows the result. np.dot(a, b) simply gives the dot product for the two arrays a and b:

```
In [16]: ry = np.dot(reg, matrix)

In [17]: plt.plot(x, f(x), 'b', label='f(x)')
         plt.plot(x, ry, 'r.', label='regression')
         plt.legend(loc=0)
         plt.grid(True)
         plt.xlabel('x')
         plt.ylabel('f(x)')
```

The result in Figure 9-5 is not really as good as expected based on our previous experience with monomials. Using the more general approach allows us to exploit our knowledge about the example function. We know that there is a sin part in the function. Therefore, it makes sense to include a sine function in the set of basis functions. For simplicity, we replace the highest-order monomial:

```
In [18]: matrix[3, :] = np.sin(x)
         reg = np.linalg.lstsq(matrix.T, f(x))[0]
         ry = np.dot(reg, matrix)
```

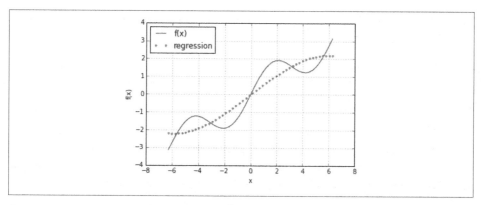

Figure 9-5. Regression via least-squares function

Figure 9-6 illustrates that the regression is now pretty close to the original function:

```
In [19]: plt.plot(x, f(x), 'b', label='f(x)')
         plt.plot(x, ry, 'r.', label='regression')
         plt.legend(loc=0)
         plt.grid(True)
         plt.xlabel('x')
         plt.ylabel('f(x)')
```

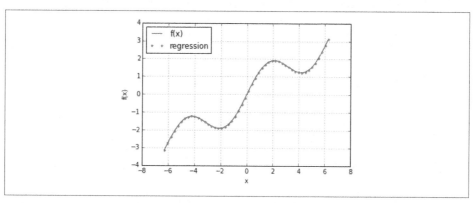

Figure 9-6. Regression using individual functions

Indeed, the regression now is "perfect" in a numerical sense:

```
In [20]: np.allclose(f(x), ry)

Out[20]: True

In [21]: np.sum((f(x) - ry) ** 2) / len(x)

Out[21]: 2.2749084503102031e-31
```

In fact, the minimization routine recovers the correct parameters of 1 for the sin part and 0.5 for the linear part:

```
In [22]: reg

Out[22]: array([  1.55428020e-16,   5.00000000e-01,   0.00000000e+00,
                  1.00000000e+00])
```

Noisy data

Regression can cope equally well with *noisy* data, be it data from simulation or from (non-perfect) measurements. To illustrate this point, let us generate both independent observations with noise and also dependent observations with noise:

```
In [23]: xn = np.linspace(-2 * np.pi, 2 * np.pi, 50)
         xn = xn + 0.15 * np.random.standard_normal(len(xn))
         yn = f(xn) + 0.25 * np.random.standard_normal(len(xn))
```

The very regression is the same:

```
In [24]: reg = np.polyfit(xn, yn, 7)
         ry = np.polyval(reg, xn)
```

Figure 9-7 reveals that the regression results are closer to the original function than the noisy data points. In a sense, the regression averages out the noise to some extent:

```
In [25]: plt.plot(xn, yn, 'b^', label='f(x)')
         plt.plot(xn, ry, 'ro', label='regression')
         plt.legend(loc=0)
         plt.grid(True)
         plt.xlabel('x')
         plt.ylabel('f(x)')
```

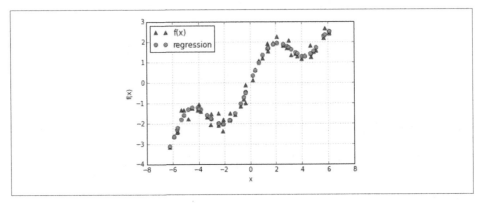

Figure 9-7. Regression with noisy data

Unsorted data

Another important aspect of regression is that the approach also works seamlessly with unsorted data. The previous examples all rely on sorted x data. This does not have to be the case. To make the point, let us randomize the independent data points as follows:

```
In [26]: xu = np.random.rand(50) * 4 * np.pi - 2 * np.pi
         yu = f(xu)
```

In this case, you can hardly identify any structure by just visually inspecting the raw data:

```
In [27]: print xu[:10].round(2)
         print yu[:10].round(2)

Out[27]: [ 4.09  0.5   1.48 -1.85  1.65  4.51 -5.7   1.83  4.42 -4.2 ]
         [ 1.23  0.72  1.74 -1.89  1.82  1.28 -2.3   1.88  1.25 -1.23]
```

As with the noisy data, the regression approach does not care for the order of the observation points. This becomes obvious upon inspecting the structure of the minimization problem in Equation 9-1. It is also obvious by the results, as presented in Figure 9-8:

```
In [28]: reg = np.polyfit(xu, yu, 5)
         ry = np.polyval(reg, xu)

In [29]: plt.plot(xu, yu, 'b^', label='f(x)')
         plt.plot(xu, ry, 'ro', label='regression')
         plt.legend(loc=0)
         plt.grid(True)
         plt.xlabel('x')
         plt.ylabel('f(x)')
```

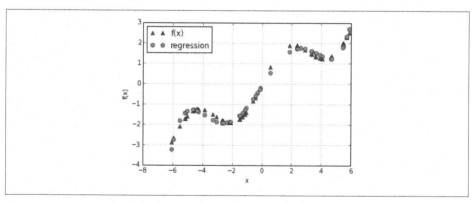

Figure 9-8. Regression with unsorted data

Multiple dimensions

Another convenient characteristic of the least-squares regression approach is that it carries over to multiple dimensions without too many modifications. As an example function we take fm, as presented next:

```
In [30]: def fm((x, y)):
             return np.sin(x) + 0.25 * x + np.sqrt(y) + 0.05 * y ** 2
```

To visualize this function, we need a grid of (independent) data points:

```
In [31]: x = np.linspace(0, 10, 20)
         y = np.linspace(0, 10, 20)
         X, Y = np.meshgrid(x, y)
           # generates 2-d grids out of the 1-d arrays
         Z = fm((X, Y))
         x = X.flatten()
         y = Y.flatten()
           # yields 1-d arrays from the 2-d grids
```

Based on the grid of independent and dependent data points as embodied now by X, Y, Z, Figure 9-9 presents the shape of the function fm:

```
In [32]: from mpl_toolkits.mplot3d import Axes3D
         import matplotlib as mpl

         fig = plt.figure(figsize=(9, 6))
         ax = fig.gca(projection='3d')
         surf = ax.plot_surface(X, Y, Z, rstride=2, cstride=2,
                 cmap=mpl.cm.coolwarm,
                 linewidth=0.5, antialiased=True)
         ax.set_xlabel('x')
         ax.set_ylabel('y')
         ax.set_zlabel('f(x, y)')
         fig.colorbar(surf, shrink=0.5, aspect=5)
```

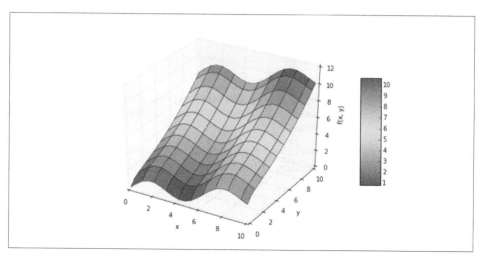

Figure 9-9. Function with two parameters

To get good regression results we compile a set of basis functions, including both a `sin` and a `sqrt` function, which leverages our knowledge of the example function:

```
In [33]: matrix = np.zeros((len(x), 6 + 1))
         matrix[:, 6] = np.sqrt(y)
         matrix[:, 5] = np.sin(x)
         matrix[:, 4] = y ** 2
         matrix[:, 3] = x ** 2
         matrix[:, 2] = y
         matrix[:, 1] = x
         matrix[:, 0] = 1
```

The `statsmodels` library offers the quite general and helpful function `OLS` for least-squares regression both in one dimension and multiple dimensions:[1]

```
In [34]: import statsmodels.api as sm
```

```
In [35]: model = sm.OLS(fm((x, y)), matrix).fit()
```

One advantage of using the `OLS` function is that it provides a wealth of additional information about the regression and its quality. A summary of the results is accessed by calling `model.summary`. Single statistics, like the *coefficient of determination*, can in general also be accessed directly:

```
In [36]: model.rsquared
```

```
Out[36]: 1.0
```

---

1. For details on the use of `OLS`, refer to the documentation (*http://bit.ly/using_ols*).

For our purposes, we of course need the optimal regression parameters, which are stored in the params attribute of our model object:

```
In [37]: a = model.params
         a

Out[37]: array([  7.14706072e-15,   2.50000000e-01,  -2.22044605e-16,
                 -1.02348685e-16,   5.00000000e-02,   1.00000000e+00,
                  1.00000000e+00])
```

The function reg_func gives back, for the given optimal regression parameters and the indpendent data points, the function values for the regression function:

```
In [38]: def reg_func(a, (x, y)):
             f6 = a[6] * np.sqrt(y)
             f5 = a[5] * np.sin(x)
             f4 = a[4] * y ** 2
             f3 = a[3] * x ** 2
             f2 = a[2] * y
             f1 = a[1] * x
             f0 = a[0] * 1
             return (f6 + f5 + f4 + f3 +
                     f2 + f1 + f0)
```

These values can then be compared with the original shape of the example function, as shown in Figure 9-10:

```
In [39]: RZ = reg_func(a, (X, Y))

In [40]: fig = plt.figure(figsize=(9, 6))
         ax = fig.gca(projection='3d')
         surf1 = ax.plot_surface(X, Y, Z, rstride=2, cstride=2,
                     cmap=mpl.cm.coolwarm, linewidth=0.5,
                     antialiased=True)
         surf2 = ax.plot_wireframe(X, Y, RZ, rstride=2, cstride=2,
                               label='regression')
         ax.set_xlabel('x')
         ax.set_ylabel('y')
         ax.set_zlabel('f(x, y)')
         ax.legend()
         fig.colorbar(surf, shrink=0.5, aspect=5)
```

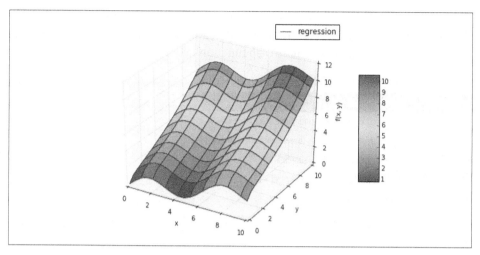

Figure 9-10. Higher-dimension regression

Regression

Least-squares regression approaches have multiple areas of application, including simple function approximation and function approximation based on noisy or unsorted data. These approaches can be applied to single as well as multidimensional problems. Due to the underlying mathematics, the application is always "almost the same."

Interpolation

Compared to regression, *interpolation* (e.g., with cubic splines), is much more involved mathematically. It is also limited to low-dimensional problems. Given an ordered set of observation points (ordered in the x dimension), the basic idea is to do a regression between two neighboring data points in such a way that not only are the data points perfectly matched by the resulting, piecewise-defined interpolation function, but also that the function is continuously differentiable at the data points. Continuous differentiability requires at least interpolation of degree 3—i.e., with *cubic* splines. However, the approach also works in general with quadratic and even linear splines. First, the importing of the respective sublibrary:

```
In [41]: import scipy.interpolate as spi
```

```
In [42]: x = np.linspace(-2 * np.pi, 2 * np.pi, 25)
```

We take again the original example function for illustration purposes:

```
In [43]: def f(x):
             return np.sin(x) + 0.5 * x
```

The application itself, given an x-ordered set of data points, is as simple as the application of polyfit and polyval. Here, the respective functions are splrep and splev. Table 9-2 lists the major parameters that the splrep function takes.

Table 9-2. Parameters of splrep function

Parameter	Description
x	(Ordered) x coordinates (independent variable values)
y	(x-ordered) y coordinates (dependent variable values)
w	Weights to apply to the y coordinates
xb, xe	Interval to fit, if None [x[0], x[-1]]
k	Order of the spline fit (1 <= k <= 5)
s	Smoothing factor (the larger, the more smoothing)
full_output	If True additional output is returned
quiet	If True suppress messages

Table 9-3 lists the parameters that the splev function takes.

Table 9-3. Parameters of splev function

Parameter	Description
x	(Ordered) x coordinates (independent variable values)
tck	Sequence of length 3 returned by splrep (knots, coefficients, degree)
der	Order of derivative (0 for function, 1 for first derivative)
ext	Behavior if x not in knot sequence (0 extrapolate, 1 return 0, 2 raise ValueError)

Applied to the current example, this translates into the following:

```
In [44]: ipo = spi.splrep(x, f(x), k=1)

In [45]: iy = spi.splev(x, ipo)
```

As Figure 9-11 shows, the interpolation already seems really good with linear splines (i.e., k=1):

```
In [46]: plt.plot(x, f(x), 'b', label='f(x)')
         plt.plot(x, iy, 'r.', label='interpolation')
         plt.legend(loc=0)
         plt.grid(True)
         plt.xlabel('x')
         plt.ylabel('f(x)')
```

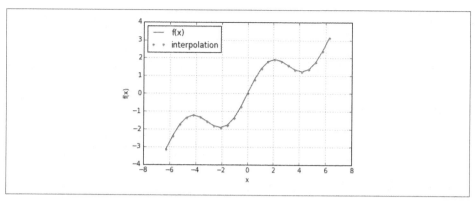

Figure 9-11. Example plot with linear interpolation

This can be confirmed numerically:

```
In [47]: np.allclose(f(x), iy)

Out[47]: True
```

Spline interpolation is often used in finance to generate estimates for dependent values of independent data points not included in the original observations. To this end, let us pick a much smaller interval and have a closer look at the interpolated values with the linear splines:

```
In [48]: xd = np.linspace(1.0, 3.0, 50)
         iyd = spi.splev(xd, ipo)
```

Figure 9-12 reveals that the interpolation function indeed interpolates *linearly* between two observation points. For certain applications this might not be precise enough. In addition, it is evident that the function is not continuously differentiable at the original data points—another drawback:

```
In [49]: plt.plot(xd, f(xd), 'b', label='f(x)')
         plt.plot(xd, iyd, 'r.', label='interpolation')
         plt.legend(loc=0)
         plt.grid(True)
         plt.xlabel('x')
         plt.ylabel('f(x)')
```

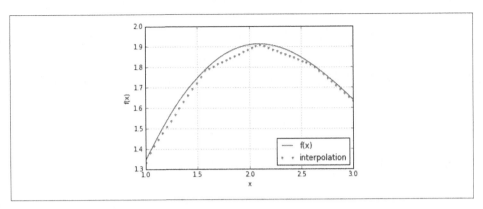

Figure 9-12. Example plot (detail) with linear interpolation

Therefore, let us repeat the complete exercise, this time using cubic splines:

```
In [50]: ipo = spi.splrep(x, f(x), k=3)
         iyd = spi.splev(xd, ipo)
```

Now, the detailed subinterval in Figure 9-13 shows a graphically perfect interpolation:

```
In [51]: plt.plot(xd, f(xd), 'b', label='f(x)')
         plt.plot(xd, iyd, 'r.', label='interpolation')
         plt.legend(loc=0)
         plt.grid(True)
         plt.xlabel('x')
         plt.ylabel('f(x)')
```

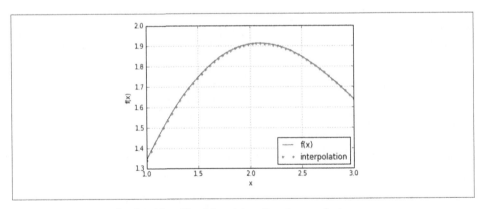

Figure 9-13. Example plot (detail) with cubic spline interpolation

Numerically, the interpolation is not perfect, but the MSE is really small:

```
In [52]: np.allclose(f(xd), iyd)
Out[52]: False
```

```
In [53]: np.sum((f(xd) - iyd) ** 2) / len(xd)

Out[53]: 1.1349319851436252e-08
```

Interpolation

In those cases where spline interpolation can be applied you can expect better approximation results compared to a least-squares regression approach. However, remember that you need to have sorted (and
"nonnoisy") data and that the approach is limited to low-dimensional
problems. It is also computationally more demanding and might
therefore take (much) longer than regression in certain use cases.

Convex Optimization

In finance and economics, *convex optimization* plays an important role. Examples are
the calibration of option pricing models to market data or the optimization of an agent's
utility. As an example function that we want to minimize, we take fm, as defined in the
following:

```
In [54]: def fm((x, y)):
             return (np.sin(x) + 0.05 * x ** 2
                 + np.sin(y) + 0.05 * y ** 2)

In [55]: x = np.linspace(-10, 10, 50)
         y = np.linspace(-10, 10, 50)
         X, Y = np.meshgrid(x, y)
         Z = fm((X, Y))
```

Figure 9-14 shows the function graphically for the defined intervals for x and y. Visual
inspection already reveals that this function has multiple local minima. The existence
of a global minimum cannot really be confirmed by this particular graphical
representation:

```
In [56]: fig = plt.figure(figsize=(9, 6))
         ax = fig.gca(projection='3d')
         surf = ax.plot_surface(X, Y, Z, rstride=2, cstride=2,
             cmap=mpl.cm.coolwarm,
             linewidth=0.5, antialiased=True)
         ax.set_xlabel('x')
         ax.set_ylabel('y')
         ax.set_zlabel('f(x, y)')
         fig.colorbar(surf, shrink=0.5, aspect=5)
```

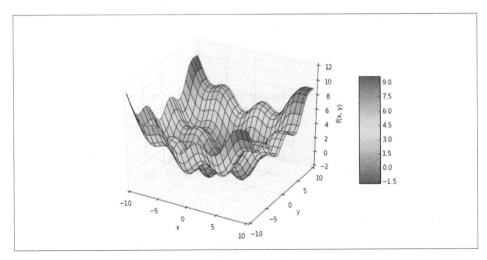

Figure 9-14. Function to minimize with two parameters

In what follows, we want to implement both a *global* minimization approach and a *local* one. The functions `brute` and `fmin` that we want to use can be found in the sublibrary `scipy.optimize`:

```
In [57]: import scipy.optimize as spo
```

Global Optimization

To have a closer look behind the scenes when we initiate the minimization procedures, we amend the original function by an option to output current parameter values as well as the function value:

```
In [58]: def fo((x, y)):
             z = np.sin(x) + 0.05 * x ** 2 + np.sin(y) + 0.05 * y ** 2
             if output == True:
                 print '%8.4f %8.4f %8.4f' % (x, y, z)
             return z
```

This allows us to keep track of all relevant information for the procedure, as the following code with its respective output illustrates. `brute` takes the parameter ranges as input. For example, providing parameter range (`-10, 10.1, 5`) for the x value will lead to "tested" values of `-10, -5, 0, 5, 10`:

```
In [59]: output = True
         spo.brute(fo, ((-10, 10.1, 5), (-10, 10.1, 5)), finish=None)

Out[59]: -10.0000 -10.0000  11.0880
         -10.0000 -10.0000  11.0880
         -10.0000  -5.0000   7.7529
         -10.0000   0.0000   5.5440
         -10.0000   5.0000   5.8351
```

```
-10.0000   10.0000   10.0000
 -5.0000  -10.0000    7.7529
 -5.0000   -5.0000    4.4178
 -5.0000    0.0000    2.2089
 -5.0000    5.0000    2.5000
 -5.0000   10.0000    6.6649
  0.0000  -10.0000    5.5440
  0.0000   -5.0000    2.2089
  0.0000    0.0000    0.0000
  0.0000    5.0000    0.2911
  0.0000   10.0000    4.4560
  5.0000  -10.0000    5.8351
  5.0000   -5.0000    2.5000
  5.0000    0.0000    0.2911
  5.0000    5.0000    0.5822
  5.0000   10.0000    4.7471
 10.0000  -10.0000   10.0000
 10.0000   -5.0000    6.6649
 10.0000    0.0000    4.4560
 10.0000    5.0000    4.7471
 10.0000   10.0000    8.9120

array([ 0.,   0.])
```

The optimal parameter values, given the initial parameterization of the function, are x
= y = 0. The resulting function value is also 0, as a quick review of the preceding output
reveals. The first parameterization here is quite rough, in that we used steps of width 5
for both input parameters. This can of course be refined considerably, leading to better
results in this case:

```
In [60]: output = False
         opt1 = spo.brute(fo, ((-10, 10.1, 0.1), (-10, 10.1, 0.1)), finish=None)
         opt1

Out[60]: array([-1.4, -1.4])

In [61]: fm(opt1)

Out[61]: -1.7748994599769203
```

The optimal parameter values are now x = y = –1.4 and the minimal function value for
the global minimization is about –1.7749.

Local Optimization

For the local convex optimization we want to draw on the results from the global optimization. The function fmin takes as input the function to minimize and the starting
parameter values. In addition, you can define levels for the input parameter tolerance
and the function value tolerance, as well as for the maximum number of iterations and
function calls:

```
In [62]: output = True
         opt2 = spo.fmin(fo, opt1, xtol=0.001, ftol=0.001, maxiter=15, maxfun=20)
         opt2

Out[62]:  -1.4000   -1.4000   -1.7749
          -1.4700   -1.4000   -1.7743
          -1.4000   -1.4700   -1.7743
          -1.3300   -1.4700   -1.7696
          -1.4350   -1.4175   -1.7756
          -1.4350   -1.3475   -1.7722
          -1.4088   -1.4394   -1.7755
          -1.4438   -1.4569   -1.7751
          -1.4328   -1.4427   -1.7756
          -1.4591   -1.4208   -1.7752
          -1.4213   -1.4347   -1.7757
          -1.4235   -1.4096   -1.7755
          -1.4305   -1.4344   -1.7757
          -1.4168   -1.4516   -1.7753
          -1.4305   -1.4260   -1.7757
          -1.4396   -1.4257   -1.7756
          -1.4259   -1.4325   -1.7757
          -1.4259   -1.4241   -1.7757
          -1.4304   -1.4177   -1.7757
          -1.4270   -1.4288   -1.7757
         Warning: Maximum number of function evaluations has been exceeded.

         array([-1.42702972, -1.42876755])
```

Again, we can observe a refinement of the solution and a somewhat lower function value:

```
In [63]: fm(opt2)

Out[63]: -1.7757246992239009
```

For many convex optimization problems it is advisable to have a global minimization before the local one. The major reason for this is that local convex optimization algorithms can easily be trapped in a local minimum (or do "basin hopping"), ignoring completely "better" local minima and/or a global minimum. The following shows that setting the starting parameterization to x = y = 2 gives a "minimum" value of above zero:

```
In [64]: output = False
         spo.fmin(fo, (2.0, 2.0), maxiter=250)

Out[64]: Optimization terminated successfully.
                  Current function value: 0.015826
                  Iterations: 46
                  Function evaluations: 86

         array([ 4.2710728 ,  4.27106945])
```

Constrained Optimization

So far, we have only considered unconstrained optimization problems. However, large classes of economic or financial optimization problems are constrained by one or multiple constraints. Such constraints can formally take on the form of equations or inequalities.

As a simple example, consider the utility maximization problem of an (expected utility maximizing) investor who can invest in two risky securities. Both securities cost $q_a = q_b$ = 10 today. After one year, they have a payoff of 15 USD and 5 USD, respectively, in state u, and of 5 USD and 12 USD, respectively, in state d. Both states are equally likely. Denote the vector payoffs for the two securities by r_a and r_b, respectively.

The investor has a budget of w_0 = 100 USD to invest and derives utility from future wealth according to the utility function $u(w) = \sqrt{w}$, where w is the wealth (USD amount) available. Equation 9-2 is a formulation of the maximization problem where a,b are the numbers of securities bought by the investor.

Equation 9-2. Expected utility maximizing problem

$$
\begin{aligned}
\max_{a,b} \mathbf{E}\big(u(w_1)\big) &= p\sqrt{w_{1u}} + (1-p)\sqrt{w_{1d}} \\
w_1 &= ar_a + br_b \\
w_0 &\geq aq_a + bq_b \\
a,b &\geq 0
\end{aligned}
$$

Putting in all numerical assumptions, we get the problem in Equation 9-3. Note that we also change to the minimization of the negative expected utility.

Equation 9-3. Expected utility maximizing problem

$$
\begin{aligned}
\min_{a,b} -\mathbf{E}\big(u(w_1)\big) &= -\Big(0.5 \cdot \sqrt{w_{1u}} + 0.5 \cdot \sqrt{w_{1d}}\Big) \\
w_{1u} &= a \cdot 15 + b \cdot 5 \\
w_{1d} &= a \cdot 5 + b \cdot 12 \\
100 &\geq a \cdot 10 + b \cdot 10 \\
a,b &\geq 0
\end{aligned}
$$

To solve this problem, we use the `scipy.optimize.minimize` function. This function takes as input—in addition to the function to be minimized—equations and inequalities (as a list of dict objects) as well as boundaries for the parameters (as a tuple of tuple objects).[2] We can translate the problem from Equation 9-3 into the following code:

```
In [65]: # function to be minimized
         from math import sqrt
         def Eu((s, b)):
             return -(0.5 * sqrt(s * 15 + b * 5) + 0.5 * sqrt(s * 5 + b * 12))

         # constraints
         cons = ({'type': 'ineq', 'fun': lambda (s, b):  100 - s * 10 - b * 10})
           # budget constraint
         bnds = ((0, 1000), (0, 1000))  # uppper bounds large enough
```

We have everything we need to use the minimize function—we just have to add an initial guess for the optimal parameters:

```
In [66]: result = spo.minimize(Eu, [5, 5], method='SLSQP',
                               bounds=bnds, constraints=cons)

In [67]: result

Out[67]:    status: 0
           success: True
              njev: 5
              nfev: 21
               fun: -9.700883611487832
                 x: array([ 8.02547122,  1.97452878])
           message: 'Optimization terminated successfully.'
               jac: array([-0.48508096, -0.48489535,  0.        ])
               nit: 5
```

The function returns a dict object. The optimal parameters can be read out as follows:

```
In [68]: result['x']

Out[68]: array([ 8.02547122,  1.97452878])
```

The optimal function value is (changing the sign again):

```
In [69]: -result['fun']

Out[69]: 9.700883611487832
```

Given the parameterization for the simple model, it is optimal for the investor to buy about eight units of security a and about two units of security b. The budget constraint is binding; i.e., the investor invests his/her total wealth of 100 USD into the securities. This is easily verified through taking the dot product of the optimal parameter vector and the price vector:

```
In [70]: np.dot(result['x'], [10, 10])
```

2. For details and examples of how to use the minimize function, refer to the documentation (*http://bit.ly/using_minimize*).

```
Out[70]: 99.999999999999986
```

Integration

Especially when it comes to valuation and option pricing, integration is an important mathematical tool. This stems from the fact that risk-neutral values of derivatives can be expressed in general as the discounted *expectation* of their payoff under the risk-neutral (martingale) measure. The expectation in turn is a sum in the discrete case and an integral in the continuous case. The sublibrary scipy.integrate provides different functions for numerical integration:

```
In [71]: import scipy.integrate as sci
```

Again, we stick to the example function comprised of a sin component and a linear one:

```
In [72]: def f(x):
             return np.sin(x) + 0.5 * x
```

We are interested in the integral over the interval [0.5, 9.5]; i.e., the integral as in Equation 9-4.

Equation 9-4. Integral of example function

$$\int_{0.5}^{9.5} \sin(x) + 0.5x \, dx$$

Figure 9-15 provides a graphical representation of the integral with a plot of the function $f(x) \equiv \sin(x) + 0.5x$:

```
In [73]: a = 0.5  # left integral limit
         b = 9.5  # right integral limit
         x = np.linspace(0, 10)
         y = f(x)
```

```
In [74]: from matplotlib.patches import Polygon

         fig, ax = plt.subplots(figsize=(7, 5))
         plt.plot(x, y, 'b', linewidth=2)
         plt.ylim(ymin=0)

         # area under the function
         # between lower and upper limit
         Ix = np.linspace(a, b)
         Iy = f(Ix)
         verts = [(a, 0)] + list(zip(Ix, Iy)) + [(b, 0)]
         poly = Polygon(verts, facecolor='0.7', edgecolor='0.5')
         ax.add_patch(poly)
```

```
# labels
plt.text(0.75 * (a + b), 1.5, r"$\int_a^b f(x)dx$",
         horizontalalignment='center', fontsize=20)

plt.figtext(0.9, 0.075, '$x$')
plt.figtext(0.075, 0.9, '$f(x)$')

ax.set_xticks((a, b))
ax.set_xticklabels(('$a$', '$b$'))
ax.set_yticks([f(a), f(b)])
```

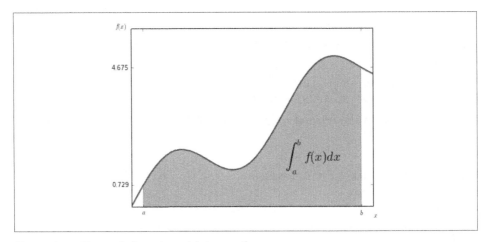

Figure 9-15. Example function with integral area

Numerical Integration

The `integrate` sublibrary contains a selection of functions to numerically integrate a given mathematical function given upper and lower integration limits. Examples are `fixed_quad` for *fixed Gaussian quadrature*, `quad` for *adaptive quadrature*, and `romberg` for *Romberg integration*:

```
In [75]: sci.fixed_quad(f, a, b)[0]

Out[75]: 24.366995967084588

In [76]: sci.quad(f, a, b)[0]

Out[76]: 24.374754718086752

In [77]: sci.romberg(f, a, b)

Out[77]: 24.374754718086713
```

There are also a number of integration functions that take as input list or ndarray objects with function values and input values. Examples in this regard are trapz, using the *trapezoidal* rule, and simps, implementing *Simpson's* rule:

```
In [78]: xi = np.linspace(0.5, 9.5, 25)

In [79]: sci.trapz(f(xi), xi)

Out[79]: 24.352733271544516

In [80]: sci.simps(f(xi), xi)

Out[80]: 24.374964184550748
```

Integration by Simulation

The valuation of options and derivatives by Monte Carlo simulation (cf. Chapter 10) rests on the insight that you can evaluate an integral by simulation. To this end, draw I random values of x between the integral limits and evaluate the integration function at every random value of x. Sum up all the function values and take the average to arrive at an average function value over the integration interval. Multiply this value by the length of the integration interval to derive an estimate for the integral value.

The following code shows how the Monte Carlo estimated integral value converges to the real one when one increases the number of random draws. The estimator is already quite close for really small numbers of random draws:

```
In [81]: for i in range(1, 20):
             np.random.seed(1000)
             x = np.random.random(i * 10) * (b - a) + a
             print np.sum(f(x)) / len(x) * (b - a)

Out[81]: 24.8047622793
         26.5229188983
         26.2655475192
         26.0277033994
         24.9995418144
         23.8818101416
         23.5279122748
         23.507857659
         23.6723674607
         23.6794104161
         24.4244017079
         24.2390053468
         24.115396925
         24.4241919876
         23.9249330805
         24.1948421203
         24.1173483782
         24.1006909297
         23.7690510985
```

Symbolic Computation

The previous sections are mainly concerned with numerical computation. This section now introduces *symbolic* computation, which can be applied beneficially in many areas of finance. To this end, let us import SymPy, the library specifically dedicated to symbolic computation:

```
In [82]: import sympy as sy
```

Basics

SymPy introduces new classes of objects. A fundamental class is the Symbol class:

```
In [83]: x = sy.Symbol('x')
         y = sy.Symbol('y')

In [84]: type(x)

Out[84]: sympy.core.symbol.Symbol
```

Like NumPy, SymPy has a number of (mathematical) function definitions. For example:

```
In [85]: sy.sqrt(x)

Out[85]: sqrt(x)
```

This already illustrates a major difference. Although x has no numerical value, the square root of x is nevertheless defined with SymPy since x is a Symbol object. In that sense, sy.sqrt(x) can be part of arbitrary mathematical expressions. Notice that SymPy in general automatically simplifies a given mathematical expression:

```
In [86]: 3 + sy.sqrt(x) - 4 ** 2

Out[86]: sqrt(x) - 13
```

Similarly, you can define arbitrary functions using Symbol objects. They are not to be confused with Python functions:

```
In [87]: f = x ** 2 + 3 + 0.5 * x ** 2 + 3 / 2

In [88]: sy.simplify(f)

Out[88]: 1.5*x**2 + 4
```

SymPy provides three basic renderers for mathematical expressions:

- LaTeX-based
- Unicode-based
- ASCII-based

When working, for example, solely in the `IPython Notebook`, LaTeX rendering is generally a good (i.e., visually appealing) choice. In what follows, we stick to the simplest option, `ASCII`, to illustrate that there is no handmade type setting involved:

```
In [89]: sy.init_printing(pretty_print=False, use_unicode=False)

In [90]: print sy.pretty(f)

Out[90]:      2
         1.5*x  + 4
```

As you can see from the output, multiple lines are used whenever needed. Also, for example, see the following for the visual representation of the square-root function:

```
In [91]: print sy.pretty(sy.sqrt(x) + 0.5)

Out[91]:     ___
         \/ x  + 0.5
```

We can not go into details here, but `SymPy` also provides many other useful mathematical functions—for example, when it comes to numerically evaluating π. The following shows the first 40 characters of the `string` representation of π up to the 400,000th digit:

```
In [92]: pi_str = str(sy.N(sy.pi, 400000))
         pi_str[:40]

Out[92]: '3.1415926535897932384626433832795028841971'
```

And here are the last 40 digits of the first 400,000:

```
In [93]: pi_str[-40:]

Out[93]: '8245672736856312185020980470362464176198'
```

You can also look up your birthday if you wish; however, there is no guarantee of a hit:

```
In [94]: pi_str.find('111272')

Out[94]: 366713
```

Equations

A strength of `SymPy` is solving equations, e.g., of the form $x^2 - 1 = 0$:

```
In [95]: sy.solve(x ** 2 - 1)

Out[95]: [-1, 1]
```

In general, `SymPy` presumes that you are looking for a solution to the equation obtained by equating the given expression to zero. Therefore, equations like $x^2 - 1 = 3$ might have to be reformulated to get the desired result:

```
In [96]: sy.solve(x ** 2 - 1 - 3)

Out[96]: [-2, 2]
```

Of course, `SymPy` can cope with more complex expressions, like $x^3 + 0.5x^2 - 1 = 0$:

```
In [97]: sy.solve(x ** 3 + 0.5 * x ** 2 - 1)
```

```
Out[97]: [0.858094329496553, -0.679047164748276 - 0.839206763026694*I,
          -0.679047164748276 + 0.839206763026694*I]
```

However, there is obviously no guarantee of a solution, either from a mathematical point
of view (i.e., the existence of a solution) or from an algorithmic point of view (i.e., an
implementation).

SymPy works similarly with functions exhibiting more than one input parameter, and
to this end also with complex numbers. As a simple example take the equation $x^2 + y^2$
= 0:

```
In [98]: sy.solve(x ** 2 + y ** 2)
```

```
Out[98]: [{x: -I*y}, {x: I*y}]
```

Integration

Another strength of SymPy is integration and differentiation. In what follows, we revisit
the example function used for numerical- and simulation-based integration and derive
now both a *symbolic* and a *numerically* exact solution. We need symbols for the integration limits:

```
In [99]: a, b = sy.symbols('a b')
```

Having defined the new symbols, we can "pretty print" the symbolic integral:

```
In [100]: print sy.pretty(sy.Integral(sy.sin(x) + 0.5 * x, (x, a, b)))
```

```
Out[100]:    b
            /
           |
           |   (0.5*x + sin(x)) dx
           |
            /
            a
```

Using integrate, we can then derive the *antiderivative* of the integration function:

```
In [101]: int_func = sy.integrate(sy.sin(x) + 0.5 * x, x)
```

```
In [102]: print sy.pretty(int_func)
```

```
Out[102]:      2
          0.25*x  - cos(x)
```

Equipped with the antiderivative, the numerical evaluation of the integral is only three
steps away. To numerically evaluate a SymPy expression, replace the respective symbol
with the numerical value using the method subs and call the method evalf on the new
expression:

```
In [103]: Fb = int_func.subs(x, 9.5).evalf()
          Fa = int_func.subs(x, 0.5).evalf()
```

The difference between Fb and Fa then yields the exact integral value:

```
In [104]: Fb - Fa  # exact value of integral
Out[104]: 24.3747547180867
```

The integral can also be solved symbolically with the symbolic integration limits:

```
In [105]: int_func_limits = sy.integrate(sy.sin(x) + 0.5 * x, (x, a, b))
          print sy.pretty(int_func_limits)
Out[105]:         2        2
          - 0.25*a  + 0.25*b  + cos(a) - cos(b)
```

As before, numerical substitution—this time using a dict object for multiple substitutions—and evaluation then yields the integral value:

```
In [106]: int_func_limits.subs({a : 0.5, b : 9.5}).evalf()
Out[106]: 24.3747547180868
```

Finally, providing quantified integration limits yields the exact value in a single step:

```
In [107]: sy.integrate(sy.sin(x) + 0.5 * x, (x, 0.5, 9.5))
Out[107]: 24.3747547180867
```

Differentiation

The derivative of the antiderivative shall yield in general the original function. Let us check this by applying the diff function to the symbolic antiderivative from before:

```
In [108]: int_func.diff()
Out[108]: 0.5*x + sin(x)
```

As with the integration example, we want to use differentiation now to derive the exact solution of the convex minimization problem we looked at earlier. To this end, we define the respective function symbolically as follows:

```
In [109]: f = (sy.sin(x) + 0.05 * x ** 2
             + sy.sin(y) + 0.05 * y ** 2)
```

For the minimization, we need the two partial derivatives with respect to both variables, x and y:

```
In [110]: del_x = sy.diff(f, x)
          del_x
Out[110]: 0.1*x + cos(x)
In [111]: del_y = sy.diff(f, y)
          del_y
Out[111]: 0.1*y + cos(y)
```

A necessary but not sufficient condition for a global minimum is that both partial derivatives are zero. As stated before, there is no guarantee of a symbolic solution. Both algorithmic and (multiple) existence issues come into play here. However, we can solve the two equations numerically, providing "educated" guesses based on the global and local minimization efforts from before:

```
In [112]: xo = sy.nsolve(del_x, -1.5)
          xo

Out[112]: mpf('-1.4275517787645941')

In [113]: yo = sy.nsolve(del_y, -1.5)
          yo

Out[113]: mpf('-1.4275517787645941')

In [114]: f.subs({x : xo, y : yo}).evalf()
              # global minimum

Out[114]: -1.77572565314742
```

Again, providing uneducated/arbitrary guesses might trap the algorithm in a local minimum instead of the global one:

```
In [115]: xo = sy.nsolve(del_x, 1.5)
          xo

Out[115]: mpf('1.7463292822528528')

In [116]: yo = sy.nsolve(del_y, 1.5)
          yo

Out[116]: mpf('1.7463292822528528')

In [117]: f.subs({x : xo, y : yo}).evalf()
              # local minimum

Out[117]: 2.27423381055640
```

This numerically illustrates that zero partial derivatives are necessary but not sufficient.

Symbolic Computations

When doing mathematics with Python, you should always think of SymPy and symbolic computations. Especially for interactive financial analytics, this can be a more efficient approach compared to non-symbolic approaches.

Conclusions

This chapter covers some mathematical topics and tools important to finance. For example, the *approximation of functions* is important in many financial areas, like yield curve interpolation and regression-based Monte Carlo valuation approaches for American options. *Convex optimization* techniques are also regularly needed in finance; for example, when calibrating parametric option pricing models to market quotes or implied volatilities of options.

Numerical integration is, for example, central to the pricing of options and derivatives. Having derived the risk-neutral probability measure for a (set of) stochastic process(es), option pricing boils down to taking the expectation of the option's payoff under the risk-neutral measure and discounting this value back to the present date. Chapter 10 covers the simulation of several types of stochastic processes under the risk-neutral measure.

Finally, this chapter introduces *symbolic computation* with SymPy. For a number of mathematical operations, like integration, differentiation, or the solving of equations, symbolic computation can prove a really useful and efficient tool.

Further Reading

For further information on the Python libraries used in this chapter, you should consult the following web resources:

- See *http://docs.scipy.org/doc/numpy/reference/* for all functions used from NumPy.
- The statsmodels library is documented here: *http://statsmodels.sourceforge.net*.
- Visit *http://docs.scipy.org/doc/scipy/reference/optimize.html* for details on scipy.op timize.
- Integration with scipy.integrate is explained here: *http://docs.scipy.org/doc/ scipy/reference/integrate.html*.
- The home of SymPy is *http://sympy.org*.

For a good reference to the mathematical topics covered, see:

- Brandimarte, Paolo (2006): *Numerical Methods in Finance and Economics,* 2nd ed. John Wiley & Sons, Hoboken, NJ.

## CHAPTER 10

Stochastics

> Predictability is not how things will go, but how they can go.
>
> — Raheel Farooq

Nowadays, stochastics is one of the most important mathematical and numerical disciplines in finance. In the beginning of the modern era of finance, mainly in the 1970s and 1980s, the major goal of financial research was to come up with closed-form solutions for, e.g., option prices given a specific financial model. The requirements have drastically changed in recent years in that not only is the correct valuation of single financial instruments important to participants in the financial markets, but also the consistent valuation of whole derivatives books, for example. Similary, to come up with consistent risk measures across a whole financial institution, like value-at-risk and credit value adjustments, one needs to take into account the whole book of the institution and all its counterparties. Such daunting tasks can only be tackled by flexible and efficient numerical methods. Therefore, stochastics in general and Monte Carlo simulation in particular have risen to prominence.

This chapter introduces the following topics from a `Python` perspective:

Random number generation
> It all starts with (pseudo)random numbers, which build the basis for all simulation efforts; although quasirandom numbers, e.g., based on Sobol sequences, have gained some popularity in finance, pseudorandom numbers still seem to be the benchmark.

Simulation
> In finance, two simulation tasks are of particular importance: simulation of *random variables* and of *stochastic processes*.

Valuation
> The two main disciplines when it comes to valuation are the valuation of derivatives with *European exercise* (at a specific date) and *American exercise* (over a specific

time interval); there are also instruments with *Bermudan exercise*, or exercise at a finite set of specific dates.

Risk measures

Simulation lends itself pretty well to the calculation of risk measures like value-at-risk, credit value-at-risk, and credit value adjustments.

Random Numbers

Throughout this chapter, to generate random numbers[1] we will work with the functions provided by the numpy.random sublibrary:

```
In [1]: import numpy as np
        import numpy.random as npr
        import matplotlib.pyplot as plt
        %matplotlib inline
```

For example, the rand function returns random numbers from the open interval [0,1) in the shape provided as a parameter to the function. The return object is an ndarray object:

```
In [2]: npr.rand(10)

Out[2]: array([ 0.40628966,  0.43098644,  0.9435419 ,  0.26760198,  0.2729951 ,
                0.67519064,  0.41349754,  0.3585647 ,  0.07450132,  0.95130158])

In [3]: npr.rand(5, 5)

Out[3]: array([[ 0.87263851,  0.8143348 ,  0.34154499,  0.56695052,  0.60645041],
               [ 0.39398181,  0.71671577,  0.63568321,  0.61652708,  0.93526172],
               [ 0.12632038,  0.35793789,  0.04241014,  0.88085228,  0.54260211],
               [ 0.14503456,  0.32939077,  0.28834351,  0.4050322 ,  0.21120017],
               [ 0.45345805,  0.29771411,  0.67157606,  0.73563706,  0.48003387]
              ])
```

Such numbers can be easily transformed to cover other intervals of the real line. For instance, if you want to generate random numbers from the interval [a,b)=[5,10), you can transform the returned numbers from rand as follows:

```
In [4]: a = 5.
        b = 10.
        npr.rand(10) * (b - a) + a

Out[4]: array([ 7.27123881,  6.51309437,  7.51380629,  7.84258434,  7.62199611,
                8.86229349,  6.78202851,  6.33248656,  8.10776244,  9.48668419])
```

This also works for multidimensional shapes due to NumPy broadcasting:

```
In [5]: npr.rand(5, 5) * (b - a) + a
```

---

1. For simplicity, we will speak of *random numbers* knowing that all numbers used will be *pseudorandom*.

```
Out[5]: array([[ 6.65649828,  6.51657569,  9.7912274 ,  8.93721206,  6.66937996],
               [ 8.97919481,  8.27547365,  5.00975386,  8.99797249,  6.05374605],
               [ 7.50268777,  8.43810167,  9.33608096,  8.5513646 ,  5.53651748],
               [ 7.04179874,  6.98111966,  8.42677435,  6.22325043,  6.39226557],
               [ 9.88334499,  7.59597546,  5.93724861,  5.39285822,  5.28435207]
              ])
```

Table 10-1 lists functions for generating *simple* random numbers.[2]

Table 10-1. Functions for simple random number generation

Function	Parameters	Description
rand	d0, d1, ..., dn	Randoms in the given shape
randn	d0, d1, ..., dn	A sample (or samples) from the standard normal distribution
randint	low[, high, size]	Random integers from *low* (inclusive) to *high* (exclusive)
random_integers	low[, high, size]	Random integers between *low* and *high*, inclusive
random_sample	[size]	Random floats in the half-open interval [0.0, 1.0)
random	[size]	Random floats in the half-open interval [0.0, 1.0)
ranf	[size]	Random floats in the half-open interval [0.0, 1.0)
sample	[size]	Random floats in the half-open interval [0.0, 1.0)
choice	a[, size, replace, p]	Random sample from a given 1D array
bytes	length	Random bytes

Let us visualize some random draws generated by selected functions from Table 10-1:

```
In [6]: sample_size = 500
        rn1 = npr.rand(sample_size, 3)
        rn2 = npr.randint(0, 10, sample_size)
        rn3 = npr.sample(size=sample_size)
        a = [0, 25, 50, 75, 100]
        rn4 = npr.choice(a, size=sample_size)
```

Figure 10-1 shows the results graphically for two continuous distributions and two discrete ones:

```
In [7]: fig, ((ax1, ax2), (ax3, ax4)) = plt.subplots(nrows=2, ncols=2,
                                                      figsize=(7, 7))
        ax1.hist(rn1, bins=25, stacked=True)
        ax1.set_title('rand')
        ax1.set_ylabel('frequency')
        ax1.grid(True)
        ax2.hist(rn2, bins=25)
        ax2.set_title('randint')
        ax2.grid(True)
        ax3.hist(rn3, bins=25)
        ax3.set_title('sample')
```

---

2. Cf. *http://docs.scipy.org/doc/numpy/reference/routines.random.html*.

```
ax3.set_ylabel('frequency')
ax3.grid(True)
ax4.hist(rn4, bins=25)
ax4.set_title('choice')
ax4.grid(True)
```

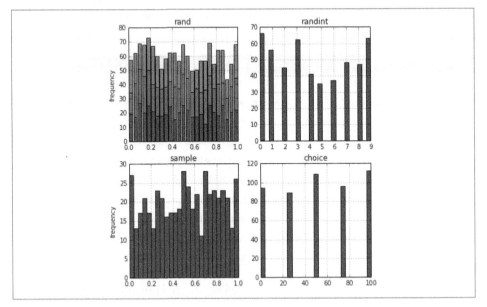

Figure 10-1. Simple pseudorandom numbers

Table 10-2 lists functions for generating random numbers according to different *distributions.*[3]

Table 10-2. Functions to generate random numbers according to different distribution laws

Function	Parameters	Description
beta	*a, b[, size]*	Samples for beta distribution over [0, 1]
binomial	*n, p[, size]*	Samples from a binomial distribution
chisquare	*df[, size]*	Samples from a chi-square distribution
dirichlet	*alpha[, size]*	Samples from the Dirichlet distribution
exponential	*[scale, size]*	Samples from the exponential distribution
f	*dfnum, dfden[, size]*	Samples from an F distribution
gamma	*shape[, scale, size]*	Samples from a gamma distribution

3. Cf. *http://docs.scipy.org/doc/numpy/reference/routines.random.html.*

Function	Parameters	Description
geometric	*p[, size]*	Samples from the geometric distribution
gumbel	*[loc, scale, size]*	Samples from a Gumbel distribution
hypergeometric	*ngood, nbad, nsample[, size]*	Samples from a hypergeometric distribution
laplace	*[loc, scale, size]*	Samples from the Laplace or double exponential distribution
logistic	*[loc, scale, size]*	Samples from a logistic distribution
lognormalv	*[mean, sigma, size]*	Samples from a log-normal distribution
logseries	*p[, size]*	Samples from a logarithmic series distribution
multinomial	*n, pvals[, size]*	Samples from a multinomial distribution
multivariate_normal	*mean, cov[, size]*	Samples from a multivariate normal distribution
negative_binomial	*n, p[, size]*	Samples from a negative binomial distribution
noncentral_chisquare	*df, nonc[, size]*	Samples from a noncentral chi-square distribution
noncentral_f	*dfnum, dfden, nonc[, size]*	samples from the noncentral F distribution
normal	*[loc, scale, size]*	Samples from a normal (Gaussian) distribution
pareto	*a[, size]*	Samples from a Pareto II or Lomax distribution with specified shape
poisson	*[lam, size]*	Samples from a Poisson distribution
power	*a[, size]*	Samples in [0, 1] from a power distribution with positive exponent *a*−1
rayleigh	*[scale, size]*	Samples from a Rayleigh distribution
standard_cauchy	*[size]*	Samples from standard Cauchy distribution with mode = 0
standard_exponential	*[size]*	Samples from the standard exponential distribution
standard_gamma	*shape[, size]*	Samples from a standard gamma distribution
standard_normal	*[size]*	Samples from a standard normal distribution (mean=0, stdev=1)
standard_t	*df[, size]*	Samples from a Student's t distribution with *df* degrees of freedom
triangular	*left, mode, right[, size]*	Samples from the triangular distribution
uniform	*[low, high, size]*	Samples from a uniform distribution
vonmises	*mu, kappa[, size]*	Samples from a von Mises distribution
wald	*mean, scale[, size]*	Samples from a Wald, or inverse Gaussian, distribution
weibull	*a[, size]*	Samples from a Weibull distribution
zipf	*a[, size]*	Samples from a Zipf distribution

Although there is much criticism around the use of (standard) normal distributions in finance, they are an indispensible tool and still the most widely used type of distribution, in analytical as well as numerical applications. One reason is that many financial models directly rest in one way or another on a normal distribution or a log-normal distribution. Another reason is that many financial models that do not rest directly on a (log-)normal assumption can be discretized, and therewith approximated for simulation purposes, by the use of the normal distribution.

As an illustration, we want to visualize random draws from the following distributions:

- **Standard normal** with mean of 0 and standard deviation of 1
- **Normal** with mean of 100 and standard deviation of 20
- **Chi square** with 0.5 degrees of freedom
- **Poisson** with lambda of 1

We do this as follows:

```
In [8]: sample_size = 500
        rn1 = npr.standard_normal(sample_size)
        rn2 = npr.normal(100, 20, sample_size)
        rn3 = npr.chisquare(df=0.5, size=sample_size)
        rn4 = npr.poisson(lam=1.0, size=sample_size)
```

Figure 10-2 shows the results for the three continuous distributions and the discrete one (Poisson). The Poisson distribution is used, for example, to simulate the arrival of (rare) external events, like a jump in the price of an instrument or an exogenic shock. Here is the code that generates it:

```
In [9]: fig, ((ax1, ax2), (ax3, ax4)) = plt.subplots(nrows=2, ncols=2,
                                                      figsize=(7, 7))
        ax1.hist(rn1, bins=25)
        ax1.set_title('standard normal')
        ax1.set_ylabel('frequency')
        ax1.grid(True)
        ax2.hist(rn2, bins=25)
        ax2.set_title('normal(100, 20)')
        ax2.grid(True)
        ax3.hist(rn3, bins=25)
        ax3.set_title('chi square')
        ax3.set_ylabel('frequency')
        ax3.grid(True)
        ax4.hist(rn4, bins=25)
        ax4.set_title('Poisson')
        ax4.grid(True)
```

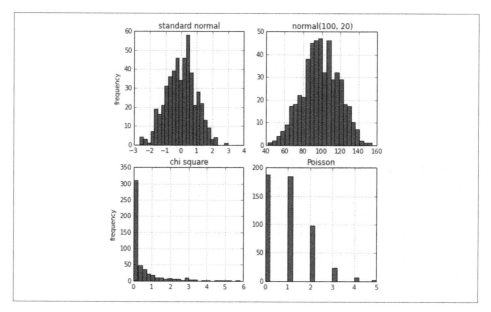

Figure 10-2. Pseudorandom numbers from different distributions

Simulation

Monte Carlo simulation (MCS) is among the most important numerical techniques in finance, if not *the* most important and widely used. This mainly stems from the fact that it is the most flexible numerical method when it comes to the evaluation of mathematical expressions (e.g., integrals), and specifically the valuation of financial derivatives. The flexibility comes at the cost of a relatively high computational burden, though, since often hundreds of thousands or even millions of complex computations have to be carried out to come up with a single value estimate.

Random Variables

Consider, for example, the Black-Scholes-Merton setup for option pricing (cf. also Chapter 3). In their setup, the level of a stock index S_T at a future date T given a level S_0 as of today is given according to Equation 10-1.

Equation 10-1. Simulating future index level in Black-Scholes-Merton setup

$$S_T = S_0 \exp\left(\left(r - \frac{1}{2}\sigma^2\right)T + \sigma\sqrt{T}z\right)$$

The variables and parameters have the following meaning:

S_T

Index level at date T

r

Constant riskless short rate

σ

Constant volatility (= standard deviation of returns) of S

z

Standard normally distributed random variable

This simple financial model is easily parameterized and simulated as follows:

```
In [10]: S0 = 100  # initial value
         r = 0.05  # constant short rate
         sigma = 0.25  # constant volatility
         T = 2.0  # in years
         I = 10000  # number of random draws
         ST1 = S0 * np.exp((r - 0.5 * sigma ** 2) * T
                      + sigma * np.sqrt(T) * npr.standard_normal(I))
```

The output of this simulation code is shown in Figure 10-3:

```
In [11]: plt.hist(ST1, bins=50)
         plt.xlabel('index level')
         plt.ylabel('frequency')
         plt.grid(True)
```

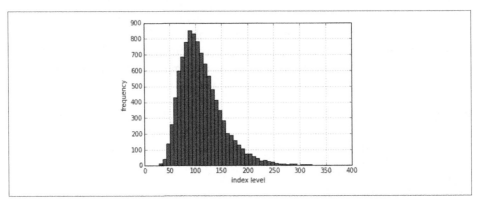

Figure 10-3. Simulated geometric Brownian motion (via standard_normal)

Figure 10-3 suggests that the distribution of the random variable as defined in Equation 10-1 is *log-normal*. We could therefore also try to use the lognormal function to directly derive the values for the random variable. In that case, we have to provide the mean and the standard deviation to the function:

```
In [12]: ST2 = S0 * npr.lognormal((r - 0.5 * sigma ** 2) * T,
                                   sigma * np.sqrt(T), size=I)
```

Figure 10-4 shows the output of the following simulation code:

```
In [13]: plt.hist(ST2, bins=50)
         plt.xlabel('index level')
         plt.ylabel('frequency')
         plt.grid(True)
```

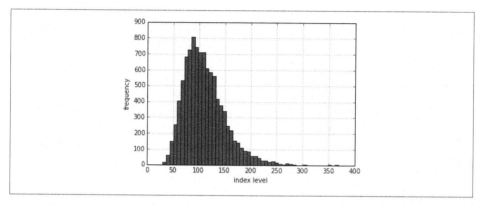

Figure 10-4. Simulated geometric Brownian motion (via lognormal)

By visual inspection, Figure 10-4 and Figure 10-3 indeed look pretty similar. But let us verify this more rigorously by comparing statistical moments of the resulting distributions.

To compare the distributional characteristics of simulation results we use the sci py.stats sublibrary and the helper function print_statistics, as defined here:

```
In [14]: import scipy.stats as scs
```

```
In [15]: def print_statistics(a1, a2):
             ''' Prints selected statistics.

             Parameters
             ==========
             a1, a2 : ndarray objects
                 results object from simulation
             '''
             sta1 = scs.describe(a1)
             sta2 = scs.describe(a2)
             print "%14s %14s %14s" % \
                 ('statistic', 'data set 1', 'data set 2')
             print 45 * "-"
             print "%14s %14.3f %14.3f" % ('size', sta1[0], sta2[0])
             print "%14s %14.3f %14.3f" % ('min', sta1[1][0], sta2[1][0])
             print "%14s %14.3f %14.3f" % ('max', sta1[1][1], sta2[1][1])
             print "%14s %14.3f %14.3f" % ('mean', sta1[2], sta2[2])
```

```
            print "%14s %14.3f %14.3f" % ('std', np.sqrt(sta1[3]),
                                                   np.sqrt(sta2[3]))
            print "%14s %14.3f %14.3f" % ('skew', sta1[4], sta2[4])
            print "%14s %14.3f %14.3f" % ('kurtosis', sta1[5], sta2[5])

In [16]: print_statistics(ST1, ST2)

Out[16]:      statistic     data set 1     data set 2
         --------------------------------------------
              size       10000.000      10000.000
               min          27.936         27.266
               max         410.795        358.997
              mean         110.442        110.528
               std          39.932         40.894
              skew           1.082          1.150
          kurtosis           1.927          2.273
```

Obviously, the statistics of both simulation results are quite similar. The differences are mainly due to what is called the *sampling error* in simulation. Error can also be introduced when *discretely* simulating *continuous* stochastic processes—namely the *discretization error*, which plays no role here due to the static nature of the simulation approach.

Stochastic Processes

Roughly speaking, a *stochastic process* is a sequence of random variables. In that sense, we should expect something similar to a sequence of repeated simulations of a random variable when simulating a process. This is mainly true, apart from the fact that the draws are in general not independent but rather depend on the result(s) of the previous draw(s). In general, however, stochastic processes used in finance exhibit the *Markov property*, which mainly says that tomorrow's value of the process only depends on today's state of the process, and not any other more "historic" state or even the whole path history. The process then is also called *memoryless*.

Geometric Brownian motion

Consider now the Black-Scholes-Merton model in its dynamic form, as described by the stochastic differential equation (SDE) in Equation 10-2. Here, Z_t is a standard Brownian motion. The SDE is called a *geometric Brownian motion*. The values of S_t are lognormally distributed and the (marginal) returns $\frac{dS_t}{S_t}$ normally.

Equation 10-2. Stochastic differential equation in Black-Scholes-Merton setup

$$dS_t = rS_t dt + \sigma S_t dZ_t$$

The SDE in Equation 10-2 can be discretized exactly by an Euler scheme. Such a scheme is presented in Equation 10-3, with Δt being the fixed discretization interval and z_t being a standard normally distributed random variable.

Equation 10-3. Simulating index levels dynamically in Black-Scholes-Merton setup

$$S_t = S_{t-\Delta t} \exp\left(\left(r - \frac{1}{2}\sigma^2\right)\Delta t + \sigma\sqrt{\Delta t}z_t\right)$$

As before, translation into `Python` and `NumPy` code is straightforward:

```
In [17]: I = 10000
         M = 50
         dt = T / M
         S = np.zeros((M + 1, I))
         S[0] = S0
         for t in range(1, M + 1):
             S[t] = S[t - 1] * np.exp((r - 0.5 * sigma ** 2) * dt
                     + sigma * np.sqrt(dt) * npr.standard_normal(I))
```

The resulting end values for the index level are log-normally distributed again, as Figure 10-5 illustrates:

```
In [18]: plt.hist(S[-1], bins=50)
         plt.xlabel('index level')
         plt.ylabel('frequency')
         plt.grid(True)
```

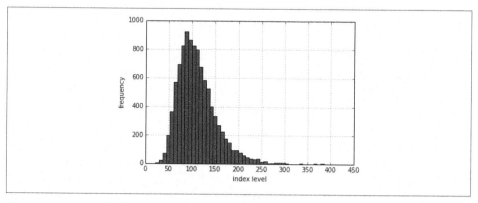

Figure 10-5. Simulated geometric Brownian motion at maturity

The first four moments are also quite close to those resulting from the static simulation approach:

```
In [19]: print_statistics(S[-1], ST2)
```

Out[19]:	statistic	data set 1	data set 2
	size	10000.000	10000.000
	min	25.531	27.266
	max	425.051	358.997
	mean	110.900	110.528
	std	40.135	40.894
	skew	1.086	1.150
	kurtosis	2.224	2.273

Figure 10-6 shows the first 10 simulated paths:

```
In [20]: plt.plot(S[:, :10], lw=1.5)
         plt.xlabel('time')
         plt.ylabel('index level')
         plt.grid(True)
```

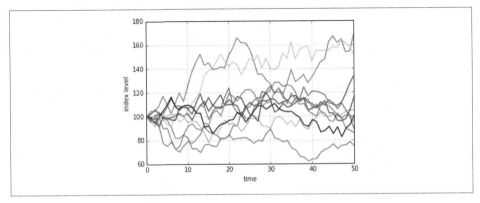

Figure 10-6. Simulated geometric Brownian motion paths

Using the dynamic simulation approach not only allows us to visualize paths as displayed in Figure 10-6, but also to value options with American/Bermudan exercise or options whose payoff is path-dependent. You get the full dynamic picture, so to say:

Square-root diffusion

Another important class of financial processes is *mean-reverting processes*, which are used to model short rates or volatility processes, for example. A popular and widely used model is the *square-root diffusion*, as proposed by Cox, Ingersoll, and Ross (1985). Equation 10-4 provides the respective SDE.

Equation 10-4. Stochastic differential equation for square-root diffusion

$$dx_t = \kappa(\theta - x_t)dt + \sigma\sqrt{x_t}dZ_t$$

The variables and parameters have the following meaning:

x_t

  Process level at date t

κ

  Mean-reversion factor

θ

  Long-term mean of the process

σ

  Constant volatility parameter

Z

  Standard Brownian motion

It is well known that the values of x_t are chi-squared distributed. However, as stated before, many financial models can be discretized and approximated by using the normal distribution (i.e., a so-called Euler discretization scheme). While the Euler scheme is exact for the geometric Brownian motion, it is biased for the majority of other stochastic processes. Even if there is an exact scheme available—one for the square-root diffusion will be presented shortly—the use of an Euler scheme might be desirable due to numerical and/or computational reasons. Defining $s \equiv t - \Delta t$ and $x^+ \equiv \max(x,0)$, Equation 10-5 presents such an Euler scheme. This particular one is generally called *full truncation* in the literature (cf. Hilpisch (2015)).

Equation 10-5. Euler discretization for square-root diffusion

$$\tilde{x}_t = \tilde{x}_s + \kappa\left(\theta - \tilde{x}_s^+\right)\Delta t + \sigma\sqrt{\tilde{x}_s^+}\sqrt{\Delta t}z_t$$
$$x_t = \tilde{x}_t^+$$

We parameterize the model for the simulations to follow with values that could represent those of a short rate model:

```
In [21]: x0 = 0.05
         kappa = 3.0
         theta = 0.02
         sigma = 0.1
```

The square-root diffusion has the convenient and realistic characteristic that the values of x_t remain strictly positive. When discretizing it by an Euler scheme, negative values cannot be excluded. That is the reason why one works always with the positive version of the originally simulated process. In the simulation code, one therefore needs two ndarray objects instead of only one:

```
In [22]: I = 10000
         M = 50
         dt = T / M
         def srd_euler():
             xh = np.zeros((M + 1, I))
             x1 = np.zeros_like(xh)
             xh[0] = x0
             x1[0] = x0
             for t in range(1, M + 1):
                 xh[t] = (xh[t - 1]
                     + kappa * (theta - np.maximum(xh[t - 1], 0)) * dt
                     + sigma * np.sqrt(np.maximum(xh[t - 1], 0)) * np.sqrt(dt)
                     * npr.standard_normal(I))
             x1 = np.maximum(xh, 0)
             return x1
         x1 = srd_euler()
```

Figure 10-7 shows the result of the simulation graphically as a histogram:

```
In [23]: plt.hist(x1[-1], bins=50)
         plt.xlabel('value')
         plt.ylabel('frequency')
         plt.grid(True)
```

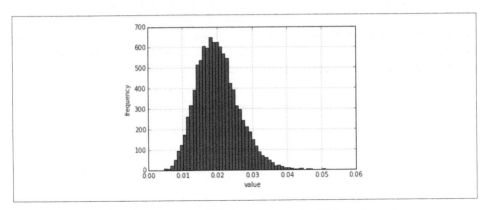

Figure 10-7. Simulated square-root diffusion at maturity (Euler scheme)

Figure 10-8 then shows the first 10 simulated paths, illustrating the resulting negative, averagef drift (due to $x_0 > \theta$) and the convergence to $\theta = 0.02$:

```
In [24]: plt.plot(x1[:, :10], lw=1.5)
         plt.xlabel('time')
         plt.ylabel('index level')
         plt.grid(True)
```

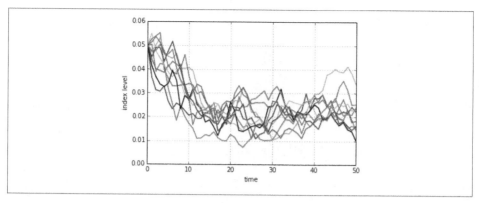

Figure 10-8. Simulated square-root diffusion paths (Euler scheme)

Let us now get more exact. Equation 10-6 presents the exact discretization scheme for the square-root diffusion based on the noncentral chi-square distribution $\chi_d'^2$ with $df = \frac{4\theta\kappa}{\sigma^2}$ degrees of freedom and noncentrality parameter $nc = \frac{4\kappa e^{-\kappa\Delta t}}{\sigma^2\left(1 - e^{-\kappa\Delta t}\right)} x_s$.

Equation 10-6. Exact discretization for square-root diffusion

$$x_t = \frac{\sigma^2\left(1 - e^{-\kappa\Delta t}\right)}{4\kappa} \chi_d'^2 \left(\frac{4\kappa e^{-\kappa\Delta t}}{\sigma^2\left(1 - e^{-\kappa\Delta t}\right)} x_s \right)$$

The Python implementation of this discretization scheme is a bit more involved but still quite concise:

```
In [25]: def srd_exact():
             x2 = np.zeros((M + 1, I))
             x2[0] = x0
             for t in range(1, M + 1):
                 df = 4 * theta * kappa / sigma ** 2
                 c = (sigma ** 2 * (1 - np.exp(-kappa * dt))) / (4 * kappa)
                 nc = np.exp(-kappa * dt) / c * x2[t - 1]
                 x2[t] = c * npr.noncentral_chisquare(df, nc, size=I)
             return x2
         x2 = srd_exact()
```

Figure 10-9 shows the output of the simulation with the exact scheme as a histogram:

```
In [26]: plt.hist(x2[-1], bins=50)
         plt.xlabel('value')
         plt.ylabel('frequency')
         plt.grid(True)
```

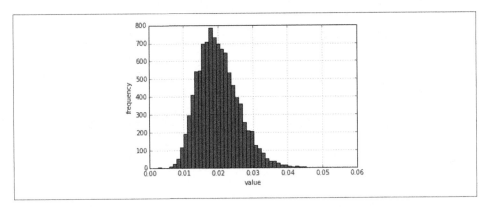

Figure 10-9. Simulated square-root diffusion at maturity (exact scheme)

Figure 10-10 presents as before the first 10 simulated paths, again displaying the negative average drift and the convergence to θ:

```
In [27]: plt.plot(x2[:, :10], lw=1.5)
         plt.xlabel('time')
         plt.ylabel('index level')
         plt.grid(True)
```

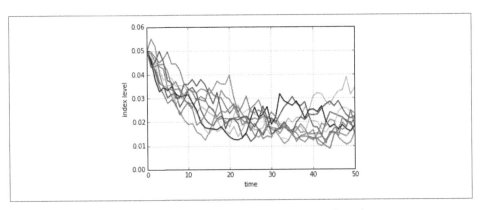

Figure 10-10. Simulated square-root diffusion paths (exact scheme)

Comparing the main statistics from the different approaches reveals that the biased Euler scheme indeed performs quite well when it comes to the desired statistical properties:

```
In [28]: print_statistics(x1[-1], x2[-1])
```

Out[28]:	statistic	data set 1	data set 2
	size	10000.000	10000.000
	min	0.004	0.005

max	0.049	0.050
mean	0.020	0.020
std	0.006	0.006
skew	0.529	0.572
kurtosis	0.418	0.503

However, a major difference can be observed in terms of execution speed, since sampling from the noncentral chi-square distribution is more computationally demanding than from the standard normal distribution. To illustrate this point, consider a larger number of paths to be simulated:

```
In [29]: I = 250000
         %time x1 = srd_euler()

Out[29]: CPU times: user 1.02 s, sys: 84 ms, total: 1.11 s
         Wall time: 1.11 s

In [30]: %time x2 = srd_exact()

Out[30]: CPU times: user 2.26 s, sys: 32 ms, total: 2.3 s
         Wall time: 2.3 s
```

The exact scheme takes roughly twice as much time for virtually the same results as with the Euler scheme:

```
In [31]: print_statistics(x1[-1], x2[-1])
         x1 = 0.0; x2 = 0.0
```

Out[31]:	statistic	data set 1	data set 2
	size	250000.000	250000.000
	min	0.003	0.004
	max	0.069	0.060
	mean	0.020	0.020
	std	0.006	0.006
	skew	0.554	0.578
	kurtosis	0.488	0.502

Stochastic volatility

One of the major simplifying assumptions of the Black-Scholes-Merton model is the *constant* volatility. However, volatility in general is neither constant nor deterministic; it is *stochastic*. Therefore, a major advancement with regard to financial modeling was achieved in the early 1990s with the introduction of so-called *stochastic volatility models*. One of the most popular models that fall into that category is that of Heston (1993), which is presented in Equation 10-7.

Equation 10-7. Stochastic differential equations for Heston stochastic volatility model

$$dS_t = rS_t dt + \sqrt{v_t}S_t dZ_t^1$$
$$dv_t = \kappa_v(\theta_v - v_t)dt + \sigma_v\sqrt{v_t}dZ_t^2$$
$$dZ_t^1 dZ_t^2 = \rho$$

The meaning of the single variables and parameters can now be inferred easily from the discussion of the geometric Brownian motion and the square-root diffusion. The parameter ρ represents the instantaneous correlation between the two standard Brownian motions Z_t^1, Z_t^2. This allows us to account for a stylized fact called the *leverage effect*, which in essence states that volatility goes up in times of stress (declining markets) and goes down in times of a bull market (rising markets).

Consider the following parameterization of the model:

```
In [32]: S0 = 100.
         r = 0.05
         v0 = 0.1
         kappa = 3.0
         theta = 0.25
         sigma = 0.1
         rho = 0.6
         T = 1.0
```

To account for the correlation between the two stochastic processes, we need to determine the Cholesky decomposition of the correlation matrix:

```
In [33]: corr_mat = np.zeros((2, 2))
         corr_mat[0, :] = [1.0, rho]
         corr_mat[1, :] = [rho, 1.0]
         cho_mat = np.linalg.cholesky(corr_mat)

In [34]: cho_mat

Out[34]: array([[ 1. ,  0. ],
                [ 0.6,  0.8]])
```

Before we start simulating the stochastic processes, we generate the whole set of random numbers for both processes, looking to use set 0 for the index process and set 1 for the volatility process:

```
In [35]: M = 50
         I = 10000
         ran_num = npr.standard_normal((2, M + 1, I))
```

For the volatility process modeled by the square-root diffusion process type, we use the Euler scheme, taking into account the correlation parameter:

```
In [36]: dt = T / M
         v = np.zeros_like(ran_num[0])
         vh = np.zeros_like(v)
         v[0] = v0
         vh[0] = v0
         for t in range(1, M + 1):
             ran = np.dot(cho_mat, ran_num[:, t, :])
             vh[t] = (vh[t - 1] + kappa * (theta - np.maximum(vh[t - 1], 0)) * dt
                     + sigma * np.sqrt(np.maximum(vh[t - 1], 0)) * np.sqrt(dt)
                     * ran[1])
         v = np.maximum(vh, 0)
```

For the index level process, we also take into account the correlation and use the exact Euler scheme for the geometric Brownian motion:

```
In [37]: S = np.zeros_like(ran_num[0])
         S[0] = S0
         for t in range(1, M + 1):
             ran = np.dot(cho_mat, ran_num[:, t, :])
             S[t] = S[t - 1] * np.exp((r - 0.5 * v[t]) * dt +
                         np.sqrt(v[t]) * ran[0] * np.sqrt(dt))
```

This illustrates another advantage of working with the Euler scheme for the square-root diffusion: *correlation is easily and consistently accounted for* since we only draw standard normally distributed random numbers. There is no simple way of achieving the same with a mixed approach, using Euler for the index and the noncentral chi square-based exact approach for the volatility process.

Figure 10-11 shows the simulation results as a histogram for both the index level process and the volatility process:

```
In [38]: fig, (ax1, ax2) = plt.subplots(1, 2, figsize=(9, 5))
         ax1.hist(S[-1], bins=50)
         ax1.set_xlabel('index level')
         ax1.set_ylabel('frequency')
         ax1.grid(True)
         ax2.hist(v[-1], bins=50)
         ax2.set_xlabel('volatility')
         ax2.grid(True)
```

An inspection of the first 10 simulated paths of each process (cf. Figure 10-12) shows that the volatility process is drifting positively on average and that it, as expected, converges to $\theta_v = 0.25$:

```
In [39]: fig, (ax1, ax2) = plt.subplots(2, 1, sharex=True, figsize=(7, 6))
         ax1.plot(S[:, :10], lw=1.5)
         ax1.set_ylabel('index level')
         ax1.grid(True)
         ax2.plot(v[:, :10], lw=1.5)
         ax2.set_xlabel('time')
         ax2.set_ylabel('volatility')
         ax2.grid(True)
```

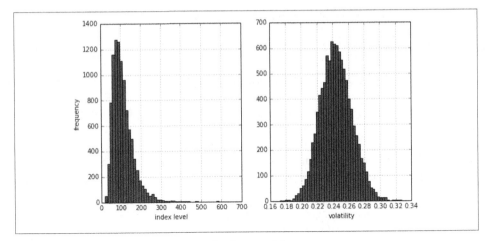

Figure 10-11. Simulated stochastic volatility model at maturity

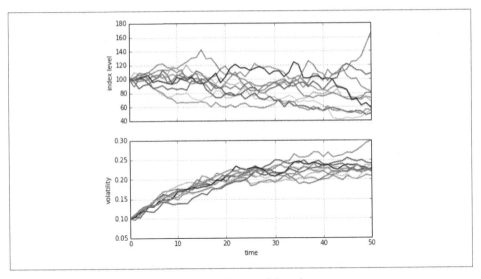

Figure 10-12. Simulated stochastic volatility model paths

Finally, let us take a brief look at the statistics for the last point in time for both data sets, showing a pretty high maximum value for the index level process. In fact, this is much higher than a geometric Brownian motion with constant volatility could ever climb, *ceteris paribus*:

```
In [40]: print_statistics(S[-1], v[-1])

Out[40]:      statistic      data set 1      data set 2
         --------------------------------------------
```

size	10000.000	10000.000
min	19.814	0.174
max	600.080	0.322
mean	108.818	0.243
std	52.535	0.020
skew	1.702	0.151
kurtosis	5.407	0.071

Jump diffusion

Stochastic volatility and the leverage effect are stylized (empirical) facts found in a number of markets. Another important stylized empirical fact is the existence of *jumps* in asset prices and, for example, volatility. In 1976, Merton published his jump diffusion model, enhancing the Black-Scholes-Merton setup by a model component generating jumps with log-normal distribution. The risk-neutral SDE is presented in Equation 10-8.

Equation 10-8. Stochastic differential equation for Merton jump diffusion model

$$dS_t = (r - r_J)S_t dt + \sigma S_t dZ_t + J_t S_t dN_t$$

For completeness, here is an overview of the variables' and parameters' meaning:

S_t

Index level at date t

r

Constant riskless short rate

$r_J \equiv \lambda \cdot \left(e^{\mu_J + \delta^2/2} - 1\right)$

Drift correction for jump to maintain risk neutrality

σ

Constant volatility of S

Z_t

Standard Brownian motion

J_t

Jump at date t with distribution ...

- ... $\log(1 + J_t) \approx \mathbf{N}\left(\log(1 + \mu_J) - \frac{\delta^2}{2}, \delta^2\right)$ with ...

- ... $\mathbf{N}$ as the cumulative distribution function of a standard normal random variable

N_t

Poisson process with intensity λ

Equation 10-9 presents an Euler discretization for the jump diffusion where the z_t^n are standard normally distributed and the y_t are Poisson distributed with intensity λ.

Equation 10-9. Euler discretization for Merton jump diffusion model

$$S_t = S_{t-\Delta t}\left(e^{\left(r-r_J-\sigma^2/2\right)\Delta t+\sigma\sqrt{\Delta t}z_t^1} + \left(e^{\mu_J+\delta z_t^2}-1\right)y_t\right)$$

Given the discretization scheme, consider the following numerical parameterization:

```
In [41]: S0 = 100.
         r = 0.05
         sigma = 0.2
         lamb = 0.75
         mu = -0.6
         delta = 0.25
         T = 1.0
```

To simulate the jump diffusion, we need to generate three sets of (independent) random numbers:

```
In [42]: M = 50
         I = 10000
         dt = T / M
         rj = lamb * (np.exp(mu + 0.5 * delta ** 2) - 1)
         S = np.zeros((M + 1, I))
         S[0] = S0
         sn1 = npr.standard_normal((M + 1, I))
         sn2 = npr.standard_normal((M + 1, I))
         poi = npr.poisson(lamb * dt, (M + 1, I))
         for t in range(1, M + 1, 1):
             S[t] = S[t - 1] * (np.exp((r - rj - 0.5 * sigma ** 2) * dt
                               + sigma * np.sqrt(dt) * sn1[t])
                               + (np.exp(mu + delta * sn2[t]) - 1)
                               * poi[t])
             S[t] = np.maximum(S[t], 0)
```

Since we have assumed a highly negative mean for the jump, it should not come as a surprise that the final values of the simulated index level are more *right-skewed* in Figure 10-13 compared to a typical log-normal distribution:

```
In [43]: plt.hist(S[-1], bins=50)
         plt.xlabel('value')
         plt.ylabel('frequency')
         plt.grid(True)
```

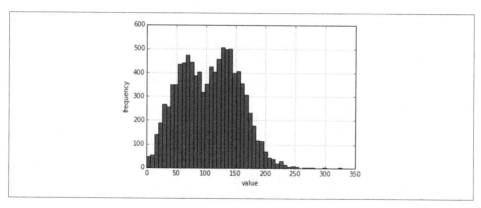

Figure 10-13. Simulated jump diffusion at maturity

The highly negative jumps can also be found in the first 10 simulated index level paths, as presented in Figure 10-14:

```
In [44]: plt.plot(S[:, :10], lw=1.5)
         plt.xlabel('time')
         plt.ylabel('index level')
         plt.grid(True)
```

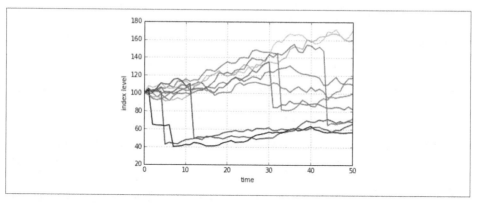

Figure 10-14. Simulated jump diffusion paths

Variance Reduction

Not only because of the fact that the Python functions we have used so far generate *pseudorandom* numbers, but also due to the varying sizes of the samples drawn, resulting sets of numbers might not exhibit statistics really close enough to the expected/desired ones. For example, you would expect a set of standard normally distributed random numbers to show a mean of 0 and a standard deviation of 1. Let us check what statistics

different sets of random numbers exhibit. To achieve a realistic comparison, we fix the
seed value for the random number generator:

```
In [45]: print "%15s %15s" % ('Mean', 'Std. Deviation')
         print 31 * "-"
         for i in range(1, 31, 2):
             npr.seed(1000)
             sn = npr.standard_normal(i ** 2 * 10000)
             print "%15.12f %15.12f" % (sn.mean(), sn.std())

Out[45]:            Mean  Std. Deviation
         -------------------------------
         -0.011870394558  1.008752430725
         -0.002815667298  1.002729536352
         -0.003847776704  1.000594044165
         -0.003058113374  1.001086345326
         -0.001685126538  1.001630849589
         -0.001175212007  1.001347684642
         -0.000803969036  1.000159081432
         -0.000601970954  0.999506522127
         -0.000147787693  0.999571756099
         -0.000313035581  0.999646153704
         -0.000178447061  0.999677277878
          0.000096501709  0.999684346792
         -0.000135677013  0.999823841902
         -0.000015726986  0.999906493379
         -0.000039368519  1.000063091949

In [46]: i ** 2 * 10000

Out[46]: 8410000
```

The results show that the statistics "somehow" get better the larger the number of draws
becomes. But they still do not match the desired ones, even in our largest sample with
more than 8,000,000 random numbers.

Fortunately, there are easy-to-implement, generic variance reduction techniques available to improve the matching of the first two moments of the (standard) normal distribution. The first technique is to use *antithetic variates*. This approach simply draws
only half the desired number of random draws, and adds the same set of random numbers with the opposite sign afterward.[4] For example, if the random number generator
(i.e., the respective Python function) draws 0.5, then another number with value –0.5
is added to the set.

With NumPy this is concisely implemented by using the function concatenate:

---

4. The described method works for symmetric median 0 random variables only, like standard normally distributed random variables, which we almost exclusively use throughout.

```
In [47]: sn = npr.standard_normal(10000 / 2)
         sn = np.concatenate((sn, -sn))
         np.shape(sn)

Out[47]: (10000,)
```

The following repeats the exercise from before, this time using antithetic variates:

```
In [48]: print "%15s %15s" % ('Mean', 'Std. Deviation')
         print 31 * "-"
         for i in range(1, 31, 2):
             npr.seed(1000)
             sn = npr.standard_normal(i ** 2 * 10000 / 2)
             sn = np.concatenate((sn, -sn))
             print "%15.12f %15.12f" % (sn.mean(), sn.std())

Out[48]:            Mean  Std. Deviation
         -------------------------------
          0.000000000000  1.009653753942
         -0.000000000000  1.000413716783
          0.000000000000  1.002925061201
         -0.000000000000  1.000755212673
          0.000000000000  1.001636910076
         -0.000000000000  1.000726758438
         -0.000000000000  1.001621265149
          0.000000000000  1.001203722778
         -0.000000000000  1.000556669784
          0.000000000000  1.000113464185
         -0.000000000000  0.999435175324
          0.000000000000  0.999356961431
         -0.000000000000  0.999641436845
         -0.000000000000  0.999642768905
         -0.000000000000  0.999638303451
```

As you immediately notice, this approach corrects the first moment perfectly—which should not come as a surprise. This follows from the fact that whenever a number n is drawn, $-n$ is also added. Since we only have such pairs, the mean is equal to 0 over the whole set of random numbers. However, this approach does not have any influence on the second moment, the standard deviation.

Using another variance reduction technique, called *moment matching*, helps correct in one step both the first and second moments:

```
In [49]: sn = npr.standard_normal(10000)

In [50]: sn.mean()

Out[50]: -0.001165998295162494

In [51]: sn.std()

Out[51]: 0.99125592020460496
```

By subtracting the mean from every single random number and dividing every single number by the standard deviation, we get a set of random numbers matching the desired first and second moments of the standard normal distribution (almost) perfectly:

```
In [52]: sn_new = (sn - sn.mean()) / sn.std()

In [53]: sn_new.mean()

Out[53]: -2.3803181647963357e-17

In [54]: sn_new.std()

Out[54]: 0.99999999999999989
```

The following function utilizes the insight with regard to variance reduction techniques and generates standard normal random numbers for process simulation using either two, one, or no variance reduction technique(s):

```
In [55]: def gen_sn(M, I, anti_paths=True, mo_match=True):
             ''' Function to generate random numbers for simulation.

             Parameters
             ==========
             M : int
                 number of time intervals for discretization
             I : int
                 number of paths to be simulated
             anti_paths: Boolean
                 use of antithetic variates
             mo_math : Boolean
                 use of moment matching
             '''
             if anti_paths is True:
                 sn = npr.standard_normal((M + 1, I / 2))
                 sn = np.concatenate((sn, -sn), axis=1)
             else:
                 sn = npr.standard_normal((M + 1, I))
             if mo_match is True:
                 sn = (sn - sn.mean()) / sn.std()
             return sn
```

Valuation

One of the most important applications of Monte Carlo simulation is the *valuation of contingent claims* (options, derivatives, hybrid instruments, etc.). Simply stated, in a risk-neutral world, the value of a contingent claim is the discounted expected payoff under the risk-neutral (martingale) measure. This is the probability measure that makes all risk factors (stocks, indices, etc.) drift at the riskless short rate. According to the Fundamental Theorem of Asset Pricing, the existence of such a probability measure is equivalent to the absence of arbitrage.

A financial option embodies the right to buy (*call option*) or sell (*put option*) a specified financial instrument at a given (maturity) date (*European option*), or over a specified period of time (*American option*), at a given price (the so-called *strike price*). Let us first consider the much simpler case of European options in terms of valuation.

European Options

The payoff of a European call option on an index at maturity is given by $h(S_T) \equiv \max(S_T - K, 0)$, where S_T is the index level at maturity date T and K is the strike price. Given a, or in complete markets *the*, risk-neutral measure for the relevant stochastic process (e.g., geometric Brownian motion), the price of such an option is given by the formula in Equation 10-10.

Equation 10-10. Pricing by risk-neutral expectation

$$C_0 = e^{-rT} \mathbf{E}_0^Q(h(S_T)) = e^{-rT} \int_0^\infty h(s)q(s)ds$$

Chapter 9 briefly sketches how to numerically evaluate an integral by Monte Carlo simulation. This approach is used in the following and applied to Equation 10-10. Equation 10-11 provides the respective Monte Carlo estimator for the European option, where $\tilde{S}_T^i$ is the ith simulated index level at maturity.

Equation 10-11. Risk-neutral Monte Carlo estimator

$$\tilde{C}_0 = e^{-rT} \frac{1}{I} \sum_{i=1}^I h(\tilde{S}_T^i)$$

Consider now the following parameterization for the geometric Brownian motion and the valuation function gbm_mcs_stat, taking as a parameter only the strike price. Here, only the index level at maturity is simulated:

```
In [56]: S0 = 100.
         r = 0.05
         sigma = 0.25
         T = 1.0
         I = 50000
         def gbm_mcs_stat(K):
             ''' Valuation of European call option in Black-Scholes-Merton
             by Monte Carlo simulation (of index level at maturity)

             Parameters
             ==========
```

```
K : float
    (positive) strike price of the option

Returns
=======
C0 : float
    estimated present value of European call option
'''
sn = gen_sn(1, I)
# simulate index level at maturity
ST = S0 * np.exp((r - 0.5 * sigma ** 2) * T
                 + sigma * np.sqrt(T) * sn[1])
# calculate payoff at maturity
hT = np.maximum(ST - K, 0)
# calculate MCS estimator
C0 = np.exp(-r * T) * 1 / I * np.sum(hT)
return C0
```

As a reference, consider the case with a strike price of $K = 105$:

```
In [57]: gbm_mcs_stat(K=105.)

Out[57]: 10.044221852841922
```

Next, we consider the dynamic simulation approach and allow for European put options in addition to the call option. The function gbm_mcs_dyna implements the algorithm:

```
In [58]: M = 50
         def gbm_mcs_dyna(K, option='call'):
             ''' Valuation of European options in Black-Scholes-Merton
             by Monte Carlo simulation (of index level paths)

             Parameters
             ==========
             K : float
                 (positive) strike price of the option
             option : string
                 type of the option to be valued ('call', 'put')

             Returns
             =======
             C0 : float
                 estimated present value of European call option
             '''
             dt = T / M
             # simulation of index level paths
             S = np.zeros((M + 1, I))
             S[0] = S0
             sn = gen_sn(M, I)
             for t in range(1, M + 1):
                 S[t] = S[t - 1] * np.exp((r - 0.5 * sigma ** 2) * dt
                         + sigma * np.sqrt(dt) * sn[t])
             # case-based calculation of payoff
             if option == 'call':
```

```
        hT = np.maximum(S[-1] - K, 0)
    else:
        hT = np.maximum(K - S[-1], 0)
    # calculation of MCS estimator
    C0 = np.exp(-r * T) * 1 / I * np.sum(hT)
    return C0
```

Now, we can compare option price estimates for a call and a put stroke at the same level:

```
In [59]: gbm_mcs_dyna(K=110., option='call')

Out[59]: 7.9500085250284336

In [60]: gbm_mcs_dyna(K=110., option='put')

Out[60]: 12.629934942682004
```

The question is how well these simulation-based valuation approaches perform relative to the benchmark value from the Black-Scholes-Merton valuation formula. To find out, let us generate respective option values/estimates for a range of strike prices, using the analytical option pricing formula for European calls in Black-Scholes-Merton found in the module BSM_Functions.py:

```
In [61]: from bsm_functions import bsm_call_value
         stat_res = []
         dyna_res = []
         anal_res = []
         k_list = np.arange(80., 120.1, 5.)
         np.random.seed(200000)
         for K in k_list:
             stat_res.append(gbm_mcs_stat(K))
             dyna_res.append(gbm_mcs_dyna(K))
             anal_res.append(bsm_call_value(S0, K, T, r, sigma))
         stat_res = np.array(stat_res)
         dyna_res = np.array(dyna_res)
         anal_res = np.array(anal_res)
```

First, we compare the results from the static simulation approach with precise analytical values:

```
In [62]: fig, (ax1, ax2) = plt.subplots(2, 1, sharex=True, figsize=(8, 6))
         ax1.plot(k_list, anal_res, 'b', label='analytical')
         ax1.plot(k_list, stat_res, 'ro', label='static')
         ax1.set_ylabel('European call option value')
         ax1.grid(True)
         ax1.legend(loc=0)
         ax1.set_ylim(ymin=0)
         wi = 1.0
         ax2.bar(k_list - wi / 2, (anal_res - stat_res) / anal_res * 100, wi)
         ax2.set_xlabel('strike')
         ax2.set_ylabel('difference in %')
         ax2.set_xlim(left=75, right=125)
         ax2.grid(True)
```

Figure 10-15 shows the results. All valuation differences are smaller than 1% absolutely. There are both negative and positive value differences.

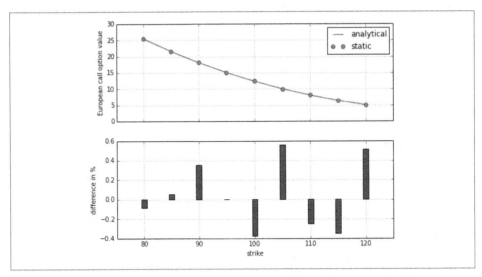

Figure 10-15. Comparison of static and dynamic Monte Carlo estimator values

A similar picture emerges for the dynamic simulation and valuation approach, whose results are reported in Figure 10-16. Again, all valuation differences are smaller than 1%, absolutely with both positive and negative deviations. As a general rule, the quality of the Monte Carlo estimator can be controlled for by adjusting the number of time intervals M used and/or the number of paths I simulated:

```
In [63]: fig, (ax1, ax2) = plt.subplots(2, 1, sharex=True, figsize=(8, 6))
         ax1.plot(k_list, anal_res, 'b', label='analytical')
         ax1.plot(k_list, dyna_res, 'ro', label='dynamic')
         ax1.set_ylabel('European call option value')
         ax1.grid(True)
         ax1.legend(loc=0)
         ax1.set_ylim(ymin=0)
         wi = 1.0
         ax2.bar(k_list - wi / 2, (anal_res - dyna_res) / anal_res * 100, wi)
         ax2.set_xlabel('strike')
         ax2.set_ylabel('difference in %')
         ax2.set_xlim(left=75, right=125)
         ax2.grid(True)
```

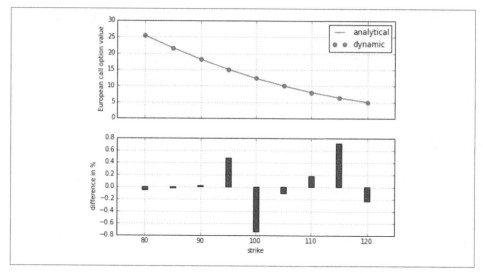

Figure 10-16. Comparison of static and dynamic Monte Carlo estimator values

American Options

The valuation of American options is more involved compared to European options. In this case, an *optimal stopping* problem has to be solved to come up with a fair value of the option. Equation 10-12 formulates the valuation of an American option as such a problem. The problem formulation is already based on a discrete time grid for use with numerical simulation. In a sense, it is therefore more correct to speak of an option value given *Bermudan* exercise. For the time interval converging to zero length, the value of the Bermudan option converges to the one of the American option.

Equation 10-12. American option prices as optimal stopping problem

$$V_0 = \sup_{\tau \in \{0, \Delta t, 2\Delta t, \dots, T\}} e^{-rT} \mathbf{E}_0^Q \big(h_\tau(S_\tau) \big)$$

The algorithm we describe in the following is called *Least-Squares Monte Carlo* (LSM) and is from the paper by Longstaff and Schwartz (2001). It can be shown that the value of an American (Bermudan) option at any given date t is given as $V_t(s) = \max(h_t(s), C_t(s))$, where $C_t(s) = \mathbf{E}_t^Q \big(e^{-r\Delta t} V_{t+\Delta t}(S_{t+\Delta t}) \big| S_t = s \big)$ is the so-called *continuation value* of the option given an index level of $S_t = s$.

Consider now that we have simulated I paths of the index level over M time intervals of equal size Δt. Define $Y_{t,i} \equiv e^{-r\Delta t} V_{t+\Delta t,i}$ to be the simulated continuation value for path i at time t. We cannot use this number directly because it would imply perfect foresight.

However, we can use the cross section of all such simulated continuation values to estimate the (expected) continuation value by least-squares regression.

Given a set of basis functions b_d, $d = 1,...,D$, the continuation value is then given by the regression estimate $\hat{C}_{t,i} = \sum_{d=1}^{D} \alpha_{d,t}^* \cdot b_d(S_{t,i})$, where the optimal regression parameters α^* are the solution of the least-squares problem stated in Equation 10-13.

Equation 10-13. Least-squares regression for American option valuation

$$\min_{\alpha_{1,t},...,\alpha_{D,t}} \frac{1}{I} \sum_{i=1}^{I} \left(Y_{t,i} - \sum_{d=1}^{D} \alpha_{d,t} \cdot b_d(S_{t,i}) \right)^2$$

The function gbm_mcs_amer implements the LSM algorithm for both American call and put options:[5]

```
In [64]: def gbm_mcs_amer(K, option='call'):
             ''' Valuation of American option in Black-Scholes-Merton
             by Monte Carlo simulation by LSM algorithm

             Parameters
             ==========
             K : float
                 (positive) strike price of the option
             option : string
                 type of the option to be valued ('call', 'put')

             Returns
             =======
             C0 : float
                 estimated present value of European call option
             '''
             dt = T / M
             df = np.exp(-r * dt)
             # simulation of index levels
             S = np.zeros((M + 1, I))
             S[0] = S0
             sn = gen_sn(M, I)
             for t in range(1, M + 1):
                 S[t] = S[t - 1] * np.exp((r - 0.5 * sigma ** 2) * dt
                                 + sigma * np.sqrt(dt) * sn[t])
             # case-based calculation of payoff
             if option == 'call':
                 h = np.maximum(S - K, 0)
             else:
                 h = np.maximum(K - S, 0)
```

---

5. For algorithmic details, refer to Hilpisch (2015).

```
# LSM algorithm
V = np.copy(h)
for t in range(M - 1, 0, -1):
    reg = np.polyfit(S[t], V[t + 1] * df, 7)
    C = np.polyval(reg, S[t])
    V[t] = np.where(C > h[t], V[t + 1] * df, h[t])
# MCS estimator
C0 = df * 1 / I * np.sum(V[1])
return C0
```

In [65]: gbm_mcs_amer(110., option='call')

Out[65]: 7.7789332794493156

In [66]: gbm_mcs_amer(110., option='put')

Out[66]: 13.614023206242445

The European value of an option represents a lower bound to the American option's value. The difference is generally called the *early exercise premium*. In what follows, we compare European and American option values for the same range of strikes as before to estimate the option premium. This time we take puts:[6]

```
In [67]: euro_res = []
         amer_res = []
         k_list = np.arange(80., 120.1, 5.)
         for K in k_list:
             euro_res.append(gbm_mcs_dyna(K, 'put'))
             amer_res.append(gbm_mcs_amer(K, 'put'))
         euro_res = np.array(euro_res)
         amer_res = np.array(amer_res)
```

Figure 10-17 shows that for the range of strikes chosen the premium can rise to up to 10%:

```
In [68]: fig, (ax1, ax2) = plt.subplots(2, 1, sharex=True, figsize=(8, 6))
         ax1.plot(k_list, euro_res, 'b', label='European put')
         ax1.plot(k_list, amer_res, 'ro', label='American put')
         ax1.set_ylabel('call option value')
         ax1.grid(True)
         ax1.legend(loc=0)
         wi = 1.0
         ax2.bar(k_list - wi / 2, (amer_res - euro_res) / euro_res * 100, wi)
         ax2.set_xlabel('strike')
         ax2.set_ylabel('early exercise premium in %')
         ax2.set_xlim(left=75, right=125)
         ax2.grid(True)
```

---

6. Since we do not assume any dividend payments (having an index in mind), there generally is no early exercise premium for call options (i.e., no incentive to exercise the option early).

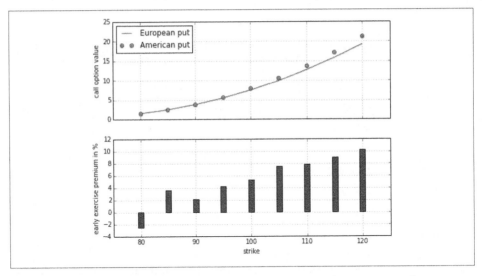

Figure 10-17. Comparison of European and LSM Monte Carlo estimator values

Risk Measures

In addition to valuation, *risk management* is another important application area of stochastic methods and simulation. This section illustrates the calculation/estimation of two of the most common risk measures applied today in the finance industry.

Value-at-Risk

Value-at-risk (VaR) is one of the most widely used risk measures, and a much debated one. Loved by practitioners for its intuitive appeal, it is widely discussed and criticized by many—mainly on theoretical grounds, with regard to its limited ability to capture what is called *tail risk* (more on this shortly). In words, VaR is a number denoted in currency units (e.g., USD, EUR, JPY) indicating a loss (of a portfolio, a single position, etc.) that is not exceeded with some confidence level (probability) over a given period of time.

Consider a stock position, worth 1 million USD today, that has a VaR of 50,000 USD at a confidence level of 99% over a time period of 30 days (one month). This VaR figure says that with a probability of 99% (i.e., in 99 out of 100 cases), the loss to be expected over a period of 30 days will *not exceed* 50,000 USD. However, it does not say anything about the size of the loss once a loss beyond 50,000 USD occurs—i.e., if the maximum loss is 100,000 or 500,000 USD what the probability of such a specific "higher than VaR loss" is. All it says is that there is a 1% probability that a loss of a *minimum of 50,000 USD or higher* will occur.

Assume again that we are in a Black-Scholes-Merton setup and consider the following parameterization and simulation of index levels at a future date $T = 30/365$ (i.e., we assume a period of 30 days):

```
In [69]: S0 = 100
         r = 0.05
         sigma = 0.25
         T = 30 / 365.
         I = 10000
         ST = S0 * np.exp((r - 0.5 * sigma ** 2) * T
                      + sigma * np.sqrt(T) * npr.standard_normal(I))
```

To estimate VaR figures, we need the simulated absolute profits and losses relative to the value of the position today in a sorted manner, i.e., from the severest loss to the largest profit:

```
In [70]: R_gbm = np.sort(ST - S0)
```

Figure 10-18 shows the histogram of the simulated absolute performance values:

```
In [71]: plt.hist(R_gbm, bins=50)
         plt.xlabel('absolute return')
         plt.ylabel('frequency')
         plt.grid(True)
```

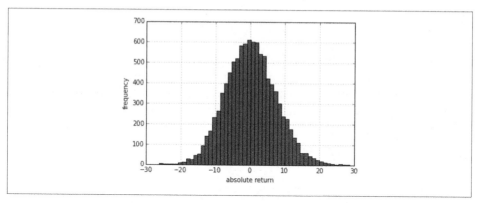

Figure 10-18. Absolute returns of geometric Brownian motion (30d)

Having the ndarray object with the sorted results, the function scoreatpercentile already does the trick. All we have to do is to define the percentiles (in percent values) in which we are interested. In the list object percs, 0.1 translates into a confidence level of 100% – 0.1% = 99.9%. The 30-day VaR given a confidence level of 99.9% in this case is 20.2 currency units, while it is 8.9 at the 90% confidence level:

```
In [72]: percs = [0.01, 0.1, 1., 2.5, 5.0, 10.0]
         var = scs.scoreatpercentile(R_gbm, percs)
         print "%16s %16s" % ('Confidence Level', 'Value-at-Risk')
         print 33 * "-"
```

```
        for pair in zip(percs, var):
            print "%16.2f %16.3f" % (100 - pair[0], -pair[1])

Out[72]: Confidence Level     Value-at-Risk
        ---------------------------------
                   99.99           26.072
                   99.90           20.175
                   99.00           15.753
                   97.50           13.265
                   95.00           11.298
                   90.00            8.942
```

As a second example, recall the jump diffusion setup from Merton, which we want to simulate dynamically:

```
In [73]: dt = 30. / 365 / M
        rj = lamb * (np.exp(mu + 0.5 * delta ** 2) - 1)
        S = np.zeros((M + 1, I))
        S[0] = S0
        sn1 = npr.standard_normal((M + 1, I))
        sn2 = npr.standard_normal((M + 1, I))
        poi = npr.poisson(lamb * dt, (M + 1, I))
        for t in range(1, M + 1, 1):
            S[t] = S[t - 1] * (np.exp((r - rj - 0.5 * sigma ** 2) * dt
                              + sigma * np.sqrt(dt) * sn1[t])
                              + (np.exp(mu + delta * sn2[t]) - 1)
                              * poi[t])
            S[t] = np.maximum(S[t], 0)

In [74]: R_jd = np.sort(S[-1] - S0)
```

In this case, with the jump component having a negative mean, we see something like a bimodal distribution for the simulated profits/losses in Figure 10-19. From a normal distribution point of view, we have a strongly pronounced left *fat tail*:

```
In [75]: plt.hist(R_jd, bins=50)
        plt.xlabel('absolute return')
        plt.ylabel('frequency')
        plt.grid(True)
```

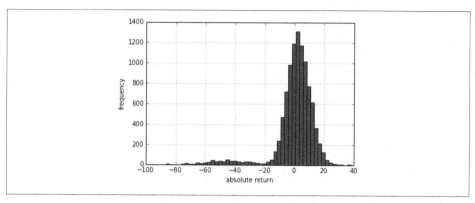

Figure 10-19. Absolute returns of jump diffusion (30d)

For this process and parameterization, the VaR over 30 days at the 90% level is almost identical, while it is more than *three times* as high at the 99.9% level as with the geometric Brownian motion (71.8 vs. 20.2 currency units):

```
In [76]: percs = [0.01, 0.1, 1., 2.5, 5.0, 10.0]
         var = scs.scoreatpercentile(R_jd, percs)
         print "%16s %16s" % ('Confidence Level', 'Value-at-Risk')
         print 33 * "-"
         for pair in zip(percs, var):
             print "%16.2f %16.3f" % (100 - pair[0], -pair[1])

Out[76]: Confidence Level     Value-at-Risk
         ---------------------------------
                    99.99            75.029
                    99.90            71.833
                    99.00            55.901
                    97.50            45.697
                    95.00            25.993
                    90.00             8.773
```

This illustrates the problem of capturing the tail risk so often encountered in financial markets by the standard VaR measure.

To further illustrate the point, we lastly show the VaR measures for both cases in direct comparison graphically. As Figure 10-20 reveals, the VaR measures behave completely differently given a range of typical confidence levels:

```
In [77]: percs = list(np.arange(0.0, 10.1, 0.1))
         gbm_var = scs.scoreatpercentile(R_gbm, percs)
         jd_var = scs.scoreatpercentile(R_jd, percs)

In [78]: plt.plot(percs, gbm_var, 'b', lw=1.5, label='GBM')
         plt.plot(percs, jd_var, 'r', lw=1.5, label='JD')
         plt.legend(loc=4)
         plt.xlabel('100 - confidence level [%]')
         plt.ylabel('value-at-risk')
```

```
plt.grid(True)
plt.ylim(ymax=0.0)
```

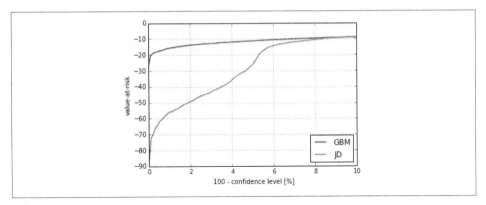

Figure 10-20. Value-at-risk for geometric Brownian motion and jump diffusion

Credit Value Adjustments

Other important risk measures are the credit value-at-risk (CVaR) and the credit value adjustment (CVA), which is derived from the CVaR. Roughly speaking, CVaR is a measure for the risk resulting from the possibility that a counterparty might not be able to honor its obligations—for example, if the counterparty goes bankrupt. In such a case there are two main assumptions to be made: *probability of default* and the (average) *loss level*.

To make it specific, consider again the benchmark setup of Black-Scholes-Merton with the following parameterization:

```
In [79]: S0 = 100.
         r = 0.05
         sigma = 0.2
         T = 1.
         I = 100000
         ST = S0 * np.exp((r - 0.5 * sigma ** 2) * T
                     + sigma * np.sqrt(T) * npr.standard_normal(I))
```

In the simplest case, one considers a fixed (average) loss level L and a fixed probability p for default (per year) of a counterparty:

```
In [80]: L = 0.5
```

```
In [81]: p = 0.01
```

Using the Poisson distribution, default scenarios are generated as follows, taking into account that a default can only occur once:

```
In [82]: D = npr.poisson(p * T, I)
         D = np.where(D > 1, 1, D)
```

Without default, the risk-neutral value of the future index level should be equal to the current value of the asset today (up to differences resulting from numerical errors):

```
In [83]: np.exp(-r * T) * 1 / I * np.sum(ST)

Out[83]: 99.981825216842921
```

The CVaR under our assumptions is calculated as follows:

```
In [84]: CVaR = np.exp(-r * T) * 1 / I * np.sum(L * D * ST)
         CVaR

Out[84]: 0.5152011134161355
```

Analogously, the present value of the asset, adjusted for the credit risk, is given as follows:

```
In [85]: S0_CVA = np.exp(-r * T) * 1 / I * np.sum((1 - L * D) * ST)
         S0_CVA

Out[85]: 99.466624103426781
```

This should be (roughly) the same as subtracting the CVaR value from the current asset value:

```
In [86]: S0_adj = S0 - CVaR
         S0_adj

Out[86]: 99.48479888658386
```

In this particular simulation example, we observe roughly 1,000 losses due to credit risk, which is to be expected given the assumed default probability of 1% and 100,000 simulated paths:

```
In [87]: np.count_nonzero(L * D * ST)

Out[87]: 1031
```

Figure 10-21 shows the complete frequency distribution of the losses due to a default. Of course, in the large majority of cases (i.e., in about 99,000 of the 100,000 cases) there is no loss to observe:

```
In [88]: plt.hist(L * D * ST, bins=50)
         plt.xlabel('loss')
         plt.ylabel('frequency')
         plt.grid(True)
         plt.ylim(ymax=175)
```

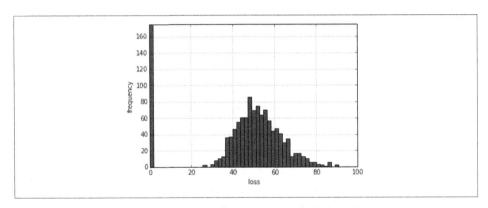

Figure 10-21. Losses due to risk-neutrally expected default (stock)

Consider now the case of a European call option. Its value is about 10.4 currency units at a strike of 100:

```
In [89]: K = 100.
         hT = np.maximum(ST - K, 0)
         C0 = np.exp(-r * T) * 1 / I * np.sum(hT)
         C0

Out[89]: 10.427336109660052
```

The CVaR is about 5 cents given the same assumptions with regard to probability of default and loss level:

```
In [90]: CVaR = np.exp(-r * T) * 1 / I * np.sum(L * D * hT)
         CVaR

Out[90]: 0.053822578452208093
```

Accordingly, the adjusted option value is roughly 5 cents lower:

```
In [91]: C0_CVA = np.exp(-r * T) * 1 / I * np.sum((1 - L * D) * hT)
         C0_CVA

Out[91]: 10.373513531207843
```

Compared to the case of a regular asset, the option case has somewhat different characteristics. We only see a little more than 500 losses due to a default, although we again have about 1,000 defaults. This results from the fact that the payoff of the option at maturity has a high probability of being zero:

```
In [92]: np.count_nonzero(L * D * hT)  # number of losses

Out[92]: 582

In [93]: np.count_nonzero(D)  # number of defaults

Out[93]: 1031

In [94]: I - np.count_nonzero(hT)  # zero payoff
```

```
Out[94]: 43995
```

Figure 10-22 shows that the CVaR for the option has a completely different frequency distribution compared to the regular asset case:

```
In [95]: plt.hist(L * D * hT, bins=50)
         plt.xlabel('loss')
         plt.ylabel('frequency')
         plt.grid(True)
         plt.ylim(ymax=350)
```

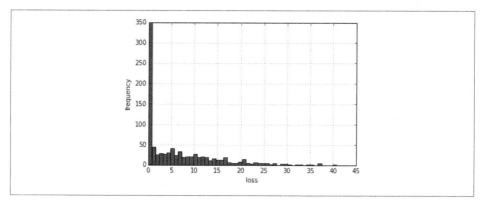

Figure 10-22. Losses due to risk-neutrally expected default (call option)

Conclusions

This chapter deals with methods and techniques important to the application of Monte Carlo simulation in finance. In particular, it shows how to *generate (pseudo)random numbers* based on different distribution laws. It proceeds with the *simulation of random variables and stochastic processes*, which is important in many financial areas. Two application areas are discussed in some depth in this chapter: *valuation of options* with European and American exercise and the *estimation of risk measures* like value-at-risk and credit value adjustments.

The chapter illustrates that Python in combination with NumPy is well suited to implementing even such computationally demanding tasks as the valuation of American options by Monte Carlo simulation. This is mainly due to the fact that the majority of functions and classes of NumPy are implemented in C, which leads to considerable speed advantages in general over pure Python code. A further benefit is the compactness and readability of the resulting code due to vectorized operations.

Further Reading

The original article introducing Monte Carlo simulation to finance is:

- Boyle, Phelim (1977): "Options: A Monte Carlo Approach." *Journal of Financial Economics*, Vol. 4, No. 4, pp. 322–338.

Other original papers cited in this chapter are (see also Chapter 16):

- Black, Fischer and Myron Scholes (1973): "The Pricing of Options and Corporate Liabilities." *Journal of Political Economy*, Vol. 81, No. 3, pp. 638–659.
- Cox, John, Jonathan Ingersoll and Stephen Ross (1985): "A Theory of the Term Structure of Interest Rates." *Econometrica*, Vol. 53, No. 2, pp. 385–407.
- Heston, Steven (1993): "A Closed-From Solution for Options with Stochastic Volatility with Applications to Bond and Currency Options." *The Review of Financial Studies*, Vol. 6, No. 2, 327–343.
- Merton, Robert (1973): "Theory of Rational Option Pricing." *Bell Journal of Economics and Management Science*, Vol. 4, pp. 141–183.
- Merton, Robert (1976): "Option Pricing When the Underlying Stock Returns Are Discontinuous." *Journal of Financial Economics*, Vol. 3, No. 3, pp. 125–144.

The books by Glassermann (2004) and Hilpisch (2015) cover all topics of this chapter in depth (however, the first one does not cover any technical implementation details):

- Glasserman, Paul (2004): *Monte Carlo Methods in Financial Engineering*. Springer, New York.
- Hilpisch, Yves (2015): *Derivatives Analytics with Python*. Wiley Finance, Chichester, England. *http://www.derivatives-analytics-with-python.com*.

It took until the turn of the century for an efficient method to value American options by Monte Carlo simulation to finally be published:

- Longstaff, Francis and Eduardo Schwartz (2001): "Valuing American Options by Simulation: A Simple Least Squares Approach." *Review of Financial Studies*, Vol. 14, No. 1, pp. 113–147.

A broad and in-depth treatment of credit risk is provided in:

- Duffie, Darrell and Kenneth Singleton (2003): *Credit Risk—Pricing, Measurement, and Management*. Princeton University Press, Princeton, NJ.

## CHAPTER 11

Statistics

I can prove anything by statistics except the truth.

— George Canning

Statistics is a vast field. The tools and results the field provides have become indispensible for finance. This also explains the popularity of domain-specific languages like R in the finance industry. The more elaborate and complex statistical models become, the more important it is to have available easy-to-use and high-performing computational solutions.

A single chapter in a book like this one cannot do justice to the richness and the broadness of the field of statistics. Therefore, the approach—as in many other chapters—is to focus on selected topics that seem of paramount importance or that provide a good starting point when it comes to the use of Python for the particular tasks at hand. The chapter has four focal points:

Normality tests

A large number of important financial models, like the mean-variance portfolio theory and the capital asset pricing model (CAPM), rest on the assumption that returns of securities are normally distributed; therefore, this chapter presents some approaches to test a given time series for normality of returns.

Portfolio theory

Modern portfolio theory (MPT) can be considered one of the biggest successes of statistics in finance; starting in the early 1950s with the work of pioneer Harry Markowitz, this theory began to replace people's reliance on judgment and experience with rigorous mathematical and statistical methods when it comes to the investment of money in financial markets. In that sense, it is maybe the first real quantitative approach in finance.

Principal component analysis

Principal component analysis (PCA) is quite a popular tool in finance, for example, when it comes to implementing equity investment strategies or analyzing the principal components that explain the movement in interest rates. Its major benefit is "complexity reduction," achieved by deriving a small set of linearly independent (noncorrelated, orthogonal) components from a potentially large set of maybe highly correlated time series components; we illustrate the application based on the German DAX index and the 30 stocks contained in that index.

Bayesian regression

On a fundamental level, Bayesian statistics introduces the notion of *beliefs* of agents and the *updating of beliefs* to statistics; when it comes to linear regression, for example, this might take on the form of having a statistical distribution for regression parameters instead of single point estimates (e.g., for the intercept and slope of the regression line). Nowadays, Bayesian methods are rather popular and important in finance, which is why we illustrate some (advanced) applications in this chapter.

Many aspects in this chapter relate to date and/or time information. Refer to Appendix C for an overview of handling such data with `Python`, `NumPy`, and `pandas`.

Normality Tests

The *normal distribution* can be considered the most important distribution in finance and one of the major statistical building blocks of financial theory. Among others, the following cornerstones of financial theory rest to a large extent on the normal distribution of stock market returns:

Portfolio theory

When stock returns are normally distributed, optimal portfolio choice can be cast into a setting where only the *mean return* and the *variance of the returns* (or the volatility) as well as the *covariances* between different stocks are relevant for an investment decision (i.e., an optimal portfolio composition).

Capital asset pricing model

Again, when stock returns are normally distributed, prices of single stocks can be elegantly expressed in relationship to a broad market index; the relationship is generally expressed by a measure for the comovement of a single stock with the market index called beta (β).

Efficient markets hypothesis

An *efficient* market is a market where prices reflect all available information, where "all" can be defined more narrowly or more widely (e.g., as in "all publicly available" information vs. including also "only privately available" information); if this hypothesis holds true, then stock prices fluctuate randomly and returns are normally distributed.

Option pricing theory

Brownian motion is *the* standard and benchmark model for the modeling of random stock (and other security) price movements; the famous Black-Scholes-Merton option pricing formula uses a geometric Brownian motion as the model for a stock's random fluctuations over time, leading to normally distributed returns.

This by far nonexhaustive list underpins the importance of the normality assumption in finance.

Benchmark Case

To set the stage for further analyses, we start with the geometric Brownian motion as one of the canonical stochastic processes used in financial modeling. The following can be said about the characteristics of paths from a geometric Brownian motion S:

Normal log returns

Log returns $\log \frac{S_t}{S_s} = \log S_t - \log S_s$ between two times $0 < s < t$ are normally distributed.

Log-normal values

At any time $t > 0$, the values S_t are log-normally distributed.

For what follows we need a number of Python libraries, including scipy.stats (*http://docs.scipy.org/doc/scipy/reference/stats.html*) and statsmodels.api (*http://statsmodels.sourceforge.net/stable/*):

```
In [1]: import numpy as np
        np.random.seed(1000)
        import scipy.stats as scs
        import statsmodels.api as sm
        import matplotlib as mpl
        import matplotlib.pyplot as plt
        %matplotlib inline
```

Let us define a function to generate Monte Carlo paths for the geometric Brownian motion (see also Chapter 10):

```
In [2]: def gen_paths(S0, r, sigma, T, M, I):
            ''' Generates Monte Carlo paths for geometric Brownian motion.

            Parameters
            ==========
            S0 : float
                initial stock/index value
            r : float
                constant short rate
            sigma : float
                constant volatility
            T : float
                final time horizon
```

```
M : int
    number of time steps/intervals
I : int
    number of paths to be simulated

Returns
=======
paths : ndarray, shape (M + 1, I)
    simulated paths given the parameters
'''
dt = float(T) / M
paths = np.zeros((M + 1, I), np.float64)
paths[0] = S0
for t in range(1, M + 1):
    rand = np.random.standard_normal(I)
    rand = (rand - rand.mean()) / rand.std()
    paths[t] = paths[t - 1] * np.exp((r - 0.5 * sigma ** 2) * dt +
                                      sigma * np.sqrt(dt) * rand)
return paths
```

The following is a possible parameterization for the Monte Carlo simulation, generating, in combination with the function gen_paths, 250,000 paths with 50 time steps each:

```
In [3]: S0 = 100.
        r = 0.05
        sigma = 0.2
        T = 1.0
        M = 50
        I = 250000
```

```
In [4]: paths = gen_paths(S0, r, sigma, T, M, I)
```

Figure 11-1 shows the first 10 simulated paths from the simulation:

```
In [5]: plt.plot(paths[:, :10])
        plt.grid(True)
        plt.xlabel('time steps')
        plt.ylabel('index level')
```

Our main interest is in the distribution of the log returns. The following code generates an ndarray object with all log returns:

```
In [6]: log_returns = np.log(paths[1:] / paths[0:-1])
```

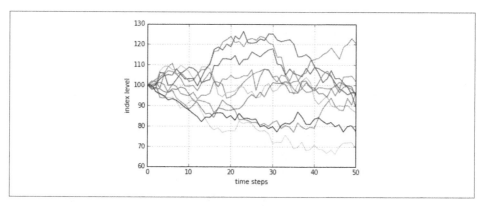

Figure 11-1. Ten simulated paths of geometric Brownian motion

Consider the very first simulated path over the 50 time steps:

```
In [7]: paths[:, 0].round(4)
```

```
Out[7]: array([ 100.    ,   97.821 ,   98.5573,  106.1546,  105.899 ,   99.8363,
                100.0145,  102.6589,  105.6643,  107.1107,  108.7943,  108.2449,
                106.4105,  101.0575,  102.0197,  102.6052,  109.6419,  109.5725,
                112.9766,  113.0225,  112.5476,  114.5585,  109.942 ,  112.6271,
                112.7502,  116.3453,  115.0443,  113.9586,  115.8831,  117.3705,
                117.9185,  110.5539,  109.9687,  104.9957,  108.0679,  105.7822,
                105.1585,  104.3304,  108.4387,  105.5963,  108.866 ,  108.3284,
                107.0077,  106.0034,  104.3964,  101.0637,   98.3776,   97.135 ,
                 95.4254,   96.4271,   96.3386])
```

A log-return series for a simulated path might then take on the form:

```
In [8]: log_returns[:, 0].round(4)
```

```
Out[8]: array([-0.022 ,  0.0075,  0.0743, -0.0024, -0.059 ,  0.0018,  0.0261,
                0.0289,  0.0136,  0.0156, -0.0051, -0.0171, -0.0516,  0.0095,
                0.0057,  0.0663, -0.0006,  0.0306,  0.0004, -0.0042,  0.0177,
               -0.0411,  0.0241,  0.0011,  0.0314, -0.0112, -0.0095,  0.0167,
                0.0128,  0.0047, -0.0645, -0.0053, -0.0463,  0.0288, -0.0214,
               -0.0059, -0.0079,  0.0386, -0.0266,  0.0305, -0.0049, -0.0123,
               -0.0094, -0.0153, -0.0324, -0.0269, -0.0127, -0.0178,  0.0104,
               -0.0009])
```

This is something one might experience in financial markets as well: days when you make a *positive return* on your investment and other days when you are *losing money* relative to your most recent wealth position.

The function `print_statistics` is a wrapper function for the `describe` function from the `scipy.stats` sublibrary. It mainly generates a more (human-)readable output for such statistics as the mean, the skewness, or the kurtosis of a given (historical or simulated) data set:

```
In [9]: def print_statistics(array):
            ''' Prints selected statistics.

            Parameters
            ==========
            array: ndarray
                object to generate statistics on
            '''
            sta = scs.describe(array)
            print "%14s %15s" % ('statistic', 'value')
            print 30 * "-"
            print "%14s %15.5f" % ('size', sta[0])
            print "%14s %15.5f" % ('min', sta[1][0])
            print "%14s %15.5f" % ('max', sta[1][1])
            print "%14s %15.5f" % ('mean', sta[2])
            print "%14s %15.5f" % ('std', np.sqrt(sta[3]))
            print "%14s %15.5f" % ('skew', sta[4])
            print "%14s %15.5f" % ('kurtosis', sta[5])
```

For example, the following shows the function in action, using a flattened version of the ndarray object containing the log returns. The method flatten returns a 1D array with all the data given in a multidimensional array:

```
In [10]: print_statistics(log_returns.flatten())
Out[10]:       statistic          value
         ----------------------------
              size   12500000.00000
               min         -0.15664
               max          0.15371
              mean          0.00060
               std          0.02828
              skew          0.00055
          kurtosis          0.00085
```

The data set in this case consists of 12,500,000 data points with the values mainly lying between +/- 0.15. We would expect annualized values of 0.05 for the mean return and 0.2 for the standard deviation (volatility). The annualized values of the data set come close to these values, if not matching them perfectly (multiply the mean value by 50 and the standard deviation by $\sqrt{50}$).

Figure 11-2 compares the frequency distribution of the simulated log returns with the probability density function (pdf) of the normal distribution given the parameterizations for r and sigma. The function used is norm.pdf from the scipy.stats sublibrary. There is obviously quite a good fit:

```
In [11]: plt.hist(log_returns.flatten(), bins=70, normed=True, label='frequency')
         plt.grid(True)
         plt.xlabel('log-return')
         plt.ylabel('frequency')
         x = np.linspace(plt.axis()[0], plt.axis()[1])
         plt.plot(x, scs.norm.pdf(x, loc=r / M, scale=sigma / np.sqrt(M)),
```

```
              'r', lw=2.0, label='pdf')
   plt.legend()
```

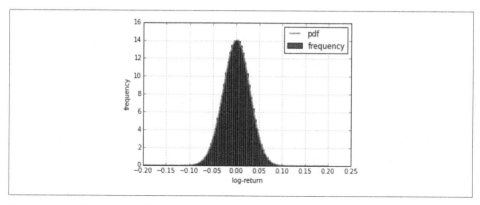

Figure 11-2. Histogram of log returns and normal density function

Comparing a frequency distribution (histogram) with a theoretical pdf is not the only way to graphically "test" for normality. So-called *quantile-quantile plots* (qq plots) are also well suited for this task. Here, sample quantile values are compared to theoretical quantile values. For normally distributed sample data sets, such a plot might look like Figure 11-3, with the absolute majority of the quantile values (dots) lying on a straight line:

```
In [12]: sm.qqplot(log_returns.flatten()[::500], line='s')
         plt.grid(True)
         plt.xlabel('theoretical quantiles')
         plt.ylabel('sample quantiles')
```

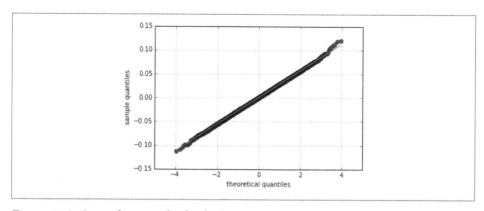

Figure 11-3. Quantile-quantile plot for log returns

However appealing the graphical approaches might be, they generally cannot replace more rigorous testing procedures. The function `normality_tests` combines three different statistical tests:

Skewness test (`skewtest`*)*
   This tests whether the skew of the sample data is "normal" (i.e., has a value close enough to zero).

Kurtosis test (`kurtosistest`*)*
   Similarly, this tests whether the kurtosis of the sample data is "normal" (again, close enough to zero).

Normality test (`normaltest`*)*
   This combines the other two test approaches to test for normality.

We define this function as follows:

```
In [13]: def normality_tests(arr):
             ''' Tests for normality distribution of given data set.

             Parameters
             ==========
             array: ndarray
                 object to generate statistics on
             '''
             print "Skew of data set  %14.3f" % scs.skew(arr)
             print "Skew test p-value %14.3f" % scs.skewtest(arr)[1]
             print "Kurt of data set  %14.3f" % scs.kurtosis(arr)
             print "Kurt test p-value %14.3f" % scs.kurtosistest(arr)[1]
             print "Norm test p-value %14.3f" % scs.normaltest(arr)[1]
```

The test values indicate that the log returns are indeed normally distributed—i.e., they show p-values of 0.05 or above:

```
In [14]: normality_tests(log_returns.flatten())

Out[14]: Skew of data set        0.001
         Skew test p-value       0.430
         Kurt of data set        0.001
         Kurt test p-value       0.541
         Norm test p-value       0.607
```

Finally, let us check whether the end-of-period values are indeed log-normally distributed. This boils down to a normality test as well, since we only have to transform the data by applying the log function to it (to then arrive at normally distributed data—or maybe not). Figure 11-4 plots both the log-normally distributed end-of-period values and the transformed ones ("log index level"):

```
In [15]: f, (ax1, ax2) = plt.subplots(1, 2, figsize=(9, 4))
         ax1.hist(paths[-1], bins=30)
         ax1.grid(True)
         ax1.set_xlabel('index level')
```

```
ax1.set_ylabel('frequency')
ax1.set_title('regular data')
ax2.hist(np.log(paths[-1]), bins=30)
ax2.grid(True)
ax2.set_xlabel('log index level')
ax2.set_title('log data')
```

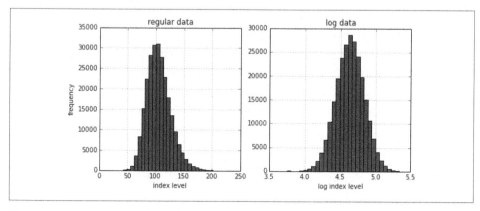

Figure 11-4. Histogram of simulated end-of-period index levels

The statistics for the data set show expected behavior—for example, a mean value close to 105 and a standard deviation (volatility) close to 20%:

```
In [16]: print_statistics(paths[-1])

Out[16]:     statistic            value
         ----------------------------
              size    250000.00000
               min        42.74870
               max       233.58435
              mean       105.12645
               std        21.23174
              skew         0.61116
          kurtosis         0.65182
```

The log index level values also have skew and kurtosis values close to zero:

```
In [17]: print_statistics(np.log(paths[-1]))

Out[17]:     statistic            value
         ----------------------------
              size    250000.00000
               min         3.75534
               max         5.45354
              mean         4.63517
               std         0.19998
              skew        -0.00092
          kurtosis        -0.00327
```

This data set also shows high p-values, providing strong support for the normal distribution hypothesis:

```
In [18]: normality_tests(np.log(paths[-1]))
```

```
Out[18]: Skew of data set            -0.001
         Skew test p-value            0.851
         Kurt of data set            -0.003
         Kurt test p-value            0.744
         Norm test p-value            0.931
```

Figure 11-5 compares again the frequency distribution with the pdf of the normal distribution, showing a pretty good fit (as now is, of course, to be expected):

```
In [19]: log_data = np.log(paths[-1])
         plt.hist(log_data, bins=70, normed=True, label='observed')
         plt.grid(True)
         plt.xlabel('index levels')
         plt.ylabel('frequency')
         x = np.linspace(plt.axis()[0], plt.axis()[1])
         plt.plot(x, scs.norm.pdf(x, log_data.mean(), log_data.std()),
                  'r', lw=2.0, label='pdf')
         plt.legend()
```

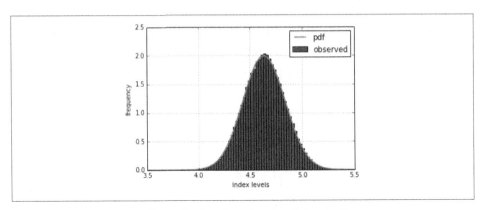

Figure 11-5. Histogram of log index levels and normal density function

Figure 11-6 also supports the hypothesis that the log index levels are normally distributed:

```
In [20]: sm.qqplot(log_data, line='s')
         plt.grid(True)
         plt.xlabel('theoretical quantiles')
         plt.ylabel('sample quantiles')
```

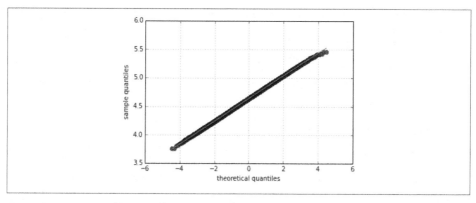

Figure 11-6. Quantile-quantile plot for log index levels

Normality

The normality assumption with regard to returns of securities is central to a number of important financial theories. Python provides efficient statistical and graphical means to test whether time series data is normally distributed or not.

Real-World Data

We are now pretty well equipped to attack real-world data and see how the normality assumption does beyond the financial laboratory. We are going to analyze four historical time series: two stock indices (the German DAX index and the American S&P 500 index) and two stocks (Yahoo! Inc. and Microsoft Inc.). The data management tool of choice is pandas (cf. Chapter 6), so we begin with a few imports:

```
In [21]: import pandas as pd
         import pandas.io.data as web
```

Here are the symbols for the time series we are interested in. The curious reader might of course replace these with any other symbol of interest:

```
In [22]: symbols = ['^GDAXI', '^GSPC', 'YHOO', 'MSFT']
```

The following reads only the Adj Close time series data into a single DataFrame object for all symbols:

```
In [23]: data = pd.DataFrame()
         for sym in symbols:
             data[sym] = web.DataReader(sym, data_source='yahoo',
                                        start='1/1/2006')['Adj Close']
         data = data.dropna()

In [24]: data.info()
```

```
Out[24]: <class 'pandas.core.frame.DataFrame'>
         DatetimeIndex: 2179 entries, 2006-01-03 00:00:00 to 2014-09-26 00:00:00
         Data columns (total 4 columns):
         ^GDAXI    2179 non-null float64
         ^GSPC     2179 non-null float64
         YHOO      2179 non-null float64
         MSFT      2179 non-null float64
         dtypes: float64(4)
```

The four time series start at rather different absolute values:

```
In [25]: data.head()

Out[25]:             ^GDAXI   ^GSPC   YHOO   MSFT
         Date
         2006-01-03  5460.68  1268.80  40.91  22.09
         2006-01-04  5523.62  1273.46  40.97  22.20
         2006-01-05  5516.53  1273.48  41.53  22.22
         2006-01-06  5536.32  1285.45  43.21  22.15
         2006-01-09  5537.11  1290.15  43.42  22.11
```

Figure 11-7 shows therefore the four time series in direct comparison, but normalized to a starting value of 100:

```
In [26]: (data / data.ix[0] * 100).plot(figsize=(8, 6))
```

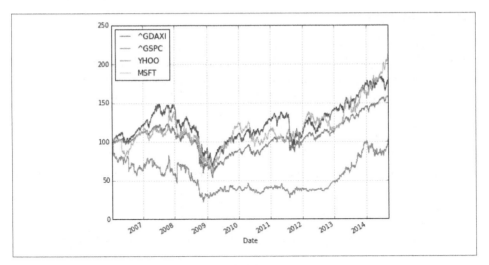

Figure 11-7. Evolution of stock and index levels over time

Calculating the log returns with pandas is a bit more convenient than with NumPy, since we can use the shift method:

```
In [27]: log_returns = np.log(data / data.shift(1))
         log_returns.head()
```

```
Out[27]:                  ^GDAXI      ^GSPC       YHOO        MSFT
         Date
         2006-01-03       NaN         NaN         NaN         NaN
         2006-01-04   0.011460   0.003666    0.001466    0.004967
         2006-01-05  -0.001284   0.000016    0.013576    0.000900
         2006-01-06   0.003581   0.009356    0.039656   -0.003155
         2006-01-09   0.000143   0.003650    0.004848   -0.001808
```

Figure 11-8 provides all log returns in the form of histograms. Although not easy to judge, one can guess that these frequency distributions might not be normal:

```
In [28]: log_returns.hist(bins=50, figsize=(9, 6))
```

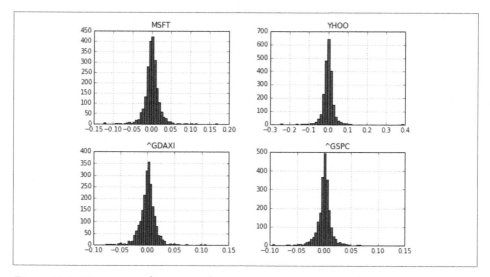

Figure 11-8. Histogram of respective log returns

As a next step, consider the different statistics for the time series data sets. The kurtosis values seem to be especially far from normal for all four data sets:

```
In [29]: for sym in symbols:
             print "\nResults for symbol %s" % sym
             print 30 * "-"
             log_data = np.array(log_returns[sym].dropna())
             print_statistics(log_data)

Out[29]: Results for symbol ^GDAXI
         ------------------------------
             statistic          value
         ------------------------------
                  size     2178.00000
                   min       -0.07739
                   max        0.10797
                  mean        0.00025
                   std        0.01462
```

```
        skew              0.02573
    kurtosis              6.52461

Results for symbol ^GSPC
- - - - - - - - - - - - - - - - - - - - - - - - - - -
    statistic               value
- - - - - - - - - - - - - - - - - - - - - - - - - - -
        size         2178.00000
         min           -0.09470
         max            0.10957
        mean            0.00020
         std            0.01360
        skew           -0.32017
    kurtosis           10.05425

Results for symbol YHOO
- - - - - - - - - - - - - - - - - - - - - - - - - - -
    statistic               value
- - - - - - - - - - - - - - - - - - - - - - - - - - -
        size         2178.00000
         min           -0.24636
         max            0.39182
        mean           -0.00000
         std            0.02620
        skew            0.56530
    kurtosis           31.98659

Results for symbol MSFT
- - - - - - - - - - - - - - - - - - - - - - - - - - -
    statistic               value
- - - - - - - - - - - - - - - - - - - - - - - - - - -
        size         2178.00000
         min           -0.12476
         max            0.17039
        mean            0.00034
         std            0.01792
        skew            0.04262
    kurtosis           10.18038
```

We will inspect the data of two symbols via a qq plot. Figure 11-9 shows the qq plot for the S&P 500. Obviously, the sample quantile values do not lie on a straight line, indicating "nonnormality." On the left and right sides there are many values that lie well below the line and well above the line, respectively. In other words, the time series data exhibits *fat tails*. This term refers to a (frequency) distribution where negative and positive outliers are observed far more often than a normal distribution would imply. The code to generate this plot is as follows:

```
In [30]: sm.qqplot(log_returns['^GSPC'].dropna(), line='s')
         plt.grid(True)
         plt.xlabel('theoretical quantiles')
         plt.ylabel('sample quantiles')
```

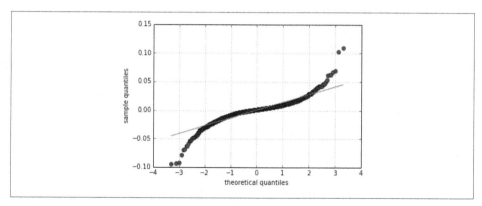

Figure 11-9. Quantile-quantile plot for S&P 500 log returns

The same conclusions can be drawn from Figure 11-10, presenting the data for the Microsoft Inc. stock. There also seems to be strong evidence for a fat-tailed distribution:

```
In [31]: sm.qqplot(log_returns['MSFT'].dropna(), line='s')
         plt.grid(True)
         plt.xlabel('theoretical quantiles')
         plt.ylabel('sample quantiles')
```

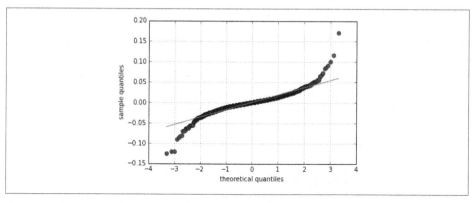

Figure 11-10. Quantile-quantile plot for Microsoft log returns

All this leads us finally to the formal normality tests:

```
In [32]: for sym in symbols:
             print "\nResults for symbol %s" % sym
             print 32 * "-"
             log_data = np.array(log_returns[sym].dropna())
             normality_tests(log_data)

Out[32]: Results for symbol ^GDAXI
         --------------------------------
```

```
Skew of data set          0.026
Skew test p-value         0.623
Kurt of data set          6.525
Kurt test p-value         0.000
Norm test p-value         0.000

Results for symbol ^GSPC
- - - - - - - - - - - - - - - - - - - - - - - - - - - - - -
Skew of data set         -0.320
Skew test p-value         0.000
Kurt of data set         10.054
Kurt test p-value         0.000
Norm test p-value         0.000

Results for symbol YHOO
- - - - - - - - - - - - - - - - - - - - - - - - - - - - - -
Skew of data set          0.565
Skew test p-value         0.000
Kurt of data set         31.987
Kurt test p-value         0.000
Norm test p-value         0.000

Results for symbol MSFT
- - - - - - - - - - - - - - - - - - - - - - - - - - - - - -
Skew of data set          0.043
Skew test p-value         0.415
Kurt of data set         10.180
Kurt test p-value         0.000
Norm test p-value         0.000
```

Throughout, the p-values of the different tests are all zero, *strongly rejecting the test hypothesis* that the different sample data sets are normally distributed. This shows that the normal assumption for stock market returns—as, for example, embodied in the geometric Brownian motion model—cannot be justified in general and that one might have to use richer models generating fat tails (e.g., jump diffusion models or models with stochastic volatility).

Portfolio Optimization

Modern or mean-variance portfolio theory (MPT) is a major cornerstone of financial theory. Based on this theoretical breakthrough the Nobel Prize in Economics was awarded to its inventor, Harry Markowitz, in 1990. Although formulated in the 1950s,[1] it is still a theory taught to finance students and applied in practice today (often with some minor or major modifications). This section illustrates the fundamental principles of the theory.

---

1. Cf. Markowitz, Harry (1952): "Portfolio Selection." *Journal of Finance*, Vol. 7, 77-91.

Chapter 5 in the book by Copeland, Weston, and Shastri (2005) provides a good introduction to the formal topics associated with MPT. As pointed out previously, the assumption of normally distributed returns is fundamental to the theory:

> By looking only at mean and variance, we are necessarily assuming that no other statistics are necessary to describe the distribution of end-of-period wealth. Unless investors have a special type of utility function (quadratic utility function), it is necessary to assume that returns have a normal distribution, which can be completely described by mean and variance.

The Data

Let us begin our Python session by importing a couple of by now well-known libraries:

```
In [33]: import numpy as np
         import pandas as pd
         import pandas.io.data as web
         import matplotlib.pyplot as plt
         %matplotlib inline
```

We pick five different assets for the analysis: American tech stocks Apple Inc., Yahoo! Inc., and Microsoft Inc., as well as German Deutsche Bank AG and gold as a commodity via an exchange-traded fund (ETF). The basic idea of MPT is *diversification* to achieve a minimal portfolio risk or maximal portfolio returns given a certain level of risk. One would expect such results for the right combination of a large enough number of assets and a certain diversity in the assets. However, to convey the basic ideas and to show typical effects, these five assets shall suffice:

```
In [34]: symbols = ['AAPL', 'MSFT', 'YHOO', 'DB', 'GLD']
         noa = len(symbols)
```

Using the DataReader function of pandas (cf. Chapter 6) makes getting the time series data rather efficient. We are only interested, as in the previous example, in the Close prices of each stock:

```
In [35]: data = pd.DataFrame()
         for sym in symbols:
             data[sym] = web.DataReader(sym, data_source='yahoo',
                                        end='2014-09-12')['Adj Close']
         data.columns = symbols
```

Figure 11-11 shows the time series data in normalized fashion graphically:

```
In [36]: (data / data.ix[0] * 100).plot(figsize=(8, 5))
```

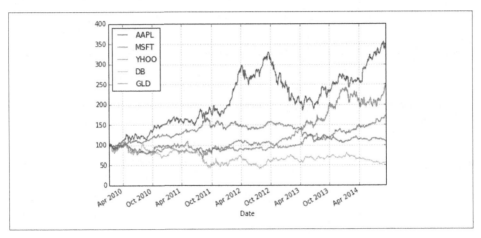

Figure 11-11. Stock prices over time

Mean-variance refers to the mean and variance of the (log) returns of the different securities, which are calculated as follows:

```
In [37]: rets = np.log(data / data.shift(1))
```

Over the period of the time series data, we see significant differences in the *annualized performance*. We use a factor of 252 trading days to annualize the daily returns:

```
In [38]: rets.mean() * 252

Out[38]: AAPL     0.266036
         MSFT     0.114476
         YHOO     0.196165
         DB      -0.125170
         GLD      0.016054
         dtype: float64
```

The *covariance matrix* for the assets to be invested in is the central piece of the whole portfolio selection process. pandas has a built-in method to generate the covariance matrix:

```
In [39]: rets.cov() * 252

Out[39]:           AAPL      MSFT      YHOO        DB       GLD
         AAPL  0.072813  0.020426  0.023254  0.041044  0.005234
         MSFT  0.020426  0.049384  0.024247  0.046100  0.002105
         YHOO  0.023254  0.024247  0.093349  0.051528 -0.000864
         DB    0.041044  0.046100  0.051528  0.177477  0.008775
         GLD   0.005234  0.002105 -0.000864  0.008775  0.032406
```

The Basic Theory

"In what follows, we assume that an investor is not allowed to set up short positions in a security. Only long positions are allowed, which means that 100% of the investor's wealth has to be divided among the available assets in such a way that all positions are long (positive) *and* that the positions add up to 100%. Given the five securities, you could for example invest equal amounts into every security (i.e., 20% of your wealth in each). The following code generates five random numbers between 0 and 1 and then normalizes the values such that the sum of all values equals 1:

```
In [40]: weights = np.random.random(noa)
         weights /= np.sum(weights)

In [41]: weights

Out[41]: array([ 0.0346395 ,  0.02726489,  0.2868883 ,  0.10396806,  0.54723926])
```

You can now check that the asset weights indeed add up to 1; i.e., $\Sigma_I w_i = 1$, where I is the number of assets and $w_i \geq 0$ is the weight of asset i. Equation 11-1 provides the formula for the *expected portfolio return* given the weights for the single securities. This is *expected* portfolio return in the sense that historical mean performance is assumed to be the best estimator for future (expected) performance. Here, the r_i are the state-dependent future returns (vector with return values assumed to be normally distributed) and μ_i is the expected return for security i. Finally, w^T is the transpose of the weights vector and μ is the vector of the expected security returns.

Equation 11-1. General formula for expected portfolio return

$$
\begin{aligned}
\mu_p &= \mathbf{E}\left(\sum_I w_i r_i\right) \\
&= \sum_I w_i \mathbf{E}(r_i) \\
&= \sum_I w_i \mu_i \\
&= w^T \mu
\end{aligned}
$$

Translated into Python this boils down to the following line of code, where we multiply again by 252 to get annualized return values:

```
In [42]: np.sum(rets.mean() * weights) * 252
         # expected portfolio return

Out[42]: 0.064385749262353215
```

The second object of choice in MPT is the *expected portfolio variance*. The covariance between two securities is defined by $\sigma_{ij} = \sigma_{ji} = \mathbf{E}(r_i - \mu_i)(r_j - \mu_j)$. The variance of a security is the special case of the covariance with itself: $\sigma_i^2 = \mathbf{E}\big((r_i - \mu_i)^2\big)$. Equation 11-2 provides the covariance matrix for a portfolio of securities (assuming an equal weight of 1 for every security).

Equation 11-2. Portfolio covariance matrix

$$\Sigma = \begin{bmatrix} \sigma_1^2 & \sigma_{12} & \cdots & \sigma_{1I} \\ \sigma_{21} & \sigma_2^2 & \cdots & \sigma_{2I} \\ \vdots & \vdots & \ddots & \vdots \\ \sigma_{I1} & \sigma_{I2} & \cdots & \sigma_I^2 \end{bmatrix}$$

Equipped with the portfolio covariance matrix, Equation 11-3 then provides the formula for the expected portfolio variance.

Equation 11-3. General formula for expected portfolio variance

$$\begin{aligned} \sigma_p^2 &= \mathbf{E}\left((r-\mu)^2\right) \\ &= \sum_{i\in I}\sum_{j\in I} w_i w_j \sigma_{ij} \\ &= w^T \Sigma w \end{aligned}$$

In Python this all again boils down to a single line of code, making heavy use of NumPy's vectorization capabilities. The dot function gives the dot product of two vectors/matrices. The T or transpose method gives the transpose of a vector or matrix:

```
In [43]: np.dot(weights.T, np.dot(rets.cov() * 252, weights))
         # expected portfolio variance

Out[43]: 0.024929484097150213
```

The (expected) portfolio standard deviation or volatility $\sigma_p = \sqrt{\sigma_p^2}$ is then only one square root away:

```
In [44]: np.sqrt(np.dot(weights.T, np.dot(rets.cov() * 252, weights)))
         # expected portfolio standard deviation/volatility

Out[44]: 0.15789073467797346
```

Language
The MPT example shows again how efficient it is with Python to translate mathematical concepts, like portfolio return or portfolio variance, into executable, vectorized code (an argument made in Chapter 1).

This mainly completes the tool set for mean-variance portfolio selection. Of paramount interest to investors is what risk-return profiles are possible for a given set of securities, and their statistical characteristics. To this end, we implement a Monte Carlo simulation (cf. Chapter 10) to generate random portfolio weight vectors on a larger scale. For every simulated allocation, we record the resulting expected portfolio return and variance:

```
In [45]: prets = []
         pvols = []
         for p in range (2500):
             weights = np.random.random(noa)
             weights /= np.sum(weights)
             prets.append(np.sum(rets.mean() * weights) * 252)
             pvols.append(np.sqrt(np.dot(weights.T,
                                  np.dot(rets.cov() * 252, weights))))
         prets = np.array(prets)
         pvols = np.array(pvols)
```

Figure 11-12 illustrates the results of the Monte Carlo simulation. In addition it provides results for the so-called Sharpe ratio, defined as $SR \equiv \frac{\mu_p - r_f}{\sigma_p}$ (i.e., the expected excess return of the portfolio) over the risk-free short rate r_f divided by the expected standard deviation of the portfolio. For simplicity, we assume $r_f = 0$:

```
In [46]: plt.figure(figsize=(8, 4))
         plt.scatter(pvols, prets, c=prets / pvols, marker='o')
         plt.grid(True)
         plt.xlabel('expected volatility')
         plt.ylabel('expected return')
         plt.colorbar(label='Sharpe ratio')
```

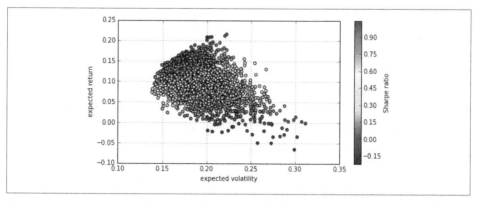

Figure 11-12. Expected return and volatility for different/random portfolio weights

It is clear by inspection of Figure 11-12 that not all weight distributions perform well when measured in terms of mean and variance. For example, for a fixed risk level of, say, 20%, there are multiple portfolios that all show different returns. As an investor one is generally interested in the maximum return given a fixed risk level or the minimum risk given a fixed return expectation. This set of portfolios then makes up the so-called *efficient frontier*. This is what we derive later in the section.

Portfolio Optimizations

To make our lives a bit easier, first we have a convenience function giving back the major portfolio statistics for an input weights vector/array:

```
In [47]: def statistics(weights):
             ''' Returns portfolio statistics.

             Parameters
             ==========
             weights : array-like
                 weights for different securities in portfolio

             Returns
             =======
             pret : float
                 expected portfolio return
             pvol : float
                 expected portfolio volatility
             pret / pvol : float
                 Sharpe ratio for rf=0
             '''
             weights = np.array(weights)
             pret = np.sum(rets.mean() * weights) * 252
             pvol = np.sqrt(np.dot(weights.T, np.dot(rets.cov() * 252, weights)))
             return np.array([pret, pvol, pret / pvol])
```

The derivation of the optimal portfolios is a constrained optimization problem for which we use the function `minimize` from the `scipy.optimize` sublibrary (cf. Chapter 9):

```
In [48]: import scipy.optimize as sco
```

The minimization function `minimize` is quite general and allows for (in)equality constraints and bounds for the parameters. Let us start with the *maximization of the Sharpe ratio*. Formally, we minimize the negative value of the Sharpe ratio:

```
In [49]: def min_func_sharpe(weights):
             return -statistics(weights)[2]
```

The constraint is that all parameters (weights) add up to 1. This can be formulated as follows using the conventions of the `minimize` function (cf. the documentation for this function (*http://bit.ly/using_minimize*)).[2]

---

2. An alternative to `np.sum(x) - 1` would be to write `np.sum(x) == 1` taking into account that with `Python` the Boolean `True` value equals 1 and the `False` value equals 0.

```
In [50]: cons = ({'type': 'eq', 'fun': lambda x:  np.sum(x) - 1})
```

We also bound the parameter values (weights) to be within 0 and 1. These values are provided to the minimization function as a tuple of tuples in this case:

```
In [51]: bnds = tuple((0, 1) for x in range(noa))
```

The only input that is missing for a call of the optimization function is a starting parameter list (initial guesses for the weights). We simply use an equal distribution:

```
In [52]: noa * [1. / noa,]

Out[52]: [0.2, 0.2, 0.2, 0.2, 0.2]
```

Calling the function returns not only optimal parameter values, but much more. We store the results in an object we call opts:

```
In [53]: %%time
         opts = sco.minimize(min_func_sharpe, noa * [1. / noa,], method='SLSQP',
                             bounds=bnds, constraints=cons)

Out[53]: CPU times: user 52 ms, sys: 0 ns, total: 52 ms
         Wall time: 50.3 ms
```

Here are the results:

```
In [54]: opts

Out[54]:    status: 0
           success: True
              njev: 6
              nfev: 42
               fun: -1.0597540702789927
                 x: array([  6.59141408e-01,   8.82635668e-02,   2.52595026e-01,
                 8.34564622e-17,  -8.91214186e-17])
           message: 'Optimization terminated successfully.'
               jac: array([  3.27527523e-05,  -1.61930919e-04,  -2.88933516e-05,
                 1.51561590e+00,   1.24186277e-03,   0.00000000e+00])
               nit: 6
```

Our main interest lies in getting the optimal portfolio composition. To this end, we access the results object by providing the key of interest—i.e., x in our case. The optimization yields a portfolio that only consists of three out of the five assets:

```
In [55]: opts['x'].round(3)

Out[55]: array([ 0.659,  0.088,  0.253,  0.    , -0.    ])
```

Using the portfolio weights from the optimization, the following statistics emerge:

```
In [56]: statistics(opts['x']).round(3)

Out[56]: array([ 0.235,  0.222,  1.06 ])
```

The expected return is about 23.5%, the expected volatility is about 22.2%, and the resulting optimal Sharpe ratio is 1.06.

Next, let us minimize the variance of the portfolio. This is the same as minimizing the volatility, but we will define a function to minimize the variance:

```
In [57]: def min_func_variance(weights):
             return statistics(weights)[1] ** 2
```

Everything else can remain the same for the call of the `minimize` function:

```
In [58]: optv = sco.minimize(min_func_variance, noa * [1. / noa,],
                             method='SLSQP', bounds=bnds,
                             constraints=cons)
```

```
In [59]: optv
```

```
Out[59]:   status: 0
          success: True
            njev: 9
            nfev: 64
             fun: 0.018286019968366075
               x: array([ 1.07591814e-01,   2.49124471e-01,   1.09219925e-01,
                  1.01101853e-17,   5.34063791e-01])
         message: 'Optimization terminated successfully.'
             jac: array([ 0.03636634,  0.03643877,  0.03613905,  0.05222051,
                  0.03676446,  0.        ])
             nit: 9
```

This time a fourth asset is added to the portfolio. This portfolio mix leads to the *absolute minimum variance portfolio*:

```
In [60]: optv['x'].round(3)
```

```
Out[60]: array([ 0.108,  0.249,  0.109,  0.   ,  0.534])
```

For the expected return, volatility, and Sharpe ratio, we get:

```
In [61]: statistics(optv['x']).round(3)
```

```
Out[61]: array([ 0.087,  0.135,  0.644])
```

Efficient Frontier

The derivation of all optimal portfolios—i.e., all portfolios with minimum volatility for a given target return level (or all portfolios with maximum return for a given risk level)—is similar to the previous optimizations. The only difference is that we have to iterate over multiple starting conditions. The approach we take is that we fix a target return level and derive for each such level those portfolio weights that lead to the minimum volatility value. For the optimization, this leads to two conditions: one for the target return level `tret` and one for the sum of the portfolio weights as before. The boundary values for each parameter stay the same:

```
In [62]: cons = ({'type': 'eq', 'fun': lambda x:  statistics(x)[0] - tret},
                 {'type': 'eq', 'fun': lambda x:  np.sum(x) - 1})
         bnds = tuple((0, 1) for x in weights)
```

For clarity, we define a dedicated function `min_func` for use in the minimization procedure. It merely returns the volatility value from the `statistics` function:

```
In [63]: def min_func_port(weights):
             return statistics(weights)[1]
```

When iterating over different target return levels (`trets`), one condition for the minimization changes. That is why the conditions dictionary is updated during every loop:

```
In [64]: %%time
         trets = np.linspace(0.0, 0.25, 50)
         tvols = []
         for tret in trets:
             cons = ({'type': 'eq', 'fun': lambda x:  statistics(x)[0] - tret},
                     {'type': 'eq', 'fun': lambda x:  np.sum(x) - 1})
             res = sco.minimize(min_func_port, noa * [1. / noa,], method='SLSQP',
                              bounds=bnds, constraints=cons)
             tvols.append(res['fun'])
         tvols = np.array(tvols)

Out[64]: CPU times: user 4.35 s, sys: 4 ms, total: 4.36 s
         Wall time: 4.36 s
```

Figure 11-13 shows the optimization results. Crosses indicate the optimal portfolios given a certain target return; the dots are, as before, the random portfolios. In addition, the figure shows two larger stars: one for the minimum volatility/variance portfolio (the leftmost portfolio) and one for the portfolio with the maximum Sharpe ratio:

```
In [65]: plt.figure(figsize=(8, 4))
         plt.scatter(pvols, prets,
                     c=prets / pvols, marker='o')
                     # random portfolio composition
         plt.scatter(tvols, trets,
                     c=trets / tvols, marker='x')
                     # efficient frontier
         plt.plot(statistics(opts['x'])[1], statistics(opts['x'])[0],
                 'r*', markersize=15.0)
                     # portfolio with highest Sharpe ratio
         plt.plot(statistics(optv['x'])[1], statistics(optv['x'])[0],
                 'y*', markersize=15.0)
                     # minimum variance portfolio
         plt.grid(True)
         plt.xlabel('expected volatility')
         plt.ylabel('expected return')
         plt.colorbar(label='Sharpe ratio')
```

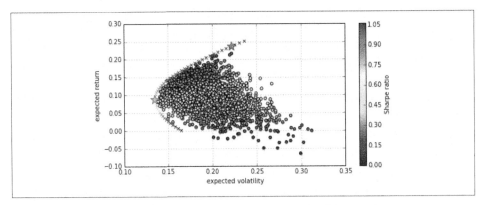

Figure 11-13. Minimum risk portfolios for given return level (crosses)

The *efficient frontier* is comprised of all optimal portfolios with a higher return than the absolute minimum variance portfolio. These portfolios dominate all other portfolios in terms of expected returns given a certain risk level.

Capital Market Line

In addition to risky securities like stocks or commodities (such as gold), there is in general one universal, riskless investment opportunity available: *cash* or *cash accounts*. In an idealized world, money held in a cash account with a large bank can be considered riskless (e.g., through public deposit insurance schemes). The downside is that such a riskless investment generally yields only a small return, sometimes close to zero.

However, taking into account such a riskless asset enhances the efficient investment opportunity set for investors considerably. The basic idea is that investors first determine an efficient portfolio of risky assets and then add the riskless asset to the mix. By adjusting the proportion of the investor's wealth to be invested in the riskless asset it is possible to achieve any risk-return profile that lies on the straight line (in the risk-return space) between the riskless asset and the efficient portfolio.

Which efficient portfolio (out of the many options) is to be taken to invest in optimal fashion? It is the one portfolio where the tangent line of the efficient frontier goes exactly through the risk-return point of the riskless portfolio. For example, consider a riskless interest rate of $r_f = 0.01$. We look for that portfolio on the efficient frontier for which the tangent goes through the point $(\sigma_f, r_f) = (0, 0.01)$ in risk-return space.

For the calculations to follow, we need a functional approximation and the first derivative for the efficient frontier. We use cubic splines interpolation to this end (cf. Chapter 9):

```
In [66]: import scipy.interpolate as sci
```

For the spline interpolation, we only use the portfolios from the efficient frontier. The following code selects exactly these portfolios from our previously used sets `tvols` and `trets`:

```
In [67]: ind = np.argmin(tvols)
         evols = tvols[ind:]
         erets = trets[ind:]
```

The new `ndarray` objects `evols` and `erets` are used for the interpolation:

```
In [68]: tck = sci.splrep(evols, erets)
```

Via this numerical route we end up being able to define a continuously differentiable function `f(x)` for the efficient frontier and the respective first derivative function `df(x)`:

```
In [69]: def f(x):
             ''' Efficient frontier function (splines approximation). '''
             return sci.splev(x, tck, der=0)
         def df(x):
             ''' First derivative of efficient frontier function. '''
             return sci.splev(x, tck, der=1)
```

What we are looking for is a function $t(x) = a + b \cdot x$ describing the line that passes through the riskless asset in risk-return space and that is tangent to the efficient frontier. Equation 11-4 describes all three conditions that the function $t(x)$ has to satisfy.

Equation 11-4. Mathematical conditions for capital market line

$$
\begin{aligned}
t(x) &= a + b \cdot x \\
t(0) &= r_f \qquad &\Longleftrightarrow \qquad a &= r_f \\
t(x) &= f(x) \qquad &\Longleftrightarrow \qquad a + b \cdot x &= f(x) \\
t'(x) &= f'(x) \qquad &\Longleftrightarrow \qquad b &= f'(x)
\end{aligned}
$$

Since we do not have a closed formula for the efficient frontier or the first derivative of it, we have to solve the system of equations in Equation 11-4 numerically. To this end, we define a `Python` function that returns the values of all three equations given the parameter set $p = (a,b,x)$:

```
In [70]: def equations(p, rf=0.01):
             eq1 = rf - p[0]
             eq2 = rf + p[1] * p[2] - f(p[2])
             eq3 = p[1] - df(p[2])
             return eq1, eq2, eq3
```

The function `fsolve` from `scipy.optimize` is capable of solving such a system of equations. We provide an initial parameterization in addition to the function `equations`. Note that success or failure of the optimization might depend on the initial parameterization, which therefore has to be chosen carefully—generally by a combination of educated guesses with trial and error:

```
In [71]: opt = sco.fsolve(equations, [0.01, 0.5, 0.15])
```

The numerical optimization yields the following values. As desired, we have $a = r_f = 0.01$:

```
In [72]: opt
Out[72]: array([ 0.01       ,  1.01498858,  0.22580367])
```

The three equations are also, as desired, zero:

```
In [73]: np.round(equations(opt), 6)
Out[73]: array([ 0., -0., -0.])
```

Figure 11-14 presents the results graphically: the star represents the optimal portfolio from the efficient frontier where the tangent line passes through the riskless asset point $(0, r_f = 0.01)$. The optimal portfolio has an expected volatility of 20.5% and an expected return of 17.6%. The plot is generated with the following code:

```
In [74]: plt.figure(figsize=(8, 4))
         plt.scatter(pvols, prets,
                     c=(prets - 0.01) / pvols, marker='o')
                     # random portfolio composition
         plt.plot(evols, erets, 'g', lw=4.0)
                     # efficient frontier
         cx = np.linspace(0.0, 0.3)
         plt.plot(cx, opt[0] + opt[1] * cx, lw=1.5)
                     # capital market line
         plt.plot(opt[2], f(opt[2]), 'r*', markersize=15.0)
         plt.grid(True)
         plt.axhline(0, color='k', ls='--', lw=2.0)
         plt.axvline(0, color='k', ls='--', lw=2.0)
         plt.xlabel('expected volatility')
         plt.ylabel('expected return')
         plt.colorbar(label='Sharpe ratio')
```

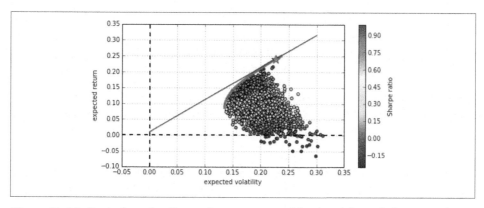

Figure 11-14. Capital market line and tangency portfolio (star) for risk-free rate of 1%

The portfolio weights of the optimal (tangent) portfolio are as follows. Only three of the five assets are in the mix:

```
In [75]: cons = ({'type': 'eq', 'fun': lambda x:  statistics(x)[0] - f(opt[2])},
                  {'type': 'eq', 'fun': lambda x:  np.sum(x) - 1})
         res = sco.minimize(min_func_port, noa * [1. / noa,], method='SLSQP',
                            bounds=bnds, constraints=cons)

In [76]: res['x'].round(3)

Out[76]: array([ 0.684,  0.059,  0.257, -0.   ,  0.   ])
```

Principal Component Analysis

Principal component analysis (PCA) has become a popular tool in finance. Wikipedia defines the technique as follows:

> Principal component analysis (PCA) is a statistical procedure that uses orthogonal transformation to convert a set of observations of possibly correlated variables into a set of values of linearly uncorrelated variables called principal components. The number of principal components is less than or equal to the number of original variables. This transformation is defined in such a way that the first principal component has the largest possible variance (that is, accounts for as much of the variability in the data as possible), and each succeeding component in turn has the highest variance possible under the constraint that it is orthogonal to (i.e., uncorrelated with) the preceding components.

Consider, for example, a stock index like the German DAX index, composed of 30 different stocks. The stock price movements of all stocks taken together determine the movement in the index (via some well-documented formula). In addition, the stock price movements of the single stocks are generally correlated, for example, due to general economic conditions or certain developments in certain sectors.

For statistical applications, it is generally quite hard to use 30 correlated factors to explain the movements of a stock index. This is where PCA comes into play. It derives single, uncorrelated *components* that are "well suited" to explain the movements in the stock index. One can think of these components as linear combinations (i.e., portfolios) of selected stocks from the index. Instead of working with 30 correlated index constituents, one can then work with maybe 5, 3, or even only 1 *principal component*.

The example of this section illustrates the use of PCA in such a context. We retrieve data for both the German DAX index and all stocks that make up the index. We then use PCA to derive principal components, which we use to construct what we call a pca_index.

First, some imports. In particular, we use the KernelPCA function of the scikit-learn machine learning library (cf. the documentation for KernelPCA (*http://bit.ly/kernelpca*)):

```
In [1]: import numpy as np
        import pandas as pd
        import pandas.io.data as web
        from sklearn.decomposition import KernelPCA
```

The DAX Index and Its 30 Stocks

The following list object contains the 30 symbols for the stocks contained in the German DAX index, as well as the symbol for the index itself:

```
In [2]: symbols = ['ADS.DE', 'ALV.DE', 'BAS.DE', 'BAYN.DE', 'BEI.DE',
                   'BMW.DE', 'CBK.DE', 'CON.DE', 'DAI.DE', 'DB1.DE',
                   'DBK.DE', 'DPW.DE', 'DTE.DE', 'EOAN.DE', 'FME.DE',
                   'FRE.DE', 'HEI.DE', 'HEN3.DE', 'IFX.DE', 'LHA.DE',
                   'LIN.DE', 'LXS.DE', 'MRK.DE', 'MUV2.DE', 'RWE.DE',
                   'SAP.DE', 'SDF.DE', 'SIE.DE', 'TKA.DE', 'VOW3.DE',
                   '^GDAXI']
```

We work only with the closing values of each data set that we retrieve (for details on how to retrieve stock data with pandas, see Chapter 6):

```
In [3]: %%time
        data = pd.DataFrame()
        for sym in symbols:
            data[sym] = web.DataReader(sym, data_source='yahoo')['Close']
        data = data.dropna()

Out[3]: CPU times: user 408 ms, sys: 68 ms, total: 476 ms
        Wall time: 5.61 s
```

Let us separate the index data since we need it regularly:

```
In [4]: dax = pd.DataFrame(data.pop('^GDAXI'))
```

The DataFrame object data now has log return data for the 30 DAX stocks:

```
In [5]: data[data.columns[:6]].head()
```

```
Out[5]:              ADS.DE  ALV.DE  BAS.DE  BAYN.DE  BEI.DE  BMW.DE
         Date
         2010-01-04   38.51   88.54   44.85    56.40   46.44   32.05
         2010-01-05   39.72   88.81   44.17    55.37   46.20   32.31
         2010-01-06   39.40   89.50   44.45    55.02   46.17   32.81
         2010-01-07   39.74   88.47   44.15    54.30   45.70   33.10
         2010-01-08   39.60   87.99   44.02    53.82   44.38   32.65
```

Applying PCA

Usually, PCA works with normalized data sets. Therefore, the following convenience function proves helpful:

```
In [6]: scale_function = lambda x: (x - x.mean()) / x.std()
```

For the beginning, consider a PCA with multiple components (i.e., we do not restrict the number of components):[3]

```
In [7]: pca = KernelPCA().fit(data.apply(scale_function))
```

The importance or explanatory power of each component is given by its Eigenvalue. These are found in an attribute of the KernelPCA object. The analysis gives too many components:

```
In [8]: len(pca.lambdas_)

Out[8]: 655
```

Therefore, let us only have a look at the first 10 components. The tenth component already has almost negligible influence:

```
In [9]: pca.lambdas_[:10].round()

Out[9]: array([ 22816.,   6559.,   2535.,   1558.,    697.,    442.,    378.,
                  255.,    183.,    151.])
```

We are mainly interested in the relative importance of each component, so we will normalize these values. Again, we use a convenience function for this:

```
In [10]: get_we = lambda x: x / x.sum()

In [11]: get_we(pca.lambdas_)[:10]

Out[11]: array([ 0.6295725 ,  0.1809903 ,  0.06995609,  0.04300101,  0.01923256,
                 0.01218984,  0.01044098,  0.00704461,  0.00505794,  0.00416612])
```

With this information, the picture becomes much clearer. The first component already explains about 60% of the variability in the 30 time series. The first five components explain about 95% of the variability:

---

3. Note that we work here—and in the section to follow on Bayesian statistics—with absolute stock prices and *not with return data*, which would be more statistically sound. The reason for this is that it simplifies intuition and makes graphical plots easier to interpret. In real-world applications, you would use return data.

```
In [12]: get_we(pca.lambdas_)[:5].sum()

Out[12]: 0.94275246704834414
```

Constructing a PCA Index

Next, we use PCA to construct a PCA (or factor) index over time and compare it with
the original index. First, we have a PCA index with a single component only:

```
In [13]: pca = KernelPCA(n_components=1).fit(data.apply(scale_function))
         dax['PCA_1'] = pca.transform(-data)
```

Figure 11-15 shows the results for normalized data—already not too bad, given the
rather simple application of the approach:

```
In [14]: import matplotlib.pyplot as plt
         %matplotlib inline
         dax.apply(scale_function).plot(figsize=(8, 4))
```

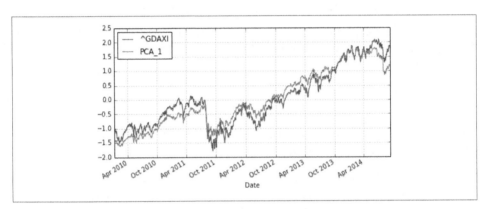

Figure 11-15. German DAX index and PCA index with one component

Let us see if we can improve the results by adding *more* components. To this end, we
need to calculate a weighted average from the single resulting components:

```
In [15]: pca = KernelPCA(n_components=5).fit(data.apply(scale_function))
         pca_components = pca.transform(-data)
         weights = get_we(pca.lambdas_)
         dax['PCA_5'] = np.dot(pca_components, weights)
```

The results as presented in Figure 11-16 are still "good," but not that much better than
before—at least upon visual inspection:

```
In [16]: import matplotlib.pyplot as plt
         %matplotlib inline
         dax.apply(scale_function).plot(figsize=(8, 4))
```

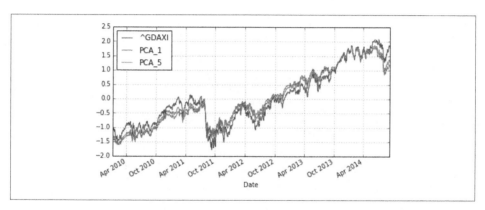

Figure 11-16. German DAX index and PCA indices with one and five components

In view of the results so far, we want to inspect the relationship between the DAX index and the PCA index in a different way—via a scatter plot, adding date information to the mix. First, we convert the DatetimeIndex of the DataFrame object to a matplotlib-compatible format:

```
In [17]: import matplotlib as mpl
         mpl_dates = mpl.dates.date2num(data.index)
         mpl_dates

Out[17]: array([ 733776.,  733777.,  733778., ...,  735500.,  735501.,  735502.])
```

This new date list can be used for a scatter plot, highlighting through different colors which date each data point is from. Figure 11-17 shows the data in this fashion:

```
In [18]: plt.figure(figsize=(8, 4))
         plt.scatter(dax['PCA_5'], dax['^GDAXI'], c=mpl_dates)
         lin_reg = np.polyval(np.polyfit(dax['PCA_5'],
                                         dax['^GDAXI'], 1),
                                         dax['PCA_5'])
         plt.plot(dax['PCA_5'], lin_reg, 'r', lw=3)
         plt.grid(True)
         plt.xlabel('PCA_5')
         plt.ylabel('^GDAXI')
         plt.colorbar(ticks=mpl.dates.DayLocator(interval=250),
                      format=mpl.dates.DateFormatter('%d %b %y'))
```

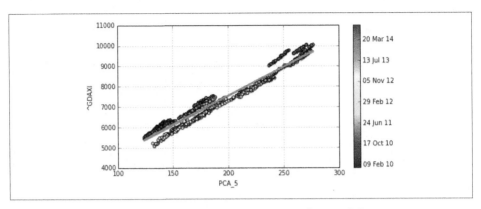

Figure 11-17. DAX return values against PCA return values with linear regression

Figure 11-17 reveals that there is obviously some kind of structural break sometime in the middle of 2011. If the PCA index were to perfectly replicate the DAX index, we would expect all the points to lie on a straight line and to see the regression line going through these points. Perfection is hard to achieve, but we can maybe do better.

To this end, let us divide the total time frame into two subintervals. We can then implement an *early* and a *late* regression:

```
In [19]: cut_date = '2011/7/1'
         early_pca = dax[dax.index < cut_date]['PCA_5']
         early_reg = np.polyval(np.polyfit(early_pca,
                         dax['^GDAXI'][dax.index < cut_date], 1),
                         early_pca)

In [20]: late_pca = dax[dax.index >= cut_date]['PCA_5']
         late_reg = np.polyval(np.polyfit(late_pca,
                         dax['^GDAXI'][dax.index >= cut_date], 1),
                         late_pca)
```

Figure 11-18 shows the new regression lines, which indeed display the high explanatory power both before our cutoff date and thereafter. This heuristic approach will be made a bit more formal in the next section on Bayesian statistics:

```
In [21]: plt.figure(figsize=(8, 4))
         plt.scatter(dax['PCA_5'], dax['^GDAXI'], c=mpl_dates)
         plt.plot(early_pca, early_reg, 'r', lw=3)
         plt.plot(late_pca, late_reg, 'r', lw=3)
         plt.grid(True)
         plt.xlabel('PCA_5')
         plt.ylabel('^GDAXI')
         plt.colorbar(ticks=mpl.dates.DayLocator(interval=250),
                         format=mpl.dates.DateFormatter('%d %b %y'))
```

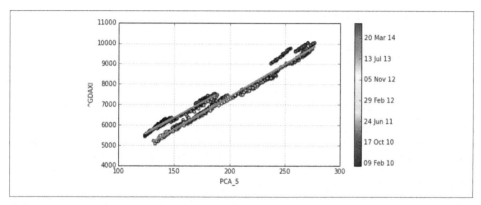

Figure 11-18. DAX index values against PCA index values with early and late regression (regime switch)

Bayesian Regression

Bayesian statistics nowadays is a cornerstone in empirical finance. This chapter cannot lay the foundations for all concepts of the field. You should therefore consult, if needed, a textbook like that by Geweke (2005) for a general introduction or Rachev (2008) for one that is financially motivated.

Bayes's Formula

The most common interpretation of Bayes' formula in finance is the *diachronic interpretation*. This mainly states that over time we learn new information about certain variables or parameters of interest, like the mean return of a time series. Equation 11-5 states the theorem formally. Here, H stands for an event, the hypothesis, and D represents the data an experiment or the real world might present.[4] On the basis of these fundamental definitions, we have:

- $p(H)$ is called the *prior* probability.
- $p(D)$ is the probability for the data under any hypothesis, called the *normalizing constant*.
- $p(D|H)$ is the *likelihood* (i.e., the probability) of the data under hypothesis H.
- $p(H|D)$ is the *posterior* probability; i.e., after we have seen the data.

---

4. For a `Python`-based introduction into these and other fundamental concepts of Bayesian statistics, refer to Downey (2013).

Equation 11-5. Bayes's formula

$$p(H|D) = \frac{p(H)p(D|H)}{p(D)}$$

Consider a simple example. We have two boxes, B_1 and B_2. Box B_1 contains 20 black balls and 70 red balls, while box B_2 contains 40 black balls and 50 red balls. We randomly draw a ball from one of the two boxes. Assume the ball is *black*. What are the probabilities for the hypotheses "H_1: Ball is from box B_1" and "H_2: Ball is from box B_2," respectively?

Before we randomly draw the ball, both hypotheses are equally likely. After it is clear that the ball is black, we have to update the probability for both hypotheses according to Bayes' formula. Consider hypothesis H_1:

- **Prior:** $p(H_1) = 0.5$
- **Normalizing constant:** $p(D) = 0.5 \cdot 0.2 + 0.5 \cdot 0.4 = 0.3$
- **Likelihood:** $p(D|H_1) = 0.2$

This gives for the updated probability of H_1 $p(H_1|D) = \frac{0.5 \cdot 0.2}{0.3} = \frac{1}{3}$.

This result also makes sense intuitively. The probability for drawing a black ball from box B_2 is twice as high as for the same event happening with box B_1. Therefore, having drawn a black ball, the hypothesis H_2 has with $p(H_2|D) = \frac{2}{3}$ an updated probability two times as high as the updated probability for hypothesis H_1.

PyMC3

With PyMC3 the Python ecosystem provides a powerful and performant library to technically implement Bayesian statistics. PyMC3 is (at the time of this writing) *not* part of the Anaconda distribution recommended in Chapter 2. On a Linux or a Mac OS X operating system, the installation comprises mainly the following steps.

First, you need to install the Theano compiler package needed for PyMC3 (cf. *http://bit.ly/install_theano*). In the shell, execute the following commands:

```
$ git clone git://github.com/Theano/Theano.git
$ sudo python Theano/python.py install
```

On a Mac OS X system you might need to add the following line to your .bash_profile file (to be found in your *home/user* directory):

```
export DYLD_FALLBACK_LIBRARY_PATH= \
$DYLD_FALLBACK_LIBRARY_PATH:/Library/anaconda/lib:
```

Once Theano is installed, the installation of PyMC3 is straightforward:

```
$ git clone https://github.com/pymc-devs/pymc.git
$ cd pymc
$ sudo python setup.py install
```

If successful, you should be able to import the library named pymc as usual:

```
In [22]: import warnings
         warnings.simplefilter('ignore')
         import pymc as pm
         import numpy as np
         np.random.seed(1000)
         import matplotlib.pyplot as plt
         %matplotlib inline
```

PyMC3

PyMC3 is already a powerful library at the time of this writing. However, it is still in its early stages, so you should expect further enhancements, changes to the API, etc. Make sure to stay up to date by regularly checking the website (*http://bit.ly/pymc3*) when using PyMC3.

Introductory Example

Consider now an example where we have noisy data around a straight line:[5]

```
In [23]: x = np.linspace(0, 10, 500)
         y = 4 + 2 * x + np.random.standard_normal(len(x)) * 2
```

As a benchmark, consider first an ordinary least-squares regression given the noisy data, using NumPy's polyfit function (cf. Chapter 9). The regression is implemented as follows:

```
In [24]: reg = np.polyfit(x, y, 1)
         # linear regression
```

Figure 11-19 shows the data and the regression line graphically:

```
In [25]: plt.figure(figsize=(8, 4))
         plt.scatter(x, y, c=y, marker='v')
         plt.plot(x, reg[1] + reg[0] * x, lw=2.0)
         plt.colorbar()
         plt.grid(True)
         plt.xlabel('x')
         plt.ylabel('y')
```

---

5. This example and the one in the following subsection are from a presentation by Thomas Wiecki (*http://bit.ly/bayesian-data-analysis-pymc3*), one of the lead developers of PyMC3; he allowed me to use them for this chapter, for which I am most grateful.

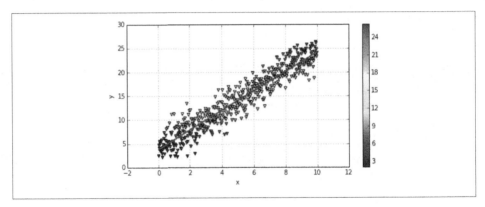

Figure 11-19. Sample data points and regression line

The result of the "standard" regression approach is fixed values for the parameters of the regression line:

```
In [26]: reg

Out[26]: array([ 2.03384161,  3.77649234])
```

Note that the highest-order monomial factor (in this case, the slope of the regression line) is at index level 0 and that the intercept is at index level 1. The original parameters 2 and 4 are not perfectly recovered, but this of course is due to the noise included in the data.

Next, the Bayesian regression. Here, we assume that the parameters are distributed in a certain way. For example, consider the equation describing the regression line $\hat{y}(x) = \alpha + \beta \cdot x$. We now assume the following *priors*:

- α is normally distributed with mean 0 and a standard deviation of 20.
- β is normally distributed with mean 0 and a standard deviation of 20.

For the *likelihood*, we assume a normal distribution with mean of $\hat{y}(x)$ and a uniformly distributed standard deviation between 0 and 10.

A major element of Bayesian regression is (Markov Chain) Monte Carlo (MCMC) sampling.[6] In principle, this is the same as drawing balls multiple times from boxes, as in the previous simple example—just in a more systematic, automated way.

For the technical sampling, there are three different functions to call:

---

6. Cf. *http://en.wikipedia.org/wiki/Markov_chain_Monte_Carlo*. For example, the Monte Carlo algorithms used throughout the book and analyzed in detail in Chapter 10 all generate so-called *Markov chains*, since the immediate next step/value only depends on the current state of the process and not on any other historic state or value.

- find_MAP finds the starting point for the sampling algorithm by deriving the *local maximum a posteriori point.*

- NUTS implements the so-called "efficient No-U-Turn Sampler with dual averaging" (NUTS) algorithm for MCMC sampling given the assumed priors.

- sample draws a number of samples given the starting value from find_MAP and the optimal step size from the NUTS algorithm.

All this is to be wrapped into a PyMC3 Model object and executed within a with statement:

```
In [27]: with pm.Model() as model:
                 # model specifications in PyMC3
                 # are wrapped in a with statement
             # define priors
             alpha = pm.Normal('alpha', mu=0, sd=20)
             beta = pm.Normal('beta', mu=0, sd=20)
             sigma = pm.Uniform('sigma', lower=0, upper=10)

             # define linear regression
             y_est = alpha + beta * x

             # define likelihood
             likelihood = pm.Normal('y', mu=y_est, sd=sigma, observed=y)

             # inference
             start = pm.find_MAP()
               # find starting value by optimization
             step = pm.NUTS(state=start)
               # instantiate MCMC sampling algorithm
             trace = pm.sample(100, step, start=start, progressbar=False)
               # draw 100 posterior samples using NUTS sampling
```

Have a look at the estimates from the first sample:

```
In [28]: trace[0]
```

```
Out[28]: {'alpha': 3.8783781152509031,
          'beta': 2.0148472296530033,
          'sigma': 2.0078134493352975}
```

All three values are rather close to the original values (4, 2, 2). However, the whole procedure yields, of course, many more estimates. They are best illustrated with the help of a *trace plot*, as in Figure 11-20—i.e., a plot showing the resulting posterior distribution for the different parameters as well as all single estimates per sample. The posterior distribution gives us an intuitive sense about the uncertainty in our estimates:

```
In [29]: fig = pm.traceplot(trace, lines={'alpha': 4, 'beta': 2, 'sigma': 2})
         plt.figure(figsize=(8, 8))
```

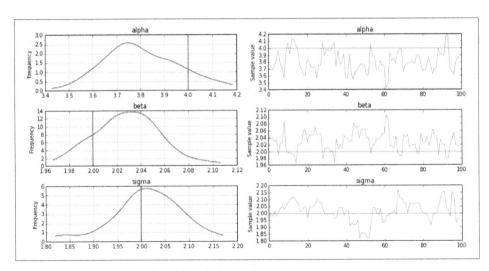

Figure 11-20. Trace plots for alpha, beta, and sigma

Taking only the `alpha` and `beta` values from the regression, we can draw all resulting regression lines as shown in Figure 11-21:

```
In [30]: plt.figure(figsize=(8, 4))
         plt.scatter(x, y, c=y, marker='v')
         plt.colorbar()
         plt.grid(True)
         plt.xlabel('x')
         plt.ylabel('y')
         for i in range(len(trace)):
             plt.plot(x, trace['alpha'][i] + trace['beta'][i] * x)
```

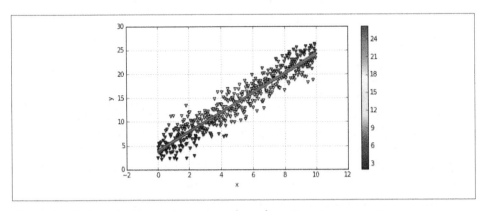

Figure 11-21. Sample data and regression lines from Bayesian regression

Real Data

Having seen Bayesian regression with PyMC3 in action with dummy data, we now move on to real market data. In this context, we introduce yet another Python library: zipline (cf. *https://github.com/quantopian/zipline* and *https://pypi.python.org/pypi/zipline*). zipline is a Python, open source algorithmic trading library that powers the community backtesting platform Quantopian (*http://www.quantopian.com*).

It is also to be installed separately, e.g., by using pip (*https://pip.readthedocs.org/en/latest/*):

```
$ pip install zipline
```

After installation, import zipline as well pytz and datetime as follows:

```
In [31]: import warnings
         warnings.simplefilter('ignore')
         import zipline
         import pytz
         import datetime as dt
```

Similar to pandas, zipline provides a convenience function to load financial data from different sources. Under the hood, zipline also uses pandas.

The example we use is a "classical" pair trading strategy, namely with gold and stocks of gold mining companies. These are represented by ETFs with the following symbols, respectively:

- GLD (*http://finance.yahoo.com/q/pr?s=GLD+Profile*)
- GDX (*http://finance.yahoo.com/q/pr?s=GDX+Profile*)

We can load the data using zipline as follows:

```
In [32]: data = zipline.data.load_from_yahoo(stocks=['GLD', 'GDX'],
             end=dt.datetime(2014, 3, 15, 0, 0, 0, 0, pytz.utc)).dropna()
         data.info()

Out[32]: GLD
         GDX
         <class 'pandas.core.frame.DataFrame'>
         DatetimeIndex: 1967 entries, 2006-05-22 00:00:00+00:00 to 2014-03-14 00
         :00:00+00:00
         Data columns (total 2 columns):
         GDX    1967 non-null float64
         GLD    1967 non-null float64
         dtypes: float64(2)
```

Figure 11-22 shows the historical data for both ETFs:

```
In [33]: data.plot(figsize=(8, 4))
```

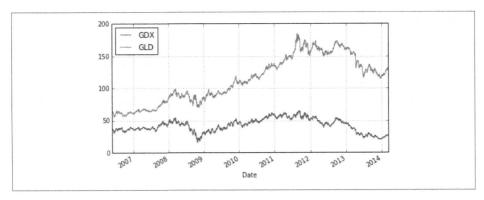

Figure 11-22. Comovements of trading pair

The absolute performance differs significantly:

```
In [34]: data.ix[-1] / data.ix[0] - 1
Out[34]: GDX    -0.216002
         GLD     1.038285
         dtype: float64
```

However, both time series seem to be quite strongly positively correlated when inspecting Figure 11-22, which is also reflected in the correlation data:

```
In [35]: data.corr()
Out[35]:              GDX       GLD
         GDX     1.000000  0.466962
         GLD     0.466962  1.000000
```

As usual, the `DatetimeIndex` object of the `DataFrame` object consists of `Timestamp` objects:

```
In [36]: data.index
Out[36]: <class 'pandas.tseries.index.DatetimeIndex'>
         [2006-05-22, ..., 2014-03-14]
         Length: 1967, Freq: None, Timezone: UTC
```

To use the date-time information with `matplotlib` in the way we want to in the following, we have to first convert it to an ordinal date representation:

```
In [37]: import matplotlib as mpl
         mpl_dates = mpl.dates.date2num(data.index)
         mpl_dates
Out[37]: array([ 732453., 732454., 732455., ...,  735304., 735305., 735306.])
```

Figure 11-23 shows a scatter plot of the time series data, plotting the GLD values against the GDX values and illustrating the dates of each data pair with different colorings:[7]

```
In [38]: plt.figure(figsize=(8, 4))
         plt.scatter(data['GDX'], data['GLD'], c=mpl_dates, marker='o')
         plt.grid(True)
         plt.xlabel('GDX')
         plt.ylabel('GLD')
         plt.colorbar(ticks=mpl.dates.DayLocator(interval=250),
                      format=mpl.dates.DateFormatter('%d %b %y'))
```

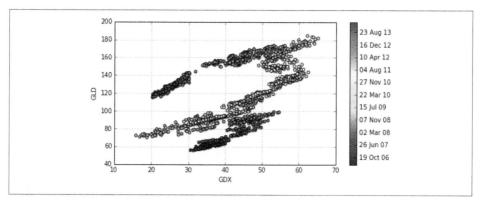

Figure 11-23. Scatter plot of prices for GLD and GDX

Let us implement a Bayesian regression on the basis of these two time series. The parameterizations are essentially the same as in the previous example with dummy data; we just replace the dummy data with the real data we now have available:

```
In [39]: with pm.Model() as model:
             alpha = pm.Normal('alpha', mu=0, sd=20)
             beta = pm.Normal('beta', mu=0, sd=20)
             sigma = pm.Uniform('sigma', lower=0, upper=50)

             y_est = alpha + beta * data['GDX'].values

             likelihood = pm.Normal('GLD', mu=y_est, sd=sigma,
                                    observed=data['GLD'].values)

             start = pm.find_MAP()
             step = pm.NUTS(state=start)
             trace = pm.sample(100, step, start=start, progressbar=False)
```

---

7. Note also here that we are working with absolute price levels and not return data, which would be statistically more sound. For a real-world (trading) application, you would rather choose the return data to implement such an analysis.

Figure 11-24 shows the results from the MCMC sampling procedure given the assumptions about the prior probability distributions for the three parameters:

```
In [40]: fig = pm.traceplot(trace)
         plt.figure(figsize=(8, 8))
```

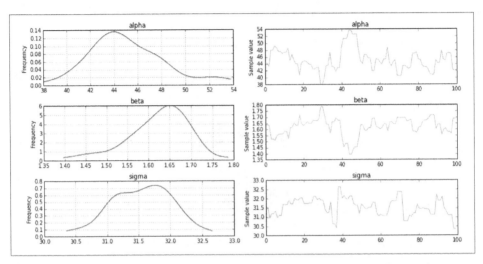

Figure 11-24. Trace plots for alpha, beta, and sigma based on GDX and GLD data

Figure 11-25 adds all the resulting regression lines to the scatter plot from before. All the regression lines are pretty close to each other:

```
In [41]: plt.figure(figsize=(8, 4))
         plt.scatter(data['GDX'], data['GLD'], c=mpl_dates, marker='o')
         plt.grid(True)
         plt.xlabel('GDX')
         plt.ylabel('GLD')
         for i in range(len(trace)):
             plt.plot(data['GDX'], trace['alpha'][i] + trace['beta'][i] * data
                     ['GDX'])
         plt.colorbar(ticks=mpl.dates.DayLocator(interval=250),
                     format=mpl.dates.DateFormatter('%d %b %y'))
```

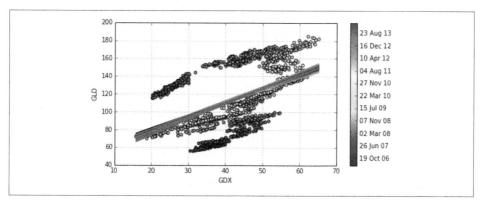

Figure 11-25. Scatter plot with "simple" regression lines

The figure reveals a major drawback of the regression approach used: the approach does not take into account evolutions over time. That is, the most recent data is treated the same way as the oldest data.

As pointed out at the beginning of this section, the Bayesian approach in finance is generally most useful when seen as diachronic—i.e., in the sense that new data revealed over time allows for better regressions and estimates.

To incorporate this concept in the current example, we assume that the regression parameters are not only random and distributed in some fashion, but that they follow some kind of random walk over time. It is the same generalization used when making the transition in finance theory from random variables to stochastic processes (which are essentially ordered sequences of random variables):

To this end, we define a new PyMC3 model, this time specifying parameter values as random walks with the variance parameter values transformed to log space (for better sampling characteristics).

```
In [42]: model_randomwalk = pm.Model()
         with model_randomwalk:
             # std of random walk best sampled in log space
             sigma_alpha, log_sigma_alpha = \
                     model_randomwalk.TransformedVar('sigma_alpha',
                                     pm.Exponential.dist(1. / .02, testval=.1),
                                     pm.logtransform)
             sigma_beta, log_sigma_beta = \
                     model_randomwalk.TransformedVar('sigma_beta',
                                     pm.Exponential.dist(1. / .02, testval=.1),
                                     pm.logtransform)
```

After having specified the distributions of the random walk parameters, we can proceed with specifying the random walks for alpha and beta. To make the whole procedure more efficient, 50 data points at a time share common coefficients:

```
In [43]: from pymc.distributions.timeseries import GaussianRandomWalk
         # to make the model simpler, we will apply the same coefficients
         # to 50 data points at a time
         subsample_alpha = 50
         subsample_beta = 50

         with model_randomwalk:
             alpha = GaussianRandomWalk('alpha', sigma_alpha**-2,
                                       shape=len(data) / subsample_alpha)
             beta = GaussianRandomWalk('beta', sigma_beta**-2,
                                       shape=len(data) / subsample_beta)

             # make coefficients have the same length as prices
             alpha_r = np.repeat(alpha, subsample_alpha)
             beta_r = np.repeat(beta, subsample_beta)
```

The time series data sets have a length of 1,967 data points:

```
In [44]: len(data.dropna().GDX.values)  # a bit longer than 1,950

Out[44]: 1967
```

For the sampling to follow, the number of data points must be divisible by 50. Therefore, only the first 1,950 data points are taken for the regression:

```
In [45]: with model_randomwalk:
             # define regression
             regression = alpha_r + beta_r * data.GDX.values[:1950]

             # assume prices are normally distributed
             # the mean comes from the regression
             sd = pm.Uniform('sd', 0, 20)
             likelihood = pm.Normal('GLD',
                                    mu=regression,
                                    sd=sd,
                                    observed=data.GLD.values[:1950])
```

All these definitions are a bit more involved than before due to the use of random walks instead of a single random variable. However, the inference steps with the MCMC remain essentially the same. Note, though, that the computational burden increases substantially since we have to estimate per random walk sample 1,950 / 50 = 39 parameter pairs (instead of 1, as before):

```
In [46]: import scipy.optimize as sco
         with model_randomwalk:
             # first optimize random walk
             start = pm.find_MAP(vars=[alpha, beta], fmin=sco.fmin_l_bfgs_b)

             # sampling
             step = pm.NUTS(scaling=start)
             trace_rw = pm.sample(100, step, start=start, progressbar=False)
```

In total, we have 100 estimates with 39 time intervals:

```
In [47]: np.shape(trace_rw['alpha'])

Out[47]: (100, 39)
```

We can illustrate the evolution of the regression factors `alpha` and `beta` over time by plotting a subset of the estimates and the average over all samples, as in Figure 11-26:

```
In [48]: part_dates = np.linspace(min(mpl_dates), max(mpl_dates), 39)

In [49]: fig, ax1 = plt.subplots(figsize=(10, 5))
         plt.plot(part_dates, np.mean(trace_rw['alpha'], axis=0),
                 'b', lw=2.5, label='alpha')
         for i in range(45, 55):
             plt.plot(part_dates, trace_rw['alpha'][i], 'b-.', lw=0.75)
         plt.xlabel('date')
         plt.ylabel('alpha')
         plt.axis('tight')
         plt.grid(True)
         plt.legend(loc=2)
         ax1.xaxis.set_major_formatter(mpl.dates.DateFormatter('%d %b %y') )
         ax2 = ax1.twinx()
         plt.plot(part_dates, np.mean(trace_rw['beta'], axis=0),
                 'r', lw=2.5, label='beta')
         for i in range(45, 55):
             plt.plot(part_dates, trace_rw['beta'][i], 'r-.', lw=0.75)
         plt.ylabel('beta')
         plt.legend(loc=4)
         fig.autofmt_xdate()
```

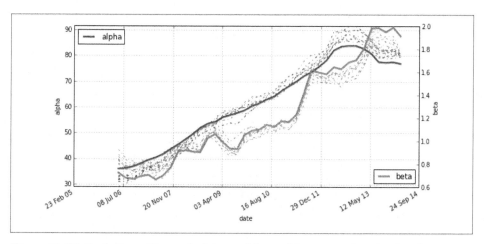

Figure 11-26. Evolution of (mean) alpha and (mean) beta over time (updated estimates over time)

Absolute Price Data Versus Relative Return Data

Both when presenting the PCA analysis implementation and for this example about Bayesian statistics, we've worked with absolute price levels instead of relative (log) return data. This is for illustration purposes only, because the respective graphical results are easier to understand and interpret (they are visually "more appealing"). However, for real-world financial applications you would instead rely on relative return data.

Using the mean `alpha` and `beta` values, we can illustrate how the regression is updated over time. Figure 11-27 again shows the data points as a scatter plot. In addition, the 39 regression lines resulting from the mean `alpha` and `beta` values are displayed. It is obvious that updating over time increases the regression fit (for the current/most recent data) tremendously—in other words, every time period needs its own regression:

```
In [50]: plt.figure(figsize=(10, 5))
         plt.scatter(data['GDX'], data['GLD'], c=mpl_dates, marker='o')
         plt.colorbar(ticks=mpl.dates.DayLocator(interval=250),
                     format=mpl.dates.DateFormatter('%d %b %y'))
         plt.grid(True)
         plt.xlabel('GDX')
         plt.ylabel('GLD')
         x = np.linspace(min(data['GDX']), max(data['GDX']))
         for i in range(39):
             alpha_rw = np.mean(trace_rw['alpha'].T[i])
             beta_rw = np.mean(trace_rw['beta'].T[i])
             plt.plot(x, alpha_rw + beta_rw * x, color=plt.cm.jet(256 * i / 39))
```

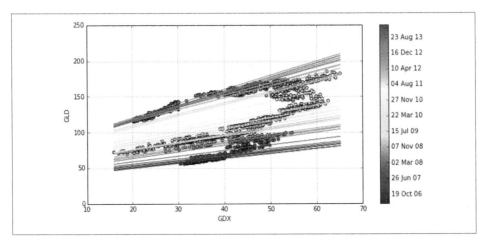

Figure 11-27. Scatter plot with time-dependent regression lines (updated estimates)

This concludes the section on Bayesian regression, which shows that Python offers with PyMC3 a powerful library to implement different approaches from Bayesian statistics. Bayesian regression in particular is a tool that has become quite popular and important recently in quantitative finance.

Conclusions

Statistics is not only an important discipline in its own right, but also provides indispensible tools for many other disciplines, like finance and the social sciences. It is impossible to give a broad overview of statistics in a single chapter. This chapter therefore concentrates on four important topics, illustrating the use of Python and several statistics libraries on the basis of realistic examples:

Normality tests

> The normality assumption with regard to financial market returns is an important one for many financial theories and applications; it is therefore important to be able to test whether certain time series data conforms to this assumption. As we have seen—via graphical and statistical means—real-world return data generally is *not* normally distributed.

Modern portfolio theory

> MPT, with its focus on the mean and variance/volatility of returns, can be considered one of the major conceptual and intellectual successes of statistics in finance; the important concept of investment *diversification* is beautifully illustrated in this context.

Principal component analysis

> PCA provides a pretty helpful method to reduce complexity for factor/component analysis tasks; we have shown that five principal components—constructed from the 30 stocks contained in the DAX index—suffice to explain more than 95% of the index's variability.

Bayesian regression

> Bayesian statistics in general (and Bayesian regression in particular) has become a popular tool in finance, since this approach overcomes shortcomings of other approaches, as introduced in Chapter 9; even if the mathematics and the formalism are more involved, the fundamental ideas—like the updating of probability/distribution beliefs over time—are easily grasped intuitively.

Further Reading

The following online resources are helpful:

- Information about the `SciPy` statistical functions is found here: *http://docs.scipy.org/doc/scipy/reference/stats.html.*

- Also consult the documentation of the `statsmodels` library: *http://statsmodels.sourceforge.net/stable/.*

- For the optimization functions used in this chapter, refer to *http://docs.scipy.org/doc/scipy/reference/optimize.html.*

- There is a short tutorial available for `PyMC3` (*http://bit.ly/pymc3_tutorial*); at the time of this writing the library is still in early release mode and not yet fully documented.

Useful references in book form are:

- Copeland, Thomas, Fred Weston, and Kuldeep Shastri (2005): *Financial Theory and Corporate Policy*, 4th ed. Pearson, Boston, MA.

- Downey, Allen (2013): *Think Bayes*. O'Reilly, Sebastopol, CA.

- Geweke, John (2005): *Contemporary Bayesian Econometrics and Statistics*. John Wiley & Sons, Hoboken, NJ.

- Rachev, Svetlozar et al. (2008): *Bayesian Methods in Finance*. John Wiley & Sons, Hoboken, NJ.

## CHAPTER 12

Excel Integration

Microsoft Excel is probably the most successful data analytics platform of all times.

— Kirat Singh

It is fair to say that Microsoft Excel—as part of Microsoft's Office suite of productivity tools—is one of the most widely used tools and applications in the finance industry and the finance functions of corporate and other institutions. What started out as a computerized version of paper spreadsheets has become a multipurpose tool for financial analysis and financial application building (in addition to the many use cases in other fields and industries).

Spreadsheet applications, like Microsoft Excel and LibreOffice Calc, are characterized by a few main features:

Organization

    A *workbook* is a spreadsheet application file that is organized in single *sheets* that in turn are organized in *cells*.

Data

    Data is generally stored in tabular form in single cells; the cells contain the data itself (e.g., a floating-point number or a text string), formatting information for display purposes (e.g., font type, color), and maybe some computer code (if, for example, the data in the cell is the result of a numerical operation).

Functionality

    Given the data stored in single cells, you can do computational and other operations with that data, like adding or multiplying integers.

Visualization

    Data can be easily visualized, for example, as a pie chart.

Programmability

Modern spreadsheet applications allow highly flexible programmability, e.g., via Visual Basic for Applications (VBA) within an Excel spreadsheet.

References

The major tool for implementing functionality or writing, e.g., VBA code is the *cell reference*; every cell has unique coordinates (workbook, sheet name, column, and row) identifying the cell.

This brief characterization might explain the popularity: all technical elements needed to implement financial analyses or applications are found in a single place. Thinking of Python and the previous chapters, you need a couple of libraries and tools (Python, NumPy, matplotlib, PyTables, etc.) combined to have available all of the features just listed.

Such convenience and one-size-fits-all approaches generally come at a cost, though. To pick just one area, spreadsheets are *not* suited to storing large amounts of data or data with complex relationships. This is the reason why Microsoft Excel in the finance industry has developed more as a *general graphical user interface* (GUI) "only." In many cases, it is mainly used to display and visualize data and aggregate information and to implement ad hoc analyses. For example, there are interfaces available to get data from leading data service providers, like Bloomberg and Thomson Reuters, into Excel (and maybe the other way around).

This chapter works on the assumption that Microsoft Excel is available on almost every desktop or notebook computer and that it is used as a general GUI. In this sense, Python can play the following roles:

Manipulation tool

Using Python, you can interact with and manipulate Excel spreadsheets.

Data processor

Python can provide data to a spreadsheet and read data from a spreadsheet.

Analytics engine

Python can provide its whole analytics capabilities to spreadsheets, becoming a full-fledged substitute for VBA programming.

Basic Spreadsheet Interaction

Fundamental Python libraries to work with Excel spreadsheet files are xlrd and xlwt (cf. *http://www.python-excel.org*). Although quite popular, a major drawback of xlwt is that it can only write spreadsheet files compatible with Microsoft Excel 97/2000/XP/2003, OpenOffice.org Calc, and Gnumeric—i.e., those with the suffix .xls. Therefore, we also use the libraries xlsxwriter (*http://xlsxwriter.readthedocs.org*) and OpenPyxl (*http://openpyxl.readthedocs.org*), which generate spreadsheet files in the current `.xslx` format. We'll begin, then, with a few imports.

```
In [1]: import numpy as np
        import pandas as pd
        import xlrd, xlwt
        import xlsxwriter
        path = 'data/'
```

Generating Workbooks (.xls)

We start by generating a workbook with two sheets.[1] First, the `Workbook` object `wb`. Note that this is an *in-memory* version of the workbook only (so far):

```
In [2]: wb = xlwt.Workbook()
```

```
In [3]: wb
```

```
Out[3]: <xlwt.Workbook.Workbook at 0x7f7dcc49df10>
```

The second step is to add one or multiple sheets to the `Workbook` object:

```
In [4]: wb.add_sheet('first_sheet', cell_overwrite_ok=True)
```

```
Out[4]: <xlwt.Worksheet.Worksheet at 0x7f7dac9dde90>
```

We now have one `Worksheet` object, which has index number 0:

```
In [5]: wb.get_active_sheet()
```

```
Out[5]: 0
```

To further work with the sheet, define an alias for it:

```
In [6]: ws_1 = wb.get_sheet(0)
        ws_1
```

```
Out[6]: <xlwt.Worksheet.Worksheet at 0x7f7dac9dde90>
```

Of course, these two steps—instantiation and alias definition—can be combined into a single step:

```
In [7]: ws_2 = wb.add_sheet('second_sheet')
```

Both `Worksheet` objects are still empty. Therefore, let us generate a `NumPy` `ndarray` object containing some numbers:

```
In [8]: data = np.arange(1, 65).reshape((8, 8))
```

```
In [9]: data
```

---

1. Note that a simple mechanism to generate `Excel` spreadsheets from `Python` is to export data in the form of a comma-separated value (`CSV`) file and to import this with `Excel`. This might sometimes be more efficient than the ways presented in the following discussion.

```
Out[9]: array([[ 1,  2,  3,  4,  5,  6,  7,  8],
               [ 9, 10, 11, 12, 13, 14, 15, 16],
               [17, 18, 19, 20, 21, 22, 23, 24],
               [25, 26, 27, 28, 29, 30, 31, 32],
               [33, 34, 35, 36, 37, 38, 39, 40],
               [41, 42, 43, 44, 45, 46, 47, 48],
               [49, 50, 51, 52, 53, 54, 55, 56],
               [57, 58, 59, 60, 61, 62, 63, 64]])
```

Using the write method and providing row and column information (with zero-based indexing), data is easily written to a certain cell in a certain worksheet:

```
In [10]: ws_1.write(0, 0, 100)
           # write 100 in cell "A1"
```

This way, the sample data can be written "in bulk" to the two Worksheet objects:

```
In [11]: for c in range(data.shape[0]):
             for r in range(data.shape[1]):
                 ws_1.write(r, c, data[c, r])
                 ws_2.write(r, c, data[r, c])
```

The save method of the Workbook class allows us to save the whole Workbook object to disk:

```
In [12]: wb.save(path + 'workbook.xls')
```

On Windows systems, the path might look like r"C:\path\data\workbook.xls".

Generating Workbooks (.xslx)

(The creation of spreadsheet files in the new format works essentially the same way. First, we create a Workbook object:

```
In [13]: wb = xlsxwriter.Workbook(path + 'workbook.xlsx')
```

Second, the Worksheet objects:

```
In [14]: ws_1 = wb.add_worksheet('first_sheet')
         ws_2 = wb.add_worksheet('second_sheet')
```

Third, we write data to the Worksheet objects:

```
In [15]: for c in range(data.shape[0]):
             for r in range(data.shape[1]):
                 ws_1.write(r, c, data[c, r])
                 ws_2.write(r, c, data[r, c])
```

Fourth, we close the Workbook file object:

```
In [16]: wb.close()

In [17]: ll $path*
```

```
Out[17]: -rw------- 1 yhilpisch 7375 Sep 28 18:18 data/chart.xlsx
         -rw------- 1 yhilpisch 5632 Sep 28 18:18 data/workbook.xls
         -rw------- 1 yhilpisch 6049 Sep 28 18:18 data/workbook.xlsx
```

If everything went well, the file opened in Microsoft Excel should look like Figure 12-1.

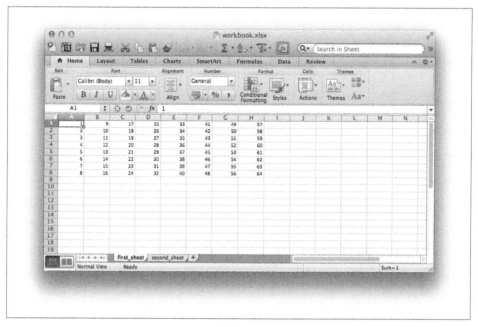

Figure 12-1. Screenshot of workbook in Excel

xlsxwriter has many more options to generate Workbook objects, for example with charts. Consider the following code (cf. the xlsxwriter documentation (*http://bit.ly/xlsxwriter*)):

```
In [18]: wb = xlsxwriter.Workbook(path + 'chart.xlsx')
         ws = wb.add_worksheet()

         # write cumsum of random values in first column
         values = np.random.standard_normal(15).cumsum()
         ws.write_column('A1', values)

         # create a new chart object
         chart = wb.add_chart({'type': 'line'})

         # add a series to the chart
         chart.add_series({'values': '=Sheet1!$A$1:$A$15',
                           'marker': {'type': 'diamond'},})
           # series with markers (here: diamond)
```

```
# insert the chart
ws.insert_chart('C1', chart)

wb.close()
```

The resulting spreadsheet file is shown as a screenshot in Figure 12-2.

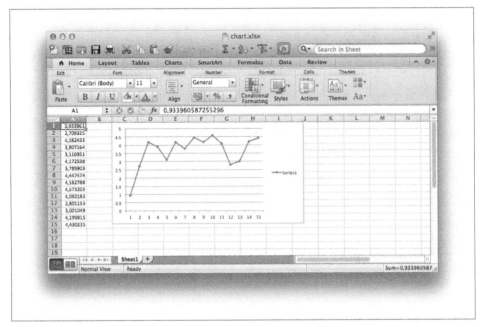

Figure 12-2. Screenshot of workbook in Excel with a chart

Reading from Workbooks

The sister library xlrd is responsible for reading data from spreadsheet files (i.e., workbooks):

```
In [19]: book = xlrd.open_workbook(path + 'workbook.xlsx')
```

```
In [20]: book
```

```
Out[20]: <xlrd.book.Book at 0x7f7dabec4890>
```

Once a workbook is opened, the sheet_names method provides the names of all Work sheet objects in this particular Workbook object:

```
In [21]: book.sheet_names()
```

```
Out[21]: [u'first_sheet', u'second_sheet']
```

Worksheets can be accessed via their names or index values:

```
In [22]: sheet_1 = book.sheet_by_name('first_sheet')
         sheet_2 = book.sheet_by_index(1)
         sheet_1

Out[22]: <xlrd.sheet.Sheet at 0x7f7dabec4a10>

In [23]: sheet_2.name

Out[23]: u'second_sheet'
```

Important attributes of a Worksheet object are ncols and nrows, indicating the number of columns and rows, respectively, that contain data:

```
In [24]: sheet_1.ncols, sheet_1.nrows

Out[24]: (8, 8)
```

Single cells—i.e. Cell objects—are accessed via the cell method, providing the numbers for both the row and the column (again, numbering is zero-based). The value attribute then gives the data stored in this particular cell:

```
In [25]: cl = sheet_1.cell(0, 0)
         cl.value

Out[25]: 1.0
```

The attribute ctype gives the cell type:

```
In [26]: cl.ctype

Out[26]: 2
```

Table 12-1 lists all Excel cell types.

Table 12-1. Excel cell types

Type	Number	Python type
XL_CELL_EMPTY	0	Empty string
XL_CELL_TEXT	1	A Unicode string
XL_CELL_NUMBER	2	float
XL_CELL_DATE	3	float
XL_CELL_BOOLEAN	4	int (1 = TRUE, 0 = FALSE)
XL_CELL_ERROR	5	int representing internal Excel codes
XL_CELL_BLANK	6	Empty string, only when formatting_info=True

Similarly, you can access whole rows by providing the number of the row to the row method:

```
In [27]: sheet_2.row(3)

Out[27]: [number:25.0,
          number:26.0,
          number:27.0,
```

```
                  number:28.0,
                  number:29.0,
                  number:30.0,
                  number:31.0,
                  number:32.0]
```

And, analogously, whole columns:

```
In [28]: sheet_2.col(3)

Out[28]: [number:4.0,
          number:12.0,
          number:20.0,
          number:28.0,
          number:36.0,
          number:44.0,
          number:52.0,
          number:60.0]
```

The methods `row_values` and `col_values` only deliver the values contained in the respective row or column:

```
In [29]: sheet_1.col_values(3, start_rowx=3, end_rowx=7)

Out[29]: [28.0, 29.0, 30.0, 31.0]

In [30]: sheet_1.row_values(3, start_colx=3, end_colx=7)

Out[30]: [28.0, 36.0, 44.0, 52.0]
```

To read out all the data in a `Worksheet` object, just iterate over all columns and rows that contain data:

```
In [31]: for c in range(sheet_1.ncols):
             for r in range(sheet_1.nrows):
                 print '%i' % sheet_1.cell(r, c).value,
             print

Out[31]: 1 2 3 4 5 6 7 8
         9 10 11 12 13 14 15 16
         17 18 19 20 21 22 23 24
         25 26 27 28 29 30 31 32
         33 34 35 36 37 38 39 40
         41 42 43 44 45 46 47 48
         49 50 51 52 53 54 55 56
         57 58 59 60 61 62 63 64
```

Using OpenPyxl

There is yet another library to generate and read `Excel` spreadsheet files in `.xlsx` format with `Python`: `OpenPyxl` (*http://openpyxl.readthedocs.org*). This library allows us to both create spreadsheet files and read from them. In addition, while basic usage is similar to the other libraries, the interface is in some cases a bit more `Pythonic` and might therefore be worth taking a look at. Import the library as follows:

```
In [32]: import openpyxl as oxl
```

Let us proceed as before. First, generate a Workbook object:

```
In [33]: wb = oxl.Workbook()
```

Second, create a Worksheet object:

```
In [34]: ws = wb.create_sheet(index=0, title='oxl_sheet')
```

Third, write the data to the worksheet:

```
In [35]: for c in range(data.shape[0]):
             for r in range(data.shape[1]):
                 ws.cell(row=r, column=c).value = data[c, r]
                 # creates a Cell object and assigns a value
```

Fourth, close the file object:

```
In [36]: wb.save(path + 'oxl_book.xlsx')
```

With OpenPyxl, you can also read workbooks:

```
In [37]: wb = oxl.load_workbook(path + 'oxl_book.xlsx')
```

Now, single cells are easily accessed via their cell names:

```
In [38]: ws = wb.get_active_sheet()

In [39]: cell = ws['B4']

In [40]: cell.column

Out[40]: 'B'

In [41]: cell.row

Out[41]: 4

In [42]: cell.value

Out[42]: 12
```

Similarly, you can access cell ranges as in Excel:

```
In [43]: ws['B1':'B4']

Out[43]: ((<Cell oxl_sheet.B1>,),
          (<Cell oxl_sheet.B2>,),
          (<Cell oxl_sheet.B3>,),
          (<Cell oxl_sheet.B4>,))

In [44]: for cell in ws['B1':'B4']:
             print cell[0].value

Out[44]: 9
         10
         11
         12
```

There is also a `range` method to which you can provide the cell range in Excel syntax as a string:

```
In [45]: ws.range('B1:C4')
         # same as ws['B1':'C4']

Out[45]: ((<Cell oxl_sheet.B1>, <Cell oxl_sheet.C1>),
          (<Cell oxl_sheet.B2>, <Cell oxl_sheet.C2>),
          (<Cell oxl_sheet.B3>, <Cell oxl_sheet.C3>),
          (<Cell oxl_sheet.B4>, <Cell oxl_sheet.C4>))

In [46]: for row in ws.range('B1:C4'):
             for cell in row:
                 print cell.value,
             print

Out[46]: 9 17
         10 18
         11 19
         12 20
```

Refer to the library's website (*http://pythonhosted.org/openpyxl/*) for more details.

Using pandas for Reading and Writing

Chapter 7 shows how to interact with Excel spreadsheet files using the `pandas` library. Let us use these approaches to read the data written with the `xlwt` library. We need a `DataFrame` object for each sheet. With `header=None`, pandas does not interpret the first data row as the header for the data set:

```
In [47]: df_1 = pd.read_excel(path + 'workbook.xlsx',
                              'first_sheet', header=None)
         df_2 = pd.read_excel(path + 'workbook.xlsx',
                              'second_sheet', header=None)
```

To recover the column names/values of the spreadsheet file, let us generate a list with capital letters as column names for the `DataFrame` objects:

```
In [48]: import string
         columns = []
         for c in range(data.shape[0]):
             columns.append(string.uppercase[c])
         columns

Out[48]: ['A', 'B', 'C', 'D', 'E', 'F', 'G', 'H']
```

We pass this list as the new column names to the two objects:

```
In [49]: df_1.columns = columns
         df_2.columns = columns
```

Indeed, the output of the two `DataFrame` objects now resembles the spreadsheet style pretty well:

```
In [50]: df_1

Out[50]:    A   B   C   D   E   F   G   H
        0   1   9  17  25  33  41  49  57
        1   2  10  18  26  34  42  50  58
        2   3  11  19  27  35  43  51  59
        3   4  12  20  28  36  44  52  60
        4   5  13  21  29  37  45  53  61
        5   6  14  22  30  38  46  54  62
        6   7  15  23  31  39  47  55  63
        7   8  16  24  32  40  48  56  64

In [51]: df_2

Out[51]:    A   B   C   D   E   F   G   H
        0   1   2   3   4   5   6   7   8
        1   9  10  11  12  13  14  15  16
        2  17  18  19  20  21  22  23  24
        3  25  26  27  28  29  30  31  32
        4  33  34  35  36  37  38  39  40
        5  41  42  43  44  45  46  47  48
        6  49  50  51  52  53  54  55  56
        7  57  58  59  60  61  62  63  64
```

Similarly, pandas allows us to write the data to Excel spreadsheet files:

```
In [52]: df_1.to_excel(path + 'new_book_1.xlsx', 'my_sheet')
```

Note that when writing DataFrame objects to spreadsheet files pandas adds both column names and index values, as seen in Figure 12-3.

Of course, pandas-generated Excel workbooks can be read as before with the xlrd library:

```
In [53]: wbn = xlrd.open_workbook(path + 'new_book_1.xlsx')
```

```
In [54]: wbn.sheet_names()
```

```
Out[54]: [u'my_sheet']
```

To write multiple DataFrame objects to a single spreadsheet file, one needs an Excel Writer object:

```
In [55]: wbw = pd.ExcelWriter(path + 'new_book_2.xlsx')
         df_1.to_excel(wbw, 'first_sheet')
         df_2.to_excel(wbw, 'second_sheet')
         wbw.save()
```

Let us inspect if we indeed have generated the two sheets in the single spreadsheet file:

```
In [56]: wbn = xlrd.open_workbook(path + 'new_book_2.xlsx')
```

```
In [57]: wbn.sheet_names()
```

```
Out[57]: [u'first_sheet', u'second_sheet']
```

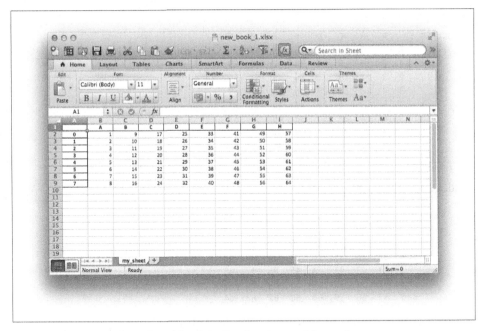

Figure 12-3. Screenshot of workbook in Excel written with pandas

As a final use case for `pandas` and `Excel`, consider the reading and writing of larger amounts of data. Although this is not a fast operation, it might be useful in some circumstances. First, the sample data to be used:

```
In [58]: data = np.random.rand(20, 100000)

In [59]: data.nbytes

Out[59]: 16000000
```

Second, generate a `DataFrame` object out of the sample data:

```
In [60]: df = pd.DataFrame(data)
```

Third, write it as an `Excel` file to the disk:

```
In [61]: %time df.to_excel(path + 'data.xlsx', 'data_sheet')

Out[61]: CPU times: user 1min 25s, sys: 460 ms, total: 1min 26s
         Wall time: 1min 25s
```

This takes quite a while. For comparison, see how fast native storage of the `NumPy` `ndarray` object is (on an SSD drive):

```
In [62]: %time np.save(path + 'data', data)

Out[62]: CPU times: user 8 ms, sys: 20 ms, total: 28 ms
         Wall time: 159 ms
```

```
In [63]: ll $path*
```

```
Out[63]: -rw------- 1 yhilpisch     7372 Sep 28 18:18 data/chart.xlsx
         -rw------- 1 yhilpisch 16000080 Sep 28 18:20 data/data.npy
         -rw------- 1 yhilpisch  3948600 Sep 28 18:20 data/data.xlsx
         -rw------- 1 yhilpisch     5828 Sep 28 18:18 data/new_book_1.xlsx
         -rw------- 1 yhilpisch     6688 Sep 28 18:18 data/new_book_2.xlsx
         -rw------- 1 yhilpisch     6079 Sep 28 18:18 data/oxl_book.xlsx
         -rw------- 1 yhilpisch     5632 Sep 28 18:18 data/workbook.xls
         -rw------- 1 yhilpisch     6049 Sep 28 18:18 data/workbook.xlsx
```

Fourth, read it from disk. This is significantly faster than writing it:

```
In [64]: %time df = pd.read_excel(path + 'data.xlsx', 'data_sheet')
```

```
Out[64]: CPU times: user 6.53 s, sys: 44 ms, total: 6.58 s
         Wall time: 6.51 s
```

However, see again the speed difference compared to native storage:

```
In [65]: %time data = np.load(path + 'data.npy')
```

```
Out[65]: CPU times: user 16 ms, sys: 8 ms, total: 24 ms
         Wall time: 40.5 ms
```

```
In [66]: data, df = 0.0, 0.0
         !rm $path*
```

Scripting Excel with Python

The previous section shows how to generate, read, and manipulate Excel spreadsheet files (i.e., workbooks). Although there are some beneficial use cases, Python is not the only way, and sometimes also not the best way, to achieve the results presented there.

Much more interesting is to expose the analytical power of Python to Excel spreadsheets. However, this is a technically more demanding task. For example, the Python library PyXLL (*http://www.pyxll.com*) provides means to expose Python functions via so-called Excel *add-ins*, Microsoft's technology to enhance the functionality of Excel. Additionally, the company DataNitro provides a solution that allows the full integration of Python and Excel and makes Python a full substitute for VBA programming. Both solutions, however, are commercial products that need to be licensed.

In what follows, we provide an overview of how to use DataNitro for Excel scripting, since this is a rather flexible approach to integrating Python with Excel.

Installing DataNitro

DataNitro works on Windows operating systems and Excel installations only. On Mac OS systems it can be used in a Windows virtual machine environment. It is compatible with Office 2007 and higher. Refer to the website *http://www.datanitro.com* for further instructions on how to get a (trial) license for the solution and how to install it.

When installing DataNitro you have the option to install Python as well. However, if you have already installed Anaconda (cf. Chapter 2), for example, there is no need to install another Python version or distribution. You then just have to customize the DataNitro solution (via the Settings menu) to use the existing Anaconda installation. DataNitro works with all Python versions 2.6 and higher as well as with versions 3.x.

If successfully installed, you then find the DataNitro ribbon within Excel, as displayed in Figure 12-4.

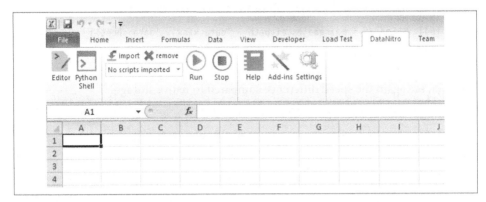

Figure 12-4. Screenshot of Excel with DataNitro ribbon

Working with DataNitro

There are two main methods to combine DataNitro with Excel:

Scripting
> With this method, you control Excel spreadsheets via Python scripts, similar to the approach presented in the previous section.

User-defined functions
> Using this approach, you expose your own Python functions to Excel in such a way that they can be called from within Excel.

Both methods need an installation of the DataNitro solution to work—i.e., you cannot distribute something that you have worked on to somebody else who does not have the DataNitro solution installed.

Scripting with DataNitro

Open the previously generated spreadsheet file workbook.xlsx in Excel. We want to work with DataNitro and this particular file. When you then click on the Python Shell symbol in the DataNitro ribbon, your screen should look like Figure 12-5.

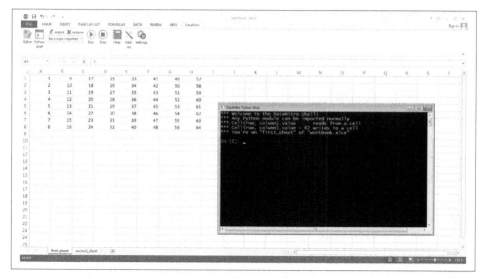

Figure 12-5. Screenshot of Excel with DataNitro IPython shell

A simple session could then look like the following:

```
In [1]: Cell("B1")
Out[1]: B1

In [2]: Cell("B1").value
Out[2]: 9

In [3]: Cell("B1").value = 'Excel with Python'
  # this immediately changes the (displayed) value
  # in the spreadsheet

In [4]: Cell("B1").value
Out[4]: u'Excel with Python'
```

In the same way as you change the `value` attribute of a `Cell` object, you can assign a formula to it:

```
In [5]: Cell("A9").formula = '=Sum(A1:A8)'

In [6]: Cell("A9").value
Out[6]: 36
```

Table 12-2 lists the attributes of the `DataNitro` `Cell` object.

Table 12-2. DataNitro Cell attributes

Attribute	Description
row	Row of the cell
col	Column of the cell

Attribute	Description
position	Position as a (*row, col*) tuple
sheet	Name of the sheet the cell is in
name	Name of the cell in Excel fashion
value	Value of the cell
vertical	All cell values including and below the cell
vertical_range	Excel range for all cells including and below the cell
horizontal	All cell values including and right of the cell
horizontal_range	Excel range for all cells including and right of the cell
table	All values including and below/right of the cell as nested list object
table_range	Excel range for table object
formula	Excel formula
comment	Comment attached to cell
hyperlink	Hyperlink or email address as string object
alignment	Text/value alignment for display
color	Cell color
df	Lets you write a pandas DataFrame object directly to the spreadsheet

Table 12-3 shows typesetting options for the Cell object. All options are attributes of the font object, which is a property of the Cell object. For example, this:

```
Cell("A1").font.size = 15
```

sets a (new) font size.

Table 12-3. DataNitro Cell typesetting options

Attribute	Description
size	Font size
color	Font color
bold	Bold font via Cell("A1").font.bold=True
italic	Italic font
underline	Underlines text
strikethrough	Puts strikethrough line through text
subscript	Subscripts text
superscript	Superscripts text

Finally, there are also a couple of methods for the Cell object. They are listed in Table 12-4.

Table 12-4. DataNitro Cell methods

Attribute	Description
clear	Resets all properties/attributes of the cell
copy_from	Copies all properties/attributes from another cell
copy_format_from	Copies all properties/attributes from another cell except `value` and `formula`
is_empty	Returns `True` if empty
offset	Returns cell object given relative offset as (*row, col*) tuple
subtraction	Subtraction gives the offset; e.g., `Cell("B4") - Cell("A2")` gives `(2, 1)`
print	Gives name and sheet of cell
set_name	Sets named range in `Excel`; e.g., `Cell("A1").set_name("upper_left")`

Often, it is helpful to work with `CellRange` instead of `Cell` objects only. One can think of this as an approach to vectorize certain operations on multiple `Cell` objects. Consider the following examples, still based on the same spreadsheet file `workbook.xlsx` with our previous changes:

```
In [6]: CellRange("A1:A8").value
Out[6]: [1, 2, 3, 4, 5, 6, 7, 8]

In [7]: CellRange("A1:A8").value = 1
  # like broadcasting

In [8]: CellRange("A1:A8").value
Out[8]: [1, 1, 1, 1, 1, 1, 1, 1]

In [9]: CellRange("A1:A8").value = 2 * [1, 2, 3, 4]

In [10]: CellRange("A1:A8").value
Out[10]: [1, 2, 3, 4, 1, 2, 3, 4]

In [11]: Cell("A9").value
Out[11]: 20
  # value of Sum function is
  # automatically updated
```

Of course, you can also use `CellRange` for iteration:

```
In [12]: for cell in CellRange("A1:B2"):
    ....:     print cell.name, cell.value
    ....:
A1 1
B1 Python with Excel
A2 2
B2 10
```

The majority of the `Cell` attributes and methods can also be used with `CellRange`.

When writing complex Python scripts for interaction with Excel spreadsheets, *performance* might be an issue. Basically, performance is bound by Excel input/output (I/O) speed. The following rules should be followed whenever possible:

Reading/writing
> Do not alternate reading with writing operations, since this might lower performance significantly.

Vectorization
> Use CellRange objects or Cell().table objects to read and write data in (large) blocks instead of loops.[2]

Use Python
> For example, when you have to transform a data block, it is better to read it in total with Python, to manipulate it with Python, and to write it back to the spreadsheet as a block; cell-by-cell operations can be really slow.

Store data in Python
> Store values in Python when possible rather than rereading them, especially for performance-critical loops or similar operations.

See the relevant sections in the DataNitro documentation for details on how to work with whole Worksheet (*http://datanitro.com/docs/sheets.html*) and Workbook (*http://datanitro.com/docs/workbook.html*) objects.

Plotting with DataNitro

A special topic when scripting Excel spreadsheets with DataNitro is plotting data contained in a spreadsheet with Python instead of using Excel's plotting capabilities. Example 12-1 shows a Python script that is only executable if DataNitro is installed. It retrieves Apple Inc. stock price data with the DataReader function from pandas (cf. Chapter 6), writes the data to a newly generated Workbook object, and then plots the data stored in the respective Worksheet object with Python—i.e., with the help of Data Nitro's matplotlib.pyplot wrapper nitroplot—and exposes the result to the spreadsheet.

Example 12-1. Plotting data stored in a spreadsheet with DataNitro and displaying a matplotlib plot in the same spreadsheet

```
#
# Plotting with DataNitro in Excel
# dn_plotting.py
#
```

---

2. Cf. Chapter 4 for a similar discussion in the context of NumPy ndarray objects and the benefits of vectorization. The rule of thumb there as well as here is to avoid loops on the Python level.

```
import pandas.io.data as web
import nitroplot as nplt
  # wrapper for matplotlib.pyplot (plt)

# make a new workbook

wb = new_wkbk()
active_wkbk(wb)
rename_sheet("Sheet1", "Apple_Stock")

# read Apple Inc. stock data

aapl = web.DataReader('aapl', data_source='yahoo')[['Open', 'Close']]

# write the data to the new workbook

Cell("A1").df = aapl

# generate matplotlib plot

nplt.figure(figsize=(8, 4))
nplt.plot(Cell("A2").vertical, Cell("C2").vertical, label='AAPL')
nplt.legend(loc=0)
nplt.grid(True)
nplt.xticks(rotation=35)

# expose plot to Excel spreadsheet

nplt.graph()
  # as plt.show()

# save the new workbook with data and plot

save('dn_plot.xlsx')
```

From a `DataNitro IPython` shell, execute the script with:

```
In [1]: %run dn_plotting.py
```

If the script is successfully executed, the workbook/worksheet in `Excel` should look as displayed in Figure 12-6.

Figure 12-6. Screenshot of Excel with DataNitro plot of Apple stock price data

User-defined functions

From a finance point of view, it seems most interesting to expose user-defined functions (UDFs) via DataNitro to Excel. This option has to be enabled in the Settings menu of DataNitro. Once this is enabled, you can import a Python script with DataNitro called functions.py. All Python functions included in this file—and they have to be in this particular file—will then be directly callable from Excel. Consider the by now well-known function to value European call options in the Black-Scholes-Merton model in Example 12-2.

Example 12-2. Python script for import with DataNitro into Excel

```
#
# Valuation of European call options in BSM model
# for use with DataNitro and Excel spreadsheets
# functions.py
#

# analytical Black-Scholes-Merton (BSM) formula


def bsm_call_value(S0, K, T, r, sigma):
    ''' Valuation of European call option in BSM model.
    Analytical formula.

    Parameters
    ==========
    S0 : float
        initial stock/index level
```

```
K : float
    strike price
T : float
    time-to-maturity (for t=0)
r : float
    constant risk-free short rate
sigma : float
    volatility factor in diffusion term

Returns
=======
value : float
    present value of the European call option
'''
from math import log, sqrt, exp
from scipy import stats
S0 = float(S0)
d1 = (log(S0 / K) + (r + 0.5 * sigma ** 2) * T) / (sigma * sqrt(T))
d2 = (log(S0 / K) + (r - 0.5 * sigma ** 2) * T) / (sigma * sqrt(T))
value = (S0 * stats.norm.cdf(d1, 0.0, 1.0)
        - K * exp(-r * T) * stats.norm.cdf(d2, 0.0, 1.0))
return value
```

If this script is imported via DataNitro, with UDFs enabled, you can use the valuation formula from Excel. In practice, you can then type the following into an Excel cell:

```
= bsm_call_value(B1, 100, 2.0, B4, B5)
```

This is the same then as with any other Excel formula. For example, have a look at Figure 12-7. In the upper-left corner you see a parameterization of the Black-Scholes-Merton model. When you click on Insert Function in the FORMULAS tab of Excel, you can enter a function dialog for the option valuation formula from Python (you find it under DataNitro functions). Once you have provided references to the cells containing the single parameter values, Python calculates the option value and returns the result to Excel.

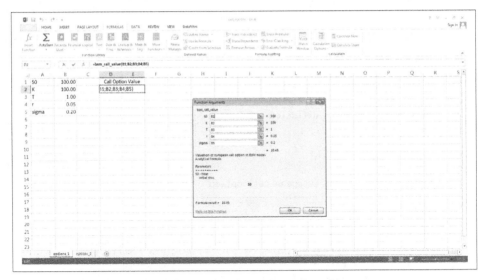

Figure 12-7. Screenshot of Excel function dialog for Python function

Although this function is not that computationally demanding, it illustrates how to harness the analytical power of Python from Excel and how to expose the results directly to Excel (cells). Similarly, see Figure 12-8. Here, we use a parameter grid to calculate multiple option values at once. The formula in cell D11 then takes on the form:

```
= bsm_call_value($B$1, $A11, D$8, $B$4, $B$5)
```

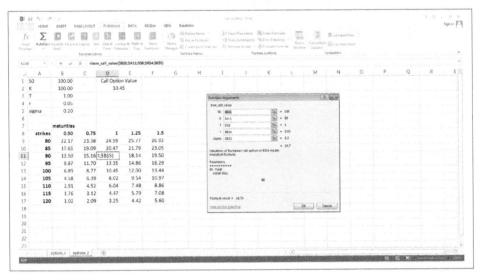

Figure 12-8. Screenshot of Excel with parameter grid for European option values

Whereas in a previous example we plotted data contained in an Excel spreadsheet, we can now also plot data generated with Python in our spreadsheet. Figure 12-9 shows a 3D plot generated with Excel for the European option value surface.

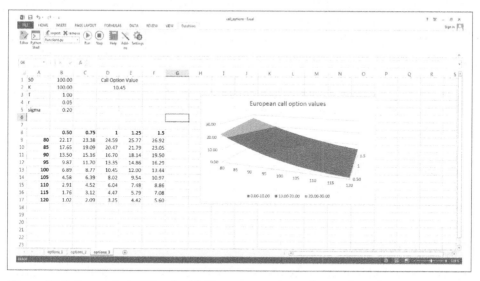

Figure 12-9. Screenshot of Excel with European option value surface plot

xlwings

At the time of this writing, a new contender in the Python-Excel integration world has emerged: xlwings (*http://www.xlwings.org*). xlwings provides almost all the functionality for interacting with and scripting Excel spreadsheets with Python. It is, in contrast to the DataNitro solution, an open source library and can be freely shipped with any spreadsheet. The receiver of an xlwings "powered" spreadsheet only needs a (minimal) Python installation. One advantage of xlwings is that it works with Excel both on Windows and Apple/Mac operating systems. In addition, it is well documented, although it is only in early release (0.3 at the time of this writing). The whole solution and approach look promising. and anybody interested in integrating Python and Excel should give it a try.

Conclusions

There are several options to integrate Python with Excel. Some Python libraries—like xlwt or xlsxwriter—allow the creation of Excel spreadsheets. Other libraries like xlrd allow the reading of arbitrary spreadsheet files, or they allow both reading and writing of spreadsheet files.

pandas is, at least for some tasks, also helpful. For example, it is useful when it comes to writing larger data sets to a spreadsheet file or when it comes to reading data stored in such a file format.

The most powerful solution, however, at the time of this writing is the one by DataNitro that offers a tight integration of both worlds. It has similar (or even better) spreadsheet manipulation capabilities than other libraries. In addition, DataNitro allows us, for example, to expose Python plots to Excel spreadsheets. More importantly, it allows us to define user-defined Python functions (UDFs) for usage with Excel that are callable in the same way as Excel's built-in functions are. xlwings, a new, open source library that has been made available recently, is similar in scope and capabilities to the DataNi tro solution.

In particular, the DataNitro and xlwings approaches allow us to use Excel as a flexible and powerful general GUI—available on almost every computer in the finance industry—and combine it with the analytical capabilities of Python. The best of both worlds, so to say.

Further Reading

For all libraries and solutions presented in this chapter, there are helpful web resources available:

- For xlrd and xlwt, see *http://www.python-excel.org* for the online documentation; there is also a tutorial available in PDF format at *http://www.simplistix.co.uk/presen tations/python-excel.pdf*.

- xlsxwriter is nicely documented on the website *http://xlsxwriter.readthedocs.org*.

- OpenPyxl has its home here: *http://pythonhosted.org/openpyxl/*.

- For detailed information about PyXLL, see *https://www.pyxll.com*.

- Free trials and detailed documentation for DataNitro can be found at *http:// www.datanitro.com*.

- You can find the documentation and everything else you need regarding xlwings at *http://xlwings.org*.

## CHAPTER 13

Object Orientation and Graphical User Interfaces

> First, solve the problem. Then, write the code.
>
> — Jon Johnson

Object orientation has its fans and critics. Referring to the quote above, object-oriented implementation styles might provide the most benefit when they are applied by programmers who really understand the problem at hand and when there is much to gain from abstraction and generalization. On the other hand, if you do not know what exactly to do, a different, more interactive and exploratory programming style, like procedural programming, might be a better choice.

In this chapter, we do not want to discuss the risks and merits of using object orientation. We take it for granted that this approach has its place when it comes to the development of more complex financial applications (cf. the project implemented in Part III of the book) and that it brings along a number of measurable benefits in these cases. When it comes to building graphical user interfaces (GUIs), object orientation in general is a *conditio sine qua non*.

Therefore, we combine the two topics in this chapter and introduce first fundamental concepts of Python classes and objects. Equipped with this knowledge, it is much easier to introduce the development of GUIs.

Object Orientation

Wikipedia (*http://bit.ly/oo_programming*) provides the following definition for *object-oriented programming*:

> Object-oriented programming (OOP) is a programming paradigm that represents concepts as "objects" that have data fields (attributes that describe the object) and associated

procedures known as methods. Objects, which are usually instances of classes, are used to interact with one another to design applications and computer programs.

This already provides the main technical terms that are also used in the Python world for classes and objects and that will be made clearer in the remainder of this section.

Basics of Python Classes

We start by defining a new class (of objects). To this end, use the statement `class`, which is applied like a `def` statement for function definitions. The following code defines a new Python class named `ExampleOne`. This class does nothing but "exist." The `pass` command simply does what its name says—it passes and does nothing:

```
In [1]: class ExampleOne(object):
            pass
```

However, the existence of the class `ExampleOne` allows us to generate instances of the class as new Python objects:

```
In [2]: c = ExampleOne()
```

In addition, since this class inherits from the general `object` class, it already has some batteries included. For example, the following provides the string representation of the newly generated object based on our class:

```
In [3]: c.__str__()
Out[3]: '<__main__.ExampleOne object at 0x7f8fcc28ef10>'
```

We can also use `type` to learn about the type of the object—in this case, an instance of the class `ExampleOne`:

```
In [4]: type(c)
Out[4]: __main__.ExampleOne
```

Let us now define a class that has two attributes, say, a and b. To this end, we define a special method called `init` that is automatically invoked at every instantiation of the class. Note that the object itself—i.e., by Python convention, `self`—is also a parameter of this function:

```
In [5]: class ExampleTwo(object):
            def __init__(self, a, b):
                self.a = a
                self.b = b
```

Instantiating the new class `ExampleTwo` now takes two values, one for attribute a and one for attribute b. Note in the preceding definition that these attributes are referenced internally (i.e., in the class definition) by `self.a` and `self.b`, respectively:

```
In [6]: c = ExampleTwo(1, 'text')
```

Similarly, we can access the values of the attributes of the object c as follows:

```
In [7]: c.a
Out[7]: 1
In [8]: c.b
Out[8]: 'text'
```

We can also overwrite our initial values by simply assigning new values to the attributes:

```
In [9]: c.a = 100
In [10]: c.a
Out[10]: 100
```

Python is quite flexible when it comes to the use of classes and objects. For example, attributes of an object can be defined even after instantiation, as the following example illustrates:

```
In [11]: c = ExampleOne()
In [12]: c.first_name = 'Jason'
         c.last_name = 'Bourne'
         c.movies = 4
In [13]: print c.first_name, c.last_name, c.movies
Out[13]: Jason Bourne 4
```

The class definition that follows introduces methods for classes. In this case, the class ExampleThree is the same as ExampleTwo apart from the fact that there is a definition for a custom method, addition:

```
In [14]: class ExampleThree(object):
             def __init__(self, a, b):
                 self.a = a
                 self.b = b
             def addition(self):
                 return self.a + self.b
```

Instantiation works as before. This time we use only integers for the attributes a and b:

```
In [15]: c = ExampleThree(10, 15)
```

A call of the method addition then returns the sum of the two attribute values (as long as it is defined, given the types of the attributes):

```
In [16]: c.addition()
Out[16]: 25
In [17]: c.a += 10
         c.addition()
Out[17]: 35
```

One of the advantages of the object-oriented programming paradigm is reusability. As pointed out, the class definitions for ExampleTwo and ExampleThree are only different with respect to the custom method definition. Another way of defining the class Exam pleThree is therefore to use the class ExampleTwo and to inherit from this class the definition of the special function init:

```
In [18]: class ExampleFour(ExampleTwo):
             def addition(self):
                 return self.a + self.b
```

The behavior of instances of class ExampleFour is now exactly the same as that of instances of class ExampleThree:

```
In [19]: c = ExampleFour(10, 15)
```

```
In [20]: c.addition()
```

```
Out[20]: 25
```

Python allows for multiple inheritances. However, one should be careful with regard to readability and maintainability, especially by others:

```
In [21]: class ExampleFive(ExampleFour):
             def multiplication(self):
                 return self.a * self.b
```

```
In [22]: c = ExampleFive(10, 15)
```

```
In [23]: c.addition()
```

```
Out[23]: 25
```

```
In [24]: c.multiplication()
```

```
Out[24]: 150
```

For example, custom method definitions do not necessarily need to be included in the class definition itself. They can be placed somewhere else, and as long as they are in the global namespace, they can be used within a class definition. The following code illustrates this approach:

```
In [25]: def multiplication(self):
                 return self.a * self.b
```

```
In [26]: class ExampleSix(ExampleFour):
             multiplication = multiplication
```

And again, the instance of the class ExampleSix behaves exactly the same as the instance of the earlier class ExampleFive:

```
In [27]: c = ExampleSix(10, 15)
```

```
In [28]: c.addition()
```

```
Out[28]: 25
```

```
In [29]: c.multiplication()

Out[29]: 150
```

It might be helpful to have (class/object) *private* attributes. These are generally indicated by one or two leading underscores, as the following class definition illustrates:

```
In [30]: class ExampleSeven(object):
             def __init__(self, a, b):
                 self.a = a
                 self.b = b
                 self.__sum = a + b
             multiplication = multiplication
             def addition(self):
                 return self.__sum
```

The behavior is the same as before when it comes to a call of the method `addition`:

```
In [31]: c = ExampleSeven(10, 15)

In [32]: c.addition()

Out[32]: 25
```

Here, you cannot directly access the private attribute `sum`. However, via the following syntax, it is still possible:

```
In [33]: c._ExampleSeven__sum

Out[33]: 25
```

As the class `ExampleSeven` is defined, one must be careful with the inner workings. For example, a change of an attribute value does not change the result of the `addition` method call:

```
In [34]: c.a += 10
         c.a

Out[34]: 20

In [35]: c.addition()

Out[35]: 25
```

This, of course, is due to the fact that the private attribute is not updated:

```
In [36]: c._ExampleSeven__sum

Out[36]: 25
```

Calling the `multiplication` method, however, works as desired:

```
In [37]: c.multiplication()

Out[37]: 300
```

To conclude the introduction into the main concepts of Python classes and objects, we want to pick one other special method of importance: the `iter` method. It is called whenever an iteration over an instance of a class is asked for. To begin with, define a list of first names as follows:

```
In [38]: name_list = ['Sandra', 'Lilli', 'Guido', 'Zorro', 'Henry']
```

In Python it is usual to iterate over such lists directly—i.e., without the use of integer counters or indexes:

```
In [39]: for name in name_list:
             print name

Out[39]: Sandra
         Lilli
         Guido
         Zorro
         Henry
```

We are now going to define a new Python class that also returns values from a list, but the list is sorted before the iterator starts returning values from the list. The class sor ted_list contains the following definitions:

init

> To initialize the attribute elements we expect a list object, which we sort at instantiation.

iter

> This special method is called whenever an iteration is desired; it needs a definition of a next method.

next

> This method defines what happens per iteration step; it starts at index value self.position = -1 and increases the value by 1 per call; it then returns the value of elements at the current index value of self.position.

The class definition looks like this:

```
In [40]: class sorted_list(object):
             def __init__(self, elements):
                 self.elements = sorted(elements)  # sorted list object
             def __iter__(self):
                 self.position = -1
                 return self
             def next(self):
                 if self.position == len(self.elements) - 1:
                     raise StopIteration
                 self.position += 1
                 return self.elements[self.position]
```

Instantiate the class now with the name_list object:

```
In [41]: sorted_name_list = sorted_list(name_list)
```

The outcome is as desired—iterating over the new object returns the elements in alphabetical order:

```
In [42]: for name in sorted_name_list:
             print name

Out[42]: Guido
         Henry
         Lilli
         Sandra
         Zorro
```

In principle, we have replicated a call of the function sorted, which takes as input a list object and returns as output a list object:

```
In [43]: type(sorted(name_list))

Out[43]: list

In [44]: for name in sorted(name_list):
             print name

Out[44]: Guido
         Henry
         Lilli
         Sandra
         Zorro
```

Our approach, however, works on a completely new type of object—namely, a **sor ted_list**:

```
In [45]: type(sorted_name_list)

Out[45]: __main__.sorted_list
```

This concludes the rather concise introduction into selected concepts of object orientation in Python. In the following discussion, these concepts are illustrated by introductory financial use cases. In addition, Part III makes extensive use of object-oriented programming to implement a derivatives analytics library.

Simple Short Rate Class

One of the most fundamental concepts in finance is *discounting*. Since it is so fundamental, it might justify the definition of a *discounting class*. In a constant short rate world with continuous discounting, the factor to discount a future cash flow due at date $t > 0$ to the present $t = 0$ is defined by $D_0(t) = e^{-rt}$.

Consider first the following function definition, which returns the discount factor for a given future date and a value for the constant short rate. Note that a NumPy universal function is used in the function definition for the exponential function to allow for vectorization:

```
In [46]: import numpy as np
         def discount_factor(r, t):
             ''' Function to calculate a discount factor.

             Parameters
             ==========
             r : float
                 positive, constant short rate
             t : float, array of floats
                 future date(s), in fraction of years;
                 e.g. 0.5 means half a year from now

             Returns
             =======
             df : float
                 discount factor
             '''
             df = np.exp(-r * t)
               # use of NumPy universal function for vectorization
             return df
```

Figure 13-1 illustrates how the discount factors behave for different values for the constant short rate over five years. The factors for $t = 0$ are all equal to 1; i.e., "no discounting" of today's cash flows. However, given a short rate of 10% and a cash flow due in five years, the cash flow would be discounted to a value slightly above 0.6 per currency unit (i.e., to 60%). We generate the plot as follows:

```
In [47]: import matplotlib.pyplot as plt
         %matplotlib inline

In [48]: t = np.linspace(0, 5)
         for r in [0.01, 0.05, 0.1]:
             plt.plot(t, discount_factor(r, t), label='r=%4.2f' % r, lw=1.5)
         plt.xlabel('years')
         plt.ylabel('discount factor')
         plt.grid(True)
         plt.legend(loc=0)
```

For comparison, now let us look at the class-based implementation approach. We call it short_rate since this is the central entity/object and the derivation of discount factors is accomplished via a method call:

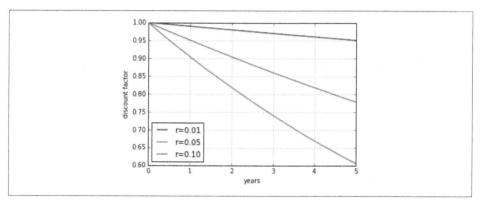

Figure 13-1. Discount factors for different short rates over five years

```
In [49]: class short_rate(object):
             ''' Class to model a constant short rate object.

             Parameters
             ==========
             name : string
                 name of the object
             rate : float
                 positive, constant short rate

             Methods
             =======
             get_discount_factors :
                 returns discount factors for given list/array
                 of dates/times (as year fractions)
             '''
             def __init__(self, name, rate):
                 self.name = name
                 self.rate = rate
             def get_discount_factors(self, time_list):
                 ''' time_list : list/array-like '''
                 time_list = np.array(time_list)
                 return np.exp(-self.rate * time_list)
```

To start with, define sr to be an instance of the class short_rate:

```
In [50]: sr = short_rate('r', 0.05)

In [51]: sr.name, sr.rate

Out[51]: ('r', 0.05)
```

To get discount factors from the new object, a time list with year fractions is needed:

```
In [52]: time_list = [0.0, 0.5, 1.0, 1.25, 1.75, 2.0]  # in year fractions

In [53]: sr.get_discount_factors(time_list)
```

```
Out[53]: array([ 1.        ,  0.97530991,  0.95122942,  0.93941306,  0.91621887,
                 0.90483742])
```

Using this object, it is quite simple to generate a plot as before (see Figure 13-2). The major difference is that we first update the attribute rate and then provide the time list t to the method get_discount_factors:

```
In [54]: for r in [0.025, 0.05, 0.1, 0.15]:
             sr.rate = r
             plt.plot(t, sr.get_discount_factors(t),
                      label='r=%4.2f' % sr.rate, lw=1.5)
         plt.xlabel('years')
         plt.ylabel('discount factor')
         plt.grid(True)
         plt.legend(loc=0)
```

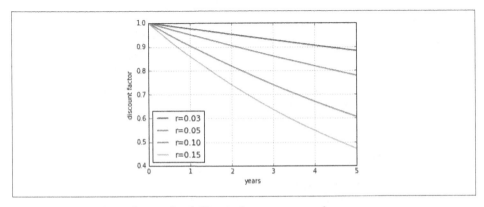

Figure 13-2. Discount factors for different short rates over five years

Generally, discount factors are "only" a means to an end. For example, you might want to use them to discount future cash flows. With our short rate object, this is an easy exercise when we have the cash flows and the dates/times of their occurrence available. Consider the following cash flow example, where there is a negative cash flow today and positive cash flows after one year and two years, respectively. This could be the cash flow profile of an investment opportunity:

```
In [55]: sr.rate = 0.05
         cash_flows = np.array([-100, 50, 75])
         time_list = [0.0, 1.0, 2.0]
```

With the time_list object, discount factors are only one method call away:

```
In [56]: disc_facts = sr.get_discount_factors(time_list)
```

```
In [57]: disc_facts
```

```
Out[57]: array([ 1.        ,  0.95122942,  0.90483742])
```

Present values for all cash flows are obtained by multiplying the discount factors by the cash flows:

```
In [58]: # present values
         disc_facts * cash_flows

Out[58]: array([-100.      ,   47.56147123,   67.86280635])
```

A typical decision rule in investment theory says that a decision maker should invest into a project whenever the net present value (NPV), given a certain (short) rate representing the opportunity costs of the investment, is positive. In our case, the NPV is simply the sum of the single present values:

```
In [59]: # net present value
         np.sum(disc_facts * cash_flows)

Out[59]: 15.424277577732667
```

Obviously, for a short rate of 5% the investment should be made. What about a rate of 15%? Then the NPV becomes negative, and the investment should not be made:

```
In [60]: sr.rate = 0.15
         np.sum(sr.get_discount_factors(time_list) * cash_flows)

Out[60]: -1.4032346276182679
```

Cash Flow Series Class

With the experience gained through the previous example, the definition of another class to model a cash flow series should be straightforward. This class should provide methods to give back a list/array of present values and also the net present value for a given cash flow series—i.e., cash flow values and dates/times:

```
In [61]: class cash_flow_series(object):
             ''' Class to model a cash flow series.

             Attributes
             ==========
             name : string
                 name of the object
             time_list : list/array-like
                 list of (positive) year fractions
             cash_flows : list/array-like
                 corresponding list of cash flow values
             short_rate : instance of short_rate class
                 short rate object used for discounting

             Methods
             =======
             present_value_list :
                 returns an array with present values
             net_present_value :
                 returns NPV for cash flow series
```

```
            '''
        def __init__(self, name, time_list, cash_flows, short_rate):
            self.name = name
            self.time_list = time_list
            self.cash_flows = cash_flows
            self.short_rate = short_rate
        def present_value_list(self):
            df = self.short_rate.get_discount_factors(self.time_list)
            return np.array(self.cash_flows) * df
        def net_present_value(self):
            return np.sum(self.present_value_list())
```

We use all objects from the previous example to instantiate the class:

```
In [62]: sr.rate = 0.05
         cfs = cash_flow_series('cfs', time_list, cash_flows, sr)

In [63]: cfs.cash_flows

Out[63]: array([-100,   50,   75])

In [64]: cfs.time_list

Out[64]: [0.0, 1.0, 2.0]
```

We can now compare the present values and the NPV with the results from before. Fortunately, we get the same results:

```
In [65]: cfs.present_value_list()

Out[65]: array([-100.        ,   47.56147123,   67.86280635])

In [66]: cfs.net_present_value()

Out[66]: 15.424277577732667
```

There is further potential to generalize the steps of the previous example. One option is to define a new class that provides a method for calculating the NPV for different short rates—i.e., a *sensitivity analysis*. We use, of course, the cash_flow_series class to inherit from:

```
In [67]: class cfs_sensitivity(cash_flow_series):
             def npv_sensitivity(self, short_rates):
                 npvs = []
                 for rate in short_rates:
                     sr.rate = rate
                     npvs.append(self.net_present_value())
                 return np.array(npvs)

In [68]: cfs_sens = cfs_sensitivity('cfs', time_list, cash_flows, sr)
```

For example, defining a list containing different short rates, we can easily compare the resulting NPVs:

```
In [69]: short_rates = [0.01, 0.025, 0.05, 0.075, 0.1, 0.125, 0.15, 0.2]
```

```
In [70]: npvs = cfs_sens.npv_sensitivity(short_rates)
         npvs

Out[70]: array([ 23.01739219,  20.10770244,  15.42427758,  10.94027255,
                  6.64667738,   2.53490386,  -1.40323463,  -8.78945889])
```

Figure 13-3 shows the result graphically. The thicker horizontal line (at 0) shows the cutoff point between a profitable investment and one that should be dismissed given the respective (short) rate:

```
In [71]: plt.plot(short_rates, npvs, 'b')
         plt.plot(short_rates, npvs, 'ro')
         plt.plot((0, max(short_rates)), (0, 0), 'r', lw=2)
         plt.grid(True)
         plt.xlabel('short rate')
         plt.ylabel('net present value')
```

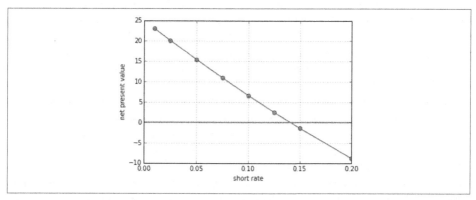

Figure 13-3. Net present values of cash flow list for different short rates

Graphical User Interfaces

For the majority of computer *users*, as compared to developers or data scientists, a graphical user interface (GUI) is what they are used to. Such a GUI does not only bring along visual appeal and simplicity; it also allows us to guide and control user interaction much better than alternative approaches like interactive scripting, or use of a command line interface or shell. In what follows, we build on the examples of the previous section and build simple GUIs for our short rate and cash flow series classes.

To build the GUIs we use the `traits` library, documentation of which you can find at *http://code.enthought.com/projects/traits/docs/html/index.html*. `traits` is generally used for rapid GUI building on top of existing classes and only seldom for more complex applications. In what follows, we will reimplement the two example classes from before, taking into account that we want to use a GUI for interacting with instances of the respective classes.

Short Rate Class with GUI

To start, we need to import the `traits.api` sublibrary:

```
In [72]: import numpy as np
         import traits.api as trapi
```

For the definition of our new `short_rate` class, we use the `HasTraits` class to inherit from. Also note in the following class definition that `traits` has its own data types, which are generally closely intertwined with visual elements of a GUI—to put it differently, `traits` knows which graphical elements (e.g., for a text field) to use to build a GUI (semi)automatically:

```
In [73]: class short_rate(trapi.HasTraits):
             name = trapi.Str
             rate = trapi.Float
             time_list = trapi.Array(dtype=np.float, shape=(5,))
             def get_discount_factors(self):
                 return np.exp(-self.rate * self.time_list)
```

Instantiation of such a `traits`-based class is done as usual:

```
In [74]: sr = short_rate()
```

However, via a call of the method `configure_traits` (inherited from `HasTraits`) a GUI is automatically generated, and we can use this GUI to input values for the attributes of the new object `sr`:

```
In [75]: sr.configure_traits()
```

Figure 13-4 shows such a simple GUI, which in this case is still empty (i.e., no input values have been put in the different fields). Note that the lower five fields all belong to "Time list"—this layout is generated by default.

Figure 13-5 shows the same simple GUI, this time however with values in every single field. Pushing the OK button assigns the values from the input fields to the respective attributes of the object.

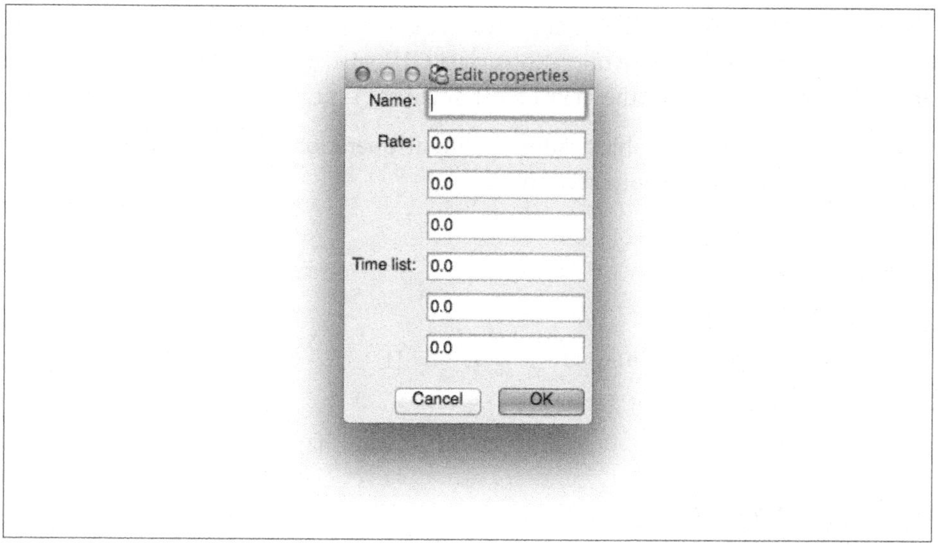

Figure 13-4. Screenshot of traits GUI (empty)

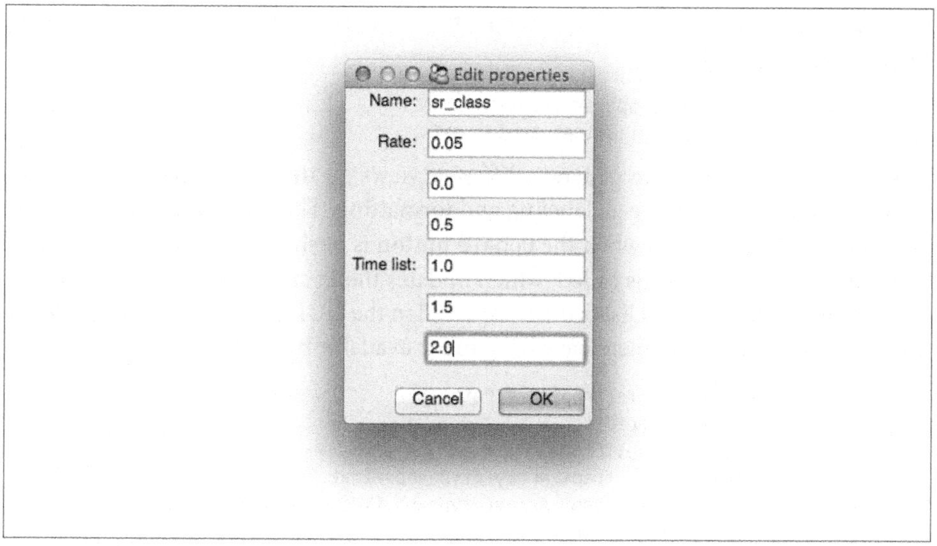

Figure 13-5. Screenshot of traits GUI (with data)

In effect, this gives the same results as the following lines of code:

```
In [76]: sr.name = 'sr_class'
         sr.rate = 0.05
         sr.time_list = [0.0, 0.5, 1.0, 1.5, 2.0]
```

By providing the traits-specific data types, traits is able to generate the correct visual elements to accomplish these operations via a GUI—i.e. a text input field for sr.name and five input elements for the list object sr.time_list.

The behavior of the new object after the input operations is the same as with our short_rate from the previous section:

```
In [77]: sr.rate

Out[77]: 0.05

In [78]: sr.time_list

Out[78]: array([ 0. ,  0.5,  1. ,  1.5,  2. ])

In [79]: sr.get_discount_factors()

Out[79]: array([ 1.         ,  0.97530991,  0.95122942,  0.92774349,  0.90483742])
```

Updating of Values

So far, the new short_rate class using traits allows us to input data for initializing attributes of an instance of the class. However, a GUI usually is also used to present results. You would generally want to avoid providing input data via a GUI and then making the user access the results via interactive scripting. To this end, we need another sublibrary, traitsui.api:

```
In [80]: import traits.api as trapi
         import traitsui.api as trui
```

This sublibrary allows us to generate different views on the same class/object. It also provides more options for, e.g., labeling and formatting. The key in the following class definition is what happens when the Update button is pushed. In this case, the private method _update_fired is called, which updates the list object containing the discount factors. This updated list is then displayed in the GUI window. A prerequisite for this is that all input parameters have been made available by the user:

```
In [81]: class short_rate(trapi.HasTraits):
             name = trapi.Str
             rate = trapi.Float
             time_list = trapi.Array(dtype=np.float, shape=(1, 5))
             disc_list = trapi.Array(dtype=np.float, shape=(1, 5))
             update = trapi.Button
             def _update_fired(self):
                 self.disc_list = np.exp(-self.rate * self.time_list)
             v = trui.View(trui.Group(trui.Item(name = 'name'),
                     trui.Item(name='rate'),
                     trui.Item(name='time_list',
                             label='Insert Time List Here'),
                     trui.Item('update', show_label=False),
                     trui.Item(name='disc_list',
                             label='Press Update for Factors'),
```

```
                    show_border=True, label='Calculate Discount Factors'),
                    buttons = [trui.OKButton, trui.CancelButton],
                    resizable = True)
```

Again, instantiation and configuration are achieved as before:

```
In [82]: sr = short_rate()
```

```
In [83]: sr.configure_traits()
```

Figure 13-6 shows the new, enhanced GUI, which is still empty. You see the new elements, like the Update button and the output fields for the discount factors.

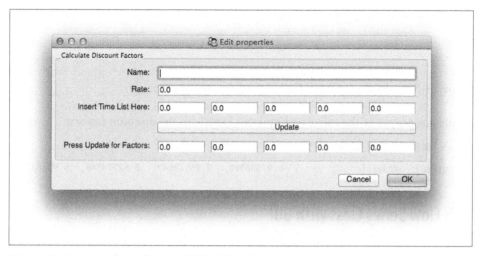

Figure 13-6. Screenshot of traits GUI with updating (empty)

Figure 13-7 illustrates what happens with this new GUI "in action." Providing values
for the object attributes and pushing the Update button returns the calculated discount
factors—this time within the GUI window.

The following Python code shows step-by-step the equivalent operations without a GUI.
First, the assigning of values to the attributes:

```
In [84]: sr.name = 'sr_class'
         sr.rate = 0.05
         sr.time_list = np.array(([0.0, 0.5, 1.0, 1.5, 2.0],), dtype=np.float32)
```

Second, the update of the list object containing the discount factors:

```
In [85]: sr._update_fired()
```

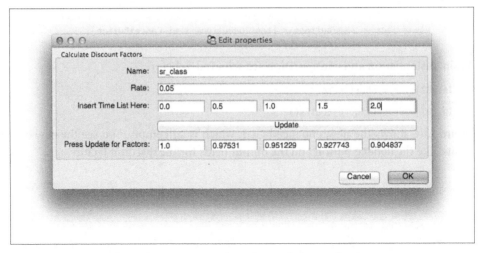

Figure 13-7. Screenshot of traits GUI with updating (after update)

Finally, the output of the calculated/updated list with the discount factors:

```
In [86]: sr.disc_list
```

```
Out[86]: array([[ 1.        ,  0.97530991,  0.95122942,  0.92774349,  0.90483742
         ]])
```

Cash Flow Series Class with GUI

The last example in this section is about the cash_flow_series class. In principle, we have seen in the previous example the basic workings of traits when it comes to presenting results within a GUI window. Here, we only want to add some twists to the story: for example, a slider to easily change the value for the short rate. In the class definition that follows, this is accomplished by using the Range function, where we provide a minimum, a maximum, and a default value. There are also more output fields to account for the calculation of the present values and the net present value:

```
In [87]: class cash_flow_series(trapi.HasTraits):
             name = trapi.Str
             short_rate = trapi.Range(0.0, 0.5, 0.05)
             time_list = trapi.Array(dtype=np.float, shape=(1, 6))
             cash_flows = trapi.Array(dtype=np.float, shape=(1, 6))
             disc_values = trapi.Array(dtype=np.float, shape=(1, 6))
             present_values = trapi.Array(dtype=np.float, shape=(1, 6))
             net_present_value = trapi.Float
             update = trapi.Button
             def _update_fired(self):
                 self.disc_values = np.exp(-self.short_rate * self.time_list)
                 self.present_values = self.disc_values * self.cash_flows
                 self.net_present_value = np.sum(self.present_values)
             v = trui.View(trui.Group(trui.Item(name = 'name'),
```

```
    trui.Item(name='short_rate'),
    trui.Item(name='time_list', label='Time List'),
    trui.Item(name='cash_flows', label='Cash Flows'),
    trui.Item('update', show_label=False),
    trui.Item(name='disc_values',
              label='Discount Factors'),
    trui.Item(name='present_values',
              label='Present Values'),
    trui.Item(name='net_present_value',
              label='Net Present Value'),
    show_border=True, label='Calculate Present Values'),
    buttons = [trui.OKButton, trui.CancelButton],
    resizable = True)
```

Apart from the slightly more complex class definition, the usage is still the same:

```
In [88]: cfs = cash_flow_series()
```

```
In [89]: cfs.configure_traits()
```

Figure 13-8 shows the new GUI without any actions taken so far (i.e., empty). Notice the slider and all the new fields for the cash flow values, the present values, and the net present value.

Figure 13-9 shows a version of the GUI where input data has been typed in already, but no other action has taken place.

Finally, Figure 13-10 presents the GUI with both input data and results data—i.e., after pushing the Update button. Although this is still quite a simple example, the result can almost be considered an *application*. We have:

Input
    The GUI allows for inputting data to initialize all object attributes.

Logic
    There is application logic that calculates discount factors, present values, and an NPV.

Output
    The GUI presents the results of applying the logic to the input data.

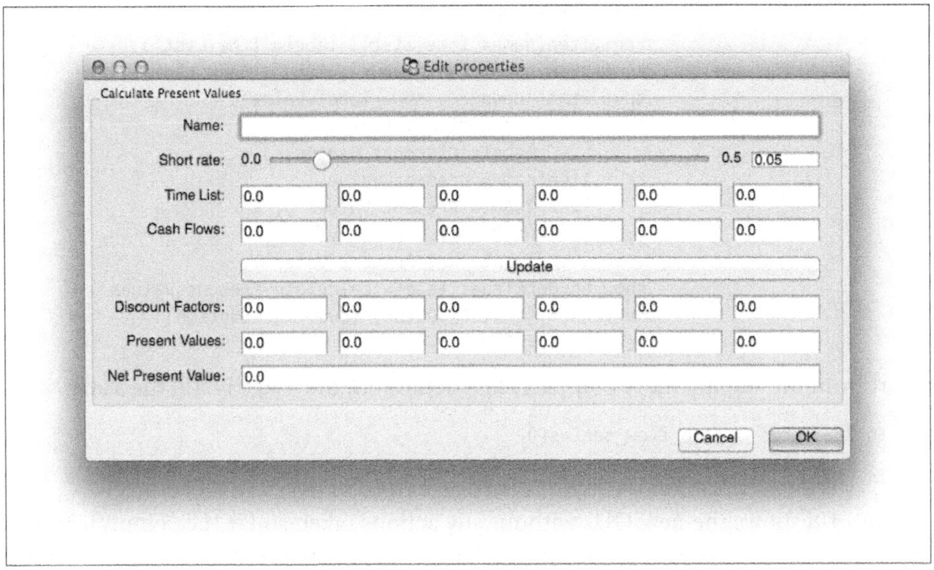

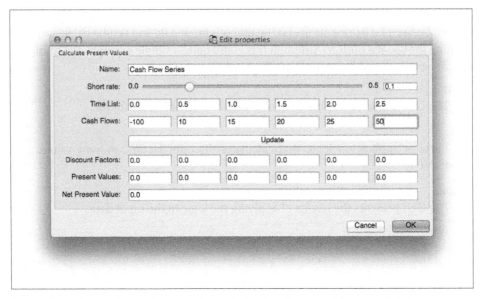

Figure 13-8. Screenshot of traits GUI for Cash Flow Series (empty)

Figure 13-9. Screenshot of traits GUI for Cash Flow Series (with input data)

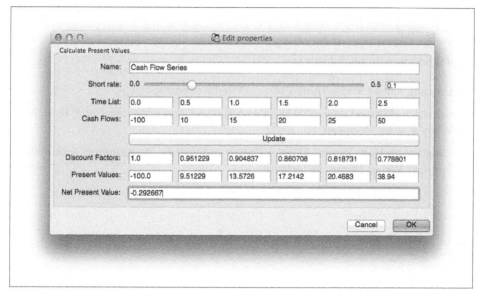

Figure 13-10. Screenshot of traits GUI for Cash Flow Series (with results)

Conclusions

Object-oriented paradigms are an indispensible tool for modern application develop-ment. Python provides a rather flexible framework for the definition of customer-defined classes and for working with instances of these classes. This chapter provides only the fundamentals of Python class definitions—Part III of the book illustrates the use of (financial) Python classes in a more complex and realistic application scenario.

Modern application design generally builds on *graphical* user interfaces. The efficient building of GUIs therefore is generally quite important, even in a rapid application development scenario. This chapter uses the traits library, which allows simple and efficient building of GUIs based on a Pythonic, object-oriented approach. The subsequent chapter shows how to build GUIs based on web technologies, a technical alternative nowadays even used for in-house applications in financial institutions.

Further Reading

The following web resources are good starting points for Python classes and object orientation, and for traits:

- The Python class documentation: *https://docs.python.org/2/tutorial/classes.html*

- The `traits` documentation: *http://code.enthought.com/projects/traits/docs/html/index.html*

Helpful resources in book form are:

- Downey, Allen (2012): *Think Python*. O'Reilly, Sebastopol, CA.
- Goodrich, Michael et al. (2013): *Data Structures and Algorithms in Python*. John Wiley & Sons, Hoboken, NJ.
- Langtangen, Hans Petter (2009): *A Primer on Scientific Programming with Python*. Springer Verlag, Berlin, Heidelberg.

## CHAPTER 14

Web Integration

> I have been quoted saying that, in the future, all companies will be
> Internet companies. I still believe that. More than ever, really.
>
> — Andrew Grove

The *Internet*, or the *Web*, has evolved from some separate world into something that is everywhere and in everything. It has become a technology platform enabling a multitude of different use cases. From a finance perspective, the following seem particularly noteworthy:

Data provision/gathering

Web technology allows the provision of data and the gathering thereof in a simplified manner and generally at reduced costs; it also speeds up in general all associated processes. Large financial data providers, like Bloomberg and Thomson Reuters, rely heavily on the Web and related technologies to provide the financial world with data in real time.

Trading/buying/selling

Using the Web also facilitates trading of financial securities; even private investors today have access to professional trading facilities (e.g., online brokers like Interactive Brokers) and can trade securities in real time.

Application providing

Models like Software-as-a-Service (SaaS) allow both small companies, like startups, and large ones to provide applications in an efficient manner; even the smallest outfit can today reach a global target audience at very little cost. Large corporations benefit from web technologies, for example, when they use them to provide internal applications that are accessible and usable via any standard web browser, instead of installing such applications on hundreds or even thousands of different machines.

Communication

Of course, the Web facilitates communication within organizations and across organizations; the majority of today's business and financial communication has moved from paper to the Web.

Commoditization/scalability

Recent web technologies also allow for better virtualization, making web servers and servers in general a commodity that everybody can rent at rather low variable costs and that is easily scalable when requirements change; computing power and storage capacity become more and more comparable to electricity, which we are all used to getting from the plug sockets at home.

Again, `Python` for the Web is a broad topic in itself that cannot be covered by a single chapter in this book. However, this chapter is able to cover a number of important topics from a finance perspective. In particular, it covers:

Web protocols

The first section shows how to transfer files via `FTP` and how to access websites via `HTTP`.

Web plotting

Web technologies generally allow for better interactivity and for better real-time support than standard approaches, for example, for plotting data; the second section introduces the plotting library `Bokeh` to generate interactive web plots and to realize real-time plotting of financial data.

Web applications

One of `Python`'s strengths is its powerful web frameworks to develop web-based applications; one that is really `Pythonic` and that has become quite popular recently is `Flask`. This chapter illustrates techniques for developing web-based applications using this framework.

Web services

Web services have become an important aspect of web-enabled applications; the last section shows how to develop a simple web service for the valuation of European options on the VSTOXX volatility index.

Web Basics

This section gives a rather brief overview of selected `Python` libraries for working with web technologies and protocols. Several topics, like the handling of email functionality with `Python`, are not touched upon.

ftplib

The File Transfer Protocol (FTP) is, as the name suggests, a protocol to transfer files over the Web.[1] Python provides a dedicated library to work with FTP called ftplib (*http://docs.python.org/2/library/ftplib.html*):

```
In [1]: import ftplib
        import numpy as np
```

In what follows, we will connect to an FTP server, log in, transfer a file to the server, transfer it back to the local machine, and delete the file on the server. First, the connection:

```
In [2]: ftp = ftplib.FTP('quant-platform.com')
```

Not every FTP server is password protected, but this one is:

```
In [3]: ftp.login(user='python', passwd='python')

Out[3]: '230 Login successful.'
```

To have a file that we can transfer, we generate a NumPy ndarray object with some random data and save it to disk:

```
In [4]: np.save('./data/array', np.random.standard_normal((100, 100)))
```

For the FTP file transfer to follow, we have to open the file for reading:

```
In [5]: f = open('./data/array.npy', 'r')
```

This open file can now be written, choosing here binary transfer, by the STOR command in combination with the target filename:

```
In [6]: ftp.storbinary('STOR array.npy', f)

Out[6]: '226 Transfer complete.'
```

Let us have a look at the directory of the FTP server. Indeed, the file was transferred:

```
In [7]: ftp.retrlines('LIST')

Out[7]: -rw-------    1 1001     1001         80080 Sep 29 11:05 array.npy

        '226 Directory send OK.'
```

The other way around is pretty similar. To retrieve a distant file and to save it to disk, we need to open a new file, this time in write mode:

```
In [8]: f = open('./data/array_ftp.npy', 'wb').write
```

Again, we choose binary transfer, and we use the RETR command for retrieving the file from the FTP server:

---

1. For details and background refer to *http://en.wikipedia.org/wiki/Ftp*.

```
In [9]: ftp.retrbinary('RETR array.npy', f)

Out[9]: '226 Transfer complete.'
```

Since we do not need the file on the server anymore, we can delete it:

```
In [10]: ftp.delete('array.npy')

Out[10]: '250 Delete operation successful.'

In [11]: ftp.retrlines('LIST')

Out[11]: '226 Directory send OK.'
```

Finally, we should close the connection to the FTP server:

```
In [12]: ftp.close()
```

In the local directory there are now two files, the one that was generated locally and the one generated by retrieving the file from the server:

```
In [13]: !ls -n ./data

<<<<<<< HEAD
Out[13]: insgesamt 156
         -rw------- 1 1000 1000 77824 Sep 15 08:14 array_ftp.npy
         -rw------- 1 1000 1000 80080 Sep 15 08:14 array.npy

=======
Out[13]: insgesamt 156
         -rw------- 1 1000 1000 77824 Sep 29 17:05 array_ftp.npy
         -rw------- 1 1000 1000 80080 Sep 29 17:05 array.npy
>>>>>>> 798603793467fffcd06a9df88edf091e339dec37

In [14]: !rm -f ./data/arr*
             # cleanup directory
```

All that has happened so far was done without encryption (i.e., was fully insecure). Both login information and data were transferred in readable form. However, for most applications such operations should be encrypted so others are not able to read the data and/or steal the login information and do even worse things.

ftplib can connect to FTP servers securely via the function FTP_TLS. Once such a secure connection is established, all other operations remain the same:

```
In [15]: ftps = ftplib.FTP_TLS('quant-platform.com')

In [16]: ftps.login(user='python', passwd='python')

Out[16]: '230 Login successful.'

In [17]: ftps.prot_p()

Out[17]: '200 PROT now Private.'

In [18]: ftps.retrlines('LIST')

Out[18]: '226 Directory send OK.'

In [19]: ftps.close()
```

httplib

Another important protocol, if not the most important one on the Web, is the HyperText Transfer Protocol (HTTP).[2] This protocol is used whenever a (HTML-based) web page is displayed in the browser. The Python library to work with HTTP is called httplib (*http://docs.python.org/2/library/httplib.html*):

```
In [20]: import httplib
```

As with FTP, we first need a connection to the HTTP server:

```
In [21]: http = httplib.HTTPConnection('hilpisch.com')
```

Once the connection is established, we can send requests, for example asking for the index.htm page (file):

```
In [22]: http.request('GET', '/index.htm')
```

To test whether this was successful, use the getresponse method:

```
In [23]: resp = http.getresponse()
```

The returned object provides status information. Fortunately, our request was successful:

```
In [24]: resp.status, resp.reason
Out[24]: (200, 'OK')
```

Equipped with the response object, we can now read the content as follows:

```
In [25]: content = resp.read()
         content[:100]
           # first 100 characters of the file
Out[25]: '<!doctype html>\n<html lang="en">\n\n\t<head>\n\t\t<meta charset="utf-
         8">\n\n\t\t<title>Dr. Yves J. Hilpisch \xe2\x80'
```

Once you have the content of a particular web page, there are many potential use cases. You might want to look up certain information, for example. You might know that you can find the email address on the page by looking for E (in this very particular case). Since content is a string object, you can apply the find method to look for E:[3]

```
In [26]: index = content.find(' E ')
         index
Out[26]: 2071
```

---

2. For details and background refer to *http://en.wikipedia.org/wiki/Http*.

3. This example is for illustration purposes only. In general, you would want to use specialized libraries such as lxml (*http://lxml.de*) or Beautiful Soup (*http://www.crummy.com/software/BeautifulSoup/*).

Equipped with the index value for the information you are looking for, you can inspect the subsequent characters of the object:

```
In [27]: content[index:index + 29]
```

```
Out[27]: ' E contact [at] dyjh [dot] de'
```

Once you are finished, you should again close the connection to the server:

```
In [28]: http.close()
```

urllib

There is another Python library that supports the use of *different* web protocols. It is called urllib (*http://docs.python.org/2/library/urllib.html*). There is also a related library called urllib2 (*http://docs.python.org/2/library/urllib2.html*). Both libraries are designed to work with arbitrary web resources, in the spirit of the "uniform" in URL (uniform resource locator).[4] A standard use case, for example, is to retrieve files, like CSV data files, via the Web. Begin by importing urllib:

```
In [29]: import urllib
```

The application of the library's functions resembles that of both ftplib and httplib. Of course, we need a URL representing the web resource of interest (HTTP or FTP server, in general). For this example, we use the URL of Yahoo! Finance to retrieve stock price information in CSV format:

```
In [30]: url = 'http://ichart.finance.yahoo.com/table.csv?g=d&ignore=.csv'
         url += '&s=YHOO&a=01&b=1c=2014&d=02&e=6&f=2014'
```

Next, one has to establish a connection to the resource:

```
In [31]: connect = urllib.urlopen(url)
```

With the connection established, read out the content by calling the read method on the connection object:

```
In [32]: data = connect.read()
```

The result in this case is historical stock price information for Yahoo! itself:

```
In [33]: print data
```

```
Out[33]: Date,Open,High,Low,Close,Volume,Adj Close
         2014-03-06,39.60,39.98,39.50,39.66,10626700,39.66
         2014-03-05,39.83,40.15,39.19,39.50,12536800,39.50
         2014-03-04,38.76,39.79,38.68,39.63,16139400,39.63
         2014-03-03,37.65,38.66,37.43,38.25,14714700,38.25
         2014-02-28,38.55,39.38,38.22,38.67,16957100,38.67
```

---

4. There are alternatives to these libraries, like Requests (*http://docs.python-requests.org*), that come with a more modern API.

```
2014-02-27,37.80,38.48,37.74,38.47,15489400,38.47
2014-02-26,37.35,38.10,37.34,37.62,15778900,37.62
2014-02-25,37.48,37.58,37.02,37.26,9756900,37.26
2014-02-24,37.23,37.71,36.82,37.42,15738900,37.42
2014-02-21,37.90,37.96,37.22,37.29,12351900,37.29
2014-02-20,37.83,38.04,37.30,37.79,11155900,37.79
2014-02-19,38.06,38.33,37.68,37.81,15851900,37.81
2014-02-18,38.31,38.59,38.09,38.31,12096400,38.31
2014-02-14,38.43,38.45,38.11,38.23,9975800,38.23
2014-02-13,37.92,38.69,37.79,38.52,12088100,38.52
2014-02-12,38.60,38.91,38.03,38.11,14088500,38.11
2014-02-11,38.15,38.86,38.09,38.50,18348000,38.50
2014-02-10,38.00,38.13,37.25,37.76,17642900,37.76
2014-02-07,36.65,37.27,36.24,37.23,16178500,37.23
2014-02-06,35.65,36.75,35.61,36.24,14250000,36.24
2014-02-05,35.60,35.94,34.99,35.49,14022900,35.49
2014-02-04,35.11,35.86,34.86,35.66,21082500,35.66
2014-02-03,35.94,36.01,34.66,34.90,22195200,34.90
```

The library also provides convenience functions to customize URL strings. For example, you might want to be able to parameterize the symbol to look up and the starting date. To this end, define a new URL string with a string replacement part where you can insert the parameters:

```
In [34]: url = 'http://ichart.finance.yahoo.com/table.csv?g=d&ignore=.csv'
         url += '&%s'  # for replacement with parameters
         url += '&d=06&e=30&f=2014'
```

The function urlencode takes as an argument a Python dictionary with the parameter names and the values to associate:

```
In [35]: params = urllib.urlencode({'s': 'MSFT', 'a': '05', 'b': 1, 'c': 2014})
```

As result, there is a string object that can be inserted into the preceding URL string to complete it:

```
In [36]: params

Out[36]: 'a=05&s=MSFT&b=1&c=2014'

In [37]: url % params

Out[37]: 'http://ichart.finance.yahoo.com/table.csv?g=d&ignore=.csv&a=05&s=MSFT&
         b=1&c=2014&d=06&e=30&f=2014'
```

Equipped with this new URL string, establish a connection and read the data from the connection:

```
In [38]: connect = urllib.urlopen(url % params)

In [39]: data = connect.read()
```

The result again is stock price data, this time for more dates and for Microsoft:

```
In [40]: print data

Out[40]: Date,Open,High,Low,Close,Volume,Adj Close
         2014-07-30,44.07,44.10,43.29,43.58,31921400,43.31
         2014-07-29,43.91,44.09,43.64,43.89,27763100,43.62
         2014-07-28,44.36,44.51,43.93,43.97,29684200,43.70
         2014-07-25,44.30,44.66,44.30,44.50,26737700,44.22
         2014-07-24,44.93,45.00,44.32,44.40,30725300,44.12
         2014-07-23,45.45,45.45,44.62,44.87,52362900,44.59
         2014-07-22,45.00,45.15,44.59,44.83,43095800,44.55
         2014-07-21,44.56,45.16,44.22,44.84,37604400,44.56
         2014-07-18,44.65,44.84,44.25,44.69,43407500,44.41
         2014-07-17,45.45,45.71,44.25,44.53,82180300,44.25
         2014-07-16,42.51,44.31,42.48,44.08,63318000,43.81
         2014-07-15,42.33,42.47,42.03,42.45,28748700,42.19
         2014-07-14,42.22,42.45,42.04,42.14,21881100,41.88
         2014-07-11,41.70,42.09,41.48,42.09,24083000,41.83
         2014-07-10,41.37,42.00,41.05,41.69,21854700,41.43
         2014-07-09,41.98,41.99,41.53,41.67,18445900,41.41
         2014-07-08,41.87,42.00,41.61,41.78,31218200,41.52
         2014-07-07,41.75,42.12,41.71,41.99,21952400,41.73
         2014-07-03,41.91,41.99,41.56,41.80,15969300,41.54
         2014-07-02,41.73,41.90,41.53,41.90,20208100,41.64
         2014-07-01,41.86,42.15,41.69,41.87,26917000,41.61
         2014-06-30,42.17,42.21,41.70,41.70,30805500,41.44
         2014-06-27,41.61,42.29,41.51,42.25,74640000,41.99
         2014-06-26,41.93,41.94,41.43,41.72,23604400,41.46
         2014-06-25,41.70,42.05,41.46,42.03,20049100,41.77
         2014-06-24,41.83,41.94,41.56,41.75,26509100,41.49
         2014-06-23,41.73,42.00,41.69,41.99,18743900,41.73
         2014-06-20,41.45,41.83,41.38,41.68,47764900,41.42
         2014-06-19,41.57,41.77,41.33,41.51,19828200,41.25
         2014-06-18,41.61,41.74,41.18,41.65,27097000,41.39
         2014-06-17,41.29,41.91,40.34,41.68,22518600,41.42
         2014-06-16,41.04,41.61,41.04,41.50,24205300,41.24
         2014-06-13,41.10,41.57,40.86,41.23,26310000,40.97
         2014-06-12,40.81,40.88,40.29,40.58,29818900,40.33
         2014-06-11,40.93,41.07,40.77,40.86,18040000,40.61
         2014-06-10,41.03,41.16,40.86,41.11,15117700,40.85
         2014-06-09,41.39,41.48,41.02,41.27,15019200,41.01
         2014-06-06,41.48,41.66,41.24,41.48,24060500,41.22
         2014-06-05,40.59,41.25,40.40,41.21,31865200,40.95
         2014-06-04,40.21,40.37,39.86,40.32,23209000,40.07
         2014-06-03,40.60,40.68,40.25,40.29,18068900,40.04
         2014-06-02,40.95,41.09,40.68,40.79,18504300,40.54
```

The function urlretrieve allows us to retrieve content and save it to disk in a single step, which is quite convenient in many circumstances:

```
In [41]: urllib.urlretrieve(url % params, './data/msft.csv')

Out[41]: ('./data/msft.csv', <httplib.HTTPMessage instance at 0x7f92ca59afc8>)
```

A brief inspection of the content of the saved file shows that we have indeed retrieved and saved the same content as before:

```
In [42]: csv = open('./data/msft.csv', 'r')
         csv.readlines()[:5]

Out[42]: ['Date,Open,High,Low,Close,Volume,Adj Close\n',
          '2014-07-30,44.07,44.10,43.29,43.58,31921400,43.31\n',
          '2014-07-29,43.91,44.09,43.64,43.89,27763100,43.62\n',
          '2014-07-28,44.36,44.51,43.93,43.97,29684200,43.70\n',
          '2014-07-25,44.30,44.66,44.30,44.50,26737700,44.22\n']

In [43]: !rm -f ./data/*
```

Web Plotting

Chapter 5 introduces `matplotlib`, the most popular plotting library for `Python`. However, as powerful as it might be for 2D and 3D plotting, its strength lies in static plotting. In fact, `matplotlib` is also able to generate interactive plots, e.g., with sliders for variables. But it is safe to say that this is not one of its strengths.[5]

This section starts with generating *static* plots, then proceeds to *interactive* plots to finally arrive at *real-time* plotting.

Static Plots

First, a brief benchmark example using the `pandas` library based on a financial time series from the Yahoo! Finance API, as used in the previous section:

```
In [44]: import numpy as np
         import pandas as pd
         %matplotlib inline
```

As shown in Chapter 6, using `pandas` makes data retrieval from the Web in general quite convenient. We do not even have to use additional libraries, such as `urllib`—almost everything happens under the hood. The following retrieves historical stock price quotes for Microsoft Inc. and stores the data in a `DataFrame` object:

```
In [45]: url = 'http://ichart.yahoo.com/table.csv?s=MSFT&a=0&b=1&c=2009'
         data = pd.read_csv(url, parse_dates=['Date'])
```

`pandas` accepts column names as parameter values for the x and y coordinates. The result is shown in Figure 14-1:

```
In [46]: data.plot(x='Date', y='Close')
```

---

5. For more information on interactive plots with `matplotlib`, refer to the library's home page (*http://www.matplotlib.org*).

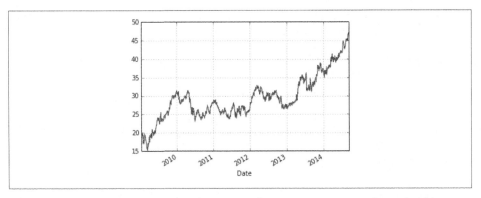

Figure 14-1. Historical stock prices for Microsoft since January 2009 (matplotlib)

Graphics and plots like Figure 14-1 can of course also be used in a web context. For example, it is straightforward to save plots generated with `matplotlib` as files in the PNG (`Portable Network Graphics`) format and to include such files in a website. However, recent web technologies typically also provide interactivity, like *panning* or *zooming*.

Bokeh (*http://bokeh.pydata.org*) is a library that explicitly aims at providing modern, interactive web-based plots to `Python`. According to its website:

> Bokeh is a Python interactive visualization library for large data sets that natively uses the latest web technologies. Its goal is to provide elegant, concise construction of novel graphics in the style of Protovis/D3, while delivering high-performance interactivity over large data to thin clients.

Three elements of this description are noteworthy:

Large data sets
 It is a "plotting problem" in itself to plot large data sets. Just imagine a scatter plot with 1,000,000 points—in general, large parts of the information get lost; Bokeh provides built-in help in this regard.

Latest web technologies
 In general, `JavaScript` is the language of choice as of today when it comes to web development and visualization; it underlies libraries such as D3 (`Data-Driven Docu ments` (*http://d3js.org*)) and also Bokeh.

High-performance interactivity
 On the Web, people are used to real-time interactivity (think modern browser games), which can become an issue when visualizing and interacting with large data sets; Bokeh also provides built-in capabilities to reach this goal.

On a fundamental level, working with Bokeh is not that different from working with matplotlib. However, the default output generally is not a standard window or, for example, an IPython Notebook (which is also an option). It is a separate HTML file:

```
In [47]: import bokeh.plotting as bp
```

```
In [48]: bp.output_file("../images/msft_1.html", title="Bokeh Example (Static)")
         # use: bp.output_notebook("default")
         # for output within an IPython Notebook
```

In terms of plotting, Bokeh provides a wealth of different plotting styles that are continuously enhanced. To start with the simplest one, consider the following code that generates a line plot similar to our pandas/matplotlib benchmark plot. The result is shown as Figure 14-2. Apart from the x and y coordinates, all other parameters are optional:

```
In [49]: bp.line(
             data['Date'],
                 # x coordinates
             data['Close'],
                 # y coordinates
             color='#0066cc',
                 # set a color for the line
             legend='MSFT',
                 # attach a legend label
             title='Historical Stock Quotes',
                 # plot title
             x_axis_type='datetime',
                 # datetime information on x-axis
             tools = ''
         )
         bp.show()
```

In the tradition of matplotlib, Bokeh also has a gallery (*http://bokeh.pydata.org/docs/gallery.html*) showcasing different plot styles.

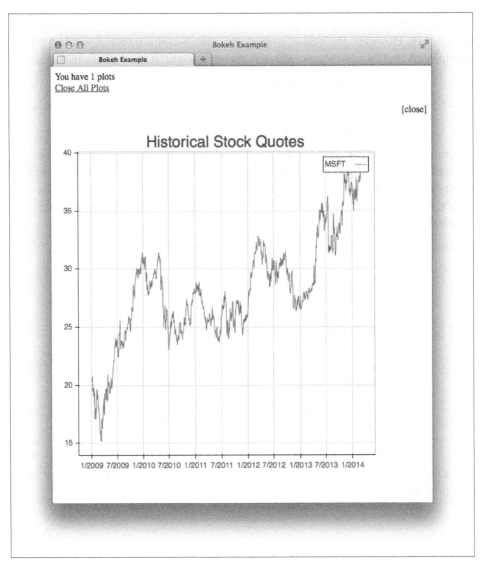

Figure 14-2. Screenshot of HTML-based Bokeh plot

Interactive Plots

The next step is to add interactivity to the web-based plot. Available interactivity elements ("tools") include:

pan

> Supports panning of the plot (like panning with a movie camera); i.e., moving the plot (including x and y coordinates) relative to the fixed plotting frame

`wheel_zoom`
   Enables zooming into the plot by using the mouse wheel

`box_zoom`
   Enables zooming into the plot by marking a box with the mouse

`reset`
   Resets the original/default view of the plot

`previewsave`
   Generates a static (bitmap) version of the plot that can be saved in PNG format

The following code demonstrates adding these tools:

```
In [50]: bp.output_file("../images/msft_2.html",
                        title="Bokeh Example (Interactive)")
         bp.line(
             data['Date'],
             data['Close'],
             color='#0066cc',
             legend='MSFT',
             title='Historical Stock Quotes',
             x_axis_type = "datetime",
             tools = 'pan, wheel_zoom, box_zoom, reset, previewsave'
                 # adding a list of interactive tools
         )
         bp.show()
```

The output of this code is shown as Figure 14-3, where the panning function is used to move the plot within the plotting frame (compare this with Figure 14-2).

In principle, all the features shown so far can also be implemented by using `matplotlib`. In fact, the interactive tools shown for Bokeh are available by default with `matplotlib` when you plot into a separate window. Figure 14-4 shows a zoomed and panned version of the `pandas` plot in Figure 14-1 in a separate (Python-controlled) window. However, in contrast to Bokeh, `matplotlib` cannot "export" this functionality to be included in a separate, standalone graphics file.[6]

---

6. The majority of graphics formats `matplotlib` can export to are static by nature (i.e., bitmaps). A counter-example is graphics in SVG (`Scalable Vector Graphics`) format, which can be programmed in `JavaScript/ECMAScript`. The library's website (*http://www.matplotlib.org*) provides some examples of how to do this.

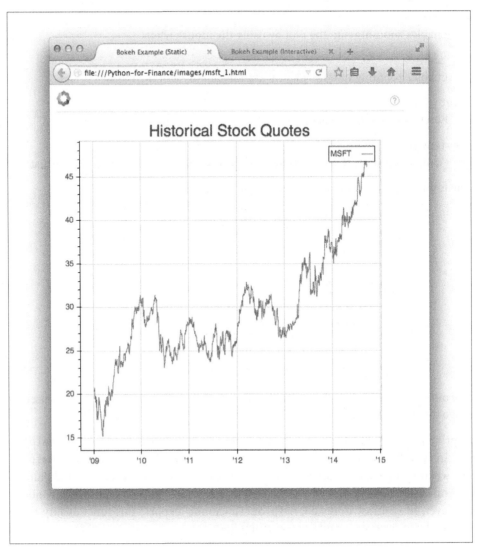

Figure 14-3. Screenshot of HTML-based Bokeh plot with interactive elements

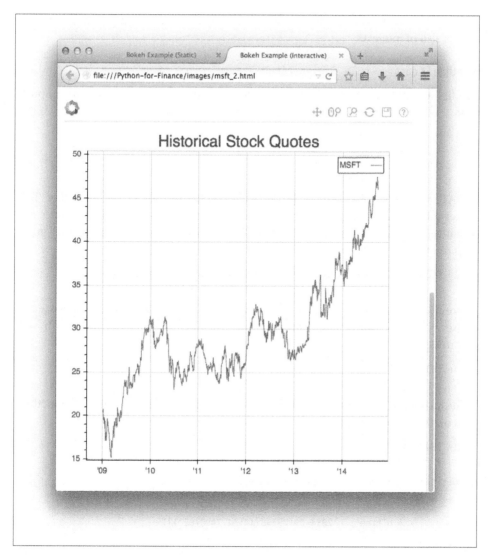

Figure 14-4. Screenshot of pandas/matplotlib-based plot with interactive elements

Real-Time Plots

The previous subsection shows how easy it is to generate interactive, web-based plots with Bokeh. However, Bokeh shines when it comes to real-time visualization of, for example, high-frequency financial data. Therefore, this subsection contains examples for two different real-time APIs, one for FX (foreign exchange) data in JSON (JavaScript Object Notation) format and one for intraday tick data for stock prices delivered in

CSV text file format. Apart from the visualization aspect, how to read out data from such APIs is also of interest.

Real-time FX data

Our first example is based on a JSON API for, among others, FX rates. Some imports first:

```
In [51]: import time
         import pandas as pd
         import datetime as dt
         import requests
```

The API we use is from OANDA (*http://www.oanda.com*), an FX online broker. This broker offers an API sandbox that provides random/dummy data that resembles real exchange rates. Our example is based on the EUR–USD exchange rate (cf. the API guide (*http://developer.oanda.com/*)):

```
In [52]: url = 'http://api-sandbox.oanda.com/v1/prices?instruments=%s'
         # real-time FX (dummy!) data from JSON API
```

To connect to the API we use the `requests` library (*http://docs.python-requests.org*) whose aim is to improve the interface for "humans" when interacting with web resources:

```
In [53]: instrument = 'EUR_USD'
         api = requests.get(url % instrument)
```

With the open connection, data in JSON format is simply read by calling the method `json` on the connection object:

```
In [54]: data = api.json()
         data
Out[54]: {u'prices': [{u'ask': 1.25829,
            u'bid': 1.2582,
            u'instrument': u'EUR_USD',
            u'time': u'2014-09-29T06:14:34.749878Z'}]}
```

Unfortunately, the data is not yet completely in the format we would like it to have. Therefore, we transform it a bit. The following code takes only the first element of the `list` object stored under the key "prices." The resulting object is a standard `dict` object:

```
In [55]: data = data['prices'][0]
         data
Out[55]: {u'ask': 1.25829,
            u'bid': 1.2582,
            u'instrument': u'EUR_USD',
            u'time': u'2014-09-29T06:14:34.749878Z'}
```

Since we collect such small data sets at a high frequency, we use a `DataFrame` object to store all the data. The following code initializes an appropriate `DataFrame` object:

```
In [56]: ticks = pd.DataFrame({'bid': data['bid'],
                               'ask': data['ask'],
                               'instrument': data['instrument'],
                               'time': pd.Timestamp(data['time'])},
                               index=[pd.Timestamp(data['time']),])
         # initialization of ticks DataFrame

In [57]: ticks[['ask', 'bid', 'instrument']]

Out[57]:                                          ask      bid instrument
         2014-09-29 06:14:34.749878+00:00  1.25829   1.2582    EUR_USD
```

Implementing a real-time plot requires two things: real-time data collection and real-time updates of the plot. With Bokeh, this is accomplished by using the Bokeh server, which handles real-time updates of a plot given new data. It has to be started via the shell or command-line interface as follows:

```
$ bokeh-server
```

With the server running in the background, let us implement the real-time data update routine:

```
In [58]: import bokeh.plotting as bp
         from bokeh.objects import Glyph
```

Before any *updating* takes place, there needs to be an object to be updated. This again is a line plot—if only with very little data at first. The output is directed to the IPython Notebook the code is executed in. However, in fact it is redirected again to the server, which in this case can be accessed locally via *http://localhost:5006/*:

```
In [59]: bp.output_notebook("default")
         bp.line(ticks['time'], ticks['bid'],
                 x_axis_type='datetime', legend=instrument)

Out[59]: Using saved session configuration for http://localhost:5006/
         To override, pass 'load_from_config=False' to Session

         <bokeh.objects.Plot at 0x7fdb7e1b2e10>
```

We need to get access to our current plot (i.e., the most recently generated plot). Calling the function curplot returns the object we are looking for:

```
In [60]: bp.curplot()

Out[60]: <bokeh.objects.Plot at 0x7fdb7e1b2e10>
```

Such a Plot object consists of a number of rendering objects that accomplish different plotting tasks, like plotting a Grid or plotting the line (= Glyph) representing the financial data. All rendering objects are stored in a list attribute called renderers:

```
In [61]: bp.curplot().renderers

Out[61]: [<bokeh.objects.DatetimeAxis at 0x7fdbaece6b50>,
          <bokeh.objects.Grid at 0x7fdb7e161190>,
          <bokeh.objects.LinearAxis at 0x7fdb7e161090>,
```

```
            <bokeh.objects.Grid at 0x7fdb7e1614d0>,
            <bokeh.objects.BoxSelectionOverlay at 0x7fdb7e161490>,
            <bokeh.objects.BoxSelectionOverlay at 0x7fdb7e161550>,
            <bokeh.objects.Legend at 0x7fdb7e161650>,
            <bokeh.objects.Glyph at 0x7fdb7e161610>]
```

The following `list` comprehension returns the first rendering object of type `Glyph`:

```
In [62]: renderer = [r for r in bp.curplot().renderers
                     if isinstance(r, Glyph)][0]
```

The `glyph` attribute of the object contains the type of the `Glyph` object—in this case, as expected, a `Line` object:

```
In [63]: renderer.glyph

Out[63]: <bokeh.glyphs.Line at 0x7fdb7e161590>
```

With the rendering object, we can access its data source directly:

```
In [64]: renderer.data_source

Out[64]: <bokeh.objects.ColumnDataSource at 0x7fdb7e1b2ed0>

In [65]: renderer.data_source.data

Out[65]: {'x': 2014-09-29 06:14:34.749878+00:00    2014-09-29 06:14:34.749878+00
         :00
          Name: time, dtype: object, 'y': 2014-09-29 06:14:34.749878+00:00    1.
         2582
          Name: bid, dtype: float64}

In [66]: ds = renderer.data_source
```

This is the object that we will work with and that is to be updated whenever new data arrives. The following `while` loop runs for a predetermined period of time only. During the loop, a new request object is generated and the `JSON` data is read. The new data is appended to the existing `DataFrame` object. The x and y coordinates of the rendering object are updated and then stored to the current session:

```
In [67]: start = time.time()
         # run for 60 seconds
         while (time.time() - start) < 60:
             data = requests.get(url % instrument).json()
               # connect and read data
             data = dict(data['prices'][0])
               # transform data to dict object
             ticks = ticks.append(pd.DataFrame({'bid': data['bid'],
                                               'ask': data['ask'],
                                               'instrument': data['instrument'],
                                               'time': pd.Timestamp(data['time'])},
                                   index=[pd.Timestamp(data['time']),]))
               # append DataFrame object with new data to existing object
             ds.data['x'] = ticks['time']
               # update x coordinates in rendering object
```

```
ds.data['y'] = ticks['bid']
  # update y coordinates in rendering object
bp.cursession().store_objects(ds)
  # store data objects
time.sleep(0.1)
  # wait for a bit
```

Figure 14-5 shows the output of the plotting exercise—i.e., a static snapshot of a real-time plot. This approach and the underlying technology of course have many interesting application areas, both in finance, with its focus today on real-time, high-frequency data, and far beyond.

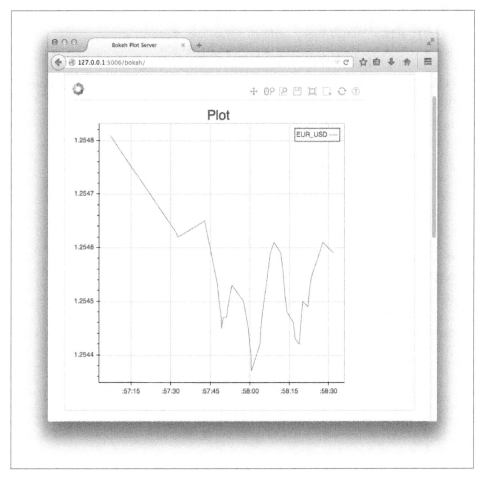

Figure 14-5. Screenshot of real-time Bokeh plot via Bokeh Server (exchange rate)

Real-time stock price quotes

The second example uses real-time, high-frequency stock price data. First, make sure to correctly direct the output (i.e., in this case to the Bokeh server for the real-time plot):

```
In [68]: bp.output_notebook("default")

Out[68]: Using saved session configuration for http://localhost:5006/
         To override, pass 'load_from_config=False' to Session
```

Chapter 6 provides an example based on the data source and API that we use in what follows. It is the stock price API for intraday real-time data provided by Netfonds (*http://www.netfonds.no*), a Norwegian online broker. The API and web service, respectively, have the following basic URL format:

```
In [69]: url1 = 'http://hopey.netfonds.no/posdump.php?'
         url2 = 'date=%s%s%s&paper=%s.O&csv_format=csv'
         url = url1 + url2
```

This URL is to be customized by providing date information and the symbol one is interested in:

```
In [70]: today = dt.datetime.now()
         y = '%d' % today.year
           # current year
         m = '%02d' % today.month
           # current month, add leading zero if needed
         d = '%02d' % (today.day)
           # current day, add leading zero if needed
         sym = 'AAPL'
           # Apple Inc. stocks

In [71]: y, m, d, sym

Out[71]: ('2014', '09', '29', 'AAPL')

In [72]: urlreq = url % (y, m, d, sym)
         urlreq

Out[72]: 'http://hopey.netfonds.no/posdump.php?date=20140929&paper=AAPL.O&csv_fo
         rmat=csv'
```

Equipped with the right URL string, retrieving data is only one line of code away:

```
In [73]: data = pd.read_csv(urlreq, parse_dates=['time'])
             # initialize DataFrame object
```

The details of what follows are known from the previous example. First, the initial plot:

```
In [74]: bp.line(data['time'], data['bid'],
                 x_axis_type='datetime', legend=sym)
             # intial plot

Out[74]: <bokeh.objects.Plot at 0x7f92bedc8dd0>
```

Second, selection of the rendering object:

```
In [75]: renderer = [r for r in bp.curplot().renderers
                     if isinstance(r, Glyph)][0]
         ds = renderer.data_source
```

Third, the while loop updating the financial data and the plot per loop:

```
In [76]: start = time.time()
         while (time.time() - start) < 60:
             data = pd.read_csv(urlreq, parse_dates=['time'])
             data = data[data['time'] > dt.datetime(int(y), int(m), int(d),
                                                    10, 0, 0)]
               # only data from trading start at 10am
             ds.data['x'] = data['time']
             ds.data['y'] = data['bid']
             ds._dirty = True
             bp.cursession().store_objects(ds)
             time.sleep(0.5)
```

Figure 14-6 shows the resulting output—again, unfortunately, only a static snapshot of a real-time plot.

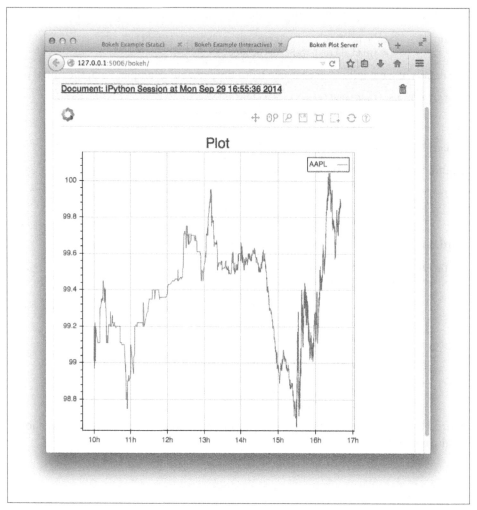

Figure 14-6. Screenshot of real-time Bokeh plot via Bokeh Server (stock quotes)

Rapid Web Applications

If the Python world were to be divided into continents, there might be, among others, the *science and finance* content, the *system administration* continent, and for sure the *web development* continent. Although not really transparent, it is highly probable that the web development continent, to stay with this concept, might be one of the largest when it comes to people (developers) populating it and houses (applications) built on it.

One of the major reasons for Python being strong in web development is the availability of different high-level, full-stack frameworks. As the Python web page (*http:// wiki.python.org/moin/WebFrameworks*) states:

> A web application may use a combination of a base HTTP application server, a storage mechanism such as a database, a template engine, a request dispatcher, an authentication module and an AJAX toolkit. These can be individual components or be provided together in a high-level framework.

Among the most popular frameworks are:

- Django (*http://www.djangoproject.com*)
- Flask (*http://flask.pocoo.org*)
- Pyramid/Pylons (*http://www.pylonsproject.org*)
- TurboGears (*http://www.turbogears.org*)
- Zope (*http://zope2.zope.org*)

It is safe to say that there is not a single framework that is best suited for everybody and every different application type.[7] All have their strengths (and sometimes weaknesses), and often it is more a matter of taste (regarding architecture, style, syntax, APIs, etc.) what framework is chosen.

One framework that has recently gained popularity quite rapidly is Flask. It is the framework we use here, mainly for the following reasons:

Pythonic
> Application development with Flask is really Pythonic, with a lot of the web-related details being taken care of behind the scenes.

Compactness
> It is not too complex and can therefore be learned quite rapidly; it is based mainly on standard components and libraries widely used elsewhere.

Documentation
> It is well documented, with both an online HTML version and a PDF with around 300 pages available at the time of this writing.[8]

The two main libraries that Flask relies on are:

---

7. See *http://wiki.python.org/moin/WebFrameworks* for further information on Python web frameworks. See *https://wiki.python.org/moin/ContentManagementSystems* for an overview of content management systems (CMSs) for Python.

8. Although the framework is still quite recent (it all started in 2010), there are already books about Flask available. Cf. Grinberg (2014).

- `Jinja2` (*http://jinja.pocoo.org/docs/*), a web templating language/engine for `Python`
- `Werkzeug` (*http://werkzeug.pocoo.org*), a `WSGI` (`Web Server Gateway Interface`) toolkit for `Python`

Traders' Chat Room

We will now dive into the example application called *Tradechat* for a traders' chat room, which basically relies on the example used in the tutorial of the `Flask` documentation but includes a couple of changes and adds some further functionality.[9]

The basic idea is to build a web-based application for which traders can register that provides one central chat room to exchange ideas and talk markets. The main screen shall allow a user who is logged in to type in text that is, after pushing a button, added to the timeline, indicating who added the comment and when this happened. The main screen also shows all the historical entries in descending order (from newest to oldest).

Data Modeling

We start by generating the needed directories. `tradechat` shall be the main directory. In addition, at a minimum, we need the two subdirectories `static` and `templates` (by `Flask` convention):

```
$ mkdir tradechat
$ mkdir tradechat/static
$ mkdir tradechat/templates
```

To store data—both for registered users and for comments made in the chat room—we use `SQLite3` (cf. *http://www.sqlite.org* and *http://docs.python.org/2/library/sqlite3.html*) as a database. Two different tables are needed that can be generated by the SQL schema presented in Example 14-1, the details of which we do not discuss here. You should store this under the filename `tables.sql` in the main directory of the application, `tradechat`.

Example 14-1. SQL schema to generate tables in SQLite3

```
drop table if exists comments;
create table comments (
  id integer primary key autoincrement,
  comment text not null,
  user text not null,
```

---

9. The example application is called `Flaskr` (*https://github.com/mitsuhiko/flask/tree/master/examples/flaskr/*) and represents a microblog application. Our example is, more or less, a mixture between `Flaskr` and `Mini twit` (*https://github.com/mitsuhiko/flask/tree/master/examples/minitwit*), another `Flask` example application resembling a simple Twitter clone.

```
  time text not null
);

drop table if exists users;
create table users (
  id integer primary key autoincrement,
  name text not null,
  password text not null
);
```

The Python Code

The SQL schema is a main input for the Python/Flask application to follow. We will go through the single elements step by step to finally arrive at the complete Python script to be stored under tradechat.py in the main directory, tradechat.

Imports and database preliminaries

At the beginning we need to import a couple of libraries and also some main functions from Flask. We import the functions directly to shorten the code throughout and increase readability somewhat:

```
# Tradechat
#
# A simple example for a web-based chat room
# based on Flask and SQLite3.
#

import os
import datetime as dt
from sqlite3 import dbapi2 as sqlite3
from flask import Flask, request, session, g, redirect, url_for, abort, \
    render_template, flash
```

The whole application hinges on a Flask object, an instance of the main class of the framework. Instantiating the class with name lets the object inherit the application name (i.e., main) when the script is executed, for example, from a shell:

```
# the application object from the main Flask class
app = Flask(__name__)
```

The next step is to do some configuration for the new application object. In particular, we need to provide a database filename:

```
# override config from environment variable
app.config.update(dict(
    DATABASE=os.path.join(app.root_path, 'tradechat.db'),
      # the SQLite3 database file ("TC database")
    DEBUG=True,
    SECRET_KEY='secret_key',
      # use secure key here for real applications
```

```
    ))
    app.config.from_envvar('TC_SETTINGS', silent=True)
      # do not complain if no config file exists
```

Having provided the path and filename of the database, the function `connect_db` connects to the database and returns the connection object:

```
def connect_db():
    ''' Connects to the TC database.'''
    rv = sqlite3.connect(app.config['DATABASE'])
    rv.row_factory = sqlite3.Row
    return rv
```

Flask uses an object called g to store global data and other objects. For example, web applications serving large numbers of users make it necessary to connect regularly to databases. It would be inefficient to instantiate a connection object every time a database operation has to be executed. One can rather store such a connection object in the attribute `sqlite_db` of the g object. The function `get_db` makes use of this approach in that a *new* database connection is opened only when there is no connection object stored in the g object already:

```
def get_db():
    ''' Opens a new connection to the TC database. '''
    if not hasattr(g, 'sqlite_db'):
        # open only if none exists yet
        g.sqlite_db = connect_db()
    return g.sqlite_db
```

At least once, we need to create the tables in the database. Calling the function `init_db` for a second time will delete all information previously stored in the database (according to the SQL schema used):

```
def init_db():
    ''' Creates the TC database tables.'''
    with app.app_context():
        db = get_db()
        with app.open_resource('tables.sql', mode='r') as f:
            db.cursor().executescript(f.read())
                # creates entries and users tables
        db.commit()
```

The function `close_db` closes the database connection if one exists in the g object. For the first time (and for sure not the last time), we encounter a Flask function decorator, i.e., `@app.teardown_appcontext`. This decorator ensures that the respective function is called whenever the application context tears down—that is, roughly speaking, when the execution of the application is terminated by the user or by an error/exception:

```
@app.teardown_appcontext
def close_db(error):
    ''' Closes the TC database at the end of the request. '''
```

```
    if hasattr(g, 'sqlite_db'):
        g.sqlite_db.close()
```

Core functionality

Building on the database infrastructure, we can now proceed and implement the core
functionality for the application. First, we have to define what happens when we connect
to the main/home page of the application. To this end, we use the Flask function decorator @app.route("/"). The function decorated in that way will be called whenever a
connection is established to the main page. The function show_entries basically es-
tablishes a database connection, retrieves all comments posted so far (maybe none,
maybe many), and sends them to a template-based rendering engine to return an HTML
document based on the template and the data provided (more on the templating
part soon):

```
@app.route('/')
def show_entries():
    ''' Renders all entries of the TC database. '''
    db = get_db()
    query = 'select comment, user, time from comments order by id desc'
    cursor = db.execute(query)
    comments = cursor.fetchall()
    return render_template('show_entries.html', comments=comments)
```

We only want to allow *registered* users to post comments in the chat room. Therefore,
we must provide functionality for a user to register. To this end, technically, we must
allow use of the POST method for the respective HTML to be rendered by the application
and to be accessed by the user. To register, a user must provide a *username* and a
password. Otherwise, an error is reported. The function register should be considered
a simple illustration only. It is missing a number of ingredients important for real-world
applications, like checking whether a username already exists and encryption of the
passwords (they are stored as plain text). Once users have successfully registered, their
status is automatically changed to logged_in and they are redirected to the main page
via redirect(url_for("show_entries")):

```
@app.route('/register', methods=['GET', 'POST'])
def register():
    ''' Registers a new user in the TC database. '''
    error = None
    if request.method == 'POST':
        db = get_db()
        if request.form['username'] == '' or request.form['password'] == '':
            error = 'Provide both a username and a password.'
            # both fields have to be nonempty
        else:
            db.execute('insert into users (name, password) values (?, ?)',
                        [request.form['username'], request.form['password']])
            db.commit()
            session['logged_in'] = True
```

```
            # directly log in new user
            flash('You were sucessfully registered.')
            app.config.update(dict(USERNAME=request.form['username']))
            return redirect(url_for('show_entries'))
    return render_template('register.html', error=error)
```

For such a web application, there are probably returning users that do not need or want to reregister anew. We therefore need to provide a form to log in with an existing account. This is what the function login does. The functionality is similar to that provided by register:

```
@app.route('/login', methods=['GET', 'POST'])
def login():
    ''' Logs in a user. '''
    error = None
    if request.method == 'POST':
        db = get_db()
        try:
            query = 'select id from users where name = ? and password = ?'
            id = db.execute(query, (request.form['username'],
                                    request.form['password'])).fetchone()[0]
              # fails if record with provided username and password
              # is not found
            session['logged_in'] = True
            flash('You are now logged in.')
            app.config.update(dict(USERNAME=request.form['username']))
            return redirect(url_for('show_entries'))
        except:
            error = 'User not found or wrong password.'
    return render_template('login.html', error=error)
```

Once users have registered or logged in again, they should be able to add comments in the chat room. The function add_entry stores the comment text, the username of the user who commented, and the exact time (to the second) of the posting. The function also checks whether the user is logged in or not:

```
@app.route('/add', methods=['POST'])
def add_entry():
    ''' Adds entry to the TC database. '''
    if not session.get('logged_in'):
        abort(401)
    db = get_db()
    now = dt.datetime.now()
    db.execute('insert into comments (comment, user, time) values (?, ?, ?)',
            [request.form['text'], app.config['USERNAME'], str(now)[:-7]])
    db.commit()
    flash('Your comment was successfully added.')
    return redirect(url_for('show_entries'))
```

Finally, to end the session, the user must log out. This is what the function logout supports:

```
@app.route('/logout')
def logout():
    ''' Logs out the current user. '''
    session.pop('logged_in', None)
    flash('You were logged out')
    return redirect(url_for('show_entries'))
```

If we want to run the Python script as a standalone application we should add the following lines, which make sure that a server is fired up and that the application is served:

```
# main routine
if __name__ == '__main__':
    init_db()  # comment out if data in current
               # TC database is to be kept
    app.run()
```

Putting all these pieces together, we end up with the Python script shown as Example 14-2.

Example 14-2. Python script embodying the core of the Tradechat application

```
# Tradechat
#
# A simple example for a web-based chat room
# based on Flask and SQLite3.
#

import os
import datetime as dt
from sqlite3 import dbapi2 as sqlite3
from flask import Flask, request, session, g, redirect, url_for, abort, \
     render_template, flash


# the application object from the main Flask class
app = Flask(__name__)

# override config from environment variable
app.config.update(dict(
    DATABASE=os.path.join(app.root_path, 'tradechat.db'),
      # the SQLite3 database file ("TC database")
    DEBUG=True,
    SECRET_KEY='secret_key',
      # use secure key here for real applications
))
app.config.from_envvar('TC_SETTINGS', silent=True)
  # do not complain if no config file exists

def connect_db():
    ''' Connects to the TC database.'''
    rv = sqlite3.connect(app.config['DATABASE'])
    rv.row_factory = sqlite3.Row
```

```
        return rv


def get_db():
    ''' Opens a new connection to the TC database. '''
    if not hasattr(g, 'sqlite_db'):
        # open only if none exists yet
        g.sqlite_db = connect_db()
    return g.sqlite_db


def init_db():
    ''' Creates the TC database tables.'''
    with app.app_context():
        db = get_db()
        with app.open_resource('tables.sql', mode='r') as f:
            db.cursor().executescript(f.read())
                # creates entries and users tables
        db.commit()


@app.teardown_appcontext
def close_db(error):
    ''' Closes the TC database at the end of the request. '''
    if hasattr(g, 'sqlite_db'):
        g.sqlite_db.close()


@app.route('/')
def show_entries():
    ''' Renders all entries of the TC database. '''
    db = get_db()
    query = 'select comment, user, time from comments order by id desc'
    cursor = db.execute(query)
    comments = cursor.fetchall()
    return render_template('show_entries.html', comments=comments)


@app.route('/register', methods=['GET', 'POST'])
def register():
    ''' Registers a new user in the TC database. '''
    error = None
    if request.method == 'POST':
        db = get_db()
        if request.form['username'] == '' or request.form['password'] == '':
            error = 'Provide both a username and a password.'
            # both fields have to be nonempty
        else:
            db.execute('insert into users (name, password) values (?, ?)',
                        [request.form['username'], request.form['password']])
            db.commit()
            session['logged_in'] = True
```

```python
            # directly log in new user
            flash('You were sucessfully registered.')
            app.config.update(dict(USERNAME=request.form['username']))
            return redirect(url_for('show_entries'))
    return render_template('register.html', error=error)


@app.route('/login', methods=['GET', 'POST'])
def login():
    ''' Logs in a user. '''
    error = None
    if request.method == 'POST':
        db = get_db()
        try:
            query = 'select id from users where name = ? and password = ?'
            id = db.execute(query, (request.form['username'],
                                    request.form['password'])).fetchone()[0]
              # fails if record with provided username and password
              # is not found
            session['logged_in'] = True
            flash('You are now logged in.')
            app.config.update(dict(USERNAME=request.form['username']))
            return redirect(url_for('show_entries'))
        except:
            error = 'User not found or wrong password.'
    return render_template('login.html', error=error)


@app.route('/add', methods=['POST'])
def add_entry():
    ''' Adds entry to the TC database. '''
    if not session.get('logged_in'):
        abort(401)
    db = get_db()
    now = dt.datetime.now()
    db.execute('insert into comments (comment, user, time) values (?, ?, ?)',
            [request.form['text'], app.config['USERNAME'], str(now)[:-7]])
    db.commit()
    flash('Your comment was successfully added.')
    return redirect(url_for('show_entries'))


@app.route('/logout')
def logout():
    ''' Logs out the current user. '''
    session.pop('logged_in', None)
    flash('You were logged out')
    return redirect(url_for('show_entries'))

# main routine
if __name__ == '__main__':
    init_db()  # comment out if data in current
```

```
                       # TC database is to be kept
app.run()
```

 Security
Although the example in this section illustrates the basic design of a
web application in `Python` with `Flask`, it barely addresses security
issues, which are of paramount importance when it comes to web
applications. However, `Flask` and other web frameworks provide
complete tool sets to tackle typical security issues (e.g., encryption)
with due diligence.

Templating

Basically, templating with `Flask` (`Jinja2`) works similarly to simple string replacements
in `Python`: you have a basic `string` indicating where to replace what and some data to
be inserted into the `string` object. Consider the following examples:

```
In [77]: '%d, %d, %d' % (1, 2, 3)

Out[77]: '1, 2, 3'

In [78]: '{}, {}, {}'.format(1, 2, 3)

Out[78]: '1, 2, 3'

In [79]: '{}, {}, {}'.format(*'123')

Out[79]: '1, 2, 3'
```

Templating to generate `HTML` pages works pretty similarly. The major difference is that
the `string` object "resembles" an `HTML` document (or a part thereof) and has commands
for replacements and also, for example, ways of controlling the flow when rendering
the template (e.g., the `for` loop). Missing information is added during the rendering
procedure, as we added the integers to the `string` object in the previous examples.
Consider now the following `string` object, containing partly standard `HTML` code and
some template-specific code:

```
In [80]: templ = '''<!doctype html>
            Just print out <b>numbers</b> provided to the template.
            <br><br>
            {% for number in numbers %}
              {{ number }}
            {% endfor %}
         '''
```

So far, this is a `string` object only. We have to generate a `Jinja2` `Template` object out
of it before proceeding:

```
In [81]: from jinja2 import Template

In [82]: t = Template(templ)
```

This `Template` object has a method called `render` to make valid HTML code out of the template and some input values—in this case, some numbers via the parameter `numbers`:

```
In [83]: html = t.render(numbers=range(5))
```

The code is again a `string` object:

```
In [84]: html
Out[84]: u'<!doctype html>\n  Just print out <b>numbers</b> provided to the temp
         late.\n  <br><br>\n  \n     0\n  \n     1\n  \n     2\n  \n     3\n  \n
         4\n  '
```

Such an object containing HTML code can be rendered in `IPython Notebook` as follows:

```
In [85]: from IPython.display import HTML
         HTML(html)

Out[85]: <IPython.core.display.HTML at 0x7fdb7e1eb890>
```

Of course, templating involves much more than this simple example can illustrate (e.g., inheritance). More details can be found at *http://jinja.pocoo.org*. However, the templates for the Tradechat application already include a number of important aspects. Specifically, we need the following templates:

layout.html
Defines the basic layout from which the other templates inherit

register.html
The template for the user registration page

login.html
The corresponding template for the user login

show_entries.html
The main page showing the comments in the chat room and, if the user is logged in, the text field for writing and posting comments

These files have to be stored in `templates`, the default (sub)directory for templates when using `Flask`.

Example 14-3 shows the template containing the basic layout and some meta-information (like the site title). This is the template all other templates inherit from.

Example 14-3. Template for basic layout of Tradechat application

```
<!doctype html>
<title>Tradechat</title>
<link rel=stylesheet type=text/css
    href="{{ url_for('static', filename='style.css') }}">
<div class=page>
  <h1>Tradechat</h1>
  <div class=metanav>
```

```
{% if not session.logged_in %}
  <a href="{{ url_for('login') }}">log in</a><br>
  <a href="{{ url_for('register') }}">register</a>
{% else %}
  <a href="{{ url_for('logout') }}">log out</a>
{% endif %}
</div>
{% for message in get_flashed_messages() %}
  <div class=flash>{{ message }}</div>
{% endfor %}
{% block body %}{% endblock %}
</div>
```

Figure 14-7 shows a screenshot of the main page after starting the application for the first time. No users are registered (or logged in, of course). No comments have been posted yet.

Figure 14-7. Screenshot of "empty" home page of Tradechat

Example 14-4 provides the templating code for the user registration page. Here, forms are used to allow users to provide information to the page via the POST method.

Example 14-4. Template for Tradechat user registration

```
{% extends "layout.html" %}
{% block body %}
  <h2>Register</h2>
```

```
{% if error %}<p class=error><strong>Error:</strong> {{ error }}{% endif %}
<form action="{{ url_for('register') }}" method=post>
  <dl>
    <dd><font size="-1">Username</font>
    <dd><input type=text name=username>
    <dd><font size="-1">Password</font>
    <dd><input type=password name=password>
    <dd><input type=submit value=Register>
  </dl>
</form>
{% endblock %}
```

Figure 14-8 shows a screenshot of the registration page.

Figure 14-8. Screenshot of Tradechat registration page

The templating code for the login page, as shown in Example 14-5, is pretty similar to the code for the registration page. Again, the user can provide login information via a form.

Example 14-5. Template for Tradechat user login

```
{% extends "layout.html" %}
{% block body %}
  <h2>Login</h2>
  {% if error %}<p class=error><strong>Error:</strong> {{ error }}{% endif %}
  <form action="{{ url_for('login') }}" method=post>
    <dl>
```

```
        <dd><font size="-1">Username</font>
        <dd><input type=text name=username>
        <dd><font size="-1">Password</font>
        <dd><input type=password name=password>
        <dd><input type=submit value=Login>
      </dl>
    </form>
{% endblock %}
```

The login page, as shown in Figure 14-9, not only looks pretty similar to the registration page but also provides mainly the same functionality.

Figure 14-9. Screenshot of Tradechat login page

Finally, Example 14-6 provides the templating code for the main page. This template does mainly two things:

Enables commenting

>If the user is logged in, a text field and a Post button are shown to allow the user to post comments.

Displays comments

>All comments found in the database are displayed in reverse chronological order (newest first, oldest last).

Example 14-6. Template for Tradechat main page with chat room comments

```
{% extends "layout.html" %}
{% block body %}
  {% if session.logged_in %}
    <form action="{{ url_for('add_entry') }}" method=post class=add-comment>
      <dl>
        <dd>What's up?
        <dd><textarea name=text rows=3 cols=40></textarea>
        <dd><input type=submit value=Post>
      </dl>
    </form>
  {% endif %}
  <ul class=comments>
  {% for comment in comments %}
    <li>{{ comment.comment|safe }}
        <font size="-2">({{ comment.user }} @ {{ comment.time }})</font>
  {% else %}
    <li><em>No comments so far.</em>
  {% endfor %}
  </ul>
{% endblock %}
```

Once a user is logged in and has posted some comments, the main page shows the text field and the Post button as well as all comments stored in the database (cf. Figure 14-10).

Just showing the screenshots in combination with the templates is cheating, in a sense. What is missing in the mix is the styling information.

Figure 14-10. Screenshot of Tradechat main page

Styling

Today's standard when it comes to the styling of web pages and web-based applications is CSS (Cascading Style Sheets). If you take a closer look at the single templates, you will find in many places parameterizations like class=comments or class=add-comment. Without a corresponding CSS file, these parameterizations are essentially meaningless.

Therefore, let us have a look at the file style.css, stored in the (sub)directory static and shown in Example 14-7. Here you find the aforementioned parameters (com ments, add-comment) again. You also find references to standard HTML tags, like h1 for the highest-ranking header. All information provided after a custom class name, like comments, or a standard tag, like h1, defines or changes certain style elements (e.g., font type and/or size) of the relevant object.

This style information is the final ingredient defining the look of the Tradechat application and explaining why, for example, the "Tradechat" heading is displayed in blue (namely, due to the line a, h1, h2 { color: #0066cc; }).

Example 14-7. CSS stylesheet for Tradechat application

```
body { font-family: sans-serif; background: #eee; }
a, h1, h2 { color: #0066cc; }
h1, h2 { font-family: 'Helvetica', sans-serif; margin: 0; }
h1 { font-size: 1.4em; border-bottom: 2px solid #eee; }
h2 { font-size: 1.0em; }

.page { margin: 2em auto; width: 35em; border: 1px solid #ccc;
                padding: 0.8em; background: white; }
.comments { list-style: none; margin: 0; padding: 0; }
.comments li { margin: 0.8em 1.2em; }
.comments li h2 { margin-left: -1em; }
.add-comment { color: #0066cc; font-size: 0.7em; border-bottom: 1px solid #ccc; }
.add-comment dl { font-weight: bold; }
.metanav { text-align: right; font-size: 0.8em; padding: 0.3em;
                margin-bottom: 1em; background: #fafafa; }
.flash { color: #b9b9b9; font-size: 0.7em; }
.error { color: #ff4629; font-size: 0.7em; padding: 0.5em; }
```

If you have followed every step, your tradechat directory should now contain the same
files listed here:

```
In [86]: import os
         for path, dirs, files in os.walk('../python/tradechat'):
             print path
             for f in files:
                 print f

Out[86]: ../python/tradechat
         tables.sql
         tradechat.db
         tradechat.py
         ../python/tradechat/static
         style.css
         ../python/tradechat/templates
         layout.html
         login.html
         register.html
         show_entries.html
```

You can now run the main script from the shell as follows and start the application:

```
$ python tradechat.py
```

You can then access the application via your web browser at *http://127.0.0.1:5000*. Click on `register` to register as a user, and after having provided a username and a password you will be able to post your comments.

Web Services

The last topic in this chapter—and a very interesting and important one—is web services. Web services provide a simple and efficient means to access server-based functionality via web protocols. For example, one of the web services with the highest traffic is the Google search functionality. We are used to visiting *http://www.google.com* and typing some words of interest into the search/text input field provided on the website. However, what happens after you press the Return key or push the Search button is that the page translates all the information it has (from the search field and maybe your personal preferences) into a more or less complex URL.

Such a URL could, for example, take on the form *http://www.google.de/search? num=5&q=yves+python*. When you click this link or copy it into your web browser, Google Search returns those five search results (`num=5`) that the engine considers the best matches given the words provided (`q=Yves+Python`). Your web browser then displays something similar to Figure 14-11.

Using web services, any kind of data- and transaction-oriented financial service can be provided via web technologies. For instance, Yahoo! Finance and Google Finance offer historical stock price information via such a web service approach. More complex services such as derivatives pricing and risk analytics are also available via such services (for example, the web-based analytics solution DEXISION; cf. *http://derivatives-analytics.com*). The following example illustrates the implementation of such a service in the context of option pricing.

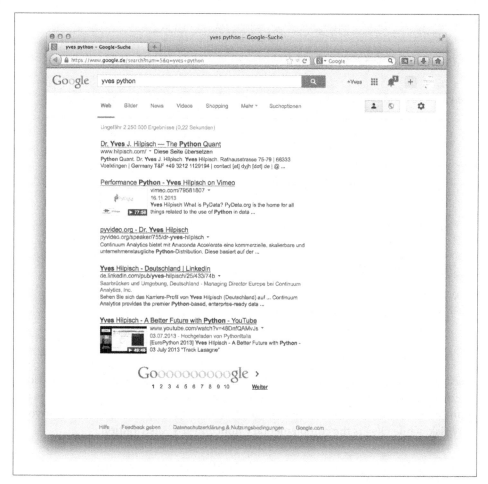

Figure 14-11. Screenshot of Google search results via web service

The Financial Model

In this section, we are going to implement a web service that allows us to value volatility options (e.g., on a volatility index). The model we use is the one of Gruenbichler and Longstaff (1996). They model the volatility process (e.g., the process of a volatility index) in direct fashion by a square-root diffusion, provided in Equation 14-1. This process is known to exhibit convenient features for volatility modeling, like positivity and mean reversion.[10]

---

10. See also the larger case study about volatility options presented in Chapter 19.

Equation 14-1. Square-root diffusion for volatility modeling

$$dV_t = \kappa_V(\theta_V - V_t)dt + \sigma_V\sqrt{V_t}dZ$$

The variables and parameters in Equation 14-1 have the following meanings:

V_t
> The time t value of the volatility index (for example, the VSTOXX)

θ_V
> The long-run mean of the volatility index

κ_V
> The rate at which V_t reverts to θ

Σ_V
> The volatility of the volatility ("vol-vol")

$\theta_V,\ \kappa_V,\ and\ \Sigma_V$
> Assumed to be constant and positive

Z_t
> A standard Brownian motion

Based on this model, Gruenbichler and Longstaff (1996) derive the formula provided in Equation 14-2 for the value of a European call option. In the formula, $D(T)$ is the appropriate discount factor. The parameter ζ denotes the expected premium for volatility risk, while $Q(\cdot)$ is the complementary noncentral χ^2 distribution.

Equation 14-2. Call option formula of Gruenbichler and Longstaff (1996)

$$
\begin{aligned}
C(V_0, K, T) \;=\;& D(T)\cdot e^{-\beta T}\cdot V_0\cdot Q(\gamma\cdot K\,|\,v+4, \lambda)\\
+\;& D(T)\cdot\left(\frac{\alpha}{\beta}\right)\cdot\left(1-e^{-\beta T}\right)\cdot Q(\gamma\cdot K\,|\,v+2, \lambda)\\
-\;& D(T)\cdot K\cdot Q(\gamma\cdot K\,|\,v, \lambda)\\
\alpha \;=\;& \kappa\theta\\
\beta \;=\;& \kappa+\zeta\\
\gamma \;=\;& \frac{4\beta}{\sigma^2\left(1-e^{-\beta T}\right)}\\
v \;=\;& \frac{4\alpha}{\sigma^2}\\
\lambda \;=\;& \gamma\cdot e^{-\beta T}\cdot V
\end{aligned}
$$

The Implementation

The translation of the formula as presented in Equation 14-2 to Python is, as usual, quite straightforward. Example 14-8 shows the code of a Python module with such a valuation function. We call the script `vol_pricing_formula.py` and store it in a sub-directory, `volservice`.

Example 14-8. Python script for volatility option valuation

```
#
# Valuation of European volatility call options
# in Gruenbichler-Longstaff (1996) model
# square-root diffusion framework
# -- semianalytical formula
#
from scipy.stats import ncx2
import numpy as np


# Semianalytical option pricing formula of GL96


def calculate_option_value(V0, kappa, theta, sigma, zeta, T, r, K):
    ''' Calculation of European call option price in GL96 model.

    Parameters
    ==========
    V0 : float
        current volatility level
    kappa : float
        mean reversion factor
    theta : float
        long-run mean of volatility
    sigma : float
        volatility of volatility
    zeta :
        volatility risk premium
    T : float
        time-to-maturity
    r : float
        risk-free short rate
    K : float
        strike price of the option

    Returns
    =======
    value : float
        net present value of volatility call option
    '''
    D = np.exp(-r * T)  # discount factor

    # variables
    alpha = kappa * theta
```

```
    beta = kappa + zeta
    gamma = 4 * beta / (sigma ** 2 * (1 - np.exp(-beta * T)))
    nu = 4 * alpha / sigma ** 2
    lamb = gamma * np.exp(-beta * T) * V0
    cx1 = 1 - ncx2.cdf(gamma * K, nu + 4, lamb)
    cx2 = 1 - ncx2.cdf(gamma * K, nu + 2, lamb)
    cx3 = 1 - ncx2.cdf(gamma * K, nu, lamb)

    # formula for European call price
    value = (D * np.exp(-beta * T) * V0 * cx1
      + D * (alpha / beta) * (1 - np.exp(-beta * T))
      * cx2 - D * K * cx3)
    return value
```

To simplify the implementation of the web service we write a convenience function, `get_option_value`, which will check for the provision of all needed parameters to calculate a call option value. The function is stored in a Python module called `vol_pricing_service.py`, the code of which is shown in Example 14-9. This script also contains a dictionary with all the necessary parameters and brief descriptions of these parameters. The function will return an error message detailing what is missing whenever one or more parameters are missing. If all necessary parameters are provided during the web service call, the function calls the pricing function `calculate_option_value` from the `vol_pricing_formula.py` script.

Example 14-9. Python script for volatility option valuation and web service helper function

```
#
# Valuation of European volatility options
# in Gruenbichler-Longstaff (1996) model
# square-root diffusion framework
# -- parameter dictionary & web service function
#
from vol_pricing_formula import calculate_option_value

# model parameters

PARAMS={
    'V0' : 'current volatility level',
    'kappa' : 'mean reversion factor',
    'theta' : 'long-run mean of volatility',
    'sigma' : 'volatility of volatility',
    'zeta' : 'factor of the expected volatility risk premium',
    'T' : 'time horizon in years',
    'r' : 'risk-free interest rate',
    'K' : 'strike'
    }

# function for web service
```

```
def get_option_value(data):
    ''' A helper function for web service. '''
    errorline = 'Missing parameter %s (%s)\n'
    errormsg = ''
    for para in PARAMS:
        if not data.has_key(para):
            # check if all parameters are provided
            errormsg += errorline % (para, PARAMS[para])
    if errormsg != '':
        return errormsg
    else:
        result = calculate_option_value(
                    float(data['V0']),
                    float(data['kappa']),
                    float(data['theta']),
                    float(data['sigma']),
                    float(data['zeta']),
                    float(data['T']),
                    float(data['r']),
                    float(data['K'])
                    )
        return str(result)
```

To begin with, we add the path of the aforementioned Python scripts:

```
In [87]: import sys
         sys.path.append("../python/volservice")
           # adjust if necessary to your path
```

We use the library Werkzeug to handle our WSGI application-based web service (recall that Werkzeug is an integral part of Flask). To this end, we need to import some functions from Werkzeug sublibraries:

```
In [88]: from werkzeug.wrappers import Request, Response
```

Furthermore, for our core WSGI application to follow, we need the function get_option_value that we defined earlier:

```
In [89]: from vol_pricing_service import get_option_value
```

The only thing that remains is to implement the WSGI application (function) itself. This function might in our case look as follows:

```
In [90]: def application(environ, start_response):
             request = Request(environ)
               # wrap environ in new object
             text = get_option_value(request.args)
               # provide all parameters of call to function
               # get back either error message or option value
             response = Response(text, mimetype='text/html')
               # generate response object based on the returned text
             return response(environ, start_response)
```

Here, environ is a dictionary containing all incoming information. The Request function wraps all information in a manner that makes accessing the environ information a bit more convenient. start_response is usually used to indicate the start of a response. However, with Werkzeug you have the Response function, which takes care of the response.

All parameters provided to the web service are found in the request.args attribute, and this is what we provide to the get_option_value function. This function returns either an error message in text form or the calculated option value in text form.

To be better able to serve this function (e.g., via a local web server), we put the function into a separate WSGI script and add the serving functionality to it. Example 14-10 shows the code of this script, called vol_pricing.py.

Example 14-10. Python script for volatility option valuation and web service helper function

```
#
# Valuation of European volatility options
# in Gruenbichler-Longstaff (1996) model
# square-root diffusion framework
# -- WSGI application for web service
#
from vol_pricing_service import get_option_value
from werkzeug.wrappers import Request, Response
from werkzeug.serving import run_simple

def application(environ, start_response):
    request = Request(environ)
      # wrap environ in new object
    text = get_option_value(request.args)
      # provide all parameters of call to function
      # get back either error message or option value
    response = Response(text, mimetype='text/html')
      # generate response object based on the returned text
    return response(environ, start_response)

if __name__=='__main__':
    run_simple('localhost', 4000, application)
```

Being in the right subdirectory (volservice), you can now start the application by executing the following command via the shell or command-line interface:

```
$ python vol_pricing.py
 * Running on http://localhost:4000/
```

This fires up a separate Python process that serves the WSGI application. Using urllib, we can now access the "full power" of the web service. Copying the URL in your web browser and pressing the Return key yields something like the result shown in Figure 14-12.

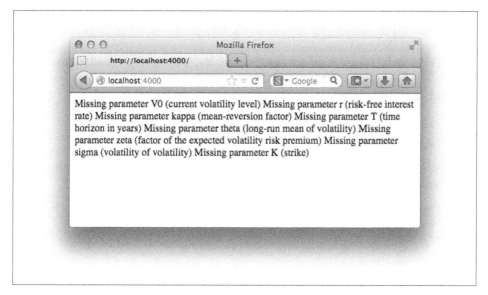

Figure 14-12. Screenshot of the error message of the web service

However, usually you want to use a web service quite a bit differently—for example, from a scripting environment like IPython. To this end, we can use the functionality the urllib library provides:

```
In [91]: import numpy as np
         import urllib
         url = 'http://localhost:4000/'
```

A simple call to the web service without providing any parameters returns the following error message, which (apart from formatting issues) is the same as in the screenshot in Figure 14-12:

```
In [92]: print urllib.urlopen(url).read()
```

```
Out[92]: Missing parameter V0 (current volatility level)
         Missing parameter r (risk-free interest rate)
         Missing parameter kappa (mean-reversion factor)
         Missing parameter T (time horizon in years)
         Missing parameter theta (long-run mean of volatility)
         Missing parameter zeta (factor of the expected volatility risk premium)
         Missing parameter sigma (volatility of volatility)
         Missing parameter K (strike)
```

Of course, we need to provide a number of parameters. Therefore, we first build a URL string object in which we can replace specific parameter values during later calls:

```
In [93]: urlpara = url + 'application?V0=%s&kappa=%s&theta=%s&sigma=%s&zeta=%s'
         urlpara += '&T=%s&r=%s&K=%s'
```

A possible parameterization might be the following one:

```
In [94]: urlval = urlpara % (25, 2.0, 20, 1.0, 0.0, 1.5, 0.02, 22.5)
         urlval

Out[94]: 'http://localhost:4000/application?V0=25&kappa=2.0&theta=20&sigma=1.0&z
         eta=0.0&T=1.5&r=0.02&K=22.5'
```

Using this particular URL string returns an option value, as desired:

```
In [95]: print urllib.urlopen(urlval).read()

Out[95]: 0.202937705934
```

With such a web service, you can of course do multiple calls to calculate multiple option values quite easily:

```
In [96]: %%time
         urlpara = 'http://localhost:4000/application?V0=25&kappa=2.0'
         urlpara += '&theta=25&sigma=1.0&zeta=0.0&T=1&r=0.02&K=%s'
         strikes = np.linspace(20, 30, 50)
         results = []
         for K in strikes:
             results.append(float(urllib.urlopen(urlpara % K).read()))
         results = np.array(results)

Out[96]: CPU times: user 64 ms, sys: 20 ms, total: 84 ms
         Wall time: 196 ms

In [97]: results

Out[97]: array([ 4.91296701,  4.71661296,  4.52120153,  4.32692516,  4.1339945 ,
                 3.94264561,  3.75313813,  3.56575972,  3.38079846,  3.19858765,
                 3.01946028,  2.8437621 ,  2.67184576,  2.50406508,  2.34078693,
                 2.18230495,  2.02898213,  1.88111287,  1.738968  ,  1.60280064,
                 1.47281111,  1.34917004,  1.23204859,  1.12141092,  1.01739405,
                 0.9199686 ,  0.82907686,  0.74462353,  0.66647327,  0.59445387,
                 0.52843174,  0.46798166,  0.41300694,  0.36319553,  0.31824647,
                 0.27785656,  0.24171678,  0.20951651,  0.18094732,  0.1557064 ,
                 0.1334996 ,  0.11414975,  0.09710449,  0.08234678,  0.06958767,
                 0.05859317,  0.04915788,  0.04109348,  0.03422854,  0.02840802])
```

One advantage of this approach is that you do not use your local resources to get the results, but rather the resources of a web server—which might also use, for example, parallelization techniques. Of course, in our example all is local and the web service uses the local computing resources. Figure 14-13 shows the valuation results graphically, concluding this section:

```
In [98]: import matplotlib.pyplot as plt
         %matplotlib inline
         plt.plot(strikes, results, 'b')
         plt.plot(strikes, results, 'ro')
         plt.grid(True)
         plt.xlabel('strike')
         plt.ylabel('European call option value')
```

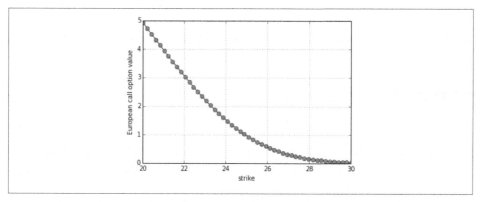

Figure 14-13. Value of European volatility call option for different strikes

Web Services Architecture

The web services architecture is often a powerful and efficient alternative to the provision of Python-based analytical functionality, or even whole applications. This holds true for the Internet as well as for models where private networks are used. This architecture also simplifies updates and maintenance, since such services are generally provided in a centralized fashion.

Conclusions

Nowadays, web technologies are an integral part of almost any application architecture. They are not only beneficial for communicating with the outside world and providing simple to sophisticated web services to external entities, but also within (financial) organizations.

This chapter first illustrates some basic techniques with regard to the most common *communication protocols* (mainly FTP and HTTP). It also shows how to implement interactive *web plotting*, how to interface in real time with web-based financial data APIs (e.g., JSON-based) and how to visualize such high frequency data in real time with Bokeh. These basic tools and techniques are helpful in almost any context.

However, the Python ecosystem also provides a number of powerful, *high level frameworks* to develop even complex web applications in rapid fashion. We use Flask, a framework which has gained some popularity recently, to implement a simple chat room for traders with simple user administration (registration and login). All elements of a typical web application—core functionality in Python, templating with Jinja2, and styling with CSS—are illustrated.

Finally, the last section in this chapter addresses the important topic of *web services*. Using the `Werkzeug` library for a somewhat simplified handling of `WSGI` applications, we implement a web-based pricing service for volatility options based on the model and formula of Gruenbichler and Longstaff (1996).

Further Reading

The following web resources are helpful with regard to the topics covered in this chapter:

- The `Python` documentation should be a starting point for the basic tools and techniques shown in this chapter: *http://docs.python.org*; see also this overview page: *http://docs.python.org/2/howto/webservers.html*.

- You should consult the home page of `Bokeh` for more on this webfocused plotting library: *http://bokeh.pydata.org*.

- For more on `Flask`, start with the home page of the framework: *http://flask.pocoo.org*; also, download the `PDF` documentation: *https://media.readthe docs.org/pdf/flask/latest/flask.pdf*.

- Apart from the `Python` documentation itself, consult the home page of the `Werkzeug` library for more on web services: *http://werkzeug.pocoo.org*.

For a `Flask` reference in book form, see the following:

- Grinberg, Miguel (2014): *Flask Web Development—Developing Web Applications with Python*. O'Reilly, Sebastopol, CA.

Finally, here is the research paper about the valuation of volatility options:

- Gruenbichler, Andreas and Francis Longstaff (1996): "Valuing Futures and Options on Volatility." *Journal of Banking and Finance*, Vol. 20, pp. 985–1001.

PART III
Derivatives Analytics Library

This part of the book is concerned with the development of a smaller, but nevertheless still powerful, real-world application for the pricing of options and derivatives by Monte Carlo simulation.[1] The goal is to have, in the end, a set of Python classes—a *library* we call DX, for *Derivatives AnalytiX*—that allows us to do the following:

Modeling

> To model short rates for discounting purposes; to model European and American options, including their underlying risk factors, as well as their relevant market environments; to model even complex portfolios consisting of multiple options with multiple, possibly correlated, underlying risk factors

Simulation

> To simulate risk factors based on geometric Brownian motions and jump diffusions as well as on square-root diffusions; to simulate a number of such risk factors simultaneously and consistently, whether they are correlated or not

Valuation

> To value, by the risk-neutral valuation approach, European and American options with arbitrary payoffs; to value portfolios composed of such options in a consistent, integrated fashion

---

1 Cf. Bittman, James (2009): *Trading Options as a Professional* (McGraw Hill, New York) for an introduction to and a comprehensive overview of options trading and related topics like market fundamentals and the role of the so-called Greeks in options risk management.

Risk management

To estimate numerically the most important Greeks—i.e., the Delta and the Vega of an option/derivative—independently of the underlying risk factor or the exercise type

Application

To use the library to value and manage a VSTOXX volatility options portfolio in a market-based manner (i.e., with a calibrated model for the VSTOXX)

The material presented in this part of the book relies on the DX Analytics library (*http://dx-analytics.com*), which is developed and offered by the author and The Python Quants GmbH (in combination with the Python Quant Platform (*http://quant-platform.com*)). The full-fledged version allows, for instance, the modeling, pricing, and risk management of complex, multi-risk derivatives and trading books composed thereof.

The part is divided into the following chapters:

- Chapter 15 presents the valuation framework in both theoretical and technical form. Theoretically, the Fundamental Theorem of Asset Pricing and the risk-neutral valuation approach are central. Technically, the chapter presents Python classes for risk-neutral discounting and for market environments.

- Chapter 16 is concerned with the simulation of risk factors based on geometric Brownian motions, jump diffusions, and square-root diffusion processes; a generic class and three specialized classes are discussed.

- Chapter 17 addresses the valuation of single derivatives with European or American exercise based on a single underlying risk factor; again, a generic and two specialized classes represent the major building blocks. The generic class allows the estimation of the Delta and the Vega independent of the option type.

- Chapter 18 is about the valuation of possibly complex derivatives portfolios with multiple derivatives based on multiple, possibly correlated underlyings; a simple class for the modeling of a derivatives position is presented as well as a more complex class for a consistent portfolio valuation.

- Chapter 19 uses the DX library developed in the other chapters to value and manage a portfolio of options on the VSTOXX volatility index.

## CHAPTER 15

Valuation Framework

Compound interest is the greatest mathematical discovery of all time.

— Albert Einstein

This chapter provides the framework for the development of the DX library by introducing the most fundamental concepts needed for such an undertaking. It briefly reviews the Fundamental Theorem of Asset Pricing, which provides the theoretical background for the simulation and valuation. It then proceeds by addressing the fundamental concepts of *date handling* and *risk-neutral discounting*. We take only the simplest case of constant short rates for the discounting, but more complex and realistic models can be added to the library quite easily. This chapter also introduces the concept of a _market environment_—i.e., a collection of constants, lists, and curves needed for the instantiation of almost any other class to come in subsequent chapters.

Fundamental Theorem of Asset Pricing

The *Fundamental Theorem of Asset Pricing* is one of the cornerstones and success stories of modern financial theory and mathematics.[1] The central notion underlying the Fundamental Theorem of Asset Pricing is the concept of a *martingale* measure; i.e., a probability measure that removes the drift from a discounted risk factor (stochastic process). In other words, under a martingale measure, all risk factors drift with the risk-free short rate—and not with any other market rate involving some kind of risk premium over the risk-free short rate.

---

1. Cf. the book by Delbaen and Schachermayer (2004) for a comprehensive review and details of the mathematical machinery involved. See also Chapter 4 of Hilpisch (2015) for a shorter introduction, in particular for the discrete time version.

A Simple Example

Consider a simple economy at the dates today and tomorrow with a risky asset, a "stock," and a riskless asset, a "bond." The bond costs 10 USD today and pays off 10 USD tomorrow (zero interest rates). The stock costs 10 USD today and, with a probability of 60% and 40%, respectively, pays off 20 USD and 0 USD tomorrow. The riskless return of the bond is 0. The expected return of the stock is $\frac{0.6 \cdot 20 + 0.4 \cdot 0}{10} - 1 = 0.2$, or 20%. This is the risk premium the stock pays for its riskiness.

Consider now a call option with strike price of 15 USD. What is the fair value of such a contingent claim that pays 5 USD with 60% probability and 0 USD otherwise? We can take the expectation, for example, and discount the resulting value back (here with zero interest rates). This approach yields a value of $0.6 \cdot 5 = 3$ USD, since the option pays 5 USD in the case where the stock price moves up to 20 USD and 0 USD otherwise.

However, there is another approach that has been successfully applied to option pricing problems like this: *replication* of the option's payoff through a portfolio of traded securities. It is easily verified that buying 0.25 of the stock perfectly replicates the option's payoff (in the 60% case we then have $0.25 \cdot 20 = 5$ USD). A quarter of the stock only costs 2.5 USD and *not* 3 USD. Taking expectations under the real-world probability measure *overvalues* the option.

Why is this case? The real-world measure implies a risk premium of 20% for the stock since the risk involved in the stock (gaining 100% or losing 100%) is "real" in the sense that it cannot be diversified or hedged away. On the other hand, there is a portfolio available that replicates the option's payoff without any risk. This also implies that someone writing (selling) such an option can completely hedge away any risk.[2] Such a perfectly hedged portfolio of an option and a hedge position must yield the riskless rate in order to avoid arbitrage opportunities (i.e., the opportunity to make some money out of no money with a positive probability).

Can we save the approach of taking expectations to value the call option? Yes, we can. We "only" have to change the probability in such a way that the risky asset, the stock, drifts with the riskless short rate of zero. Obviously, a (martingale) measure giving equal mass of 50% to both scenarios accomplishes this; the calculation is $\frac{0.5 \cdot 20 + 0.5 \cdot 0}{10} - 1 = 0$. Now, taking expectations of the option's payoff under the new martingale measure yields the correct (arbitrage-free) fair value: $0.5 \cdot 5 + 0.5 \cdot 0 = 2.5$ USD.

---

2. The strategy would involve selling an option at a price of 2.5 USD and buying 0.25 stocks for 2.5 USD. The payoff of such a portfolio is 0 no matter what scenario plays out in the simple economy.

The General Results

The beauty of this approach is that it carries over to even the most complex economies with, for example, continuous time modeling (i.e., a continuum of points in time to consider), large numbers of risky assets, complex derivative payoffs, etc.

Therefore, consider a general market model in discrete time:[3]

A *general market model* $\mathcal{M}$ in discrete time is a collection of:

- A finite state space Ω
- A filtration $\mathbb{F}$
- A strictly positive probability measure P defined on $\wp(\Omega)$
- A terminal date $T \in \mathbb{N}$, $T < \infty$
- A set $\mathbb{S} \equiv \left\{ \left(S_t^k\right)_{t \in \{0,\ldots,T\}} : k \in \{0,\ldots,K\} \right\}$ of $K+1$ strictly positive security price processes

We write $\mathcal{M} = \{(\Omega,\wp(\Omega),\mathbb{F},P),T,\mathbb{S}\}$.

Based on such a general market model, we can formulate the Fundamental Theorem of Asset Pricing as follows:[4]

Consider the general market model $\mathcal{M}$. According to the *Fundamental Theorem of Asset Pricing*, the following three statements are equivalent:

- There are no arbitrage opportunities in the market model $\mathcal{M}$.
- The set $\mathbb{Q}$ of P-equivalent martingale measures is nonempty.
- The set $\mathbb{P}$ of consistent linear price systems is nonempty.

When it comes to valuation and pricing of contingent claims (i.e., options, derivatives, futures, forwards, swaps, etc.), the importance of the theorem is illustrated by the following corollary:

If the market model $\mathcal{M}$ is arbitrage-free, then there exists a *unique price V_0* associated with any attainable (i.e., replicable) contingent claim (option, derivative, etc.) V_T. It satisfies $\forall Q \in \mathbb{Q}: V_0 = \mathbf{E}_0^Q\left(e^{-rT} V_T\right)$, where e^{-rT} is the relevant risk-neutral discount factor for a constant short rate r.

This result illustrates the importance of the theorem, and shows that our simple reasoning from the introductory above indeed carries over to the general market model.

Due to the role of the martingale measure, this approach to valuation is also often called the *martingale approach*, or—since under the martingale measure all risky assets drift with the riskless short rate—the *risk-neutral valuation approach*. The second term

---

3. Cf. Williams (1991) on the probabilistic concepts.

4. Cf. Delbaen and Schachermayer (2004).

might, for our purposes, be the better one because in numerical applications, we "simply" let the risk factors (stochastic processes) drift by the risk-neutral short rate. One does not have to deal with the probability measures directly for our applications—they are, however, what theoretically justifies the central theoretical results we apply and the technical approach we implement.

Finally, consider market completeness in the general market model:

> The market model $\mathcal{M}$ is *complete* if it is arbitrage-free and if every contingent claim (option, derivative, etc.) is attainable (i.e., replicable).

> Suppose that the market model $\mathcal{M}$ is arbitrage-free. The market model is complete if and only if $\mathbb{Q}$ is a singleton; i.e., if there is a unique *P*-equivalent martingale measure.

This mainly completes the discussion of the theoretical background for what follows. For a detailed exposition of the concepts, notions, definitions, and results, refer to Chapter 4 of Hilpisch (2015).

Risk-Neutral Discounting

Obviously, risk-neutral discounting is central to the risk-neutral valuation approach. We therefore start by developing a Python class for risk-neutral discounting. However, it pays to first have a closer look at the modeling and handling of *relevant dates* for a valuation.

Modeling and Handling Dates

A necessary prerequisite for discounting is the modeling of dates (see also Appendix C). For valuation purposes, one typically divides the time interval between today and the final date of the general market model *T* into discrete time intervals. These time intervals can be homogenous (i.e., of equal length), or they can be heterogenous (i.e., of varying length). A valuation library should be able to handle the more general case of heterogeneous time intervals, since the simpler case is then automatically included. Therefore, we work with lists of dates, assuming that the smallest relevant time interval is *one day*. This implies that we do not care about intraday events, for which we would have to model *time* (in addition to dates).[5]

To compile a list of relevant dates, one can basically take one of two approaches: constructing a list of concrete *dates* (e.g., as `datetime.datetime` objects in `Python`) or of *year fractions* (as decimal numbers, as is often done in theoretical works).

For example, the following two definitions of `dates` and `fractions` are (roughly) equivalent:

---

5. Adding a time component is actually a straightforward undertaking, which is nevertheless not done here for the ease of the exposition.

```
In [1]: import datetime as dt

In [2]: dates = [dt.datetime(2015, 1, 1), dt.datetime(2015, 7, 1),
                                dt.datetime(2016, 1, 1)]

In [3]: (dates[1] - dates[0]).days / 365.
Out[3]: 0.4958904109589041

In [4]: (dates[2] - dates[1]).days / 365.
Out[4]: 0.5041095890410959

In [5]: fractions = [0.0, 0.5, 1.0]
```

They are only *roughly* equivalent since year fractions seldom lie on the beginning (0 a.m.) of a certain day. Just consider the result of dividing a year by 50.

Sometimes it is necessary to get year fractions out of a list of dates. The function get_year_deltas presented in Example 15-1 does the job.

Example 15-1. Function to get year fractions from a list or array of datetime objects

```
#
# DX Library Frame
# get_year_deltas.py
#
import numpy as np

def get_year_deltas(date_list, day_count=365.):
    ''' Return vector of floats with day deltas in years.
    Initial value normalized to zero.

    Parameters
    ==========
    date_list : list or array
        collection of datetime objects
    day_count : float
        number of days for a year
        (to account for different conventions)

    Results
    =======
    delta_list : array
        year fractions
    '''

    start = date_list[0]
    delta_list = [(date - start).days / day_count
                    for date in date_list]
    return np.array(delta_list)
```

This function can then be applied as follows:

```
In [1]: import datetime as dt

In [2]: dates = [dt.datetime(2015, 1, 1), dt.datetime(2015, 7, 1),
                             dt.datetime(2016, 1, 1)]

In [3]: get_year_deltas(dates)
Out[4]: array([ 0.        ,  0.49589041,  1.        ])
```

When modeling the short rate, it becomes clear what the benefit of this is.

Constant Short Rate

We focus on the simplest case for discounting by the short rate; namely, the case where
the short rate is *constant through time*. Many option pricing models, like the ones of
Black-Scholes-Merton (1973), Merton (1976), and Cox-Ross-Rubinstein (1979), make
this assumption.[6] We assume continuous discounting, as is usual for option pricing
applications. In such a case, the general discount factor as of today, given a future date
t and a constant short rate of r, is then given by $D_0(t) = e^{-rt}$. Of course, for the end of the
economy we have the special case $D_0(T) = e^{-rT}$. Note that here both t and T are in year
fractions.

The discount factors can also be interpreted as the value of a *unit zero-coupon bond*
(ZCB) as of today, maturing at t and T, respectively.[7] Given two dates $t \geq s \geq 0$, the
discount factor relevant for discounting from t to s is then given by the equation $D_s(t)$
$= D_0(t) / D_0(s) = e^{-rt} / e^{-rs} = e^{-rt} \cdot e^{rs} = e^{-r(t-s)}$.

Example 15-2 presents a Python class that translates all these considerations into Python
code.[8]

Example 15-2. Class for risk-neutral discounting with constant short rate

```
#
# DX Library Frame
# constant_short_rate.py
#
from get_year_deltas import *


class constant_short_rate(object):
    ''' Class for constant short rate discounting.
```

---

6. For the pricing of, for example, short-dated options, this assumption seems satisfied in many circumstances.

7. A *unit zero-coupon bond* pays exactly one currency unit at its maturity and no coupons between today and
   maturity.

8. See Chapter 13 for the basics of object-oriented development in Python. Here, and for the rest of this part,
   we deviate from the standard PEP 8 naming conventions with regard to Python class names. PEP 8 recom-
   mends using "CapWords" or "CamelCase" convention in general for Python class names. We rather use the
   function name convention as mentioned in PEP 8 as a valid alternative "in cases where the interface is documented and used primarily as a callable."

```
Attributes
==========
name : string
    name of the object
short_rate : float (positive)
    constant rate for discounting

Methods
=======
get_discount_factors :
    get discount factors given a list/array of datetime objects
    or year fractions
'''

def __init__(self, name, short_rate):
    self.name = name
    self.short_rate = short_rate
    if short_rate < 0:
        raise ValueError('Short rate negative.')

def get_discount_factors(self, date_list, dtobjects=True):
    if dtobjects is True:
        dlist = get_year_deltas(date_list)
    else:
        dlist = np.array(date_list)
    dflist = np.exp(self.short_rate * np.sort(-dlist))
    return np.array((date_list, dflist)).T
```

The application of the class constant_short_rate is best illustrated by a simple, concrete example. We stick to the same list of datetime objects as before:

```
In [1]: import datetime as dt

In [2]: dates = [dt.datetime(2015, 1, 1), dt.datetime(2015, 7, 1),
   ...:          dt.datetime(2016, 1, 1)]

In [3]: from constant_short_rate import *

In [4]: csr = constant_short_rate('csr', 0.05)

In [5]: csr.get_discount_factors(dates)
Out[5]:
array([[datetime.datetime(2015, 1, 1, 0, 0), 0.95122942450071402],
       [datetime.datetime(2015, 7, 1, 0, 0), 0.9755103387657228],
       [datetime.datetime(2016, 1, 1, 0, 0), 1.0]], dtype=object)
```

The main result is a two-dimensional ndarray object containing pairs of a datetime object and the relevant discount factor. The class in general and the object csr in particular work with year fractions as well:

```
In [7]: deltas = get_year_deltas(dates)

In [8]: csr.get_discount_factors(deltas, dtobjects=False)
Out[8]:
array([[ 0.        ,  0.95122942],
       [ 0.49589041,  0.97551034],
       [ 1.        ,  1.        ]])
```

This class will take care of all discounting operations needed in other classes.

Market Environments

Market environment is "just" a name for a collection of other data and `Python` objects. However, it is rather convenient to work with this abstraction since it simplifies a number of operations and also allows for a consistent modeling of recurring aspects.[9] A market environment mainly consists of three dictionaries to store the following types of data and `Python` objects:

Constants
These can be, for example, model parameters or option maturity dates.

Lists
These are sequences of objects in general, like a `list` object of objects modeling (risky) securities.

Curves
These are objects for discounting; for example, like an instance of the `con stant_short_rate` class.

Example 15-3 presents the `market_environment` class. Refer to Chapter 4 for a refresher on the handling of `dict` objects.

Example 15-3. Class for modeling a market environment with constants, lists, and curves

```
#
# DX Library Frame
# market_environment.py
#

class market_environment(object):
    ''' Class to model a market environment relevant for valuation.

    Attributes
    ==========
    name: string
```

---

9. On this concept see also Fletcher and Gardner (2009), who use market environments extensively.

```
        name of the market environment
pricing_date : datetime object
        date of the market environment

Methods
=======
add_constant :
        adds a constant (e.g. model parameter)
get_constant :
        gets a constant
add_list :
        adds a list (e.g. underlyings)
get_list :
        gets a list
add_curve :
        adds a market curve (e.g. yield curve)
get_curve :
        gets a market curve
add_environment :
        adds and overwrites whole market environments
        with constants, lists, and curves
'''

    def __init__(self, name, pricing_date):
        self.name = name
        self.pricing_date = pricing_date
        self.constants = {}
        self.lists = {}
        self.curves = {}

    def add_constant(self, key, constant):
        self.constants[key] = constant

    def get_constant(self, key):
        return self.constants[key]

    def add_list(self, key, list_object):
        self.lists[key] = list_object

    def get_list(self, key):
        return self.lists[key]

    def add_curve(self, key, curve):
        self.curves[key] = curve

    def get_curve(self, key):
        return self.curves[key]

    def add_environment(self, env):
        # overwrites existing values, if they exist
        for key in env.constants:
            self.constants[key] = env.constants[key]
```

```
for key in env.lists:
    self.lists[key] = env.lists[key]
for key in env.curves:
    self.curves[key] = env.curves[key]
```

Although there is nothing special in the `market_environment` class, a simple example shall illustrate how convenient it is to work with instances of the class:

```
In [1]: from market_environment import *

In [2]: import datetime as dt

In [3]: dates = [dt.datetime(2015, 1, 1), dt.datetime(2015, 7, 1),
                 dt.datetime(2016, 1, 1)]

In [4]: csr = constant_short_rate('csr', 0.05)

In [5]: me_1 = market_environment('me_1', dt.datetime(2015, 1, 1))

In [6]: me_1.add_list('symbols', ['AAPL', 'MSFT', 'FB'])

In [7]: me_1.get_list('symbols')
Out[7]: ['AAPL', 'MSFT', 'FB']

In [8]: me_2 = market_environment('me_2', dt.datetime(2015, 1, 1))

In [9]: me_2.add_constant('volatility', 0.2)

In [10]: me_2.add_curve('short_rate', csr)  # add instance of discounting class

In [11]: me_2.get_curve('short_rate')
Out[11]: <constant_short_rate.constant_short_rate at 0x104ac3c90>

In [12]: me_1.add_environment(me_2)  # add complete environment

In [13]: me_1.get_curve('short_rate')
Out[13]: <constant_short_rate.constant_short_rate at 0x104ac3c90>

In [14]: me_1.constants
Out[14]: {'volatility': 0.2}

In [15]: me_1.lists
Out[15]: {'symbols': ['AAPL', 'MSFT', 'FB']}

In [16]: me_1.curves
Out[16]: {'short_rate': <constant_short_rate.constant_short_rate at 0x104ac3c90>}

In [17]: me_1.get_curve('short_rate').short_rate
Out[17]: 0.05
```

This illustrates the basic handling of this rather generic "storage" class. For practical applications, market data and other data as well as Python objects are first collected, then a `market_environment` object is instantiated and filled with the relevant data and objects. This is then delivered in a single step to other classes that need the data and objects stored in the respective `market_environment` object.

A major advantage of this object-oriented modeling approach is, for example, that instances of the `constant_short_rate` class can live in multiple environments. Once the instance is updated—for example, when a new constant short rate is set—all the instances of the `market_environment` class containing that particular instance of the discounting class will be updated automatically.

Conclusions

This chapter provides the framework for the larger project of building a `Python` library to value options and other derivatives by Monte Carlo simulation. The chapter introduces the Fundamental Theorem of Asset Pricing, illustrating it by a rather simple numerical example. Important results in this regard are provided for a general market model in discrete time.

The chapter also develops a `Python` class for risk-neutral discounting purposes to make numerical use of the machinery of the Fundamental Theorem of Asset Pricing. Based on a list of either `Python` `datetime` objects or `floats` representing year fractions, instances of the class `constant_short_rate` provide the respective discount factors (present values of unit zero-coupon bonds).

The chapter concludes with the rather generic `market_environment` class, which allows for the collection of relevant data and `Python` objects for modeling, simulation, valuation, and other purposes.

To simplify future imports we will use a wrapper module called `dx_frame.py`, as presented in Example 15-4.

Example 15-4. Wrapper module for framework components

```
#
# DX Library Frame
# dx_frame.py
#
import datetime as dt

from get_year_deltas import get_year_deltas
from constant_short_rate import constant_short_rate
from market_environment import market_environment
```

A single `import` statement like the following then makes all framework components available in a single step:

```
    from dx_frame import *
```

Thinking of a `Python` library and a package of modules, there is also the option to store all relevant `Python` modules in a (sub)directory and to put in that directory a special init file that does all the imports. For example, when storing all modules in a directory called dx, say, the file presented in Example 15-5 does the job. However, notice the naming convention for this particular file.

Example 15-5. Python packaging file

```
#
# DX Library
# packaging file
# __init__.py
#
import datetime as dt

from get_year_deltas import get_year_deltas
from constant_short_rate import constant_short_rate
from market_environment import market_environment
```

In that case you can just use the directory name to accomplish all the imports at once:

```
from dx import *
```

Or via the alternative approach:

```
import dx
```

Further Reading

Useful references in book form for the topics covered in this chapter are:

- Delbaen, Freddy and Walter Schachermayer (2004): *The Mathematics of Arbitrage.* Springer Verlag, Berlin, Heidelberg.
- Fletcher, Shayne and Christopher Gardner (2009): *Financial Modelling in Python.* John Wiley & Sons, Chichester, England.
- Hilpisch, Yves (2015): *Derivatives Analytics with Python.* Wiley Finance, Chichester, England. *http://derivatives-analytics-with-python.com.*
- Williams, David (1991): *Probability with Martingales.* Cambridge University Press, Cambridge, England.

For the original research papers defining the models cited in this chapter, refer to the "Further Reading" sections in subsequent chapters.

## CHAPTER 16

Simulation of Financial Models

> The purpose of science is not to analyze or
> describe but to make useful models of the world.
>
> — Edward de Bono

Chapter 10 introduces in some detail the Monte Carlo simulation of stochastic processes using Python and NumPy. This chapter applies the basic techniques presented there to implement simulation classes as a central component of the DX library. We restrict our attention to three widely used stochastic processes:

Geometric Brownian motion

This is the process that was introduced to the option pricing literature by the seminal work of Black and Scholes (1973); it is used several times throughout this book and still represents—despite its known shortcomings and given the mounting empirical evidence from financial reality—a benchmark process for option and derivative valuation purposes.

Jump diffusion

The jump diffusion, as introduced by Merton (1976), adds a log-normally distributed jump component to the geometric Brownian motion (GBM); this allows us to take into account that, for example, short-term out-of-the-money (OTM) options often seem to have priced in the possibility of large jumps. In other words, relying on GBM as a financial model often cannot explain the market values of such OTM options satisfactorily, while a jump diffusion may be able to do so.

Square-root diffusion

The square-root diffusion, popularized for finance by Cox, Ingersoll, and Ross (1985), is used to model mean-reverting quantities like interest rates and volatility; in addition to being mean-reverting, the process stays positive, which is generally a desirable characteristic for those quantities.

The chapter proceeds in the first section with developing a function to generate standard normally distributed random numbers using variance reduction techniques.[1] Subsequent sections then develop a generic simulation class and three specific simulation classes, one for each of the aforementioned stochastic processes of interest.

For further details on the simulation of the models presented in this chapter, refer also to Hilpisch (2015). In particular, that book also contains a complete case study based on the jump diffusion model of Merton (1976).

Random Number Generation

Random number generation is a central task of Monte Carlo simulation.[2] Chapter 10 shows how to use Python and libraries such as numpy.random to generate random numbers with different distributions. For our project at hand, *standard normally distributed random numbers* are the most important ones. That is why it pays off to have a convenience function available for generating this particular type of random numbers. Example 16-1 presents such a function.

Example 16-1. Function to generate standard normally distributed random numbers

```
import numpy as np

def sn_random_numbers(shape, antithetic=True, moment_matching=True,
                      fixed_seed=False):
    ''' Returns an array of shape shape with (pseudo)random numbers
    that are standard normally distributed.

    Parameters
    ==========
    shape : tuple (o, n, m)
        generation of array with shape (o, n, m)
    antithetic : Boolean
        generation of antithetic variates
    moment_matching : Boolean
        matching of first and second moments
    fixed_seed : Boolean
        flag to fix the seed

    Results
    =======
    ran : (o, n, m) array of (pseudo)random numbers
    '''
    if fixed_seed:
        np.random.seed(1000)
    if antithetic:
```

---

1. We speak of "random" numbers knowing that they are in general "pseudorandom" only.

2. Cf. Glasserman (2004), Chapter 2, on generating random numbers and random variables.

```
    ran = np.random.standard_normal((shape[0], shape[1], shape[2] / 2))
    ran = np.concatenate((ran, -ran), axis=2)
else:
    ran = np.random.standard_normal(shape)
if moment_matching:
    ran = ran - np.mean(ran)
    ran = ran / np.std(ran)
if shape[0] == 1:
    return ran[0]
else:
    return ran
```

The variance reduction techniques used in this function, namely *antithetic paths* and *moment matching*, are also illustrated in Chapter 10.[3]

The application of the function is straightforward:

```
In [1]: from sn_random_numbers import *

In [2]: snrn = sn_random_numbers((2, 2, 2), antithetic=False,
   ...:                            moment_matching=False,
   ...:                            fixed_seed=True)

In [3]: snrn
Out[3]:
array([[[-0.8044583 ,  0.32093155],
        [-0.02548288,  0.64432383]],

       [[-0.30079667,  0.38947455],
        [-0.1074373 , -0.47998308]]])

In [4]: snrn_mm = sn_random_numbers((2, 3, 2), antithetic=False,
   ...:                              moment_matching=True,
   ...:                              fixed_seed=True)

In [5]: snrn_mm
Out[5]:
array([[[-1.47414161,  0.67072537],
        [ 0.01049828,  1.28707482],
        [-0.51421897,  0.80136066]],

       [[-0.14569767, -0.85572818],
        [ 1.19313679, -0.82653845],
        [ 1.3308292 , -1.47730025]]])

In [6]: snrn_mm.mean()
Out[6]: 1.8503717077085941e-17
```

---

3. Glasserman (2004) presents in Chapter 4 an overview and theoretical details of different variance reduction techniques.

```
In [7]: snrn_mm.std()
Out[7]: 1.0
```

This function will prove a workhorse for the simulation classes to follow.

Generic Simulation Class

Object-oriented modeling—as introduced in Chapter 13—allows inheritance of attributes and methods. This is what we want to make use of when building our simulation classes: we start with a *generic* simulation class containing those attributes and methods that all other simulation classes share.

To begin with, it is noteworthy that we instantiate an object of any simulation class by "only" providing three attributes:

name
> A `string` object as a name for the model simulation object

mar_env
> An instance of the `market_environment` class

corr
> A flag (`bool`) indicating whether the object is correlated or not

This again illustrates the role of a *market environment*: to provide in a single step all data and objects required for simulation and valuation. The methods of the generic class are:

generate_time_grid
> This method generates the time grid of relevant dates used for the simulation; this task is the same for every simulation class.

get_instrument_values
> Every simulation class has to return the `ndarray` object with the simulated instrument values (e.g., simulated stock prices, commodities prices, volatilities).

Example 16-2 presents such a generic model simulation class. The methods make use of other methods that the model-tailored classes will provide, like `self.gener ate_paths`. All details in this regard will become clear when we have the full picture of a specialized, nongeneric simulation class.

Example 16-2. Generic financial model simulation class

```
#
# DX Library Simulation
# simulation_class.py
#
import numpy as np
import pandas as pd
```

```
class simulation_class(object):
    ''' Providing base methods for simulation classes.

    Attributes
    ==========
    name : string
        name of the object
    mar_env : instance of market_environment
        market environment data for simulation
    corr : Boolean
        True if correlated with other model object

    Methods
    =======
    generate_time_grid :
        returns time grid for simulation
    get_instrument_values :
        returns the current instrument values (array)
    '''

    def __init__(self, name, mar_env, corr):
        try:
            self.name = name
            self.pricing_date = mar_env.pricing_date
            self.initial_value = mar_env.get_constant('initial_value')
            self.volatility = mar_env.get_constant('volatility')
            self.final_date = mar_env.get_constant('final_date')
            self.currency = mar_env.get_constant('currency')
            self.frequency = mar_env.get_constant('frequency')
            self.paths = mar_env.get_constant('paths')
            self.discount_curve = mar_env.get_curve('discount_curve')
            try:
                # if time_grid in mar_env take this
                # (for portfolio valuation)
                self.time_grid = mar_env.get_list('time_grid')
            except:
                self.time_grid = None
            try:
                # if there are special dates, then add these
                self.special_dates = mar_env.get_list('special_dates')
            except:
                self.special_dates = []
            self.instrument_values = None
            self.correlated = corr
            if corr is True:
                # only needed in a portfolio context when
                # risk factors are correlated
                self.cholesky_matrix = mar_env.get_list('cholesky_matrix')
                self.rn_set = mar_env.get_list('rn_set')[self.name]
                self.random_numbers = mar_env.get_list('random_numbers')
```

```
        except:
            print "Error parsing market environment."

    def generate_time_grid(self):
        start = self.pricing_date
        end = self.final_date
        # pandas date_range function
        # freq = e.g. 'B' for Business Day,
        # 'W' for Weekly, 'M' for Monthly
        time_grid = pd.date_range(start=start, end=end,
                              freq=self.frequency).to_pydatetime()
        time_grid = list(time_grid)
        # enhance time_grid by start, end, and special_dates
        if start not in time_grid:
            time_grid.insert(0, start)
            # insert start date if not in list
        if end not in time_grid:
            time_grid.append(end)
            # insert end date if not in list
        if len(self.special_dates) > 0:
            # add all special dates
            time_grid.extend(self.special_dates)
            # delete duplicates
            time_grid = list(set(time_grid))
            # sort list
            time_grid.sort()
        self.time_grid = np.array(time_grid)

    def get_instrument_values(self, fixed_seed=True):
        if self.instrument_values is None:
            # only initiate simulation if there are no instrument values
            self.generate_paths(fixed_seed=fixed_seed, day_count=365.)
        elif fixed_seed is False:
            # also initiate resimulation when fixed_seed is False
            self.generate_paths(fixed_seed=fixed_seed, day_count=365.)
        return self.instrument_values
```

Parsing of the market environment is embedded in a *single* try-except clause, which raises an exception whenever the parsing fails. To keep the code concise, there are *no* sanity checks implemented. For example, the following line of code is considered a "success," no matter if the content is indeed an instance of a discounting class or not. Therefore, one has to be rather careful when compiling and passing market_environment objects to any simulation class:

```
self.discount_curve = mar_env.get_curve('discount_curve')
```

Table 16-1 shows all components that a market_environment object must contain for the generic and therefore for all other simulation classes.

Table 16-1. Elements of market environment for all simulation classes

Element	Type	Mandatory	Description
initial_value	Constant	Yes	Initial value of process at pricing_date
volatility	Constant	Yes	Volatility coefficient of process
final_date	Constant	Yes	Simulation horizon
currency	Constant	Yes	Currency of the financial entity
frequency	Constant	Yes	Date frequency, as pandas freq parameter
paths	Constant	Yes	Number of paths to be simulated
discount_curve	Curve	Yes	Instance of constant_short_rate
time_grid	List	No	Time grid of relevant dates (in portfolio context)
random_numbers	List	No	Random number array (for correlated objects)
cholesky_matrix	List	No	Cholesky matrix (for correlated objects)
rn_set	List	No	dict object with pointer to relevant random number set

Everything that has to do with the correlation of model simulation objects is explained in subsequent chapters. In this chapter, we focus on the simulation of single, uncorrelated processes. Similarly, the option to pass a time_grid is only relevant in a portfolio context, something also explained later.

Geometric Brownian Motion

Geometric Brownian motion is a stochastic process as described in Equation 16-1 (see also Equation 10-2 in Chapter 10, in particular for the meaning of the parameters and variables). The drift of the process is already set equal to the riskless, constant short rate *r*, implying that we operate under the equivalent martingale measure (see Chapter 15).

Equation 16-1. Stochastic differential equation of geometric Brownian motion

$$dS_t = rS_t dt + \sigma S_t dZ_t$$

Equation 16-2 presents an Euler discretization of the stochastic differential equation for simulation purposes (see also Equation 10-3 in Chapter 10 for further details). We work in a discrete time market model, such as the general market model $\mathcal{M}$ from Chapter 15, with a finite set of relevant dates $0 < t_1 < t_2 < \ldots < T$.

Equation 16-2. Difference equation to simulate the geometric Brownian motion

$$S_{t_{m+1}} = S_{t_m} \exp\left(\left(r - \frac{1}{2}\sigma^2\right)(t_{m+1} - t_m) + \sigma\sqrt{t_{m+1} - t_m}z_t\right)$$

$$0 \leq t_m < t_{m+1} \leq T$$

The Simulation Class

Example 16-3 now presents the specialized class for the GBM model. We present it in its entirety first and highlight selected aspects afterward.

Example 16-3. Simulation class for geometric Brownian motion

```
#
# DX Library Simulation
# geometric_brownian_motion.py
#
import numpy as np

from sn_random_numbers import sn_random_numbers
from simulation_class import simulation_class

class geometric_brownian_motion(simulation_class):
    ''' Class to generate simulated paths based on
    the Black-Scholes-Merton geometric Brownian motion model.

    Attributes
    ==========
    name : string
        name of the object
    mar_env : instance of market_environment
        market environment data for simulation
    corr : Boolean
        True if correlated with other model simulation object

    Methods
    =======
    update :
        updates parameters
    generate_paths :
        returns Monte Carlo paths given the market environment
    '''

    def __init__(self, name, mar_env, corr=False):
        super(geometric_brownian_motion, self).__init__(name, mar_env, corr)

    def update(self, initial_value=None, volatility=None, final_date=None):
        if initial_value is not None:
            self.initial_value = initial_value
        if volatility is not None:
```

```
            self.volatility = volatility
        if final_date is not None:
            self.final_date = final_date
        self.instrument_values = None

    def generate_paths(self, fixed_seed=False, day_count=365.):
        if self.time_grid is None:
            self.generate_time_grid()
                # method from generic simulation class
        # number of dates for time grid
        M = len(self.time_grid)
        # number of paths
        I = self.paths
        # array initialization for path simulation
        paths = np.zeros((M, I))
        # initialize first date with initial_value
        paths[0] = self.initial_value
        if not self.correlated:
            # if not correlated, generate random numbers
            rand = sn_random_numbers((1, M, I),
                                     fixed_seed=fixed_seed)
        else:
            # if correlated, use random number object as provided
            # in market environment
            rand = self.random_numbers
        short_rate = self.discount_curve.short_rate
          # get short rate for drift of process
        for t in range(1, len(self.time_grid)):
            # select the right time slice from the relevant
            # random number set
            if not self.correlated:
                ran = rand[t]
            else:
                ran = np.dot(self.cholesky_matrix, rand[:, t, :])
                ran = ran[self.rn_set]
            dt = (self.time_grid[t] - self.time_grid[t - 1]).days / day_count
                # difference between two dates as year fraction
            paths[t] = paths[t - 1] * np.exp((short_rate - 0.5
                                    * self.volatility ** 2) * dt
                          + self.volatility * np.sqrt(dt) * ran)
            # generate simulated values for the respective date
        self.instrument_values = paths
```

In this particular case, the market_environment object has to contain only the data and objects shown in Table 16-1—i.e., the minimum set of components.

The method update does what its name suggests: it allows the updating of selected important parameters of the model. The method generate_paths is, of course, a bit more involved. However, it has a number of inline comments that should make clear the most important aspects. Some complexity is brought into this method by, in principle, allowing for the correlation between different model simulation objects. This will become clearer, especially in Example 18-2.

A Use Case

The following interactive IPython session illustrates the use of the `geometric_browni an_motion` class. First, we have to generate a `market_environment` object with all mandatory elements:

```
In [1]: from dx import *

In [2]: me_gbm = market_environment('me_gbm', dt.datetime(2015, 1, 1))

In [3]: me_gbm.add_constant('initial_value', 36.)
        me_gbm.add_constant('volatility', 0.2)
        me_gbm.add_constant('final_date', dt.datetime(2015, 12, 31))
        me_gbm.add_constant('currency', 'EUR')
        me_gbm.add_constant('frequency', 'M')
            # monthly frequency (respective month end)
        me_gbm.add_constant('paths', 10000)

In [4]: csr = constant_short_rate('csr', 0.05)

In [5]: me_gbm.add_curve('discount_curve', csr)
```

Second, we instantiate a model simulation object:

```
In [6]: from dx_simulation import *

In [7]: gbm = geometric_brownian_motion('gbm', me_gbm)
```

Third, we can work with the object. For example, let us generate and inspect the `time_grid`. You will notice that we have 13 `datetime` objects in the `time_grid` array object (all the month ends in the relevant year, plus the `pricing_date`):

```
In [8]: gbm.generate_time_grid()

In [9]: gbm.time_grid

Out[9]: array([datetime.datetime(2015, 1, 1, 0, 0),
               datetime.datetime(2015, 1, 31, 0, 0),
               datetime.datetime(2015, 2, 28, 0, 0),
               datetime.datetime(2015, 3, 31, 0, 0),
               datetime.datetime(2015, 4, 30, 0, 0),
               datetime.datetime(2015, 5, 31, 0, 0),
               datetime.datetime(2015, 6, 30, 0, 0),
               datetime.datetime(2015, 7, 31, 0, 0),
               datetime.datetime(2015, 8, 31, 0, 0),
               datetime.datetime(2015, 9, 30, 0, 0),
               datetime.datetime(2015, 10, 31, 0, 0),
               datetime.datetime(2015, 11, 30, 0, 0),
               datetime.datetime(2015, 12, 31, 0, 0)], dtype=object)
```

Next, we might ask for the simulated instrument values:

```
In [10]: %time paths_1 = gbm.get_instrument_values()
```

```
Out[10]: CPU times: user 10.7 ms, sys: 2.91 ms, total: 13.6 ms
         Wall time: 12.8 ms
```

```
In [11]: paths_1
```

```
Out[11]: array([[ 36.          ,  36.          ,  36.          , ...,  36.          ,
                  36.          ,  36.          ],
                [ 37.37221481,  38.08890977,  34.37156575, ...,  36.22258915,
                  35.05503522,  39.63544014],
                [ 39.45866146,  42.18817025,  32.38579992, ...,  34.80319951,
                  33.60600939,  37.62733874],
                ...,
                [ 40.15717404,  33.16701733,  23.32556112, ...,  37.5619937 ,
                  29.89282508,  30.2202427 ],
                [ 42.0974104 ,  36.59006321,  21.70771374, ...,  35.70950512,
                  30.64670854,  30.45901309],
                [ 43.33170027,  37.42993532,  23.8840177 , ...,  35.92624556,
                  27.87720187,  28.77424561]])
```

Let us generate instrument values for a higher volatility as well:

```
In [12]: gbm.update(volatility=0.5)
```

```
In [13]: %time paths_2 = gbm.get_instrument_values()
```

```
Out[13]: CPU times: user 9.78 ms, sys: 1.36 ms, total: 11.1 ms
         Wall time: 10.2 ms
```

The difference in the two sets of paths is illustrated in Figure 16-1:

```
In [14]: import matplotlib.pyplot as plt
         %matplotlib inline
         plt.figure(figsize=(8, 4))
         p1 = plt.plot(gbm.time_grid, paths_1[:, :10], 'b')
         p2 = plt.plot(gbm.time_grid, paths_2[:, :10], 'r-.')
         plt.grid(True)
         l1 = plt.legend([p1[0], p2[0]],
                         ['low volatility', 'high volatility'], loc=2)
         plt.gca().add_artist(l1)
         plt.xticks(rotation=30)
```

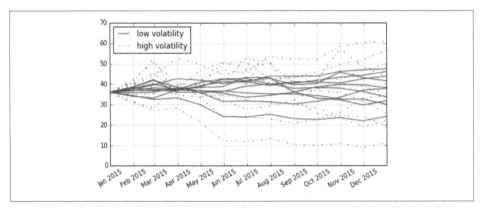

Figure 16-1. Simulated paths from GBM simulation class

Jump Diffusion

Equipped with the background knowledge from the `geometric_brownian_motion` class, it is now straightforward to implement a class for the jump diffusion model described by Merton (1976). Recall the stochastic differential equation of the jump diffusion, as shown in Equation 16-3 (see also Equation 10-8 in Chapter 10, in particular for the meaning of the parameters and variables).

Equation 16-3. Stochastic differential equation for Merton jump diffusion model

$$dS_t = (r - r_J)S_t dt + \sigma S_t dZ_t + J_t S_t dN_t$$

An Euler discretization for simulation purposes is presented in Equation 16-4 (see also Equation 10-9 in Chapter 10 and the more detailed explanations given there).

Equation 16-4. Euler discretization for Merton jump diffusion model

$$S_{t_{m+1}} = S_{t_m}\left(\exp\left(\left(r - r_J - \frac{1}{2}\sigma^2\right)(t_{m+1} - t_m) + \sigma\sqrt{t_{m+1} - t_m}z_t^1\right) + \left(e^{\mu_J + \delta z_t^2} - 1\right)y_t\right)$$
$$0 \leq t_m < t_{m+1} \leq T$$

The Simulation Class

Example 16-4 presents the Python code for the `jump_diffusion` simulation class. This class should by now contain no surprises. Of course, the model is different, but the design and the methods are essentially the same.

Example 16-4. Simulation class for jump diffusion

```
#
# DX Library Simulation
# jump_diffusion.py
#
import numpy as np

from sn_random_numbers import sn_random_numbers
from simulation_class import simulation_class

class jump_diffusion(simulation_class):
    ''' Class to generate simulated paths based on
    the Merton (1976) jump diffusion model.

    Attributes
    ==========
    name : string
        name of the object
    mar_env : instance of market_environment
        market environment data for simulation
    corr : Boolean
        True if correlated with other model object

    Methods
    =======
    update :
        updates parameters
    generate_paths :
        returns Monte Carlo paths given the market environment
    '''

    def __init__(self, name, mar_env, corr=False):
        super(jump_diffusion, self).__init__(name, mar_env, corr)
        try:
            # additional parameters needed
            self.lamb = mar_env.get_constant('lambda')
            self.mu = mar_env.get_constant('mu')
            self.delt = mar_env.get_constant('delta')
        except:
            print "Error parsing market environment."

    def update(self, initial_value=None, volatility=None, lamb=None,
                mu=None, delta=None, final_date=None):
        if initial_value is not None:
            self.initial_value = initial_value
        if volatility is not None:
            self.volatility = volatility
        if lamb is not None:
            self.lamb = lamb
        if mu is not None:
            self.mu = mu
        if delta is not None:
```

```
        self.delt = delta
        if final_date is not None:
            self.final_date = final_date
        self.instrument_values = None

    def generate_paths(self, fixed_seed=False, day_count=365.):
        if self.time_grid is None:
            self.generate_time_grid()
                # method from generic simulation class
        # number of dates for time grid
        M = len(self.time_grid)
        # number of paths
        I = self.paths
        # array initialization for path simulation
        paths = np.zeros((M, I))
        # initialize first date with initial_value
        paths[0] = self.initial_value
        if self.correlated is False:
            # if not correlated, generate random numbers
            sn1 = sn_random_numbers((1, M, I),
                                    fixed_seed=fixed_seed)
        else:
            # if correlated, use random number object as provided
            # in market environment
            sn1 = self.random_numbers

        # standard normally distributed pseudorandom numbers
        # for the jump component
        sn2 = sn_random_numbers((1, M, I),
                                fixed_seed=fixed_seed)

        rj = self.lamb * (np.exp(self.mu + 0.5 * self.delt ** 2) - 1)

        short_rate = self.discount_curve.short_rate
        for t in range(1, len(self.time_grid)):
            # select the right time slice from the relevant
            # random number set
            if self.correlated is False:
                ran = sn1[t]
            else:
                # only with correlation in portfolio context
                ran = np.dot(self.cholesky_matrix, sn1[:, t, :])
                ran = ran[self.rn_set]
            dt = (self.time_grid[t] - self.time_grid[t - 1]).days / day_count
                # difference between two dates as year fraction
            poi = np.random.poisson(self.lamb * dt, I)
                # Poisson-distributed pseudorandom numbers for jump component
            paths[t] = paths[t - 1] * (np.exp((short_rate - rj
                                      - 0.5 * self.volatility ** 2) * dt
                        + self.volatility * np.sqrt(dt) * ran)
                        + (np.exp(self.mu + self.delt *
```

```
                        sn2[t]) - 1) * poi)
        self.instrument_values = paths
```

Of course, since we are dealing now with a different model, we need a different set of elements in the `market_environment` object. In addition to those for the `geomet ric_brownian_motion` class (see Table 16-1), there are three additions, as outlined in Table 16-2: namely, the parameters of the log-normal jump component, `lambda`, `mu`, and `delta`.

Table 16-2. Specific elements of market environment for jump_diffusion class

Element	Type	Mandatory	Description
lambda	Constant	Yes	Jump intensity (probability p.a.)
mu	Constant	Yes	Expected jump size
delta	Constant	Yes	Standard deviation of jump size

For the generation of the paths, this class of course needs further random numbers because of the jump component. Inline comments in the method `generate_paths` highlight the two spots where these additional random numbers are generated. For the generation of Poisson-distributed random numbers, see also Chapter 10.

A Use Case

In what follows, we again illustrate the use of the simulation class `jump_diffusion` interactively. We make use of the `market_environment` object defined for the GBM object in the previous section:

```
In [15]: me_jd = market_environment('me_jd', dt.datetime(2015, 1, 1))
```

```
In [16]: # add jump diffusion specific parameters
         me_jd.add_constant('lambda', 0.3)
         me_jd.add_constant('mu', -0.75)
         me_jd.add_constant('delta', 0.1)
```

To this environment, we add the complete environment of the GBM simulation class, which completes the input needed:

```
In [17]: me_jd.add_environment(me_gbm)
```

Based on this `market_environment` object, we can instantiate the simulation class for the jump diffusion:

```
In [18]: from jump_diffusion import jump_diffusion
```

```
In [19]: jd = jump_diffusion('jd', me_jd)
```

Due to the modeling approach we have implemented, the generation of instrument values is now formally the same. The method call in this case is a bit slower, however, since we need to simulate more numerical values due to the jump component:

```
In [20]: %time paths_3 = jd.get_instrument_values()

Out[20]: CPU times: user 19.7 ms, sys: 2.92 ms, total: 22.6 ms
         Wall time: 21.9 ms
```

With the aim of again comparing two different sets of paths, change, for example, the jump probability:

```
In [21]: jd.update(lamb=0.9)
```

```
In [22]: %time paths_4 = jd.get_instrument_values()
```

```
Out[22]: CPU times: user 26.3 ms, sys: 2.07 ms, total: 28.4 ms
         Wall time: 27.7 ms
```

Figure 16-2 compares a couple of simulated paths from the two sets with low and high intensity (jump probability), respectively. You can spot a few jumps for the low intensity case and multiple jumps for the high intensity case in the figure:

```
In [23]: plt.figure(figsize=(8, 4))
         p1 = plt.plot(gbm.time_grid, paths_3[:, :10], 'b')
         p2 = plt.plot(gbm.time_grid, paths_4[:, :10], 'r-.')
         plt.grid(True)
         l1 = plt.legend([p1[0], p2[0]],
                         ['low intensity', 'high intensity'], loc=3)
         plt.gca().add_artist(l1)
         plt.xticks(rotation=30)
```

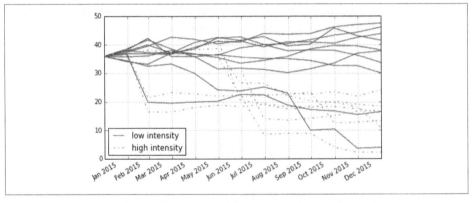

Figure 16-2. Simulated paths from jump diffusion simulation class

Square-Root Diffusion

The third stochastic process to be simulated is the square-root diffusion as used by Cox, Ingersoll, and Ross (1985) to model stochastic short rates. Equation 16-5 shows the stochastic differential equation of the process (see also Equation 10-4 in Chapter 10 for further details).

Equation 16-5. Stochastic differential equation of square-root diffusion

$$dx_t = \kappa(\theta - x_t)dt + \sigma\sqrt{x_t}dZ_t$$

We use the discretization scheme as presented in Equation 16-6 (see also Equation 10-5 in Chapter 10, as well as Equation 10-6, for an alternative, exact scheme).

Equation 16-6. Euler discretization for square-root diffusion (full truncation scheme)

$$
\begin{aligned}
\tilde{x}_{t_{m+1}} &= \tilde{x}_{t_m} + \kappa\left(\theta - \tilde{x}_s^+\right)\left(t_{m+1} - t_m\right) + \sigma\sqrt{\tilde{x}_s^+}\sqrt{t_{m+1} - t_m}\,z_t \\
x_{t_{m+1}} &= \tilde{x}_{t_{m+1}}^+
\end{aligned}
$$

The Simulation Class

Example 16-5 presents the Python code for the `square_root_diffusion` simulation class. Apart from, of course, a different model and discretization scheme, the class does not contain anything new compared to the other two specialized classes.

Example 16-5. Simulation class for square-root diffusion

```
#
# DX Library Simulation
# square_root_diffusion.py
#
import numpy as np

from sn_random_numbers import sn_random_numbers
from simulation_class import simulation_class


class square_root_diffusion(simulation_class):
    ''' Class to generate simulated paths based on
    the Cox-Ingersoll-Ross (1985) square-root diffusion model.

    Attributes
    ==========
    name : string
        name of the object
    mar_env : instance of market_environment
        market environment data for simulation
    corr : Boolean
        True if correlated with other model object

    Methods
    =======
```

```
    update :
        updates parameters
    generate_paths :
        returns Monte Carlo paths given the market environment
    '''

    def __init__(self, name, mar_env, corr=False):
        super(square_root_diffusion, self).__init__(name, mar_env, corr)
        try:
            self.kappa = mar_env.get_constant('kappa')
            self.theta = mar_env.get_constant('theta')
        except:
            print "Error parsing market environment."

    def update(self, initial_value=None, volatility=None, kappa=None,
               theta=None, final_date=None):
        if initial_value is not None:
            self.initial_value = initial_value
        if volatility is not None:
            self.volatility = volatility
        if kappa is not None:
            self.kappa = kappa
        if theta is not None:
            self.theta = theta
        if final_date is not None:
            self.final_date = final_date
        self.instrument_values = None

    def generate_paths(self, fixed_seed=True, day_count=365.):
        if self.time_grid is None:
            self.generate_time_grid()
        M = len(self.time_grid)
        I = self.paths
        paths = np.zeros((M, I))
        paths_ = np.zeros_like(paths)
        paths[0] = self.initial_value
        paths_[0] = self.initial_value
        if self.correlated is False:
            rand = sn_random_numbers((1, M, I),
                                     fixed_seed=fixed_seed)
        else:
            rand = self.random_numbers

        for t in range(1, len(self.time_grid)):
            dt = (self.time_grid[t] - self.time_grid[t - 1]).days / day_count
            if self.correlated is False:
                ran = rand[t]
            else:
                ran = np.dot(self.cholesky_matrix, rand[:, t, :])
                ran = ran[self.rn_set]

            # full truncation Euler discretization
```

```
            paths_[t] = (paths_[t - 1] + self.kappa
                        * (self.theta - np.maximum(0, paths_[t - 1, :])) * dt
                        + np.sqrt(np.maximum(0, paths_[t - 1, :]))
                        * self.volatility * np.sqrt(dt) * ran)
            paths[t] = np.maximum(0, paths_[t])
        self.instrument_values = paths
```

Table 16-3 lists the two elements of the market environment that are specific to this class.

Table 16-3. Specific elements of market environment for square_root_diffusion class

Element	Type	Mandatory	Description
kappa	Constant	Yes	Mean reversion factor
theta	Constant	Yes	Long-term mean of process

A Use Case

A rather brief use case illustrates the use of the simulation class. As usual, we need a market environment, for example to model a volatility (index) process:

```
In [35]: me_srd = market_environment('me_srd', dt.datetime(2015, 1, 1))
```

```
In [36]: me_srd.add_constant('initial_value', .25)
         me_srd.add_constant('volatility', 0.05)
         me_srd.add_constant('final_date', dt.datetime(2015, 12, 31))
         me_srd.add_constant('currency', 'EUR')
         me_srd.add_constant('frequency', 'W')
         me_srd.add_constant('paths', 10000)
```

Two components of the market environment are specific to the class:

```
In [37]: # specific to simualation class
         me_srd.add_constant('kappa', 4.0)
         me_srd.add_constant('theta', 0.2)
```

Although we do not need it here to implement the simulation, the generic simulation class requires a discounting object. This requirement can be justified from a risk-neutral valuation perspective, which is the overarching goal of the whole DX analytics library:

```
In [38]: # required but not needed for the class
         me_srd.add_curve('discount_curve', constant_short_rate('r', 0.0))
```

```
In [39]: from square_root_diffusion import square_root_diffusion
```

```
In [40]: srd = square_root_diffusion('srd', me_srd)
```

As before, we get simulation paths, given the `market_environment` object as input, by calling the `get_instrument_values` method:

```
In [41]: srd_paths = srd.get_instrument_values()[:, :10]
```

Figure 16-3 illustrates the mean-reverting characteristic by showing how the single simulated paths on average revert to the long-term mean theta (dashed line):

```
In [42]: plt.figure(figsize=(8, 4))
         plt.plot(srd.time_grid, srd.get_instrument_values()[:, :10])
         plt.axhline(me_srd.get_constant('theta'), color='r', ls='--', lw=2.0)
         plt.grid(True)
         plt.xticks(rotation=30)
```

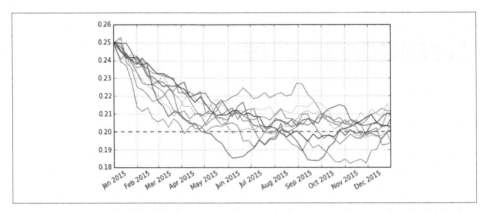

Figure 16-3. Simulated paths from square-root diffusion simulation class (dashed line = long-term mean theta)

Conclusions

This chapter develops all the tools and classes needed for the simulation of the three stochastic processes of interest: geometric Brownian motions, jump diffusions, and square-root diffusions. The chapter presents a function to conveniently generate standard normally distributed random numbers. It then proceeds by introducing a generic model simulation class. Based on this foundation, the chapter introduces three specialized simulation classes and presents use cases for these classes.

To simplify future imports, we can again use a wrapper module called dx_simula tion.py, as presented in Example 16-6.

Example 16-6. Wrapper module for simulation components

```
#
# DX Library Simulation
# dx_simulation.py
#
import numpy as np
import pandas as pd

from dx_frame import *
from sn_random_numbers import sn_random_numbers
```

```
from simulation_class import simulation_class
from geometric_brownian_motion import geometric_brownian_motion
from jump_diffusion import jump_diffusion
from square_root_diffusion import square_root_diffusion
```

As with the first wrapper module, dx_frame.py, the benefit is that a single import statement makes available all simulation components in a single step:

```
from dx_simulation import *
```

Since dx_simulation.py also imports everything from dx_frame.py, this single import in fact exposes *all functionality* developed so far. The same holds true for the enhanced init file in the dx directory, as shown in Example 16-7.

Example 16-7. Enhanced Python packaging file

```
#
# DX Library
# packaging file
# __init__.py
#
import numpy as np
import pandas as pd
import datetime as dt

# frame
from get_year_deltas import get_year_deltas
from constant_short_rate import constant_short_rate
from market_environment import market_environment

# simulation
from sn_random_numbers import sn_random_numbers
from simulation_class import simulation_class
from geometric_brownian_motion import geometric_brownian_motion
from jump_diffusion import jump_diffusion
from square_root_diffusion import square_root_diffusion
```

Further Reading

Useful references in book form for the topics covered in this chapter are:

- Glasserman, Paul (2004): *Monte Carlo Methods in Financial Engineering.* Springer, New York.

- Hilpisch, Yves (2015): *Derivatives Analytics with Python.* Wiley Finance, Chichester, England. *http://derivatives-analytics-with-python.com.*

Original papers cited in this chapter are:

- Black, Fischer and Myron Scholes (1973): "The Pricing of Options and Corporate Liabilities." *Journal of Political Economy*, Vol. 81, No. 3, pp. 638–659.

- Cox, John, Jonathan Ingersoll, and Stephen Ross (1985): "A Theory of the Term Structure of Interest Rates." *Econometrica*, Vol. 53, No. 2, pp. 385–407.

- Merton, Robert (1973): "Theory of Rational Option Pricing." *Bell Journal of Economics and Management Science*, Vol. 4, pp. 141–183.

- Merton, Robert (1976): "Option Pricing When the Underlying Stock Returns Are Discontinuous." *Journal of Financial Economics*, Vol. 3, No. 3, pp. 125–144.

## CHAPTER 17

Derivatives Valuation

> Derivatives are a huge, complex issue.
>
> — Judd Gregg

Options and derivatives valuation has long been the domain of so-called *rocket scientists* on Wall Street—i.e., people with a Ph.D. in physics or a similarly demanding discipline when it comes to the mathematics involved. However, the application of the models by the means of numerical methods like Monte Carlo simulation is generally a little less involved than the theoretical models themselves.

This is particularly true for the valuation of options and derivatives with *European exercise*—i.e., where exercise is only possible at a certain, predetermined date. It is a bit less true for options and derivatives with *American exercise*, where exercise is allowed at any point over a prespecified period of time. This chapter introduces and uses the *Least-Squares Monte Carlo* (LSM) algorithm, which has become a benchmark algorithm when it comes to American options valuation based on Monte Carlo simulation.

The current chapter is similar in structure to Chapter 16 in that it first introduces a generic valuation class and then provides two specialized valuation classes, one for European exercise and another one for American exercise.

The generic valuation class contains methods to numerically estimate the most important Greeks of an option: the *Delta* and the *Vega*. Therefore, the valuation classes are important not only for valuation purposes, but also for *risk management* purposes.

Generic Valuation Class

As with the generic simulation class, we instantiate an object of the valuation class by providing only a few inputs (in this case, four):

name
> A `string` object as a name for the model simulation object

underlying
> An instance of a simulation class representing the underlying

mar_env
> An instance of the `market_environment` class

payoff_func
> A Python string containing the payoff function for the option/derivative

The generic class has three methods:

update
> This method updates selected valuation parameters (attributes).

delta
> This method calculates a numerical value for the Delta of an option/derivative.

vega
> This method calculates the Vega of an option/derivative.

Equipped with the background knowledge from the previous chapters about the DX library, the generic valuation class as presented in Example 17-1 should be almost self-explanatory; where appropriate, inline comments are also provided. We again present the class in its entirety first and highlight selected topics immediately afterward and in the subsequent sections.

Example 17-1. Generic valuation class

```
#
# DX Library Valuation
# valuation_class.py
#

class valuation_class(object):
    ''' Basic class for single-factor valuation.

    Attributes
    ==========
    name : string
        name of the object
    underlying :
        instance of simulation class
    mar_env : instance of market_environment
        market environment data for valuation
    payoff_func : string
        derivatives payoff in Python syntax
        Example: 'np.maximum(maturity_value - 100, 0)'
        where maturity_value is the NumPy vector with
```

```
        respective values of the underlying
        Example: 'np.maximum(instrument_values - 100, 0)'
        where instrument_values is the NumPy matrix with
        values of the underlying over the whole time/path grid

Methods
=======
update:
    updates selected valuation parameters
delta :
    returns the Delta of the derivative
vega :
    returns the Vega of the derivative
'''

def __init__(self, name, underlying, mar_env, payoff_func=''):
    try:
        self.name = name
        self.pricing_date = mar_env.pricing_date
        try:
            self.strike = mar_env.get_constant('strike')
              # strike is optional
        except:
            pass
        self.maturity = mar_env.get_constant('maturity')
        self.currency = mar_env.get_constant('currency')
        # simulation parameters and discount curve from simulation object
        self.frequency = underlying.frequency
        self.paths = underlying.paths
        self.discount_curve = underlying.discount_curve
        self.payoff_func = payoff_func
        self.underlying = underlying
        # provide pricing_date and maturity to underlying
        self.underlying.special_dates.extend([self.pricing_date,
                                              self.maturity])
    except:
        print "Error parsing market environment."

def update(self, initial_value=None, volatility=None,
           strike=None, maturity=None):
    if initial_value is not None:
        self.underlying.update(initial_value=initial_value)
    if volatility is not None:
        self.underlying.update(volatility=volatility)
    if strike is not None:
        self.strike = strike
    if maturity is not None:
        self.maturity = maturity
        # add new maturity date if not in time_grid
        if not maturity in self.underlying.time_grid:
            self.underlying.special_dates.append(maturity)
            self.underlying.instrument_values = None
```

```
def delta(self, interval=None, accuracy=4):
    if interval is None:
        interval = self.underlying.initial_value / 50.
    # forward-difference approximation
    # calculate left value for numerical Delta
    value_left = self.present_value(fixed_seed=True)
    # numerical underlying value for right value
    initial_del = self.underlying.initial_value + interval
    self.underlying.update(initial_value=initial_del)
    # calculate right value for numerical delta
    value_right = self.present_value(fixed_seed=True)
    # reset the initial_value of the simulation object
    self.underlying.update(initial_value=initial_del - interval)
    delta = (value_right - value_left) / interval
    # correct for potential numerical errors
    if delta < -1.0:
        return -1.0
    elif delta > 1.0:
        return 1.0
    else:
        return round(delta, accuracy)

def vega(self, interval=0.01, accuracy=4):
    if interval < self.underlying.volatility / 50.:
        interval = self.underlying.volatility / 50.
    # forward-difference approximation
    # calculate the left value for numerical Vega
    value_left = self.present_value(fixed_seed=True)
    # numerical volatility value for right value
    vola_del = self.underlying.volatility + interval
    # update the simulation object
    self.underlying.update(volatility=vola_del)
    # calculate the right value for numerical Vega
    value_right = self.present_value(fixed_seed=True)
    # reset volatility value of simulation object
    self.underlying.update(volatility=vola_del - interval)
    vega = (value_right - value_left) / interval
    return round(vega, accuracy)
```

One topic covered by the generic `valuation_class` class is the estimation of Greeks. This is something we should take a closer look at. To this end, consider that we have a continuously differentiable function $V(S_0, \sigma_0)$ available that represents the present value of an option. The *Delta* of the option is then defined as the first partial derivative with respect to the current value of the underlying S_0; i.e., $\Delta = \frac{\partial V(\cdot)}{\partial S_0}$.

Suppose now that we have from Monte Carlo valuation (see Chapter 10 and subsequent sections in this chapter) a numerical Monte Carlo estimator $\bar{V}(S_0, \sigma_0)$ for the option value. A numerical approximation for the Delta of the option is then given in

Equation 17-1.[1] This is what the delta method of the generic valuation class implements. The method assumes the existence of a present_value method that returns the Monte Carlo estimator given a certain set of parameter values.

Equation 17-1. Numerical Delta of an option

$$\bar{\Delta} = \frac{\bar{V}(S_0 + \Delta S, \sigma_0) - \bar{V}(S_0, \sigma_0)}{\Delta S}, \Delta S > 0$$

Similarly, the *Vega* of the instrument is defined as the first partial derivative of the present value with respect to the current (instantaneous) volatility σ_0, i.e., $\mathbf{V} = \frac{\partial V(\cdot)}{\partial \sigma_0}$. Again assuming the existence of a Monte Carlo estimator for the value of the option, Equation 17-2 provides a numerical approximation for the Vega. This is what the vega method of the valuation_class class implements.

Equation 17-2. Numerical Vega of an option

$$\mathbf{V} = \frac{\bar{V}(S_0, \sigma_0 + \Delta\sigma) - \bar{V}(S_0, \sigma_0)}{\Delta\sigma}, \Delta\sigma > 0$$

Note that the discussion of Delta and Vega is based only on the *existence* of either a differentiable function or a Monte Carlo estimator for the present value of an option. This is the very reason why we can define methods to numerically estimate these quantities without knowledge of the exact definition and numerical implementation of the Monte Carlo estimator.

European Exercise

The first case to which we want to specialize the generic valuation class is *European exercise*. To this end, consider the following simplified recipe to generate a Monte Carlo estimator for an option value:

1. Simulate the relevant underlying risk factor S under the risk-neutral measure I times to come up with as many simulated values of the underlying at the maturity of the option T—i.e., $\bar{S}_T(i), i \in \{1, 2, \ldots, I\}$

---

1. For details on how to estimate Greeks numerically by Monte Carlo simulation, refer to Chapter 7 of Glasserman (2004). We only use *forward-difference* schemes here since this leads to only *one* additional simulation and revaluation of the option. For example, a *central-difference* approximation would lead to *two* option revaluations and therefore a higher computational burden.

2. Calculate the payoff h_T of the option at maturity for every simulated value of the underlying—i.e., $h_T(\bar{S}_T(i)), i \in \{1, 2, \dots, I\}$

3. Derive the Monte Carlo estimator for the option's present value as $\bar{V}_0 \equiv e^{-rT} \frac{1}{I} \sum_{i=1}^{I} h_T(\bar{S}_T(i))$

The Valuation Class

Example 17-2 shows the class implementing the present_value method based on this recipe. In addition, it contains the method generate_payoff to generate the simulated paths and the payoff of the option given the simulated paths. This, of course, builds the very basis for the Monte Carlo estimator.

Example 17-2. Valuation class for European exercise

```
#
# DX Library Valuation
# valuation_mcs_european.py
#
import numpy as np

from valuation_class import valuation_class

class valuation_mcs_european(valuation_class):
    ''' Class to value European options with arbitrary payoff
    by single-factor Monte Carlo simulation.

    Methods
    =======
    generate_payoff :
        returns payoffs given the paths and the payoff function
    present_value :
        returns present value (Monte Carlo estimator)
    '''

    def generate_payoff(self, fixed_seed=False):
        '''
        Parameters
        ==========
        fixed_seed : Boolean
            use same/fixed seed for valuation
        '''
        try:
            # strike defined?
            strike = self.strike
        except:
            pass
        paths = self.underlying.get_instrument_values(fixed_seed=fixed_seed)
        time_grid = self.underlying.time_grid
        try:
```

```
            time_index = np.where(time_grid == self.maturity)[0]
            time_index = int(time_index)
        except:
            print "Maturity date not in time grid of underlying."
        maturity_value = paths[time_index]
        # average value over whole path
        mean_value = np.mean(paths[:time_index], axis=1)
        # maximum value over whole path
        max_value = np.amax(paths[:time_index], axis=1)[-1]
        # minimum value over whole path
        min_value = np.amin(paths[:time_index], axis=1)[-1]
        try:
            payoff = eval(self.payoff_func)
            return payoff
        except:
            print "Error evaluating payoff function."

    def present_value(self, accuracy=6, fixed_seed=False, full=False):
        '''

        Parameters
        ==========
        accuracy : int
            number of decimals in returned result
        fixed_seed : Boolean
            use same/fixed seed for valuation
        full : Boolean
            return also full 1d array of present values
        '''
        cash_flow = self.generate_payoff(fixed_seed=fixed_seed)
        discount_factor = self.discount_curve.get_discount_factors(
                        (self.pricing_date, self.maturity))[0, 1]
        result = discount_factor * np.sum(cash_flow) / len(cash_flow)
        if full:
            return round(result, accuracy), discount_factor * cash_flow
        else:
            return round(result, accuracy)
```

The `generate_payoff` method provides some special objects to be used for the definition of the payoff of the option:

- `strike` is the *strike* of the option.

- `maturity_value` represents the 1D ndarray object with the simulated values of the *underlying at maturity* of the option.

- `mean_value` is the *average* of the underlying over a whole path from today until maturity.

- `max_value` is the *maximum value* of the underlying over a whole path.

- `min_value` gives the *minimum value* of the underlying over a whole path.

The last three especially allow for the efficient handling of options with Asian (i.e., lookback) features.

A Use Case

The application of the valuation class `valuation_mcs_european` is best illustrated by a specific use case. However, before a valuation class can be instantiated, we need a simulation object—i.e., an underlying for the option to be valued. From Chapter 16, we use the `geometric_brownian_motion` class to model the underlying. We also use the example parameterization of the respective use case there:

```
In [1]: from dx import *

In [2]: me_gbm = market_environment('me_gbm', dt.datetime(2015, 1, 1))

In [3]: me_gbm.add_constant('initial_value', 36.)
        me_gbm.add_constant('volatility', 0.2)
        me_gbm.add_constant('final_date', dt.datetime(2015, 12, 31))
        me_gbm.add_constant('currency', 'EUR')
        me_gbm.add_constant('frequency', 'M')
        me_gbm.add_constant('paths', 10000)

In [4]: csr = constant_short_rate('csr', 0.06)

In [5]: me_gbm.add_curve('discount_curve', csr)

In [6]: gbm = geometric_brownian_motion('gbm', me_gbm)
```

In addition to a simulation object, we need to provide a market environment for the option itself. It has to contain at least a `maturity` and a `currency`. Optionally, we can provide a `strike`:

```
In [7]: me_call = market_environment('me_call', me_gbm.pricing_date)

In [8]: me_call.add_constant('strike', 40.)
        me_call.add_constant('maturity', dt.datetime(2015, 12, 31))
        me_call.add_constant('currency', 'EUR')
```

A central element, of course, is the payoff function, provided here as a `string` object containing Python code that the `eval` function can evaluate. We want to define a European *call* option. Such an option has a payoff of $h_T = \max(S_T - K, 0)$, with S_T being the value of the underlying at maturity and K being the strike price of the option. In Python and NumPy—i.e., with vectorized storage of all simulated values—this takes on the following form:

```
In [9]: payoff_func = 'np.maximum(maturity_value - strike, 0)'
```

We can now put all the ingredients together to instantiate the `valuation_mcs_european` class:

```
In [10]: from valuation_mcs_european import valuation_mcs_european
```

```
In [11]: eur_call = valuation_mcs_european('eur_call', underlying=gbm,
                                            mar_env=me_call, payoff_func=payoff_func)
```

With this valuation object available, all quantities of interest are only one method call away. Let us start with the present value of the option:

```
In [12]: %time eur_call.present_value()

Out[12]: CPU times: user 41.7 ms, sys: 11 ms, total: 52.7 ms
         Wall time: 44.6 ms


Out[12]: 2.180511
```

The Delta of the option is, as expected for a European call option, positive—i.e., the present value of the option increases with increasing initial value of the underlying:

```
In [13]: %time eur_call.delta()

Out[13]: CPU times: user 10.9 ms, sys: 1.09 ms, total: 12 ms
         Wall time: 11.1 ms


         0.4596
```

The Vega is calculated similarly. It shows the increase in the present value of the option given an increase in the initial volatility of 1%; e.g., from 24% to 25%. The Vega is positive for both European put and call options:

```
In [14]: %time eur_call.vega()

Out[14]: CPU times: user 15.2 ms, sys: 1.34 ms, total: 16.5 ms
         Wall time: 15.6 ms


         14.2782
```

Once we have the valuation object, a more comprehensive analysis of the present value and the Greeks is easily implemented. The following code calculates the present value, Delta, and Vega for initial values of the underlying ranging from 34 to 46 EUR:

```
In [15]: %%time
         s_list = np.arange(34., 46.1, 2.)
         p_list = []; d_list = []; v_list = []
         for s in s_list:
             eur_call.update(initial_value=s)
             p_list.append(eur_call.present_value(fixed_seed=True))
             d_list.append(eur_call.delta())
             v_list.append(eur_call.vega())

Out[15]: CPU times: user 239 ms, sys: 8.18 ms, total: 248 ms
         Wall time: 248 ms
```

Equipped with all these values, we can graphically inspect the results. To this end, we use a helper function as shown in Example 17-3.

Example 17-3. Helper function to plot options statistics

```
#
# DX Library Valuation
# plot_option_stats.py
#
import matplotlib.pyplot as plt

def plot_option_stats(s_list, p_list, d_list, v_list):
    ''' Plots option prices, Deltas, and Vegas for a set of
    different initial values of the underlying.

    Parameters
    ==========
    s_list : array or list
        set of initial values of the underlying
    p_list : array or list
        present values
    d_list : array or list
        results for Deltas
    v_list : array or list
        results for Vegas
    '''
    plt.figure(figsize=(9, 7))
    sub1 = plt.subplot(311)
    plt.plot(s_list, p_list, 'ro', label='present value')
    plt.plot(s_list, p_list, 'b')
    plt.grid(True); plt.legend(loc=0)
    plt.setp(sub1.get_xticklabels(), visible=False)
    sub2 = plt.subplot(312)
    plt.plot(s_list, d_list, 'go', label='Delta')
    plt.plot(s_list, d_list, 'b')
    plt.grid(True); plt.legend(loc=0)
    plt.ylim(min(d_list) - 0.1, max(d_list) + 0.1)
    plt.setp(sub2.get_xticklabels(), visible=False)
    sub3 = plt.subplot(313)
    plt.plot(s_list, v_list, 'yo', label='Vega')
    plt.plot(s_list, v_list, 'b')
    plt.xlabel('initial value of underlying')
    plt.grid(True); plt.legend(loc=0)
```

Importing this function and providing the valuation results to it generates a picture like that shown in Figure 17-1:

```
In [16]: from plot_option_stats import plot_option_stats
         %matplotlib inline

In [17]: plot_option_stats(s_list, p_list, d_list, v_list)
```

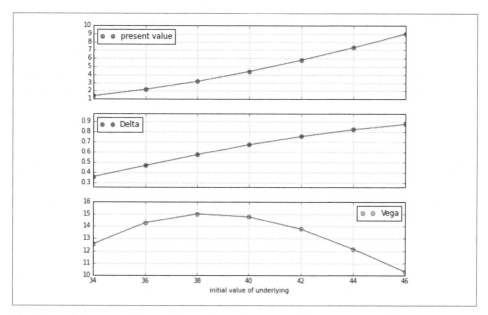

Figure 17-1. Present value, Delta, and Vega estimates for European call option

This illustrates that working with the DX library—although heavy numerics are involved—boils down to an approach that is comparable to having a closed-form option pricing formula available. However, this approach does not only apply to such simple payoffs as the one considered so far. With exactly the same approach, we can handle much more complex payoffs. To this end, consider the following payoff, a *mixture of a regular and an Asian payoff*:

```
In [18]: payoff_func = 'np.maximum(0.33 * (maturity_value + max_value) - 40, 0)'
         # payoff dependent on both the simulated maturity value
         # and the maximum value
```

Everything else shall remain the same:

```
In [19]: eur_as_call = valuation_mcs_european('eur_as_call', underlying=gbm,
                             mar_env=me_call, payoff_func=payoff_func)
```

All statistics, of course, change in this case:

```
In [20]: %%time
         s_list = np.arange(34., 46.1, 2.)
         p_list = []; d_list = []; v_list = []
         for s in s_list:
             eur_as_call.update(s)
             p_list.append(eur_as_call.present_value(fixed_seed=True))
             d_list.append(eur_as_call.delta())
             v_list.append(eur_as_call.vega())
```

```
Out[20]: CPU times: user 286 ms, sys: 14.5 ms, total: 300 ms
         Wall time: 303 ms
```

Figure 17-2 shows that Delta becomes 1 when the initial value of the underlying reaches the strike price of 40 in this case. Every (marginal) increase of the initial value of the underlying leads to the same (marginal) increase in the option's value from this particular point on:

```
In [21]: plot_option_stats(s_list, p_list, d_list, v_list)
```

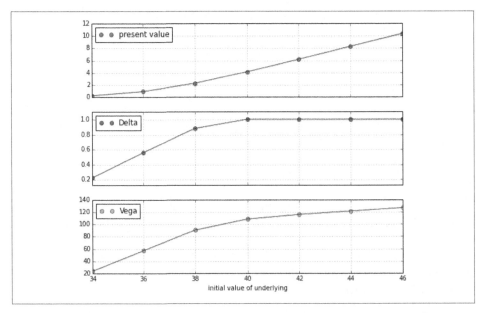

Figure 17-2. Present value, Delta, and Vega estimates for European–Asian call option

American Exercise

The valuation of options with *American exercise*—or *Bermudan exercise*, to this end[2]—is much more involved than with European exercise. Therefore, we have to introduce a bit more valuation theory first before proceeding to the valuation class.

---

2. *American* exercise refers to a situation where exercise is possible at every instant of time over a fixed time interval (at least during trading hours). *Bermudan* exercise generally refers to a situation where there are multiple, discrete exercise dates. In numerical applications, American exercise is approximated by Bermudan exercise, and maybe letting the number of exercise dates go to infinity in the limit.

Least-Squares Monte Carlo

Although Cox, Ross, and Rubinstein (1979) presented with their binomial model a simple numerical method to value European and American options in the same framework, only with the Longstaff-Schwartz (2001) model was the valuation of American options by Monte Carlo simulation (MCS) satisfactorily solved. The major problem is that MCS per se is a forward-moving algorithm, while the valuation of American options is generally accomplished by backward induction, estimating the continuation value of the American option starting at maturity and working *back* to the present.

The major insight of the Longstaff-Schwartz (2001) model is to use an ordinary least-squares regression[3] to estimate the continuation value based on the cross section of all available simulated values—taking into account, per path:

- The simulated value of the underlying(s)
- The inner value of the option
- The actual continuation value given the specific path

In discrete time, the value of a Bermudan option (and in the limit of an American option) is given by the *optimal stopping problem*, as presented in Equation 17-3 for a finite set of points in time $0 < t_1 < t_2 < ... < T.$[4]

Equation 17-3. Optimal stopping problem in discrete time for Bermudan option

$$V_0 = \sup_{\tau \in \{0, t_1, t_2, ..., T\}} e^{-r\tau} \mathbf{E}_0^Q \big(h_\tau(S_\tau) \big)$$

Equation 17-4 presents the continuation value of the American option at date $0 \le t_m < T$. It is just the risk-neutral expectation at date t_{m+1} under the martingale measure of the value of the American option $V_{t_{m+1}}$ at the subsequent date.

Equation 17-4. Continuation value for the American option

$$C_{t_m}(s) = e^{-r(t_{m+1} - t_m)} \mathbf{E}_{t_m}^Q \big(V_{t_{m+1}} \big(S_{t_{m+1}} \big) \big| S_{t_m} = s \big)$$

---

3. That is why their algorithm is generally abbreviated as LSM, for *Least-Squares Monte Carlo*.

4. Kohler (2010) provides a concise overview of the theory of American option valuation in general and the use of regression-based methods in particular.

The value of the American option V_{t_m} at date t_m can be shown to equal the formula in Equation 17-5—i.e., the maximum of the payoff of immediate exercise (inner value) and the expected payoff of not exercising (continuation value).

Equation 17-5. Value of American option at any given date

$$V_{t_m} = \max\left(h_{t_m}(s), C_{t_m}(s)\right)$$

In Equation 17-5, the inner value is of course easily calculated. The continuation value is what makes it a bit trickier. The Longstaff-Schwartz (2001) model approximates this value by a regression, as presented in Equation 17-6. There, i stands for the current simulated path, D is the number of basis functions for the regression used, α^* are the optimal regression parameters, and b_d is the regression function numbered d.

Equation 17-6. Regression-based approximation of continuation value

$$\overline{C}_{t_m,i} = \sum_{d=1}^{D} \alpha^*_{d,t_m} \cdot b_d\left(S_{t_m,i}\right)$$

The optimal regression parameters are the result of the solution of the least-squares regression problem presented in Equation 17-7. Here, $Y_{t_m,i} \equiv e^{-r(t_{m+1}-t_m)}V_{t_{m+1},i}$ is the actual continuation value at date t_m for path i (and not a regressed/estimated one).

Equation 17-7. Ordinary least-squares regression

$$\min_{\alpha_{1,t_m},\dots,\alpha_{D,t_m}} \frac{1}{I}\sum_{i=1}^{I}\left(Y_{t_m,i} - \sum_{d=1}^{D} \alpha_{d,t_m} \cdot b_d\left(S_{t_m,i}\right)\right)^2$$

This completes the basic (mathematical) tool set to value an American option by MCS.

The Valuation Class

Example 17-4 presents the class for the valuation of options and derivatives with American exercise. There is one noteworthy step in the implementation of the LSM algorithm in the present_value method (which is also commented on inline): the *optimal decision step*. Here, it is important that, based on the decision that is made, the LSM algorithm takes either the inner value or the *actual* continuation value—and *not* the estimated continuation value.[5]

Example 17-4. Valuation class for American exercise

```
#
# DX Library Valuation
# valuation_mcs_american.py
#
import numpy as np

from valuation_class import valuation_class

class valuation_mcs_american(valuation_class):
    ''' Class to value American options with arbitrary payoff
    by single-factor Monte Carlo simulation.

    Methods
    =======
    generate_payoff :
        returns payoffs given the paths and the payoff function
    present_value :
        returns present value (LSM Monte Carlo estimator)
        according to Longstaff-Schwartz (2001)
    '''

    def generate_payoff(self, fixed_seed=False):
        '''
        Parameters
        ==========
        fixed_seed :
            use same/fixed seed for valuation
        '''
        try:
            strike = self.strike
        except:
            pass
        paths = self.underlying.get_instrument_values(fixed_seed=fixed_seed)
        time_grid = self.underlying.time_grid
        try:
            time_index_start = int(np.where(time_grid == self.pricing_date)[0])
            time_index_end = int(np.where(time_grid == self.maturity)[0])
        except:
            print "Maturity date not in time grid of underlying."
        instrument_values = paths[time_index_start:time_index_end + 1]
        try:
            payoff = eval(self.payoff_func)
            return instrument_values, payoff, time_index_start, time_index_end
        except:
```

5. See also Chapter 6 of Hilpisch (2015).

```
        print "Error evaluating payoff function."

def present_value(self, accuracy=6, fixed_seed=False, bf=5, full=False):
    '''

    Parameters
    ==========
    accuracy : int
        number of decimals in returned result
    fixed_seed : boolean
        use same/fixed seed for valuation
    bf : int
        number of basis functions for regression
    full : Boolean
        return also full 1d array of present values
    '''
    instrument_values, inner_values, time_index_start, time_index_end = \
            self.generate_payoff(fixed_seed=fixed_seed)
    time_list = self.underlying.time_grid[time_index_start:time_index_end + 1]
    discount_factors = self.discount_curve.get_discount_factors(
                        time_list, dtobjects=True)
    V = inner_values[-1]
    for t in range(len(time_list) - 2, 0, -1):
        # derive relevant discount factor for given time interval
        df = discount_factors[t, 1] / discount_factors[t + 1, 1]
        # regression step
        rg = np.polyfit(instrument_values[t], V * df, bf)
        # calculation of continuation values per path
        C = np.polyval(rg, instrument_values[t])
        # optimal decision step:
        # if condition is satisfied (inner value > regressed cont. value)
        # then take inner value; take actual cont. value otherwise
        V = np.where(inner_values[t] > C, inner_values[t], V * df)
    df = discount_factors[0, 1] / discount_factors[1, 1]
    result = df * np.sum(V) / len(V)
    if full:
        return round(result, accuracy), df * V
    else:
        return round(result, accuracy)
```

A Use Case

As has become by now the means of choice, a use case shall illustrate how to work with
the valuation_mcs_american class. The use case replicates all American option values
as presented in Table 1 of the seminal paper by Longstaff and Schwartz (2001). The
underlying is the same as before, a geometric_brownian_motion object. The starting
parameterization for the underlying is as follows:

```
In [22]: from dx_simulation import *

In [23]: me_gbm = market_environment('me_gbm', dt.datetime(2015, 1, 1))
```

```
In [24]: me_gbm.add_constant('initial_value', 36.)
         me_gbm.add_constant('volatility', 0.2)
         me_gbm.add_constant('final_date', dt.datetime(2016, 12, 31))
         me_gbm.add_constant('currency', 'EUR')
         me_gbm.add_constant('frequency', 'W')
           # weekly frequency
         me_gbm.add_constant('paths', 50000)

In [25]: csr = constant_short_rate('csr', 0.06)

In [26]: me_gbm.add_curve('discount_curve', csr)

In [27]: gbm = geometric_brownian_motion('gbm', me_gbm)
```

The *option type* is an American put option with payoff:

```
In [28]: payoff_func = 'np.maximum(strike - instrument_values, 0)'
```

The first option in Table 1 of the paper has a maturity of one year, and the strike price is 40 throughout:

```
In [29]: me_am_put = market_environment('me_am_put', dt.datetime(2015, 1, 1))

In [30]: me_am_put.add_constant('maturity', dt.datetime(2015, 12, 31))
         me_am_put.add_constant('strike', 40.)
         me_am_put.add_constant('currency', 'EUR')
```

The next step is to instantiate the valuation object based on the numerical assumptions:

```
In [31]: from valuation_mcs_american import valuation_mcs_american

In [32]: am_put = valuation_mcs_american('am_put', underlying=gbm,
                         mar_env=me_am_put, payoff_func=payoff_func)
```

The valuation of the American put option takes much longer than the same task for the European options. Not only have we increased the number of paths and the frequency for the valuation, but the algorithm is much more computationally demanding due to the backward induction and the regression per induction step. Our numerical value is pretty close to the correct one reported in the original paper of 4.478:

```
In [33]: %time am_put.present_value(fixed_seed=True, bf=5)

Out[33]: CPU times: user 1.36 s, sys: 239 ms, total: 1.6 s
         Wall time: 1.6 s

         4.470627
```

Due to the very construction of the LSM Monte Carlo estimator, it represents a *lower bound* of the mathematically correct American option value.[6] Therefore, we would expect the numerical estimate to lie under the true value in any numerically realistic case.

---

6. The main reason is that the "optimal exercise policy" based on the regression estimates of the continuation value is only "suboptimal."

Alternative dual estimators can provide *upper bounds* as well.[7] Taken together, two such different estimators then define an interval for the true American option value.

The main stated goal of this use case is to replicate all American option values of Table 1 in the original paper. To this end, we only need to combine the valuation object with a nested loop. During the innermost loop, the valuation object has to be updated according to the then-current parameterization:

```
In [34]: %%time
         ls_table = []
         for initial_value in (36., 38., 40., 42., 44.):
             for volatility in (0.2, 0.4):
                 for maturity in (dt.datetime(2015, 12, 31),
                                  dt.datetime(2016, 12, 31)):
                     am_put.update(initial_value=initial_value,
                                   volatility=volatility,
                                   maturity=maturity)
                     ls_table.append([initial_value,
                                      volatility,
                                      maturity,
                                      am_put.present_value(bf=5)])

Out[34]: CPU times: user 31.1 s, sys: 3.22 s, total: 34.3 s
         Wall time: 33.9 s
```

Following is our simplified version of Table 1 in the paper by Longstaff and Schwartz (2001). Overall, our numerical values come pretty close to those reported in the paper, where some different parameters have been used (they use, for example, double the number of paths):

```
In [35]: print "S0  | Vola | T | Value"
         print 22 * "-"
         for r in ls_table:
             print "%d  | %3.1f  | %d | %5.3f" % \
                   (r[0], r[1], r[2].year - 2014, r[3])

Out[35]: S0  | Vola | T | Value
         ----------------------
         36  | 0.2  | 1 | 4.444
         36  | 0.2  | 2 | 4.769
         36  | 0.4  | 1 | 7.000
         36  | 0.4  | 2 | 8.378
         38  | 0.2  | 1 | 3.210
         38  | 0.2  | 2 | 3.645
         38  | 0.4  | 1 | 6.066
         38  | 0.4  | 2 | 7.535
         40  | 0.2  | 1 | 2.267
         40  | 0.2  | 2 | 2.778
```

7. Cf. Chapter 6 in Hilpisch (2015) for a dual algorithm leading to an upper bound and a Python implementation thereof.

```
40  |  0.4  |  1  |  5.203
40  |  0.4  |  2  |  6.753
42  |  0.2  |  1  |  1.554
42  |  0.2  |  2  |  2.099
42  |  0.4  |  1  |  4.459
42  |  0.4  |  2  |  6.046
44  |  0.2  |  1  |  1.056
44  |  0.2  |  2  |  1.618
44  |  0.4  |  1  |  3.846
44  |  0.4  |  2  |  5.494
```

To conclude the use case, note that the estimation of Greeks for American options is formally the same as for European options—a major advantage of our approach over alternative numerical methods (like the binomial model):

```
In [36]: am_put.update(initial_value=36.)
         am_put.delta()

Out[36]: -0.4655

In [37]: am_put.vega()

Out[37]: 17.3411
```

Conclusions

This chapter is about the numerical valuation of both *European* and *American* options based on Monte Carlo simulation. The chapter introduces a generic valuation class, called valuation_class. This class provides methods, for example, to estimate the most important Greeks (Delta, Vega) for both types of options, independent of the simulation object (risk factor/stochastic process) used for the valuation.

Based on the generic valuation class, the chapter presents two specialized classes, valuation_mcs_european and valuation_mcs_american. The class for the valuation of European options is mainly a straightforward implementation of the risk-neutral valuation approach presented in Chapter 15 in combination with the numerical estimation of an expectation term (i.e., an integral by Monte Carlo simulation, as discussed in Chapter 9).

The class for the valuation of American options needs a certain kind of regression-based valuation algorithm. This is due to the fact that for American options an optimal exercise policy has to be derived for a valuation. This is theoretically and numerically a bit more involved. However, the respective present_value method of the class is still concise.

The approach taken with the DX derivatives analytics library proves to be beneficial. Without too much effort we are able to value a pretty large class of options with the following features:

- Single risk factor options
- European or American exercise

- Arbitrary payoff

In addition, we can estimate the most important Greeks for this class of options. To simplify future imports, we will again use a wrapper module, this time called dx_valu ation.py, as presented in Example 17-5.

Example 17-5. Wrapper module for all components of the library including valuation classes

```
#
# DX Library Valuation
# dx_valuation.py
#
import numpy as np
import pandas as pd

from dx_simulation import *
from valuation_class import valuation_class
from valuation_mcs_european import valuation_mcs_european
from valuation_mcs_american import valuation_mcs_american
```

Again, let us enhance the init file in the dx directory (see Example 17-6) to stay consistent here.

Example 17-6. Enhanced Python packaging file

```
#
# DX Library
# packaging file
# __init__.py
#
import numpy as np
import pandas as pd
import datetime as dt

# frame
from get_year_deltas import get_year_deltas
from constant_short_rate import constant_short_rate
from market_environment import market_environment
from plot_option_stats import plot_option_stats

# simulation
from sn_random_numbers import sn_random_numbers
from simulation_class import simulation_class
from geometric_brownian_motion import geometric_brownian_motion
from jump_diffusion import jump_diffusion
from square_root_diffusion import square_root_diffusion

# valuation
from valuation_class import valuation_class
from valuation_mcs_european import valuation_mcs_european
from valuation_mcs_american import valuation_mcs_american
```

Further Reading

References for the topics of this chapter in book form are:

- Glasserman, Paul (2004): *Monte Carlo Methods in Financial Engineering*. Springer, New York.
- Hilpisch, Yves (2015): *Derivatives Analytics with Python*. Wiley Finance, Chichester, England. *http://derivatives-analytics-with-python.com*.

Original papers cited in this chapter:

- Cox, John, Stephen Ross, and Mark Rubinstein (1979): "Option Pricing: A Simplified Approach." *Journal of Financial Economics*, Vol. 7, No. 3, pp. 229–263.
- Kohler, Michael (2010): "A Review on Regression-Based Monte Carlo Methods for Pricing American Options." In Luc Devroye et al. (eds.): *Recent Developments in Applied Probability and Statistics*. Physica-Verlag, Heidelberg, pp. 37–58.
- Longstaff, Francis and Eduardo Schwartz (2001): "Valuing American Options by Simulation: A Simple Least Squares Approach." *Review of Financial Studies*, Vol. 14, No. 1, pp. 113–147.

## CHAPTER 18

Portfolio Valuation

> Price is what you pay. Value is what you get.
>
> — Warren Buffet

By now, the whole approach for building the DX derivatives analytics library—and its associated benefits—should be rather clear. By strictly relying on Monte Carlo simulation as the only numerical method, we accomplish an almost complete modularization of the analytics library:

Discounting
The relevant risk-neutral discounting is taken care of by an instance of the con stant_short_rate class.

Relevant data
Relevant data, parameters, and other input are stored in (several) instances of the market_environment class.

Simulation objects
Relevant risk factors (underlyings) are modeled as instances of one of three simulation classes:

- geometric_brownian_motion
- jump_diffusion
- square_root_diffusion

Valuation objects
Options and derivatives to be valued are modeled as instances of one of two valuation classes:

- valuation_mcs_european
- valuation_mcs_american

One last step is missing: the valuation of possibly complex *portfolios* of options and derivatives. To this end, we require the following:

Nonredundancy
> Every risk factor (underlying) is modeled only once and potentially used by multiple valuation objects.

Correlations
> Correlations between risk factors have to be accounted for.

Positions
> An options position, for example, can consist of certain multiples of an options contract.

However, although we have in principle allowed (and even required) providing a currency for both simulation and valuation objects, we assume that we value portfolios denominated in a *single currency* only. This simplifies the aggregation of values within a portfolio significantly, because we can abstract from exchange rates and currency risks.

The chapter presents two new classes: a simple one to model a *derivatives position*, and a more complex one to model and value a *derivatives portfolio*.

Derivatives Positions

In principle, a *derivatives position* is nothing more than a combination of a valuation object and a quantity for the instrument modeled.

The Class

Example 18-1 presents the class to model a derivatives position. It is mainly a container for other data and objects. In addition, it provides a `get_info` method, printing the data and object information stored in an instance of the class.

Example 18-1. A simple class to model a derivatives position

```
#
# DX Library Portfolio
# derivatives_position.py
#

class derivatives_position(object):
    ''' Class to model a derivatives position.

    Attributes
    ==========

    name : string
        name of the object
    quantity : float
```

```
        number of assets/derivatives making up the position
    underlying : string
        name of asset/risk factor for the derivative
    mar_env : instance of market_environment
        constants, lists, and curves relevant for valuation_class
    otype : string
        valuation class to use
    payoff_func : string
        payoff string for the derivative

    Methods
    =======
    get_info :
        prints information about the derivative position
    '''


    def __init__(self, name, quantity, underlying, mar_env, otype, payoff_func):
        self.name = name
        self.quantity = quantity
        self.underlying = underlying
        self.mar_env = mar_env
        self.otype = otype
        self.payoff_func = payoff_func


    def get_info(self):
        print "NAME"
        print self.name, '\n'
        print "QUANTITY"
        print self.quantity, '\n'
        print "UNDERLYING"
        print self.underlying, '\n'
        print "MARKET ENVIRONMENT"
        print "\n**Constants**"
        for key, value in self.mar_env.constants.items():
            print key, value
        print "\n**Lists**"
        for key, value in self.mar_env.lists.items():
            print key, value
        print "\n**Curves**"
        for key in self.mar_env.curves.items():
            print key, value
        print "\nOPTION TYPE"
        print self.otype, '\n'
        print "PAYOFF FUNCTION"
        print self.payoff_func
```

To define a derivatives position we need to provide the following information, which is almost the same as for the instantiation of a valuation class:

name
: Name of the position as a `string` object

quantity
: Quantity of options/derivatives

underlying
: Instance of simulation object as a risk factor

mar_env
: Instance of `market_environment`

otype
: `string`, either "European" or "American"

payoff_func
: Payoff as a `Python` `string` object

A Use Case

The following interactive session illustrates the use of the class. However, we need to first define a simulation object—but not in full; only the most important, object-specific information is needed. Here, we basically stick to the numerical examples from the previous two chapters:

```
In [1]: from dx import *
```

For the definition of the derivatives position, we do not need a "full" `market_environ` `ment` object. Missing information is provided later (during the portfolio valuation), when the simulation object is instantiated:

```
In [2]: me_gbm = market_environment('me_gbm', dt.datetime(2015, 1, 1))
```

```
In [3]: me_gbm.add_constant('initial_value', 36.)
        me_gbm.add_constant('volatility', 0.2)
        me_gbm.add_constant('currency', 'EUR')
```

However, for the portfolio valuation, one additional constant is needed—namely, for the *model* to be used. This will become clear in the subsequent section:

```
In [4]: me_gbm.add_constant('model', 'gbm')
```

With the simulation object available, we can proceed to define a derivatives position as follows:

```
In [5]: from derivatives_position import derivatives_position
```

```
In [6]: me_am_put = market_environment('me_am_put', dt.datetime(2015, 1, 1))
```

```
In [7]: me_am_put.add_constant('maturity', dt.datetime(2015, 12, 31))
        me_am_put.add_constant('strike', 40.)
        me_am_put.add_constant('currency', 'EUR')
```

```
In [8]: payoff_func = 'np.maximum(strike - instrument_values, 0)'

In [9]: am_put_pos = derivatives_position(
                    name='am_put_pos',
                    quantity=3,
                    underlying='gbm',
                    mar_env=me_am_put,
                    otype='American',
                    payoff_func=payoff_func)
```

Information about such an object is provided by the get_info method:

```
In [10]: am_put_pos.get_info()

Out[10]: NAME
         am_put_pos

         QUANTITY
         3

         UNDERLYING
         gbm

         MARKET ENVIRONMENT

         **Constants**
         strike 40.0
         maturity 2015-12-31 00:00:00
         currency EUR

         **Lists**

         **Curves**

         OPTION TYPE
         American

         PAYOFF FUNCTION
         np.maximum(strike - instrument_values, 0)
```

Derivatives Portfolios

From a portfolio perspective, a "relevant market" is mainly composed of the relevant risk factors (underlyings) and their correlations, as well as the derivatives and derivatives positions, respectively, to be valued. Theoretically, we are now dealing with a general market model $\mathcal{M}$ as defined in Chapter 15, and applying the Fundamental Theorem of Asset Pricing (with its corollaries) to it.[1]

---

1. In practice, the approach we choose here is sometimes called *global valuation* instead of *instrument-specific valuation*. Cf. the article by Albanese, Gimonet, and White (2010a) in *Risk Magazine*.

The Class

A somewhat complex Python class implementing a *portfolio valuation* based on the Fundamental Theorem of Asset Pricing—taking into account multiple relevant risk factors and multiple derivatives positions—is presented as Example 18-2. The class is rather comprehensively documented inline, especially during passages that implement functionality specific to the purpose at hand.

Example 18-2. A class to value a derivatives portfolio

```
#
# DX Library Portfolio
# derivatives_portfolio.py
#
import numpy as np
import pandas as pd

from dx_valuation import *

# models available for risk factor modeling
models = {'gbm' : geometric_brownian_motion,
          'jd' : jump_diffusion,
          'srd' : square_root_diffusion}

# allowed exercise types
otypes = {'European' : valuation_mcs_european,
          'American' : valuation_mcs_american}


class derivatives_portfolio(object):
    ''' Class for building portfolios of derivatives positions.

    Attributes
    ==========
    name : str
        name of the object
    positions : dict
        dictionary of positions (instances of derivatives_position class)
    val_env : market_environment
        market environment for the valuation
    assets : dict
        dictionary of market environments for the assets
    correlations : list
        correlations between assets
    fixed_seed : Boolean
        flag for fixed rng seed

    Methods
    =======
    get_positions :
        prints information about the single portfolio positions
    get_statistics :
```

```
        returns a pandas DataFrame object with portfolio statistics
    '''

    def __init__(self, name, positions, val_env, assets,
                 correlations=None, fixed_seed=False):
        self.name = name
        self.positions = positions
        self.val_env = val_env
        self.assets = assets
        self.underlyings = set()
        self.correlations = correlations
        self.time_grid = None
        self.underlying_objects = {}
        self.valuation_objects = {}
        self.fixed_seed = fixed_seed
        self.special_dates = []
        for pos in self.positions:
            # determine earliest starting_date
            self.val_env.constants['starting_date'] = \
                    min(self.val_env.constants['starting_date'],
                        positions[pos].mar_env.pricing_date)
            # determine latest date of relevance
            self.val_env.constants['final_date'] = \
                    max(self.val_env.constants['final_date'],
                        positions[pos].mar_env.constants['maturity'])
            # collect all underlyings
            # add to set; avoids redundancy
            self.underlyings.add(positions[pos].underlying)

        # generate general time grid
        start = self.val_env.constants['starting_date']
        end = self.val_env.constants['final_date']
        time_grid = pd.date_range(start=start,end=end,
                    freq=self.val_env.constants['frequency']
                    ).to_pydatetime()
        time_grid = list(time_grid)
        for pos in self.positions:
            maturity_date = positions[pos].mar_env.constants['maturity']
            if maturity_date not in time_grid:
                time_grid.insert(0, maturity_date)
                self.special_dates.append(maturity_date)
        if start not in time_grid:
            time_grid.insert(0, start)
        if end not in time_grid:
            time_grid.append(end)
        # delete duplicate entries
        time_grid = list(set(time_grid))
        # sort dates in time_grid
        time_grid.sort()
        self.time_grid = np.array(time_grid)
        self.val_env.add_list('time_grid', self.time_grid)
```

```
if correlations is not None:
    # take care of correlations
    ul_list = sorted(self.underlyings)
    correlation_matrix = np.zeros((len(ul_list), len(ul_list)))
    np.fill_diagonal(correlation_matrix, 1.0)
    correlation_matrix = pd.DataFrame(correlation_matrix,
                            index=ul_list, columns=ul_list)
    for i, j, corr in correlations:
        corr = min(corr, 0.999999999999)
        # fill correlation matrix
        correlation_matrix.loc[i, j] = corr
        correlation_matrix.loc[j, i] = corr
    # determine Cholesky matrix
    cholesky_matrix = np.linalg.cholesky(np.array(correlation_matrix))

    # dictionary with index positions for the
    # slice of the random number array to be used by
    # respective underlying
    rn_set = {asset: ul_list.index(asset)
                for asset in self.underlyings}

    # random numbers array, to be used by
    # all underlyings (if correlations exist)
    random_numbers = sn_random_numbers((len(rn_set),
                                len(self.time_grid),
                                self.val_env.constants['paths']),
                                fixed_seed=self.fixed_seed)


    # add all to valuation environment that is
    # to be shared with every underlying
    self.val_env.add_list('cholesky_matrix', cholesky_matrix)
    self.val_env.add_list('random_numbers', random_numbers)
    self.val_env.add_list('rn_set', rn_set)

for asset in self.underlyings:
    # select market environment of asset
    mar_env = self.assets[asset]
    # add valuation environment to market environment
    mar_env.add_environment(val_env)
    # select right simulation class
    model = models[mar_env.constants['model']]
    # instantiate simulation object
    if correlations is not None:
        self.underlying_objects[asset] = model(asset, mar_env,
                                                corr=True)
    else:
        self.underlying_objects[asset] = model(asset, mar_env,
                                                corr=False)

for pos in positions:
    # select right valuation class (European, American)
```

```
            val_class = otypes[positions[pos].otype]
            # pick market environment and add valuation environment
            mar_env = positions[pos].mar_env
            mar_env.add_environment(self.val_env)
            # instantiate valuation class
            self.valuation_objects[pos] = \
                val_class(name=positions[pos].name,
                          mar_env=mar_env,
                          underlying=self.underlying_objects[
                                            positions[pos].underlying],
                          payoff_func=positions[pos].payoff_func)

    def get_positions(self):
        ''' Convenience method to get information about
        all derivatives positions in a portfolio. '''
        for pos in self.positions:
            bar = '\n' + 50 * '-'
            print bar
            self.positions[pos].get_info()
            print bar

    def get_statistics(self, fixed_seed=False):
        ''' Provides portfolio statistics. '''
        res_list = []
        # iterate over all positions in portfolio
        for pos, value in self.valuation_objects.items():
            p = self.positions[pos]
            pv = value.present_value(fixed_seed=fixed_seed)
            res_list.append([
                p.name,
                p.quantity,
                # calculate all present values for the single instruments
                pv,
                value.currency,
                # single instrument value times quantity
                pv * p.quantity,
                # calculate Delta of position
                value.delta() * p.quantity,
                # calculate Vega of position
                value.vega() * p.quantity,
            ])
        # generate a pandas DataFrame object with all results
        res_df = pd.DataFrame(res_list,
                    columns=['name', 'quant.', 'value', 'curr.',
                             'pos_value', 'pos_delta', 'pos_vega'])
        return res_df
```

A Use Case

In terms of the DX analytics library, the modeling capabilities are, on a high level, restricted to a combination of a simulation and a valuation class. There are a total of six possible combinations:

```
models = {'gbm' : geometric_brownian_motion,
          'jd' : jump_diffusion
          'srd': square_root_diffusion}

otypes = {'European' : valuation_mcs_european,
          'American' : valuation_mcs_american}
```

In the interactive use case that follows, we combine selected elements to define two different derivatives positions that we then combine into a portfolio.

We build on the use case for the `derivatives_position` class with the gbm and am_put_pos objects from the previous section. To illustrate the use of the `deriva tives_portfolio` class, let us define both an additional underlying and an additional options position. First, a `jump_diffusion` object:

```
In [11]: me_jd = market_environment('me_jd', me_gbm.pricing_date)
```

```
In [12]: # add jump diffusion-specific parameters
         me_jd.add_constant('lambda', 0.3)
         me_jd.add_constant('mu', -0.75)
         me_jd.add_constant('delta', 0.1)
         # add other parameters from gbm
         me_jd.add_environment(me_gbm)
```

```
In [13]: # needed for portfolio valuation
         me_jd.add_constant('model', 'jd')
```

Second, a European call option based on this new simulation object:

```
In [14]: me_eur_call = market_environment('me_eur_call', me_jd.pricing_date)
```

```
In [15]: me_eur_call.add_constant('maturity', dt.datetime(2015, 6, 30))
         me_eur_call.add_constant('strike', 38.)
         me_eur_call.add_constant('currency', 'EUR')
```

```
In [16]: payoff_func = 'np.maximum(maturity_value - strike, 0)'
```

```
In [17]: eur_call_pos = derivatives_position(
                         name='eur_call_pos',
                         quantity=5,
                         underlying='jd',
                         mar_env=me_eur_call,
                         otype='European',
                         payoff_func=payoff_func)
```

From a portfolio perspective, the relevant market now is:

```
In [18]: underlyings = {'gbm': me_gbm, 'jd' : me_jd}
         positions = {'am_put_pos' : am_put_pos, 'eur_call_pos' : eur_call_pos}
```

For the moment we abstract from correlations between the underlyings. Compiling a market_environment for the portfolio valuation is the last step before we can instantiate a derivatives_portfolio class:

```
In [19]: # discounting object for the valuation
         csr = constant_short_rate('csr', 0.06)
```

```
In [20]: val_env = market_environment('general', me_gbm.pricing_date)
         val_env.add_constant('frequency', 'W')
           # monthly frequency
         val_env.add_constant('paths', 25000)
         val_env.add_constant('starting_date', val_env.pricing_date)
         val_env.add_constant('final_date', val_env.pricing_date)
           # not yet known; take pricing_date temporarily
         val_env.add_curve('discount_curve', csr)
           # select single discount_curve for whole portfolio
```

```
In [21]: from derivatives_portfolio import derivatives_portfolio
```

```
In [22]: portfolio = derivatives_portfolio(
                       name='portfolio',
                       positions=positions,
                       val_env=val_env,
                       assets=underlyings,
                       fixed_seed=True)
```

Now we can harness the power of the valuation class and get a bunch of different statistics for the derivatives_portfolio object just defined:

```
In [23]: portfolio.get_statistics()
```

```
Out[23]:
             name    quant.    value   curr.   pos_value   pos_delta   pos_vega
0     eur_call_pos        5   2.814638    EUR   14.073190      3.3605    42.7900
1       am_put_pos        3   4.472021    EUR   13.416063     -2.0895    30.5181
```

The *sum* of the position values, Deltas, and Vegas is also easily calculated. This portfolio is slightly long Delta (almost neutral) and long Vega:

```
In [24]: portfolio.get_statistics()[['pos_value', 'pos_delta', 'pos_vega']].sum()
         # aggregate over all positions
```

```
Out[24]: pos_value    27.489253
         pos_delta     1.271000
         pos_vega     73.308100
         dtype: float64
```

A complete overview of all positions is conveniently obtained by the get_positions method—such output can, for example, be used for reporting purposes (but is omitted here due to reasons of space):

```
In [25]: portfolio.get_positions()
```

Of course, you can also access and use all (simulation, valuation, etc.) objects of the derivatives_portfolio object in direct fashion:

```
In [26]: portfolio.valuation_objects['am_put_pos'].present_value()

Out[26]: 4.450573

In [27]: portfolio.valuation_objects['eur_call_pos'].delta()

Out[27]: 0.6498
```

This derivatives portfolio valuation is conducted based on the assumption that the risk
factors are *not* correlated. This is easily verified by inspecting two simulated paths, one
for each simulation object:

```
In [28]: path_no = 777
         path_gbm = portfolio.underlying_objects['gbm'].get_instrument_values()[
                                                                   :, path_no]
         path_jd = portfolio.underlying_objects['jd'].get_instrument_values()[
                                                                   :, path_no]
```

Figure 18-1 shows the selected paths in direct comparison—no jump occurs for the
jump diffusion:

```
In [29]: import matplotlib.pyplot as plt
         %matplotlib inline

In [30]: plt.figure(figsize=(7, 4))
         plt.plot(portfolio.time_grid, path_gbm, 'r', label='gbm')
         plt.plot(portfolio.time_grid, path_jd, 'b', label='jd')
         plt.xticks(rotation=30)
         plt.legend(loc=0); plt.grid(True)
```

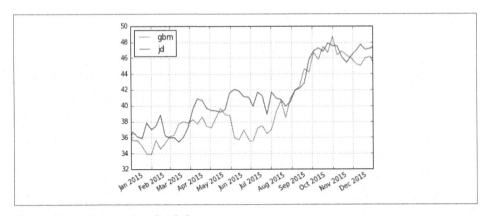

Figure 18-1. Noncorrelated risk factors

Now consider the case where the two risk factors are highly positively correlated:

```
In [31]: correlations = [['gbm', 'jd', 0.9]]
```

With this additional information, a new `derivatives_portfolio` object is to be
instantiated:

```
In [32]: port_corr = derivatives_portfolio(
                        name='portfolio',
                        positions=positions,
                        val_env=val_env,
                        assets=underlyings,
                        correlations=correlations,
                        fixed_seed=True)
```

In this case, there is no direct influence on the values of the positions in the portfolio:

```
In [33]: port_corr.get_statistics()
```

```
Out[33]:
            name  quant.     value  curr.  pos_value  pos_delta  pos_vega
0   eur_call_pos       5  2.804464    EUR  14.022320     3.3760   42.3500
1     am_put_pos       3  4.458565    EUR  13.375695    -2.0313   30.1416
```

However, the correlation takes place behind the scenes. For the graphical illustration, we take the same two paths as before:

```
In [34]: path_gbm = port_corr.underlying_objects['gbm'].\
                        get_instrument_values()[:, path_no]
         path_jd = port_corr.underlying_objects['jd'].\
                        get_instrument_values()[:, path_no]
```

Figure 18-2 now shows a development almost in perfect parallelism between the two risk factors:

```
In [35]: plt.figure(figsize=(7, 4))
         plt.plot(portfolio.time_grid, path_gbm, 'r', label='gbm')
         plt.plot(portfolio.time_grid, path_jd, 'b', label='jd')
         plt.xticks(rotation=30)
         plt.legend(loc=0); plt.grid(True)
```

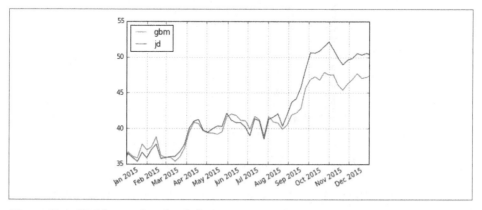

Figure 18-2. Highly correlated risk factors

As a last numerical and conceptual example, consider the *frequency distribution of the portfolio present value*. This is something impossible to generate in general with other approaches, like the application of analytical formulae or the binomial option pricing model. We get the complete set of present values per option position by calculating a present value and passing the parameter flag full=True:

```
In [36]: pv1 = 5 * port_corr.valuation_objects['eur_call_pos'].\
                 present_value(full=True)[1]
         pv1

Out[36]: array([  0.        ,  22.55857473,   8.2552922 , ...,   0.        ,
                  0.        ,   0.        ])

In [37]: pv2 = 3 * port_corr.valuation_objects['am_put_pos'].\
                 present_value(full=True)[1]
         pv2

Out[37]: array([ 22.04450095,  10.90940926,  20.25092898, ...,  21.68232889,
                 17.7583897 ,   0.        ])
```

First, we compare the frequency distribution of the two positions. The payoff profiles of the two positions, as displayed in Figure 18-3, are quite different. Note that we limit both the x- and y-axes for better readability:

```
In [38]: plt.hist([pv1, pv2], bins=25,
                 label=['European call', 'American put']);
         plt.axvline(pv1.mean(), color='r', ls='dashed',
                   lw=1.5, label='call mean = %4.2f' % pv1.mean())
         plt.axvline(pv2.mean(), color='r', ls='dotted',
                   lw=1.5, label='put mean = %4.2f' % pv2.mean())
         plt.xlim(0, 80); plt.ylim(0, 10000)
         plt.grid(); plt.legend()
```

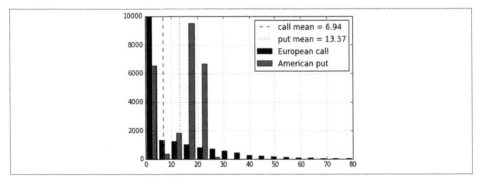

Figure 18-3. Portfolio frequency distribution of present values

The following figure finally shows the full frequency distribution of the portfolio present values. You can clearly see in Figure 18-4 the offsetting diversification effects of combining a call with a put option:

```
In [39]: pvs = pv1 + pv2
         plt.hist(pvs, bins=50, label='portfolio');
```

```
plt.axvline(pvs.mean(), color='r', ls='dashed',
            lw=1.5, label='mean = %4.2f' % pvs.mean())
plt.xlim(0, 80); plt.ylim(0, 7000)
plt.grid(); plt.legend()
```

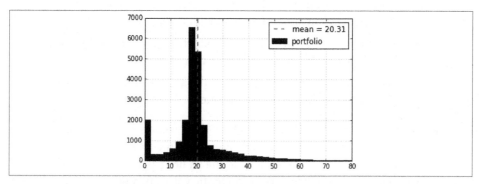

Figure 18-4. Portfolio frequency distribution of present values

What impact does the correlation between the two risk factors have on the risk of the portfolio, measured in the standard deviation of the present values? The statistics for the portfolio with correlation are easily calculated as follows:

```
In [40]: # portfolio with correlation
         pvs.std()
```

```
Out[40]: 16.736290069957963
```

Similarly, for the portfolio without correlation, we have:

```
In [41]: # portfolio without correlation
         pv1 = 5 * portfolio.valuation_objects['eur_call_pos'].\
                   present_value(full=True)[1]
         pv2 = 3 * portfolio.valuation_objects['am_put_pos'].\
                   present_value(full=True)[1]
         (pv1 + pv2).std()
```

```
Out[41]: 21.71542409437863
```

Although the mean value stays constant (ignoring numerical deviations), correlation obviously significantly decreases the portfolio risk when measured in this way. Again, this is an insight that it is not really possible to gain when using alternative numerical methods or valuation approaches.

Conclusions

This chapter addresses the valuation and risk management of a portfolio of multiple derivatives positions dependent on multiple, possibly correlated, risk factors. To this end, a new class called derivatives_position is introduced to model an options/

derivatives position. The main focus, however, lies on the `derivatives_portfolio` class, which implements some rather complex tasks. For example, the class takes care of:

- *Correlations* between risk factors (the class generates a single, consistent set of random numbers for the simulation of all risk factors)
- *Instantiation of simulation objects* given the single market environments and the general valuation environment, as well as the derivatives positions
- *Generation of portfolio statistics* based on all the assumptions, the risk factors involved, and the terms of the derivatives positions

The examples presented in this chapter can only show some simple versions of derivatives portfolios that can be managed and valued with the DX library and the `derivatives_portfolio` class. Natural extensions to the DX library would be the addition of more *sophisticated financial models*, like a stochastic volatility model, and the addition of *multirisk valuation classes* to model and value derivatives dependent on multiple risk factors, like a European basket option or an American maximum call option, to name just two. At this stage, the modular modeling and the application of a valuation framework as general as the Fundamental Theorem of Asset Pricing (or "Global Valuation") plays out its strengths: the nonredundant modeling of the risk factors and the accounting for the correlations between them will then also have a direct influence on the values and Greeks of multirisk derivatives.

Example 18-3 is a final, brief wrapper module bringing all components of the DX analytics library together for a single `import` statement.

Example 18-3. The final wrapper module bringing all DX components together

```
#
# DX Library Simulation
# dx_library.py
#
from dx_valuation import *
from derivatives_position import derivatives_position
from derivatives_portfolio import derivatives_portfolio
```

Also, the now-complete `init` file for the dx directory is in Example 18-4.

Example 18-4. Final Python packaging file

```
#
# DX Library
# packaging file
# __init__.py
#
import numpy as np
import pandas as pd
```

```
import datetime as dt

# frame
from get_year_deltas import get_year_deltas
from constant_short_rate import constant_short_rate
from market_environment import market_environment
from plot_option_stats import plot_option_stats

# simulation
from sn_random_numbers import sn_random_numbers
from simulation_class import simulation_class
from geometric_brownian_motion import geometric_brownian_motion
from jump_diffusion import jump_diffusion
from square_root_diffusion import square_root_diffusion

# valuation
from valuation_class import valuation_class
from valuation_mcs_european import valuation_mcs_european
from valuation_mcs_american import valuation_mcs_american

# portfolio
from derivatives_position import derivatives_position
from derivatives_portfolio import derivatives_portfolio
```

Further Reading

As for the preceding chapters on the DX derivatives analytics library, Glasserman (2004) is a comprehensive resource for Monte Carlo simulation in the context of financial engineering and applications. Hilpisch (2015) also provides Python-based implementations of the most important Monte Carlo algorithms:

- Glasserman, Paul (2004): *Monte Carlo Methods in Financial Engineering*. Springer, New York.

- Hilpisch, Yves (2015): *Derivatives Analytics with Python*. Wiley Finance, Chichester, England. *http://derivatives-analytics-with-python.com*.

However, there is hardly any research available when it comes to the valuation of (complex) portfolios of derivatives in a consistent, nonredundant fashion by Monte Carlo simulation. A notable exception, at least from a conceptual point of view, is the brief article by Albanese, Gimonet, and White (2010a). A bit more detailed is the white paper by the same team of authors:

- Albanese, Claudio, Guillaume Gimonet, and Steve White (2010a): "Towards a Global Valuation Model." *Risk Magazine*, May issue. *http://bit.ly/risk_may_2010*.

- Albanese, Claudio, Guillaume Gimonet, and Steve White (2010b): "Global Valuation and Dynamic Risk Management." *http://www.albanese.co.uk/Global_Valuation_and_Dynamic_Risk_Management.pdf.*

## CHAPTER 19

Volatility Options

> We are facing extreme volatility.
>
> — Carlos Ghosn

Volatility derivatives have become an important risk management and trading tool. While first-generation financial models for option pricing take volatility as just one of a number of input parameters, second-generation models and products consider *volatility as an asset class of its own*. For example, the VIX volatility index (cf. *http://en.wiki pedia.org/wiki/CBOE_Volatility_Index*), introduced in 1993, has since 2003 been calculated as a weighted implied volatility measure of certain out-of-the-money put and call options with a constant maturity of 30 days on the S&P 500 index. Generally, the fixed 30-day maturity *main index* values can only be calculated by interpolating between a shorter and a longer maturity value for the index—i.e., between *two subindices* with varying maturity.

The VSTOXX volatility index—introduced in 2005 by Eurex, the derivatives exchange operated by Deutsche Börse AG in Germany (cf. *http://www.eurexchange.com/ advanced-services/*)—is calculated similarly; however, it is based on implied volatilities from options on the EURO STOXX 50 index.[1]

This chapter is about the use of the DX derivatives analytics library developed in Chapters 15 to 18 to value a *portfolio of American put options on the VSTOXX volatility index*. As of today, Eurex only offers futures contracts and *European* call and put options on the VSTOXX. There are no American options on the VSTOXX available on public markets.

This is quite a typical situation for a bank marketing and writing options on indices that are not offered by the respective exchanges themselves. For simplicity, we assume that

---

1. For details on how the VSTOXX is calculated and how you can calculate it by yourself—using Python to collect the necessary data and to do the calculations—see the Python-based tutorial (*http://www.eurex change.com/advanced-services/vstoxx/*).

the maturity of the American put options coincides with the maturity of one of the traded options series.

As a model for the VSTOXX volatility index, we take the `square_root_diffusion` class from the DX library. This model satisfies the major requirements when it comes to the modeling of a quantity like volatility—i.e., mean reversion and positivity (see also Chapters 10, 14, and 16).[2]

In particular, this chapter implements the following major tasks:

Data collection
   We need three types of data, namely for the VSTOXX index itself, the futures on the index, and options data.

Model calibration
   To value the nontraded options in a market-consistent fashion, one generally first calibrates the chosen model to quoted option prices in such a way that the model based on the optimal parameters replicates the market prices as well as possible.

Portfolio valuation
   Equipped with all the data and a market-calibrated model for the VSTOXX volatility index, the final task then is to model and value the nontraded options.

The VSTOXX Data

This section collects step by step the necessary data to value the American put options on the VSTOXX. First, let us import our libraries of choice when it comes to the gathering and management of data:

```
In [1]: import numpy as np
        import pandas as pd
```

VSTOXX Index Data

In Chapter 6, there is a regression example based on the VSTOXX and EURO STOXX 50 indices. There, we also use the following public source for VSTOXX daily closing data:

```
In [2]: url = 'http://www.stoxx.com/download/historical_values/h_vstoxx.txt'
        vstoxx_index = pd.read_csv(url, index_col=0, header=2,
                                   parse_dates=True, dayfirst=True)
```

---

2. One of the earlier volatility option pricing models by Gruenbichler and Longstaff (1996) is also based on the square-root diffusion. However, they only consider European options, for which they come up with a closed-form solution. For a review of the model and a Python implementation of it, refer to *http://www.eurex change.com/advanced-services/vstoxx/*. See also the web service example in Chapter 14, which is based on their model and analytical valuation formula.

```
In [3]: vstoxx_index.info()

Out[3]: <class 'pandas.core.frame.DataFrame'>
        DatetimeIndex: 4010 entries, 1999-01-04 00:00:00 to 2014-09-26 00:00:00
        Data columns (total 9 columns):
        V2TX    4010 non-null float64
        V6I1    3591 non-null float64
        V6I2    4010 non-null float64
        V6I3    3960 non-null float64
        V6I4    4010 non-null float64
        V6I5    4010 non-null float64
        V6I6    3995 non-null float64
        V6I7    4010 non-null float64
        V6I8    3999 non-null float64
        dtypes: float64(9)
```

For the options analysis to follow, we only need VSTOXX index data for the first quarter of 2014. Therefore, we can delete both older and newer data contained now in the DataFrame vstoxx_index:

```
In [4]: vstoxx_index = vstoxx_index[('2013/12/31' < vstoxx_index.index)
                                     & (vstoxx_index.index < '2014/4/1')]
```

Taking a look at the data reveals that the data set not only contains daily closing values for the main index V2TX, but also for all subindices from V6I1 to V6I8, where the last figure represents the maturity (1 = closest maturity, 8 = longest maturity). As pointed out before, the main index generally is an interpolation of two subindices, in particular V6I1 and V6I2, representing in the first case a maturity of under 30 days and in the second case of between 30 and 60 days:

```
In [5]: np.round(vstoxx_index.tail(), 2)

Out[5]:             V2TX   V6I1   V6I2   V6I3   V6I4   V6I5   V6I6   V6I7   V6I8
        Date
        2014-03-25  18.26  18.23  18.31  19.04  19.84  20.31  18.11  20.83  21.20
        2014-03-26  17.59  17.48  17.70  18.45  19.42  20.00  20.26  20.45  20.86
        2014-03-27  17.64  17.50  17.76  18.62  19.49  20.05  20.11  20.49  20.94
        2014-03-28  17.03  16.68  17.29  18.33  19.30  19.83  20.14  20.38  20.82
        2014-03-31  17.66  17.61  17.69  18.57  19.43  20.04  19.98  20.44  20.90
```

VSTOXX Futures Data

The data set we use for the futures and options data is not publicly available in this form. It is a complete data set with daily prices for all instruments traded on the VSTOXX volatility index provided by Eurex. The data set covers the complete first quarter of 2014:

```
In [6]: vstoxx_futures = pd.read_excel('./source/vstoxx_march_2014.xlsx',
                                       'vstoxx_futures')

In [7]: vstoxx_futures.info()

Out[7]: <class 'pandas.core.frame.DataFrame'>
        Int64Index: 504 entries, 0 to 503
```

```
Data columns (total 8 columns):
A_DATE                        504 non-null datetime64[ns]
A_EXP_YEAR                    504 non-null int64
A_EXP_MONTH                   504 non-null int64
A_CALL_PUT_FLAG              504 non-null object
A_EXERCISE_PRICE             504 non-null int64
A_SETTLEMENT_PRICE_SCALED    504 non-null int64
A_PRODUCT_ID                 504 non-null object
SETTLE                        504 non-null float64
dtypes: datetime64[ns](1), float64(1), int64(4), object(2)
```

Several columns are not populated or not needed, such that we can delete them without loss of any relevant information:

```
In [8]: del vstoxx_futures['A_SETTLEMENT_PRICE_SCALED']
        del vstoxx_futures['A_CALL_PUT_FLAG']
        del vstoxx_futures['A_EXERCISE_PRICE']
        del vstoxx_futures['A_PRODUCT_ID']
```

For brevity, we rename the remaining columns:

```
In [9]: columns = ['DATE', 'EXP_YEAR', 'EXP_MONTH', 'PRICE']
        vstoxx_futures.columns = columns
```

As is common market practice, exchange-traded options expire on the *third Friday* of the expiry month. To this end, it is helpful to have a helper function `third_friday` available that gives, for a given year and month, the date of the third Friday:

```
In [10]: import datetime as dt
         import calendar

         def third_friday(date):
             day = 21 - (calendar.weekday(date.year, date.month, 1) + 2) % 7
             return dt.datetime(date.year, date.month, day)
```

For both VSTOXX futures and options, there are at any time eight relevant maturities with monthly differences starting either on the third Friday of the *current* month (before this third Friday) or on the third Friday of the *next* month (one day before, on, or after this third Friday).[3] In our data set, there are 11 relevant maturities, ranging from January 2014 to November 2014:

```
In [11]: set(vstoxx_futures['EXP_MONTH'])

Out[11]: {1, 2, 3, 4, 5, 6, 7, 8, 9, 10, 11}
```

We calculate the specific dates of all third Fridays once to reuse them later. Note that April 18, 2014 was a public holiday in Germany, although that is irrelevant for the following analysis:

---

3. VSTOXX volatility derivatives have their last trading day two days before expiry.

```
In [12]: third_fridays = {}
         for month in set(vstoxx_futures['EXP_MONTH']):
             third_fridays[month] = third_friday(dt.datetime(2014, month, 1))

In [13]: third_fridays

Out[13]: {1: datetime.datetime(2014, 1, 17, 0, 0),
          2: datetime.datetime(2014, 2, 21, 0, 0),
          3: datetime.datetime(2014, 3, 21, 0, 0),
          4: datetime.datetime(2014, 4, 18, 0, 0),
          5: datetime.datetime(2014, 5, 16, 0, 0),
          6: datetime.datetime(2014, 6, 20, 0, 0),
          7: datetime.datetime(2014, 7, 18, 0, 0),
          8: datetime.datetime(2014, 8, 15, 0, 0),
          9: datetime.datetime(2014, 9, 19, 0, 0),
          10: datetime.datetime(2014, 10, 17, 0, 0),
          11: datetime.datetime(2014, 11, 21, 0, 0)}
```

Wrapping the maturity date dict object in a lambda function allows for easy application to the respective EXP_MONTH column of the DataFrame object. For convenience, we store the maturity dates alongside the other futures data:

```
In [14]: tf = lambda x: third_fridays[x]
         vstoxx_futures['MATURITY'] = vstoxx_futures['EXP_MONTH'].apply(tf)

In [15]: vstoxx_futures.tail()

Out[15]:          DATE  EXP_YEAR  EXP_MONTH  PRICE    MATURITY
         499 2014-03-31     2014          7  20.40  2014-07-18
         500 2014-03-31     2014          8  20.70  2014-08-15
         501 2014-03-31     2014          9  20.95  2014-09-19
         502 2014-03-31     2014         10  21.05  2014-10-17
         503 2014-03-31     2014         11  21.25  2014-11-21
```

VSTOXX Options Data

At any time, there are eight futures traded on the VSTOXX. In comparison, there are of course many more options, such that we expect a much larger data set for the volatility options. In fact, we have almost 47,000 option quotes for the first quarter of 2014:

```
In [16]: vstoxx_options = pd.read_excel('./source/vstoxx_march_2014.xlsx',
                                        'vstoxx_options')

In [17]: vstoxx_options.info()

Out[17]: <class 'pandas.core.frame.DataFrame'>
         Int64Index: 46960 entries, 0 to 46959
         Data columns (total 8 columns):
         A_DATE                      46960 non-null datetime64[ns]
         A_EXP_YEAR                  46960 non-null int64
         A_EXP_MONTH                 46960 non-null int64
         A_CALL_PUT_FLAG             46960 non-null object
         A_EXERCISE_PRICE            46960 non-null int64
         A_SETTLEMENT_PRICE_SCALED   46960 non-null int64
```

```
A_PRODUCT_ID                    46960 non-null object
SETTLE                          46960 non-null float64
dtypes: datetime64[ns](1), float64(1), int64(4), object(2)
```

As before, not all columns are needed:

```
In [18]: del vstoxx_options['A_SETTLEMENT_PRICE_SCALED']
         del vstoxx_options['A_PRODUCT_ID']
```

A renaming of the columns simplifies later queries a bit:

```
In [19]: columns = ['DATE', 'EXP_YEAR', 'EXP_MONTH', 'TYPE', 'STRIKE', 'PRICE']
         vstoxx_options.columns = columns
```

We use the tf function to again store the maturity dates alongside the options data:

```
In [20]: vstoxx_options['MATURITY'] = vstoxx_options['EXP_MONTH'].apply(tf)
```

```
In [21]: vstoxx_options.head()
```

```
Out[21]:          DATE EXP_YEAR  EXP_MONTH TYPE  STRIKE  PRICE    MATURITY
         0  2014-01-02     2014          1    C    1000   7.95  2014-01-17
         1  2014-01-02     2014          1    C    1500   3.05  2014-01-17
         2  2014-01-02     2014          1    C    1600   2.20  2014-01-17
         3  2014-01-02     2014          1    C    1700   1.60  2014-01-17
         4  2014-01-02     2014          1    C    1800   1.15  2014-01-17
```

A single options contract is on 100 times the index value. Therefore, the strike price is also scaled up accordingly. To have a view of a single unit, we rescale the strike price by dividing it by 100:

```
In [22]: vstoxx_options['STRIKE'] = vstoxx_options['STRIKE'] / 100.
```

All data from the external resources has now been collected and prepared. If needed, one can save the three DataFrame objects for later reuse:

```
In [23]: save = False
         if save is True:
             import warnings
             warnings.simplefilter('ignore')
             h5 = pd.HDFStore('./source/vstoxx_march_2014.h5',
                              complevel=9, complib='blosc')
             h5['vstoxx_index'] = vstoxx_index
             h5['vstoxx_futures'] = vstoxx_futures
             h5['vstoxx_options'] = vstoxx_options
             h5.close()
```

Model Calibration

The next important step is the calibration of the financial model used to value the VSTOXX options to available market data. For an in-depth discussion of this topic and example code in Python see Hilpisch (2015), in particular Chapter 11.

Relevant Market Data

The first step when calibrating a model is to decide on the relevant market data to be used. For the example, let us assume the following:

- *Pricing date* shall be 31 March 2014.
- *Option maturity* shall be October 2014.

The following Python code defines the `pricing_date` and `maturity`, reads the `initial_value` for the VSTOXX from the respective `DataFrame` object, and also reads the corresponding value `forward` for the VSTOXX future with the appropriate maturity.

```
In [24]: pricing_date = dt.datetime(2014, 3, 31)
            # last trading day in March 2014
         maturity = third_fridays[10]
            # October maturity
         initial_value = vstoxx_index['V2TX'][pricing_date]
            # VSTOXX on pricing_date
         forward = vstoxx_futures[(vstoxx_futures.DATE == pricing_date)
                 & (vstoxx_futures.MATURITY == maturity)]['PRICE'].values[0]
```

Out of the many options quotes in the data set, we take only those that are:

- From the pricing date
- For the right maturity date
- For call options that are less than 20% out-of-the-money or in-the-money

We therefore have:

```
In [25]: tol = 0.20
         option_selection = \
             vstoxx_options[(vstoxx_options.DATE == pricing_date)
                     & (vstoxx_options.MATURITY == maturity)
                     & (vstoxx_options.TYPE == 'C')
                     & (vstoxx_options.STRIKE > (1 - tol) * forward)
                     & (vstoxx_options.STRIKE < (1 + tol) * forward)]
```

This leaves the following option quotes for the calibration procedure:

```
In [26]: option_selection
```

```
Out[26]:           DATE EXP_YEAR EXP_MONTH TYPE STRIKE PRICE   MATURITY
         46482 2014-03-31     2014        10    C     17   4.85 2014-10-17
         46483 2014-03-31     2014        10    C     18   4.30 2014-10-17
         46484 2014-03-31     2014        10    C     19   3.80 2014-10-17
         46485 2014-03-31     2014        10    C     20   3.40 2014-10-17
         46486 2014-03-31     2014        10    C     21   3.05 2014-10-17
         46487 2014-03-31     2014        10    C     22   2.75 2014-10-17
         46488 2014-03-31     2014        10    C     23   2.50 2014-10-17
```

```
46489 2014-03-31       2014           10    C       24   2.25 2014-10-17
46490 2014-03-31       2014           10    C       25   2.10 2014-10-17
```

Option Modeling

For the calibration of the `square_root_diffusion` model, the options selected before have to be modeled. This is the first time that the DX analytics library comes into play; everything else so far was "just" preparation for the following derivatives analytics tasks. We begin by importing the library:

```
In [27]: from dx import *
```

The first task is then the definition of a `market_environment` object for the VSTOXX index, in which we mainly store the previously collected and/or defined data:

```
In [28]: me_vstoxx = market_environment('me_vstoxx', pricing_date)
```

```
In [29]: me_vstoxx.add_constant('initial_value', initial_value)
         me_vstoxx.add_constant('final_date', maturity)
         me_vstoxx.add_constant('currency', 'EUR')
```

```
In [30]: me_vstoxx.add_constant('frequency', 'B')
         me_vstoxx.add_constant('paths', 10000)
```

```
In [31]: csr = constant_short_rate('csr', 0.01)
             # somewhat arbitrarily chosen here
```

```
In [32]: me_vstoxx.add_curve('discount_curve', csr)
```

The major goal of the calibration procedure is to derive optimal parameters for the `square_root_diffusion` simulation class, namely `kappa`, `theta`, and `volatility`. These are the, so to say, *degrees of freedom* that this class offers. All other parameters are in general dictated by the market or the task at hand.

Although the three (optimal) parameters are to be numerically derived, we need to provide some dummy values to instantiate the simulation class. For the `volatility` parameter, we take the historical volatility given our data set:

```
In [33]: # parameters to be calibrated later
         me_vstoxx.add_constant('kappa', 1.0)
         me_vstoxx.add_constant('theta', 1.2 * initial_value)
         vol_est = vstoxx_index['V2TX'].std() \
                     * np.sqrt(len(vstoxx_index['V2TX']) / 252.)
         me_vstoxx.add_constant('volatility', vol_est)
```

```
In [34]: vol_est
```

```
Out[34]: 1.0384283035169406
```

Then we provide the `market_environment` object to the simulation class:

```
In [35]: vstoxx_model = square_root_diffusion('vstoxx_model', me_vstoxx)
```

Although the DX library is designed to be completely modular, to model risk factors independently (and nonredundantly) from the derivatives to be valued, this does not necessarily have to be the case when it comes to a `market_environment` object. A single such object can be used for both the underlying risk factor and the option to be valued. To complete the market environment for use with a valuation class, just add values for the `strike` and the option `maturity`:

```
In [36]: me_vstoxx.add_constant('strike', forward)
         me_vstoxx.add_constant('maturity', maturity)
```

Of course, a payoff function is also needed to instantiate the valuation class:

```
In [37]: payoff_func = 'np.maximum(maturity_value - strike, 0)'
```

```
In [38]: vstoxx_eur_call = valuation_mcs_european('vstoxx_eur_call',
                              vstoxx_model, me_vstoxx, payoff_func)
```

A brief sanity check to see if the modeling so far works "in principle":

```
In [39]: vstoxx_eur_call.present_value()
```

```
Out[39]: 0.379032
```

To calibrate the model to the previously selected option quotes, we need to model all relevant European call options. They only differentiate themselves by the relevant strike price; everything else in the market environment is the same. We store the single valuation objects in a `dict` object. As keys for the `dict` object, we take the index values of the option quotes in the `DataFrame` object `option_selection` for unique identification:

```
In [40]: option_models = {}
         for option in option_selection.index:
             strike = option_selection['STRIKE'].ix[option]
             me_vstoxx.add_constant('strike', strike)
             option_models[option] = \
                             valuation_mcs_european(
                                 'eur_call_%d' % strike,
                                 vstoxx_model,
                                 me_vstoxx,
                                 payoff_func)
```

A single step in the calibration routine makes the updating of all valuation objects and a revaluation of all options necessary. For convenience, we put this functionality into a separate function:

```
In [41]: def calculate_model_values(p0):
             ''' Returns all relevant option values.

             Parameters
             ==========
             p0 : tuple/list
                 tuple of kappa, theta, volatility

             Returns
```

```
=======
model_values : dict
    dictionary with model values
'''
kappa, theta, volatility = p0
vstoxx_model.update(kappa=kappa,
                    theta=theta,
                    volatility=volatility)
model_values = {}
for option in option_models:
    model_values[option] = \
        option_models[option].present_value(fixed_seed=True)
return model_values
```

Providing a parameter tuple of `kappa`, `theta`, and `volatility` to the function `calculate_model_values` gives back, *ceteris paribus*, model option values for all relevant options:

```
In [42]: calculate_model_values((0.5, 27.5, vol_est))

Out[42]: {46482: 3.206401,
          46483: 2.412354,
          46484: 1.731028,
          46485: 1.178823,
          46486: 0.760421,
          46487: 0.46249,
          46488: 0.263662,
          46489: 0.142177,
          46490: 0.07219}
```

Calibration Procedure

Calibration of an option pricing model is, in general, a convex optimization problem. The most widely used function used for the calibration—i.e., the minimization—is the *mean-squared error* (MSE) for the model option values given the market quotes of the options. Assume there are N relevant options, and also model and market quotes. The problem of calibrating a financial model to the market quotes based on the MSE is then given in Equation 19-1. There, C_n^* and C_n^{mod} are the market price and the model price of the nth option, respectively. p is the parameter set provided as input to the option pricing model.

Equation 19-1. Model calibration based on mean-squared error

$$\min_{p} \frac{1}{N} \sum_{n=1}^{N} \left(C_n^* - C_n^{mod}(p) \right)^2$$

The `Python` function `mean_squared_error` implements this approach to model calibration technically. A global variable is used to control the output of intermediate parameter `tuple` objects and the resulting MSE:

```
In [43]: i = 0
         def mean_squared_error(p0):
             ''' Returns the mean-squared error given
             the model and market values.

             Parameters
             ===========
             p0 : tuple/list
                 tuple of kappa, theta, volatility

             Returns
             =======
             MSE : float
                 mean-squared error
             '''
             global i
             model_values = np.array(calculate_model_values(p0).values())
             market_values = option_selection['PRICE'].values
             option_diffs = model_values - market_values
             MSE = np.sum(option_diffs ** 2) / len(option_diffs)
               # vectorized MSE calculation
             if i % 20 == 0:
                 if i == 0:
                     print '%4s  %6s  %6s  %6s --> %6s' % \
                         ('i', 'kappa', 'theta', 'vola', 'MSE')
                 print '%4d  %6.3f  %6.3f  %6.3f --> %6.3f' % \
                     (i, p0[0], p0[1], p0[2], MSE)
             i += 1
             return MSE
```

Again, a brief check to see if the function works in principle:

```
In [44]: mean_squared_error((0.5, 27.5, vol_est))

Out[44]:    i   kappa   theta    vola -->    MSE
            0   0.500  27.500   1.038 -->  4.390

         4.3899900376937779
```

Chapter 9 introduces the `Python` and `SciPy` functions for convex optimization problems. We will apply these here as well, so we begin with an import:

```
In [45]: import scipy.optimize as spo
```

The following calibration uses both *global* optimization via the `brute` function and *local* optimization via the `fmin` function. First, the global optimization:

```
In [46]: %%time
         i = 0
```

```
            opt_global = spo.brute(mean_squared_error,
                             ((0.5, 3.01, 0.5),  # range for kappa
                              (15., 30.1, 5.),   # range for theta
                              (0.5, 5.51, 1)),   # range for volatility
                             finish=None)

Out[46]:    i   kappa   theta   vola -->    MSE
            0   0.500  15.000   0.500 --> 10.393
           20   0.500  30.000   1.500 -->  2.071
           40   1.000  25.000   3.500 -->  0.180
           60   1.500  20.000   5.500 -->  0.718
           80   2.000  20.000   1.500 -->  5.501
          100   2.500  15.000   3.500 -->  5.571
          120   2.500  30.000   5.500 --> 22.992
          140   3.000  30.000   1.500 --> 14.493
          CPU times: user 18.6 s, sys: 1.68 s, total: 20.3 s
          Wall time: 20.3 s
```

The intermediate optimal results are as follows. The MSE is already quite low:

```
In [47]: i = 0
         mean_squared_error(opt_global)

Out[47]:    i   kappa   theta   vola -->    MSE
            0   1.500  20.000   4.500 -->  0.008


         0.0076468730485555626
```

Next, we use the intermediate optimal parameters as input for the local optimization:

```
In [48]: %%time
         i = 0
         opt_local = spo.fmin(mean_squared_error, opt_global,
                             xtol=0.00001, ftol=0.00001,
                             maxiter=100, maxfun=350)

Out[48]:    i   kappa   theta   vola -->    MSE
            0   1.500  20.000   4.500 -->  0.008
           20   1.510  19.235   4.776 -->  0.008
           40   1.563  18.926   4.844 -->  0.005
           60   1.555  18.957   4.828 -->  0.005
           80   1.556  18.947   4.832 -->  0.005
          100   1.556  18.948   4.831 -->  0.005
          120   1.556  18.948   4.831 -->  0.005
          Optimization terminated successfully.
                   Current function value: 0.004654
                   Iterations: 64
                   Function evaluations: 138
          CPU times: user 17.7 s, sys: 1.67 s, total: 19.3 s
          Wall time: 19.4 s
```

This time the results are:

```
In [49]: i = 0
         mean_squared_error(opt_local)
```

```
Out[49]:    i    kappa    theta    vola -->    MSE
            0    1.556   18.948   4.831 -->   0.005

            0.0046542736439999875
```

The resulting model values are:

```
In [50]: calculate_model_values(opt_local)
```

```
Out[50]: {46482: 4.746597,
          46483: 4.286923,
          46484: 3.863346,
          46485: 3.474144,
          46486: 3.119211,
          46487: 2.793906,
          46488: 2.494882,
          46489: 2.224775,
          46490: 1.98111}
```

Let us store these in the option_selection DataFrame and calculate the differences from the market prices:

```
In [51]: option_selection['MODEL'] = \
                 np.array(calculate_model_values(opt_local).values())
         option_selection['ERRORS'] = \
                 option_selection['MODEL'] - option_selection['PRICE']
```

We get the following results:

```
In [52]: option_selection[['MODEL', 'PRICE', 'ERRORS']]
```

```
Out[52]:             MODEL   PRICE    ERRORS
         46482     4.746597    4.85  -0.103403
         46483     4.286923    4.30  -0.013077
         46484     3.863346    3.80   0.063346
         46485     3.474144    3.40   0.074144
         46486     3.119211    3.05   0.069211
         46487     2.793906    2.75   0.043906
         46488     2.494882    2.50  -0.005118
         46489     2.224775    2.25  -0.025225
         46490     1.981110    2.10  -0.118890
```

The average pricing error is relatively low, at less than 1 cent:

```
In [53]: round(option_selection['ERRORS'].mean(), 3)
```

```
Out[53]: -0.002
```

Figure 19-1 shows all the results graphically. The largest difference is observed for the call option that is farthest out of the money:

```
In [54]: import matplotlib.pyplot as plt
         %matplotlib inline
         fix, (ax1, ax2) = plt.subplots(2, sharex=True, figsize=(8, 8))
         strikes = option_selection['STRIKE'].values
         ax1.plot(strikes, option_selection['PRICE'], label='market quotes')
```

```
ax1.plot(strikes, option_selection['MODEL'], 'ro', label='model values')
ax1.set_ylabel('option values')
ax1.grid(True)
ax1.legend(loc=0)
wi = 0.25
ax2.bar(strikes - wi / 2., option_selection['ERRORS'],
        label='market quotes', width=wi)
ax2.grid(True)
ax2.set_ylabel('differences')
ax2.set_xlabel('strikes')
```

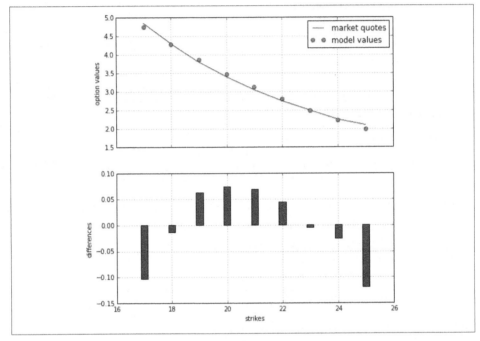

Figure 19-1. Calibrated model values for VSTOXX call options vs. market quotes

American Options on the VSTOXX

A major prerequisite for valuing and managing options not traded at exchanges is a calibrated model that is as consistent as possible with market realities—i.e., quotes for liquidly traded options in the relevant market. This is what the previous section has as the main result. This main result is used in this section to value American put options on the VSTOXX, a kind of derivative instrument not traded in the market. We assume a portfolio consisting of American put options with the same maturity and strikes as the European call options used for the model calibration.

Modeling Option Positions

The first step when valuing a derivatives portfolio with the DX analytics library is to define the relevant risk factors by a market_environment object. At this stage, it does not necessarily have to be complete; missing data and objects might be added during the portfolio valuation (e.g., paths or frequency):

```
In [55]: me_vstoxx = market_environment('me_vstoxx', pricing_date)
         me_vstoxx.add_constant('initial_value', initial_value)
         me_vstoxx.add_constant('final_date', pricing_date)
         me_vstoxx.add_constant('currency', 'NONE')
```

Of course, we use the optimal parameters from the model calibration:

```
In [56]: # adding optimal parameters to environment
         me_vstoxx.add_constant('kappa', opt_local[0])
         me_vstoxx.add_constant('theta', opt_local[1])
         me_vstoxx.add_constant('volatility', opt_local[2])
```

In a portfolio context, the specification of a simulation class/model is necessary:

```
In [57]: me_vstoxx.add_constant('model', 'srd')
```

To define the valuation classes for the American put options, we are mainly missing an appropriate payoff function:

```
In [58]: payoff_func = 'np.maximum(strike - instrument_values, 0)'
```

As before, all American options differ only with respect to their strike prices. It therefore makes sense to define a shared market_environment object first:

```
In [59]: shared = market_environment('share', pricing_date)
         shared.add_constant('maturity', maturity)
         shared.add_constant('currency', 'EUR')
```

It remains to loop over all relevant options, pick the relevant strike, and define one derivatives_position after the other, using the defining market_environment object:

```
In [60]: option_positions = {}
           # dictionary for option positions
         option_environments = {}
           # dictionary for option environments
         for option in option_selection.index:
             option_environments[option] = \
                 market_environment('am_put_%d' % option, pricing_date)
                 # define new option environment, one for each option
             strike = option_selection['STRIKE'].ix[option]
               # pick the relevant strike
             option_environments[option].add_constant('strike', strike)
               # add it to the environment
             option_environments[option].add_environment(shared)
               # add the shared data
             option_positions['am_put_%d' % strike] = \
                         derivatives_position(
```

```
                        'am_put_%d' % strike,
                        quantity=100.,
                        underlying='vstoxx_model',
                        mar_env=option_environments[option],
                        otype='American',
                        payoff_func=payoff_func)
```

Note that we use 100 as the position quantity throughout, which is the typical contract size for VSTOXX options.

The Options Portfolio

To compose the portfolio, we need to specify a couple of parameters that together define our valuation environment—i.e., those parameters shared by all objects in the portfolio:

```
In [61]: val_env = market_environment('val_env', pricing_date)
         val_env.add_constant('starting_date', pricing_date)
         val_env.add_constant('final_date', pricing_date)
           # temporary value, is updated during valuation
         val_env.add_curve('discount_curve', csr)
         val_env.add_constant('frequency', 'B')
         val_env.add_constant('paths', 25000)
```

The market is rather simple; it consists of a single risk factor:

```
In [62]: underlyings = {'vstoxx_model' : me_vstoxx}
```

Taking all this together allows us to define a `derivatives_portfolio` object:

```
In [63]: portfolio = derivatives_portfolio('portfolio', option_positions,
                                           val_env, underlyings)
```

The valuation takes quite a bit of time, since multiple American options are valued by the Least-Squares Monte Carlo approach and multiple Greeks also have to be estimated by revaluations using the same computationally demanding algorithm:

```
In [64]: %time results = portfolio.get_statistics(fixed_seed=True)

Out[64]: CPU times: user 38.6 s, sys: 1.96 s, total: 40.6 s
         Wall time: 40.6 s
```

The `results` `DataFrame` object is best sorted by the `name` column to have a better comparative view of the statistics:

```
In [65]: results.sort(columns='name')
```

```
Out[65]:        name quant.    value curr.  pos_value  pos_delta  pos_vega
         8  am_put_17   100  4.575197  EUR    457.5197     -24.85    102.77
         1  am_put_18   100  5.203648  EUR    520.3648     -30.62    107.93
         0  am_put_19   100  5.872686  EUR    587.2686     -33.31    107.79
         2  am_put_20   100  6.578714  EUR    657.8714     -34.82    110.01
         6  am_put_21   100  7.320523  EUR    732.0523     -39.46    105.20
         7  am_put_22   100  8.081625  EUR    808.1625     -40.61    102.38
         3  am_put_23   100  8.871962  EUR    887.1962     -43.26    104.37
```

```
4  am_put_24   100   9.664272   EUR   966.4272    -40.14   101.04
5  am_put_25   100  10.475168   EUR  1047.5168    -45.74   102.81
```

This portfolio is, as expected for a portfolio of long American put options, short (negative) Delta and long (positive) Vega:

```
In [66]: results[['pos_value','pos_delta','pos_vega']].sum()

Out[66]: pos_value    6664.3795
         pos_delta    -332.8100
         pos_vega      944.3000
         dtype: float64
```

Conclusions

This chapter presents a larger, realistic use case for the application of the DX analytics library to the valuation of a portfolio of nontraded American options on the VSTOXX volatility index. The chapter addresses three main tasks involved in any real-world application:

Data gathering

Current, correct market data builds the basis of any modeling and valuation effort in derivatives analytics; we need index data and futures data, as well as options data for the VSTOXX.

Model calibration

To value, manage, and hedge nontraded options and derivatives in a market-consistent fashion, one needs to calibrate the model parameters to the relevant option market quotes (relevant with regard to maturity and strikes). Our model of choice is the square-root diffusion, which is appropriate for modeling a volatility index; the calibration results are quite good although the model only offers three degrees of freedom (kappa as the mean-reversion factor, theta as the long-term volatility, and volatility as the volatility of the volatility, or so-called "vol-vol").

Portfolio valuation

Based on the market data and the calibrated model, a portfolio with the American put options on the VSTOXX is modeled and major statistics (position values, Deltas, and Vegas) are generated.

The realistic use case in this chapter shows the flexibility and the power of the DX library; it essentially allows us to address any analytical task with regard to derivatives. The very approach and architecture make the application largely comparable to the benchmark case of a Black-Scholes-Merton analytical formula for European options. Once the valuation objects are defined, you can use them similarly to an analytical formula—and this despite the fact that underneath the surface, heavy numerical routines and algorithms are applied.

Further Reading

Eurex's "VSTOXX Advanced Services" tutorial pages provide a wealth of information about the VSTOXX index and related volatility derivatives. These pages also provide lots of readily usable Python scripts to replicate the results and analyses presented in the tutorials:

- The VSTOXX Advanced Services tutorial pages from Eurex are available at *http://www.eurexchange.com/advanced-services/vstoxx/*, while a backtesting application is provided at *http://www.eurexchange.com/advanced-services/app2/*.

The following book is a good general reference for the topics covered in this chapter, especially when it comes to the calibration of option pricing models:

- Hilpisch, Yves (2015): *Derivatives Analytics with Python*. Wiley Finance, Chichester, England. *http://derivatives-analytics-with-python.com*.

With regard to the consistent valuation and management of derivatives portfolios, see also the hints at the end of Chapter 18.

Selected Best Practices

Best practices in general are those rules, either written down formally or just practiced in daily life, that may distinguish the expert Python developer from the casual Python user. There are many of these, and this appendix will introduce some of the more important ones.

Python Syntax

One really helpful feature of Spyder (*http://code.google.com/p/spyderlib/*) as an integrated development environment is its automatic syntax and code checking, which checks Python code for compliance with the PEP 8 recommendations for Python syntax (*http://www.python.org/dev/peps/pep-0008*). But what is codified in "Python Enhancement Proposal 8"? Principally, there are some code formatting rules that should both establish a common standard and allow for better readability of the code. In that sense, this approach is not too dissimilar from a written or printed natural language where certain syntax rules also apply.

For example, consider the code in Example 1-1 of Chapter 1 for the valuation of a European call option via Monte Carlo simulation. First, have a look at the version of this code in Example A-1 that does not conform to PEP 8. It is rather packed, because there are blank lines and spaces missing (sometimes there are also too many spaces or blank lines).

Example A-1. A Python script that does not conform to PEP 8

```
#   Monte Carlo valuation of European call option
# in Black-Scholes-Merton model
# bsm_mcs_euro_syntax_false.py
import numpy as np
#Parameter Values
S0=100.#initial index level
K=105.#strike price
```

```
T= 1.0#time-to-maturity
r=0.05#riskless short rate
sigma    =0.2#volatility
I=100000  # number of simulations
# Valuation Algorithm
z=np.random.standard_normal(I)#pseudorandom numbers
ST=S0*np.exp((r-   0.5*sigma** 2)+sigma*sqrt(T)*   z)#index values at maturity


hT=np.maximum(ST-K,0)#inner values at maturity
C0=np.exp(-r*T)*sum(hT)/I# Monte Carlo estimator
# Result Output
print"Value of the European Call Option %5.3f"%C0
```

Now, take a look at the version in Example A-2 that conforms to PEP 8 (i.e., exactly the one found in Example 1-1). The main difference in readability stems from two facts:

- Use of blank lines to indicate code blocks
- Use of spaces around Python operators (e.g., = or *) as well as before any hash character for comments (here: two spaces)

Example A-2. A Python script that conforms to PEP 8

```
#
# Monte Carlo valuation of European call option
# in Black-Scholes-Merton model
# bsm_mcs_euro_syntax_correct.py
#

import numpy as np

# Parameter Values
S0 = 100.  # initial index level
K = 105.  # strike price
T = 1.0  # time-to-maturity
r = 0.05  # riskless short rate
sigma = 0.2  # volatility

I = 100000  # number of simulations

# Valuation Algorithm
z = np.random.standard_normal(I)  # pseudorandom numbers
ST = S0 * np.exp((r - 0.5 * sigma ** 2) * T + sigma * np.sqrt(T) * z)
  # index values at maturity
hT = np.maximum(ST - K, 0)  # inner values at maturity
C0 = np.exp(-r * T) * np.sum(hT) / I  # Monte Carlo estimator

# Result Output
print "Value of the European Call Option %5.3f" % C0
```

Although the first version is perfectly executable by the Python interpreter, the second version for sure is more readable for both the programmer and any others who may try to understand it.

Some special rules apply to functions and classes when it comes to formatting. In general, there are supposed to be *two* blank lines before any new function (method) definition as well as any new class definition. With functions, *indentation* also comes into play. In general, indentation is achieved through *spaces* and *not* through tabulators. As a general rule, take *four spaces* per level of indentation.[1] Consider now Example A-3.

Example A-3. A Python function with multiple indentations

```
#
# Function to check prime characteristic of integer
# is_prime_no_doc.py
#


def is_prime(I):
    if type(I) != int:
        raise TypeError("Input has not the right type.")
    if I <= 3:
        raise ValueError("Number too small.")
    else:
        if I % 2 == 0:
            print "Number is even, therefore not prime."
        else:
            end = int(I / 2.) + 1
            for i in range(3, end, 2):
                if I % i == 0:
                    print "Number is not prime, it is divided by %d." % i
                    break
                if i >= end - 2:
                    print "Number is prime."
```

We immediately notice the role indentation plays in Python. There are multiple levels of indentation to indicate code blocks, here mainly "caused" by control structure elements (e.g., if or else) or loops (e.g., the for loop).

Control structure elements are explained in Chapter 4, but the basic working of the function should be clear even if you are not yet used to Python syntax. Table A-1 lists a number of heavily used Python operators. Whenever there is a question mark in the description column of Table A-1, the operation returns a Boolean object (i.e., True or False).

---

1. The majority of (Python) editors allow us to configure the use of a certain number of spaces even when pushing the Tab key. Some editors also allow semiautomatic replacement of tabs with spaces.

Table A-1. Selected Python operators

Symbol	Description
+	Addition
-	Subtraction
/	Division
*	Multiplication
%	Modulo
==	Is equal?
!=	Is not equal?
<	Is smaller?
<=	Is equal or smaller?
>	Is larger?
>=	Is equal or larger?

Documentation

The two main elements of Python documentation are:

Inline documentation

Inline documentation can in principle be placed anywhere in the code; it is indicated by the use of one or more leading hash characters (#). In general, there should be at least two spaces before a hash.

Documentation strings

Such strings are used to provide documentation for Python functions (methods) and classes, and are generally placed within their definition (at the beginning of the indented code).

The code in Example A-2 contains multiple examples of inline documentation. Example A-4 shows the same function definition as in Example A-3, but this time with a documentation string added.

Example A-4. The Python function is_prime with documentation string

```
#
# Function to check prime characteristic of integer
# is_prime_with_doc.py
#


def is_prime(I):
    ''' Function to test for prime characteristic of an integer.

    Parameters
    ==========
```

```
I : int
    number to be checked for prime characteristc

Returns
=======
output: string
    states whether number is prime or not;
    if not, provide a prime factor

Raises
======
TypeError
    if argument is not an integer
ValueError
    if the integer is too small (2 or smaller)

Examples
========
>>> is_prime(11)
Number is prime.
>>> is_prime(8)
Number is even, therefore not prime.
>>> is_prime(int(1e8 + 7))
Number is prime.
>>>
'''
if type(I) != int:
    raise TypeError("Input has not the right type.")
if I <= 3:
    raise ValueError("Number too small.")
else:
    if I % 2 == 0:
        print "Number is even, therefore not prime."
    else:
        end = int(I / 2.) + 1
        for i in range(3, end, 2):
            if I % i == 0:
                print "Number is not prime, it is divided by %d." % i
                break
            if i >= end - 2:
                print "Number is prime."
```

In general, such a documentation string provides information about the following elements:

Input

Which parameters/arguments to provide, and in which format (e.g., int)

Output

What the function/method returns, and in which format

Errors

Which ("special") errors might be raised

Examples

Example usage of the function/methods

The use of documentation strings is not only helpful for those who take a look at the code itself. The majority of Python tools, like IPython and Spyder, allow direct access to this documentation and help source. Figure A-1 shows a screenshot of Spyder, this time with the function is_prime shown in the editor and the rendered documentation string of the function in the object inspector (upper right). This illustrates how helpful it is to always include meaningful documentation strings in functions and classes.

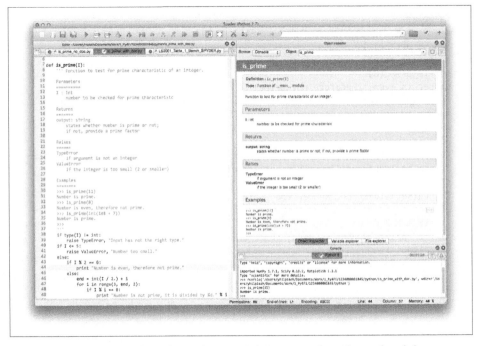

Figure A-1. Screenshot of Spyder with custom function and nicely rendered documentation string

Unit Testing

As a final best practice, we want to consider *unit testing*. Among the different testing approaches, unit testing can indeed be considered a best practice because it tests Python code on a rather fundamental level—i.e., the single *units*. What it does not test, however, is the *integration* of the single units. Typically, such units are functions, classes, or methods of classes. As a pretty simple example of a Python function that is also easily testable, consider the one in Example A-5.

Example A-5. A rather simple Python function

```
#
# Simple function to calculate
# the square of the square root
# of a positive number
# simple_function.py
#
from math import sqrt


def f(x):
    ''' Function to calculate the square of the square root.

    Parameters
    ==========
    x : float or int
        input number

    Returns
    =======
    fx : float
        square of the square root, i.e. sqrt(x) ** 2

    Raises
    ======
    TypeError
        if argument is neither float nor integer
    ValueError
        if argument is negative

    Examples
    ========
    >>> f(1)
    1
    >>> f(10.5)
    10.5
    '''
    if type(x) != float and type(x) != int:
        raise TypeError("Input has not the right type.")
    if x < 0:
        raise ValueError("Number negative.")
    fx = sqrt(x) ** 2
    return fx
```

There are many tools available that help support unit tests. We will make use of nose (*https://nose.readthedocs.org/en/latest/*) in what follows. Example A-6 contains a small test suite for the simple function f from Example A-5.

Example A-6. A test suite for the function f

```
#
# Test suite for simple function f
# nose_test.py
#
import nose.tools as nt
from simple_function import f


def test_f_calculation():
    ''' Tests if function f calculates correctly. '''
    nt.assert_equal(f(4.), 4.)
    nt.assert_equal(f(1000), 1000)
    nt.assert_equal(f(5000.5), 5000.5)


def test_f_type_error():
    ''' Tests if type error is raised. '''
    nt.assert_raises(TypeError, f, 'test string')
    nt.assert_raises(TypeError, f, [3, 'string'])


def test_f_value_error():
    ''' Tests if value error is raised. '''
    nt.assert_raises(ValueError, f, -1)
    nt.assert_raises(ValueError, f, -2.5)


def test_f_test_fails():
    ''' Tests if function test fails. '''
    nt.assert_equal(f(5.), 10)
```

Table A-2 describes the test functions that are implemented.

Table A-2. Test functions for simple function f

Function	Description
test_f_calculation	Tests if the function generates correct results
test_f_type_error	Checks if the function raises a type error when expected
test_f_value_error	Checks if the function raises a value error when expected
test_f_test_fails	Tests if the calculation test fails as expected (for illustration)

From the command line/shell, you can run the following tests:

```
$ nosetests nose_test.py
...F
======================================================================
FAIL: Test if function test fails.
----------------------------------------------------------------------
    Traceback (most recent call last):
```

```
File "/Library/anaconda/lib/python2.7/site-packages/nose/case.py",
line 197, in runTest self.test(*self.arg)
File "//Users/yhilpisch/Documents/Work/Python4Finance/python/nose_test.py",
line 30, in test_f_test_fails
  nt.assert_equal(f(5.), 10)
AssertionError: 5.000000000000001 != 10

-------------------------------------------------------------------
Ran 4 tests in 0.002s

FAILED (failures=1)
$
```

Obviously, the first three tests are successful, while the last one fails as expected. Using such tools—and more importantly, implementing a rigorous approach to unit testing—may require more effort up front, but you and those working with your code will benefit in the long run.

Call Option Class

Example B-1 contains a class definition for a European call option in the Black-Scholes-Merton (1973) model (cf. Chapter 3, and in particular Example 3-1).

Example B-1. Implementation of a Black-Scholes-Merton call option class

```
#
# Valuation of European call options in Black-Scholes-Merton Model
# incl. Vega function and implied volatility estimation
# -- class-based implementation
# bsm_option_class.py
#

from math import log, sqrt, exp
from scipy import stats

class call_option(object):
    ''' Class for European call options in BSM model.

    Attributes
    ==========
    S0 : float
        initial stock/index level
    K : float
        strike price
    T : float
        maturity (in year fractions)
    r : float
        constant risk-free short rate
    sigma : float
        volatility factor in diffusion term

    Methods
    =======
    value : float
        return present value of call option
```

```
    vega : float
        return Vega of call option
    imp_vol: float
        return implied volatility given option quote
    '''

    def __init__(self, S0, K, T, r, sigma):
        self.S0 = float(S0)
        self.K = K
        self.T = T
        self.r = r
        self.sigma = sigma

    def value(self):
        ''' Returns option value. '''
        d1 = ((log(self.S0 / self.K)
            + (self.r + 0.5 * self.sigma ** 2) * self.T)
            / (self.sigma * sqrt(self.T)))
        d2 = ((log(self.S0 / self.K)
            + (self.r - 0.5 * self.sigma ** 2) * self.T)
            / (self.sigma * sqrt(self.T)))
        value = (self.S0 * stats.norm.cdf(d1, 0.0, 1.0)
            - self.K * exp(-self.r * self.T) * stats.norm.cdf(d2, 0.0, 1.0))
        return value

    def vega(self):
        ''' Returns Vega of option. '''
        d1 = ((log(self.S0 / self.K)
            + (self.r + 0.5 * self.sigma ** 2) * self.T)
            / (self.sigma * sqrt(self.T)))
        vega = self.S0 * stats.norm.cdf(d1, 0.0, 1.0) * sqrt(self.T)
        return vega

    def imp_vol(self, C0, sigma_est=0.2, it=100):
        ''' Returns implied volatility given option price. '''
        option = call_option(self.S0, self.K, self.T, self.r, sigma_est)
        for i in range(it):
            option.sigma -= (option.value() - C0) / option.vega()
        return option.sigma
```

This class can be used in an interactive IPython session as follows:

```
In [1]: from bsm_option_class import call_option

In [2]: o = call_option(100., 105., 1.0, 0.05, 0.2)
        type(o)

Out[2]: bsm_option_class.call_option

In [3]: value = o.value()
        value

Out[3]: 8.0213522351431763

In [4]: o.vega()
```

```
Out[4]: 54.222833358480528

In [5]: o.imp_vol(C0=value)

Out[5]: 0.20000000000000001
```

The option class can be easily used to visualize, for example, the value and Vega of the option for different strikes and maturities. This is, in the end, one of the major advantages of having such formulae available. The following Python code generates the option statistics for different maturity-strike combinations:

```
In [6]: import numpy as np
        maturities = np.linspace(0.05, 2.0, 20)
        strikes = np.linspace(80, 120, 20)
        T, K = np.meshgrid(strikes, maturities)
        C = np.zeros_like(K)
        V = np.zeros_like(C)
        for t in enumerate(maturities):
            for k in enumerate(strikes):
                o.T = t[1]
                o.K = k[1]
                C[t[0], k[0]] = o.value()
                V[t[0], k[0]] = o.vega()
```

First, let us have a look at the option values. For plotting, we need to import some libraries and functions:

```
In [7]: import matplotlib.pyplot as plt
        from mpl_toolkits.mplot3d import Axes3D
        from pylab import cm
        %matplotlib inline
```

The output of the following code is presented in Figure B-1:

```
In [8]: fig = plt.figure(figsize=(12, 7))
        ax = fig.gca(projection='3d')
        surf = ax.plot_surface(T, K, C, rstride=1, cstride=1,
                    cmap=cm.coolwarm, linewidth=0.5, antialiased=True)
        ax.set_xlabel('strike')
        ax.set_ylabel('maturity')
        ax.set_zlabel('European call option value')
        fig.colorbar(surf, shrink=0.5, aspect=5)
```

Second, we have the results for the Vega of the call option, as shown in Figure B-2:

```
In [9]: fig = plt.figure(figsize=(12, 7))
        ax = fig.gca(projection='3d')
        surf = ax.plot_surface(T, K, V, rstride=1, cstride=1,
                    cmap=cm.coolwarm, linewidth=0.5, antialiased=True)
        ax.set_xlabel('strike')
        ax.set_ylabel('maturity')
        ax.set_zlabel('Vega of European call option')
        fig.colorbar(surf, shrink=0.5, aspect=5)
        plt.show()
```

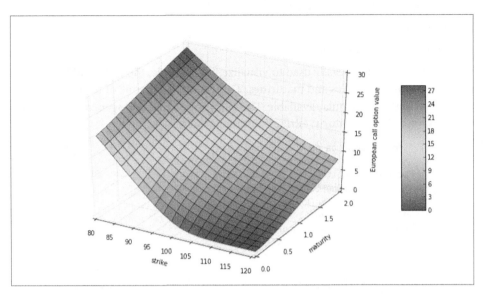

Figure B-1. Value of European call option

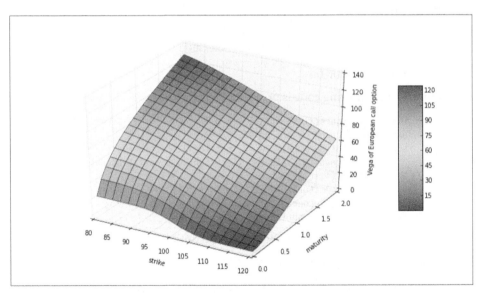

Figure B-2. Vega of European call option

Compared with the code in Example 3-1 of Chapter 3, the code in Example B-1 of this appendix shows a number of advantages:

- Better overall code structure and readability
- Avoidance of redundant definitions as far as possible
- Better reusability and more compact method calls

The option class also lends itself pretty well to the visualization of option statistics.

Dates and Times

As in the majority of scientific disciplines, dates and times play an important role in finance. This appendix introduces different aspects of this topic when it comes to Python programming. It cannot, of course, not be exhaustive. However, it provides an introduction into the main areas of the Python ecosystem that support the modeling of date and time information.

Python

The `datetime` module from the Python standard library allows for the implementation of the most important date and time-related tasks.[1] We start by importing the module:

```
In [1]: import datetime as dt
```

Two different functions provide the exact current date and time:

```
In [2]: dt.datetime.now()

Out[2]: datetime.datetime(2014, 9, 14, 19, 22, 24, 366619)

In [3]: to = dt.datetime.today()
        to

Out[3]: datetime.datetime(2014, 9, 14, 19, 22, 24, 491234)
```

The resulting object is a `datetime` object:

```
In [4]: type(to)

Out[4]: datetime.datetime
```

---

1. For more information on this module, see the online documentation (*https://docs.python.org/2/library/date time.html*).

The method weekday provides the number for the day of the week, given a datetime object:

```
In [5]: dt.datetime.today().weekday()
        # zero-based numbering; 0 = Monday

Out[5]: 6
```

Such an object can, of course, be directly constructed:

```
In [6]: d = dt.datetime(2016, 10, 31, 10, 5, 30, 500000)
        d

Out[6]: datetime.datetime(2016, 10, 31, 10, 5, 30, 500000)

In [7]: print d

Out[7]: 2016-10-31 10:05:30.500000

In [8]: str(d)

Out[8]: '2016-10-31 10:05:30.500000'
```

From such an object you can easily extract, for example, year, month, day information, and so forth:

```
In [9]: d.year

Out[9]: 2016

In [10]: d.month

Out[10]: 10

In [11]: d.day

Out[11]: 31

In [12]: d.hour

Out[12]: 10
```

Via the method toordinal, you can translate the date information to ordinal number representation:

```
In [13]: o = d.toordinal()
         o

Out[13]: 736268
```

This also works the other way around. However, you lose the time information during this process:

```
In [14]: dt.datetime.fromordinal(o)

Out[14]: datetime.datetime(2016, 10, 31, 0, 0)
```

On the other hand, you can separate out the time information from the datetime object, which then gives you a time object:

```
In [15]: t = dt.datetime.time(d)
         t

Out[15]: datetime.time(10, 5, 30, 500000)

In [16]: type(t)

Out[16]: datetime.time
```

Similarly, you can separate out the date information only, ending up with a date object:

```
In [17]: dd = dt.datetime.date(d)
         dd

Out[17]: datetime.date(2016, 10, 31)
```

Often, a certain degree of precision is sufficient. To this end, you can simply replace certain attributes of the datetime object with literal:

```
In [18]: d.replace(second=0, microsecond=0)

Out[18]: datetime.datetime(2016, 10, 31, 10, 5)
```

timedelta is another class of objects that result from arithmetic operations on the other date-time-related objects:

```
In [19]: td = d - dt.datetime.now()
         td

Out[19]: datetime.timedelta(777, 52983, 863732)

In [20]: type(td)

Out[20]: datetime.timedelta
```

Again, you can access the attributes directly to extract detailed information:

```
In [21]: td.days

Out[21]: 777

In [22]: td.seconds

Out[22]: 52983

In [23]: td.microseconds

Out[23]: 863732

In [24]: td.total_seconds()

Out[24]: 67185783.863732
```

There are multiple ways to transform a datetime object into different representations, as well as to generate datetime objects out of, say, a string object. Details are found in the documentation of the datetime module. Here are a few examples:

```
In [25]: d.isoformat()

Out[25]: '2016-10-31T10:05:30.500000'
```

```
In [26]: d.strftime("%A, %d. %B %Y %I:%M%p")

Out[26]: 'Monday, 31. October 2016 10:05AM'

In [27]: dt.datetime.strptime('2017-03-31', '%Y-%m-%d')
            # year first and four-digit year

Out[27]: datetime.datetime(2017, 3, 31, 0, 0)

In [28]: dt.datetime.strptime('30-4-16', '%d-%m-%y')
            # day first and two-digit year

Out[28]: datetime.datetime(2016, 4, 30, 0, 0)

In [29]: ds = str(d)
         ds

Out[29]: '2016-10-31 10:05:30.500000'

In [30]: dt.datetime.strptime(ds, '%Y-%m-%d %H:%M:%S.%f')

Out[30]: datetime.datetime(2016, 10, 31, 10, 5, 30, 500000)
```

In addition to the now and today functions, there is also the utcnow function, which gives the exact date and time information in UTC (Coordinated Universal Time, formerly known as Greenwich Mean Time, or GMT). This represents a two-hour difference from the author's time zone (CET):

```
In [31]: dt.datetime.now()

Out[31]: datetime.datetime(2014, 9, 14, 19, 22, 28, 123943)

In [32]: dt.datetime.utcnow()
            # Coordinated Universal Time

Out[32]: datetime.datetime(2014, 9, 14, 17, 22, 28, 240319)

In [33]: dt.datetime.now() - dt.datetime.utcnow()
            # UTC + 2h = CET (summer)

Out[33]: datetime.timedelta(0, 7199, 999982)
```

Another class of the datetime module is the tzinfo class, a generic time zone class with methods utcoffset, dst, and tzname. dst stands for Daylight Saving Time (DST). A definition for UTC time might look as follows:

```
In [34]: class UTC(dt.tzinfo):
             def utcoffset(self, d):
                 return dt.timedelta(hours=0)
             def dst(self, d):
                 return dt.timedelta(hours=0)
             def tzname(self, d):
                 return "UTC"
```

This can be used as an attribute to a datetime object and be defined via the replace method:

```
In [35]: u = dt.datetime.utcnow()
         u = u.replace(tzinfo=UTC())
           # attach time zone information
         u

Out[35]: datetime.datetime(2014, 9, 14, 17, 22, 28, 597383, tzinfo=<__main__.UTC
           object at 0x7f59e496ec10>)
```

Similarly, the following definition is for CET during the summer:

```
In [36]: class CET(dt.tzinfo):
             def utcoffset(self, d):
                 return dt.timedelta(hours=2)
             def dst(self, d):
                 return dt.timedelta(hours=1)
             def tzname(self, d):
                 return "CET + 1"
```

Making use of the astimezone method then makes it straightforward to transform the UTC-based datetime object u into a CET-based one:

```
In [37]: u.astimezone(CET())

Out[37]: datetime.datetime(2014, 9, 14, 19, 22, 28, 597383, tzinfo=<__main__.CET
           object at 0x7f59e79d8f10>)
```

There is a Python module available called pytz (*http://pytz.sourceforge.net*) that implements the most important time zones from around the world:

```
In [38]: import pytz
```

country_names and country_timezones are dictionaries containing the countries and time zones covered:

```
In [39]: pytz.country_names['US']

Out[39]: u'United States'

In [40]: pytz.country_timezones['BE']

Out[40]: [u'Europe/Brussels']

In [41]: pytz.common_timezones[-10:]

Out[41]: ['Pacific/Wake',
          'Pacific/Wallis',
          'US/Alaska',
          'US/Arizona',
          'US/Central',
          'US/Eastern',
          'US/Hawaii',
          'US/Mountain',
          'US/Pacific',
          'UTC']
```

With pytz, there is generally no need to define your own tzinfo objects:

```
In [42]: u = dt.datetime.utcnow()
         u = u.replace(tzinfo=pytz.utc)
         u

Out[42]: datetime.datetime(2014, 9, 14, 17, 22, 29, 503702, tzinfo=<UTC>)

In [43]: u.astimezone(pytz.timezone("CET"))

Out[43]: datetime.datetime(2014, 9, 14, 19, 22, 29, 503702, tzinfo=<DstTzInfo 'C
         ET' CEST+2:00:00 DST>)

In [44]: u.astimezone(pytz.timezone("GMT"))

Out[44]: datetime.datetime(2014, 9, 14, 17, 22, 29, 503702, tzinfo=<StaticTzInfo
         'GMT'>)

In [45]: u.astimezone(pytz.timezone("US/Central"))

Out[45]: datetime.datetime(2014, 9, 14, 12, 22, 29, 503702, tzinfo=<DstTzInfo 'U
         S/Central' CDT-1 day, 19:00:00 DST>)
```

NumPy

Since NumPy 1.7, there has been native date-time information support in NumPy (*http:// docs.scipy.org/doc/numpy/reference/arrays.datetime.html*). The basic class is called da tetime64:

```
In [46]: import numpy as np

In [47]: nd = np.datetime64('2015-10-31')
         nd

Out[47]: numpy.datetime64('2015-10-31')
```

Like datetime objects, datetime64 objects can be represented as string objects:

```
In [48]: np.datetime_as_string(nd)

Out[48]: '2015-10-31'
```

Every such object has metadata stored with it, which can be accessed via the date time_data method. The two main components are the frequency information (e.g., D for day) and the unit (e.g., 1 for one day in our case):

```
In [49]: np.datetime_data(nd)

Out[49]: ('D', 1)
```

A datetime64 object can easily be constructed from a datetime object:

```
In [50]: d

Out[50]: datetime.datetime(2016, 10, 31, 10, 5, 30, 500000)

In [51]: nd = np.datetime64(d)
         nd

Out[51]: numpy.datetime64('2016-10-31T11:05:30.500000+0100')
```

Similarly, using the `astype` method, a `datetime64` object can be converted into a `date time` object:

```
In [52]: nd.astype(dt.datetime)

Out[52]: datetime.datetime(2016, 10, 31, 10, 5, 30, 500000)
```

Another way to construct such an object is by providing a `string` object, e.g., with year and month, and the frequency information. Note that in the following case, the object value defaults to the first day of the month:

```
In [53]: nd = np.datetime64('2015-10', 'D')
         nd

Out[53]: numpy.datetime64('2015-10-01')
```

Comparing two `datetime64` objects yields a `True` value whenever the information given is the same—even if the level of detail is different:

```
In [54]: np.datetime64('2015-10') == np.datetime64('2015-10-01')

Out[54]: True
```

Of course, you can also define `ndarray` objects containing multiple `datetime64` objects:

```
In [55]: np.array(['2016-06-10', '2016-07-10', '2016-08-10'], dtype='datetime64')

Out[55]: array(['2016-06-10', '2016-07-10', '2016-08-10'], dtype='datetime64[D]')

In [56]: np.array(['2016-06-10T12:00:00', '2016-07-10T12:00:00',
                   '2016-08-10T12:00:00'], dtype='datetime64[s]')

Out[56]: array(['2016-06-10T12:00:00+0200', '2016-07-10T12:00:00+0200',
                '2016-08-10T12:00:00+0200'], dtype='datetime64[s]')
```

You can also generate ranges of dates by using the function `arange`. Different frequencies (e.g., days, months, or weeks) are easily taken care of:

```
In [57]: np.arange('2016-01-01', '2016-01-04', dtype='datetime64')
             # daily frequency as default in this case

Out[57]: array(['2016-01-01', '2016-01-02', '2016-01-03'], dtype='datetime64[D]')

In [58]: np.arange('2016-01-01', '2016-10-01', dtype='datetime64[M]')
             # monthly frequency

Out[58]: array(['2016-01', '2016-02', '2016-03', '2016-04', '2016-05', '2016-06',
                '2016-07', '2016-08', '2016-09'], dtype='datetime64[M]')

In [59]: np.arange('2016-01-01', '2016-10-01', dtype='datetime64[W]')[:10]
             # weekly frequency

Out[59]: array(['2015-12-31', '2016-01-07', '2016-01-14', '2016-01-21',
                '2016-01-28', '2016-02-04', '2016-02-11', '2016-02-18',
                '2016-02-25', '2016-03-03'], dtype='datetime64[W]')
```

You can also easily use subday frequencies, like hours or seconds (refer to the documentation for all options):

```
In [60]: dtl = np.arange('2016-01-01T00:00:00', '2016-01-02T00:00:00',
                          dtype='datetime64[h]')
             # hourly frequency
         dtl[:10]

Out[60]: array(['2016-01-01T00+0100', '2016-01-01T01+0100', '2016-01-01T02+0100',
                 '2016-01-01T03+0100', '2016-01-01T04+0100', '2016-01-01T05+0100',
                 '2016-01-01T06+0100', '2016-01-01T07+0100', '2016-01-01T08+0100',
                 '2016-01-01T09+0100'], dtype='datetime64[h]')
```

Plotting date-time and/or time series data can sometimes be tricky. matplotlib has good support for standard datetime objects. Transforming datetime64 information into datetime information generally does the trick, as the following example, whose result is shown in Figure C-1, illustrates:

```
In [61]: import matplotlib.pyplot as plt
         %matplotlib inline

In [62]: np.random.seed(3000)
         rnd = np.random.standard_normal(len(dtl)).cumsum() ** 2

In [63]: fig = plt.figure()
         plt.plot(dtl.astype(dt.datetime), rnd)
             # convert np.datetime to datetime.datetime
         plt.grid(True)
         fig.autofmt_xdate()
             # autoformatting of datetime x-ticks
```

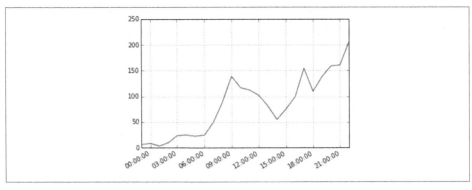

Figure C-1. Plot with datetime.datetime x-ticks autoformatted

Finally, we also have an illustration of using arange with seconds and milliseconds as frequencies:

```
In [64]: np.arange('2016-01-01T00:00:00', '2016-01-02T00:00:00',
                    dtype='datetime64[s]')[:10]
             # seconds as frequency

Out[64]: array(['2016-01-01T00:00:00+0100', '2016-01-01T00:00:01+0100',
                 '2016-01-01T00:00:02+0100', '2016-01-01T00:00:03+0100',
```

```
                '2016-01-01T00:00:04+0100', '2016-01-01T00:00:05+0100',
                '2016-01-01T00:00:06+0100', '2016-01-01T00:00:07+0100',
                '2016-01-01T00:00:08+0100', '2016-01-01T00:00:09+0100'], dtype='
        datetime64[s]')

In [65]: np.arange('2016-01-01T00:00:00', '2016-01-02T00:00:00',
                    dtype='datetime64[ms]')[:10]
         # milliseconds as frequency

Out[65]: array(['2016-01-01T00:00:00.000+0100', '2016-01-01T00:00:00.001+0100',
                '2016-01-01T00:00:00.002+0100', '2016-01-01T00:00:00.003+0100',
                '2016-01-01T00:00:00.004+0100', '2016-01-01T00:00:00.005+0100',
                '2016-01-01T00:00:00.006+0100', '2016-01-01T00:00:00.007+0100',
                '2016-01-01T00:00:00.008+0100', '2016-01-01T00:00:00.009+0100'],
               dtype='datetime64[ms]')
```

pandas

The pandas library was specifically designed with time series data in mind. Therefore, the library provides classes that are able to efficiently handle date-time information, like the DatetimeIndex class for time indices (cf. the documentation (*http://pandas.pyda ta.org/pandas-docs/stable/timeseries.html*)):

```
In [66]: import pandas as pd
```

Date-time information in pandas is generally stored as a Timestamp object:

```
In [67]: ts = pd.Timestamp('2016-06-30')
         ts

Out[67]: Timestamp('2016-06-30 00:00:00')
```

Such objects are easily transformed into regular datetime objects with the to_datetime method:

```
In [68]: d = ts.to_datetime()
         d

Out[68]: datetime.datetime(2016, 6, 30, 0, 0)
```

Similarly, a Timestamp object is straightforwardly constructed from a datetime object:

```
In [69]: pd.Timestamp(d)

Out[69]: Timestamp('2016-06-30 00:00:00')
```

or from a NumPy datetime64 object:

```
In [70]: pd.Timestamp(nd)

Out[70]: Timestamp('2015-10-01 00:00:00')
```

Another important class is the DatetimeIndex class, which is a collection of Timestamp objects with a number of powerful methods attached (cf. *http://bit.ly/date_range_doc* and *http://bit.ly/datetimeindex_doc*). Such an object can be instantiated with the date_range function, which is rather flexible and powerful for constructing time indices (see Chapter 6 for more details on this function):

```
In [71]: dti = pd.date_range('2016/01/01', freq='M', periods=12)
         dti

Out[71]: <class 'pandas.tseries.index.DatetimeIndex'>
         [2016-01-31, ..., 2016-12-31]
         Length: 12, Freq: M, Timezone: None
```

Single elements of the object are accessed by the usual indexing operations:

```
In [72]: dti[6]

Out[72]: Timestamp('2016-07-31 00:00:00', offset='M')
```

DatetimeIndex objects can be transformed into arrays of datetime objects through the method to_pydatetime:

```
In [73]: pdi = dti.to_pydatetime()
         pdi

Out[73]: array([datetime.datetime(2016, 1, 31, 0, 0),
                 datetime.datetime(2016, 2, 29, 0, 0),
                 datetime.datetime(2016, 3, 31, 0, 0),
                 datetime.datetime(2016, 4, 30, 0, 0),
                 datetime.datetime(2016, 5, 31, 0, 0),
                 datetime.datetime(2016, 6, 30, 0, 0),
                 datetime.datetime(2016, 7, 31, 0, 0),
                 datetime.datetime(2016, 8, 31, 0, 0),
                 datetime.datetime(2016, 9, 30, 0, 0),
                 datetime.datetime(2016, 10, 31, 0, 0),
                 datetime.datetime(2016, 11, 30, 0, 0),
                 datetime.datetime(2016, 12, 31, 0, 0)], dtype=object)
```

Using the DatetimeIndex constructor also allows the opposite operation:

```
In [74]: pd.DatetimeIndex(pdi)

Out[74]: <class 'pandas.tseries.index.DatetimeIndex'>
         [2016-01-31, ..., 2016-12-31]
         Length: 12, Freq: None, Timezone: None
```

In the case of NumPy datetime64 objects, the astype method has to be used:

```
In [75]: pd.DatetimeIndex(dtl.astype(pd.datetime))

Out[75]: <class 'pandas.tseries.index.DatetimeIndex'>
         [2015-12-31 23:00:00, ..., 2016-01-01 22:00:00]
         Length: 24, Freq: None, Timezone: None
```

pandas takes care of proper plotting of date-time information (see Figure C-2 and also Chapter 6):

```
In [76]: rnd = np.random.standard_normal(len(dti)).cumsum() ** 2

In [77]: df = pd.DataFrame(rnd, columns=['data'], index=dti)
```

```
In [78]: df.plot()
```

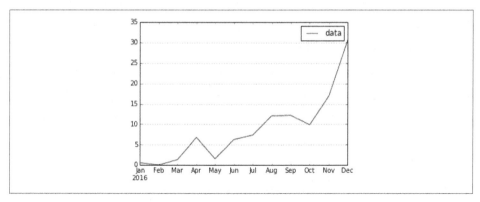

Figure C-2. pandas plot with Timestamp x-ticks autoformatted

pandas also integrates well with the `pytz` module to manage time zones:

```
In [79]: pd.date_range('2016/01/01', freq='M', periods=12,
                        tz=pytz.timezone('CET'))

Out[79]: <class 'pandas.tseries.index.DatetimeIndex'>
         [2016-01-31 00:00:00+01:00, ..., 2016-12-31 00:00:00+01:00]
         Length: 12, Freq: M, Timezone: CET

In [80]: dti = pd.date_range('2016/01/01', freq='M', periods=12, tz='US/Eastern')
         dti

Out[80]: <class 'pandas.tseries.index.DatetimeIndex'>
         [2016-01-31 00:00:00-05:00, ..., 2016-12-31 00:00:00-05:00]
         Length: 12, Freq: M, Timezone: US/Eastern
```

Using the `tz_convert` method, `DatetimeIndex` objects can be transformed from one
time zone to another:

```
In [81]: dti.tz_convert('GMT')

Out[81]: <class 'pandas.tseries.index.DatetimeIndex'>
         [2016-01-31 05:00:00+00:00, ..., 2016-12-31 05:00:00+00:00]
         Length: 12, Freq: M, Timezone: GMT
```

Index

Symbols
64-bit double precision standard, 83

A
absolute minimum variance portfolio, 330
actual continuation value, 502
adaptive quadrature, 256
American exercise
    definition of, 489, 500
    Least-Squares Monte Carlo (LSM) algo-
        rithm, 501
    use case, 504–507
    valuation class, 502
American options
    definition of, 291
    on the VSTOXX, 542–545
    valuation of contingent claims, 295
Anaconda, 26–32
    benefits of, 26
    conda package manager, 30
    downloading, 26
    installing, 27
    libraries/packages available, 27
    multiple Python environments, 31
analytics
    basic, 146
    derivatives analytics library
        derivatives valuation, 489–507

    extensions to, 526
    modularization offered by, 511
    portfolio valuation, 511–525
    simulation of financial models, 467–486
    valuation framework, 455–465
    volatility options, 529–545
financial
    definition of, 12
    implied volatilities example, 50–59
    Monte Carlo simulation example, 59–68
    retrieving data, 151–156
    size of data sets, 173
    technical analysis example, 68–74
interactive
    benefits of Python for, 18–21
    publishing platform for sharing, 39
    tools for, 34–47
real-time, 12
annualized performance, 324
antithetic paths, 469
antithetic variates, 288
application development
    benefits of Python for end-to-end, 21
    documentation best practices, 550
    rapid web applications, 424–442
    syntax best practices, 547
    tools for, 34–47
    unit testing best practices, 553

We'd like to hear your suggestions for improving our indexes. Send email to index@oreilly.com.

approximation of functions, 234–249
    interpolation, 245
    regression, 234–245
arbitrary precision floats, 83
arrays
    DataFrames and, 146
    input-output operations with PyTables, 197
    memory layout and, 105
    regular NumPy arrays, 97–101
    structure of, 95
    structured arrays, 101
    with Python lists, 96
    writing/reading NumPy, 181
average loss level, 302

B

basic analytics, 146
Bayesian regression, 341–355
    diachronic interpretation of Bayes's formula, 341
    introductory example, 343
    overview of, 308, 355
    PyMC3 library, 342
    real data, 347–355
beliefs of agents, 308
Bermudan exercises, 295, 500
best practices
    documentation, 550
    functional programming tools, 92
    syntax, 547
    unit testing, 553
bfill parameter, 162
big data, 12, 173
binomial model, 501
binomial option pricing, 218–223
Black-Scholes-Merton model
    class definition for European call option, 557–561
    European call option, 14–16
    formula for, 50
    LaTeX code for, 42
    parameters meanings, 50
    simulating future index level, 271
    stochastic differential equation, 60
    Vega of a European option, 51
Bokeh library
    benefits of, 412
    default output, 413
    interactive plots, 414
    plotting styles, 413
    real-time plots, 417
    stand-alone graphics files, 415
boxplots, 125
broadcasting, 103
brute function, 250, 539

C

call options
    class definition for European, 557–561
    definition of, 291
candlestick plots, 128
capital asset pricing model, 308
capital market line, 332
cash flow series, 391, 398
cells
    in DataNitro, 371
    in Excel spreadsheets, 363
    in IPython, 37
characters, symbols for, 114
classes
    accessing attribute values, 383
    assigning new attribute values, 383
    attributes and, 382
    cash flow series example, 391
    defining, 382
    defining object attributes, 383
    for risk-neutral discounting, 460
    generic simulation class, 470
    generic valuation class, 489
    geometric Brownian motion, 473
    inheritance in, 382
    iteration over, 385
    jump diffusion, 478
    private attributes, 385
    readability and maintainability of, 384
    reusability and, 384
    simple short rate class example, 387
    square-root diffusion, 482
    to model derivatives portfolios, 516
    to model derivatives positions, 512
    valuation class for American exercise, 502
    valuation class for European exercise, 494
coefficient of determination, 243
color abbreviations, 114
comma-separated value (CSV) files
    generating Excel spreadsheets with, 359
    input-output operations with pandas, 188
    parameters of read_csv function, 161

reading/writing, 177
regular expressions and, 85
retrieving via the Web, 408
communication protocols
file transfer protocol, 404
hypertext transfer protocol, 407
providing web services via, 442–451
secure connections, 406
uniform resource locators, 408
compilation
dynamic, 217–223
static, 223–226
compiled languages, 80
compressed tables, working with, 196
concatenate function, 288
conda package manager, 30
configure_traits method, 394
constant short rate, 460
constrained optimization, 253
contingent claims, valuation of, 290–297
American options, 295
European options, 291
continuation value, 295, 501
control structures, 89
convenience methods, 146
convex optimization, 249–254
constrained, 253
functions for, 539
global, 250
local, 251
covariance matrix, 324
covariances, 308
Cox-Ingersoll-Ross SDE, 276
Cox-Ross-Rubinstein binomial model, 501
credit value adjustment (CVA), 302
credit value-at-risk (CVaR), 302
CSS (Cascading Style Sheets), 440
cubic splines, 245
Cython library, 80, 223

D

data
basic data structures, 86–95
basic data types, 80–86
big data, 12, 173
formats supported by pandas library, 183
high frequency, 166
high-frequency, 422
missing data, 141, 147

noisy data, 240
NumPy data structures, 95–102
provision/gathering with web technology,
403
quality of web sources, 129, 151
real-time foreign exchange, 418
real-time stock price quotes, 422
resampling of, 168
retrieving, 151–156
sources of, 152
storage of, 173
unsorted data, 241
VSTOXX data, 530–534
data visualization
3D plotting, 132
Bokeh library for, 412
financial plots, 128
for implied volatilities, 57
graphical analysis of Monte Carlo simulation, 67
interactive plots, 414
panning/zooming, 414
plot_surface parameters, 134
plt.axis options, 112
plt.candlestick parameters, 130
plt.hist parameters, 124
plt.legend options, 116
real-time plots, 417
standard color abbreviations, 114
standard style characters, 114
static plots, 411
two-dimensional plotting, 109–128
DataFrame class, 138–146
arrays and, 146
features of, 139
frequency parameters for date-range function, 145
line plot of DataFrame object, 147
parameters of DataFrame function, 143, 183
parameters of date-range function, 144
similarity to SQL database table, 138
vectorization with, 154
DataNitro
benefits of, 369
cell attributes, 371
cell methods, 372
cell typesetting options, 372
combining with Excel, 370
installing, 369

optimizing performance, 374
plotting with, 374
scripting with, 370
user-defined functions, 376
DataReader function, 152
dates and times
described by regular expressions, 85
implied volatilities example, 50–59
in risk-neutral discounting, 458
Monte Carlo simulation example, 59–68
NumPy support for, 568–571
pandas support for, 571–573
Python datetime module, 563–568
technical analysis example, 68–74
(see also financial time series data)
datetime module, 563–568
datetime64 class, 568–571
date_range function, 144
default, probability of, 302
Deltas, 492
dependent observations, 234
deployment
Anaconda, 26–32
Python Quant platform, 32
via web browser, 32
derivatives analytics library
derivatives valuation, 489–507
extensions to, 526
goals for, 453
modularization offered by, 511
portfolio valuation, 511–525
simulation of financial models, 467–486
valuation framework, 455–465
volatility options, 529–545
derivatives portfolios
class for valuation, 516
relevant market for, 515
use case, 520–525
derivatives positions
definition of, 512
modeling class, 512
use case, 514
derivatives valuation
American exercise, 500–507
European exercise, 493–500
generic valuation class, 489
methods available, 489
deserialization, 174

diachronic interpretation (of Bayes's formula),
341
dicts, 92
differentiation, 261
discounting, 387, 458
discretization error, 274
diversification, 323
documentation
best practices, 550
documentation strings, 550
IPython Notebook for, 38
dot function, 238, 326
DX (Derivatives AnalytiX) library, 453
dynamic compiling, 217–223
binomial option pricing, 218–223
example of, 217
dynamically typed languages, 80

E
early exercise premium, 297
editors
configuring, 45
Spyder, 46
efficiency, 17–21
efficient frontier, 330
efficient markets hypothesis, 308
encryption, 406
errors
discretization error, 274
mean-squared error (MSE), 538
sampling error, 274
estimated continuation value, 502
Euler scheme, 65, 277, 483
European exercise
definition of, 489
Monte Carlo estimator for option values, 493
use case, 496–500
valuation class, 494
European options
definition of, 291
valuation of contingent claims, 291
Excel
basic spreadsheet interaction, 358–369
benefits of, 357
cell types in, 363
drawbacks of, 358
features of, 357
file input-output operations, 189
integration with Python, 358

integration with xlwings, 379
    scripting with Python, 369–379
excursion
    control structures, 89
    functional programming, 91
expected portfolio return, 325
expected portfolio variance, 325

F

fat tails, 300, 320
ffill parameter, 162
file transfer protocol, 404
fillna method, 162
finance
    mathematical tools for, 233–262
    role of Python in, 13–22
    role of technology in, 9–13
    role of web technologies in, 403
financial analytics
    basic analytics, 146
        (see also financial time series data)
    definition of, 12
    implied volatilities example, 50–59
    Monte Carlo simulation example, 59–68
    retrieving data, 151–156
    size of data sets, 173
    technical analysis example, 68–74
financial plots, 128–131
financial time series data
    definition of, 137
    financial data, 151–156
    high frequency data, 166
    pandas library, 138–151
    regression analysis, 157–166
first in, first out (FIFO) principle, 177
fixed Gaussian quadrature, 256
flash trading, 11
Flask framework
    benefits of, 425
    commenting functionality, 430
    connection/log in, 429
    data modeling, 426
    database infrastructure, 428
    importing libraries, 427
    libraries required, 425
    security issues, 434
    styling web pages in, 440
    templating in, 434
    traders' chat room application, 426

floats, 81–83
fmin function, 250, 539
frequency distribution, 523
ftplib library, 404
full truncation, 277, 483
functional programming, 91
Fundamental Theorem of Asset Pricing, 290,
    455, 515
FX (foreign exchange) data, 418

G

general market model, 457, 515
General Purpose Graphical Processing Units
    (GPGPUs), 226
generate_payoff method, 494
geometric Brownian motion, 467, 473
get_info method, 512
global optimization, 250, 539
graphical analysis, 67
    (see also matplotlib library)
graphical user interfaces (GUIs)
    cash flow series with, 398
    libraries required, 393
    Microsoft Excel as, 358
    short rate class with, 394
    updating values, 396
Greeks, estimation of, 492
groupby operations, 150
Gruenbichler and Longstaff model, 443
Guassian quadrature, 256

H

HDF5 database format, 198
Heston stochastic volatility model, 281
high frequency data, 166
histograms, 123
HTML-based web pages, 407
httplib library, 407
hypertext transfer protocol, 407

I

immutability, 88
implied volatilities
    Black-Scholes-Merton formula, 50
    definition of, 50
    futures data, 54
    Newton scheme for, 51

option quotes, 54
visualizing data, 57
volatility smile, 57
importing, definition of, 6
independent observations, 234
inline documentation, 550
input-output operations
  with pandas
    data as CSV file, 188
    data as Excel file, 189
    from SQL to pandas, 185
    SQL databases, 184
  with PyTables
    out-of-memory computations, 198
    working with arrays, 197
    working with compressed tables, 196
    working with tables, 190
  with Python
    reading/writing text files, 177
    SQL databases, 179
    writing objects to disk, 174
    writing/reading Numpy arrays, 181
input/output operations
  importance of, 173
integer index, 58
integers, 80
integrate sublibrary, 256
integration
  by simulation, 257
  numerical, 256
  scipy.integrate sublibrary, 255
  symbolic computation, 260
interactive analytics
  benefits of Python for, 18–21
  publishing platform for sharing, 39
  rise of real-time, 12
  tools for, 34–47
interactive web plots, 414
interpolation, 245–249
interpreters
  IPython, 35–45
  standard, 34
IPython, 35–45
  basic usage, 37
  benefits of, 7
  documentation with, 38
  help functions in, 44
  importing libraries, 36
  invoking, 35

IPython.parallel library, 209–214
  magic commands, 43
  Markdown commands, 41
  rendering capabilities, 41
  system shell commands, 45
  versions of, 35
iter method, 385

J

Jinja2 library, 425
jump diffusion, 285, 467, 478

K

KernelPCA function, 336
killer application, 7
kurtosis test, 314

L

large integers, 81
LaTeX
  commands, 41
  IPython Notebook cells and, 40
least-squares function, 238
Least-Squares Monte Carlo (LSM) algorithm, 295, 489, 501
leverage effect, 155, 282
libraries
  available in Anaconda, 27
  Cython library, 80
  importing, 6, 105, 234
  importing to IPython, 36
  standard, 6
list comprehensions, 91
lists, 88, 96
LLVM compiler infrastructure, 217
local maximum a posteriori point, 344
local optimization, 251, 539
lognormal function, 272
Longstaff-Schwartz model, 501, 504
loss level, 302

M

magic commands/functions, 43
Markdown commands, 41
market environments, 462
(Markov Chain) Monte Carlo (MCMC) sampling, 344

Markov property, 274
martingale measures, 455, 501
mathematical syntax, 17
mathematical tools
    approximation of functions, 234–262
    convex optimization, 249–254
    integration, 255
    symbolic computation, 258
matplotlib library
    3D plotting, 132
    benefits of, 8
    financial plots, 128–131
    importing matplotlib.pyplot, 234
    NumPy arrays and, 111
    pandas library wrapper for, 148
    strengths of, 411
    two-dimensional plotting, 109–128
maximization of Sharpe ratio, 328
mean returns, 308
mean-squared error (MSE), 538
mean-variance, 324
mean-variance portfolio theory (MPT), 322
memory layout, 105
memory-less processes, 274
Microsoft Excel (see Excel)
minimization function, 328
missing data, 141, 147
model calibration
    option modeling, 536
    procedure for, 538
    relevant market data, 535
modern portfolio theory (MPT), 307, 322
moment matching, 289, 469
Monte Carlo simulation
    approaches to, 59
    benefits of, 59
    BSM stochastic differential equation, 60
    drawbacks of, 59, 501
    for European call option, 61
    full vectorization with log Euler scheme, 65
    graphical analysis of, 67
    importance of, 271
    integration by simulation, 257
    Least-Squares Monte Carlo (LSM) algo-
        rithm, 295, 489
    pure Python approach, 61
    valuation of contingent claims, 290–297
    vectorization with NumPy, 63
moving averages, 155

multiple dimensions, 242
multiprocessing module, 215
mutability, 88

N

ndarray class, 63
Newton scheme, 51
noisy data, 240
normality tests, 308–322
    benchmark case, 309
    importance of, 308
    normality assumption, 317
    overview of, 307, 355
    real-world data, 317
Numba library, 217–223
NumbaPro library, 226
numexpr library, 205
NumPy
    benefits of, 8
    concatenate function, 288
    data structures, 95–102
    date-time information support in, 568
    importing, 234
    Monte Carlo simulation with, 63
    numpy.linalg sublibrary, 238
    numpy.random sublibrary, 266
    universal functions, 147
    writing/reading arrays, 181
NUTS algorithm, 344

O

OANDA online broker, 418
object orientation, 381–393
    cash flow series class example, 391
    definition of, 381
    Python classes, 382
    simple short rate class example, 387
observation points, 234, 241
OpenPyxl library, 364
operators, 550
optimal decision step, 502
optimal stopping problems, 295, 501
optimization
    constrained, 253
    convex, 249–254
    global, 250
    local, 251
option pricing theory, 309

ordinary least-squares regression (OLS), 157, 243, 501
out-of-memory computations, 198

P

pandas library, 138–151
  basic analytics, 146
  benefits of, 9, 74
  data formats supported, 183
  data sources supported, 152
  DataFrame class, 138–146
  date-time information support in, 571–573
  development of, 137
  error tolerance in, 147
  groupby operations, 150
  hierarchically indexed data sets and, 58
  input-output operations
    data as CSV file, 188
    data as Excel file, 189
    from SQL to pandas, 185
    SQL databases, 184
  reading/writing spreadsheets with, 366
  Series class, 149
  working with missing data, 141
  wrapper for matplotlib library, 148
parallel computing, 209–214
  Monte Carlo algorithm, 209
  parallel calculation, 211
  performance comparison, 214
  sequential calculation, 210
PEP (Python Enhancement Proposal) 20, 4
PEP (Python Enhancement Proposal) 8, 547
performance computing
  benefits of Python for, 19
  dynamic compiling, 217–223
  memory layout and, 207
  multiprocessing module, 215
  parallel computing, 209–214
  Python paradigms and, 204
  random number generation on GPUs, 226
  static compiling with Cython, 223
petascale processing, 173
pickle module, 174
plot function, 110
plot method, 148
plot_surface function, 134
plt.axis method, 112
plt.candlestick, 130
plt.hist function, 124

plt.legend function, 116
PNG (portable network graphics) format, 412
Poisson distribution, 270
polyfit function, 235
portfolio theory/portfolio optimization
  basic idea of, 323
  basic theory, 324
  capital market line, 332
  data collection for, 323
  efficient frontier, 330
  importance of, 322
  overview of, 308, 355
  portfolio covariance matrix, 325
  portfolio optimizations, 328
portfolio valuation
  benefits of analytics library for, 511
  derivatives portfolios, 515–525
  derivatives positions, 512–515
  requirements for complex portfolios, 512
precision floats, 83
presentation, IPython Notebook for, 38
present_value method, 494
principal component analysis (PCA), 335–340
  applying, 337
  constructing PCA indices, 338
  DAX index stocks, 336
  definition of, 335
  overview of, 308, 355
print_statistics helper function, 273
private attributes, 385
probability of default, 302
productivity, 17–21
pseudocode, 17
pseudorandom numbers, 266, 287
publishing platform, 39
put options, definition of, 291
PyMC3 library, 342
pyplot sublibrary, 110
PyTables
  benefits of, 8, 190
  importing, 190
  input-output operations
    out-of-memory computations, 198
    working with arrays, 197
    working with compressed tables, 196
    working with tables, 190
Python
  as ecosystem vs. language, 6
  benefits for finance, 13–22, 174, 404

benefits of, 3
classes in, 382–393, 460
deployment, 26–33
features of, 3
history of, 5
input-output operations
    reading/writing text files, 177
    SQL databases, 179
    writing objects to disk, 174
    writing/reading Numpy arrays, 181
invoking interpreter, 34
multiple environments for, 31
Quant platform, 32, 454
rapid web application development, 424–442
scientific stack, 8, 69
user spectrum, 7
zero-based numbering in, 87
Python Quants GmbH
benefits of, 32
features of, 33, 454

Q

quadratures, fixed Gaussian and adaptive, 256
Quant platform
benefits of, 32
features of, 33, 454
quantile-quantile (qq) plots, 313
queries, 195

R

random number generation, 226, 266–270, 468
    functions according to distribution laws, 268
    functions for simple, 267
random variables, 271
rapid web application development
benefits of Python for, 425
commenting functionality, 430
connection/log in, 429
data modeling, 426
database infrastructure, 428
Flask framework for, 425
importing libraries, 427
popular frameworks for, 425
security issues, 434
styling web pages, 440
templating, 434
traders' chat room, 426
read_csv function, 161

real-time analytics, 12
real-time economy, 12
real-time plots, 417
real-time stock price quotes, 422
regression analysis
    mathematical tools for
        individual basis functions, 238
        monomials as basis functions, 235
        multiple dimensions and, 242
        noisy data and, 240
        strengths of, 234
        unsorted data and, 241
    of financial time series data, 157–166
regular expressions, 85
reg_func function, 244
requests library, 418
resampling, 168
risk management, 489
    (see also derivatives valuation; risk measures)
risk measures, 298–305
    credit value adjustments, 302
    value-at-risk (VaR), 298
risk-neutral discounting, 458
risk-neutral valuation approach, 457
rolling functions, 155
Romberg integration, 256

S

sampling error, 274
scatter plots, 121
scientific stack, 8, 69
scikit-learn library, 336
SciPy
    benefits of, 8
    scipy.integrate sublibrary, 255
    scipy.optimize sublibrary, 250
    scipy.optimize.minimize function, 253
    scipy.stats sublibrary, 273, 309
sensitivity analysis, 392
serialization, 174
Series class, 149
sets, 94
Sharpe ratio, 328
short rates, 387, 394, 460
simple random number generation, 267
Simpson's rule, 257
simulation
    discretization error in, 274

generic simulation class, 470
geometric Brownian motion, 272–273, 473
jump diffusion, 478
noisy data from, 240
numerical integration by, 257
random number generation, 468
random variables, 271
sampling error in, 274
square-root diffusion, 482
stochastic processes, 274–290, 467
variance reduction, 287
skewness test, 314
Software-as-a-Service (SaaS), 403
splev function, 246
spline interpolation, 245
splrep function, 246
spreadsheets
    Excel cell types, 363
    generating xls workbooks, 359
    generating xlsx workbooks, 360
    OpenPyxl library for, 364
    Python libraries for, 358
    reading from workbooks, 362
    reading/writing with pandas, 366
Spyder
    benefits of, 45
    features of, 46
SQL databases
    input-output operations with pandas, 184
    input-output operations with Python, 179
square-root diffusion, 276, 467, 482, 536
standard color abbreviations, 114
standard interpreter, 34
standard normally distributed random num-
    bers, 468
standard style characters, 114
star import, 6, 105
static plots, 411
statically typed languages, 80
statistics, 307–355
    Bayesian regression, 308, 341–355
    focus areas covered, 307
    normality tests, 307–322
    portfolio theory, 307, 322–335
    principal component analysis, 308, 335–340
statmodels library, 243
stochastic differential equation (SDE), 274
stochastic processes, 274–290
    definition of, 274

geometric Brownian motion, 274, 467, 473
importance of, 265
jump diffusion, 285, 467, 478
square-root diffusion, 276, 467, 482
stochastic volatility model, 281
strings
    documentation strings, 550
    Python string class, 84–86
    selected string methods, 84
    string objects, 84
structured arrays, 101
Symbol class, 258
symbolic computation
    basics of, 258
    differentiation, 261
    equations, 259
    integration, 260
SymPy library
    benefits for symbolic computations, 262
    differentiation with, 261
    equation solving with, 259
    integration with, 260
    mathematical function definitions, 258
    Symbol class, 258
syntax
    benefits of Python for finance, 14–17
    best practices, 4, 547
    mathematical, 17
    Python 2.7 vs. 3.x, 31

T

tables
    compressed, 196
    working with, 190
tail risk, 298
technical analysis
    backtesting example, 69
    definition of, 68
    retrieving time series data, 69
    testing investment strategy, 73
    trading signal rules, 71
    trend strategy, 70
technology, role in finance, 9–13
templating, 434
testing, unit testing, 553
text
    reading/writing text files, 177
    representation with strings, 84
three-dimensional plotting, 132

tools, 34–47
    IPython, 35–45
    Python interpreter, 34
    Spyder, 45–47
        (see also mathematical tools)
traders' chat room application
    basic idea of, 426
    commenting functionality, 430
    connection/log in, 429
    data modeling, 426
    database infrastructure, 428
    importing libraries, 427
    security issues, 434
    styling, 440
    templating, 434
traits library, 393
traitsui.api library, 396
trapezoidal rule, 257
tuples, 87
two-dimensional plotting
    importing libraries, 109
    one-dimensional data set, 110–115
    other plot styles, 121–128
    two-dimensional data set, 115–120

U

unit testing best practices, 553
universal functions, 104, 147
unsorted data, 241
updating of beliefs, 308
urllib library, 408
URLs (uniform resource locators), 408
user-defined functions (UDF), 376

V

valuation framework
    Fundamental Theorem of Asset Pricing, 455
    overview of, 455
    risk-neutral discounting, 458
valuation of contingent claims, 290–297
    American options, 295
    European options, 291
valuation theory, 501
value-at-risk (VaR), 298
values, updating in GUI, 396
variance of returns, 308
variance reduction, 287

vectorization
    basic, 102
    full with log Euler scheme, 65
    fundamental idea of, 102
    memory layout, 105
    speed increase achieved by, 65
    with DataFrames, 154
    with NumPy, 63
Vega
    definition of, 493
    of a European option in BSM model, 51
visualization (see data visualization)
VIX volatility index, 529
volatility clustering, 155
volatility index, 443
volatility options
    American on the VSTOXX, 542–545
    main index, 529
    model calibration, 534–541
    tasks undertaken, 530
    VSTOXX data, 530–534
volatility smile, 57
volatility, stochastic model, 281
VSTOXX data
    futures data, 531
    index data, 530
    libraries required, 530
    options data, 533

W

web browser deployment, 32
web technologies
    communication protocols, 404–411
    rapid web applications, 424–442
    role in finance, 403
    web plotting, 411–423
    web services, 442–451
Werkzeug library, 425
workbooks
    generating xls workbooks, 359
    generating xlsx workbooks, 360
    OpenPyxl library for, 364
    pandas generated, 366
    reading from, 362

X

xlrd library, 358
xlsxwriter library, 358

xlwings library, 379
xlwt library, 358

Y

Yahoo! Finance, 129, 152

Z

Zen of Python, 4
zero-based numbering schemes, 87

About the Author

Yves Hilpisch is founder and managing partner of The Python Quants GmbH, Germany, as well as cofounder of The Python Quants LLC, New York City. The group provides Python-based financial and derivatives analytics software (cf. *http://python quants.com, http://quant-platform.com,* and *http://dx-analytics.com*), as well as consulting, development, and training services related to Python and finance.

Yves is also author of the book *Derivatives Analytics with Python* (Wiley Finance, 2015). As a graduate in Business Administration with a Dr.rer.pol. in Mathematical Finance, he lectures on Numerical Methods in Computational Finance at Saarland University.

Colophon

The animal on the cover of *Python for Finance* is a Hispaniolan solenodon. The Hispaniolan solenodon (*Solenodon paradoxus*) is an endangered mammal that lives on the Caribbean island of Hispaniola, which comprises Haiti and the Dominican Republic. It's particularly rare in Haiti and a bit more common in the Dominican Republic.

Solenodons are known to eat arthropods, worms, snails, and reptiles. They also consume roots, fruit, and leaves on occasion. A solenodon weighs a pound or two and has a foot-long head and body plus a ten-inch tail, give or take. This ancient mammal looks somewhat like a big shrew. It's quite furry, with reddish-brown coloring on top and lighter fur on its undersides, while its tail, legs, and prominent snout lack hair.

It has a rather sedentary lifestyle and often stays out of sight. When it does come out, its movements tend to be awkward, and it sometimes trips when running. However, being a night creature, it has developed an acute sense of hearing, smell, and touch. Its own distinctive scent is said to be "goatlike."

It gets toxic saliva from a groove in the second lower incisor and uses it to paralyze and attack its invertebrate prey. As such, it is one of few venomous mammals. Sometimes the venom is released when fighting among each other, and can be fatal to the solenodon itself. Often, after initial conflict, they establish a dominance relationship and get along in the same living quarters. Families tend to live together for a long time. Apparently, it only drinks while bathing.

Many of the animals on O'Reilly covers are endangered; all of them are important to the world. To learn more about how you can help, go to *animals.oreilly.com*.

The cover image is from Wood's *Illustrated Natural History*. The cover fonts are URW Typewriter and Guardian Sans. The text font is Adobe Minion Pro; the heading font is Adobe Myriad Condensed; and the code font is Dalton Maag's Ubuntu Mono.

Have it your way.

Get even more for your money.

Join the O'Reilly Community, and register the O'Reilly books you own. It's free, and you'll get:

- $4.99 ebook upgrade offer
- 40% upgrade offer on O'Reilly print books
- Membership discounts on books and events
- Free lifetime updates to ebooks and videos
- Multiple ebook formats, DRM FREE
- Participation in the O'Reilly community
- Newsletters
- Account management
- 100% Satisfaction Guarantee

Signing up is easy:

1. Go to: oreilly.com/go/register
2. Create an O'Reilly login.
3. Provide your address.
4. Register your books.

Note: English-language books only

To order books online:
oreilly.com/store

For questions about products or an order:
orders@oreilly.com

To sign up to get topic-specific email announcements and/or news about upcoming books, conferences, special offers, and new technologies:
elists@oreilly.com

For technical questions about book content:
booktech@oreilly.com

To submit new book proposals to our editors:
proposals@oreilly.com

O'Reilly books are available in multiple DRM-free ebook formats. For more information:
oreilly.com/ebooks

9 781491 945285